What's New in This Editio

Since the introduction of Visual Basic version 1.0 just a
has gone through quite an evolution! And naturally, ‍
in 21 Days follows this evolution.

Like previous editions of this book, this edition includes all the "standard" Visual
Basic topics that enable you to write powerful Windows applications in a very
short time. But naturally, all the programs of this edition of the book are
implemented with the new Visual Basic package—version 4.0.

Many of the new features that are incorporated in version 4.0 of Visual Basic are
discussed in this book.

Previous editions of this book assumed that you were using the 16-bit Windows
version 3.1*x*. The figures in this edition of the book, however, are pictures of
programs that are executed using the new 32-bit Windows 95. Nevertheless, this
edition of the book was written in a way that enables you to learn the book's
material even if you are using the 16-bit package of Visual Basic 4.0, and even if
you are using Windows NT or Windows 3.1*x*. Throughout this edition of the
book, the minor differences that exist between the various Windows operating
systems are indicated.

One of the main differences between Visual Basic 4 and the previous versions of
Visual Basic is the introduction of the powerful OLE controls. So of course, this
new edition of the book utilizes the new OLE technology.

Teach Yourself
Visual Basic 4
in 21 Days,
Third Edition

Teach Yourself
Visual Basic 4
in 21 Days,
Third Edition

Nathan Gurewich
Ori Gurewich

SAMS
PUBLISHING

201 West 103rd Street
Indianapolis, Indiana 46290

Copyright © 1995 by Sams Publishing

THIRD EDITION

International Standard Book Number: 0-672-30620-4

Library of Congress Catalog Card Number: 94-67506

98   97

Interpretation of the printing code: the rightmost double-digit number is the year of the book's printing; the rightmost single-digit, the number of the book's printing. For example, a printing code of 95-1 shows that the first printing of the book occurred in 1995.

Composed in AGaramond, Bodoni, and MCPdigital by Macmillan Computer Publishing

Printed in the United States of America

Publisher	*Richard K. Swadley*
Acquisitions Manager	*Greg Wiegand*
Development Manager	*Dean Miller*
Managing Editor	*Cindy Morrow*
Marketing Manager	*Gregg Bushyeager*

Acquisitions Editor
Christopher Denny

Development Editor
L. Angelique Brittingham

Production Editor
Kitty Wilson

Copy Editor
Lisa Lord

Technical Reviewer
Robert Bogue

Editorial Coordinator
Bill Whitmer

Technical Edit Coordinator
Lynette Quinn

Formatter
Frank Sinclair

Editorial Assistant
Sharon Cox

Cover Designer
Tim Amrhein

Book Designer
Alyssa Yesh

Production Team Supervisor
Brad Chinn

Production
Carol Bowers
Michael Brumitt
Charlotte Clapp
Jeanne Clark
Terrie Deemer
Mike Henry
Kevin Laseau
Paula Lowell
Donna Martin
Steph Mineart
Brian-Kent Proffitt
Bobbi Satterfield
SA Springer
Susan Van Ness
Mark Walchle

Indexer
Jeanne Clark

Overview

Contents

Week 3 at a Glance   525

Day   15   Arrays, OLE, and Other Topics   527

SAMS
Sams
Learning
Center
SAMS
PUBLISHING

Acknowledgments

We would like to thank Chris Denny, the acquisitions editor of this book; Angelique Brittingham, the development editor; Robert Bogue, the technical editor; and Kitty Wilson, the production editor.

We would also like to thank all the other people at Sams Publishing who contributed to this book.

Thanks also to Microsoft Corporation, which supplied us with technical information and various betas and upgrades of the software product.

About the Authors

Nathan Gurewich and **Ori Gurewich** are the authors of several best-selling books in the areas of Visual Basic, C/C++ programming, multimedia programming, database design and programming, and other topics.

Nathan Gurewich holds a master's degree in electrical engineering from Columbia University, New York, and a bachelor's degree in electrical engineering from Hofstra University, Long Island, New York. Since the introduction of the PC, the author has been involved in the design and implementation of commercial software packages for the PC. He is an expert in the field of PC programming and in providing consulting services in the area of local area networks, wide area networks, database management and design, and software marketing. Nathan Gurewich can be contacted via CompuServe (CompuServe ID 75277,2254).

Ori Gurewich holds a bachelor's degree in electrical engineering from Stony Brook University, Stony Brook, New York. His background includes working as a senior software engineer and as a software consultant engineer for companies, and developing professional multimedia and Windows applications. He is an expert in the field of PC programming and network communications, and has developed various multimedia algorithms for the PC. Ori Gurewich can be contacted via CompuServe (CompuServe ID 72072,312).

Introduction

This book teaches you how to use the Microsoft Visual Basic for Windows package. After reading this book you'll be able to write advanced Windows programs using the Visual Basic programming language.

Basic Doesn't Mean Simple

The word *Basic* in Visual Basic may be misleading. You might think that all serious Windows applications should be written using the C/C++ compiler and SDK for Windows.

However, this is not the case. After reading this book, you'll be able to write advanced Windows programs in a fraction of the time that it takes to write the same programs using other programming languages.

Visual Means Visual

As its name suggests, a big portion of the programming with Visual Basic is accomplished visually. This means that during design time, you are able to see how your program will look during runtime. This is a great advantage over other programming languages because you are able to change and experiment with your design until you are satisfied with the colors, sizes, and images that are included in your program.

Using Third-Party OLE Controls

Perhaps the most powerful feature of Visual Basic is its capability to incorporate third-party controls (known as OLE controls or OCXs). If you are unfamiliar with the concept of third-party OLE controls, be patient, this topic is covered in the book. For now, however, just remember this: Third-party OLE controls extend the capabilities of Visual Basic. No matter what application you are developing, if the programming feature you need is not included in the out-of-the-box Visual Basic package, you'll be able to add the feature by using a third-party control. For example, in this book you'll learn how to use a third-party OLE control to extend the capability of Visual Basic so your program will be able to play real voice and real music through the PC speaker without any additional hardware and without any drivers.

21 Chapters, 21 Days

The book is divided into 21 chapters, and you are expected to read and learn a chapter each day. However, many readers may feel confident enough to take 2 (or more) chapters in one day. The number of chapters you should read each day depends on your previous programming experience with Windows and/or any other programming language.

This book assumes no prior experience in Visual Basic. So take your time when reading the chapters, and be sure to learn and enter the code of all the programs covered in each chapter. Once you understand the programs, experiment with them for a while. That is, change and modify the code to see what happens when you alter the programs in some way. Remember, the only way to learn a programming language is to actually write programs.

At the end of each chapter you'll find quizzes and exercises. Be sure to perform these quizzes and exercises. (This book includes the solutions to all the quizzes and exercises.)

About Windows 16-Bit and 32-Bit Operating Systems

At first, there was the Intel 8086. This integrated circuit served as the CPU of the PC. As the popularity of PCs increased, Intel developed new CPUs such as the 80286, the 80386, the 80486, and the Pentium. Now here is the problem: When a programmer develops a program, he or she wants the program to work on every PC, no matter what CPU is used by the PC. This is also true with the operating system Windows. That is, Windows should work on an 80286, an 80386, an 80486, and a Pentium. The problem with this is that by making the program compatible with older CPUs, you are penalizing the newer CPUs.

To understand why that is, consider the case of maintaining speed limits when driving. Very old cars (say, from the beginning of the 20th Century) cannot exceed a speed of 40 miles per hour. Newer cars can drive safely at 55 miles per hour and more. Now suppose that the state keeps the laws compatible with very old cars as well as newer cars. Because it is unsafe to allow slow-moving vehicles on highways, the speed limits on highways would be 40 mph, so that it will be safe for old as well as new cars to drive. As you know, this is not the case. That is, when you enter a highway, typically you'll see a maximum speed limit sign as well as a minimum speed limit sign. So in a fact, the law penalizes the very old cars, so that the newer cars will be able to perform the way they were designed to perform.

This is exactly the situation with Windows. The so-called 16-bit Windows (such as Windows 3.1 and Windows for Workgroups 3.11) are designed for older CPUs. Sure, they will work well for the newer CPUs, but in a fact, it is as if you are driving a new car on a highway that was designed for very old cars.

The solution is to rewrite Windows. The new Windows is the so-called 32-bit Windows (such as Windows 95 and Windows NT). These operating systems do not work on PCs with older CPUs, but the advantage is that these 32-bit Windows are much more powerful than the 16-bit Windows. The terms 16-bit and 32-bit come from the fact that older CPUs were designed to process data in groups of 16 bits. Newer CPUs, on the other hand, process data in groups of 32 bits.

Because many people are still using 16-bit Windows, the Visual Basic package comes with two versions of Visual Basic: the 16-bit Visual Basic version (which was designed to work on 16-bit Windows), and the 32-bit Visual Basic version (which was designed to work on 32-bit Windows). So if you are using 16-bit Windows, install the 16-bit Visual Basic version, and if you are using 32-bit Windows, install the 32-bit Visual Basic.

As far as this book is concerned, it does not matter which version (16-bit or 32-bit) of Visual Basic you are using. Why? The 16-bit and 32-bit versions of Visual Basic are identical in the way you use them. Of course, the Visual Basic package and the programs you write with Visual Basic are faster when 32-bit technology is used.

As stated, it does not matter which version of Visual Basic or Windows you are using. There is, however, one small difference: The border and the title of the windows in 32-bit Windows are slightly different than the border and titles of the windows in 16-bit Windows. Also, some of the dialog boxes—such as the dialog boxes that let you select a file—look different in the 16-bit environment than in the 32-bit environment. However, this is a very minor difference, and as stated, you can use this book no matter which version (16- or 32-bit) you are using.

Device Independence

Windows is a very popular operating system. Why? It is a device-independent operating system. This means that no matter what printer you are using, as long as Windows accepted the printer at the time you installed the printer, the printer should work fine with every program you design. In fact, you the programmer do not care which printer is used. Again, as long as Windows has accepted the printer, your program should work fine with the installed printer. And this device-independent concept applies to other pieces of hardware. Therefore, no matter what sound card is used by your users, your programs will be able to work with the sound card without you knowing the name of the sound card's type. You'll realize this during the course of this book when you write programs that utilize the sound card. That is, there will be no mention of the type of the sound card or who manufactured the sound card.

Another thing that makes Windows so popular is the fact that the user interface is the same for all Windows applications. That is, the programs that you'll learn to design in this book are typical standard Windows programs that use regular Windows user interface. Therefore, you don't have to tell your user how to operate your programs. Your programs are Windows programs, so your user can use the Clipboard to cut, copy, and paste text and graphics; minimize and maximize the windows of your programs; and complete other conventional Windows operations.

WinG and Sprite Technology

So far, we have only said good things about Windows. However, until recently, Windows had a major flaw: It was too slow when it came to doing powerful graphics operations such as animation.

As you know, Windows is called a *graphics-based operating system.* This term means, for example, that the pushbutton is a graphic object, the check box is a graphic object, and so on. The term graphics-based does not mean that the graphics can move on the screen as is the case with animation programs. In fact, some of the better PC games on the market are designed to work on DOS (not on Windows). This is because DOS is very fast when it comes to moving graphics on the screen.

The slow graphic performances of Windows was solved by introducing the *WinG technology,* which enables you to design Windows graphics programs that let you move graphics at a very high speed (as fast as DOS). As you'll see in Chapter 20, "Sprite Animation, WinG, and 3D Virtual Reality," you can now design animation and 3D virtual reality programs in Windows by using WinG technology.

Final Words...

Visual Basic is interesting and fun because it enables you to write sophisticated professional programs for Windows in a very short time.

So relax, and prepare yourself for a very enjoyable journey.

During the course of this book, you'll write many Visual Basic programs. Therefore, you must install the Visual Basic package (if you haven't installed it yet). If you're using a 32-bit operating system such as Windows 95 or Windows NT, you need to install the 32-bit version of Visual Basic. If you're using a 16-bit operating system such as Windows 3.1 or Windows for Workgroups version 3.11, you need to install the 16-bit version of Visual Basic.

Where You're Going

Okay, you've installed Visual Basic successfully. Now what? In Chapter 1, "Writing Your First Program," you'll write your first Visual Basic program. This will give you insight into how easy it is to write a real Windows program with Visual Basic and why the package is called Visual Basic.

During the rest of the first week, you'll learn to write many more programs. Each program teaches you a new concept in Visual Basic and shows you how to apply the concept in your programs. As always, the only way to learn programming is to actually write programs, and Visual Basic is no exception.

1

Writing Your
First Program

In this chapter you'll write your first Visual Basic program. Writing Visual Basic programs involves two steps:

- The visual programming step
- The code programming step

During the *visual programming step,* you design your programs by using the tools that come with the Visual Basic package. These tools let you design your programs by using the mouse and the keyboard. To do visual programming, you don't have to do any code writing! All you have to know is how to operate and use the software tools of Visual Basic. As you'll soon see, the visual programming step amounts to a lot of clicking with your mouse, and it's a lot of fun! This chapter concentrates on learning how to use the visual tools of Visual Basic.

In the *code programming step* you write programs using a text editor. The programs are composed of statements written in the Visual Basic programming language. Writing code with Visual Basic is similar to writing code for other programming languages. However, writing code with Visual Basic is easier than with many other programming languages.

About This Chapter

If you browse through subsequent chapters of this book, you may notice that this chapter is not a typical chapter. This chapter concentrates on the visual programming aspect of Visual Basic, so it mainly emphasizes teaching you how to use the Visual Basic software tools. It is the job of subsequent chapters to teach you how to write code in the Visual Basic programming language.

Creating the Working Directory

Before starting the process of writing a Visual Basic program, you have to create a directory that will contain the files of your program. Throughout this chapter, it is assumed that you already have a directory called C:\VB4PRG\CH01 on your hard drive. You will be instructed to save files into this directory.

The Hello Program

In this chapter you'll write a Visual Basic program called Hello. Before writing the Hello program yourself, review its specifications. This way, you'll gain a better understanding of what the Hello program is supposed to do.

When you start the program, the window shown in Figure 1.1 appears. As you can see, the window contains three command buttons (Display Hello, Clear, and Exit) and an empty text box.

Figure 1.1.
The Hello program.

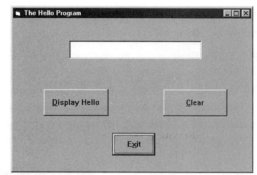

☐ When you click the Display Hello button, the text Hello World! is displayed in the text box. (See Figure 1.2.)

Figure 1.2.
Displaying text in the text box.

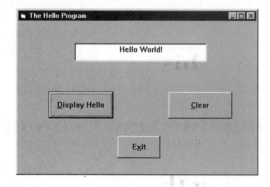

☐ When you click the Clear button, the Hello program clears the text in the text box.

☐ When you click the Exit button, the Hello program beeps and then terminates.

Creating a New Project

Now that you know what the Hello program is supposed to do, you can write the program.

Note: The Hello program is a very simple program; nevertheless, you must understand how to write the Hello program yourself because it's a typical Visual Basic program. In fact, once you learn how to write the Hello program yourself, you can say that you know Visual Basic! Sure, there's plenty of other Visual Basic information you need to know, but writing the Hello program by yourself means that you know the essentials of Visual Basic.

The very first thing that you need to do is create a new project for the Hello program by using the following steps:

☐ Start Visual Basic.

☐ Select New project from the File menu of Visual Basic.

> *Visual Basic responds by displaying various windows on the desktop. One of the windows displayed is a blank form with a caption, Form1. (See Figure 1.3.) Your job is to use the various tools of Visual Basic until the blank form looks like the form shown in Figure 1.1.*

Figure 1.3.
The blank form.

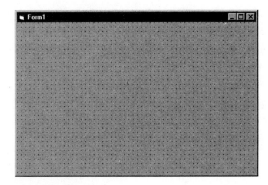

Saving the New Project

Although you haven't made any changes or modifications to the blank form yet, you should save the project at this early stage of the design. When you save the project, two files are saved:

- The project file. This file has the .VBP file extension, and it contains information Visual Basic uses for building the project.

- The form file. This file has the .FRM file extension, and it contains information about the form.

Now use the following steps to save the two files of the Hello project, Hello.vbp (the project file) and Hello.frm (the form file):

☐ Select Save Project As from the File menu.

> *Visual Basic displays the dialog box shown in Figure 1.4, asking if you want to save the form.*

Figure 1.4.
Saving the form.

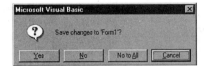

☐ Select the Yes button to indicate that you want to save the form.

Visual Basic responds by displaying a Save File As dialog box.

☐ Select the directory C:\VB4PRG\CH01 as the directory where the file will be saved, and change the default filename of the form from Form1.frm to Hello.frm. (See Figure 1.5.)

Figure 1.5.
Saving the form as Hello.frm.

☐ Click the Save button of the Save File As dialog box.

Visual Basic now displays the Save Project As dialog box.

DO	DON'T

DON'T use the default name that Visual Basic supplies when saving a form. Instead, save the form by a name appropriate to the application you're designing. For example, now you are designing the Hello program. Therefore, it is appropriate to name the form of the program Hello.frm.

The default filename that Visual Basic supplies is Project1.vbp. However, you need to name the project file with a name that is more appropriate to the particular application you're developing.

☐ Save the project file as Hello.vbp in the directory C:\VB4PRG\CH01. (See Figure 1.6.)

☐ Click the Save button of the Save Project As dialog box.

Figure 1.6.
Saving the project file as Hello.vbp.

DO	DON'T

DON'T use the default name that Visual Basic supplies when you save a project file. Instead, save the file by a name appropriate to the application you're designing. For example, now you are designing a program that displays the text Hello. So an appropriate name for the project is Hello.vbp.

Now you have saved two files: Hello.vbp (the project file) and Hello.frm (the form file).

Examining the Project Window

At this point, your project is called Hello.vbp, and it consists of a single form file: the Hello.frm file. However, in subsequent chapters your project will contain more files.

One of the tools that Visual Basic offers is the project window, which enables you to see the various files that are included in the project. (You'll learn to appreciate this feature as your projects get more complicated.)

Use the following steps to examine the project window:

☐ Select Project from the View menu. (See Figure 1.7.)

The project window pops up, as shown in Figure 1.8.

The title of the project window contains part of the name of the project. Because you saved the project as Hello.vbp, the title of the project window is Hello.

The files that appear in the project window are the names of the forms that the project contains. Because you saved the form as Hello.frm, this is the file that appears in the project window.

Figure 1.7.
The View menu.

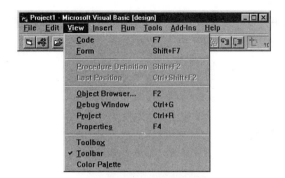

Figure 1.8.
The project window.

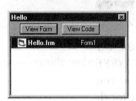

Changing the Caption Property of the Form

The blank form that was created by Visual Basic has the caption Form1, shown in Figure 1.3. This is the default caption that Visual Basic assigned to the new blank form. Although you may leave the caption of the form as Form1, it is a good idea to assign a friendlier caption to the form. As shown in Figure 1.1, the caption of the finished form should be The Hello Program.

Here is how you change the caption of the blank form to The Hello Program:

☐ Make sure the blank form is selected. You can easily recognize whether the form is selected by examining its caption. If the caption is highlighted, the form is selected. (In Visual Basic, the *title* of the window is also called the *caption* of the window.)

If the form is not selected, simply click anywhere inside the form, or you can select Project from the View menu, highlight the Hello.frm item in the project window, and click the View Form button that appears in the project window.

☐ Select Properties from the View menu.

Visual Basic responds by displaying the properties window. (See Figure 1.9.)

☐ Click the cell that appears to the right of the Caption cell in the properties window.

Figure 1.9.

The properties window.

☐ This cell currently has in it the text Form1. Use the Delete and arrow keys on your keyboard to delete the text Form1 and replace it by typing the text The Hello Program. The properties window should now look like the one shown in Figure 1.10.

Figure 1.10.

Changing the Caption property of the form.

Congratulations! You have just completed changing the Caption property of the form. Take a look at the blank form. Now its caption is The Hello Program.

What Is a Property?

The caption is just one of the properties of the form. As you can see from the properties window, the form has many other properties. To understand what a property is, you have to understand that Visual Basic programs deal with *objects,* such as forms, command buttons, scroll bars, and pictures.

The *properties* of an object define how the object looks and behaves. For example, a form is an object. The Caption property of the form defines the text that appears in the title (caption) of

the form. Another property of the form object is BackColor, which defines the background color of the form. Use the following steps to change the form's BackColor property:

☐ Make sure the form is selected by clicking anywhere inside the form.

☐ To display the properties window, select Properties from the View menu.

☐ Click the cell to the right of the BackColor property in the properties window.

> *When you click this cell, Visual Basic places a down-arrow icon in the cell. (See Figure 1.11.)*

Figure 1.11.
The BackColor property.

☐ Click the down-arrow icon that appears in the cell.

> *Visual Basic responds by displaying a color palette window. (See Figure 1.12.)*

Figure 1.12.
The color palette.

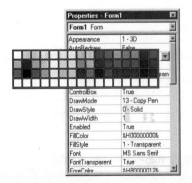

☐ Select the color of your choice by clicking on it.

DO	**DON'T**

DO examine the cell that appears to the right of the property cell that you want to set. If the cell has an arrow icon in it, clicking the arrow icon displays a window or a list that lets you select a value with the mouse.

Try a few colors by repeating the process until you are happy with your color selection.

Changing the Name Property of the Form

Each object in Visual Basic must have a name, which is defined in the Name property of the object. When you created the new form of the Hello program, Visual Basic automatically set the Name property of the form as Form1.

Now change the Name property of the form:

☐ Make sure the form is selected by clicking anywhere inside the form.

☐ Select Properties from the View menu.

☐ Highlight the Name property in the properties window. (You might have to use the vertical scroll bar of the properties window to scroll the list until you see the Name property on the left column. Note that the properties are sorted alphabetically.)

☐ Click in the cell that appears to the right of the Name property. Visual Basic now lets you edit the Name property.

☐ Replace the name Form1 by typing the name frmHello.

In the preceding step, you changed the Name property of the form from Form1 to frmHello. Throughout this book, the first three characters of the Name property of objects are three letters that indicate the type of object. Therefore, the first three characters of the Name property of a form are *frm,* as in frmHello.

DO	**DON'T**

DO change the default names of objects so their names reflect their purposes in the program. For example, frmHello is the name of a form used by the Hello program. This is not a Visual Basic requirement, but it will make the program easier to read and understand.

Saving Your Work

You haven't finished preparing the form yet. (Remember that upon completion, the form should look like the one shown in Figure 1.1.) Nevertheless, it's a good idea to save the work you have done so far, because you'll have to start designing the form all over again if your PC system collapses before you your work. This is especially true when working in the Windows environment. And, as you'll see in subsequent chapters, designing forms may involve opening and executing other Windows applications such as Paint and Word for Windows. If one of these other applications collapses, it may take down the whole system with it. So be safe—save your work from time to time.

Use the following step to save your work:

☐ Select Save Project from the File menu.

Adding the Exit Button to the frmHello Form

As shown in Figure 1.1, the final form should have three command buttons in it: Display Hello, Clear, and Exit.

Note: In some Windows literature, command buttons are also referred to as *push buttons*. However, this book calls them command buttons, because this is the terminology used in Visual Basic.

To place a command button in your form, you have to pick it up from the toolbox window.

The Toolbox Window

The toolbox window contains icons of various objects. It is your job to pick up an object from the toolbox window and place it in your form.

To display the toolbox window, select Toolbox from the View menu of Visual Basic.

Figure 1.13 shows the toolbox window. Depending on the particular version of Visual Basic you are using, the toolbox window may have fewer (or more) items in it.

One of the objects in the toolbox window—the command button—is shown magnified in Figure 1.13. You can easily recognize the various objects in the toolbox window by placing the mouse cursor (without clicking the mouse) on the object you want to examine. Visual Basic responds by displaying a small yellow rectangle with the object's name in it.

Figure 1.13.
The toolbox window, with the command button magnified.

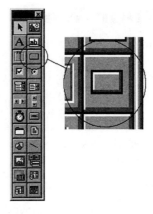

Placing the Exit Button in the Form

Use the following step to place a command button in the form:

☐ Double-click the command button icon in the toolbox window. (Figure 1.13 shows the icon of the command button in the toolbox window.)

> *Visual Basic responds by placing a command button in the center of the form. (See Figure 1.14.)*

Visual Basic assigns various default properties to the command button you placed in the form. For example, the default Caption property of this command button is Command1.

Visual Basic also assigns the default name Command1 to the Name property of the command button.

Figure 1.14.
Placing a command button in the frmHello form.

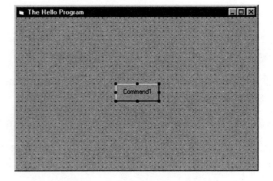

Changing the Name Property of the Exit Button

Because the command button that you just placed in the form serves as the Exit button, change its Name property to cmdExit:

☐ Select Properties from the View menu.

☐ Make sure that the object box of the properties window displays the Command1 command button. (See Figure 1.15 for the location of the object box.)

Figure 1.15.
The properties of the command button.

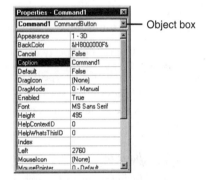

Object box

Note: Currently, the form has two objects: the form frmHello and the command button Command1. The properties window lists the properties of the object whose name currently appears in the object box shown in Figure 1.15. To switch to another object, click on the down-arrow icon of the object box and select the desired object from the list that drops down. (See Figure 1.16.)

Figure 1.16.
Selecting an object.

Click this down-arrow icon to drop down a list of all the objects in the form.

☐ Change the Name property of Command1 from Command1 to cmdExit.

Note the naming convention for the Name property of the command button. Because the object is a command button, the first three characters of its name are *cmd*. Also, because this command button serves as the Exit button, its full name is cmdExit. This naming convention is not a Visual Basic requirement, but it makes your program easier to read and understand.

Changing the Caption Property of the Exit Button

The default caption that Visual Basic assigns to the command button is Command1. Because this command button is the Exit button, a more appropriate caption is Exit.

☐ Change the Caption property of cmdExit from Command1 to E&xit.

The & character (which you type by pressing Shift+7) before the *x* in E&xit causes Visual Basic to display the *x* underlined, as shown in Figure 1.1. When you execute the program, pressing Alt+x produces the same result as clicking the Exit button.

Note: When setting the Caption property of a button, always insert an & character as a prefix before one of the characters in the caption's name. This underlines the prefixed character, and during execution time, your users will be able to either click the button or press Alt+*key* (where *key* is the underlined character).

Changing the Location of the Exit Button

As you can see from Figure 1.1, the Exit button should be near the bottom of the form.

☐ Drag the Exit button to the desired location by clicking anywhere inside the Exit button and, without releasing the mouse's left button, moving the mouse.

Changing the Font Properties of the Exit Button

As shown in Figure 1.1, the font of the Exit button is different from the default font that Visual Basic assigned to the caption of the button that you placed in the form. Use the following steps to change the font of the cmdExit button:

☐ Click the cell to the right of the Font property. As you can see, the cell has an icon with three dots in it.

> *Clicking the three-dots icon will open a new dialog box that lets you select certain values from it.*

☐ Click the three-dots icon of the Font property of the cmdExit button.

> *Visual Basic responds by displaying the Font dialog box.*

☐ Change the font to System.

☐ Change the size of the font to 10.

☐ Click the OK button of the Font dialog box.

Take a look at the Exit button. Its caption has the text font you set with the Font dialog box!

Note: One of the main advantages of Visual Basic is that you instantly see the results of your visual programming. Always experiment and try different options (that is, try different fonts, different sizes, different colors, and so on) until you are satisfied with the results.

Adding the Other Buttons to the frmHello Form

Now it's time to add two more command buttons to the form: the Display Hello button and the Clear button.

Placing the Buttons in the Form

☐ Add the Display Hello button to the form by double-clicking the command button icon in the toolbox window. Now drag the new command button to the left. (This button serves as the Display Hello button.)

☐ Double-click the command button icon in the toolbox window again, then drag the new command button to the right. (This button serves as the Clear button.)

Resizing the Buttons

The default sizes of the Display Hello and the Clear buttons are smaller than the size of the buttons shown in Figure 1.1.

☐ Enlarge the new two buttons that you placed in the form. To enlarge or shrink an object, select the object by clicking on it. Once an object is selected, Visual Basic encloses the selected object with a rectangle. The rectangle has eight little black squares on it, which are called *handles*. Drag one of the handles until the object reaches the size you want. For example, to resize an object horizontally, drag one of its handles horizontally; to resize an object vertically, drag one of its handles vertically. (See Figure 1.17.)

Figure 1.17.
Resizing an object.

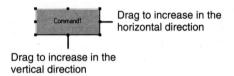

Drag to increase in the horizontal direction

Drag to increase in the vertical direction

Changing the Name Properties

The default names that Visual Basic assigned to the command buttons you just placed in the form are Command1 and Command2. More appropriate names are cmdHello and cmdClear.

☐ Change the Name property of the left command button to cmdHello.

☐ Change the Name property of the right command button to cmdClear.

Changing the Caption Properties

As shown in Figure 1.1, the left button should have the caption Display Hello, and the right button should have the caption Clear.

☐ Change the Caption property of the left button to &Display Hello.

☐ Change the Caption property of the right button to &Clear.

Changing the Font Properties

As shown in Figure 1.1, the Display Hello and Clear buttons should have a different font and font size from the default font that Visual Basic assigned to your command buttons.

☐ Change the Font property of the cmdHello button to System and the font size to 10.

☐ Change the Font property of the cmdClear button to System and the font size to 10.

After setting the font, you may discover that the button's area is too small. In this case, simply enlarge the size of the button by dragging its handles.

Adding the Text Box Object to the frmHello Form

There is one more object to add to the form: the *text box object*. A text box object is a rectangular area in which text is displayed. Its text may be inserted in the text box during design time or at execution time. In Windows terminology, a text box is also referred to as an edit box.

Placing the Text Box in the Form

In Figure 1.13, the text box object is the second object from the top in the right column of the toolbox window. Depending on your particular edition of Visual Basic, the locations of the objects in the toolbox window may be different from the locations shown in Figure 1.13.

Use the following steps to place the text box in the form:

☐ Double-click the text box icon object in the toolbox window.

☐ Move and resize the text box until it looks like the text box shown in Figure 1.1.

Changing the Properties of the Text Box

Use the following steps to modify several properties of the text box:

☐ Change the Name property of the text box from the default name Text1 to txtDisplay.

☐ The default Text property of the text box is Text1, so when you execute the Hello program, the text Text1 appears in the text box. Because you want the text box to be empty when you start the program, delete the text that appears in the cell to the right of the Text property of the txtDisplay object.

☐ Change the Font property of the txtDisplay text box to System and the font size to 10.

☐ The default Alignment property of the text box is 0-Left Justify, which means that the text in the text box is aligned to the left. Because you want the text to appear in the center of the text box, change the alignment property to 2-Center.

☐ As it turns out, Visual Basic refuses to place the text in the center of the text box unless the MultiLine property of the text box is set to True. So, besides setting the Alignment property to 2-Center, you must also change the MultiLine property to True. If you set the MultiLine property to True, Visual Basic can display more than one line in the text box. So go ahead and change the MultiLine property of the txtDisplay text box to True.

Building Forms from Figures and Tables

The visual programming portion is now completed. To save your work, select Save Project from the File menu.

Throughout this book you will be instructed to build many other forms. However, this book does not teach you to construct the form the same way you were taught to build the frmHello form. Instead, you'll have to build the form by looking at a completed form, such as the one shown in Figure 1.1, and following a properties table. A *properties table* contains all the objects included in the form and lists objects' properties that are different from the default properties.

Your job is to follow the table, line by line, and change the properties' values to the values that appear in the table. Table 1.1 is the properties table of the frmHello Form.

Table 1.1. The properties table of the frmHello program.

Object	Property	Setting
Form	**Name**	**frmHello**
	BackColor	Gray
	Caption	The Hello Program
Command Button	**Name**	**cmdExit**
	Caption	E&xit
	FontName	System
	FontSize	10
Command Button	**Name**	**cmdClear**
	Caption	&Clear
	FontName	System
	FontSize	10
Command Button	**Name**	**cmdHello**
	Caption	&Display Hello
	FontName	System
	FontSize	10
Text Box	**Name**	**txtDisplay**
	Alignment	2-Center
	FontName	System
	FontSize	10
	MultiLine	True

Attaching Code to the Objects

Because you placed the objects in the form and set their properties, the visual programming part of the job is completed. Now it's time to attach some code to the objects.

Visual Basic is an event-driven programming language. This means that code is executed as a response to an event. For example, if you click the Exit button during the execution of the Hello program, a Click event is automatically generated, and the code that corresponds to the Exit button's Click event is executed.

Likewise, if you click the Display Hello button, a Click event is generated, and the code that corresponds to the Click event of the Display Hello button is automatically executed.

Your job is to write the appropriate code and attach it to the object and event. Does this sound complicated? Well, it's actually very easy! Start by attaching some code to the Exit button.

Attaching Code to the Exit Button

Use the following steps to attach code to the cmdExit button:

☐ Double-click the cmdExit button.

Visual Basic responds by displaying the code window (you write code in this window) shown in Figure 1.18.

Figure 1.18.
Attaching code to the cmdExit button in the code window.

Visual Basic makes it very easy for you to recognize which code is currently being displayed in the code window. As shown in Figure 1.18, the top-left combo box displays the name of the object (cmdExit) and the top-right combo box displays the name of the event (Click).

As you can see from Figure 1.18, Visual Basic already placed two lines of code in the code window:

```
Private Sub cmdExit_Click ()

End Sub
```

You'll write your code between these two lines.

The First and Last Lines of the Code

The first line of code, which Visual Basic already wrote for you, starts with the words `Private Sub`. `Sub` is a keyword indicating where a procedure starts. A *procedure* is code dedicated for a particular event. The name of this procedure is `cmdExit_Click()`.

The last line of code, also written by Visual Basic, is `End Sub`, which marks the end of the procedure.

The Name of the Procedure

The name of the procedure is `cmdExit_Click()`. Why did Visual Basic assign this name to the procedure? Because you double-clicked the cmdExit button, Visual Basic knows that you are attempting to attach code to the Exit button. Therefore, the first half of the procedure name is `cmdExit_`.

The second half of the procedure name is `_Click()`. Why did Visual Basic assign this name? Because the event you're writing code for is the `Click` event.

As you can see, the last two characters of the procedure name are the parentheses.

The Code of the cmdExit_Click() Procedure

What code should you write in the `cmdExit_Click()` procedure? Because this procedure is executed whenever you click the Exit button, the code to be inserted in this procedure should cause the program to exit, or *terminate*. The code that causes a Visual Basic program to terminate is the `End` statement.

☐ Type `End` in the `cmdExit_Click()` procedure. After typing the `End` statement, the `cmdExit_Click()` procedure should look as follows:

```
Sub cmdExit_Click()

    End

End Sub
```

That's all—you've just finished attaching code to the `cmdExit_Click()` procedure.

Executing the Hello Program

Although you haven't finished attaching code to the rest of the objects, you can now execute the Hello program and see how the code you attached to the Exit button works for you.

☐ Save your work by selecting Save Project from the File menu.

☐ Select Start from the Run menu of Visual Basic.

> *Visual Basic responds by executing your program. The window of the application pops up, as shown in Figure 1.1.*

You may now click the Display Hello button, but nothing will happen. Why? Because you haven't attached any code to this button. If you click the Clear button, nothing happens because you haven't attached any code to this object either.

Now click the Exit button. In response to the clicking, the code of the procedure cmdExit_Click() is executed.

Because the code in this procedure consists of code that causes the program to terminate, the Hello program terminates.

Attaching More Code to the *cmdExit_Click()* Procedure

Use the following steps to attach more code in the cmdExit_Click() procedure:

☐ Double-click the cmdExit button.

> *Visual Basic responds by displaying the cmdExit_Click() procedure.*

☐ Add the Beep statement before the End statement as follows:

```
Private Sub cmdExit_Click()

    Beep
    End

End Sub
```

☐ Save your work by selecting Save Project from the File menu.

☐ Execute the Hello program by selecting Start from the Run menu of Visual Basic.

The Beep statement causes the PC to beep. So whenever you click the Exit button, the PC beeps and then the End statement is executed, causing the Hello program to terminate.

☐ Click the Exit button and verify that the program beeps and then the program terminates itself.

Attaching Code to the Display Hello Button

Use the following steps to attach code to the Display Hello button.

☐ Double-click the Display Hello button.

Visual Basic responds by displaying the `cmdHello_Click()` *procedure with two lines of code already written:*

```
Private Sub cmdHello_Click ()

End Sub
```

The preceding procedure is executed whenever you click the Display Hello button during the execution of the Hello program.

So what code should you insert in this procedure? It depends on what you want to happen when you click the Display Hello button. In the Hello program, you want the program to display the words `Hello World!` in the text box.

☐ Type the code

```
txtDisplay.Text = "Hello World!"
```

in the `cmdHello_Click()` procedure. When you finish, the procedure should look like this:

```
Private Sub cmdHello_Click()

    txtDisplay.Text = "Hello World!"

End Sub
```

`txtDisplay` is the name of the text box object (the text box in which the words `Hello World!` will be displayed).

The statement

```
txtDisplay.Text = "Hello World!"
```

assigns the value `Hello World!` to the Text property of txtDisplay. (The Text property of a text box contains the text it displays.)

Note: To assign a new value to a property from within the program's code, use the following format:

```
ObjectName.Property = "New value of the property"
```

For example, to change the Text property of the txtDisplay text box to `Hello World!`, use the following code:

```
txtDisplay.Text = "Hello World!"
```
Note the dot (.) that appears between the name of the object (txtDisplay) and the name of the property (Text).

Attaching Code to the Clear Button

Use the following steps to attach code to the Clear button.

☐ Double-click the Clear button.

>   *Visual Basic responds by displaying the code window with the* cmdClear_Click() *procedure in it.*

The code of this procedure should clear the text box. In other words, the Text property of the txtDisplay text box should change to null. You do this by inserting the following statement in the procedure:

```
txtDisplay.Text = ""
```

☐ Type the statement

```
    txtDisplay.Text = ""
```

in the procedure so that the procedure looks as follows:

```
Private Sub cmdClear_Click()

        txtDisplay.Text = ""

End Sub
```

☐ Save your work by selecting Save Project from the File menu.

Executing the Hello Program

The Hello program is complete. Use the following steps to execute the program:

☐ Select Start from the Run menu or press F5 to start the program.

☐ Click the Display Hello and Clear buttons to display and clear the words Hello World! in the text box.

☐ You can use the keys Alt+D and Alt+C to get the same results as clicking the Display Hello and Clear buttons.

☐ To terminate the program, click the Exit button.

Note that the text box displays the text centered in System font, because during the design time, you set the Font property to System and the Alignment property to 2-Center.

Other Events

The Hello program uses the Click event of the command buttons. There are other events that a Visual Basic program can use. Each event has its own procedure.

The *KeyDown* Event

Let's look at the procedure that corresponds to the KeyDown event, which occurs whenever you press a key on the keyboard.

To see the KeyDown procedure of the Exit button do the following:

☐ Double-click the Exit button.

> *By default, Visual Basic displays the procedure that corresponds to the Click event.*

☐ Because you want to look at the procedure that corresponds to the KeyDown event, switch to the KeyDown procedure by clicking the Proc combo box.

> *Visual Basic responds by dropping down a list that contains all the possible events associated with the cmdExit object. (See Figure 1.19.)*

Figure 1.19.

Selecting the event for the cmdExit button.

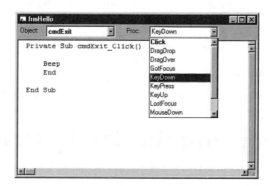

☐ Click the KeyDown item in the list.

> *Visual Basic responds by displaying the cmdExit_KeyDown procedure:*

```
Private Sub cmdExit_KeyDown(KeyCode As Integer, _
                            Shift As Integer)

End Sub
```

The first line of the procedure that Visual Basic automatically writes for the KeyDown event is a little different from the first line for the Click event. That is, the parentheses of the cmdExit_Click() procedure do not have anything in them. However, the parentheses of the cmdExit_KeyDown() procedure do contain code. We'll discuss this difference in later chapters of this book.

At this point, do not add any code to the cmdExit_KeyDown() procedure. (You went through this exercise to become familiar with accessing the procedures of other events.)

Creating an Executable File (HELLO.EXE)

Earlier, you executed the Hello program by selecting Start from the Run menu. Naturally, you don't want your users to execute the program this way (your users may not even own the Visual Basic package).

To be able to distribute the Hello program, you need to generate the EXE file HELLO.EXE:

☐ Select Make EXE File from the File menu.

> *Visual Basic responds by displaying the Make EXE File dialog box. (Don't click the OK button in the dialog box yet.)*

☐ Save the file as HELLO.EXE in the C:\VB4PRG\CH01\HELLO.EXE directory and then click the OK button.

> *Visual Basic responds by saving the file HELLO.EXE in the directory C:\VB4PRG\CH01.*

You may now execute HELLO.EXE just as you would any other Windows program!

Summary

In this chapter you have written your first Visual Basic program. You have learned about the steps necessary to write a Visual Basic program: the visual programming step and the code programming step.

In the visual programming step, you place objects in the form and set their properties.

In the code programming step, you select a procedure by selecting the object and the event, and then you insert code in the procedure. This code is executed during runtime whenever the event occurs.

Q&A

Q The title of this book is *Teach Yourself Visual Basic 4 in 21 Days.* **Can I read and learn the book in fewer (or more) days?**

A Yes. Some people work through a couple of chapters each day. You should learn at your own pace.

Q **Can I write professional programs using Visual Basic?**

A Yes. Visual Basic is designed so you can write fancy, advanced Windows applications in a very short time.

Q **What is the difference between a command button and a push button?**

A Push buttons and command buttons are the same thing. Visual Basic literature refers to these objects as command buttons (other Windows literature sometimes calls them push buttons).

Q **I get confused! There are many windows on the desktop: form, project, properties, toolbox, color palette, and so on. Is there any good trick for finding and selecting a particular window?**

A At any point during your design, you can select Project from the View menu. This pops up the project window.

You can now highlight the Form item in the project window, then click either the View Form button to display the form or the View Code button to display the code window.

If you click View Form, the form is selected, and you may then pop up the properties window by selecting Properties from the View menu, or pop up the toolbox window by selecting the Toolbox item from the View menu.

After practicing for a while, you'll be able to maneuver among the various windows without any difficulty.

Quiz

1. What are the two steps in the design process of a Visual Basic program?
2. What is the first thing you have to do when writing a new Visual Basic program?
3. Give several examples of objects and their properties.
4. Which of the following is not a Visual Basic object?
   a. command button
   b. form
   c. variable
   d. text box

5. Describe how you attach code to an object.

6. BUG BUSTER: There is something wrong in the following statement:

   ```
   txtDisplay.Text = Hi there!
   ```

   What's wrong with it?

Exercise

Build the form shown in Figure 1.20 from Table 1.2. After you finish, attach code to the Click event of the Exit button so that when the user clicks the Exit button, the program terminates.

Table 1.2. The properties table of Exercise 1.

Object	Property	Setting
Form	**Name**	**frmEX1**
	Caption	The Exercise 1 Program
Horizontal Scroll Bar	**Name**	**hsbMyScrollBar**
	Max	100
	Min	0
Command Button	**Name**	**cmdExit**
	Caption	E&xit
	FontName	System
	FontSize	10
Check Box	**Name**	**chkMyCheckBox**
	Caption	Check1
	FontName	System
	FontSize	10
Check Box	**Name**	**chkOurCheckBox**
	Caption	Check2
	FontName	System
	FontSize	10

Figure 1.20.
The form of Exercise 1 in design mode.

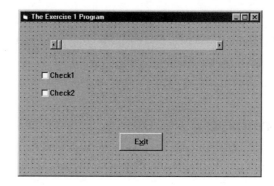

Quiz Answers

1. These are the two steps:

   The visual programming step. In this step, you place objects in the form and set their properties.

   The code programming step. In this step, you write and attach code to objects and events.

2. The first thing you have to do when writing a new Visual Basic program is open a new project from the File menu.

3. A command button is an example of an object. Use the following steps to see its properties:

   ☐ Open a new project.

   ☐ Double-click the command button icon in the toolbox.

   > *Visual Basic responds by placing the button in the form.*

   ☐ Open the properties window for the command button (that is, select Properties from the View menu) and browse through the properties of the command button. As you can see, the command button has many properties.

   Repeat the above process for other objects.

4. c. A variable is not an object. (Variables are discussed in later chapters.)

5. Do the following to attach code to an object:

   ☐ Double-click the object you placed in the form.

   > *Visual Basic responds by displaying the code window for this object.*

   ☐ Select the event by clicking the Proc combo box shown in Figure 1.19.

You can now attach code to the object by typing it between the `Private Sub` and `End Sub` lines of the procedure.

6. This is the correct syntax:

```
txtDisplay.Text = "Hi there!"
```

That is, you must enclose the text within double quotation marks.

Exercise Answer

☐ Start a new project.

☐ Select Save Project As from the File menu.

Visual Basic responds by asking if you want to save the form.

☐ Click the Yes button (that is, you want to save the form).

Visual Basic responds by displaying the Save File As dialog box.

☐ Save the form as EX1.FRM in the C:\VB4PRG\CH01 directory.

Visual Basic responds by saving the file and displaying another dialog box that lets you save the project file.

☐ Save the project file as EX1.VBP in the C:\VB4PRG\CH01 directory.

The first item in Table 1.2 is the form. As you can see from Table 1.2, you need to set two properties for the form. Use the following steps to set the form's Name property to frmEX1:

☐ Make sure the form is selected (that is, the title of the form is highlighted). To select the form, click anywhere inside the form.

☐ Select Properties from the View menu.

Visual Basic responds by displaying the properties window of the form.

☐ Select the Name property in the properties window and set its value to frmEX1.

Use the following steps to change the Caption property of the form:

☐ Select the Caption property from the properties window and set its value to The Exercise 1 Program.

The next item in the properties table of Table 1.2 is the horizontal scroll bar.

Use the following steps to place the horizontal scroll bar in the form:

☐ Double-click the horizontal scroll bar icon in the toolbox. In Figure 1.13, this icon is shown in the toolbox on the left column, sixth from the top.

Visual Basic responds by placing the horizontal scroll bar in the form.

☐ Drag and size the scroll bar so that it looks like the one shown in Figure 1.20.

☐ Make sure the scroll bar is selected and then select Properties from the View menu.

Visual Basic responds by displaying the properties window of the scroll bar.

You may now set the Name, Min, and Max properties of the horizontal scroll bar according to the specifications in Table 1.2.

In a similar manner, place all the other objects listed in Table 1.2 and set their properties. The icon of the check box object is shown in Figure 1.13 on the left column, fourth from the top.

To attach code to the cmdExit button do the following:

☐ Double click the Exit button.

Visual Basic responds by displaying the cmdExit_Click() *procedure for you to edit.*

☐ Type the code in the cmdExit_Click() procedure. After typing the code, the cmdExit_Click() procedure should look like this:

```
Private Sub cmdExit_Click()

    End

End Sub
```

☐ Save your work by selecting Save Project from the File menu.

☐ Select Start from the Run menu to execute the EX1 program.

☐ Experiment with the EX1 program, and then click the Exit button to terminate the program. Note that you didn't attach any code to the scroll bar and the check boxes. The point of the exercise is just to demonstrate how you place objects in the form.

2

Properties and Controls

This chapter focuses on Visual Basic *controls,* such as scroll bars, text boxes, option buttons, and command buttons. You'll learn how to include these controls in your programs, how to change their properties, and how to attach code to them.

Most programs output information to the user and get information from the user. The process of outputting and inputting information is called the *user interface* aspect of the program. Windows programs use controls to provide easy and pleasant user interface (that's one of the reasons for the popularity of Windows). In this chapter you'll learn that implementing a fancy user interface is very easy in Visual Basic.

The Scroll Bar Control

The scroll bar is a commonly used control in Windows programs. Using this object enables the user to select a value by positioning the thumb (the square tab) of the scroll bar to a desired position (instead of typing the desired value).

Note: In Chapter 1, "Writing Your First Program," the scroll bar was called an *object.* In this chapter and in the remaining chapters of this book, it will usually be referred to as a *control.*

In most cases, an object is also a control, but not always. For example, a form is an object, but it isn't a control. Typically, you call an object a control if the object can be placed in a form.

The Speed Program

The Speed program illustrates how a scroll bar is used for getting a value from the user.

The Speed program should do the following things:

- When the Speed program is started, the form shown in Figure 2.1 should pop up. The thumb of the scroll bar should be positioned at the center of the scroll bar (the default position), and the text box should display a speed value of 50 mph (the default value).
- When you change the thumb's position on the scroll bar, the text box should reflect the change. For example, when the thumb is placed at the extreme left, the text box should display the value 0; when the thumb is placed at the extreme right, the text box should display the value 100.
- To exit the program, click the Exit button.

Figure 2.1.
The Speed program.

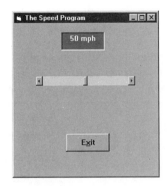

The Visual Implementation of the Speed Program

The Speed program uses the horizontal scroll bar control. To see which item in the toolbox window represents the horizontal scroll bar control, refer to Figure 1.13 in Chapter 1. The exact location of the icon in the toolbox varies from version to version, but in Figure 1.13, the horizontal scroll bar icon is shown on the left column, sixth from the top.

☐ Open a new project by selecting New Project from the File menu.

☐ Save the new form of the project as SPEED.FRM in the C:\VB4PRG\CH02 directory, and save the project file of the project as SPEED.VBP in the C:\VB4PRG\CH02 directory. (That is, select Save Project As from the File menu. When Visual Basic asks if you want to save the form, click the Yes button, and when the Save File As dialog box pops up, save the file as SPEED.FRM. When Visual Basic displays the Save As dialog box for saving the project file, save it as SPEED.VBP.)

☐ Build the frmSpeed form using the specifications in Table 2.1.

The completed form should look like the one shown in Figure 2.1.

☐ From Chapter 1 you should recall that to place a control in a form, you have to double-click the control's icon in the toolbox.

Visual Basic responds by placing the control in the middle of the form. You then move the control by dragging it with the mouse. You enlarge or shrink the control by dragging its handles.

☐ To access the properties of the control, make sure that the control you placed in the form is selected and select Properties from the View menu or press F4.

Visual Basic responds by displaying the properties window for the control. You can then change the control's properties.

☐ Save the project by selecting Save Project from the File menu.

Table 2.1. The properties table of the frmSpeed form.

Object	Property	Setting
Form	Name	frmSpeed
	BackColor	Light gray
	Caption	The Speed Program
	Height	4545
	Left	1080
	Top	1170
	Width	4125
Command Button	Name	cmdExit
	Caption	E&xit
	Height	495
	Left	1440
	Top	3000
	Width	1215
Horizontal Scroll Bar	Name	hsbSpeed
	Height	255
	Left	600
	Min	0
	Max	100
	Top	1440
	Value	50
	Width	2775
Text Box	Name	txtSpeed
	Alignment	2-Center
	BackColor	Red
	ForeColor	White
	Height	495
	Left	1320

Object	Property	Setting
	MultiLine	True
	Text	50 mph
	Top	240
	Width	1215

Entering the Code of the Speed Program

Now enter the code of the Speed program:

☐ Enter the following code in the cmdExit_Click() procedure of the frmSpeed form:

```
Private Sub cmdExit_Click()

    End

End Sub
```

Note: To enter the code, double-click the Exit button. Visual Basic responds by displaying the code window of the cmdExit_Click() procedure, where you can type the code.

☐ Save the project by selecting Save Project from the File menu.

Executing the Speed Program

Although you haven't finished writing the code of the Speed program yet, execute the Speed program to see what you have accomplished so far:

☐ To execute the Speed program, you may press F5, select Start from the Run menu, or click the Start icon. (See Figure 2.2 for the location of the Run icon.)

The form of the Speed program pops up, as shown in Figure 2.1.

☐ Change the scroll bar's thumb position by clicking the right- and left-arrow icons of the scroll bar.

As you can see, nothing is happening in the text box! Why? Because you haven't attached any code that changes the contents of the text box in accordance with the scroll bar position.

☐ Click the Exit button to terminate the program.

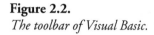
Figure 2.2.

The toolbar of Visual Basic.

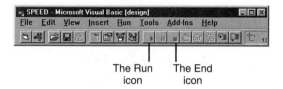

The Min, Max, and Value Properties of the Scroll Bar

Table 2.1 lists some new properties not covered in Chapter 1. The following sections review these properties.

The Min and Max Properties

A scroll bar represents a set of values. The Min property represents the minimum value, and the Max property represents the maximum value. As shown in Table 2.1, the Min property is set to 0, and the Max property is set to 100. This means that the scroll bar may be set to any value between 0 and 100.

The Value Property

The Value property of the scroll bar represents the current value of the scroll bar, so the Value property of the scroll bar may be any integer number between 0 and 100. When you execute the Speed program, the scroll bar's thumb is set to the position that corresponds to the Value property. During design time you set the Value property of the scroll bar to 50, so when you start the Speed program, the scroll bar's thumb is positioned at the middle of the bar (that is, midway between 0 and 100).

Note that the Text property of the text box is set to 50 mph in Table 2.1. When you start the program, the string displayed in the text box (50 mph) reflects the current setting of the scroll bar (Value=50).

The Keyboard Focus

While the program is running, you can press the Tab key on your keyboard to move the *focus* from control to control. Each time the Tab key is pressed, the focus shifts from one control to another. You can easily recognize which control has the focus because it will usually have a blinking cursor on it. For example, when the text box has the focus, a cursor in the text box blinks; when the scroll bar has the focus, its thumb is blinking. However, when the Exit button has the focus, a dashed rectangle surrounds the button's caption (instead of a blinking cursor).

What does it mean when a control has the focus? When a control has the focus, you can use the keyboard to control it. To understand keyboard focus, try the following:

☐ Execute the Speed program.

☐ Press the Tab key until the scroll bar has the focus (that is, until you see the scroll bar's thumb blinking).

☐ While the scroll bar has the focus, use the right-arrow and left-arrow keys on the keyboard to move the thumb of the scroll bar. Because the scroll bar now has the focus, pressing the arrow keys on the keyboard has the same effect as clicking the right-arrow and left-arrow scroll bar icons.

☐ Press the Tab key until the Exit button has the focus.

☐ While the Exit button has the focus, press the space bar or Enter key. Pressing the space bar or Enter key while the button has the focus has the same effect as clicking the button.

See how much you can do with the Speed program! You can change the scroll bar position, shrink and enlarge the window of the program, move the window of the program by dragging its caption, and perform many other Windows operations. The beauty of it is that you didn't have to write any code to use these features. Indeed, this is one of the main advantages of writing Windows programs—the "standard" Windows features are already incorporated into your programs, and you don't need to write any code.

Enhancing the Speed Program

Now enhance the Speed program by attaching more code to it.

☐ To access the hsbSpeed_Change() procedure, double-click the scroll bar control that you placed in the form.

> *Visual Basic responds by displaying the* hsbSpeed_Change() *procedure, where you can type the code.*

☐ Enter the following code in the hsbSpeed_Change() procedure:

```
Private Sub hsbSpeed_Change()

    txtSpeed.Text = Str(hsbSpeed.Value) + " mph"

End Sub
```

As implied by the name hsbSpeed_Change(), this procedure is executed whenever you change the position of the scroll bar. As you change the position of the scroll bar, the Value property of the scroll bar changes automatically. For example, if you place the scroll bar's thumb to the extreme left, the Value property of the scroll bar is automatically set to 0 (because this is the value you set for the Min property).

Whenever you change the position of the scroll bar, the text box should display the new position of the scroll bar. In other words, you need to assign the Value property of the scroll bar to the

Text property of the text box. You do this in the `hsbSpeed_Change()` procedure with the following statement:

```
txtSpeed.Text = Str(hsbSpeed.Value) + " mph"
```

For example, if the Value property of the scroll bar is 20, the Text property of the text box is set to 20 mph.

The Text property of the text box expects a character string; however, the Value property of the scroll bar is numeric. This means you must use the `Str()` function to convert the numeric value of the Value property to a character string. Inside the parentheses of the `Str()` function you type the numeric value that you want to convert to a character string. For example, to convert the number 11 to the string `"11"` you use `Str(11)`, and to convert the number 12345 to the string `"12345"` you use `Str(12345)`. In this case, you want to convert the numeric `hsbSpeed.Value` to a string, so you use the following statement:

```
Str(hsbSpeed.Value)
```

So to put it all together, if the current position of the scroll bar is at 32 (that is, `hsbSpeed.Value` is equal to 32), then the statement

```
txtSpeed.Text = Str(hsbSpeed.Value) + " mph"
```

fills the Text property of the text box with

```
22 mph
```

Now watch your code in action!

☐ Save the project by selecting Save Project from the File menu.

☐ Execute the Speed program.

☐ Play with the scroll bar. As you change the scroll bar's thumb position, the content of the text box changes accordingly.

There is, however, a cosmetic problem with the current version of the Speed program. Can you tell what the problem is? You are able to type text in the text box. This creates a problem because you may type a number in the text box that doesn't correspond to the position of the scroll bar.

☐ While the Speed program is running, click inside the text box and type `Blah Blah Blah`.

Because the text box should always display the current speed as indicated by the scroll bar, your program shouldn't allow you to enter text in the text box.

To prevent the user from entering text in the text box, you need to change the Enabled property of the text box:

☐ Terminate the Speed program by clicking the Exit button or clicking the End icon that appears on the toolbar, as shown in Figure 2.2.

☐ Display the properties window for the text box and change the Enabled property of the text box object to False.

☐ Execute the program again and verify that the text box cannot be edited.

Note: To prevent the user from entering text in a text box, set the Enabled property of the text box to False.

Always make sure you are setting the property of the correct object. For example, in the preceding steps you were instructed to set the Enabled property of the text box to False. This prevents the user from typing in the text box. If by mistake you set the Enabled property of the frmSpeed form to False, all the objects in the form will be disabled. You won't be able to type in the text box, change the scroll bar position, or click the Exit button. In this case, to exit the program you'll have to click the icon that appears in the upper-left corner of the window, and then select Close from the system menu that pops up.

Changing the Text Box While Dragging the Scroll Bar Thumb

You are almost done with the Speed program. There is, however, one more problem to solve. To see the problem, use the following steps:

☐ Execute the Speed program.

☐ Try to drag the thumb of the scroll bar. As you drag the thumb, the text box content does not change! It changes only after you release the thumb.

It would be nice if the text box would change its content while you drag the scroll bar's thumb.

☐ To make this change, enter the following code in the hsbSpeed_Scroll() procedure:

```
Private Sub hsbSpeed_Scroll()

    txtSpeed.Text = Str(hsbSpeed.Value) + " mph"

End Sub
```

☐ To place code in the hsbSpeed_Scroll() procedure, double-click the scroll bar.

> *Visual Basic responds by displaying the code window with the procedure* hsbSpeed_Change() *in it.*

☐ Because you need to enter code in the hsbSpeed_Scroll() procedure, select the Scroll item from the Proc list box that appears in the top-right portion of the code window.

As implied by the name hsbSpeed_Scroll(), this procedure is automatically executed whenever you change the position of the scroll bar. As you change the position of the scroll bar, the Value property of the scroll bar is updated automatically.

Note that the code in the hsbSpeed_Scroll() procedure is identical to the code in the hsbSpeed_Change() procedure.

☐ Execute the Speed program.

☐ Drag the thumb of the scroll bar and verify that the text in the text box changes according to the position of the scroll bar.

☐ Click the Exit button to terminate the Speed program.

Final Words About the Speed Program

The Speed program illustrates how you can create an elegant user interface for entering numbers. Instead of telling the user to type an integer number between 0 and 100, you give your user a scroll bar. Your user can set any integer in the allowed range by using the scroll bar, and your user gets visual feedback on the range of numbers that can be entered.

The Option Program

The Option program demonstrates how you can write programs that let your user select an option.

The Visual Implementation of the Option Program

The Option program uses the option button control. To see which icon represents the option button in the toolbox window, refer to Figure 1.13 in Chapter 1. The exact location of the icon in the toolbox varies from version to version. In Figure 1.13 the Option control is in the right column, fourth from the top.

☐ Open a new project by selecting New Project from the File menu.

☐ Save the form of the project as OPTION.FRM in the C:\VB4PRG\CH02 directory. Save the project file of the project as OPTION.VBP in the C:\VB4PRG\CH02 directory.

☐ Build the frmOption form according to the specifications in Table 2.2.

When the form is complete, it should look like the one shown in Figure 2.3.

Table 2.2. The properties table of the frmOption form.

Object	Property	Setting
Form	**Name**	**frmOption**
	BackColor	Red
	Caption	The Option Program
	Height	4545
	Left	1080
	Top	1170
	Width	6810
Command Button	**Name**	**cmdExit**
	Caption	E&xit
	FontName	System
	FontSize	10
	Height	1095
	Left	4800
	Top	1200
	Width	1215
Check Box	**Name**	**chkSound**
	BackColor	Red
	Caption	&Sound
	FontName	System
	FontSize	10
	ForeColor	White
	Height	495
	Left	3000
	Top	1440
	Width	1215

continues

Table 2.2. continued

Object	Property	Setting
Check Box	**Name**	**chkMouse**
	BackColor	Red
	Caption	&Mouse
	FontName	System
	FontSize	10
	ForeColor	White
	Height	495
	Left	3000
	Top	960
	Width	1215
Check Box	**Name**	**chkColors**
	BackColor	Red
	Caption	&Colors
	FontName	System
	FontSize	10
	ForeColor	White
	Height	495
	Left	3000
	Top	480
	Width	1215
Option Button	**Name**	**optLevel1**
	BackColor	Red
	Caption	Level &1
	FontName	System
	FontSize	10
	ForeColor	White
	Height	495
	Left	360
	Top	480
	Width	1215

Object	Property	Setting
Option Button	**Name**	**optLevel2**
	BackColor	Red
	Caption	Level &2
	FontName	System
	FontSize	10
	ForeColor	White
	Height	495
	Left	360
	Top	960
	Width	1215
Option Button	**Name**	**optLevel3**
	BackColor	Red
	Caption	Level &3
	FontName	System
	FontSize	10
	ForeColor	White
	Height	495
	Left	360
	Top	1440
	Width	1215
Label	**Name**	**lblChoice**
	Alignment	2-Center
	BorderStyle	1-Fixed Single
	FontName	System
	FontSize	10
	Height	1455
	Left	360
	Top	2280
	Width	3015

2

Figure 2.3.
The frmOption form in design mode.

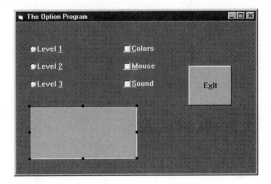

Entering the Code of the Option Program

You'll now enter code in the *general declarations section* of the frmOption form.

What is the general declarations section? It is an area in the code window where you type various general statements.

The Option Explicit statement is an example of a general statement. The exact meaning of the Option Explicit statement is discussed later in this chapter. For now, you'll just learn how to examine the general declarations section and how to type code in it.

To examine the general declarations section do the following:

☐ Double-click in the form to display the code window.

    Visual Basic responds by displaying the code window.

☐ Click the down-arrow icon of the Object list box to drop down a list of objects in the frmOption form. (See Figure 2.4.)

Figure 2.4.
Displaying the list of objects in the frmOption form.

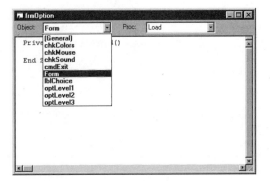

You want to examine the general declarations section, so do the following:

☐ Click the General item, which is the first item in the list of objects, and make sure that the Proc box is set to declarations.

Visual Basic responds by displaying the general declarations section, shown in Figure 2.5.

Figure 2.5.
The general declarations section.

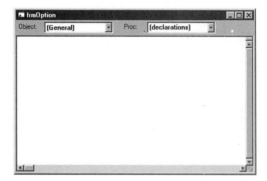

☐ You can now click in the general declarations section and type code in it. If you don't see the Option Explicit statement in the general declarations section, then click inside it and type the following code:

```
Option Explicit
```

The general declarations section should now look like the one shown in Figure 2.6.

Figure 2.6.
The general declarations section with code in it.

☐ Enter the following code in the cmdExit_Click() procedure of the frmOption form:

```
Private Sub cmdExit_Click()

    End

End Sub
```

47

Executing the Option Program

Although there's more code to be entered, execute the Option program now:

☐ Execute the Option program.

☐ Click the Level 1 option button.

> *The program responds by selecting the Level 1 option button (a dot appears in the Level 1 option button).*

☐ Click the Level 2 option button.

> *The program responds by deselecting the Level 1 button (removing the dot from the Level 1 option button) and selecting the Level 2 button (placing a dot in the Level 2 option button).*

☐ Click the Level 3 option button.

> *The program responds by deselecting the Level 2 button and selecting the Level 3 button.*

Only one option button is selected at any time. Option buttons are used in programs when you want your user to select a single option out of several options. (Note that some Windows literature refer to an option button as a radio button.)

☐ Click the Sound check box.

> *The program responds by placing an × in the Sound check box.*

☐ Click the other check boxes.

As you can see, it's possible to check more than one check box. Check boxes are used when you want the user to be able to select various settings. For example, if the program is a game application, you may select to play with or without sound, with or without the mouse, and with or without colors.

However, the user can play the game with level 1, or level 2, or level 3. It does not make sense to have both level 1 and level 2 selected at the same time.

To deselect a check box, click it again. (When a check box is not selected, it does not have an × in it.)

☐ Terminate the program by clicking the Exit button.

Entering More Code in the Option Program

Now enter more code in the Option program to detect which check boxes are selected and which option button is selected and responds to the selection.

☐ Enter the following code in the chkColors_Click() procedure of the frmOption form:

```
Private Sub chkColors_Click()

    UpdateLabel

End Sub
```

☐ Enter the following code in the chkMouse_Click() procedure of the frmOption form:

```
Private Sub chkMouse_Click()

    UpdateLabel

End Sub
```

☐ Enter the following code in the chkSound_Click() procedure of the frmOption form:

```
Private Sub chkSound_Click()

    UpdateLabel

End Sub
```

☐ Enter the following code in the optLevel1_Click() procedure of the frmOption form:

```
Private Sub optLevel1_Click()

    UpdateLabel

End Sub
```

☐ Enter the following code in the optLevel2_Click() procedure of the frmOption form:

```
Private Sub optLevel2_Click()

    UpdateLabel

End Sub
```

☐ Enter the following code in the optLevel3_Click() procedure of the frmOption form:

```
Private Sub optLevel3_Click()

    UpdateLabel

End Sub
```

What did you do in the preceding steps? You wrote the statement

UpdateLabel

in various procedures.

For example, you typed it in the optLevel3_Click() procedure. UpdateLabel is the name of a procedure you are going to write in the following steps. So whenever the user clicks the Level 3 option button, the optLevel3_Click() procedure is executed, which means the UpdateLabel procedure will be executed. The same thing happens when the user clicks the Level 2 option button because you also typed the `UpdateLabel` statement in the `optLevel2_Click()` procedure.

Now use the following steps to add the `UpdateLabel` procedure:

☐ Double-click in the form.

Visual Basic responds by displaying the code window.

☐ Select Procedure from the Insert menu.

Visual Basic responds by displaying the Insert Procedure dialog box. Note that the Procedure item in the Insert menu is available (not dimmed) if the code window is the active window.

☐ Inside the Name box type `UpdateLabel` (because this is the name of the new procedure you are adding). Also, make sure that the option buttons of the Insert Procedure dialog box are set as shown in Figure 2.7.

Figure 2.7.

Adding the `UpdateLabel` procedure.

☐ Click the OK button of the Insert Procedure dialog box.

Visual Basic responds by displaying the code window with the `UpdateLabel` procedure ready for you to edit. Visual Basic inserted the `UpdateLabel` procedure in the general section of the form.

Visual Basic wrote the first and last lines of the new `UpdateLabel` procedure for you, but it is your responsibility to write the code of the `UpdateLabel` procedure.

☐ Enter the following code in the `UpdateLabel` procedure:

```
Public Sub UpdateLabel()

    ' Declare the variables
    Dim Info
    Dim LFCR

    LFCR = Chr(13) + Chr(10)

    ' Sound
    If chkSound.Value = 1 Then
        Info = "Sound: ON"
```

```
    Else
       Info = "Sound: OFF"
    End If

    ' Mouse
    If chkMouse.Value = 1 Then
       Info = Info + LFCR + "Mouse: ON"
    Else
       Info = Info + LFCR + "Mouse: OFF"
    End If

    ' Colors
    If chkColors.Value = 1 Then
       Info = Info + LFCR + "Colors: ON"
    Else
       Info = Info + LFCR + "Colors: OFF"
    End If

   ' Level 1
   If optLevel1.Value = True Then
       Info = Info + LFCR + "Level:1"
   End If

   ' Level 2
   If optLevel2.Value = True Then
       Info = Info + LFCR + "Level:2"
   End If

    ' Level 3
   If optLevel3.Value = True Then
       Info = Info + LFCR + "Level:3"
   End If

   lblChoice.Caption = Info


End Sub
```

☐ Save the project by selecting Save Project from the File menu.

Executing the Option Program

☐ Execute the Option program.

☐ Click the various check boxes and option buttons.

> *The program responds by displaying the status of the check boxes and radio buttons in the* lblChoice *label. (See Figure 2.8.)*

☐ Terminate the program by clicking the Exit button.

Figure 2.8.
The Option window,
showing the current settings
for the check boxes and
option buttons.

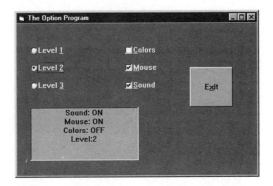

How the Option Program Works

The Option program executes the UpdateLabel procedure whenever you click any of the check boxes or radio buttons.

The Code in the *chkColors_Click()* Procedure of the frmOption Form

The chkColors_Click() procedure is executed whenever you click the chkColors check box:

```
Private Sub chkColors_Click()

    UpdateLabel

End Sub
```

What makes this procedure happen? It is executed automatically whenever you click the chkColors check box. That's how programs written with Visual Basic work!

The code in the chkColors_Click() procedure executes the UpdateLabel procedure. The code in the UpdateLabel procedure is covered later in this chapter.

The Code in the *chkMouse_Click()* Procedure of the frmOption Form

The chkMouse_Click() procedure is executed automatically whenever you click the chkMouse check box:

```
Private Sub chkMouse_Click()

    UpdateLabel

End Sub
```

Just like the chkColors_Click() procedure, this procedure also executes the UpdateLabel procedure.

The Code in the *chkSound_Click()* Procedure of the frmOption Form

The chkSound_Click() procedure is executed automatically whenever you click the chkSound check box:

```
Private Sub chkSound_Click()

    UpdateLabel

End Sub
```

Just like the chkColors_Click() and chkMouse_Click() procedures, this procedure also executes the UpdateLabel procedure.

The Code in the *optLevel1_Click()* Procedure of the frmOption Form

The optLevel1_Click() procedure is executed automatically whenever you click the optLevel1 procedure:

```
Private Sub optLevel1_Click()

    UpdateLabel

End Sub
```

This procedure also executes the UpdateLabel procedure.

The optLevel2_Click() and optLevel3_Click() procedures are executed automatically whenever you click the optLevel2 and optLevel3 option buttons. These procedures also execute the UpdateLabel procedure.

The Code in the *UpdateLabel* Procedure

As discussed, whenever you click a check box or an option button, the UpdateLabel procedure is executed.

The UpdateLabel procedure is not an event procedure; it was created from the Insert menu.

Declaring the *Info* Variable

The first statement in the UpdateLabel procedure declares the Info variable:

```
Dim Info
```

The word `Dim` is an instruction to Visual Basic that the following word—`Info`—is the name of a variable. The variable `Info` is used as a string variable during the execution of the `UpdateLabel` procedure. So you can declare this variable as follows:

```
Dim Info As String
```

However, Visual Basic is liberal in this respect and does not force you to declare the type of variable at the time of the declaration.

If you have experience with other programming languages, you probably know that some programming languages don't require you to declare variables. However, it's a good programming habit to declare all variables. To see why, assume that your procedure includes the following calculations:

```
Time = 10
Velocity = 50
Distance  = Velocity * Time
lblDistance.Caption = "Distance = " + Str(Distance)
```

The preceding four statements assign 10 to the `Time` variable, 50 to the `Velocity` variable, calculate the distance by multiplying `Velocity` by `Time`, and display `Distance` by assigning its value to the Caption property of the lblDistance label.

Now suppose that by mistake you typed the following (that is, there is an *a* missing after the *t* in `Distance`):

```
lblDistance.Caption = "Distance = " + Str(Distnce)
```

Visual Basic considers `Distnce` as a new variable, and it automatically assigns the value 0 to it. Therefore, the lblVelocity label displays the following:

```
Distance: 0
```

This, of course, is an error. You can avoid such foolish errors by instructing Visual Basic to complain whenever a variable is not declared. In the preceding example, the statements that calculate and display the distance should be the following:

```
Dim Time
Dim Velocity
Dim Distance

Time = 10
Velocity = 50
Distance  = Velocity * Time
lblDistance.Caption = "Distance = " + Str(Distnce)
```

If Visual Basic is set to complain whenever your code includes a variable that is not declared, Visual Basic will prompt you with an error message during the execution of the program, telling you that the `Distnce` variable is unknown. Visual Basic highlights the variable `Distnce`, letting you know that there is something wrong with it.

To instruct Visual Basic to complain whenever there is a variable in the code that is not declared, you have to place the following statement in the general declarations section of the form:

```
Option Explicit
```

This is the reason you were instructed at the beginning of this tutorial to type the `Option Explicit` statement in the general declarations section.

Declaring the *LFCR* Variable

You also declared the `LFCR` variable:

```
Dim LFCR
```

and then you set the value of the `LFCR` variable as follows:

```
LFCR = Chr(13) + Chr(10)
```

`Chr(13)` is the return carriage character, and `Chr(10)` is the line feed character. As you'll soon see, the `lblChoice` label displays a long string that is spread over several lines. You'll spread the string over several lines by inserting the `LFCR` variable in between the lines.

Checking the Value Property of the Check Box

The next statements that you typed in the `UpdateLabel` procedure are a block of `If…Else…End If` statements:

```
' Sound
If chkSound.Value = 1 Then
   Info = "Sound: ON"
Else
   Info = "Sound: OFF"
End If
```

In Visual Basic, you can insert *comments* in the code by using the apostrophe (') character or the `Rem` word. The following line:

```
' Sound
```

is identical to this line:

```
Rem Sound
```

This book uses the apostrophe as the character that starts a comment line. Comments also can be inserted in a line of code as follows:

```
MyVariable = 1 ' Initialize the variable.
```

It's a good programming habit to insert comments that give a brief description of the code; they make the program easier to read and debug. You can write anything you want after the ' character. Visual Basic simply ignores all the characters that follow the ' character.

The `UpdateLabel` procedure checks whether the Value property of the chkSound check box is equal to 1. If the Value property is equal to 1, the statements between `If` and `Else` are executed. In this case, you have only one statement between the `If` and the `Else`, so if the Value property of the chkSound box is equal to 1, the following statement is executed:

```
Info = "Sound: ON"
```

This statement assigns the string `"Sound: ON"` to the variable `Info`.

Note that `Then` in the `If` statement must be included.

If the Value property of the Sound check box is equal to 1 it means that there is an × in the chkSound check box. Therefore, whenever there is an × in the chkSound check box, the variable `Info` is set to `"Sound: ON"`.

The statements between `Else` and `End If` are executed if the Value property of the chkSound Check property is not equal to 1. Whenever there is no × in the check box, the Value property of the check box is equal to 0. If there is no × in the chkSound check box, the statement between `Else` and `End If` is executed, which sets the contents of the `Info` variable to `"Sound: OFF"`.

To summarize, the `Info` variable is set to either `Sound: ON` or `Sound: OFF`.

In a similar way, the next `If…Else…End If` block checks the Value property of the chkMouse check box:

```
' Mouse
If chkMouse.Value = 1 Then
    Info = Info + LFCR + "Mouse: ON"
Else
    Info = Info + LFCR + "Mouse: OFF"
End If
```

For example, if the chkSound check box has an × in it and the chkMouse check box does not, the first two `If…Else…End If` blocks in the `UpdateLabel` procedure assign the following string to the `Info` variable:

```
"Sound: ON" + LFCR + "Mouse: OFF"
```

This is later displayed on two lines:

```
Sound: ON
Mouse: OFF
```

because of the `LFCR` that was inserted between the two strings.

The next `If…Else…End If` block in the `UpdateLabel` procedure checks the Value property of the chkColors check box and updates the `Info` variable accordingly:

```
' Colors
If chkColors.Value = 1 Then
    Info = Info + LFCR + "Colors: ON"
```

```
Else
    Info = Info + LFCR + "Colors: OFF"
End If
```

The next If…End If block in the UpdateLabel procedure checks the Value property of the optLevel1 option button:

```
' Level
If optLevel1.Value = True Then
    Info = Info + LFCR + "Level:1"
End If
```

Again, the Value property of the control specifies its status. However, for the option button control, a Value property that equals True means that the option button is selected and the Info variable is updated accordingly. If the Value property of the optLevel1 does not equal True, it means that this option button is not selected. In Visual Basic, True is defined as -1, and False is defined as 0. Therefore, the state of the option button may be either True (-1) or False (0).

> **Note:** The Value property of a check box can be 0, 1, or 2. The Value property of a check box that has an × in it is 1. The Value property of a check box that does not have an × in it is 0. The Value property of a check box is 2 whenever the check box is grayed, or dimmed (unavailable). To make the check box gray, set its Enabled property to False.

> **Note:** The Value property of an option button may be True or False. If it has a dot in it, the Value property is True; if it doesn't, the Value property is False.
>
> In Visual Basic, True is defined as -1, and False is defined as 0.

The next two If…End If blocks update the Info variable according to the Value properties of the optLevel2 and optLevel3 option buttons:

```
If optLevel2.Value = True Then
    Info = Info + LFCR + "Level:2"
End If

If optLevel3.Value = True Then
    Info = Info + LFCR + "Level:3"
End If
```

The last statement in the UpdateLabel procedure updates the Caption property of the lblChoice label with the contents of the Info variable:

```
lblChoice.Caption = Info
```

This displays the contents of the Info variable in the lblChoice label, as shown in Figure 2.8.

What Else?

As you may realize by now, programming with Visual Basic amounts to understanding the meaning of each of the controls in the toolbox and the meaning and purpose of the controls' properties. The same property means different things for different controls. For example, the Caption property of the form contains the text displayed in the title of the form, while the Caption property of the label control contains the text displayed in the label. Likewise, the Value property of the check box indicates whether the check box has an × in it, while the Value property of the option button indicates whether the option button has a dot in it. Also, the Value property of the scroll bar indicates the current position of the scroll bar.

The toolbox contains the icons of the controls, and each control has its own set of properties. Some of the controls in the toolbox are standard Windows controls, such as horizontal scroll bars, vertical scroll bars, text boxes, labels, check boxes, option buttons, and command buttons. On the other hand, some of the controls in the toolbox are very special. During the course of this book, you'll have a chance to experiment with them.

Generally speaking, Visual Basic is not a difficult programming language to learn, but there is a lot to learn. The key to successful learning is practicing and experimenting. After writing and experimenting with the book's programs, you can master Visual Basic. After you enter the code of the book's programs and understand the code, experiment on your own. Try to change the properties of the control during design time (during the time you implement the visual portion of the program) and at runtime. Changing properties during runtime means that the value of the property changes from within the code of the program. For example, the last statement in the UpdateLabel procedure updates the Caption property of the lblChoice label during runtime. On the other hand, the Caption property of the form was set to The Option Program during design time.

Some properties can be changed during runtime or at design time, but some properties may be set only during runtime. For example, the Caption property of the label control may be set during design time as well as at runtime. During the course of this book, you'll learn about properties that can be changed only during runtime.

Chapter 3, "Programming Building Blocks," explores programming topics such as loops and decision statements. You'll make extensive use of these topics in subsequent chapters. The chapters that follow Chapter 3 discuss special controls, special properties, and special programming topics.

Naming Conventions Used in This Book

In this book, controls are named according to the specifications in Table 2.3. For example, names of the command buttons start with the characters *cmd* (as in cmdMyButton), and the names of the text boxes start with the characters *txt* (as in txtMyTextBox).

Table 2.3. Naming conventions for controls.

Control	Name Starts with These Characters	Example
Form	frm	frmMyForm
Check Box	chk	chkSound
Combo box	cbo	cboSelection
Command Button	cmd	cmdExit
Directory List	dir	dirFiles
Drive List	drv	drvSource
File List	fil	filTarget
Frame	fra	fraChoices
Grid	grd	grdTV
Horizontal Scroll Bar	hsb	hsbSpeed
Image	img	imgMyImage
Label	lbl	lblInfo
Line	lin	linDiagonal
List Box	lst	lstChapters
Menu	mnu	mnuFile
Option Button	opt	optLevel1
Picture Box	pic	picMyPicture
Shape	shp	shpMyShape
Text Box	txt	txtUserArea
Timer	tmr	tmrMoveIt
Vertical Scroll Bar	vsb	vsbSpeed

Assigning names to the controls' Name properties according to Table 2.3 is not a Visual Basic requirement. For example, you assigned the name lblChoice to the label control that displays information about the user's choice. However, you could have set the Name property of this label to Choice; if you had done this, the last statement in the UpdateLabel procedure would be this:

```
Choice.Caption = Info
```

However, because you set the Name property of the label to lblChoice, the last statement in UpdateLabel looks like this:

```
lblChoice.Caption = Info
```

Note that naming the controls according to Table 2.3 makes the program easy to read. For example, take a look at this statement:

```
Choice.Caption = Info
```

By just looking at this statement, you, or others who read your program, won't be able to tell that Choice is a label control. Therefore, the preceding statement might be misunderstood by someone reading the statement as updating the Caption property of a form whose Name property was set to Choice. On the other hand, look how easy it is to read this statement:

```
lblChoice.Caption = Info
```

Since you preceded the name of the label with the *lbl* characters, someone reading the statement can figure out that lblChoice is a name of a label. Therefore, the statement means: Update the Caption property of the label (whose Name property was set to lblChoice) to the value of the Info variable.

Statements That Cannot Fit on a Single Line in This Book

Starting with Visual Basic Version 4.0, a statement can be typed so that it can be spread on more than one line. For example, the statement

```
MyVariable = 1 + 2 + 3
```

can be typed this way:

```
MyVariable = 1 _
        + 2 + 3
```

or this way:

```
MyVariable = 1 _
        + 2 _
        + 3
```

In Visual Basic, you can continue the statement on the following line if you end the current line with a space followed by the underscore (_) character.

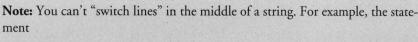

> **Note:** You can't "switch lines" in the middle of a string. For example, the statement
>
> ```
> lblMyLabel.Caption "This is my string"
> ```
>
> cannot be written as follows:
>
> ```
> ' This statement has an error in it.
> lblMyLabel.Caption "This is _
>                     my string"
> ```

Summary

In this chapter you have jumped into the water! Yes, you have actually built true Windows programs that include a scroll bar, a text box, a label, a command button, check boxes, and option buttons. You have learned how to incorporate these controls into your Visual Basic programs, how to determine their Value properties, and how to insert code in the event procedures that correspond to these controls.

Q&A

Q **The visual implementation portion took me a long time. Any suggestions?**

A Yes. Practice. You should be fluent with the visual implementation portion of the programs, and the only way to be fluent is to practice.

Q **I can't recognize the icons in the toolbox. Any suggestions?**

A Yes. Consult Figure 1.13 in Chapter 1. After practicing for a while, you won't need to refer to Figure 1.13!

You can also place the mouse cursor, without clicking, on the icons of the toolbox window. After a second or two, Visual Basic will display a small yellow rectangle that tells you the icon's purpose.

Quiz

1. A certain statement appears in this book as follows:

   ```
   Info = "ABC" + _
          + "DEF" + "GH"
   ```

   How would you type it in your Visual Basic program?

   a. `Info = "ABC" + "DEF" + "GH"`
   b. Exactly as shown in the book

2. Suppose your program includes a vertical scroll bar with the name vsbVolume. Write a statement that places the thumb of the scroll bar at position 37.

3. Suppose your program includes a horizontal scroll bar with the name hsbDistance. How do you change the Min and Max properties of the scroll bar to 10 and 200, respectively?

Exercise

Enhance the Option program so it accomplishes the following:

- When you check the chkSound check box, the PC beeps.
- When you uncheck the chkColors check box, the form's background changes to purple, and when you check the chkColors check box, the form's background changes to yellow.

Note: To make the PC beep, use the Beep statement.

To change the form's background to purple, use the following statement:

```
frmOption.BackColor = QBColor(13)
```

To change the form's background to yellow, use the following statement:

```
frmOption.BackColor = QBColor(14)
```

Quiz Answers

1. a or b. Both answers are correct.

2. To place the thumb of the vsbVolume scroll bar at position 37, use the following statement:

```
vsbVolume.Value = 37
```

3. You can change the Min and Max properties of the scroll bar at design time or runtime.

   Use the following steps to change the properties at design time:

   ☐ Select the scroll bar that you placed in the from.

   ☐ Select Properties from the View menu or press F4.

   Visual Basic responds by displaying the properties window for the scroll bar.

☐ Select the Min property and change its value to 10.

☐ Select the Max property and change its value to 200.

Or you can set these properties at runtime by using the following statements:

```
hsbDistance.Min = 10
hsbDistance.Max = 200
```

Exercise Answer

Change the `chkSound_Click()` procedure so that it looks like the following:

```
Private Sub chkSound_Click()

    If chkSound.Value = 1 Then
        Beep
    End If
    UpdateLabel

End Sub
```

Change the `chkColors_Click()` procedure so that it looks like the following:

```
Private Sub chkColors_Click ()

    If chkColors.Value = 1 Then
        frmOption.BackColor = QBColor(13)
    Else
        frmOption.BackColor = QBColor(14)
    End If

    UpdateLabel

End Sub
```

The `If…End If` block in the `chkSound_Click()` procedure checks the Value property of the check box. If it's 1, it means that the user checked the box (put an × in this check box), and the `Beep` statement is executed.

The `If…Else…End If` block in the `chkColors_Click()` procedure checks the Value property of the chkColors check box. If the Value property is equal to 1, it means that the user checked the box, and the form's BackColor property is set to QBColor(13). If the Value property of the check box isn't equal to 1, it means that the user unchecked the check box, and the form's BackColor property is set to QBColor(14).

The `QBColor()` function is discussed in detail later in the book.

3

Programming
Building Blocks

This chapter focuses on Visual Basic's programming building blocks. Just like any other programming language, Visual Basic uses programming building blocks such as procedures, functions, If statements, Do loops, variables, and other important programming language concepts.

The Multiply Program

The Multiply program illustrates how to use procedures and functions in your programs.

The Visual Implementation of the Multiply Program

☐ Open a new project, save the form of the project as MULTIPLY.FRM in the C:\VB4PRG \CH03 directory, and save the project file as MULTIPLY.VBP in the C:\VB4PRG \CH03 directory.

☐ Build the frmMultiply form according to the specifications in Table 3.1.

The completed form should look like the one shown in Figure 3.1.

Table 3.1. The properties table of the frmMultiply form.

Object	Property	Setting
Form	**Name**	**frmMultiply**
	Caption	The Multiply Program
	Height	4545
	Left	1080
	Top	1170
	Width	6225
Text Box	**Name**	**txtResult**
	Height	495
	Left	480
	Text	(empty)
	Top	600
	Width	5055

Object	Property	Setting
Command Button	**Name**	**cmdExit**
	Caption	E&xit
	Height	495
	Left	2280
	Top	3360
	Width	1215
Command Button	**Name**	**cmdCalculate**
	Caption	&Calculate
	Height	1095
	Left	2280
	Top	1440
	Width	1215
Label	**Name**	**lblResult**
	Caption	Result:
	Height	255
	Left	480
	Top	360
	Width	1215

Figure 3.1.
The frmMultiply form.

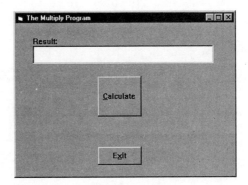

Entering the Code of the Multiply Program

☐ Enter the following code in the general declarations section of the frmMultiply form:

```
' All variables MUST be declared.
Option Explicit
```

Add the preceding statement only if Visual Basic did not write this statement for you.

☐ Enter the following code in the cmdCalculate_Click() procedure of the frmMultiply form:

```
Private Sub cmdCalculate_Click()

    Multiply 2, 3

End Sub
```

☐ Enter the following code in the cmdExit_Click() procedure of the frmMultiply form:

```
Private Sub cmdExit_Click()

    End

End Sub
```

Add a new procedure to the form and name it Multiply. You do this as follows:

☐ Double-click the frmMultiply form to display the code window and then select Procedure from the Insert menu of Visual Basic.

Visual Basic responds by displaying the Insert Procedure dialog box.

☐ Set the Name box in the Insert Procedure dialog box to Multiply.

☐ Set the Type of the procedure to Sub.

☐ Set the Scope of the procedure to Public.

Your Insert Procedure dialog box should now look like the one shown in Figure 3.2.

Figure 3.2.

Adding the Multiply() *procedure.*

☐ Click the OK button of the Insert Procedure dialog box.

Visual Basic responds by adding the Multiply() *procedure to the general declarations section of the frmMultiply form and displaying the code window of the* Multiply() *procedure.*

☐ Change the heading (the first line) of the Multiply() procedure so that it looks like this:

```
Public Sub Multiply(X As Integer, Y As Integer)

End Sub
```

That is, the default heading line of the procedure is

```
Public Sub Multiply()
```

and you insert code between the parentheses so that it looks like this:

```
Public Sub Multiply(X As Integer, Y As Integer)
```

☐ Enter the following code in the Multiply() procedure:

```
Public Sub Multiply(X As Integer, Y As Integer)

    Dim Z

    Z = X * Y
    txtResult.Text = Str(Z)

End Sub
```

Executing the Multiply Program

☐ Execute the Multiply program.

☐ Click the Calculate button.

The program responds by displaying the number 6 in the text box. (When you press the Calculate button, the program multiplies 2 by 3 and displays the result in the text box.)

How the Multiply Program Works

The Multiply program executes the Multiply() procedure to multiply two numbers.

The Code in the *cmdCalculate_Click()* Procedure

The cmdCalculate_Click() procedure is executed whenever the user clicks the cmdCalculate button:

```
Private Sub cmdCalculate_Click()

    Multiply 2, 3

End Sub
```

The statement in this procedure executes the `Multiply()` procedure with two arguments: 2 and 3. That is, the `Multiply()` procedure needs to know which numbers to multiply. You supply the numbers 2 and 3 as the arguments, so now the `Multiply()` procedure knows that it should multiply 2 by 3.

The Code in the *Multiply()* Procedure

The `Multiply()` procedure has two arguments:

```
Public Sub Multiply(X As Integer, Y As Integer)

    Dim Z

    Z = X * Y
    txtResult.Text = Str(Z)

End Sub
```

The first argument is called X, and it is declared As Integer. The second argument is called Y and it is also declared As Integer.

The `Multiply()` procedure declares a variable called Z and then assigns to it the result of the X*Y multiplication.

The procedure then assigns the value of the Z variable to the Text property of the txtResult text box. The Str() function is used to convert the value of Z to a string.

Note that the UpdateLabel procedure used in the Option program in Day 2, "Properties and Controls," did not have any arguments, so its heading was as follows:

```
Public Sub UpdateLabel ()

End Sub
```

To execute the UpdateLabel procedure, the following statement was used:

```
UpdateLabel
```

On the other hand, the `Multiply()` procedure has two arguments (both are integers), so its heading is as follows:

```
Public Sub Multiply (X As Integer, Y As Integer)

End Sub
```

To execute the `Multiply()` procedure, the following statement is used:

```
Multiply 2, 3
```

In Visual Basic, you can also execute procedures using the Call statement. For example, you can rewrite the cmdCalculate_Click() procedure as follows:

```
Private Sub cmdCalculate_Click ()

   Call Multiply (2, 3)

End Sub
```

When using the Call statement, you must include the arguments in parentheses. (It doesn't matter which method you use to execute procedures; use whichever method is more convenient for you.)

Note: When you added the Multiply() procedure using the Insert Procedure dialog box (refer back to Figure 3.2), you set the scope of the procedure to Public. Therefore, Visual Basic declared the Multiply() procedure as public:

```
Public Sub Multiply()
```

If you had set the scope of the Multiply() procedure to Private, Visual Basic would have declared the Multiply() procedure as private:

```
Private Sub Multiply()
```

What's the difference between a public and private procedure?

A *private* procedure can be used only by another procedure in the same file. For example, if you had declared the Multiply() procedure as private, then only procedures in the frmMultiply form (the MULTIPLY.FRM file) could use the Multiply() procedure.

On the other hand, a *public* procedure can be used by any procedure in any file of the program. As you'll learn in later chapters in this book, a program can include several files (for example, several forms). When you declare a procedure as public, any procedure in any of the program's files can use the public procedure.

Using a Function in the Multiply Program

The Multiply() procedure is called a procedure because it does not return any value. A *function* is similar to a procedure, but a function does return a value. To see a function in action, use the following steps. Remove the Multiply() procedure from the Multiply program as follows:

☐ Display the code window by highlighting the frmMultiply form in the project window and clicking the View Code button in the project window. (Or you can double-click anywhere inside the frmMultiply form.)

☐ Locate the `Multiply()` procedure in the code window. You'll find it in the general declarations area.

☐ Highlight the whole procedure (including its heading and last line) and press Delete on your keyboard.

That's it—you don't have the `Multiply()` procedure in your program anymore.

Use the following steps to add a new function to the Multiply program:

☐ Display the code window of the frmMultiply form.

☐ Select Procedure from the Insert menu of Visual Basic.

> *Visual Basic responds by displaying the Insert Procedure dialog box.*

☐ Set the Name in the Insert Procedure dialog box to Multiply.

☐ Set the Type of the procedure to Function (because you're adding a new function).

☐ Set the Scope of the procedure to Public.

Your Insert Procedure dialog box should now look like the one shown in Figure 3.3.

Figure 3.3.
Adding the `Multiply()`
function.

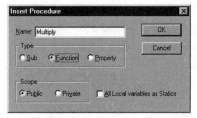

☐ Click the OK button of the Insert Procedure dialog box.

> *Visual Basic responds by adding the* `Multiply()` *function to the general declarations section of the frmMultiply form and displaying the code window with the* `Multiply()` *function ready for editing:*

```
Public Function Multiply ()

End Function
```

☐ Change the heading of the `Multiply()` function so that it looks like the following:

```
Public Function Multiply (X As Integer, Y As Integer)

End Function
```

☐ Add the following code in the `Multiply()` function:

```
Public Function Multiply (X As Integer, Y As Integer)
```

```
Dim Z
Z = X * Y
Multiply = Z
```

End Function

Don't forget to modify the first line of the function so that the Multiply() function has two arguments.

☐ Change the cmdCalculate_Click() procedure so that it looks like the following:

Private Sub cmdCalculate_Click ()

```
txtResult.Text = Str( Multiply(2, 3) )
```

End Sub

☐ Save the project by selecting Save Project from the File menu.

☐ Execute the Multiply program.

☐ Click the Calculate button.

As you can see, the program behaves in the same manner as it did when the Multiply() procedure was used.

☐ Click the Exit button to terminate the program.

The Code in the *Multiply()* Function

The code in the Multiply() function declares the Z variable and assigns the result of the X*Y multiplication to it:

Public Function Multiply (X As Integer, Y As Integer)

```
Dim Z
Z = X * Y
Multiply = Z
```

End Function

The last statement in the Multiply() procedure assigns the value of Z to Multiply:

Multiply = Z

Multiply is the returned value of the Multiply() function. That is, by setting the name of the function (Multiply) to Z:

Multiply = Z

you are specifying that the returned value of the Multiply() function is the value of Z.

Whoever executes the Multiply() function can use the returned value of the Multiply() function, as explained in the next section.

The Code in the *cmdCalculate_Click()* Procedure

The code in the cmdCalculate_Click() procedure assigns the returned value from the Multiply() function to the Text property of the txtResult text box:

```
Private Sub cmdCalculate_Click ()

    txtResult.Text = Str( Multiply(2, 3) )

End Sub
```

As you can see, using a function is a little bit more complicated than using procedures. However, after using functions for a while, you'll get used to them and learn to appreciate them, because they make your program easier to read and understand. Consider the following statement:

```
txtResult.Text = Str( Multiply(2, 3) )
```

This statement says the following: Execute the Multiply() function with two arguments, 2 and 3; convert the returned value of Multiply to a string (using the Str() function); and assign the string to the Text property of the txtResult text box. Therefore, the txtResult text box will be filled with the string "6" because 2×3=6.

Procedures, Functions, and Methods

As discussed earlier in this chapter, the difference between a procedure and a function is that a procedure does not return a value and a function does. In subsequent chapters of this book you will also encounter the term *method*. A method works similarly to how procedures and functions work. However, usually a method performs some type of functionality on a particular object. For example, the following statement clears the frmMyForm form:

```
frmMyForm.Cls
```

Note that in the preceding statement, Cls is the name of the method. From a programmer's point of view, methods can be seen as procedures with a strange syntax.

Decision Makers' Statements

The following sections describe the main programming building blocks that are available in Visual Basic. The rest of this chapter shows you how to write programs that make use of these programming building blocks.

Specifying Controls

As you may have noticed by now, you can refer to a control's property by typing the name of the control, a dot (.), and then the name of the property. For example, this is how you refer to the Text property of the txtResult text box control:

```
txtResult.Text
```

You can also refer to the property by including the name of the form on which the control is located. For example, this is how you can refer to the Text property of the txtResult text box that is located in the frmMultiply form:

```
frmMultiply.txtResult.Text
```

In most cases, you can omit the name of the form (this saves you some typing). However, if your program includes more than one form, you may have to specify the name of the form. You'll see examples of situations where you must include the name of the form later in this book.

3

The *If* Statement

You've already encountered the If…End If block of statements in Chapter 2. In the following If…End If block, the statements between the If line and the End If line are executed only if A is equal to 1:

```
If A = 1 Then

... This code is executed only if A
... is equal to 1.

End If
```

The following statements illustrate the If…Else…End If statements:

```
If A = 1 Then

    ... This code is executed only if A
    ... is equal to 1.

else

    ... This code is executed only if A
    ... is NOT equal to 1.

End If
```

The *Select Case* Statement

Select Case is sometimes more convenient to use than the If…Else…End If. The following block of statements illustrates how Select Case works:

```
Select Case X
      Case 0
            ... Write here code that will be ...
            ... executed if X = 0.          ...
            ....................................
      Case 1
            ....................................
            ... Write here code that will be ...
            ... executed if X = 1.          ...
            ....................................
      Case 2
            ....................................
            ... Write here code that will be ...
            ... executed if X = 2.          ...
End  Select
```

As you can see, Select Case works in a similar way to the If statement.

The *Do While...Loop* Method

The Do...Loop is used to execute statements until a certain condition is satisfied. The following Do...Loop counts from 1 to 1000:

```
Counter = 1
Do While Counter < 1001
   Counter = Counter + 1
Loop
```

The variable Counter is initialized to 1, and then the Do While loop starts.

The first line of the loop checks whether the Counter variable is less than 1001. If it is, the statements between the Do While line and the Loop line are executed. In the preceding example, there is only one statement between these lines:

```
Counter = Counter + 1
```

which increases the Counter variable by 1.

The program then returns to the Do While line and examines the value of the Counter variable again. Now Counter is equal to 2, so again the statement between the Do While line and the Loop line is executed. This process continues until Counter equals 1001. In this case, the Do While line finds that Counter is no longer less than 1001, and the program continues with the statement after the Loop line.

The *Do...Loop While* Method

The statements in the Do While...Loop described in the previous section may or may not be executed. For example, in the following Do While...Loop, the statements between the Do While line and the Loop line are never executed:

```
Counter = 2000
Do While Counter < 1001
   Counter = Counter + 1
Loop
```

When the program reaches the Do While line, it discovers that Counter is equal to 2000; therefore, the statement between the Do While line and the Loop line is not executed.

Sometimes, you may want the program to enter the loop at least once. In this case, use the Do...Loop While statements:

```
Counter = 2000
Do
     txtUserArea.Text = Str(Counter)
     Counter = Counter + 1
Loop While Counter < 1001
```

The program executes the statements between the Do line and the Loop While line in any case. Then the program determines whether Counter is less then 1001. If it is, the program again executes the statements between the Do line and the Loop While line.

When the program discovers that the Counter variable is no longer less than 1001, it continues by executing the statement that appears after the Loop While line.

The following Do...Loop While method counts from 50 to 300:

```
Counter = 50
Do
     Counter = Counter + 1
Loop While Counter < 301
```

The *For...Next* Method

The For...Next loop is another way to make loops in Visual Basic. The following loop counts from 1 to 100:

```
For I =1 to 100 Step 1

   txtMyTextArea.Text = Str(I)

Next
```

To count from 1 to 100 in steps of 2, you can use the following For...Next loop:

```
For I =1 to 100 Step 2

   txtMyTextArea.Text = Str(I)

Next
```

This loop counts as follows: 1,3,5,...

If you omit the Step word, Visual Basic uses Step 1 as the default. So the following two For…Next blocks produce the same results:

```
For I =1 to 100 Step 1

    txtMyTextArea.Text = Str(I)

Next

For I =1 to 100

    txtMyTextArea.Text = Str(I)

Next
```

The *Exit For* Statement

You can exit a For…Next loop by using the Exit For statement as follows:

```
For I = 1 To 1000
    txtResult.Text = Str(I)
    If I = 500 Then
        Exit For
    End If
Next
```

The preceding code counts in increments of 1, starting from 1. In each repetition of the loop, I is increased by 1.

When I equals 500, the condition of the If statement (If I=500) is satisfied; as a result, the Exit For statement is executed, which terminates the For…Next loop.

The *Exit Do* Statement

Do While…Loop may be terminated by using the Exit Do statement as follows:

```
I = 1
Do While I < 10001
    txtResult.Text = Str(I)
    I = I + 2
    If I > 500 Then
        Exit Do
    End If
Loop
```

The preceding loops count in increments of 2, starting from 1. When I is greater than 500, Do While…Loop terminates.

Oops...

Occasionally, you might make errors like the one shown in the following loop:

```
I = 1
Do While I < 10001
    txtResult.Text = Str(I)
    If I > 500 Then
        Exit Do
    End If
Loop
```

That is, you might forget to include the following statement:

```
I = I + 2
```

In the preceding Do While…Loop, the Counter variable remains at its current value (Counter = 1), because you forgot to increment its value. In this case, the program stays in the loop forever, because I is always less than 10,001 and is never greater than 500. In fact I is always equal to 1.

To get out of the loop, press Ctrl+Break to stop the program.

The *With* Statement

The With statement enables you to set several properties of an object without typing the name of the object for each property.

For example, the following With statement sets several properties of the cmdMyButton push-button:

```
With cmdMyButton
    .Height = 300
    .Width  = 900
    .Caption = "&My Button"
End With
```

This With statement has the same effect as the following statements:

```
cmdMyButton.Height = 300
cmdMyButton.Width  = 900
cmdMyButton.Caption = "&My Button"
```

As you can see, the With statement saves you typing time. It lets you write code that sets several properties of a control without typing the name of the control for each property—you type the name of the control only at the first line of the With statement.

The Sum Program

The Sum program allows the user to select a number and then adds all the integers from 1 to the selected number. For example, if the user selects the number 5, the program makes the following calculation:

1 + 2 + 3 + 4 + 5 = 15

and displays the result.

The Visual Implementation of the Sum Program

☐ Open a new project, save the form of the project as SUM.FRM in the C:\VBPRG\CH03 directory, and save the project file as SUM.VBP in the C:\VBPRG\CH03 directory.

☐ Build the frmSum form according to the specifications in Table 3.2.

The completed form should look like the one shown in Figure 3.4.

Table 3.2. The properties table of the frmSum form.

Object	Property	Setting
Form	**Name**	**frmSum**
	Caption	The Sum Program
	Height	4545
	Left	1080
	Top	1170
	Width	4410
Command Button	**Name**	**cmdExit**
	Caption	E&xit
	FontName	System
	FontSize	10
	Height	495
	Left	1560
	Top	3480
	Width	1215
Text Box	**Name**	**txtResult**
	Alignment	2-Center
	Enabled	0-False

Object	Property	Setting
	Height	495
	Left	1440
	MultiLine	-1-True
	Text	(empty)
	Top	720
	Width	2655
Vertical Scroll Bar	**Name**	**vsbNum**
	Height	2775
	Left	840
	Max	500
	Min	1
	Top	720
	Value	1
	Width	255
Command Button	**Name**	**cmdSumIt**
	Caption	&Sum It
	FontName	System
	FontSize	10
	Height	1575
	Left	2040
	Top	1560
	Width	1455
Label	**Name**	**lblNum**
	Caption	Selected Number: 1
	FontName	System
	FontSize	10
	Height	255
	Left	120
	Top	360
	Width	2175

3

Figure 3.4.
The frmSum form.

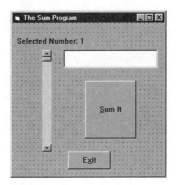

Entering the Code of the Sum Program

☐ Enter the following code in the general declarations section of the frmSum form:

```
' All variables MUST be declared.
Option Explicit
```

☐ Enter the following code in the cmdExit_Click() procedure of the frmSum form:

```
Private Sub cmdExit_Click ()

    End

End Sub
```

☐ Enter the following code in the cmdSumIt_Click() procedure of the frmSum form:

```
Private Sub cmdSumIt_Click ()

    Dim I
    Dim R

    For I = 1 To vsbNum.Value Step 1
        R = R + I
    Next

    txtResult.Text = Str(R)

End Sub
```

☐ Enter the following code in the vsbNum_Change() procedure of the frmSum form:

```
Private Sub vsbNum_Change ()

    lblNum = "Selected number: " + Str(vsbNum.Value)

End Sub
```

☐ Enter the following code in the vsbNum_Scroll() procedure of the frmSum form:

```
Private Sub vsbNum_Scroll ()
```

```
        lblNum = "Selected number: " + Str(vsbNum.Value)

End Sub
```

Executing the Sum Program

☐ Execute the Sum program.

☐ Select a number by clicking the arrow icons of the vertical scroll bar or by dragging the thumb of the scroll bar.

The program responds by displaying the selected number. (See Figure 3.5.)

☐ Click the Sum It button.

The program responds by making the calculations and displaying the result in the text box. (See Figure 3.5.)

For example, select the number 5 with the scroll bar and click the Sum It button. The program should display the number 15 (that is, 1+2+3+4+5=15).

☐ Terminate the program by clicking the Exit button.

Figure 3.5.
The Sum program.

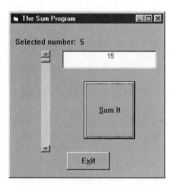

How the Sum Program Works

The Sum program uses a For…Next loop to perform the calculations.

The Code in the *cmdSumIt_Click()* Procedure

The cmdSumIt_Click() procedure is executed whenever the user clicks the cmdSumIt button:

```
Private Sub cmdSumIt_Click ()
```

```
Dim I
Dim R

For I = 1 To vsbNum.Value Step 1
    R = R + I
Next

txtResult.Text = Str(R)
```

End Sub

The procedure declares two variables, I and R.

The For...Next loop then calculates the sum:

```
1 + 2 + 3 + ...+ vsbNum.Value
```

Initially, the R variable is equal to 0, because Visual Basic initializes variables to 0 at the time of the declaration. Some programmers like to include the redundant statement

```
R = 0
```

before the For statement to make the code easier to read.

The last statement in this procedure updates the Text property of the text box with the content of the R variable.

The Code in the *vsbNum_Change()* Procedure

The vsbNum_Change() procedure is executed whenever the user changes the scroll bar position:

Private Sub vsbNum_Change ()

```
    lblNum = "Selected number: " + Str(vsbNum.Value)
```

End Sub

The procedure updates the Caption property of the lblNum label with the Value property of the scroll bar so the user can read the position of the scroll bar.

Note that the statement

```
lblNum = "Selected number: " + Str(vsbNum.Value)
```

is the same as the statement

```
lblNum.Caption = "Selected number: " + Str(vsbNum.Value)
```

That is, when you set a label control to a value without specifying a property name, Visual Basic assumes that you want to set the value of the label's Caption property, since the Caption property is the default property for a label control.

Like the label control, other controls also have a default property. For example, the default property of the Text Box control is the Text property. Therefore, the statement

```
txtMyTextBox = "Hello"
```

is the same as the statement

```
txtMyTextBox.Text = "Hello"
```

The Code in the *vsbNum_Scroll()* Procedure

The vsbNum_Scroll() procedure is executed whenever the user drags the thumb of the scroll bar:

```
Private Sub vsbNum_Scroll ()

    lblNum = "Selected number: " + Str(vsbNum.Value)

End Sub
```

This procedure has the same code as the vsbNum_Change() procedure, so while the user drags the thumb of the scroll bar, the label is updated with the Value property of the scroll bar.

The Timer Program

The Timer program illustrates the concept of *variable visibility*. This program also introduces a new control: the Timer control.

The Visual Implementation of the Timer Program

The Timer program uses the Timer control. To see which icon in the toolbox window represents the Timer control, refer back to Figure 1.13 in Chapter 1, "Writing Your First Program." The exact location of the icon in the toolbox window varies from version to version. In Figure 1.13, the icon of the Timer control is located on the left column, seventh from the top.

☐ Open a new project, save the form of the project as TIMER.FRM in the C:\VB4PRG \CH03 directory, and save the project file as TIMER.VBP in the C:\VB4PRG \CH03 directory.

☐ Build the frmTimer form according to the specifications in Table 3.3.

The completed form should look like the one shown in Figure 3.6.

Table 3.3. The properties table of the frmTimer form.

Object	Property	Setting
Form	**Name**	**frmTimer**
	Caption	The Timer Program
	Height	4290
	Left	1080
	Top	1170
	Width	3330
Command Button	**Name**	**cmdExit**
	Caption	E&xit
	Height	495
	Left	960
	Top	3120
	Width	1215
Timer	**Name**	**tmrTimer**
	Enabled	0-False
	Interval	2000
	Left	240
	Top	2040

Figure 3.6.
The frmTimer form.

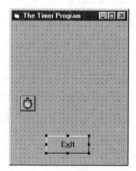

Entering the Code of the Timer Program

☐ Enter the following code in the general declarations section of the frmTimer form:

```
' All variables MUST be declared.
Option Explicit
```

☐ Enter the following code in the cmdExit_Click() procedure of the frmTimer form:

```
Private Sub cmdExit_Click ()

    End

End Sub
```

☐ Enter the following code in the tmrTimer_Timer() procedure of the frmTimer form:

```
Private Sub tmrTimer_Timer ()

    Beep

End Sub
```

Executing the Timer Program

☐ Execute the Timer program.

As you can hear, the Timer program beeps every 2 seconds. During the execution of the Timer program, the timer control icon is not shown. As you'll see during the course of this book, some controls are invisible during runtime.

☐ Click the Exit button to terminate the program.

How the Timer Program Works

The Timer program uses the timer control. The program automatically executes the tmrTimer_Timer() procedure every 2000 milliseconds.

The Code in the *tmrTimer_Timer()* Procedure

The Interval property of tmrTimer was set to 2000 at design time, so the tmrTimer_Timer() procedure is executed automatically every 2000 milliseconds (2 seconds):

```
Private Sub tmrTimer_Timer ()

    Beep

End Sub
```

Therefore, every 2 seconds the PC beeps.

Because the Timer control icon is not shown during the execution of the program, its position in the form is not important, and you may place it anywhere in the form.

Enhancing the Timer Program

☐ Add a command button to the frmTimer form, as shown in Figure 3.7. The command button should have the following properties: The Name property should be cmdEnableDisable and the Caption property should be &Enable.

Figure 3.7.

Adding the Enable button to the frmTimer form.

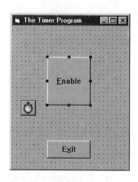

☐ Modify the general declarations section of the frmTimer form so that it looks like the following:

```
' All variables MUST be declared.
Option Explicit

' Declare the gKeepTrack variable
Dim gKeepTrack
```

☐ Modify the tmrTimer_Timer() procedure so that it looks like the following:

```
Private Sub tmrTimer_Timer ()

    ' If the gKeepTrack variable is equal to 1,
    ' then beep.
    If gKeepTrack = 1 Then
        Beep
    End If

End Sub
```

☐ Add the following code in the cmdEnableDisable_Click() procedure:

```
Private Sub cmdEnableDisable_Click ()

    If gKeepTrack = 1 Then
        gKeepTrack = 0
        cmdEnableDisable.Caption = "&Enable"
    Else
        gKeepTrack = 1
        cmdEnableDisable.Caption = "&Disable"
    End If

End Sub
```

Executing the Timer Program

☐ Execute the Timer program.

The program does not beep every 2 seconds.

☐ To enable the beeping, click the Enable button. (See Figure 3.8.)

The caption of the Enable button changes to Disable, and the program now beeps every 2 seconds. (See Figure 3.9.)

☐ Click the Disable button.

The caption of the Disable button changes to Enable, and the program does not beep every 2 seconds.

Figure 3.8.
The cmdEnableDisable button as an Enable button.

Figure 3.9.
The cmdEnableDisable button as a Disable button.

☐ You can keep clicking the Enable/Disable button to enable or disable the beeping.

☐ Click the Exit button to terminate the program.

The Code in the General Declarations Section of the frmTimer Form

The code in the general declarations section of the frmTimer form includes the declaration of the gKeepTrack variable:

```
' Declare the gKeepTrack variable
Dim gKeepTrack
```

Why do you declare this variable in the general declarations section? You want this variable to be visible by all the procedures of this form. If you declare this variable in the tmrTimer_Timer() procedure, you can access this variable in the code of the tmrTimer_Timer() procedure, but you can't access it from any other procedure. By declaring this variable in the general declarations area of the form, you make it accessible by all the procedures and functions that exist in this form.

Note that the first letter of the gKeepTrack variable is *g* to signify that the gKeepTrack variable is declared in the general declarations area of the form. Including the *g* is not a Visual Basic requirement, but it is a good programming habit.

Note: It's a good programming habit to make the first letter of a variable declared in the general declarations section *g* because the program's code will be easier to understand.

Someone who goes through the code of the form and encounters a variable whose first letter is *g*, such as gMyVariable, knows immediately that it is declared in the general declarations area of the form and is accessible by all the procedures of the form.

The Code in the *tmrTimer_Timer()* Procedure

The tmrTimer_Timer() procedure is executed every 2 seconds because you set the Interval property of the tmrTimer control to 2000:

```
Private Sub tmrTimer_Timer ()

    ' If the gKeepTrack variable is equal to 1,
    ' then beep.
    If gKeepTrack = 1 Then
       Beep
    End If

End Sub
```

If the variable gKeepTrack is equal to 1, the statement between the If line and the End If line is executed, and the Beep statement is executed. If, however, the variable gKeepTrack is not equal

to 1, the Beep statement is not executed. Note that the gKeepTrack variable is not declared in this procedure; nevertheless, this procedure recognizes this variable because it was declared in the general declarations section of the form.

When you start the program, the variable gKeepTrack is created and its value is initialized to 0 by Visual Basic.

The Code in the *cmdEnableDisable_Click()* Procedure

The cmdEnableDisable_Click() procedure is executed whenever the user clicks the cmdEnableDisable button:

```
Private Sub cmdEnableDisable_Click ()

    If gKeepTrack = 1 Then
        gKeepTrack = 0
        cmdEnableDisable.Caption = "&Enable"
    Else
        gKeepTrack = 1
        cmdEnableDisable.Caption = "&Disable"
    End If

End Sub
```

If the current value of the gKeepTrack variable is 1, the statements between the If line and the Else line change the value of gKeepTrack to 0 and change the Caption property of the cmdEnableDisable button to Enable.

If, however, the current value of the gKeepTrack variable is not equal to 1, the statements between the Else line and the End If line are executed. These statements toggle the value of the gKeepTrack variable to 1 and change the Caption property of the cmdEnableDisable button to Disable.

The cmdEnableDisable_Click() procedure recognizes the gKeepTrack variable because it was declared in the general declarations section of the frmTimer form.

Modifying the Timer Program

The gKeepTrack variable was used to demonstrate how a variable is declared in the general declarations section so it can be accessed by all the procedures of the form. However, you can run the Timer program without using the gKeepTrack variable. Use the following steps to see how this is accomplished:

☐ Remove the declaration of the gKeepTrack variable from the general declarations section of the frmTimer form (that is, the program will not use this variable). This is the only code that should be in the general declarations area of the form:

```
' All variables MUST be declared.
Option Explicit
```

Visual Basic assigns the value True as the default value for the Enabled property of the Timer control. Now change the setting of this property as follows:

☐ Change the Enabled property of the tmrTimer control to False. That is, display the frmTimer form in design time, click the tmrTimer control, press F4 to display the properties window, and change the Enabled property of the tmrTimer control to False.

☐ Change the cmdEnableDisable_Click() procedure so it looks like the following:

```
Private Sub cmdEnableDisable_Click ()

    If tmrTimer.Enabled = True Then
        tmrTimer.Enabled = False
        cmdEnableDisable.Caption = "&Enable"
    Else
        tmrTimer.Enabled = True
        cmdEnableDisable.Caption = "&Disable"
    End If

End Sub
```

☐ Change the tmrTimer_Timer() procedure so that it looks like the following:

```
Private Sub tmrTimer_Timer ()

    Beep

End Sub
```

☐ Save the project.

Executing the Timer Program

☐ Execute the Timer program and verify that it works the same way it worked when the gKeepTrack variable was used.

☐ Terminate the program by clicking the Exit button.

The Code in the *tmrTimer_Timer()* Procedure

The code in the tmrTimer_Timer() procedure is executed every 2000 milliseconds (2 seconds) if the Enabled property of the tmrTimer control is set to True. (Recall that the interval of the timer is 2000 milliseconds because in design time you set the Interval property of the tmrTimer control to 2000.)

At design time you set the Enabled property of the tmrTimer timer to False, so when you start the program, the tmrTimer_Timer() procedure is not executed every 2 seconds.

The code of the `tmrTimer_Timer()` procedure simply beeps:

```
Private Sub tmrTimer_Timer ()

   Beep

End Sub
```

Therefore, every 2000 milliseconds, if the Enabled property of the tmrTimer control is set to True, the program will beep.

The Code in the *cmdEnableDisable_Click()* Procedure

The `cmdEnableDisable_Click()` procedure is executed whenever the user clicks the cmdEnableDisable button:

```
Private Sub cmdEnableDisable_Click ()

   If tmrTimer.Enabled = True Then
      tmrTimer.Enabled = False
      cmdEnableDisable.Caption = "&Enable"
   Else
      tmrTimer.Enabled = True
      cmdEnableDisable.Caption = "&Disable"
   End If

End Sub
```

The If statement checks the value of the Enabled property of the timer control. If the timer is enabled, the statements between the If line and the Else line are executed. These statements set the Enabled property of the timer to False and change the Caption property of the cmdEnableDisable button to Enable.

If, however, the current value of the Enabled property of the timer control is not True, the statements between the Else line and the End If line are executed. These statements set the Enabled property of the timer to True and change the Caption property of the cmdEnableDisable button to Disable.

Many Windows programs use the preceding technique for changing the Caption of the button according to the current status of the program.

Summary

This chapter discusses the decision-maker statements of Visual Basic and the various loop statements. These statements are considered the programming building blocks of Visual Basic, which, added to your knowledge of controls and properties, enable you to write Visual Basic programs for Windows.

This chapter also focuses on the timer control, the visibility of the variables, and procedures, functions, and methods.

Q&A

Q **The Timer program illustrates that I can run the program with or without the `gKeepTrack` variable declared in the general declarations section. Which way is preferred?**

A Generally speaking, if you can run a program without using variables declared in the general declarations section, that's the preferred way because the program is easier to read and understand.

However, when writing programs, if you find that it is necessary to use such variables, then use them. The problem with such variables is that if you have many variables declared in the general declarations section, you might lose track of their purpose, and the program will become difficult to read and understand.

Quiz

1. What's wrong with the following `If…End If` statement:

```
If B = 3
    B = 2
End If
```

2. Suppose that the variable `MyVariable` is currently equal to 3. What will be the contents of the lblMyLabel label after the following code is executed:

```
Select Case MyVariable
        Case 0
        lblMyLabel.Caption = "Hi, Have a nice day"
        Case 1
        lblMyLabel.Caption = ""
        Case 2
        lblMyLabel.Caption = "Are you having fun?"
        Case 3
        lblMyLabel.Caption = "Good-bye"
        Case 4
        lblMyLabel.Caption = "Good morning"
End  Select
```

Exercises

1. Change the Sum program so that it uses the `Do While…Loop` statements instead of the `For…Next` loop.

2. Enhance the Sum program as follows:

   Add a command button with the following properties: The Name property should be cmdSqr and the Caption property should be Square Root.

Whenever the user clicks the Square Root button, the program should calculate and display the square root of the number selected by the scroll bar.

Hint: Use the Sqr() function of Visual Basic to calculate the square root of a number.

Quiz Answers

1. You must include the Then word. The correct syntax is as follows:

```
If B = 3 Then
   B = 2
End If
```

2. Because the current value of MyVariable is equal to 3, the statements under Case 3 are executed. In this example, there is only one statement under the Case 3 line:

```
Case 3
lblMyLabel.Caption = "Good-bye"
```

The lblMyLabel label contains the text Good-bye.

Exercise Answers

1. Change the cmdSumIt_Click() procedure so that it looks like the following:

```
Private Sub cmdSumIt_Click ()

    Dim I
    Dim R

    I = 1
    Do While I <= vsbNum.Value
        R = R + I
        I = I + 1
    Loop

    txtResult.Text = Str(R)

End Sub
```

The procedure initializes the variable I to 1 and starts the Do While…Loop. The statements between the Do While line and the Loop line are executed as long as I is less than or equal to the Value property of the vsbNum scroll bar.

3

2. Use the following steps:

☐ Add a pushbutton to the form.

☐ Set the Name property of the pushbutton to cmdSqr.

☐ Add the following code in the `cmdSqr_Click()` procedure:

```
Private Sub cmdSqr_Click ()

    txtResult.Text = Str( Sqr(vsbNum.Value) )

End Sub
```

☐ Save the project.

☐ Execute the Sum program.

☐ Select the number 4 by clicking the scroll bar.

☐ Click the Square Root button.

The program responds by displaying the result.

☐ Terminate the program by clicking the Exit button.

The `cmdSqr_Click()` procedure is executed whenever the user clicks the Square Root button. The statement in this procedure executes the `Sqr()` function:

```
txtResult.Text = Str( Sqr(vsbNum.Value) )
```

The returned value of the `Sqr()` function is assigned to the Text property of the txtResult text box. The `Sqr()` function returns the square root of the number specified as its argument. Note that the `Str()` function is used to convert the returned value of the `Sqr()` function from numeric to a string.

The `Sqr()` function is one of the many functions that Visual Basic includes, so you don't have to write the `Sqr()` function yourself.

4

The Mouse

Many Windows programs make heavy use of the mouse. In this chapter you'll learn how to detect and use events that occur in response to mouse movements, mouse clicking, and combining mouse clicking and keyboard pressing. You'll also learn about dragging and dropping objects with the mouse.

The Move Program

The Move program illustrates how to move objects by responding to mouse events.

The Visual Implementation of the Move Program

To build the Move program, use the following steps:

☐ Start a new project.

☐ Save the form of the project as MOVE.FRM in the C:\VB4PRG\CH04 directory, and save the project file as MOVE.VBP in the C:\VB4PRG\CH04 directory.

☐ Build the form of the Move program according to the specifications in Table 4.1. Some new objects you'll be placing in the frmMove form are *image controls*. See Figure 1.13 (in Chapter 1, "Writing Your First Program") for the location of the image control's icon—on the left column, third from the bottom.

The completed form should look like the one shown in Figure 4.1.

Table 4.1. The properties table of the Move program.

Object	Property	Setting
Form	**Name**	**frmMove**
	BackColor	Yellow
	Caption	The Move Program
	Height	4545
	Left	1080
	Top	1170
	Width	6810
Command Button	**Name**	**cmdExit**
	Caption	E&xit
	FontName	System

Object	Property	Setting
	FontSize	10
	Height	495
	Left	2520
	Top	3360
	Width	1215
Option Button	**Name**	**optCup**
	BackColor	Yellow
	Caption	&Cup
	FontName	System
	FontSize	10
	Height	495
	Left	360
	Top	840
	Value	-1-True
	Width	1215
Option Button	**Name**	**optClub**
	BackColor	Yellow
	Caption	C&lub
	FontName	System
	FontSize	10
	Height	495
	Left	360
	Top	1440
	Width	1215
Option Button	**Name**	**optBell**
	BackColor	Yellow
	Caption	&Bell
	FontName	System
	FontSize	10
	Height	495
	Left	360

4

continues

Table 4.1. continued

Object	Property	Setting
	Top	1920
	Width	1215
Image	**Name**	**imgCup**
	Height	330
	Left	2400
	Picture	C:\VB\BITMAPS\ASSORTED\CUP.BMP
	Top	240
	Width	360
Image	**Name**	**imgClub**
	Height	330
	Left	2880
	Picture	C:\VB\BITMAPS\ASSORTED\CLUB.BMP
	Top	240
	Width	360
Image	**Name**	**imgBell**
	Height	330
	Left	3360
	Picture	C:\VB\BITMAPS\ASSORTED\BELL.BMP
	Top	240
	Width	360

Depending on which version of Visual Basic you are using, the BMP files listed in Table 4.1 may not appear in your Visual Basic directory. If your Visual Basic directory doesn't contain these files, use any other small BMP files. For example, start Paintbrush (usually in the Accessories group) and draw small pictures of a bell, a cup, and a club.

Figure 4.1.
The Move program.

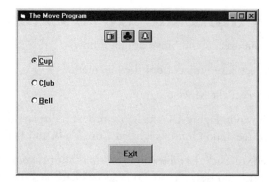

Entering the Code of the Move Program

You'll now write the code of the Move program. As usual, let's start with the general declarations section of the form.

☐ Enter the following code in the general declarations section of the frmMove form:

```
' All variables MUST be declared.
Option Explicit
```

☐ Enter the following code in the Form_MouseDown() procedure:

```
Private Sub Form_MouseDown(Button As Integer, _
                           Shift As Integer, _
                           X As Single, _
                           Y As Single)

    ' Move the checked object to coordinate X,Y
    If optBell.Value = True Then
       imgBell.Move X, Y
    ElseIf optClub.Value = True Then
       imgClub.Move X, Y
    Else
       imgCup.Move X, Y
    End If

End Sub
```

☐ Enter the following code in the cmdExit_Click() procedure:

```
Private Sub cmdExit_Click()

    End

End Sub
```

Executing the Move Program

You can execute the Move program now.

☐ Select Save Project from the File menu.

☐ Execute the Move program.

As shown in Figure 4.1, the Move program displays three images—a cup, a club, and a bell—and three option buttons labeled Cup, Club, and Bell.

When you click the mouse in the form of the program, one of the images moves to the location where the mouse is clicked. You select which image moves by selecting one of the option buttons.

For example, if the bell's option button is currently checked, clicking the mouse anywhere inside a free area of the form moves the bell image to the position where the mouse was clicked. (See Figure 4.2.)

To terminate the Move program, click the Exit button.

Figure 4.2.
The Move program, after you move the bell.

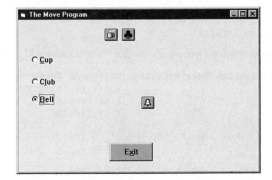

How the Move Program Works

During the discussion of the Move program, you'll encounter the term *form coordinates,* so the discussion of the Move program starts with this topic.

Form Coordinates

A form's coordinates may be specified in various units set by the ScaleMode property. The default measurement that Visual Basic sets for this property is a *twip* (there are 1440 twips in 1 inch).

Note: The ScaleMode property may be set to any of the following units:

Twips (1440 twips in 1 inch)
Points (72 points in 1 inch)
Pixels (the number per inch depends on your monitor's resolution)
Inches
Millimeters
Centimeters

The origin of the form coordinate system is defined by the ScaleTop and ScaleLeft properties of the form. The default value that Visual Basic assigns to the ScaleTop and ScaleLeft properties is 0. This means that the upper-left corner of the form's area has the coordinate 0,0. As you know, a form has borders and a title bar. However, the term *form's area* means the usable area of the form, which doesn't include its borders or title bar.

The Code in the *cmdExit_Click()* Procedure

Whenever the user clicks the Exit button, the cmdExit_Click() procedure is executed. The End statement in this procedure causes the program to terminate:

```
Private Sub cmdExit_Click()

    End

End Sub
```

The Code in the *Form_MouseDown()* Procedure

Mouse devices may have one to three buttons. Whenever you push any of the mouse buttons inside the form's area, the Form_MouseDown() procedure is executed.

Note: *Pushing* the mouse button means pressing down the mouse button. *Clicking* the mouse means pushing and then releasing the mouse button. The Form_MouseDown() procedure is executed whenever you push the mouse button. That is, the procedure is executed even before you release the mouse button.

Because the form's area doesn't include its title bar, this procedure is not executed if the mouse is clicked in the title bar. The procedure is executed only if the mouse button is clicked inside a free area of the form. For example, if the mouse button is clicked inside the area of the option buttons or the Exit button, the Form_MouseDown() procedure is not executed.

The Arguments of the *Form_MouseDown()* Procedure

The Form_MouseDown() procedure has four arguments: Button, Shift, X, and Y. These arguments contain information about the mouse's condition when the mouse button is clicked:

```
Private Sub Form_MouseDown(Button As Integer, _
                           Shift As Integer, _
                           X As Single, _
                           Y As Single)
    …
    …
    …
End Sub
```

The first argument of the Form_MouseDown() procedure is an integer called Button. The value of this argument indicates whether the clicked button was the left, right, or middle mouse button. The Move program doesn't care which button was clicked, so the value of this argument is not used in the procedure.

The second argument of the Form_MouseDown() procedure is an integer called Shift. The value of this argument indicates whether the mouse button was clicked simultaneously with the Shift key, Ctrl key, or Alt key. A better name for this argument would be ShiftCtrlAlt, but you have to work with whatever name the designers of Visual Basic decided to use. The Move program doesn't care whether the mouse button was clicked simultaneously with any of these keys, so the value of the Shift argument is not used in the procedure.

The third and fourth arguments of the Form_MouseDown() procedure are the X and Y variables. These variables contain the coordinates of the mouse location at the time the mouse button was clicked. Because the Form_MouseDown() procedure is automatically executed whenever the mouse button is clicked inside the form's area, the X,Y coordinates are referenced to the form. (For example, when the ScaleMode property is set to twips, X=0, Y=0 means that the mouse button was clicked on the upper-left corner of the form. X=10, Y=20 means that the mouse button was clicked 10 twips from the left side of the form and 20 twips from the top of the form, and so on.)

The *If...Else* Statements in the Code of the *Form_MouseDown()* Procedure

The If…Else statements in the Form_MouseDown() procedure check which option button is currently checked.

For example, if the currently checked option button is the Bell button, the first If condition

```
If optBell.Value = True Then
```

is met, and the statement

```
imgBell.Move X, Y
```

is executed. This statement uses the Move method to move the bell image from its current position to the X,Y coordinate where the mouse button was clicked.

The *Move* Method

You use the Move method to move objects. Forms and controls are the objects you can move with the Move method.

To move the Cup object from its current location to a new location that has the X,Y coordinate, use this statement:

```
imgCup.Move X, Y
```

> **Note:** After using the statement
> ```
> imgCup.Move X, Y
> ```
> the new location of the upper-left corner of the image is at coordinate X,Y.
>
> To move the image so that its center has the X,Y coordinate, use the following statement:
> ```
> imgCup.Move(X-imgCup.Width/2), _
>           (Y-imgCup.Height/2)
> ```

4

Important Information About Option Buttons

You have completed the Move program. However, there is one more thing you need to know about the option buttons.

In the Move program, you have three option buttons, but only one option button can be selected at any time. Therefore, you can select the cup, the bell, or the club, but you cannot select, for example, the cup and the bell together.

However, sometimes you'll need to have two or more groups of option buttons in the same form. You can add a second group of option buttons to the frmMove form as follows:

☐ Double-click the frame control in the toolbox. (See Figure 1.13 for the location of the frame control's icon—on the left column, third row from the top.)

Visual Basic responds by placing the frame control in the frmMove form.

☐ Move the frame control to the right and enlarge its area.

Your frmMove form should now look like the one shown in Figure 4.3.

Figure 4.3.
The frmMove form with a frame control added.

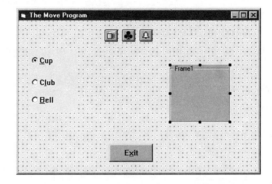

☐ Double-click the frame control in the toolbox again.

   Visual Basic responds by placing a second frame control in the frmMove form.

☐ Move the second frame control to the right and enlarge its area.

Your frmMove form should now look like the one shown in Figure 4.4.

Figure 4.4.
The frmMove form with two frame controls added.

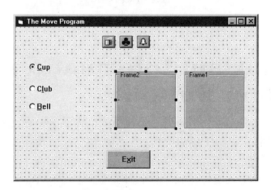

Now place two option buttons in the right frame control:

☐ Click (do not double-click) the option button icon in the toolbox.

☐ Place the mouse cursor in the right frame control and drag the mouse.

   Visual Basic responds by placing an option button in the frame control.

Your frmMove form should now look like the one shown in Figure 4.5.

Figure 4.5.

*The frmMove form with an
option button added in the
right frame control.*

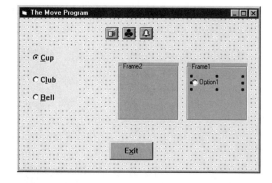

☐ Now repeat the steps for placing an option button in the frame. Remember not to
double-click the option button in the toolbox. Place a second option button in the right
frame control, and place three option buttons in the left frame control.

When you're done placing the option buttons, your frmMove form should look like the one
shown in Figure 4.6.

Figure 4.6.

*The frmMove form with
option buttons in the two
frame controls.*

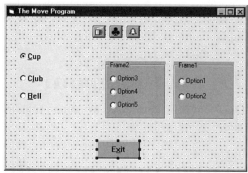

☐ Select Save Project from the File menu to save your work.

☐ Execute the Move program.

The important point to note is that the frmMove from has three independent option button
groups. That is, when you select an option button inside the Bell/Club/Cup group, it does not
influence the other two groups. Also, when you select Option1 or Option2, it does not influence
the other groups. And the same is true for the Option3/Option4/Option5 group. You can verify
this as follows:

☐ Select the Option1, Option3, and Cup option buttons. (See Figure 4.7.)

Figure 4.7.
Selecting a group of option buttons.

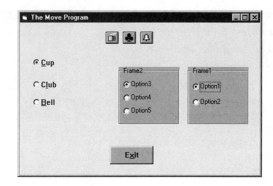

☐ Now change the selections in each of the option button groups and note that the other groups remain the same.

☐ Click the Exit button to terminate the program.

You have finished experimenting with the Move program. If you wish, you can delete the Frame1 and Frame2 frames and the Option1, Option2, Option3, Option4, and Option 5 option buttons. To remove an option button or a frame, select the control and then press Delete on your keyboard. You can delete each option button in the frame and later delete the frame itself, or you can just delete the frame, which will also delete all the controls inside it.

The Draw Program

The Draw program illustrates how your program can use mouse events to run a drawing program.

The Visual Implementation of the Draw Program

☐ Start a new project.

☐ Save the form of the project as DRAW.FRM in the C:\VB4PRG\CH04 directory and save the project file as DRAW.VBP in the C:\VB4PRG\CH04 directory.

☐ Build the form of the Draw program according to the specifications in Table 4.2.

The completed form should look like the one shown in Figure 4.8.

Table 4.2. The properties table of the Draw program.

Object	Property	Setting
Form	**Name**	**frmDraw**
	Caption	The Draw Program
	Height	4545
	Left	1080
	Top	1170
	Width	6810
Command Button	**Name**	**cmdExit**
	Caption	E&xit
	FontName	System
	FontSize	10
	Height	495
	Left	2640
	Top	3600
	Width	1215

Figure 4.8.
The Draw program.

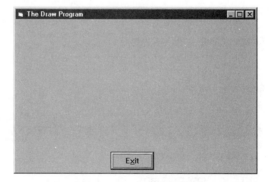

Entering the Code of the Draw Program

You'll now enter the code of the Draw program.

☐ Enter the following code in the general declarations area of the frmDraw form:

```
' All variables MUST be declared.
Option Explicit
```

☐ Enter the following code in the Form_MouseDown() event procedure:

```
Private Sub Form_MouseDown(Button As Integer, _
                           Shift As Integer, _
                           X As Single, _
                           Y As Single)

    ' Change CurrentX and CurrentY to the coordinates
    ' where the mouse button was just clicked.
    frmDraw.CurrentX = X
    frmDraw.CurrentY = Y

End Sub
```

☐ Enter the following code in the Form_MouseMove() event procedure:

```
Private Sub Form_MouseMove(Button As Integer, _
                           Shift As Integer, _
                           X As Single, _
                           Y As Single)

 ' If the left mouse button is currently clicked
 ' then draw a line.
  If Button = 1 Then
    Line (frmDraw.CurrentX, frmDraw.CurrentY)-(X, Y), _
         QBColor(0)
  End If

End Sub
```

☐ Enter the following code in the cmdExit_Click() procedure:

```
Private Sub cmdExit_Click()

    End

End Sub
```

Executing the Draw Program

Let's execute the Draw program.

☐ Start the Draw program.

An empty form pops up, as shown in Figure 4.8.

When you click and hold the mouse button while moving the mouse in the form, a line is drawn corresponding to the mouse's movement. Releasing the mouse button stops the drawing process. Figure 4.9 shows a drawing done with the Draw program.

Figure 4.9.
The Draw program with lines drawn in it.

☐ Draw something with the Draw program.

☐ To terminate the Draw program, click the Exit button.

How the Draw Program Works

The Draw program uses two graphics-related Visual Basic concepts: the Line method and the CurrentX and CurrentY properties. To understand the Draw program, you need to understand these concepts first.

The *Line* Method

To draw a line in a form, use the Line method. For example, to draw a line from the coordinate X=2000,Y=1500 to X=5000,Y=6000, use the following statement:

```
Line (2000,1500) - (5000,6000)
```

Figure 4.10 shows the line drawn by this Line method statement. The line starts 2000 twips from the left side of the form and 1500 twips from the top of the form. The line ends 5000 twips from the left side of the form and 6000 twips from the top of the form.

Figure 4.10.
Drawing a line with the Line method.

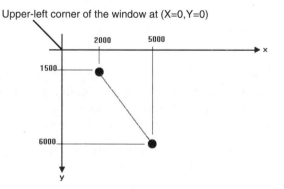

You may also specify the color for the line you draw by using the QBColor() function, which uses the numbers shown in Table 4.3.

Table 4.3. Numbers used in the QBColor() function.

Color	Number
Black	0
Blue	1
Green	2
Cyan	3
Red	4
Magenta	5
Yellow	6
White	7
Gray	8
Light blue	9
Light green	10
Light cyan	11
Light red	12
Light magenta	13
Light yellow	14
Bright white	15

For example, to draw the line in Figure 4.10 in black, use this statement:

```
Line (2000,1500) - (5000,6000), QBColor(0)
```

To draw the line in red, use this statement:

```
Line (2000,1500) - (5000,6000), QBColor(4)
```

The CurrentX and CurrentY Properties of a Form

If you examine the properties window of a form, you won't find the CurrentX and CurrentY properties because Visual Basic does not let you set these properties at design time. You can change the values of these properties only at runtime.

The CurrentX and CurrentY properties are automatically updated by Visual Basic after using various graphics methods. For example, after using the Line method to draw a line in a form,

Visual Basic automatically assigns the coordinate of the line's endpoint to the CurrentX and CurrentY properties of the form on which the line was drawn. Therefore, after the following statement is executed, CurrentX equals 5000 and CurrentY equals 6000.

```
Line (2000,1500) - (5000,6000), QBColor(0)
```

The Code in the *Form_MouseDown()* Procedure

Whenever the mouse button is clicked in the form's area, the Form_MouseDown() procedure is automatically executed:

```
Private Sub Form_MouseDown(Button As Integer, _
                           Shift As Integer, _
                           X As Single, _
                           Y As Single)

    ' Change CurrentX and CurrentY to the coordinates
    ' where the mouse button was just clicked.
    frmDraw.CurrentX = X
    frmDraw.CurrentY = Y

End Sub
```

The Form_MouseDown() procedure assigns the values of the X and Y arguments to the CurrentX and CurrentY properties of the frmDraw form. Therefore, after you click the mouse button, the CurrentX and CurrentY properties are updated with the coordinate of the mouse at the time you clicked the mouse button.

The Code in the *Form_MouseMove()* Procedure

The procedure Form_MouseMove() is executed whenever you move the mouse over the form.

The X and Y arguments of this procedure have the same meanings as the X and Y arguments of the Form_MouseDown() procedure (that is, X,Y is the mouse's coordinates):

```
Private Sub Form_MouseMove(Button As Integer, _
                           Shift As Integer, _
                           X As Single, _
                           Y As Single)

    ' If the left mouse button is currently clicked
    ' then draw a line.
    If Button = 1 Then
      Line (frmDraw.CurrentX, frmDraw.CurrentY)-(X, Y), _
           QBColor(0)
    End If

End Sub
```

The code in the Form_MouseMove() procedure checks to see whether the left mouse button is currently being clicked by examining the value of the Button argument. If the Button argument is equal to 1, it means that the left mouse button is clicked.

4

If the left button is clicked, the Line method statement is executed:

```
Line (frmDraw.CurrentX, frmDraw.CurrentY)-(X, Y), _
      QBColor(0)
```

This Line statement draws a black line from the location specified by the CurrentX and CurrentY properties to the current location of the mouse.

Remember, Visual Basic automatically updates the CurrentX and CurrentY properties with the line's endpoint after the Line method is executed. This means that the next time the Form_MouseMove() procedure is executed, the line's starting point is already updated. So on the next execution of the Form_MouseMove() procedure, a line is drawn starting from the endpoint of the previous line.

As you move the mouse, Visual Basic executes the Form_MouseMove() procedure; if the mouse button is held down, a new line is drawn from the end of the previous line to the current location of the mouse.

The Code in the *cmdExit_Click()* Procedure

Whenever you click the Exit button, the cmdExit_Click() procedure is automatically executed. The End statement in this procedure causes the program to terminate:

```
Private Sub cmdExit_Click()

    End

End Sub
```

The AutoRedraw Property

There is a small flaw in the Draw program. Use the following steps to see the problem:

☐ Execute the Draw program and draw several lines with it.

☐ Minimize the window of the program. (Click the icon that appears on the upper-left corner of the form, then select Minimize from the system menu that pops up.)

    The Draw program responds by displaying itself as an icon.

☐ Restore the window of the Draw program. (Click the minimized icon of the program, and then select Restore from the system menu that pops up.)

    As you can see, your drawing disappears!

The same problem occurs if you hide part of the Draw window by placing another window on top of it. To solve this problem, at design time simply set the AutoRedraw property of the frmDraw form to True. As implied by the name of this property, if it is set to True, Visual Basic automatically redraws the window whenever necessary.

The HowOften Program

Visual Basic cannot occupy itself by constantly executing the `Form_MouseMove()` procedure whenever the mouse is moved. If it did, your program couldn't execute any other procedure while you moved the mouse. Visual Basic checks the status of the mouse only at fixed intervals so it can execute other tasks while the mouse is moving. If Visual Basic finds that the mouse was moved since the last check, the `Form_MouseMove()` procedure is executed. The HowOften program illustrates how often `Form_MouseMove()` is executed.

The Visual Implementation of the HowOften Program

☐ Start a new project.

☐ Save the form of the project as HOWOFTEN.FRM in the C:\VB4PRG\CH04 directory and save the project file as HOWOFTEN.VBP in the C:\VB4PRG\CH04 directory.

☐ Build the form according to the specifications in Table 4.4.

The completed form should look like the one shown in Figure 4.11.

Table 4.4. The properties table of the HowOften program.

Object	Property	Setting
Form	**Name**	**frmHowOften**
	Caption	The HowOften Program
	Height	4545
	Left	1080
	Top	1170
	Width	6810
Command Button	**Name**	**cmdExit**
	Caption	E&xit
	FontName	System
	FontSize	10
	Height	495
	Left	2640
	Top	3480
	Width	1215

Figure 4.11.
The HowOften program.

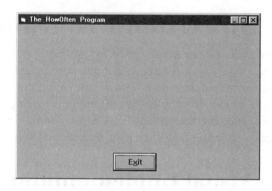

Entering the Code of the HowOften Program

☐ Enter the following code in the general declarations section of the frmHowOften form:

```
' All variables MUST be declared.
Option Explicit
```

☐ Enter the following code in the Form_MouseMove() event procedure:

```
Private Sub Form_MouseMove(Button As Integer, _
                           Shift As Integer, _
                           X As Single, _
                           Y As Single)

    ' Draw a circle with radius 40
    Circle (X, Y), 40

End Sub
```

☐ Enter the following code in the cmdExit_Click() event procedure:

```
Private Sub cmdExit_Click()

    End

End Sub
```

Executing the HowOften Program

☐ Execute the HowOften program.

When you execute the HowOften program, the window shown in Figure 4.11 is displayed. As you move the mouse, the Form_MouseMove() procedure draws small circles at the current location of the mouse; however, you will notice you that the Form_MouseMove() procedure is not executed for each and every movement of the mouse. (See Figure 4.12.)

When you move the mouse quickly, the trail of circles that the Form_MouseMove() procedure draws is spaced widely along the path of the mouse. However, if you move the mouse slowly, the Form_MouseMove() procedure leaves a dense trail of circles.

Remember, each small circle is an indication that the MouseMove event occurred and the Form_MouseMove() procedure was executed.

Figure 4.12.
Moving the mouse in the HowOften program.

Mouse was
moved slowly

Mouse was
moved fast

How the HowOften Program Works

The HowOften program uses the Form_MouseMove() procedure for performing the work.

The Code in the *Form_MouseMove()* Procedure

Whenever Visual Basic checks the mouse status and finds that the mouse moved since the last check, the Form_MouseMove() procedure is executed:

```
Private Sub Form_MouseMove(Button As Integer, _
                           Shift As Integer, _
                           X As Single, _
                           Y As Single)

    ' Draw a circle with radius 40
    Circle (X, Y), 40

End Sub
```

The Form_MouseMove() procedure simply draws a small circle at the mouse's current location by using the Circle method.

The *Circle* Method

As implied by its name, the Circle method draws a circle. To draw a circle with a radius of 40 units at coordinate X,Y, use the following statement:

```
Circle (X, Y), 40
```

The Circle method uses the units indicated by the ScaleMode property. Because the ScaleMode property of the form is Twip, the Circle method uses twip units (that is, the radius is measured in units of twips, and the center is set at X,Y coordinates measured in units of twips).

The Code in the *cmdExit_Click()* Procedure

Whenever you click the Exit button, the cmdExit_Click() procedure is executed. The End statement in this procedure causes the program to terminate:

```
Private Sub cmdExit_Click()

    End

End Sub
```

The Button Program

Now write a program called Button that uses the Button argument of the Form_MouseDown() and Form_MouseUp() procedures for determining which mouse button was clicked or released.

The Visual Implementation of the Button Program

☐ Start a new project.

☐ Save the form of the project as BUTTON.FRM in the C:\VB4PRG\CH04 directory and save the project file as BUTTON.VBP in the C:\VB4PRG\CH04 directory.

☐ Build the form of the Button program according to the specifications in Table 4.5.

The completed form should look like the one shown in Figure 4.13.

Table 4.5. The properties table of the Button program.

Object	Property	Setting
Form	**Name**	**frmButton**
	BackColor	White
	Caption	The Button Program
	Height	4545
	Left	1080
	Top	1170
	Width	6810

Object	Property	Setting
Command Button	**Name**	**cmdExit**
	Caption	E&xit
	FontName	System
	FontSize	10
	Height	495
	Left	2520
	Top	3240
	Width	1215
Text Box	**Name**	**txtResult**
	Alignment	2-Center
	Enabled	0-False
	FontName	System
	FontSize	10
	Height	495
	Left	1440
	MultiLine	-1-True
	Top	720
	Width	4215
Label	**Name**	**lblInstructions**
	Alignment	2-Center
	BackColor	White
	Caption	Push any of the mouse buttons
	FontName	System
	FontSize	10
	ForeColor	Red
	Height	375
	Left	1680
	Top	120
	Width	3975
Image	**Name**	**imgMouse**
	Height	1215
	Left	240

continues

Table 4.5. continued

Object	Property	Setting
	Picture	C:\VB\ICONS\COMPUTER \MOUSE04.ICO
	Stretch	-1-True
	Top	1680
	Width	1815

Figure 4.13.

The frmButton form in design mode.

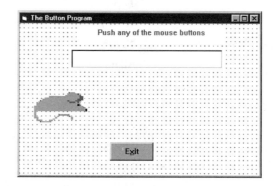

Table 4.5 instructs you to set the Picture property of imgMouse to C:\VB\ICONS \COMPUTER\MOUSE04.ICO. If your Visual Basic directory does not contain the MOUSE04.ICO file, then use a different ICO file.

Entering the Code of the Button Program

☐ Enter the following code in the general declarations section of the frmButton form:

```
' All variables must be declared
Option Explicit
```

☐ Enter the following code in the Form_MouseDown() procedure:

```
Private Sub Form_MouseDown(Button As Integer, _
                           Shift As Integer, _
                           X As Single, _
                           Y As Single)

  ' Is the left mouse down?
  If Button = 1 Then
     txtResult.Text = "Left button is currently clicked"
  End If

  ' Is the right mouse down?
  If Button = 2 Then
    txtResult.Text = "Right button is currently clicked"
```

```
        End If

        ' Is the middle mouse down?
        If Button = 4 Then
         txtResult.Text = "Middle button is currently clicked"
        End If

    End Sub
```

☐ Enter the following code in the `Form_MouseUp()` procedure:

```
Private Sub Form_MouseUp(Button As Integer, _
                         Shift As Integer, _
                         X As Single, _
                         Y As Single)

     ' Clear the content of the text box
     txtResult.Text = ""

End Sub
```

☐ Enter the following code in the `cmdExit_Click()` procedure:

```
Private Sub cmdExit_Click()

    End

End Sub
```

Executing the Button Program

☐ Execute the Button program.

When you start the Button program, the window in Figure 4.13 is displayed.

Whenever you click any of the mouse buttons in a free area of the form, the text box displays the name of the currently clicked button. For example, Figure 4.14 shows the content of the text box when the right button is clicked, and Figure 4.15 shows the content of the text box when the left button is clicked. The Button program displays the status of the mouse button only if the button is clicked in a free area of the form.

Figure 4.14.
Displaying the clicked (right) button.

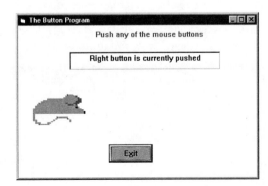

Figure 4.15.
*Displaying the clicked
(left) button.*

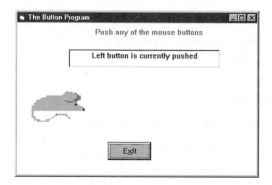

Note: An area inside the form not covered by an enabled control is called a *free area*. For example, the Enabled property of the lblInstruction label is True. Therefore, the area that this label occupies is not considered a free area of the form. On the other hand, the Enabled property of the txtResult text box is False, so the area that this text box occupies is considered a free area of the form.

Even if your mouse has three buttons, if it isn't installed as a three-button mouse, the Button program does not respond to clicking the middle mouse button.

How the Button Program Works

The Button program responds to the MouseDown event in the Form_MouseDown() procedure and to the MouseUp event in the Form_MouseUp() procedure.

The Code in the *Form_MouseDown()* Procedure

Whenever you click any of the mouse buttons inside a free area of the form, the Form_MouseDown() procedure is automatically executed. This procedure detects which button was clicked by examining the value of the Button argument.

When the Button argument equals 1, it means that the left button is being clicked; 2 means the right button is being clicked, and 4 means the middle button is being clicked:

```
Private Sub Form_MouseDown(Button As Integer, _
                           Shift As Integer, _
                           X As Single, _
                           Y As Single)

   ' Is the left mouse down?
   If Button = 1 Then
```

```
      txtResult.Text = "Left button is currently clicked"
   End If

   ' Is the right mouse down?
   If Button = 2 Then
      txtResult.Text = "Right button is currently clicked"
   End If

   ' Is the middle mouse down?
   If Button = 4 Then
      txtResult.Text = "Middle button is currently clicked"
   End If

End Sub
```

The Code in the *Form_MouseUp()* Procedure

Whenever the mouse button is released, the `Form_MouseUp()` procedure is executed. The code in this procedure clears the contents of the text box:

```
Private Sub Form_MouseUp(Button As Integer, _
                         Shift As Integer, _
                         X As Single, _
                         Y As Single)

   ' Clear the content of the text box
   txtResult.Text = ""

End Sub
```

The *Button* Argument of the *MouseMove* Event

The `Button` argument of the mouse procedures specifies which mouse button was clicked at the time of the event. As stated, the `Button` argument in the `Form_MouseDown()` procedure may be 1, 2, or 4, but it cannot have any other values, which means you can't use the `MouseDown` event to detect whether more than one mouse button has been clicked.

The `Button` argument of the `Form_MouseMove()` procedure, however, can have any value between 0 and 7, indicating all the possible combinations of pushing the mouse buttons. For example, when both the left and right buttons are clicked, the `Button` argument of the `Form_MouseMove()` procedure is equal to 3, with the equivalent binary number 00000011. (See Figure 4.16.)

Figure 4.16.

A visual representation of the `Button` argument of the `Form_MouseMove()` procedure.

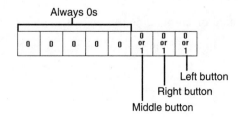

Note: Look over the following list if you're not familiar with the binary system:

Binary Notation	Decimal Notation
00000000	0
00000001	1
00000010	2
00000011	3
00000100	4
00000101	5
00000110	6
00000111	7

For example, when the Button argument is equal to 0, the binary value is 00000000. Looking at Figure 4.16, it means that none of the mouse buttons is pressed. When the Button argument is equal to 7, the binary value is 00000111, which means that all three mouse buttons are pressed. And when the Button argument is equal to 4, the binary value is 0000100, which means that the middle button is pressed.

The Button2 Program

The Button2 program illustrates how to use the Button argument of the Form_MouseMove() procedure.

The Visual Implementation of the Button2 Program

☐ Start a new project.

☐ Save the form as BUTTON2.FRM in the C:\VB4PRG\CH04 directory and save the project file as BUTTON2.VBP in the C:\VB4PRG\CH04 directory.

☐ Build the form of the Button2 program according to the specifications in Table 4.6.

The completed form should look like the one shown in Figure 4.17.

Table 4.6. The properties table of the Button2 program.

Object	Property	Setting
Form	**Name**	**frmButton2**
	BackColor	White
	Caption	The Button2 Program
	Height	4545
	Left	1080
	Top	1170
	Width	6810
Command Button	**Name**	**cmdExit**
	Caption	E&xit
	FontName	System
	FontSize	10
	Height	495
	Left	2760
	Top	3480
	Width	1215
Check Box	**Name**	**chkLeft**
	BackColor	White
	Caption	Left
	Enabled	0-False
	FontName	System
	FontSize	10
	Height	495
	Left	2040
	Top	360
	Width	1215
Check Box	**Name**	**chkMiddle**
	BackColor	White
	Caption	Middle
	Enabled	0-False
	FontName	System

continues

Table 4.6. continued

Object	Property	Setting
	FontSize	10
	Height	495
	Left	2760
	Top	960
	Width	1215
Check Box	**Name**	**chkRight**
	BackColor	White
	Caption	Right
	Enabled	0-False
	FontName	System
	FontSize	10
	Height	495
	Left	3480
	Top	360
	Width	1215
Label	**Name**	**lblInstruction**
	Alignment	2-Center
	BorderStyle	1-Fixed Single
	Caption	Press any of the mouse buttons and move the mouse
	FontName	System
	FontSize	10
	Height	375
	Left	240
	Top	1680
	Width	6255
Image	**Name**	**imgMouse**
	Height	1095
	Left	2640
	Picture	C:\VB\ICONS\COMPUTER \MOUSE04.ICO

Object	Property	Setting
	Stretch	-1-True
	Top	2040
	Width	1455

Figure 4.17.
The Button2 program.

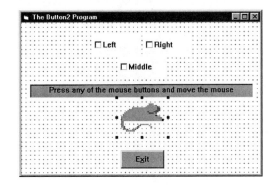

Entering the Code of the Button2 Program

☐ Enter the following code in the general declarations area of the frmButton2 form:

```
' All variables MUST be declared.
Option Explicit
```

☐ Enter the following code in the Form_MouseMove() procedure:

```
Private Sub Form_MouseMove(Button As Integer, _
                           Shift As Integer, _
                           X As Single, _
                           Y As Single)

    ' Is the left button clicked?
    If (Button And 1) = 1 Then
        chkLeft.Value = 1
    Else
        chkLeft.Value = 0
    End If

    ' Is the right button clicked?
    If (Button And 2) = 2 Then
        chkRight.Value = 1
    Else
        chkRight.Value = 0
    End If

    ' Is the middle button clicked?
    If (Button And 4) = 4 Then
        chkMiddle.Value = 1
    Else
```

```
            chkMiddle.Value = 0
        End If

    End Sub
```

☐ Enter the following code in the Form_MouseUp() event procedure:

```
Private Sub Form_MouseUp(Button As Integer, _
                         Shift As Integer, _
                         X As Single, _
                         Y As Single)

    ' Was the left button just released?
    If Button = 1 Then
        chkLeft.Value = 0
    End If

    ' Was the right button just released?
    If Button = 2 Then
        chkRight.Value = 0
    End If

    ' Was the middle button just released?
    If Button = 4 Then
        chkMiddle.Value = 0
    End If

End Sub
```

☐ Enter the following code in the cmdExit_Click() procedure:

```
Private Sub cmdExit_Click()

    End

End Sub
```

Executing the Button2 Program

☐ Execute the Button2 program. As shown in Figure 4.17, the window of the Button2 program includes three check boxes: Left, Middle, and Right.

The Button2 program checks and unchecks the check boxes according to the status of the mouse buttons while the mouse is moving.

For example, if you click the left and right mouse buttons together and move the mouse, the program checks the Left and Right check boxes. (See Figure 4.18.)

Figure 4.18.
*The Button2 program
showing the status of the
mouse buttons.*

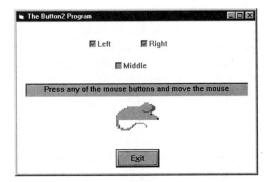

How the Button2 Program Works

The Button2 program uses the `Button` argument of the `Form_MouseMove()` procedure to report any combination of mouse buttons being clicked.

The Code in the *Form_MouseMove()* Procedure

Whenever you move the mouse, the `Form_MouseMove()` procedure is automatically executed:

```
Private Sub Form_MouseMove(Button As Integer, _
                           Shift As Integer, _
                           X As Single, _
                           Y As Single)

    ' Is the left button clicked?
    If (Button And 1) = 1 Then
        chkLeft.Value = 1
    Else
        chkLeft.Value = 0
    End If

    ' Is the right button clicked?
    If (Button And 2) = 2 Then
        chkRight.Value = 1
    Else
        chkRight.Value = 0
    End If

    ' Is the middle button clicked?
    If (Button And 4) = 4 Then
        chkMiddle.Value = 1
    Else
        chkMiddle.Value = 0
    End If

End Sub
```

The code in this procedure checks and unchecks the check boxes based on the value of the Button argument. For example, the first If...Else statement determines whether the left button is clicked by ANDing the Button argument with 1. If the result of the AND operation is 1, the left mouse button is clicked. Similarly, if the result of ANDing Button with 2 is equal to 2, the right button was clicked; if the result of ANDing Button with 4 is 4, the middle button was clicked. Don't worry if you're not familiar with the AND operation and binary notation; you just need to know what results the code will have on clicking and moving the mouse.

The Code in the *Form_MouseUp()* Procedure

Whenever you release any of the mouse buttons, the Form_MouseUp() procedure is executed:

```
Private Sub Form_MouseUp(Button As Integer, _
                        Shift As Integer, _
                        X As Single, _
                        Y As Single)

    ' Was the left button just released?
    If Button = 1 Then
        chkLeft.Value = 0
    End If

    ' Was the right button just released?
    If Button = 2 Then
        chkRight.Value = 0
    End If

    ' Was the middle button just released?
    If Button = 4 Then
        chkMiddle.Value = 0
    End If

End Sub
```

This code checks which mouse button was released, then unchecks the corresponding check box. For example, if the mouse button that was just released is the left button, the first If condition is met and the Left check box is unchecked.

Pressing the Shift, Ctrl, and Alt Keys with the Mouse Buttons

The MouseDown, MouseUp, and MouseMove events have the Shift integer as their second argument, which indicates whether the Shift, Ctrl, or Alt keys were pressed with the mouse buttons.

Figure 4.19 shows how the Shift argument indicates which key was pressed.

Figure 4.19.
The Shift *argument.*

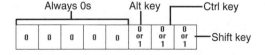

As shown in Figure 4.19, the three least significant bits of the Shift argument (the three bits on the left side) represent the status of the Shift, Ctrl, and Alt keys when you click the mouse button(s).

Table 4.7 shows the meaning of the eight possible values the Shift argument can have.

Table 4.7. The Shift argument.

Binary Value of the Shift Argument	Decimal Value of the Shift Argument	Alt Key Pressed	Ctrl Key Pressed	Shift Key Pressed
00000000	0	No	No	No
00000001	1	No	No	Yes
00000010	2	No	Yes	No
00000011	3	No	Yes	Yes
00000100	4	Yes	No	No
00000101	5	Yes	No	Yes
00000110	6	Yes	Yes	No
00000111	7	Yes	Yes	Yes

For example, when the Shift argument of the Form_MouseDown(), Form_MouseUp(), or Form_MouseMove() procedures is equal to 6, it means you clicked the mouse button while holding down the Alt and Ctrl keys but not the Shift key.

Note that the Button argument of the Form_MouseDown() procedure may have the value 1, 2, or 4. In contrast, the Shift argument of the Form_MouseDown() procedure may have any of the values listed in Table 4.7.

The Drag Program

You have learned how to use mouse events that occur when you click the mouse button (MouseDown), release the mouse button (MouseUp), and move the mouse (MouseMove). You'll now learn how to use mouse events related to dragging and dropping controls with the mouse.

Dragging is the process of clicking the left mouse button in a control and moving the mouse while holding down the mouse button. The action of releasing the mouse button after the dragging is called *dropping*.

You'll now write a program called Drag; it illustrates how easy it is to use dragging in a program.

The Visual Implementation of the Drag Program

☐ Start a new project.

☐ Save the form of the project as DRAG.FRM in the C:\VB4PRG\CH04 directory and save the project file as DRAG.VBP in the C:\VB4PRG\CH04 directory.

☐ Build the form of the Drag program according to the specifications in Table 4.8.

The completed form should look like the one shown in Figure 4.20.

Table 4.8. The properties table of the Drag program.

Object	Property	Setting
Form	Name	frmDrag
	Caption	The Drag Program
	Height	4545
	Left	1080
	Top	1170
	Width	6810
Command Button	Name	cmdExit
	Caption	E&xit
	FontName	System
	Font	10
	Height	495
	Left	2880
	Top	3360
	Width	1215
Command Button	Name	cmdDragMe
	Caption	&Drag Me
	DragMode	1-Automatic
	FontName	System
	FontSize	10
	Height	495
	Left	1080
	Top	840
	Width	1215

Figure 4.20.
The Drag program.

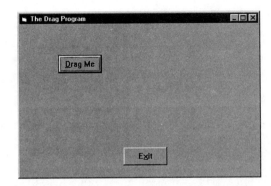

Entering the Code of the Drag Program

☐ Enter the following code in the general declarations section of the frmDrag form:

```
' All variables MUST be declared.
Option Explicit
```

☐ Enter the following code in the cmdExit_Click() procedure:

```
Private Sub cmdExit_Click()

    End

End Sub
```

Executing the Drag Program

During design time you set the DragMode property of the Drag Me button to 1-Automatic, so the Drag Me button may be dragged.

Use the following steps to see how the Drag Me button is dragged:

☐ Execute the Drag program.

☐ Click the left mouse button in the Drag Me button and hold the mouse button down while moving the mouse.

> *As you can see, a rectangle the size of the Drag Me button pops up and follows the mouse movements.*

☐ Try to drag the Drag Me button outside the form.

> *The program responds by displaying the illegal icon, which is an indication that you dragged the control to a forbidden zone.*

When you release the mouse button (called *dropping*), the rectangle disappears. Note that the Drag Me button remains in its original position.

Enhancing the Drag Program

In the Drag program, while you move a control with its DragMode property set to 1-Automatic, a rectangle the same size as the control moves in response to the mouse movements. This rectangle enables you to see where the control is being dragged.

To produce a different image while the control is being dragged, use the following steps:

☐ Select the Drag Me button and display its properties window.

☐ Change the DragIcon property of the cmdDragMe button to C:\VB\ICONS\DRAGDROP\DRAG1PG.ICO. (If your VB directory doesn't contain the DRAG1PG.ICO icon, use another ICO file.)

Use the following steps to see the effect of setting the DragIcon property:

☐ Execute the Drag program.

☐ Drag the Drag Me button.

> *The program responds by displaying the DRAG1PG.ICO icon while the Drag Me button is dragged.*

The Drop Program

The Drop program illustrates how dropping, the action of releasing the mouse button, is used in a program.

The Visual Implementation of the Drop Program

☐ Start a new project.

☐ Save the form of the project as DROP.FRM in the C:\VB4PRG\CH04 directory and save the project file as DROP.VBP in the C:\VB4PRG\CH04 directory.

☐ Build the form of the Drop program according to the specifications in Table 4.9. Table 4.9 instructs you to set the Picture property of the imgWater control to the WATER.ICO icon. If the Visual Basic version that you are using does not include this icon file, use a different icon.

The completed form should look like the one shown in Figure 4.21.

Table 4.9. The properties table of the Drop program.

Object	Property	Setting
Form	**Name**	**frmDrop**
	Caption	The Drop Program
	Height	4545
	Left	1080
	Top	1170
	Width	6810
Command Button	**Name**	**cmdExit**
	Caption	E&xit
	FontName	System
	FontSize	10
	Height	495
	Left	2760
	Top	3360
	Width	1215
Text Box	**Name**	**txtInfo**
	Alignment	2-Center
	Enabled	0-False
	FontName	System
	FontSize	10
	Height	495
	Left	1200
	MultiLine	-1-True
	Top	240
	Width	4455
Image	**Name**	**imgWater**
	DragMode	1-Automatic
	Height	1080
	Left	2760
	Picture	C:\VB\ICONS\ELEMENTS \WATER.ICO

continues

Table 4.9. continued

Object	Property	Setting
	Stretch	-1-True
	Tag	Water image
	Top	1320
	Width	1095

Figure 4.21.
The Drop program.

Entering the Code of the Drop Program

☐ Enter the following code in the general declarations area of the frmDrop form:

```
' All variables MUST be declared.
Option Explicit
```

☐ Enter the following code in the `Form_DragOver()` procedure:

```
Private Sub Form_DragOver(Source As Control, _
                          X As Single, _
                          Y As Single, _
                          State As Integer)

    Dim sInfo As String

    ' Display the dragging information.
    sInfo = "Now dragging "
    sInfo = sInfo + Source.Tag
    sInfo = sInfo + " over the Form."
    sInfo = sInfo + " State = "
    sInfo = sInfo + Str(State)
    txtInfo.Text = sInfo

End Sub
```

☐ Enter the following code in the `cmdExit_Click()` event procedure:

```
Private Sub cmdExit_Click()

    End

End Sub
```

☐ Enter the following code in the `Form_DragDrop()` procedure:

```
Private Sub Form_DragDrop(Source As Control, _
                          X As Single, _
                          Y As Single)

    ' Clear the text box.
    txtInfo.Text = ""
    ' Move the control.
    Source.Move X, Y

End Sub
```

☐ Enter the following code in the `cmdExit_DragOver()` procedure:

```
Private Sub cmdExit_DragOver(Source As Control, _
                             X As Single, _
                             Y As Single, _
                             State As Integer)

    Dim sInfo As String

    ' Display the dragging information.
    sInfo = "Now dragging "
    sInfo = sInfo + Source.Tag
    sInfo = sInfo + " over the Exit button."
    sInfo = sInfo + " State = "
    sInfo = sInfo + Str(State)
    txtInfo.Text = sInfo

End Sub
```

Executing the Drop Program

☐ Execute the Drop program.

☐ Drag the Water image.

As you drag the Water image, the text box displays a message that indicates the status of the dragging. Releasing the mouse button, or dropping, causes the Water image to move to the point of the drop.

☐ Terminate the program by clicking the Exit button.

How the Drop Program Works

The Drop program uses the `Form_DragOver()`, `cmdExit_DragOver()`, and `Form_DragDrop()` procedures.

The Code in the *Form_DragOver()* Procedure

In the Drop program, the control being dragged is the Water image. Therefore, whenever you drag the Water image over the form, the `Form_DragOver()` procedure is executed. This procedure has four arguments—`Source`, `X`, `Y`, and `State`:

```
Private Sub cmdExit_DragOver(Source As Control, _
                             X As Single, _
                             Y As Single, _
                             State As Integer)

    ...
    ...
    ...

End Sub
```

The `Source` argument is the name of the control being dragged. Because the dragged control is the Water image, the `Source` argument is automatically set to imgWater.

The `X` and `Y` arguments are the current X,Y coordinate of the mouse (referenced to the form coordinate system).

The `State` argument is an integer that has a value of 0, 1, or 2:

☐ When the `State` argument equals 2, the Water image is dragged from one free point to another on the form.

☐ When the `State` argument equals 1, the Water image is dragged from a free point on the form to an illegal point (such as to a point outside the form's free area).

☐ When the `State` argument equals 0, the Water image is dragged from an illegal point to a free point in the form.

The `Form_DragOver()` procedure prepares a string called sInfo and displays this string in the txtInfo text box:

```
Dim sInfo As String

' Display the dragging information.
sInfo = "Now dragging "
sInfo = sInfo + Source.Tag
sInfo = sInfo + " over the Form."
sInfo = sInfo + " State = "
sInfo = sInfo + Str(State)
txtInfo.Text = sInfo
```

For example, when the Water image is dragged from one free point in the form to another, the content of the sInfo string is the following:

```
Now dragging Water image over the Form. State=2
```

The following statement is one used in preparing the sInfo string:

```
sInfo = sInfo + Source.Tag
```

During design time, you set the Tag property of the Water image to Water image. Therefore, the value of Source.Tag is equal to Water image.

The Tag Property

The Tag property is often used as a storage area for data. For example, the Tag property of imgWater contains a string that identifies the control. In the Form_DragOver() procedure, you use this string to identify the dragged control. You can set the Tag property to anything you want, such as My Water for the imgWater control.

The Code in the *cmdExit_DragOver()* Procedure

The cmdExit_DragOver() procedure is executed whenever you drag a control over the Exit button. Therefore, whenever you drag the Water image over the Exit button, this procedure is executed.

The code in this procedure is similar to the code in the Form_DragOver() procedure, only now the sInfo string shows the Water image being dragged over the Exit button:

```
Private Sub cmdExit_DragOver(Source As Control, _
                             X As Single, _
                             Y As Single, _
                             State As Integer)

    Dim sInfo As String

    ' Display the dragging information.
    sInfo = "Now dragging "
    sInfo = sInfo + Source.Tag
    sInfo = sInfo + " over the Form."
    sInfo = sInfo + " State = "
    sInfo = sInfo + Str(State)
    txtInfo.Text = sInfo

End Sub
```

For example, when dragging the Water image from a point in the form to the Exit button, sInfo is filled with the string:

```
Now dragging Water image over the Exit button. State = 0
```

State is 0 in this string because the Water image is dragged from outside the Exit button into the Exit button. From the Exit button's point of view, any point outside the Exit button is an illegal point.

The Code in the *Form_DragDrop()* Procedure

The Form_DragDrop() procedure is executed whenever you drop the control in the form. There are two things to do when this occurs: clear the txtInfo text box and move the Water image to the drop point. You use the following two statements to perform this procedure:

```
Private Sub Form_DragDrop(Source As Control, _
                          X As Single, _
                          Y As Single)

    ' Clear the text box.
    txtInfo.Text = ""

    ' Move the control.
    Source.Move X, Y

End Sub
```

The Water image is moved to the drop point by using the Move method. The drop point is specified by the X and Y arguments of the procedure.

Summary

This chapter discusses mouse events. You have learned about the MouseDown, MouseUp, MouseMove, DragOver, and DragDrop events. The arguments of their procedures give you information about the state of the mouse at the time of the event. The Button argument tells you which mouse button was clicked or released; the Shift argument tells you whether the Shift, Ctrl, or Alt keys were pressed with the mouse button(s); and the X and Y arguments tell you where the mouse was at the time of the event.

Q&A

Q Dragging and dropping a control is nice. But where can I use it?

A Suppose that you are developing a program that lets your user design forms. In such a program, the user should be able to drag and move controls. (Of course, there are many other applications for the drag and drop features.)

Q During the execution of the Button program in this chapter, I clicked the mouse button on the lblHeading label, but the program did not recognize this click. Why?

A The Form_MouseDown() procedure is executed only if the mouse button is clicked in a free area of the form. During design time, you left the Enabled property of the label in its default value (True). This means that the area occupied by this label belongs to the label and is not considered part of the free area of the form.

Q I assigned an icon to the DragIcon property of a control. Later I changed my mind about this icon. How do I take it off?

A During design time, you may select the DragIcon property in the properties window and then click on the three dots; Visual Basic will then let you select another icon.

If you want to return the default icon (an empty rectangle), press the Delete key. The DragIcon property changes from (icon) to (none).

Quiz

1. When is the Form_MouseDown() procedure executed?

   a. When the user clicks the mouse on the Exit button
   b. When any of the mouse buttons is clicked in a free area of the form
   c. Whenever the mouse moves in a free area of the form

2. What is the ScaleMode property?

3. What method is used for moving objects during runtime?

   a. The Move method
   b. The Line method
   c. The Circle method

4. What is the meaning of the X and Y arguments in mouse event procedures?

5. When is the Form_MouseMove() procedure executed?

   a. When the user moves the mouse in a free area of the form
   b. When any of the mouse buttons is released
   c. When the left mouse button is released

6. When is the Form_DragDrop() procedure executed?

   a. When the mouse drops down on the floor
   b. When you release the mouse button over a free area of the form after dragging the mouse
   c. When a control is dragged outside the form

7. What is the value of the Source argument of the Form_DragDrop() procedure?

   a. Source = 0
   b. Source = the Name property of the control that was dropped
   c. Source = the Tag property of the control that was dropped

4

Exercises

1. Enhance the Drag program so that whenever you drag the Drag Me button outside the free area of the form, the PC beeps.

2. Currently, the Draw program uses the left mouse button for drawing in black. Enhance the Draw program so that the right mouse button is used for drawing in red.

Quiz Answers

1. b

2. The ScaleMode property defines the units of the coordinate system of the object. For example, if the ScaleMode property of a form is set to twips, the width, height, and all other length-related properties are measured in twips.

3. a

4. The X and Y arguments contain the values of the mouse location when the event occurred.

5. a

6. b

7. b

Exercise Answers

1. The program may detect that you dragged the control to a point outside the free area of the form by using the State argument of the Form_DragOver() procedure. If the State argument is equal to 1, the control was dragged outside the free area of the form:

```
Private Sub Form_DragOver(Source As Control, _
                          X As Single, _
                          Y As Single, _
                          State As Integer)

        If State = 1 Then
            Beep
        End If

End Sub
```

2. Modify the Form_MouseMove() procedure as follows:

```
Private Sub Form_MouseMove(Button As Integer, _
                           Shift As Integer, _
                           X As Single, _
                           Y As Single)
```

```
If Button = 1 Then
    ' Draw the line in black.
    Line(frmDraw.CurrentX, _
         frmDraw.CurrentY)-(X,Y),QBColor(0)
End If

If Button = 2 Then
    ' Draw the line in red.
    Line(frmDraw.CurrentX, _
         frmDraw.CurrentY)-(X,Y),QBColor(4)
End If
```

End Sub

The first If statement checks whether the left mouse button is currently clicked. If this is the case, a line is drawn in black.

The second If statement checks to see whether the right mouse button is currently clicked. If this is the case, a line is drawn in red.

5

Menus

This chapter focuses on incorporating a menu into a program. You'll learn how to design the menu and attach code to it.

The Colors Program

You'll now write a program that includes a menu. The program, called Colors, lets you choose a color from a menu and fill the program's form with the selected color. The program also lets you select the size of the program's form from a menu.

Before you start writing the Colors program, you need to specify how the menu system of the program should look and what it should do.

☐ When you start the program, a menu bar with two menu titles appears: Colors and Size. (See Figure 5.1.)

Figure 5.1.
The Colors program.

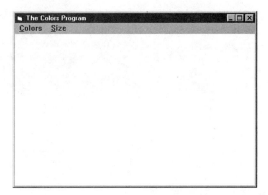

☐ The Colors menu has two items: Set Color and Exit. (See Figure 5.2.)

Figure 5.2.
The Colors menu.

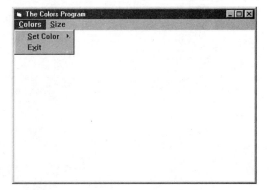

☐ The Size menu has two items: Small and Large. (See Figure 5.3.)

Figure 5.3.
The Size menu.

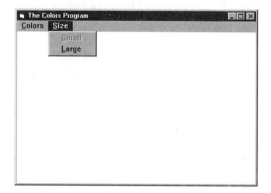

☐ When you select Set Color from the Colors menu, another menu pops up with a list of colors. (See Figure 5.4.) Once you select a color, the form of the program is filled with that color.

Figure 5.4.
The submenu of the Set Color menu item.

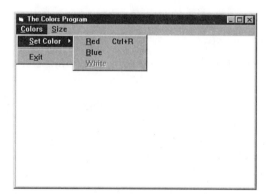

☐ When you select any of the sizes from the Size menu, the program window is sized to the selected size.

☐ When you select Exit from the Colors menu, the program terminates.

The Visual Implementation of the Colors Program

☐ Start a new project.

☐ Save the form of the project as COLORS.FRM in the C:\VB4PRG\CH05 directory, and save the project file as COLORS.VBP in the C:\VB4PRG\CH05 directory.

☐ Build the form of the Colors program according to the specifications in Table 5.1.

Table 5.1. The properties table of the Colors program.

Object	Property	Value
Form	**Name**	**frmColors**
	BackColor	White
	Caption	The Colors Program

Creating the Menu of the Colors Program

You'll now create the menus of the Colors program.

In Visual Basic, a menu is attached to a form. So, before creating the menu you must first select the form you want to attach it to.

☐ Select the frmColors form (highlight COLORS.FRM in the project window, then click the View Form button in the project window). For the Colors program this step may seem redundant since the project has only one form, but when your project includes more than one form, this step is necessary because you have to attach the menu to the form you select.

COLORS.FRM is now selected. In the following steps, Visual Basic attaches the menu to the COLORS.FRM form.

☐ Select Menu Editor from the Tools menu.

Visual Basic responds by displaying the Menu Editor. (See Figure 5.5.)

You'll now use the Menu Editor to create the menu system shown in Figures 5.1 through 5.4.

Figure 5.5.
The Menu Editor.

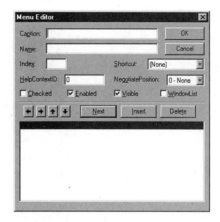

Creating Menu Controls

As you can see from Figure 5.5, the Menu Editor has two parts: the menu control list box (the lower part of the window) and the menu control properties (the upper part of the window).

When you finish creating the menus of the Colors program, the menu control list box will contain all the menu controls in the Colors program. What are menu controls? *Menu controls* could be menu titles (such as the Colors and Size menu titles shown in Figure 5.1) or menu items (such as the Set Color and Exit items shown in Figure 5.2).

The Colors program has two pull-down menus: the Colors menu shown in Figure 5.2 and the Size menu shown in Figure 5.3.

As you can see from Figure 5.2, the Colors menu has three menu controls:

- Colors (the menu title)
- Set Color (a menu item)
- Exit (a menu item)

At this point, a blank row is highlighted in the menu control list box of the Menu Editor, as shown in Figure 5.5. This means that Visual Basic is ready for you to create a menu control.

Use the following steps to create the Colors menu title:

☐ In the Caption text box of the Menu Editor, type &Colors.

☐ In the Name text box of the Menu Editor, type mnuColors.

The & character in &Colors causes Visual Basic to underline the *C*. (See Figure 5.1.) When you run the program, pressing Alt+C has the same result as clicking the Colors menu title.

You have just created the menu title of the Colors menu. The Menu Editor should now look like the one shown in Figure 5.6.

Figure 5.6.
*Creating the Colors
menu title.*

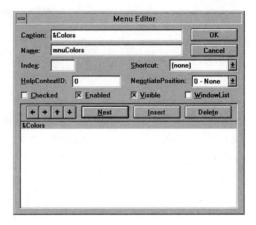

Next, create the two menu items in the Colors menu.

Use the following step to create the Set Color menu item:

☐ Click the Next button.

> *Visual Basic responds by highlighting the next row in the menu control list.*

☐ In the Caption text box, type &Set Color.

☐ In the name text box, type mnuSetColor.

Because Set Color is an item in the Colors menu, it must be indented. Use the following step to indent Set Color:

☐ Click the right-arrow button.

The Menu Editor should now look like the one shown in Figure 5.7.

Figure 5.7.
*Creating the Set Color
menu item.*

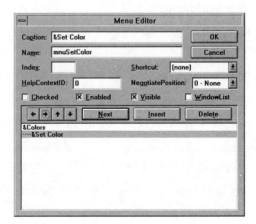

The & character in &Set Color causes Visual Basic to underline the *S*. When you run the program, pressing *S* when the Colors menu is displayed has the same result as clicking the Set Color item.

Use the following steps to create the second item in the Colors menu:

☐ Click the Next button.

> *Visual Basic responds by highlighting the next row in the menu control list.*

☐ In the Caption text box, type E&xit.

☐ In the Name text box, type mnuExit.

> *Visual Basic indented this item for you automatically, so you don't need to indent it.*

That's it for the Colors menu. Now create the Size menu. As you can see from Figure 5.3, the Size menu has three menu controls:

- Size (the menu title)
- Small (a menu item)
- Large (a menu item)

Use the following step to create the Size menu title:

☐ Click the Next button.

> *Visual Basic responds by highlighting the next row in the menu control list.*

☐ In the Caption text box, type &Size.

☐ In the Name text box, type mnuSize.

> *Visual Basic indented this item for you automatically, but since Size is a menu title, not a menu item, you need to remove the indent.*

Use this step to remove the indent before Size:

☐ Click the left-arrow button.

The Menu Editor should now look like the one shown in Figure 5.8.

Now use the following steps to create the two menu items in the Size menu:

☐ Click the Next button.

> *Visual Basic responds by highlighting the next row in the menu control list.*

☐ In the Caption text box, type &Small.

☐ In the Name text box, type mnuSmall.

Figure 5.8.
Creating the Size menu
title.

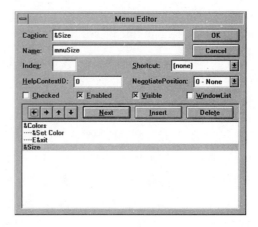

Since Small is an item in the Size menu, use this step to indent it:

☐ Click the right-arrow button.

Use the following steps to create the second item in the Size menu:

☐ Click the Next button.

☐ In the Caption text box, type &Large.

☐ In the Name text box, type mnuLarge.

> *Visual Basic indented this item for you automatically, so you don't need to indent it.*

The Size menu is ready! The Menu Editor should now look like the one shown in Figure 5.9.

Figure 5.9.
Creating the items in the
Size menu.

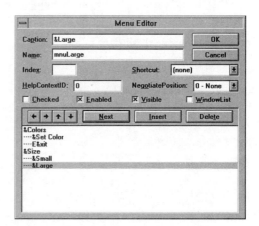

You have finished creating the Colors menu and the Size menu, but you still need to create the Set Color menu.

When you select Set Color from the Colors menu, a submenu with three items—Red, Blue, and White—should pop up. (See Figure 5.4.) Since this submenu is displayed whenever Set Color is selected, you should insert those three items below the Set Color item.

Use the following steps to insert Red below Set Color:

☐ Select the Exit item (because you are about to insert an item in the line above the Exit item).

☐ Click the Insert button.

> *Visual Basic responds by inserting a blank row below Set Color.*

☐ In the Caption text box, type &Red.

☐ In the Name text box, type mnuRed.

Currently, Red is indented at the same level as Set Color, but it should be indented further because Red is an item in the Set Color submenu.

Use the following step to indent Red further:

☐ Click the right-arrow button.

Use the following steps to insert the Blue item:

☐ Insert a blank row below the Red submenu item by selecting the Exit menu item and clicking the Insert button.

☐ In the Caption text box, type &Blue.

☐ In the Name text box, type mnuBlue.

☐ Click the right-arrow button to indent Blue at the same level as Red.

Use the following steps to insert the White submenu item:

☐ Insert a blank row below the Blue submenu item by selecting the Exit menu item and clicking the Insert button.

☐ In the Caption text box, type &White.

☐ In the Name text box, type mnuWhite.

☐ Click the right-arrow button to indent White at the same level as Red and Blue.

Congratulations! The menu of the Colors program is complete! The Menu Editor should now look like the one shown in Figure 5.10.

5

Figure 5.10.

The Menu Editor after the Colors menu is complete.

Use the following step to exit the Menu Editor:

☐ Click the OK button.

> *Visual Basic responds by closing the Menu Editor, and the frmColors form is displayed onscreen. As you can see, the menu that you just designed is attached to the form.*

The visual implementation of the Colors program is done. Use the following step to save your work:

☐ Select Save Project from the File menu.

Following a Menu Table

Because the Colors program is your first menu program, the preceding instructions were a step-by-step tutorial of how to create a menu. However, later in this chapter and in subsequent chapters, you will be instructed to create other menus by following a *menu table*.

A menu table is made up of two columns. The left column lists the captions and indentation levels of the menu controls, and the right column lists the names of the menu controls.

A typical menu table is shown in Table 5.2. As you can see, it is the menu table of the Colors program.

Table 5.2. The menu table of the Colors program.

Caption	Name
&Colors	mnuColors
...&Set Color	mnuSetColor
......&Red	mnuRed

Caption	Name
......&Blue	mnuBlue
......&White	mnuWhite
...E&xit	mnuExit
&Size	mnuSize
...&Small	mnuSmall
...&Large	mnuLarge

Entering the Code of the Colors Program

Each of the menu controls that you designed has a Click event, which is executed whenever you select that menu item. For example, when you select the Exit item of the Colors menu, the event procedure mnuExit_Click() is automatically executed. The name of this event procedure starts with the characters mnuExit_ because mnuExit is the name that you assigned to the Exit menu item.

Although the event is called Click, this event procedure is executed whether you select the menu item by clicking or by using the keyboard.

As you can see, the program's menu is displayed onscreen during design time. To display the procedure of a menu item, simply click on the menu item. For example, to see the procedure that is executed whenever you select the Exit menu item, simply click this item.

Another way to display the procedure of a menu item is to display the form's code window by double-clicking anywhere in the form and selecting the desired menu object from the Object list box at the top of the code window.

Note: To display the Form_Load() procedure, double-click any free area inside the frmColors form.

Or you can display the Form_Load() procedure as follows:

☐ Display the code window.

☐ Set the Object list box of the code window to Form.

☐ Set the Proc list box of the code window to Load.

Now enter the code of the Colors program.

☐ Enter the following code in the general declarations section of the frmColors form:

```
' All variables MUST be declared.
Option Explicit
```

☐ Enter the following code in the Form_Load() procedure:

```
Private Sub Form_Load ()

    'Because initially the window is white,
    'disable the White menu item.
    mnuWhite.Enabled = False

    'Because initially the window is small,
    'disable the Small menu item.
    mnuSmall.Enabled = False

End Sub
```

Note: To display the mnuRed_Click() procedure, display the frmColors form, select the Set Color item in the Colors menu, and then select Red from the submenu that pops up.

Or you can display the mnuRed_Click() procedure as follows:

☐ Display the code window.

☐ Set the Object list box of the code window to mnuRed.

☐ Set the Proc list box of the code window to Click.

☐ Enter the following code in the mnuRed_Click() procedure:

```
Private Sub mnuRed_Click ()

    ' Set the color of the form to red.
    frmColors.BackColor = QBColor(4)

    ' Disable the Red menu item.
    mnuRed.Enabled = False

    ' Enable the Blue and White menu items.
    mnuBlue.Enabled = True
    mnuWhite.Enabled = True

End Sub
```

☐ Enter the following code in the mnuBlue_Click() procedure:

```
Private Sub mnuBlue_Click ()

    ' Set the color of the form to blue.
```

```
frmColors.BackColor = QBColor(1)

' Disable the Blue menu item.
mnuBlue.Enabled = False

' Enable the Red and White menu items.
mnuRed.Enabled = True
mnuWhite.Enabled = True
```

End Sub

☐ Enter the following code in the mnuWhite_Click() procedure:

Private Sub mnuWhite_Click ()

```
' Set the color of the form to bright white.
frmColors.BackColor = QBColor(15)

' Disable the White menu item.
mnuWhite.Enabled = False

' Enable the Red and Blue menu items.
mnuRed.Enabled = True
mnuBlue.Enabled = True
```

End Sub

☐ Enter the following code in the mnuSmall_Click() procedure:

Private Sub mnuSmall_Click ()

```
' Set the size of the form to small.
frmColors.WindowState = 0

' Disable the Small menu item.
mnuSmall.Enabled = False

' Enable the Large menu item.
mnuLarge.Enabled = True
```

End Sub

☐ Enter the following code in the mnuLarge_Click() procedure:

Private Sub mnuLarge_Click ()

```
' Set the size of the form to large.
frmColors.WindowState = 2

' Disable the Large menu item.
mnuLarge.Enabled = False

' Enable the Small menu item.
mnuSmall.Enabled = True
```

End Sub

5

Enter the following code in the mnuExit_Click() procedure:

```
Private Sub mnuExit_Click ()

    End

End Sub
```

Executing the Colors Program

Execute the Colors program and select the various items of the menu. While you run the program, notice the following features:

- When you execute the program, the menu item White of the Set Color submenu is dimmed (that is, not available). This menu item is dimmed because the color of the form is already white, so it makes no sense to change white to white. Similarly, the Small menu item of the Size menu is dimmed because the form is already small.

- After you select Large from the Size menu, the form becomes large and the menu item Large is dimmed.

- After you select a color from the Set Color submenu, the form changes its color and the menu item of the selected color is dimmed.

Select Exit from the Colors menu to terminate the Colors program.

How the Colors Program Works

The Colors program uses the Form_Load() procedure and the Click event of the various menu items.

The Code in the *Form_Load()* Procedure

When you start the program, the Form_Load() procedure is automatically executed, which disables the menu item White of the Set Color submenu and the menu item Small of the Size menu.

The Form_Load() procedure disables the White and Small menu items by setting their Enabled properties to False:

```
Private Sub Form_Load ()

    ' Because initially the window is white,
    ' disable the White menu item.
    mnuWhite.Enabled = False

    ' Because initially the window is small,
    ' disable the Small menu item.
```

```
mnuSmall.Enabled = False
```

End Sub

The Code in the *mnuRed_Click()* Procedure

When you select Red from the Set Color submenu, the mnuRed_Click() procedure is executed, which changes the color of the form to red and disables the Red menu item:

Private Sub mnuRed_Click ()

```
' Set the color of the form to red.
frmColors.BackColor = QBColor(4)

'Disable the Red menu item.
mnuRed.Enabled = False

'Enable the Blue and White menu items.
mnuBlue.Enabled = True
mnuWhite.Enabled = True
```

End Sub

After the procedure disables the Red menu item, the procedure enables the Blue and White menu items. The Blue and White menu items are enabled because now the form's color is red, and you should be able to change it to either blue or white.

The mnuBlue_Click() and mnuWhite_Click() procedures are similar to the mnuRed_Click() procedure.

The Code in the *mnuSmall_Click()* Procedure

When you select Small from the Size menu, the mnuSmall_Click() procedure is executed, which changes the size of the form to small and disables the Small menu item:

Private Sub mnuSmall_Click ()

```
' Set the size of the form to small.
frmColors.WindowState = 0

' Disable the Small menu item.
mnuSmall.Enabled = False

' Enable the Large menu item.
mnuLarge.Enabled = True
```

End Sub

You change the size of the form by setting the WindowState property of the form. When the WindowState property of the form is set to 0, the form is sized to its default normal size (the size set at design time). When it is set to 2, the form is its maximum size.

After the procedure disables the Small menu item, it enables the Large menu item because when the form is small, you should be able to change it to large.

The `mnuLarge_Click()` procedure is similar to the `mnuSmall_Click()` procedure.

The Code in the *mnuExit_Click()* Procedure

When you select Exit from the Colors menu, the `mnuExit_Click()` procedure is executed, which terminates the program:

```
Private Sub mnuExit_Click ()

    End

End Sub
```

Adding Shortcut Keys

You can enhance the Colors program by adding *shortcut keys*. They enable you to execute a menu item by pressing a combination of keys on the keyboard.

For example, in the Colors program you may assign the shortcut key Ctrl+R to the Red menu item of the Set Color submenu. By doing so, whenever you press Ctrl+R, the form will change its color to red.

Use the following steps to assign the shortcut key Ctrl+R to the Red menu item:

☐ Select the frmColors form by clicking anywhere inside the form or by highlighting frmColors in the project window and clicking the View Form button.

☐ Select Menu Editor from the Tools menu.

Visual Basic responds by displaying the Menu Editor.

☐ Highlight the Red menu item.

Visual Basic responds by displaying the properties of the Red menu item.

As you can see, the Shortcut combo box of the Red menu item is currently set to (none).

Use the following steps to set the shortcut to Ctrl+R:

☐ Click the down arrow of the Shortcut combo box and select the shortcut Ctrl+R.

☐ Click the OK button to close the Menu Editor.

Use the following steps to see the Ctrl+R shortcut that you attached to the Red menu item in action:

☐ Execute the Colors program.

☐ Press Ctrl+R.

The Colors program responds by changing the color of the form to red.

You can now assign the shortcut Ctrl+B to the Blue menu item and the shortcut Ctrl+W to the White menu item.

Adding a Separator Bar to a Menu

A *separator bar* is a horizontal line that separates menu items. Its only purpose is cosmetic. Figure 5.11 shows the Colors menu of the Colors program after a separator bar was inserted between the Set Color item and the Exit item.

Figure 5.11.

A separator bar.

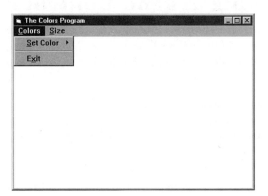

Use the following steps to insert a separator bar between the Set Color item and the Exit item:

☐ Select the frmColors form by clicking anywhere inside the form or by highlighting frmColors in the project window and clicking View Form.

☐ Select Menu Editor from the Tools menu.

Visual Basic responds by displaying the Menu Editor.

☐ Highlight the Exit menu item and click the Insert button.

Visual Basic responds by inserting a blank row above the Exit item.

☐ In the Caption text box, type -.

☐ In the name text box, type mnuSep1.

☐ Click the OK button to close the Menu Editor.

The hyphen character (-) you entered in the Caption text box is the symbol for a separator bar.

You named the separator bar mnuSep1. If you have to add more separator bars to the menu, you could name them mnuSep2, mnuSep3, and so on. Of course, you can give a separator bar any name you wish, but it's a good idea to give it a name that distinguishes it as a separator.

You cannot select the separator bar during runtime, so the mnuSep1_Click() procedure is never executed.(Why do you need a name for a menu item that is never executed? Visual Basic requires that you name all menu items.)

☐ Execute the Colors program.

As you can see, the separator bar that you just created appears.

Making a Menu Control Invisible

In the Colors program you enabled and disabled menu items at runtime by setting the Enabled property of the item to True or False. When the item is disabled (that is, the Enabled property is set to False), it becomes dimmed and you cannot select it. However, you can still see the disabled menu item.

In some programs you may need to hide a menu item completely, not just dim it. You use the Visible property to do this. For example, to make a menu item called mnuMyItem invisible during runtime, use the following statement:

```
mnuMyItem.Visible = False
```

After issuing this statement, the mnuMyItem menu item disappears, and all the menu items under it move up to fill its space.

To make a whole menu invisible, you need to set the Visible property of the menu's title to False. After making a menu invisible, it disappears and all the menus to its right move to the left to fill its space.

Using Check Marks

In some programs you may need to mark menu items. You can use check marks to do this. Figure 5.12 shows a menu item with a check mark next to it.

To place a check mark next to a menu item, set the Checked property to True; to remove the check mark, set the Checked property to False. For example, to place a check mark next to the L.A. menu item shown in Figure 5.12, you need to issue the following statement:

```
mnuLA.Checked = True
```

To uncheck the L.A. menu item, issue the following statement:

```
mnuLA.Checked = False
```

Figure 5.12.
A check mark next to a menu item.

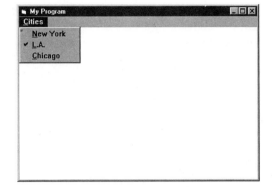

The Grow Program

You'll now write a program called Grow that illustrates how items can be added to or removed from a menu during runtime. Before you start writing the Grow program, you need to specify what the program should do:

☐ When you start the program, a menu bar with the menu title Grow appears, as shown in Figure 5.13.

Figure 5.13.
The Grow program.

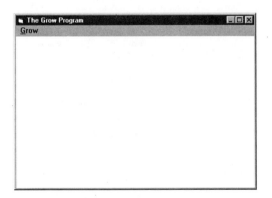

☐ The Grow menu initially has three menu items—Add, Remove, and Exit—and a separator bar. (See Figure 5.14.) Note that the Remove menu item is dimmed.

☐ Every time you select Add, a new item is added to the Grow menu. For example, after you select Add three times, the Grow menu should look like the one shown in Figure 5.15.

Figure 5.14.
The Grow menu without added items.

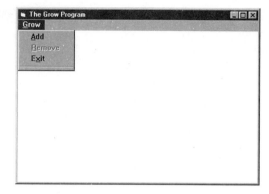

Figure 5.15.
The Grow menu with three added items.

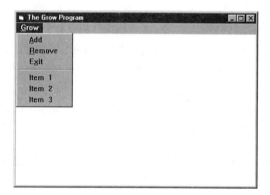

☐ Every time you select Remove, the last item of the Grow menu is removed.

☐ When you select one of the items that was added to the menu, a message box pops up with the name of the selected item. For example, if you select Item 2, the message box shown in Figure 5.16 appears.

Figure 5.16.
The message box after you select Item 2 from the Grow menu.

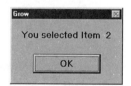

The Visual Implementation of the Grow Program

☐ Start a new project.

☐ Save the form of the project as GROW.FRM in the C:\VB4PRG\CH05 directory, and save the project file as GROW.VBP in the C:\VB4PRG\CH05 directory.

☐ Build the form according to the specifications in Table 5.3.

Table 5.3. The properties table of the frmGrow form.

Object	Property	Value
Form	Name	frmGrow
	Caption	The Grow Program
	BackColor	White

Creating the Menu of the Grow Program

Now attach a menu to the frmGrow form:

☐ Select the frmGrow form by clicking anywhere in the form or by highlighting frmColors in the project window and clicking View Form.

☐ Select Menu Editor from the Tools menu.

Visual Basic responds by displaying the Menu Editor.

☐ Design the menu according to the specifications in Table 5.4.

Table 5.4. The menu table of the frmGrow form.

Caption	Name
&Grow	mnuGrow
...&Add	mnuAdd
...&Remove	mnuRemove
...E&xit	mnuExit
...-	mnuItems

☐ Highlight the last item of the menu, the separator bar, and type 0 in the Index text box. (See Figure 5.17.)

☐ Click the OK button.

The visual implementation of the Grow program is complete!

Figure 5.17.
Setting the Index property of the separator bar.

Creating a Menu Control Array

By setting the Index property of the separator bar to 0, you created a menu control array. Because you set the Name property to mnuItems, the control array you created is called `mnuItems`.

So far, the `mnuItems` array has only one element: the separator bar (that is, `mnuItems(0)` is the separator bar). During runtime, every time you select Add from the Grow menu, the program's code will add a new element to the `mnuItems` array. As a result, more menu items will appear below the separator bar.

Entering the Code of the Grow Program

☐ Enter the following code in the general declarations section of the frmGrow form:

```
' All variables MUST be declared.
Option Explicit

' Declare the gLastElement variable.
Dim gLastElement As Integer
```

☐ Enter the following code in the `Form_Load()` procedure:

```
Private Sub Form_Load ()

    ' Initially the last element in the
    ' mnuItems[] array is 0.
    gLastElement = 0

    ' Initially no items are added to the
```

```
' Grow menu, so disable the Remove option.
mnuRemove.Enabled = False
```

End Sub

☐ Enter the following code in the `mnuAdd_Click()` procedure:

Private Sub mnuAdd_Click ()

```
' Increment the gLastElement variable.
gLastElement = gLastElement + 1

' Add a new element to the mnuItems[] array.
Load mnuItems(gLastElement)

' Assign a caption to the item that
' was just added.
mnuItems(gLastElement).Caption = _
            "Item "+Str(gLastElement)

' Because an element was just added to the
' mnuItems array, the Remove option should be
' enabled.
mnuRemove.Enabled = True
```

End Sub

☐ Enter the following code in the `mnuRemove_Click()` procedure:

Private Sub mnuRemove_Click ()

```
' Remove the last element of the mnuItems array.
Unload mnuItems(gLastElement)

' Decrement the gLastElement variable.
gLastElement = gLastElement - 1

' If only element 0 is left in the array,
' disable the Remove menu item.
If gLastElement = 0 Then
   mnuRemove.Enabled = False
End If
```

End Sub

☐ Enter the following code in the `mnuItems_Click()` procedure:

Private Sub mnuItems_Click (Index As Integer)

```
' Display the item that was selected.
MsgBox "You selected Item " + Str(Index)
```

End Sub

5

☐ Enter the following code in the mnuExit_Click() procedure:

```
Private Sub mnuExit_Click ()

    End

End Sub
```

Executing the Grow Program

Execute the Grow program and select the various items in the menu. While you run the program, notice the following features:

- When you execute the program, the menu item Remove is dimmed (that is, not available because no items have been added to the menu at this point, so there is nothing to remove).
- Every time Add is selected, a new item is added to the menu. Whenever there is at least one added item in the menu, the Remove option is available.
- Every time Remove is selected, the last added menu item is removed. When there are no more added items in the menu, the Remove option is dimmed.

☐ Select Exit from the menu to terminate the Grow program.

How the Grow Program Works

The Grow program uses the variable gLastElement to keep count of the number of elements in the mnuItems array. Because this variable should be visible in all the procedures of the form, it is declared in the general declarations section of the form.

The Code in the *Form_Load()* Procedure

When you start the program, the Form_Load() procedure is automatically executed.

In this procedure, gLastElement is initialized to 0 and the Remove menu item is disabled:

```
Private Sub Form_Load ()

    ' Initially the last element in the
    ' mnuItems[] array is 0.
    gLastElement = 0

    ' Initially no items are added to the
    ' Grow menu, so disable the Remove option.
    mnuRemove.Enabled = False

End Sub
```

The first statement in this procedure initializes the gLastElement variable to 0 because the mnuItems array has only one element in it: the 0th element. You created the 0th element of the array, the separator bar, at design time.

The next statement in this procedure disables the Remove menu item because you haven't added any items to the menu yet.

The Code in the *mnuAdd_Click()* Procedure

The mnuAdd_Click() procedure is executed when you select Add from the Grow menu. This procedure is responsible for adding a new element to the mnuItems array and setting its Caption property:

```
Private Sub mnuAdd_Click ()

    ' Increment the gLastElement variable.
    gLastElement = gLastElement + 1

    ' Add a new element to the mnuItems[] array.
    Load mnuItems(gLastElement)

    ' Assign a caption to the item that
    ' was just added.
    mnuItems(gLastElement).Caption = "Item "+Str(gLastElement)

    ' Because an element was just added to the
    ' mnuItems array, the Remove option should be
    ' enabled.
    mnuRemove.Enabled = True

End Sub
```

The first thing the procedure does is increment the value of the variable gLastElement:

```
gLastElement = gLastElement + 1
```

Then a new element is added to the mnuItems array with the Load statement:

```
Load mnuItems(gLastElement)
```

The Caption property of the new element is set with the following statement:

```
mnuItems(gLastElement).Caption = "Item "+Str(gLastElement)
```

Finally, the Remove menu item is enabled:

```
mnuRemove.Enabled = True
```

The Remove menu item is enabled because the procedure just added an item to the menu, and you should be able to remove it.

The Code in the *mnuRemove_Click()* Procedure

The mnuRemove_Click() procedure is executed whenever you select Remove from the menu:

```
Private Sub mnuRemove_Click ()

    ' Remove the last element of the mnuItems array.
    Unload mnuItems(gLastElement)

    ' Decrement the gLastElement variable.
    gLastElement = gLastElement - 1

    ' If only element 0 is left in the array,
    ' disable the Remove menu item.
    If gLastElement = 0 Then
       mnuRemove.Enabled = False
    End If

End Sub
```

In this procedure, the last element of the mnuItems array is removed with the Unload statement:

```
Unload mnuItems(gLastElement)
```

Then the variable gLastElement is decremented.

After removing the last element of the array, if it is left with only element 0, the Remove menu item is disabled:

```
If gLastElement = 0 Then
   mnuRemove.Enabled = False
End If
```

The Code in the *mnuItems_Click()* Procedure

The mnuItems_Click() procedure is executed whenever you select any of the added items from the Grow menu:

```
Private Sub mnuItems_Click (Index As Integer)

    ' Display the item that was selected.
    MsgBox "You selected Item " + Str(Index)

End Sub
```

The Index argument of this procedure indicates which item was selected. For example, if you selected Item 1, the Index argument is equal to 1 (that is, Item 1 is element number 1 in the mnuItems array). If you selected Item 2, the Index argument is equal to 2, and so on. Visual Basic automatically updates the Index argument for you.

Summary

This chapter teaches you how to write programs that include a menu, how to attach a menu to a form using the Menu Editor, and how to attach code to the menu controls. The different properties of the menu controls, such as the Visible property and the Checked property, give you the power and flexibility to change the appearance of the menu during runtime. By creating a menu control array, you can even add items to and remove them from a menu during runtime.

Q&A

Q **In the Colors program, the Enabled properties of the White and Small menu items were set to False in the `Form_Load()` procedure. Can I set these properties at design time?**

A Yes, you can set these properties during design time by using the Menu Editor dialog box.

Q **I learned how to disable menu items during runtime from the examples of this chapter. How can I disable a complete menu?**

A You need to set the Enabled property of the menu title to False to disable a complete menu. By doing so, the disabled title becomes dimmed, and the menu will not pop up. For example, to disable the Size menu of the Colors program you need to issue the following statement:

```
mnuSize.Enabled = False
```

The entire Size menu is disabled after issuing this statement.

Q **How many levels of submenus can a menu include?**

A A menu can include a maximum of four levels of submenus, as shown in Figure 5.18.

Figure 5.18.

Four levels of submenus.

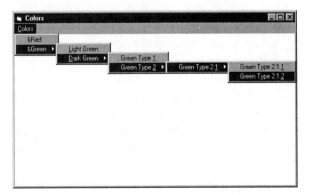

Quiz

1. What is the difference between the Enabled property and the Visible property of a menu control?
2. How do you create a menu control array, and what is it used for?
3. What are shortcut keys and how do you create them?
4. What are check marks and how do you use them in a program?
5. What is a separator bar?

Exercises

1. Enhance the Colors program so that when a color is selected, a check mark is placed next to the selected color menu item.
2. Enhance the Grow program so that you will be limited to adding a maximum of 15 items to the Grow menu (at this point, you can add an unlimited number of items).

Quiz Answers

1. When the Enabled property of a menu item is set to False, the menu item is disabled (dimmed), but you can still see it. On the other hand, when the Visible property of a menu item is set to False, the menu item completely disappears (that is, it is not just dimmed). You may need to completely hide a menu item or an entire menu in some programs.
2. A menu control array is created during design time by setting the Index property of a menu item to 0. This menu item becomes element number 0 of the array. During runtime, the program can add items to the menu by adding more elements to the array. (The items are added below the item created in design time.)
3. A shortcut key enables you to execute a menu item by pressing a combination of keys on the keyboard (for example, Ctrl+C, Ctrl+A). You assign a shortcut key to a menu item during design time by setting the Shortcut property to the desired key combination.
4. A check mark is used to mark menu items. To place a check mark next to a menu item during runtime, set the Checked property of the item to True. To remove a check mark, set the Checked property of the item to False.
5. A separator bar is a horizontal line used to separate menu items. The Caption property of a separator bar is the hyphen character (-).

Exercise Answers

1. To enhance the Colors program so that it will place a check mark next to the selected color menu item, modify the procedures mnuRed_Click(), mnuBlue_Click(), and mnuWhite_Click() as follows:

   ☐ Add the following statements to the mnuRed_Click() procedure:

   ```
   ' Put a check mark next to the Red menu item.
   mnuRed.Checked = True

   ' Uncheck the Blue and White menu items.
   mnuWhite.Checked = False
   mnuBlue.Checked = False
   ```

   ☐ Add the following statements to the mnuBlue_Click() procedure:

   ```
   ' Put a check mark next to the Blue menu item.
   mnuBlue.Checked = True

   ' Uncheck the White and Red menu items.
   mnuWhite.Checked = False
   mnuRed.Checked = False
   ```

   ☐ Add the following statements to the mnuWhite_Click() procedure:

   ```
   ' Put a check mark next to the White menu item.
   mnuWhite.Checked = True

   ' Uncheck the Blue and Red menu items.
   mnuBlue.Checked = False
   mnuRed.Checked = False
   ```

2. To limit the number of items that you can add to the Grow menu to 15, insert the following code at the beginning of the mnuAdd_Click() procedure:

   ```
   Private Sub mnuAdd_Click ()

       ' If the last element is 15 then beep and end
       ' this procedure.
       If gLastElement = 15 Then
          Beep
          Exit Sub
       End If
       ..................................
       ... The rest of the procedure ...
       ... remains the same.        ...
       ..................................
   End Sub
   ```

5

Dialog Boxes

This chapter shows you how to incorporate dialog boxes into your programs. Dialog boxes are used to display and get information. In Visual Basic there are three types of dialog boxes: predefined dialog boxes, custom dialog boxes, and common dialog boxes.

Predefined Dialog Boxes

As the name implies, *predefined dialog boxes* are predefined by Visual Basic. To display a predefined dialog box, you use a Visual Basic statement with parameters that specify how and when the dialog box should appear. You can display a predefined dialog box by using

- The MsgBox statement and MsgBox() function.
- The InputBox() function.

The Message Program

You can use the MsgBox statement and MsgBox() function to display messages to the user and to get the user's response to yes/no questions. The Message program shows how the MsgBox statement and MsgBox() function are used in a program.

The Visual Implementation of the Message Program

☐ Start a new project.

☐ Save the form of the project as MESSAGE.FRM in the C:\VB4PRG\CH06 directory, and save the project file as MESSAGE.VBP in the C:\VB4PRG\CH06 directory.

☐ Build the form according to the specifications in Table 6.1.

The completed form should look like the one shown in Figure 6.1.

Table 6.1. The properties table of the frmMessage form.

Object	Property	Value
Form	**Name**	**frmMessage**
	Caption	The Message Program
	Height	4545
	Left	1080
	Top	1170
	Width	6810

Object	Property	Value
Command Button	**Name**	**cmdMessage**
	Caption	&Message
	FontName	System
	FontSize	10
	Height	975
	Left	1920
	Top	1320
	Width	2775
Command Button	**Name**	**cmdExit**
	Caption	E&xit
	FontName	System
	FontSize	10
	Height	495
	Left	2640
	Top	3480
	Width	1215

Figure 6.1.
The form of the Message program.

Entering the Code of the Message Program

☐ Enter the following code in the general declarations area of the frmMessage form:

```
' All variables MUST be declared.
Option Explicit
```

☐ Enter the following code in the cmdMessage_Click() procedure:

```
Private Sub cmdMessage_Click()

    Dim Message As String
    Dim DialogType As Integer
    Dim Title As String

    ' The message of the dialog box.
    Message = "This is a sample message!"

    ' The dialog box should have an OK button and
    ' an exclamation icon.
    DialogType = vbOKOnly + vbExclamation

    ' The title of the dialog box.
    Title = "Dialog Box Demonstration"

    ' Display the dialog box.
    MsgBox Message, DialogType, Title

End Sub
```

☐ Enter the following code in the cmdExit_Click() procedure:

```
Private Sub cmdExit_Click()

    Dim Message As String
    Dim DialogType As Integer
    Dim Title As String
    Dim Response As Integer

    ' The message of the dialog box.
    Message = "Are you sure you want to quit?"

    ' The dialog box should have Yes and No buttons,
    ' and a question icon.
    DialogType = vbYesNo + vbQuestion

    ' The title of the dialog box.
    Title = "The Message Program"

    ' Display the dialog box and get user's response.
    Response = MsgBox(Message, DialogType, Title)

    ' Evaluate the user's response.
    If Response = vbYes Then
        End
    End If

End Sub
```

Executing the Message Program

Execute the Message program. While you run it, note the following features:

- When you click the Message button, a dialog box with a sample message, an OK button, and an exclamation point icon are displayed. (See Figure 6.2.) This message box is modal, which means that the program won't continue until you close the dialog box. For example, if you try to click the mouse on the Exit button while the dialog box is displayed, the program beeps.

- When you click the Exit button, a dialog box with a question, a Yes button, a No button, and a question mark icon are displayed. (See Figure 6.3.) This dialog box asks you to confirm whether you want to exit the program. If you press the Yes button, the program terminates. If you press the No button, the dialog box closes and the program does not terminate. This dialog box is also modal (that is, you must click the Yes or No button for the program to continue).

Figure 6.2.
A dialog box with an OK button and an exclamation point icon.

Figure 6.3.
A dialog box with Yes and No buttons and a question mark icon.

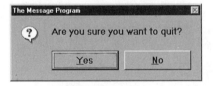

How the Message Program Works

The Message program uses the MsgBox statement and MsgBox() function to display message boxes.

Displaying a Dialog Box with the *MsgBox* Statement

Whenever the user clicks the Message button, the cmdMessage_Click() procedure is automatically executed. The code in this procedure uses the MsgBox statement to display a dialog box with an OK button and an exclamation point icon:

```
Private Sub cmdMessage_Click()

    Dim Message As String
    Dim DialogType As Integer
    Dim Title As String

    ' The message of the dialog box.
    Message = "This is a sample message!"

    ' The dialog box should have an OK button and
    ' an exclamation icon.
    DialogType = vbOKOnly + vbExclamation

    ' The title of the dialog box.
    Title = "Dialog Box Demonstration"

    ' Display the dialog box.
    MsgBox Message, DialogType, Title

End Sub
```

The `cmdMessage_Click()` procedure passes three parameters to the `MsgBox` statement:

- The message to be displayed (a string)
- The dialog box type (a numeric value)
- The title of the dialog box (a string)

Before executing the `MsgBox` statement, the `cmdMessage_Click()` procedure updates three variables that will be used as the parameters of the `MsgBox` statement.

The first variable that the `cmdMessage()` procedure updates is the string variable `Message`, which is updated with the message of the dialog box:

```
Message = "This is a sample message!"
```

`Message` is used as the first parameter of the `MsgBox` statement.

The second variable that is updated by the `cmdMessage_Click()` procedure is the integer variable `DialogType`, which is updated with a number that determines the dialog box type:

```
DialogType = vbOKOnly + vbExclamation
```

`DialogType` is used as the second parameter of the `MsgBox` statement.

`vbOKOnly` and `vbExclamation` are Visual Basic constants. `vbOKOnly` is a constant that represents the OK button, and `vbExclamation` is a constant that represents the exclamation point icon. By specifying `DialogType` as the sum of `vbOKOnly` and `vbExclamation`, you specify that the dialog box should have an OK button and an exclamation point icon, as shown in Figure 6.2.

Tables 6.2 and 6.3 list all the button constants and icon constants you can use to specify a dialog type. For example, to specify a dialog box with an OK button and a critical icon, the second parameter of the `MsgBox` statement should be the sum of the two constants `vbOKOnly` and `vbCritical`.

Table 6.2. Button constants.

Constant Name	Value	Displayed Buttons
vbOKOnly	0	OK
vbOKCancel	1	OK, Cancel
vbAbortRetryIgnore	2	Abort, Retry, Ignore
vbYesNoCancel	3	Yes, No, Cancel
vbYesNo	4	Yes, No
vbRetryCancel	5	Retry, Cancel

Table 6.3. Icon constants.

Constant Name	Value	Displayed Icon
vbCritical	16	Critical icon
vbQuestion	32	Warning query icon
vbExclamation	48	Warning message icon
vbInformation	64	Information icon

The third variable that the cmdMessage_Click() procedure updates is Title, which is updated with the title of the dialog box:

```
Title = "Dialog Box Demonstration"
```

Finally, the variables Message, DialogType, and Title are used as the parameters of the MsgBox statement:

```
MsgBox Message, DialogType, Title
```

As a result, the message box shown in Figure 6.2 is displayed.

Displaying a Dialog Box with the *MsgBox()* Function

Whenever you click the Exit button, the cmdExit_Click() procedure is executed. The code in this procedure uses the MsgBox() function to display a dialog box with a question message, Yes and No buttons, and a question mark icon:

```
Private Sub cmdExit_Click()

    Dim Message As String
    Dim DialogType As Integer
    Dim Title As String
    Dim Response As Integer
```

```
' The message of the dialog box.
Message = "Are you sure you want to quit?"

' The dialog box should have Yes and No buttons,
' and a question icon.
DialogType = vbYesNo + vbQuestion

' The title of the dialog box.
Title = "The Message Program"

' Display the dialog box and get user's response.
Response = MsgBox(Message, DialogType, Title)

' Evaluate the user's response.
If Response = vbYes Then
    End
End If

End Sub
```

The MsgBox() function takes the same parameters as the MsgBox statement. The only difference between the MsgBox statement and the MsgBox() function is that the MsgBox() function returns a value. The returned value of the MsgBox() function indicates which button in the dialog box was clicked.

Before executing the MsgBox() function, the cmdExit_Click() procedure updates the three variables Message, DialogType, and Title:

```
Message = "Are you sure you want to quit?"
DialogType = vbYesNo + vbQuestion
Title = "The Message Program"
```

The variable DialogType is updated with the sum of the constants vbYesNo and vbQuestion, because the dialog box should have Yes and No buttons and a question mark icon.

Once the variables Message, DialogType, and Title are updated, the MsgBox() function is executed and its returned value is assigned to the variable Response:

```
Response = MsgBox(Message, DialogType, Title)
```

The returned value of the MsgBox() function indicates which button was clicked. Table 6.4 lists all possible constants that can be returned by the MsgBox() function. For example, if the returned value of the MsgBox() function is the constant vbYes, then you clicked the Yes button of the message box.

Table 6.4. The output constants of the MsgBox() function.

Constant Name	Value	Clicked Button
vbOK	1	OK button
vbCancel	2	Cancel button

Constant Name	Value	Clicked Button
vbAbort	3	Abort button
vbRetry	4	Retry button
vbIgnore	5	Ignore button
vbYes	6	Yes button
vbNo	7	No button

To determine which button was clicked (the Yes button or the No button), the value of the Response variable is examined with an If statement:

```
If Response = vbYes Then
    End
End If
```

If you clicked the Yes button, Response is equal to vbYes and the program is terminated with the End statement. That is, you answered Yes to the question "Are you sure you want to quit?" and so the program ended.

Application Modal Versus System Modal

Dialog boxes that are displayed with the MsgBox statement and MsgBox() function are modal; however, a modal dialog box can be either application modal or system modal.

If the dialog box is *application modal*, you can't keep working with the current application until you respond to the dialog box. However, you can work in other applications.

If the dialog box is *system modal*, you can't keep working with any application until you respond to the dialog box. As long as the dialog box is displayed, you can't work with the current application or any other application.

The Message program's dialog boxes are application modal. To check this, use the following steps:

☐ Execute the Message program.

☐ Click the Message button.

   The program responds by displaying the dialog box shown in Figure 6.2.

☐ While the dialog box is displayed, try to click the Exit button of the Message program.

   The program responds by beeping, which is an indication that you must respond to the dialog box.

☐ While the dialog box is displayed, try to switch to another Windows application.

Windows will respond by switching to that program and you'll be able to work with it.

As you can see, the Message program's dialog box is application modal, not system modal. That is, while the dialog box is displayed, you cannot continue with the Message program but you can switch to other applications.

Is it possible to make the dialog box system modal? Yes. The following steps show you how to modify the Message program so the displayed dialog box is system modal:

☐ Switch back to the Message program, close the dialog box, and terminate the program.

☐ Change the line in the `cmdMessage_Click()` procedure that updates the `DialogType` variable from this:

```
' The dialog box should have an OK button and
' an exclamation icon.
DialogType = vbOKOnly + vbExclamation
```

to this:

```
' The dialog box should have an OK button,
' an exclamation icon, and it should be system-modal.
DialogType = vbExclamation + vbSystemModal
```

☐ Save the project.

By adding the constant `vbSystemModal` to the `DialogType` variable, you are specifying that the dialog type should be system modal. Check that it is system modal by using the following steps:

☐ Execute the Message program.

☐ Click the Message button.

The program responds by displaying the dialog box.

☐ While the dialog box is displayed, try to click the Exit button of the Message program. The program responds by doing nothing! It doesn't even beep.

☐ While the dialog box is displayed, try to switch to another Windows application. Again, nothing happens.

As you can see, the dialog box is now system modal. While the dialog box is displayed, you can't work with the current application or switch to other applications. As long as the dialog box is displayed, all the system's applications are suspended.

The Dialogs Program

The Message program illustrates how you can use the MsgBox statement and MsgBox() function to display a dialog box with an OK button and a dialog box with Yes and No buttons. As shown in Table 6.2, you can display other standard buttons in the dialog box.

The Dialogs program illustrates how you can use the MsgBox() function to display various buttons in dialog boxes and how you can use the returned value of the MsgBox() function to determine which button was clicked.

The Visual Implementation of the Dialogs Program

☐ Start a new project.

☐ Save the form of the project as DIALOGS.FRM in the C:\VB4PRG\CH06 directory, and save the project file as DIALOGS.VBP in the C:\VB4PRG\CH06 directory.

☐ Build the form according to the specifications in Table 6.5 and Table 6.6. (Table 6.6 is the menu table of the frmDialogs form.)

The completed form should look like the one shown in Figure 6.4.

Table 6.5. The properties table of the frmDialogs form.

Object	Property	Value
Form	Name	frmDialogs
	BackColor	White
	Caption	The Dialogs Program
Menu	(See Table 6.6.)	(See Table 6.6.)

Table 6.6. The menu table of the frmDialogs form.

Caption	Name
Dialogs	mnuDialogs
...OK-Cancel dialog	mnuOkCancel
...Abort-Retry-Ignore dialog	mnuAbortRetryIgnore
...Yes-No-Cancel dialog	mnuYesNoCancel
...Yes-No dialog	mnuYesNo
...Retry-Cancel dialog	mnuRetryCancel
...-	mnuSep1
...E&xit	mnuExit

6

Figure 6.4.
The frmDialogs form.

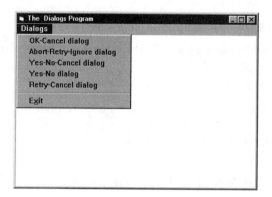

Entering the Code of the Dialogs Program

☐ Enter the following code in the general declarations area of the frmDialogs form:

```
' All variables MUST be declared.
Option Explicit
```

☐ Enter the following code in the mnuAbortRetryIgnore_Click() procedure of the frmDialogs form:

```
Private Sub mnuAbortRetryIgnore_Click ()

    Dim DialogType As Integer
    Dim DialogTitle As String
    Dim DialogMsg As String
    Dim Response As Integer

    ' Dialog should have Abort, Retry, Ignore buttons,
    ' and an Exclamation icon.
    DialogType = vbAbortRetryIgnore + vbExclamation

    ' The dialog title.
    DialogTitle = "MsgBox Demonstration"

    ' The dialog message.
    DialogMsg = "This is a sample message!"

    ' Display the dialog box, and get user's response.
    Response = MsgBox(DialogMsg, DialogType, DialogTitle)

    ' Evaluate the user's response.
    Select Case Response
            Case vbAbort
                MsgBox "You clicked the Abort button!"
            Case vbRetry
                MsgBox "You clicked the Retry button!"
            Case vbIgnore
                MsgBox "You clicked the Ignore button!"
    End Select

End Sub
```

☐ Enter the following code in the `mnuExit_Click()` procedure of the frmDialogs form:

```
Private Sub mnuExit_Click ()

    Dim DialogType As Integer
    Dim DialogTitle As String
    Dim DialogMsg As String
    Dim Response As Integer

    ' Dialog should have Yes & No buttons,
    ' and a Critical Message icon.
    DialogType = vbYesNo + vbCritical

    ' The dialog title.
    DialogTitle = "The Dialogs Program"

    ' The dialog message.
    DialogMsg = "Are you sure you want to exit?"

    ' Display the dialog box, and get user's response.
    Response = MsgBox(DialogMsg, DialogType, DialogTitle)

    ' Evaluate the user's response.
    If Response = vbYes Then
        End
    End If

End Sub
```

☐ Enter the following code in the `mnuOkCancel_Click()` procedure of the frmDialogs form:

```
Private Sub mnuOkCancel_Click ()

    Dim DialogType As Integer
    Dim DialogTitle As String
    Dim DialogMsg As String
    Dim Response As Integer

    ' Dialog should have OK & Cancel buttons,
    ' and an Exclamation icon.
    DialogType = vbOkCancel + vbExclamation

    ' The dialog title.
    DialogTitle = "MsgBox Demonstration"

    ' The dialog message.
    DialogMsg = "This is a sample message!"

    ' Display the dialog box, and get user's response.
    Response = MsgBox(DialogMsg, DialogType, DialogTitle)

    ' Evaluate the user's response.
    If Response = vbOK Then
        MsgBox "You clicked the OK button!"
    Else
        MsgBox "You clicked the Cancel button!"
    End If

End Sub
```

6

Enter the following code in the `mnuRetryCancel_Click()` procedure of the frmDialogs form:

```
Private Sub mnuRetryCancel_Click ()

    Dim DialogType As Integer
    Dim DialogTitle As String
    Dim DialogMsg As String
    Dim Response As Integer

    ' Dialog should have Retry & Cancel buttons,
    ' and an Exclamation icon.
    DialogType = vbRetryCancel + vbExclamation

    ' The dialog title.
    DialogTitle = "MsgBox Demonstration"

    ' The dialog message.
    DialogMsg = "This is a sample message!"

    ' Display the dialog box, and get user's response.
    Response = MsgBox(DialogMsg, DialogType, DialogTitle)

    ' Evaluate the user's response.
    If Response = vbRetry Then
        MsgBox "You clicked the Retry button!"
    Else
        MsgBox "You clicked the Cancel button!"
    End If

End Sub
```

Enter the following code in the `mnuYesNo_Click()` procedure of the frmDialogs form:

```
Private Sub mnuYesNo_Click ()

    Dim DialogType As Integer
    Dim DialogTitle As String
    Dim DialogMsg As String
    Dim Response As Integer

    ' Dialog should have Yes & No buttons,
    ' and a question mark icon.
    DialogType = vbYesNo + vbQuestion

    ' The dialog title.
    DialogTitle = "MsgBox Demonstration"

    ' The dialog message.
    DialogMsg = "Is this a sample message?"

    ' Display the dialog box, and get user's response.
    Response = MsgBox(DialogMsg, DialogType, DialogTitle)
```

```
' Evaluate the user's response.
If Response = vbYes Then
   MsgBox "You clicked the Yes button!"
Else
   MsgBox "You clicked the No button!"
End If
```

End Sub

☐ Enter the following code in the mnuYesNoCancel_Click() procedure of the frmDialogs form:

Private Sub mnuYesNoCancel_Click ()

```
Dim DialogType As Integer
Dim DialogTitle As String
Dim DialogMsg As String
Dim Response As Integer

' Dialog should have Yes, No, and Cancel buttons,
' and an Exclamation icon.
DialogType = vbYesNoCancel + vbExclamation

' The dialog title.
DialogTitle = "MsgBox Demonstration"

' The dialog message.
DialogMsg = "This is a sample message!"

' Display the dialog box, and get user's response.
Response = MsgBox(DialogMsg, DialogType, DialogTitle)

' Evaluate the user's response.
Select Case Response
        Case vbYes
                MsgBox "You clicked the Yes button!"
        Case vbNo
                MsgBox "You clicked the No button!"
        Case vbCancel
                MsgBox "You clicked the Cancel button!"
End Select
```

End Sub

Executing the Dialogs Program

Execute the Dialogs program and experiment with the various dialog boxes. For example, do this to display the Abort-Retry-Ignore dialog box:

☐ Select Abort-Retry-Ignore dialog from the Dialogs menu.

The program responds by displaying a dialog box with Abort, Retry, and Ignore buttons. (See Figure 6.5.)

Figure 6.5.

A dialog box with Abort, Retry, and Ignore buttons.

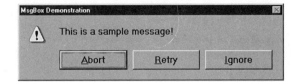

☐ Click one of the buttons in the dialog box.

The program responds by displaying a message with the name of the button you clicked.

Use the following steps to terminate the Dialogs program:

☐ Select Exit from the Dialogs menu.

The program responds by displaying a Yes/No dialog box, asking if you're sure you want to quit.

☐ Click the Yes button.

How the Dialogs Program Works

The Dialogs program uses the `MsgBox()` function to display various dialog boxes with different buttons. The program uses the returned value of the `MsgBox()` function to determine which button was clicked.

The *mnuAbortRetryIgnore_Click()* Procedure

Whenever you select Abort-Retry-Ignore dialog from the Dialogs menu, the `mnuAbortRetryIgnore_Click()` procedure is executed. The code in this procedure uses the `MsgBox()` function to display a dialog box with Abort, Retry, and Ignore buttons:

```
Private Sub mnuAbortRetryIgnore_Click ()

    Dim DialogType As Integer
    Dim DialogTitle As String
    Dim DialogMsg As String
    Dim Response As Integer

    ' Dialog should have Abort, Retry, Ignore buttons,
    ' and an Exclamation icon.
    DialogType = vbAbortRetryIgnore + vbExclamation

    ' The dialog title.
    DialogTitle = "MsgBox Demonstration"

    ' The dialog message.
    DialogMsg = "This is a sample message!"

    ' Display the dialog box, and get user's response.
    Response = MsgBox(DialogMsg, DialogType, DialogTitle)
```

```
' Evaluate the user's response.
Select Case Response
      Case vbAbort
            MsgBox "You clicked the Abort button!"
      Case vbRetry
            MsgBox "You clicked the Retry button!"
      Case vbIgnore
            MsgBox "You clicked the Ignore button!"
End Select
```

End Sub

Before executing the MsgBox() function, the mnuAbortRetryIgnore_Click() procedure updates the variables DialogType, DialogMsg, and DialogTitle:

```
DialogType = vbAbortRetryIgnore + vbExclamation
DialogTitle = "MsgBox Demonstration"
DialogMsg = "This is a sample message!"
```

The variable DialogType is updated with the sum of vbAbortRetryIgnore and vbExclamation, because the dialog box should have Abort, Retry, and Ignore buttons and an exclamation point icon.

Once the variables Message, DialogType, and Title are updated, the MsgBox() function is executed, and its returned value is assigned to the variable Response:

```
Response = MsgBox(DialogMsg, DialogType, DialogTitle)
```

To determine which button was clicked (that is, the Abort button, the Retry button, or the Ignore button), the value of the Response variable is examined with a Select Case statement:

```
Select Case Response
      Case vbAbort
            MsgBox "You clicked the Abort button!"
      Case vbRetry
            MsgBox "You clicked the Retry button!"
      Case vbIgnore
            MsgBox "You clicked the Ignore button!"
End Select
```

If, for example, you clicked the Ignore button, the variable Response is equal to vbIgnore, and the statement under vbIgnore Case is executed. (The meanings of the vbAbort, vbRetry, and vbIgnore constants are listed in Table 6.4.)

The MsgBox statements under the Select Case statement specify only one parameter. For example, under the Case vbAbort line, the MsgBox statement is as follows:

```
MsgBox "You clicked the Abort button!"
```

When the second and third parameters of the MsgBox statement are not specified, the dialog box is displayed with an OK button and without any icon. The title of the dialog box is set to the name of the program.

6

The rest of the procedures of the Dialogs program are similar to the mnuAbortRetryIgnore_Click() procedure. They update the variables DialogMsg, DialogType, and DialogTitle and then use the MsgBox() function to display a dialog box. The returned value of the MsgBox() function is used to determine which button was clicked.

The *InputBox()* Function

You can use the InputBox() function to get information from the user. The InputBox() function displays a dialog box with a message, a text box, an OK button, and a Cancel button. The user can type in the text box and then close the dialog box by clicking the OK button.

The first parameter of the InputBox() function is the message of the dialog box, and the second parameter is the title of the dialog box. The InputBox() function returns whatever the user typed in the text box. For example, the following statement displays a dialog box, shown in Figure 6.6, that asks the user to enter a name:

```
Name = _
  InputBox ("Enter your name:", "InputBox Demonstration")
```

Figure 6.6.

A dialog box that asks the user to enter a name.

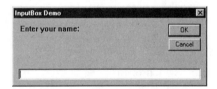

The user may type a name in the text box and then click OK to close the dialog box. In this example, the returned value of the InputBox() function is assigned to the variable Name. After the user clicks the OK button, the variable Name is updated with the user's name.

Now enhance the Dialogs program to show how you can use the InputBox() function to get a string, a number, and a date from the user.

☐ Add four new items with the following characteristics to the menu of the Dialogs program (insert them above the Exit menu item):

Caption	Name
...Get A String	mnuGetString
...Get A Number	mnuGetNumber
...Get A Date	mnuGetDate
...-	mnuSep2

After you insert these items, the menu table of the Dialogs program should look like the one shown in Table 6.7.

Table 6.7. The new menu table of the Dialogs program.

Caption	Name
Dialogs	mnuDialogs
...OK-Cancel dialog	mnuOkCancel
...Abort-Retry-Ignore dialog	mnuAbortRetryIgnore
...Yes-No-Cancel dialog	mnuYesNoCancel
...Yes-No dialog	mnuYesNo
...Retry-Cancel dialog	mnuRetryCancel
...-	mnuSep1
...Get A String	mnuGetString
...Get A Number	mnuGetNumber
...Get A Date	mnuGetDate
...-	mnuSep2
...Exit	mnuExit

☐ Enter the following code in the mnuGetString_Click() procedure of the frmDialogs form:

```
Private Sub mnuGetString_Click ()

Dim UserInput

' Get a string from the user.
UserInput = InputBox("Type anything:", "InputBox Demo")

' If the user did not enter anything, or if the user
' pressed Cancel, exit the procedure.
If UserInput = "" Then
   MsgBox "You did not type anything or pressed Cancel."
   Exit Sub
End If

' Display whatever the user typed.
MsgBox "You typed: " + UserInput

End Sub
```

☐ Enter the following code in the `mnuGetNumber_Click()` procedure of the frmDialogs form:

```
Private Sub mnuGetNumber_Click ()

Dim UserInput

' Get a number from the user.
UserInput = InputBox("Enter a number:", "InputBox Demo")

' If the user did not enter anything, or if the user
' pressed Cancel, exit the procedure.
If UserInput = "" Then
   MsgBox "You did not type anything or pressed Cancel."
   Exit Sub
End If

' If the user did not enter a number,
' exit the procedure.
If Not IsNumeric(UserInput) Then
   MsgBox "Invalid number!"
   Exit Sub
End If

' Display the number that the user entered.
MsgBox "You entered the number: " + UserInput

End Sub
```

☐ Enter the following code in the `mnuGetDate_Click()` procedure of the frmDialogs form:

```
Private Sub mnuGetDate_Click ()

Dim UserInput, DayOfWeek, Msg

' Get a date from the user.
UserInput = InputBox("Enter a date:", "InputBox Demo")

' If the user did not enter anything, or if the user
' pressed Cancel, exit the procedure.
If UserInput = "" Then
   MsgBox "You did not type anything or pressed Cancel."
   Exit Sub
End If

' If the user did not enter a date, exit the procedure.
If Not IsDate(UserInput) Then
   MsgBox "Invalid date!"
   Exit Sub
End If

' Calculate the day of week of the entered date.
DayOfWeek = Format(UserInput, "dddd")

' Display the date that the user entered and the day
' of week of that date.
Msg = "You entered the date: " + UserInput
```

```
    Msg = Msg + " Day of week of this date is: "+ DayOfWeek
    MsgBox Msg

        End Sub
```

☐ Save your work!

Execute the Dialogs program and experiment with the new menu items:

☐ Select Get A String from the menu.

The program responds by displaying the dialog box shown in Figure 6.7.

Figure 6.7.
*The Get A String
dialog box.*

☐ Type anything in the dialog box and click the OK button.

The program responds by displaying whatever you typed.

☐ Select Get A String again, but this time click the Cancel button instead of the OK button.

The program responds by displaying a message telling you that you either typed nothing or pressed Cancel.

☐ Select Get A Number from the menu.

The program responds by displaying a dialog box that asks you to enter a number.

☐ Enter any valid number, such as 1234, and click the OK button.

The program responds by displaying a message with the number you typed.

☐ Select Get A Number again, but this time type an invalid number, such as ABCD.

The program responds by displaying a message telling you that you entered an invalid number.

☐ Now experiment with the Get A Date menu item by entering both valid and invalid dates in the Get A Date dialog box. Valid dates might be, for example, January 1, 1994; July 4, 1776; and 01/01/94. Examples of invalid dates are 1234, ABCD, and 14/77/93.

Notice that after you enter a valid date in the Get A Date dialog box, the program displays a message box with the date you entered as well as the day of the week of that date. For example, if you enter the date July 4, 1776, the program responds by displaying this message:

```
You entered the date: July 4, 1776   Day of week of this date is: Thursday
```

The Code in the *mnuGetString_Click()* Procedure

Whenever you select Get A String from the menu, the `mnuGetString_Click()` procedure is executed to get a string. The procedure begins by executing the `InputBox()` function:

```
UserInput = InputBox("Type anything:", "InputBox Demo")
```

This statement displays the dialog box shown in Figure 6.7. The returned value of the `InputBox()` function is assigned to the variable `UserInput`. If you pressed the Cancel button, the returned value of the `InputBox()` function is null. If, however, you typed something and clicked the OK button, the returned value of the `InputBox()` function is whatever you typed.

To see if the Cancel button was clicked, an `If` statement is used:

```
If UserInput = "" Then
    MsgBox "You did not type anything or pressed Cancel."
    Exit Sub
End If
```

If you typed nothing or pressed the Cancel button, the condition `UserInput=""` is satisfied. As a result, the message `You did not type anything or pressed Cancel` is displayed, and the procedure is terminated with the `Exit Sub` statement.

If, however, the condition `UserInput=""` is not met, the last statement of the procedure is executed:

```
MsgBox "You typed: " + UserInput
```

This statement displays whatever you entered.

The Code in the *mnuGetNumber_Click()* Procedure

Whenever you select Get A Number from the menu, the procedure is executed. The code in this procedure asks you to enter a number and then verifies that the number is valid. The procedure begins by executing the `InputBox()` function:

```
UserInput = InputBox("Enter a number:", "InputBox Demo")
```

An `If` statement is used to determine if you pressed Cancel:

```
If UserInput = "" Then
    MsgBox "You did not type anything or pressed Cancel."
    Exit Sub
End If
```

If you typed nothing and clicked the Cancel button, the condition `UserInput=""` is satisfied. As a result, the message `You did not type anything or pressed Cancel` is displayed, and the procedure is terminated with the `Exit Sub` statement.

After verifying that you typed something and didn't press Cancel, the procedure determines whether you typed a valid number by using the `IsNumeric()` function:

```
If Not IsNumeric(UserInput) Then
   MsgBox "Invalid number!"
   Exit Sub
End If
```

If the variable UserInput is filled with characters such as ABC, the condition Not IsNumeric(UserInput) is satisfied. As a result, you are prompted with the message Invalid number! and the procedure is terminated with the Exit Sub statement.

If, however, the variable UserInput is filled with characters such as 123, the condition Not IsNumeric(UserInput) is not satisfied, and the last statement of the procedure is executed:

```
MsgBox "You entered the number: " + UserInput
```

This statement displays the number you entered.

The Code in the *mnuGetDate_Click()* Procedure

Whenever you select Get A Date from the menu, the mnuGetDate_Click() procedure is executed. The code in this procedure asks you to enter a date and then verifies whether the date is valid. The procedure begins by executing the InputBox() function:

```
UserInput = InputBox("Enter a date:", "InputBox Demo")
```

An If statement is used to determine whether you pressed Cancel:

```
If UserInput = "" Then
   MsgBox "You did not type anything or pressed Cancel."
   Exit Sub
End If
```

If you typed nothing or clicked the Cancel button, the condition UserInput="" is satisfied. As a result, the message You did not type anything or pressed Cancel is displayed, and the procedure is terminated with the Exit Sub statement.

After verifying that you typed something and didn't press Cancel, the procedure determines whether you typed a valid date by using the IsDate() function:

```
If Not IsDate(UserInput) Then
   MsgBox "Invalid date!"
   Exit Sub
End If
```

If the variable UserInput is filled with characters such as 123 or ABC, the condition Not IsDate(UserInput) is satisfied. As a result, you are prompted with the message Invalid date!, and the procedure is terminated with the Exit Sub statement. If, however, the variable UserInput is filled with characters such as 12/01/94, the condition Not IsDate(UserInput) is not satisfied, and the last four statements of the procedure are executed:

```
DayOfWeek = Format(UserInput, "dddd")
Msg = "You entered the date: " + UserInput
Msg = Msg + " Day of week of this date is: "+ DayOfWeek
MsgBox Msg
```

6

These statements display the date you entered (that is, UserInput) as well as the day of the week of that date (that is, DayOfWeek). The variable DayOfWeek is updated by using the Format() function. If, for example, UserInput is equal to July 4, 1776, Format(UserInput, "dddd") returns Thursday.

Using Other Parameters of the *InputBox()* Function

The Dialogs program used the InputBox() function with only two parameters (the message to be displayed and the title of the dialog box). You can also use other optional parameters of the InputBox() function. The third parameter specifies the default string that appears in the text box of the dialog box. The fourth and fifth parameters specify the X and Y positions (in twips) at which the dialog box appears.

For example, use the following statement:

```
MyNumber = InputBox("Enter a number:","Demo","7",100,200)
```

to display a dialog box with the following characteristics:

- The message is Enter a number:
- The title is Demo
- The default string in the text box is 7
- The left edge of the dialog box is 100 twips from the screen's left edge
- The upper edge of the dialog box is 200 twips from the top of the screen

As a result, the dialog box appears at the screen coordinate X=100,Y=200 and the default value in the text box is 7.

Custom Dialog Boxes

As the name implies, *custom dialog boxes* are customized by the user. Designing a custom dialog box is the same as designing a form. In fact, a custom dialog box is a regular form used to display and get information; it is designed so it can be used by any application.

To illustrate how to design a custom dialog box and use it in a program, you'll now enhance the Dialogs program further. You'll design a custom dialog box called GetMonth.FRM that lets you select a month. After you finish designing the GetMonth.FRM dialog box, you'll add code to the Dialogs program that uses the GetMonth.FRM dialog box.

Designing a Custom Dialog Box

To design the GetMonth.FRM dialog box, use the following steps:

☐ Open the DIALOGS.VBP project.

☐ Select Form from the Insert menu.

Visual Basic responds by displaying a new blank form.

☐ Save the form as GetMonth.FRM (that is, select Save File As from the File menu and save the file as GetMonth.FRM in the C:\VB4PRG\CH06 directory).

☐ Build the GetMonth.FRM dialog box according to the specifications in Table 6.8. The Picture property of the frmGetMonth form is set for cosmetic reasons only, to make the frmGetMonth form attractive. Use Paintbrush, Paint, or another drawing program to draw a picture such as the GLOBE.BMP picture, save the picture as a BMP file, and then set the Picture property of the frmGetMonth form to the BMP file that you drew.

The completed dialog box should look like the one shown in Figure 6.8.

☐ Save the project.

Table 6.8. The properties table of the GetMonth.FRM dialog box.

Object	Property	Value
Form	**Name**	**frmGetMonth**
	BackColor	Dark gray
	BorderStyle	1-Fixed Single
	Caption	Select a month
	ControlBox	0-False
	Height	5325
	Left	1020
	MaxButton	0-False
	MinButton	0-False
	Picture	C:\VB4PRG\BMP\GLOBE.BMP
	Top	645
	Width	7365

continues

6

Table 6.8. continued

Object	Property	Value
Option Button	**Name**	**optJan**
	Caption	&Jan.
	FontName	System
	FontSize	10
	Height	495
	Left	5520
	Top	840
	Value	True
	Width	1215
Option Button	**Name**	**optFeb**
	Caption	&Feb.
	FontName	System
	FontSize	10
	Height	495
	Left	5520
	Top	1320
	Width	1215
Option Button	**Name**	**optMar**
	Caption	&Mar.
	FontName	System
	FontSize	10
	Height	495
	Left	5520
	Top	1800
	Width	1215
Option Button	**Name**	**optApr**
	Caption	&Apr.
	FontName	System
	FontSize	10
	Height	495
	Left	5520

Object	Property	Value
	Top	2280
	Width	1215
Command Button	**Name**	**cmdOK**
	Cancel	False
	Caption	&OK
	Default	True
	FontName	System
	FontSize	10
	Height	495
	Left	5880
	Top	4080
	Width	1215
Command Button	**Name**	**cmdCancel**
	Cancel	True
	Caption	&Cancel
	Default	False
	FontName	System
	FontSize	10
	Height	495
	Left	4560
	Top	4080
	Width	1215

6

Figure 6.8.
The GetMonth.FRM dialog box in design mode.

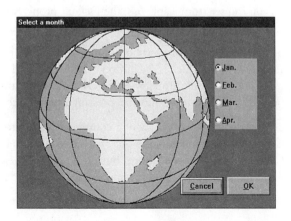

> **Note:** Table 6.8 instructs you to place only four option buttons for four months, so the user will be able to select January, February, March, or April.
>
> You are instructed to place only four option buttons because this will save you a lot of design time. At a later time, you can enhance the frmGetMonth form to include all 12 months.

Standard Dialog Box Properties

A typical dialog box is designed so that you can't change its appearance during runtime. As you can see from Table 6.8, the properties of the frmGetMonth dialog box are set so that you can't size, maximize, or minimize the frmGetMonth dialog box during runtime:

- The Border Style property of the frmGetMonth dialog box is set to Fixed Single so you can't change the size of the dialog box during runtime.

- The Control Box property of the frmGetMonth dialog box is set to False so the dialog box is displayed without the Control Menu box. (The Control Menu box is the small icon that appears in the top-left corner of a form.)

- The Max Button property of the frmGetMonth dialog box is set to False so the dialog box is displayed without the Maximize button on its upper-right corner. This prevents you from maximizing the dialog box during runtime.

- The Min Button property of the frmGetMonth dialog box is set to False so the dialog box is displayed without the Minimize button on its upper-right corner. This prevents you from minimizing the dialog box during runtime.

The Cancel Property and Default Property of the Command Buttons

As you can see from Table 6.8, the Default property of the OK button is set to True, and the Cancel property of the Cancel button is set to True.

Setting the Default property of a command button to True makes this command button the Default button, which is the button that's considered clicked when you press Enter. Therefore, because the Default property of the OK button is set to True, when the frmGetMonth dialog box is displayed during runtime, pressing Enter has the same effect as clicking the OK button.

Setting the Cancel property of a command button to True makes this command button the Cancel button, which is the one that's selected when you press Esc. Therefore, because the Cancel property of the Cancel button is set to True, when the frmGetMonth dialog box is displayed during runtime, pressing Esc has the same effect as clicking the Cancel button.

Displaying and Hiding a Custom Dialog Box

To display a custom dialog box, use the Show method. The dialog box should be displayed as modal (the user must respond to the dialog box before the program continues). To display the dialog box as modal, use the Show method with its argument equal to 1. For example, to display the dialog box frmMyDialog as modal, use the following statement:

```
frmMyDialog.Show 1
```

To hide a dialog box, use the Hide method. For example, if the dialog box frmMyDialog is displayed, the following statement hides it from view:

```
frmMyDialog.Hide
```

To see the Show method and Hide method in action, add code to the Dialogs program. This code displays the frmGetMonth dialog box whenever you select the menu item Get A Month and hides the dialog box whenever you respond to the dialog box by clicking the OK button or Cancel button in the dialog box.

☐ Add two new items with the following characteristics to the menu of the frmDialogs form (insert them above the Exit menu item):

Caption	Name
…Get A Month (custom dialog)	mnuGetMonth
…-	mnuSep3

After inserting these items, the menu table of the Dialogs program should look like the one shown in Table 6.9.

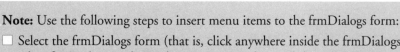

Note: Use the following steps to insert menu items to the frmDialogs form:

☐ Select the frmDialogs form (that is, click anywhere inside the frmDialogs form or select frmDialogs in the Dialogs project window and then click the View Form button).

☐ Select Menu Editor from the Tools menu.

Visual Basic will respond by displaying the Menu Editor with the menu of the frmDialogs form.

If the frmGetMonth form is currently selected and you don't select the frmDialogs form before selecting Menu Editor from the Tools menu, Visual Basic will "think" that you want to use the Menu Editor for editing the menu of the frmGetMonth form.

6

Table 6.9. The menu table of the Dialogs program after you add the Get Month item.

Caption	Name
Dialogs	mnuDialogs
...OK-Cancel dialog	mnuOkCancel
...Abort-Retry-Ignore dialog	mnuAbortRetryIgnore
...Yes-No-Cancel dialog	mnuYesNoCancel
...Yes-No dialog	mnuYesNo
...Retry-Cancel dialog	mnuRetryCancel
...-	mnuSep1
...Get A String	mnuGetString
...Get A Number	mnuGetNumber
...Get A Date	mnuGetDate
...-	mnuSep2
...Get A Month (custom dialog)	mnuGetMonth
...-	mnuSep3
...Exit	mnuExit

☐ Enter the following code in the `mnuGetMonth_Click()` procedure of the frmDialogs form:

```
Private Sub mnuGetMonth_Click ()

    ' Display the frmGetMonth dialog box.
    frmGetMonth.Show 1

    ' Display the month that the user selected (if any).
    If frmGetMonth.Tag = "" Then
       MsgBox "You cancelled the dialog box!"
    Else
       MsgBox "You selected: " + frmGetMonth.Tag
    End If

End Sub
```

Whenever you select Get A Month from the Dialogs menu, the `mnuGetMonth_Click()` procedure is executed. The code of this procedure uses the Show method to display the frmGetMonth dialog box and displays the month you selected by displaying the Tag property of the frmGetMonth dialog box. As you will soon see, the code of the frmGetMonth dialog box uses `frmGetMonth.Tag` to store the name of the month you selected.

☐ Enter the following code in the general declarations section of the frmGetMonth dialog box:

```
' All variables must be declared.
Option Explicit
```

> **Note:** To display the code window of the frmGetMonth form, double-click anywhere inside the frmGetMonth form or select frmGetMonth in the dialog's project window and then click the View Code button. Visual Basic then displays the code window of the frmGetMonth form.

☐ Enter the following code in the cmdOK_Click() procedure of the frmGetMonth form:

```
Private Sub cmdOK_Click ()

    ' Update frmGetMonth.Tag with the month that the
    ' user selected. (frmGetMonth.Tag is used as the
    ' output of the form).
    If optJan = True Then frmGetMonth.Tag = "January"
    If optFeb = True Then frmGetMonth.Tag = "February"
    If optMar = True Then frmGetMonth.Tag = "March"
    If optApr = True Then frmGetMonth.Tag = "April"

    ' Hide the frmGetMonth form.
    frmGetMonth.Hide

End Sub
```

Whenever you click the OK button of the frmGetMonth dialog box, the cmdOK_Click() procedure is executed. The code of this procedure uses a series of four If statements to see which option button is currently selected and accordingly updates the Tag property of the dialog box (frmGetMonth.Tag) with the name of the selected month. After the four If statements, the procedure uses the Hide method to hide the frmGetMonth dialog box from view.

The Tag property of the frmGetMonth dialog box is used as the output of the dialog box. That is, whoever displays the frmGetMonth dialog box can use frmGetMonth.Tag to know which month the user selected.

☐ Enter the following code in the cmdCancel_Click() procedure of the frmGetMonth dialog box:

```
Private Sub cmdCancel_Click ()

    ' Set frmGetMonth.Tag to null.
    frmGetMonth.Tag = ""
```

6

```
' Hide the frmGetMonth form.
frmGetMonth.Hide

End Sub
```

Whenever you click the Cancel button of the frmGetMonth dialog box, the `cmdCancel_Click()` procedure is executed. The code of this procedure sets the Tag property of the dialog box (frmGetMonth.Tag) to null and then uses the `Hide` method to hide the frmGetMonth dialog box from view. Setting frmGetMonth.Tag to null indicates that the user clicked the Cancel button.

☐ Save the project.

☐ Execute the Dialogs program, select Get A Month from the Dialogs menu, and experiment with the Get A Month custom dialog box.

☐ Terminate the Dialogs program by selecting Exit from the Dialogs menu.

Common Dialog Boxes

Visual Basic includes a control called *common dialog custom control*. You can use it to display common dialog boxes during runtime by simply setting its properties. The common dialog box is used as a dialog box that lets the user select and save files.

The Common Program

To illustrate how to use the common dialog custom control in a program, you'll now write the Common program to display two common dialog boxes: the Color Selection dialog box and the Open File dialog box.

The Visual Implementation of the Common Program

☐ Start a new project.

☐ Save the form of the project as COMMON.FRM in the C:\VB4PRG\CH06 directory, and save the project file as COMMON.VBP in the C:\VB4PRG\CH06 directory.

Because the common dialog control is a custom control, you must first make sure that the OCX file of this custom control is included in your project before you can place it in a form. The OCX file of the common dialog custom control is COMDLG16.OCX if you are using 16-bit Visual Basic, or COMDLG32.OCX if you are using 32-bit Visual Basic.

To see if the COMDLG16.OCX or COMDLG32.OCX file is included in the COMMON.VBP project do the following:

☐ Select Custom Controls from the Tools menu.

Visual Basic responds by displaying the Custom Controls dialog box. (See Figure 6.9.)

Figure 6.9.
The Custom Controls dialog box.

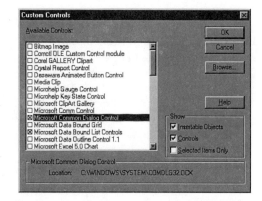

As you can see, the Custom Controls dialog box lists check boxes with names of various custom controls. The custom controls that have check marks in their check boxes are currently included in the project.

As shown in Figure 6.9, the Microsoft Common Dialog Control check box has a check mark in it. This means that the Common Dialog custom control is included in the project.

☐ Make sure that the Microsoft Common Dialog Control check box has a check mark in it. If it doesn't, place a check mark in it by clicking it.

☐ Click the OK button of the Custom Controls dialog box.

Visual Basic responds by closing the Custom Controls dialog box.

Note: If you don't see Microsoft Common Dialog Control in the Available Controls list of the Custom Controls dialog box, then add it to the list as follows:

☐ Click the Browse button of the Custom Controls dialog box.

☐ Select the COMDLG16.OCX file if you are using 32-bit Windows or the COMDLG16.OCX file if you are using 16-bit Windows. The OCX files should be in your Windows system directory.

Now that you've made sure the common dialog custom control is included in the project, you can place the common dialog custom control in the COMMON.FRM form:

☐ Select the COMMON.FRM form by clicking anywhere inside the COMMON.FRM form or by selecting COMMON.FRM in the project window, and then clicking the View Form button.

Visual Basic responds by displaying the COMMON.FRM form.

☐ Double-click the icon of the common dialog custom control in the toolbox window shown in Figure 6.10. (The exact location of the icon in the toolbox window varies from version to version.)

Visual Basic responds by placing the common dialog custom control in the COMMON.FRM form. The default name that Visual Basic assigns to this control is CommonDialog1.

Figure 6.10.
The icon of the common dialog custom control.

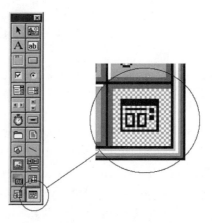

☐ Build the COMMON.FRM form according to the specifications in Table 6.10 and Table 6.11. (Table 6.11 is the menu table of the frmCommon form.)

The completed form should look like the one shown in Figure 6.11.

Table 6.10. The properties table of the COMMON.FRM form.

Object	Property	Value
Form	**Name**	**frmCommon**
	Caption	The Common Program
Common Dialog	**Name**	**CommonDialog1**
	CancelError	True
Menu	**(See Table 6.11.)**	**(See Table 6.11.)**

Table 6.11. The menu table of the frmCommon form.

Caption	Name
&File	mnuFile
...Color...	mnuColor
...Open...	mnuOpen
...-	mnuSep1
...E&xit	mnuExit

Figure 6.11.
The form of the Common program.

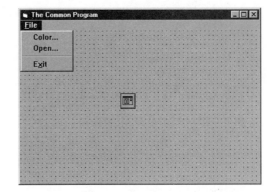

Entering the Code of the Common Program

☐ Enter the following code in the general declarations area of the frmCommon form:

```
' All variables must be declared.
Option Explicit
```

☐ Enter the following code in the mnuColor_Click() procedure of the frmCommon form:

```
Private Sub mnuColor_Click ()

    ' Set an error trap to detect the pressing of the
    ' Cancel button of the Color dialog box.
    On Error GoTo ColorError

    ' Display the Color dialog box.
    CommonDialog1.Action = 3

    ' Change the color of the form to the color that the
    ' user selected in the color dialog box.
    frmCommon.BackColor = CommonDialog1.Color

    ' Exit the procedure.
    Exit Sub
```

```
ColorError:
    ' The user pressed the Cancel button of the Color
    ' dialog box.
    MsgBox "You cancelled the dialog box!"
    Exit Sub

End Sub
```

☐ Enter the following code in the mnuOpen_Click() procedure of the frmCommon form:

```
Private Sub mnuOpen_Click ()

    Dim Filter As String

    ' Set an error trap to detect the pressing of the
    ' Cancel key of the Open dialog box.
    On Error GoTo OpenError

    ' Fill the items of the File Type list box of
    ' the Open dialog box.
    Filter = "All Files (*.*)¦*.* ¦"
    Filter = Filter + "Text Files (*.txt)¦*.txt ¦"
    Filter = Filter + "Batch Files (*.bat)¦*.bat"
    CommonDialog1.Filter = Filter

    ' Set the default File Type to Text Files (*.txt).
    CommonDialog1.FilterIndex = 2

    ' Display the Open dialog box.
    CommonDialog1.Action = 1

    ' Display the name of the file that the user selected.
    MsgBox "You selected: " + CommonDialog1.Filename

    ' Exit the procedure.
    Exit Sub

OpenError:
    ' The user pressed the Cancel key.
    MsgBox "You cancelled the dialog box!"
    Exit Sub

End Sub
```

☐ Enter the following code in the mnuExit_Click() procedure of the frmCommon form:

```
Private Sub mnuExit_Click ()

    End

End Sub
```

Executing the Common Program

Execute the Common program. Note that the common dialog custom control is invisible. The control comes to life as soon as you select Color or Open from the File menu. (Remember that during design time you cannot modify the size of the control.)

☐ Select Color from the File menu.

The Common program responds by displaying the Color dialog box. (See Figure 6.12.)

Figure 6.12.
The Color dialog box.

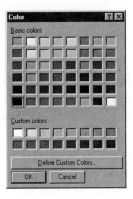

☐ Select a color from the Color dialog box by clicking the desired color and pressing the OK button.

The Common program responds by closing the Color dialog box and changing the color of the form to the selected color.

☐ Select Open from the File menu.

The Common program responds by displaying the Open dialog box. (See Figure 6.13.)

Figure 6.13.
The Open dialog box.

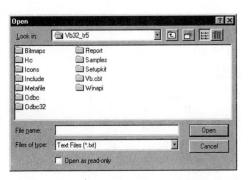

☐ Select a file from the Open dialog box.

The Common program responds by displaying the name of the selected file.

☐ Experiment with the Common program and then terminate the program by selecting Exit from the File menu.

How the Common Program Works

The Common program uses the common dialog custom control to display a Color dialog box and an Open dialog box. The Color dialog box lets you select a color, and the Open dialog box lets you select a file.

The Color Dialog Box

Whenever you select Color from the File menu, the `mnuColor_Click()` procedure is executed. The code in this procedure uses the common dialog custom control to display a Color dialog box:

```
Private Sub mnuColor_Click ()

    ' Set an error trap to detect the pressing of the
    ' Cancel button of the Color dialog box.
    On Error GoTo ColorError

    ' Display the Color dialog box.
    CommonDialog1.Action = 3

    ' Change the color of the form to the color that the
    ' user selected in the color dialog box.
    frmCommon.BackColor = CommonDialog1.Color

    ' Exit the procedure.
    Exit Sub

ColorError:
    ' The user pressed the Cancel button of the Color
    ' dialog box.
    MsgBox "You canceled the dialog box!"
    Exit Sub

End Sub
```

Before displaying the dialog box, the `mnuColor_Click()` procedure sets an error trap:

```
On Error GoTo ColorError
```

The purpose of this error trap is to detect an error during the display of the dialog box. Recall that during design time you set the CancelError property of the CommonDialog1 common dialog custom control to True. Therefore, if you press the Cancel button while the dialog box

is displayed, an error is generated; as a result of the above error trap, the program branches to the ColorError label.

After setting the error trap, the procedure displays the Color dialog box by setting the Action property of the CommonDialog1 common dialog custom control to 3:

```
CommonDialog1.Action = 3
```

If you press the Cancel button while the dialog box is displayed, an error is generated and, as a result, the code under the ColorError label is executed. The code under the ColorError label displays a message and terminates the procedure:

```
ColorError:
    MsgBox "You canceled the dialog box!"
    Exit Sub
```

However, if you don't press the Cancel button, but select a color from the dialog box and press the OK button, the procedure executes the following two statements:

```
frmCommon.BackColor = CommonDialog1.Color
Exit Sub
```

The first statement changes the BackColor property of the form to the color you selected, which is in the Color property of the CommonDialog1 control (`CommonDialog1.Color`). The second statement terminates the procedure.

The Open Dialog Box

Whenever you select Open from the File menu, the mnuOpen_Click() procedure is executed. The code in this procedure uses the common dialog custom control to display an Open dialog box:

```
Private Sub mnuOpen_Click ()

    Dim Filter As String

    ' Set an error trap to detect the pressing of the
    ' Cancel key of the Open dialog box.
    On Error GoTo OpenError

    ' Fill the items of the File Type list box of
    ' the Open dialog box.
    Filter = "All Files (*.*)¦*.* ¦"
    Filter = Filter + "Text Files (*.txt)¦*.txt ¦"
    Filter = Filter + "Batch Files (*.bat)¦*.bat"
    CommonDialog1.Filter = Filter

    ' Set the default File Type to Text Files (*.txt).
    CommonDialog1.FilterIndex = 2

    ' Display the Open dialog box.
    CommonDialog1.Action = 1
```

```
' Display the name of the file that the user selected.
MsgBox "You selected: " + CommonDialog1.Filename

' Exit the procedure.
Exit Sub

OpenError:
    ' The user pressed the Cancel key.
    MsgBox "You canceled the dialog box!"
    Exit Sub
```

End Sub

The first statement of the procedure sets an error trap:

```
On Error GoTo OpenError
```

As a result of this error trap, if you press the Cancel button while the Open dialog box is displayed, the procedure branches to the OpenError label.

After setting the error trap, the procedure uses the Filter property of the CommonDialog1 control to fill the items in the Files of type list box of the Open dialog box. The Files of type list box is filled with three file types:

```
Filter = "All Files (*.*)¦*.* ¦"
Filter = Filter + "Text Files (*.txt)¦*.txt ¦"
Filter = Filter + "Batch Files (*.bat)¦*.bat"
CommonDialog1.Filter = Filter
```

Figure 6.14 shows the Files of type list box that is created with this statement.

Figure 6.14.

A Files of type list box.

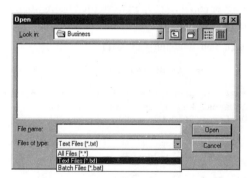

The preceding statements fill the Filter property of the CommonDialog1 control with a string that specifies the text of each of the items appearing in the Files of type list box, as well as the skeleton of the files that are displayed.

For example, the first item that appears in the Files of type list box is specified with the following string:

```
All Files (*.*)¦*.*
```

This string is made of two parts separated by the pipe character (|). (You type the pipestem character by pressing Shift+\.) The first part indicates the text that appears in the list box:

```
All Files (*.*)
```

The second part indicates the skeleton of the files that are displayed when this item is selected:

```
*.*
```

That is, when the first item of the Files of type list box is selected, the files with the skeleton *.* (that is, all the files) are displayed in the dialog box.

Notice that for clarity, the preceding statements fill the Filter property of the CommonDialog1 control in steps. First, the string variable `Filter` is filled:

```
Filter = "All Files (*.*)¦*.* ¦"
Filter = Filter + "Text Files (*.txt)¦*.txt ¦"
Filter = Filter + "Batch Files (*.bat)¦*.bat"
```

Then the Filter property of the CommonDialog1 control is set to the value of the `Filter` variable:

```
CommonDialog1.Filter = Filter
```

After the Files of type list box of the dialog box is filled, the default item that appears in the Files of type list box is set to item number 2. This is done by setting the FilterIndex property of CommonDialog1 to 2:

```
CommonDialog1.FilterIndex = 2
```

Because item number 2 of the Files of type list box is Text Files (*.txt), the default files listed in the Open dialog box are files with a .TXT extension.

6

The procedure displays the Open dialog box by setting the Action property of the CommonDialog1 common dialog custom control to 1:

```
CommonDialog1.Action = 1
```

If you press the Cancel button while the dialog box is displayed, an error is generated and, as a result, the code under the OpenError label is executed. The code under the OpenError label displays a message and terminates the procedure:

```
OpenError:
   MsgBox "You canceled the dialog box!"
   Exit Sub
```

However, if you don't press the Cancel button but select a file from the dialog box, the name of the selected file is displayed and the procedure is terminated:

```
MsgBox "You selected: " + CommonDialog1.Filename
Exit Sub
```

The file you selected is in the FileName property of the CommonDialog1 control (`CommonDialog1.FileName`).

Other Common Dialog Boxes

The Common program used the common dialog custom control to display a Color dialog box and an Open dialog box. You may use the common dialog custom control to display other common dialog boxes. Table 6.12 lists the common dialog boxes that may be displayed and the values that should be assigned to the Action property of the common dialog custom control to display a particular dialog box. For example, to display the Save As common dialog box, you should set the Action property of the common dialog custom control to 2:

```
CommonDialog1.Action=2
```

Table 6.12. The common dialog boxes.

Displayed Common Dialog Box	Action Property
Open	1
Save As	2
Color	3
Font	4
Print	5

Like the Color and Open dialog boxes, you may use the properties of the common dialog custom control to determine the user's response to the dialog box.

Summary

This chapter discusses dialog boxes. You have learned how to display predefined dialog boxes with the MsgBox statement, the MsgBox() function, and the InputBox() function. These dialog boxes are ideal for cases when you need to inform the user with short messages, get the user's response to yes/no questions, or get text data, such as a name, from the user.

You have also learned how to design your own custom dialog boxes and use them in a program. When you design a custom dialog box, there is no limit to the number of buttons or controls you can have in the dialog box.

The last section of this chapter covers the common dialog custom control used to display common dialog boxes such as Open, Save As, Print, Color, and Font.

Q&A

Q This chapter covers three types of dialog boxes (predefined, custom, and common). Which type should I use?

A The advantage of designing your own custom dialog box, such as the frmGetMonth form, is that there is no limit to the buttons or controls you can place in the dialog box. For example, you can place any picture in the custom dialog box to improve the way it looks.

The disadvantage of designing your own custom control is that you need to spend some time designing it. If a predefined dialog box or a common dialog box can already do what your custom dialog box does, you will be "reinventing the wheel."

Remember that the common dialog boxes can be very powerful. For example, when you use a common dialog box to select a color, the control knows which color is supported by your PC, or when you use a common dialog box to select a font, the control knows which fonts are available on your system.

Quiz

1. What is the difference between the MsgBox statement and MsgBox() function?

2. What does the following statement do?

   ```
   MsgBox "File is missing!", vbOKOnly, "ERROR"
   ```

3. What does the following code do?

   ```
   If MsgBox("Exit program?",vbYesNo,"DEMO")=vbYes Then
       End
   Endif
   ```

4. What does the following code do?

   ```
   UserName = InputBox ("Enter your name:", "Demo")
   If UserName<>"" Then
       MsgBox "Hello "+Username
   Endif
   ```

5. Assume that you designed a custom dialog box called frmMyDialog. What does the following statement do?

   ```
   frmMyDialog.Show 1
   ```

6. Assume that you designed a custom dialog box called frmMyDialog. What does the following statement do?

   ```
   frmMyDialog.Hide
   ```

7. Assume that you have a common dialog custom control called CommonDialog1. What does the following statement do? (Use Table 6.12 to answer this question.)

```
CommonDialog1.Action = 2
```

Exercises

1. Write code that displays a dialog box with the title ERROR, the message `Disk error!`, an OK button, and an exclamation point icon.

2. Write code that displays a dialog box with the title QUESTION, the question message `Are you sure you want to quit?`, Yes and No buttons, and a question mark icon. If the user's response to the question is Yes (the user clicked the Yes button), terminate the program.

3. Write code that displays a dialog box asking the user to enter a number between 1 and 10. If the user enters a number in the range 1 to 10, the code should display a dialog box with the selected number. If, however, the user enters a number that is not in the range 1 to 10 (or the user enters nonnumeric characters), the code should display an error message. If the user presses the Cancel button of the dialog box, the code should not display anything. (Hint: This code is similar to the code in the `mnuGetNumber_Click()` procedure of the Dialogs program.)

Quiz Answers

1. The `MsgBox` statement and `MsgBox()` function take the same parameters and display the same dialog boxes. The only difference between them is that the `MsgBox()` function returns a value that represents the button selected in the dialog box. The `MsgBox` statement does not return any value.

2. This statement displays a dialog box with the title ERROR, the message `File is missing!`, and an OK button.

3. This code displays a message box with the title DEMO, the question message `Exit program?`, and Yes and No buttons. If you click the Yes button of the dialog box, the `MsgBox()` function returns the value `vbYes`, in which case the condition of the `If` statement is satisfied and the program is terminated by executing the `End` statement.

4. This code uses the `InputBox()` function to display a dialog box prompting you to enter a name. The returned value of the `InputBox()` function is assigned to the variable `UserName`. If you enter a name and don't press the Cancel button, the variable `UserName` is not null, in which case the condition of the `If` statement `If UserName<>""` is satisfied and you are prompted with a Hello message displaying your name.

5. This statement uses the `Show` method to display the frmMyDialog dialog box as modal.

6. This statement uses the Hide method to hide the frmMyDialog dialog box from view. After executing this statement, the frmMyDialog dialog box disappears. Typically, this statement is used in the code of the terminating button of the dialog box. For example, after you respond to the dialog box by pressing the OK or Cancel button, use the Hide method to hide the dialog box from view.

7. This statement displays the Save As common dialog box.

Exercise Answers

1. To display such a dialog box, use the following statement:

```
MsgBox "Disk error!", vbOKOnly+vbExclamation, "ERROR"
```

2. To display such a dialog box, use the following code:

```
If MsgBox ( "Are you sure you want to quit?", _
            vbYesNo + vbQuestion, _
            "QUESTION" ) = vbYes Then
    End
End If
```

3. The following code is one possible solution:

```
Dim UserInput

' Get a number from the user.
UserInput = _
 InputBox("Enter a number between 1 and 10", "Demo")

' If the user did not enter anything, or if the user
' pressed Cancel, exit the procedure.
If UserInput = "" Then
    Exit Sub
End If

' If the user did not enter numeric characters,
' then display an error message and exit the procedure.
If Not IsNumeric(UserInput) Then
    MsgBox "Invalid number!"
    Exit Sub
End If

' If the number that the user entered is not in the range
' of 1 through 10, then display an error message and exit.
If UserInput<1 Or UserInput>10 Then
    MsgBox "The number is not between 1 and 10!"
    Exit Sub
End If

' Display the number that the user entered.
MsgBox "You entered the number: " + UserInput
```

7

Graphics Controls

One of the advantages of using Visual Basic for Windows is that it enables you to easily create programs that include graphics. In this chapter you'll learn how to write programs that include graphics controls.

The Twip

In Visual Basic you can display graphic objects such as lines, circles, bitmap files, and so on. You need to specify the dimensions, such as length of line or radius of circle, for these objects. Although Visual Basic may use a variety of units for specifying the dimensions and locations of these graphic objects, the most commonly used unit is called a *twip*. There are 1440 twips in 1 inch.

Colors

An important characteristic of a graphic object is its color. You can use the RGB() function or QBColor() function to specify the color of objects.

Specifying Colors with the *RGB()* Function

The RGB() function enables you to specify colors. The letters *RGB* stand for *red, green,* and *blue* because all colors can be displayed by mixing these three basic colors. The RGB() function has three arguments: the value of the first argument represents the amount of red in the final color; the second argument represents the amount of green in the final color; and the third argument represents the amount of blue in the final color. For example, the following statement uses the RGB() function to return the color red:

```
RGB(255, 0, 0)
```

The maximum value of each argument in the RGB() function is 255 and the minimum value is 0, so RGB(255,0,0) represents red, RGB(0,255,0) represents green, and RGB(0,0,255) represents blue.

For example, to change the BackColor property of a form called frmMyForm to blue, use the following statement:

```
frmMyForm.BackColor = RGB(0,0,255)
```

To generate yellow, use RGB(255,255,0). How can you tell that this combination of numbers yields the color yellow? Well, if you have a Ph.D. in physics, you probably know the answer and can explain it in terms of wavelength and other light properties. Otherwise, you have to generate the color by trial and error. But there are two RGB() combinations you should remember: RGB(255,255,255) represents white, and RGB(0,0,0) represents black.

Specifying Colors with the *QBColor()* Function

Another easy way to specify colors is by using the QBColor() function. It has one argument that may have any integer value between 0 and 15.

To change the BackColor property of the form frmMyForm to gray, use the following statement:

```
frmMyForm.BackColor = QBColor(8)
```

Table 4.3 in Chapter 4, "The Mouse," lists the 16 possible colors and their corresponding values. (This table is also shown on the book's tear-out card.)

The QBColor() function is easier to use than the RGB() function, but you can generate only 16 colors with it.

The Line Control

The line control is used for drawing lines. The Line program demonstrates how to use it in a program.

The Visual Implementation of the Line Program

Use the following steps to build the form of the Line program:

☐ Create a new project by selecting New Project from the File menu.

☐ Save the form of the project as LINE.FRM in the C:\VB4PRG\CH07 directory, and save the project file as LINE.VBP in the C:\VB4PRG\CH07 directory.

☐ Build the form of the Line program according to the specifications in Table 7.1.

The completed form should look like the one shown in Figure 7.1.

Table 7.1. The properties table of the Line program.

Object	Property	Setting
Form	Name	frmLine
	BackColor	White
	Caption	The Line Program
	Height	4545

continues

Table 7.1. continued

Object	Property	Setting
	Left	1080
	Top	1170
	Width	6810
Command Button	**Name**	**cmdStart**
	Caption	&Start
	FontName	System
	FontSize	10
	Height	495
	Left	2640
	Top	120
	Width	1215
Command Button	**Name**	**cmdExit**
	Caption	E&xit
	FontName	System
	FontSize	10
	Height	495
	Left	2640
	Top	3600
	Width	1215
Line	**Name**	**linLine**
	X1	2760
	X2	3960
	Y1	1800
	Y2	2280

Figure 7.1.
The form of the Line program.

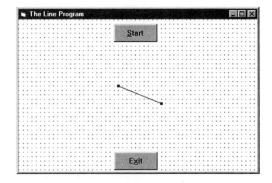

Entering the Code of the Line Program

☐ Enter the following code in the general declarations section of the frmLine form:

```
' All variables MUST be declared.
Option Explicit
```

☐ Enter the following code in the cmdExit_Click() procedure:

```
Private Sub cmdExit_Click()

    End

End Sub
```

☐ Enter the following code in the cmdStart_Click() procedure:

```
Private Sub cmdStart_Click()

    ' Set the start and endpoints of the line
' control to random values.
    linLine.X1 = Int(frmLine.Width * Rnd)
    linLine.Y1 = Int(frmLine.Height * Rnd)
    linLine.X2 = Int(frmLine.Width * Rnd)
    linLine.Y2 = Int(frmLine.Height * Rnd)

End Sub
```

Executing the Line Program

☐ Execute the Line program.

Click the Start button several times and notice that every time you click the button, the line control changes its location and its length. Since you set the Caption property of the Start button to &Start, you can press Alt+S on your keyboard. This will produce the same result as clicking the Start button.

How the Line Program Works

The Line program uses the `cmdStart_Click()` procedure to display the line control at a different location every time you click the Start button.

The Code in the *cmdStart_Click()* Procedure

The `cmdStart_Click()` procedure is executed whenever you click the Start button:

```
Private Sub cmdStart_Click()

    ' Set the start and endpoints of the line
    ' control to random values.
    linLine.X1 = Int(frmLine.Width * Rnd)
    linLine.Y1 = Int(frmLine.Height * Rnd)
    linLine.X2 = Int(frmLine.Width * Rnd)
    linLine.Y2 = Int(frmLine.Height * Rnd)

End Sub
```

The `Rnd` function returns a random number between 0 and 1, and the Width property gives the width of the frmLine form. Therefore, the product

```
frmLine.Width * Rnd
```

is equal to a number between 0 and the width of the form.

For example, if the `Rnd` function returns 0, the product equals 0. If the `Rnd` function returns 1, the product equals the width of the form. If the `Rnd` function returns 0.75, the product equals $^{3}/_{4}$ the width of the form.

The `Int()` function converts its argument to an integer. For example, `Int(3.5)` returns 3, and `Int(7.999)` returns 7. Therefore, the product `Int(frmLine.Width * Rnd)` returns a random integer between 0 and the width of the form.

The first statement in the `cmdStart_Click()` procedure assigns an integer to the X1 property of the line control. This integer is between 0 and the width of the form:

```
linLine.X1 = Int(frmLine.Width * Rnd)
```

The X1 property of the line control is the horizontal coordinate of the point where the line begins. Because the line is drawn on the form, the coordinate system is referenced to the form. Visual Basic's default coordinate system defines the coordinate X1=0,Y1=0 as the top-left corner of the form.

The second statement in the `cmdStart_Click()` procedure assigns a value to the Y1 property of the line control. The assigned value may be an integer between 0 and the height of the form:

```
linLine.Y1 = Int(frmLine.Height * Rnd)
```

The Y1 property of the line control is the vertical coordinate of the point where the line begins.

The last two statements of the cmdStart_Click() procedure assign values to the X2 and Y2 properties of the line control. The X2 and Y2 properties are the coordinates of the endpoints of the line control:

```
linLine.X2 = Int(frmLine.Width * Rnd)
linLine.Y2 = Int(frmLine.Height * Rnd)
```

Whenever you click the Start button, the line moves to a new location that depends on random numbers.

More About the Properties of the Line Control

Experiment with some of the properties of the line control at design time:

☐ Select the line control at design time.

☐ Change the BorderColor property of the line control to red.

Visual Basic responds by changing the color of the line to red.

☐ Change the BorderWidth property of the line control to 10.

Visual Basic responds by changing the width of the line to 10 twips.

☐ Save the project by selecting Save Project from the File menu.

☐ Execute the Line program and then click the Start button several times.

The Line program now displays the line control as a red line that is 10 twips wide. (See Figure 7.2.)

Figure 7.2.
Changing the BorderColor and BorderWidth properties of the line control.

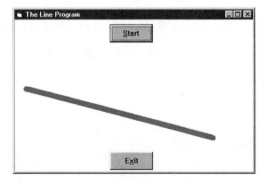

You can also change the color of the line and the size of the line at runtime:

☐ Insert the following statement at the beginning of the cmdStart_Click() procedure:

```
linLine.BorderColor=RGB(Int(255*Rnd), _
                        Int(255*Rnd), _
                        Int(255*Rnd))

linLine.BorderWidth = Int(100 * Rnd) + 1
```

The first statement assigns a new value to the BorderColor property of the line control. The new value is the returned value from the RGB() function in which all three arguments of the function are random numbers between 0 and 255, so the returned value from this RGB() function is a random color.

The second statement assigns a new value to the BorderWidth property of the line control. This new value is a random number between 0 and 100 plus 1. This means that the width of the line is assigned a new width between 1 and 101 twips. You add 1 to Int(100 * Rnd) because the minimum value for the BorderWidth cannot be 0.

☐ Execute the program.

As you can see, the line changes its color and its width every time you click the Start button or press Alt+S. Of course, if the random color is the same color as the form's background, you will not see the line.

The Shape Control

The shape control is used for drawing several shapes: rectangle, square, rounded rectangle, rounded square, circle, and oval. The Shape program illustrates how to display these shapes.

The Visual Implementation of the Shape Program

Use the following steps to build the form of the Shape program:

☐ Create a new project.

☐ Save the form of the project as SHAPE.FRM in the C:\VB4PRG\CH07 directory and save the project file of the project as SHAPE.VBP in the C:\VB4PRG\CH07 directory.

☐ Build the form of the Shape program according to the specifications in Table 7.2.

The completed form should look like the one shown in Figure 7.3.

Table 7.2. The properties table of the Shape program.

Object	Property	Setting
Form	**Name**	**frmShape**
	Caption	The Shape Program
	Height	4920
	Left	1080
	Top	1170
	Width	6810
Horizontal Scroll Bar	**Name**	**hsbWidth**
	Height	255
	Left	1560
	Max	10
	Min	1
	Top	3000
	Value	1
	Width	4935
Command Button	**Name**	**cmdRndRect**
	Caption	Rounded Rectan&gle
	FontName	System
	FontSize	10
	Height	495
	Left	3960
	Top	3960
	Width	2535
Command Button	**Name**	**cmdRndSqr**
	Caption	Rounded S&quare
	FontName	System
	FontSize	10
	Height	495
	Left	1560
	Top	3960
	Width	2295

continues

7

Table 7.2. continued

Object	Property	Setting
Command Button	**Name**	**cmdCircle**
	Caption	&Circle
	FontName	System
	FontSize	10
	Height	495
	Left	5280
	Top	3360
	Width	1215
Command Button	**Name**	**cmdOval**
	Caption	&Oval
	FontName	System
	FontSize	10
	Height	495
	Left	1560
	Top	3360
	Width	975
Command Button	**Name**	**cmdSquare**
	Caption	&Square
	FontName	System
	FontSize	10
	Height	495
	Left	2640
	Top	3360
	Width	1095
Command Button	**Name**	**cmdRectangle**
	Caption	&Rectangle
	FontName	System
	FontSize	10
	Height	495
	Left	3840
	Top	3360
	Width	1335

Object	Property	Setting
Command Button	**Name**	**cmdExit**
	Caption	E&xit
	FontName	System
	FontSize	10
	Height	495
	Left	240
	Top	3720
	Width	1215
Label	**Name**	**lblInfo**
	Caption	Change Width:
	FontName	System
	FontSize	10
	Height	375
	Left	1560
	Top	2640
	Width	1695
Shape	**Name**	**shpAllShapes**
	Height	495
	Left	2640
	Top	720
	Width	1215

Figure 7.3.
The frmShape form.

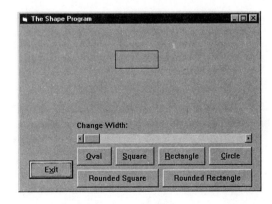

Entering the Code of the Shape Program

☐ Enter the following code in the general declarations section of the frmShape form:

```
' All variables MUST be declared.
Option Explicit
```

☐ Enter the following code in the cmdExit_Click() procedure:

```
Private Sub cmdExit_Click()

    End

End Sub
```

☐ Enter the following code in the cmdRectangle_Click() procedure:

```
Private Sub cmdRectangle_Click()

    ' The user clicked the Rectangle button,
    ' so set the Shape property of shpAllShapes to
    ' rectangle (0).
    shpAllShapes.Shape = 0

End Sub
```

☐ Enter the following code in the cmdSquare_Click() procedure:

```
Private Sub cmdSquare_Click()

    ' The user clicked the Square button,
    ' so set the Shape property of shpAllShapes to
    ' square (1).
    shpAllShapes.Shape = 1

End Sub
```

☐ Enter the following code in the cmdOval_Click() procedure:

```
Private Sub cmdOval_Click()

    ' The user clicked the Oval button,
    ' so set the Shape property of shpAllShapes to
    ' oval (2).
    shpAllShapes.Shape = 2

End Sub
```

☐ Enter the following code in the cmdCircle_Click() procedure:

```
Private Sub cmdCircle_Click()

    ' The user clicked the Circle button,
    ' so set the Shape property of shpAllShapes to
    ' circle (3).
    shpAllShapes.Shape = 3

End Sub
```

☐ Enter the following code in the `cmdRndRect_Click()` procedure:

```
Private Sub cmdRndRect_Click()

    ' The user clicked the Rounded Rectangle button,
    ' so set the Shape property of shpAllShapes to
    ' rounded rectangle (4).
    shpAllShapes.Shape = 4

End Sub
```

☐ Enter the following code in the `cmdRndSqr()` procedure:

```
Private Sub cmdRndSqr_Click()

    ' The user clicked the Rounded Square button,
    ' so set the Shape property of shpAllShapes to
    ' rounded square (5).
    shpAllShapes.Shape = 5

End Sub
```

☐ Enter the following code in the `hsbWidth_Change()` procedure:

```
Private Sub hsbWidth_Change()

    ' The user changed the scroll bar position,
    ' so set the BorderWidth property of
    ' shpAllShapes to the new value of the scroll
    ' bar.
    shpAllShapes.BorderWidth = hsbWidth.Value

End Sub
```

☐ Enter the following code in the `hsbWidth_Scroll()` procedure:

```
Private Sub hsbWidth_Scroll()

    ' The user changed the scroll bar position,
    ' so set the BorderWidth property of
    ' shpAllShapes to the new value of the scroll
    ' bar.
    shpAllShapes.BorderWidth = hsbWidth.Value

End Sub
```

Executing the Shape Program

When you execute the Shape program, the form shown in Figure 7.3 is displayed. When you click a button, the shape changes to the shape indicated by the button. For example, when you click the Circle button, the shape becomes a circle.

The width of the shape is changed whenever you change the scroll bar position. Figure 7.4 shows the shape after the Circle button was clicked and the scroll bar was set to its middle point.

Figure 7.4.
*Changing the shape and
width of the shape.*

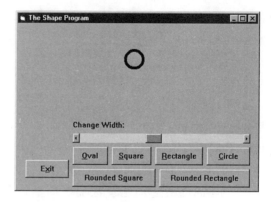

How the Shape Program Works

The code of the Shape program changes the shape and the width of the shpAllShapes control.

The Code in the *cmdRectangle_Click()* Procedure

The cmdRectangle_Click() procedure is executed whenever you click the Rectangle button. The statement in this procedure sets the Shape property of shpAllShapes to 0, which means a rectangle:

```
shpAllShapes.Shape = 0
```

In a similar manner, the cmdSquare_Click() procedure is executed whenever you click the Square button. The statement in the cmdSquare_Click() procedure sets the Shape property of shpAllShapes to 1, which means a square.

Table 7.3 lists the possible values the Shape property may have.

Table 7.3. Possible values for the shape control's Shape property.

Value	Meaning
0	Rectangle
1	Square
2	Oval
3	Circle
4	Rounded rectangle
5	Rounded square

The Code in the *hsbWidth_Change()* Procedure

The hsbWidth_Change() procedure is executed whenever you change the scroll bar position. As indicated in the properties table of the Shape program, the Min property of the scroll bar is 1 and the Max property is 10. Therefore, you can change the Value property of hsbWidth to a value between 1 and 10. This value is assigned to the BorderWidth property of shpAllShapes in the hsbWidth_Change() procedure as follows:

```
shpAllShapes.BorderWidth = hsbWidth.Value
```

Therefore, shpAllShapes changes its width according to the scroll bar position.

Other Properties of the Shape Control

The Shape program demonstrates only two properties of the shape control. You can experiment with other properties of the shape control by placing a shape in a form and changing its properties. Use the following steps as a guideline:

☐ Place a shape control in the form.

Visual Basic responds by assigning the default rectangle shape.

☐ Change the Shape property to Circle.

Visual Basic responds by changing the shape from a rectangle to a circle.

☐ Change the FillColor property to red.

Visual Basic does not fill the circle with red because the default FillStyle property of the shape is Transparent.

☐ Change the FillStyle property to Solid.

Visual Basic responds by filling the circle with solid red.

Pictures

The line control and the shape control are capable of drawing simple geometric shapes such as lines, circles, squares, and so on. To display more complex shapes, you need to use a picture file. You can place picture files on a form, in an image control, or in a picture control.

To place a picture file in one of these objects, you have to change the Picture property of the object. For example, to place a picture file in an image control, set the Picture property of the image control to the desired picture file.

You can create a picture file by using Paintbrush or Paint to draw the picture and then saving your picture as a BMP file. Or if you don't think you have the talent to draw pictures yourself, you can buy professional pictures from a variety of vendors. These third-party picture products are called *clip art.*

Placing Pictures on a Form During Design Time

You may place pictures on a form during both design time and runtime. Use the following steps to place a picture on a form at design time:

☐ Start Paintbrush.

☐ Select Image Attributes from the Options menu.

> *Paintbrush responds by displaying the Image Attributes dialog box.*

☐ Set the Width and Height fields in the Image Attribute dialog box to three inches each; these settings determine the size of the picture.

☐ Use the Paintbrush tools to draw your picture.

☐ Save your work by saving the file as MyPic.BMP.

You now have a BMP picture file that you can place on a form:

☐ Start a new Visual Basic project.

> *Visual Basic responds by displaying a blank form called Form1.frm.*

☐ Click in the Picture property of Form1, click the three dots on the right side of the Picture property, and select the MyPic.BMP file that you created.

Figure 7.5 shows the form with the picture created with Paintbrush or Paint.

Figure 7.5.
Placing a picture created with Paintbrush or Paint on a form.

As shown in Figure 7.5, the picture is displayed on the form with its upper-left corner at the X=0,Y=0 coordinate of the form. You cannot stretch the picture with Visual Basic. It has the same dimensions you specified in the Paintbrush Image Attributes.

The picture that is placed on the form serves as a background picture. You can place command buttons and other controls directly on the picture. Figure 7.6 shows the picture with several command buttons placed on the picture.

Figure 7.6.
Placing buttons on the background picture of the form.

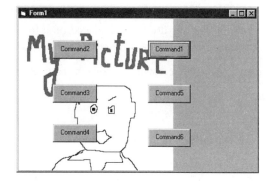

Since you can't stretch the picture, you can resize the form by dragging its handles at design time so that it will fit nicely around the picture, as shown in Figure 7.7. To prevent your user from enlarging or shrinking the form at runtime, set the BorderStyle property to Fixed Dialog, Fixed Single, or Fixed Tool Window. In each case, your user is prevented from sizing the form, and the border of the form is made of either double lines or a single line.

Figure 7.7.
The form with its BorderStyle property set to Fixed Double.

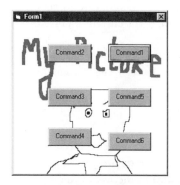

There are several applications in which you may want to place a background picture on the form. For example, some programs start by displaying a form with a picture in it, often the logo of the company that distributes the software.

Placing Pictures on a Form During Runtime

You can also place pictures on a form during runtime. To load the picture C:\VB \BITMAPS\ASSORTED\BALLOON.BMP and place it on the frmMyForm form, use the following statement:

```
frmMyForm.Picture = _
    LoadPicture("c:\vb\bitmaps\assorted\balloon.bmp")
```

Because only one picture may be placed on a form at any time, the LoadPicture() function replaces the current picture if there's already one on the form.

To clear a picture already on the form at runtime, use the following statement:

```
frmMyForm.Picture = LoadPicture("")
```

The Image Control

You can also place picture files created with Paintbrush in the image control, which supports the Stretch property. This property enables you to stretch the picture to any desired size. (The form and the picture controls do not support the Stretch property.)

To load the picture C:\VB\BITMAPS\ASSORTED\BALLOON.BMP and place it in the imgMyImage image control, use the following statement:

```
imgMyImage.Picture = _
    LoadPicture("c:\vb\bitmaps\assorted\balloon.bmp")
```

Because only one picture can be placed in an image control at any time, the LoadPicture() function replaces the current picture if there's already one in the image control.

To clear a picture already in the image control at runtime, use the following statement:

```
imgMyImage.Picture = LoadPicture("")
```

To set the Stretch property of imgMyImage to True, use the following statement:

```
imgMyImage.Stretch = True
```

After you set the Stretch property to True, the picture file is automatically stretched so that the picture fills the entire area of the image control. In other words, Visual Basic automatically enlarges or shrinks the size of the image control. For example, if the image control holds the HerPic.BMP picture and the image control is 2 inches by 3 inches, then Visual Basic sizes the HerPic.BMP picture to 2 inches by 3 inches.

You can also set the Stretch property of the image control to True or False at design time.

The Picture Control

The picture control is very similar to the image control, except that it supports more properties, more events, and more methods than the image control does. However, the picture control does not support the Stretch property (only the image control supports the Stretch property).

The picture control supports the AutoSize property. If you set the picture control AutoSize property to True, Visual Basic adjusts the size of the picture control to the size of the picture file (that is, if the picture file is 3 inches by 2 inches, Visual Basic adjusts the size of the picture control to 3 inches by 3 inches). The form and the image control do not support the AutoSize property.

The image control uses fewer resources than the picture control uses, so it is repainted faster.

Incorporating the Picture Files into the EXE Files

As stated, the LoadPicture() function may be used to load a picture into an image control, a picture control, or a form at runtime. However, using the LoadPicture() function has a drawback: You must have the picture, or BMP, file in the directory specified by the argument of the LoadPicture() function. Therefore, your distribution disk (the disk that contains your complete program) must include the picture files that your program uses.

On the other hand, any picture file that was assigned to a picture holder control (form, picture control, or image control) during design time becomes an integral part of the final EXE file, so you don't have to distribute the picture file as a separate file. The picture files that are supported by Visual Basic are bitmap files, icon files, metafiles, and cursor files.

Bitmap Files

A bitmap file has either a .BMP or .DIB file extension. The bitmap file contains bytes that describe the locations and colors of the picture's pixels.

Icon Files

An icon file has an .ICO file extension. Icon files are similar to BMP and DIB files, but icon files may represent images that have a maximum size of 32 pixels by 32 pixels.

Metafiles

A metafile has a .WMF file extension. It contains a list of instructions that describe how to generate the picture.

Cursor Files

A cursor file has a .CUR file extension and is similar to an icon file. It is a small file usually used to represent the mouse cursor, such as the familiar hourglass icon and arrow icon.

The MoveEye Program

You can move a control at runtime either by changing its Left and Top properties or by using the Move method.

Now write a program called MoveEye. This program illustrates how to move an object by changing its Left and Top properties.

The Visual Implementation of the MoveEye Program

☐ Create a new project by selecting New Project from the File menu.

☐ Save the form of the project as MOVEEYE.FRM in the C:\VB4PRG\CH07 directory, and save the project file as MOVEEYE.VBP in the C:\VB4PRG\CH07 directory.

☐ Build the form of the MoveEye program according to the specifications in Table 7.4.

The completed form should look like the one shown in Figure 7.8.

Table 7.4. The properties table of the MoveEye program.

Object	Property	Setting
Form	**Name**	**frmMoveEye**
	BackColor	Gray
	Caption	The MoveEye Program
	Height	4545
	Left	1080
	Top	1170
	Width	6810
Command Button	**Name**	**cmdMove**
	Caption	&Move
	FontName	System
	FontSize	10
	Height	495

Object	Property	Setting
	Left	3600
	Top	3480
	Width	1215
Command Button	**Name**	**cmdExit**
	Caption	E&xit
	FontName	System
	FontSize	10
	Height	495
	Left	1320
	Top	3480
	Width	1215
Image	**Name**	**imgEye**
	Height	480
	Left	5640
	Picture	C:\VB\ICONS\MISC\EYE.ICO
	Stretch	-1-True
	Top	3000
	Width	480

Table 7.4 instructs you to set the EYE.ICO icon file as the Picture property of the imgEye image. If your VB directory does not contain this ICO file, then use any other ICO file.

Figure 7.8.
The frmMoveEye form.

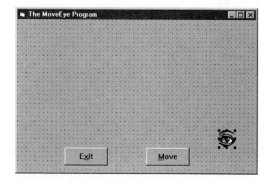

7

Entering the Code of the MoveEye Program

☐ Enter the following code in the general declarations section of the frmMoveEye form:

```
' All variables MUST be declared.
Option Explicit
```

☐ Enter the following code in the cmdExit_Click() procedure:

```
Private Sub cmdExit_Click()

    End

End Sub
```

☐ Enter the following code in the cmdMove_Click() procedure:

```
Private Sub cmdMove_Click()

    ' Declare Counter as an integer.
    Dim Counter As Integer

    ' Execute the For loop 100 times.
    For Counter = 1 To 100 Step 1

        ' Raise the Top of the image 20 twips
        ' upward.
        imgEye.Top = imgEye.Top - 20

        ' Shift the Left edge of the image 20 twips
        ' to the left.
        imgEye.Left = imgEye.Left - 20

    Next Counter

End Sub
```

Executing the MoveEye Program

☐ Execute the MoveEye program.

As you click the Move button, the eye image is moved to a new location. You can keep clicking the Move button until the eye disappears from the form.

The Code of the MoveEye Program

The MoveEye program moves the image control by changing its Top and Left properties.

The Code in the *cmdMove_Click()* Procedure

Whenever you click the Move button, the cmdMove_Click() procedure is automatically executed:

```
Private Sub cmdMove_Click()

    ' Declare Counter as an integer.
    Dim Counter As Integer

    ' Execute the For loop 100 times.
    For Counter = 1 To 100 Step 1

        ' Raise the Top of the image 20 twips
        ' upward.
        imgEye.Top = imgEye.Top - 20

        ' Shift the Left edge of the image 20 twips
        ' to the left.
        imgEye.Left = imgEye.Left - 20

    Next Counter

End Sub
```

The first statement in the For loop decreases the vertical coordinate of the top-left corner of the image by 20 twips:

```
imgEye.Top = imgEye.Top - 20
```

The second statement in the For loop decreases the horizontal coordinate of the top-left corner of the image by 20 twips:

```
imgEye.Left = imgEye.Left - 20
```

Figure 7.9 shows the effect of these two statements.

Figure 7.9.

Moving the image 20 twips upward and 20 twips to the left.

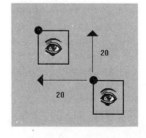

Because the For loop is executed 100 times, the image is moved 100 times, giving the illusion of continuous motion.

Moving a Control by Using the *Move* Method

The MoveEye program that was discussed in the previous section moves the image by changing its Top and Left properties. The Move method is another way to move the control.

☐ Replace the code of the cmdMove_Click() procedure with the following code:

```
Private Sub cmdMove_Click()

    ' Declare the variables.
    Dim Counter As Integer
    Dim LeftEdge As Single
    Dim TopEdge As Single

    ' Initialize the variables with the current
    ' location of the image.
    LeftEdge = imgEye.Left
    TopEdge = imgEye.Top

    ' Use the For loop to move the image 100
    ' times. In each Move, the image moves 20 twips
    ' upward and 20 twips to the left.
    For Counter = 1 To 100 Step 1
        LeftEdge = LeftEdge - 20
        TopEdge = TopEdge - 20
        imgEye.Move LeftEdge, TopEdge
    Next Counter

End Sub
```

The code in the procedure initializes the two variables, LeftEdge and TopEdge, to the current location of the top-left corner of the image, and the For loop is executed 100 times.

In each iteration of the For loop, the variables LeftEdge and TopEdge are decremented by 20. The Move method is used with the variable LeftEdge as the new horizontal coordinate and the variable TopEdge as the new vertical coordinate.

More About the *Move* Method

The full syntax of the Move method is as follows:

```
[Object name].Move. left, top, width, height
```

This means that you can also specify the new width and height that the object will have after the movement. Here is an example:

☐ Replace the cmdMove_Click() procedure of the MoveEye program with the following code:

```
Private Sub cmdMove_Click()
```

```
    Dim Counter As Integer
    Dim LeftEdge As Single
    Dim TopEdge As Single
    Dim WidthOfImage As Single
    Dim HeightOfImage As Single
    imgEye.Stretch = True
    LeftEdge = imgEye.Left
    TopEdge = imgEye.Top
    WidthOfImage = imgEye.Width
    HeightOfImage = imgEye.Height
    For Counter = 1 To 100 Step 1
       LeftEdge = LeftEdge - 20
       TopEdge = TopEdge - 20
       WidthOfImage = WidthOfImage + 10
       HeightOfImage = HeightOfImage + 10
       imgEye.Move LeftEdge, TopEdge, _
                   WidthOfImage, HeightOfImage
    Next Counter

End Sub
```

☐ Execute the program and note how the eye moves and grows. After 100 moves, the form looks like the one shown in Figure 7.10.

Figure 7.10.

Using the Move *method to move and enlarge the eye.*

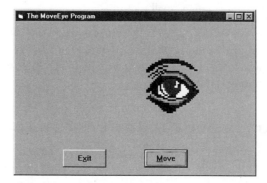

The first statement after the declaration statement is this:

```
imgEye.Stretch = True
```

This statement sets the Stretch property of imgEye to True so that the program can stretch the image. (You already set the Stretch property of the imgEye image to True during design time. So why are you instructed to set this property again during runtime? Just to illustrate that the Stretch property can be set during runtime as well as design time.)

The variables `WidthOfImage` and `HeightOfImage` are initialized to the current width and height of the image:

```
WidthOfImage = imgEye.Width
HeightOfImage = imgEye.Height
```

Then the `Move` method is executed 100 times. In each iteration of the `For` loop, the `WidthOfImage` and `HeightOfImage` variables are increased by 10 twips.

The `Move` method specifies the new coordinates for the top-left corner of the image and the new width and height the image should have after the movement:

```
imgEye.Move LeftEdge, TopEdge, WidthOfImage, HeightOfImage
```

Comparing the Moving Techniques

If you compare the performance of the MoveEye program using both moving techniques—using the `Move` method and changing the Top and Left properties—you might notice that the `Move` method is better. Changing the Top and Left properties produces a jerky movement. However, if you are using a fast computer, such as a Pentium 99-MHz, you may not notice any differences between the two moving techniques in the MoveEye program because the picture you're moving is a small picture.

However, while using the `Move` method, you may notice some flickering on the screen. In fact, the larger the image becomes, the more flickering you'll see. The flickering can be eliminated by using a WinG technology. In Chapter 21, "Multimedia," you'll learn about this sophisticated technology.

Moving a Picture Control

The previous program illustrated that using the `Move` method to move a control produces smoother motion than changing the Top and Left properties. But you can get even better results by using a picture control instead of an image control. To prove it, change the frmMoveEye form as follows:

☐ Delete the imgEye image control from the form by selecting the imgEye control and pressing Delete.

☐ Create a picture control by double-clicking the picture control in the toolbox window.

   Visual Basic responds by placing a picture control in the form.

☐ Change the Name property of the picture control to picEye.

☐ Set the Picture property of picEye to C:\VB\ICONS\MISC\EYE.ICO.

☐ Set the BorderStyle property of picEye to None so the picture will not be enclosed with a border.

□ Set the Appearance property of the picEye control to 0-Flat so that the picture control will appear flat, not three dimensional.

□ Set the AutoSize property of the picEye control to True so that the picture control will resize itself to the size of the eye picture.

□ Replace the cmdMove_Click procedure with the following code:

```
Private Sub cmdMove_Click()

    ' Declare the variables.
    Dim Counter As Integer
    Dim LeftEdge As Single
    Dim TopEdge As Single

    ' Initialize the variables with the current
    ' location of the picture.
    LeftEdge = picEye.Left
    TopEdge = picEye.Top

    ' Use the For loop to move the image 100
    ' times. In each Move, the picture moves 20
    ' twips upward and 20 twips to the left.
    For Counter = 1 To 100 Step 1
        LeftEdge = LeftEdge - 20
        TopEdge = TopEdge - 20
        picEye.Move LeftEdge, TopEdge
    Next Counter

End Sub
```

□ Execute the program, click the Start button, and notice how the eye moves.

Control Arrays

A *control array* is an array that contains controls as its elements. For example, you can create an array whose elements are image controls.

The Moon Program

You'll now write a program called Moon. The Moon program makes use of arrays of images.

The Visual Implementation of the Moon Program

You'll now visually implement the form of the Moon program.

□ Create a new project.

☐ Save the form of the project as MOON.FRM in the C:\VB4PRG\CH07 directory and save the project file as MOON.VBP in the C:\VB4PRG\CH07 directory.

☐ Set the Name property of the form to frmMoon and set the Caption property of the form to The Moon Program.

☐ Place an image control in the form by double-clicking the image control in the toolbox window.

> *Visual Basic responds by placing the image control in the form.*

☐ Drag the image control to the upper-left portion of the form.

☐ Change the Name property of the image to imgMoon.

☐ Change the Visible property of the image to False.

☐ Make sure the Stretch property of imgMoon is set to False.

☐ Set the Picture property of imgMoon to C:\VB\ICONS\ELEMENTS\MOON01.ICO.

Your frmMoon form should now look like the one in Figure 7.11.

Figure 7.11.
The first element of the image control array.

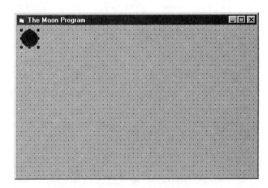

You have completed placing the image control in the form. This image will soon serve as element number 0 in the array of images. Currently, the image that you placed is a "regular" (nonarray) control. You can check this by examining the Index property of the imgMoon image. It should be blank.

Use the following steps to place the second element of the array:

☐ Double-click the image control of the toolbox window.

> *Visual Basic responds by placing the control in the form. The form now contains two image controls.*

☐ Drag the image to the right of the first image control.

☐ Change the Visible property of the image to False.

☐ Make sure that the Stretch property of the image is set to False.

☐ Set the Picture property of the image to C:\VB\ICONS\ELEMENTS\MOON2.ICO.

Your frmMoon form should now look like the one in Figure 7.12.

Figure 7.12.
The first and second elements of the image control array.

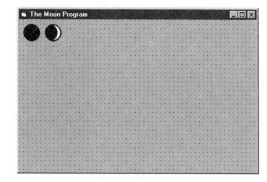

☐ Change the Name property of the second image to imgMoon and then click anywhere in the form.

> *Visual Basic responds by displaying the dialog box in Figure 7.13; that is, Visual Basic makes sure you intend to name the second image with the same name as the first image.*

Figure 7.13.
Creating a control array.

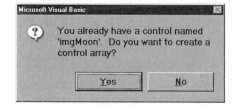

☐ Click the Yes button of the dialog box.

You are informing Visual Basic that you are creating a control array.

☐ Examine the Index properties of the first two images.

The Index property is 0 for the first image and 1 for the second image. This means that you now have a control array called imgMoon(). The first element of the array, imgMoon(0), is MOON01.ICO, which is the first image you placed on the form. The second element of the array is the image MOON02.ICO—the imgMoon(1) element.

☐ Now repeat this process and add six more elements to the control array. When you are finished, you should have a total of eight elements in the array, as shown in Figure 7.14

Graphics Controls

and Table 7.5. Don't forget to set the Name, Stretch, and Visible properties of the remaining six images. Note that when you add additional elements to the imgMoon() array, Visual Basic does not prompt you with the dialog box in Figure 7.13 because Visual Basic already knows that imgMoon is a control array.

Figure 7.14.

The eight moons of the control array.

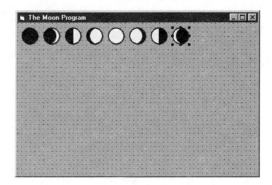

Table 7.5. The imgMoon() control array.

Element	Content of the Element
imgMoon(0)	C:\VB\ICONS\ELEMENTS\MOON01.ICO
imgMoon(1)	C:\VB\ICONS\ELEMENTS\MOON02.ICO
imgMoon(2)	C:\VB\ICONS\ELEMENTS\MOON03.ICO
imgMoon(3)	C:\VB\ICONS\ELEMENTS\MOON04.ICO
imgMoon(4)	C:\VB\ICONS\ELEMENTS\MOON05.ICO
imgMoon(5)	C:\VB\ICONS\ELEMENTS\MOON06.ICO
imgMoon(6)	C:\VB\ICONS\ELEMENTS\MOON07.ICO
imgMoon(7)	C:\VB\ICONS\ELEMENTS\MOON08.ICO

☐ Continue building the form according to the specifications in Table 7.6.

The completed form should look like the one shown in Figure 7.15.

Figure 7.15.
The frmMoon form.

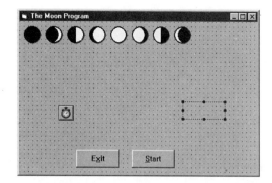

Table 7.6. The properties table of the Moon program.

Object	Property	Setting
Form	**Name**	**frmMoon**
	Caption	The Moon Program
	Height	4545
	Left	1080
	Top	1170
	Width	6810
Timer	**Name**	**tmrTimer**
	Interval	250
	Left	1080
	Top	2280
Command Button	**Name**	**cmdStart**
	Caption	&Start
	FontName	System
	FontSize	10
	Height	495
	Left	3120
	Top	3480
	Width	1215
Command Button	**Name**	**cmdExit**
	Caption	E&xit
	FontName	System

continues

Table 7.6. continued

Object	Property	Setting
	FontSize	10
	Height	495
	Left	1560
	Top	3480
	Width	1215
Image	**Name**	**imgCurrentMoon**
	Height	495
	Left	4560
	Top	2160
	Width	1215
Image Control	**(See Table 7.5.)**	**(See Table 7.5.)**

Note: Leave the Picture property of imgCurrentMoon at its default value (None). You'll assign a value to this property in the program's code. This image control is not part of the imgMoon image control array.

The Timer control is not visible during runtime, so it doesn't matter where you place it in the form.

Entering the Code of the Moon Program

☐ Enter the following code in the general declarations section of the Moon program:

```
' All variables MUST be declared.
Option Explicit
' Declaration of variables that are visible from any
' procedure in the form.
Dim gRotateFlag As Integer
Dim gCurrentMoon As Integer
```

☐ Enter the following code in the cmdExit_Click() procedure:

```
Private Sub cmdExit_Click()

    End

End Sub
```

Enter the following code in the cmdStart_Click() procedure:

```
Private Sub cmdStart_Click()

    ' Toggle the gRotateFlag, and toggle
    ' the caption of the Start/Stop button.
    If gRotateFlag = 0 Then
        gRotateFlag = 1
        cmdStart.Caption = "&Stop"
    Else
        gRotateFlag = 0
        cmdStart.Caption = "&Start"
    End If

End Sub
```

Enter the following code in the Form_Load() procedure:

```
Private Sub Form_Load()

    ' Initialize the flags.
    gRotateFlag = 0
    gCurrentMoon = 0

End Sub
```

Enter the following code in the tmrTimer_Timer() procedure:

```
Private Sub tmrTimer_Timer()

    If gRotateFlag = 1 Then
        imgCurrentMoon.Picture = _
                imgMoon(gCurrentMoon).Picture
        gCurrentMoon = gCurrentMoon + 1

        If gCurrentMoon = 8 Then
            gCurrentMoon = 0
        End If

    End If

End Sub
```

Executing the Moon Program

Execute the Moon program.

Click the Start button.

As you can see, the image of the moon seems to rotate around its axis.

Click the Exit button to terminate the Moon program.

The Code of the Moon Program

The code of the Moon program uses a control array of images to display the elements (images) of the array one after the other, giving the illusion of a rotating moon.

The Code in the General Declarations Section

The code in the general declarations section declares two integers: gRotateFlag and gCurrentMoon. These variables are visible by all the procedures of the frmMoon form.

The Code in the *Form_Load()* Procedure

The Form_Load() procedure is automatically executed when you start the program, and it's a good place for performing various initializations. The two variables that were declared in the general declarations section are initialized to 0:

```
gRotateFlag = 0
gCurrentMoon = 0
```

Note: When you create variables, Visual Basic automatically initializes the variables to 0. However, including the initialization in the Form_Load() procedure makes the program easier to read.

The Code in the *cmdStart_Click()* Procedure

The cmdStart_Click() procedure is executed whenever you click the Start button. This procedure executes an If...Else statement. The If statement checks to see the current value of the gRotateFlag variable:

```
Private Sub cmdStart_Click()

    ' Toggle the gRotateFlag, and toggle
    ' the caption of the Start/Stop button.
    If gRotateFlag = 0 Then
       gRotateFlag = 1
       cmdStart.Caption = "&Stop"
    Else
       gRotateFlag = 0
       cmdStart.Caption = "&Start"
    End If

End Sub
```

If the current value of gRotateFlag is 0, it is changed to 1 and the caption of the cmdStart button changes to &Stop. If, however, the current value of gRotateFlag is 1, this procedure changes the value of gRotateFlag to 0 and the caption of the cmdStart button is changed to &Start.

The gRotateFlag variable is used in the timer procedure discussed in the following section.

The Code in the *tmrTimer_Timer()* Procedure

Because you set the Interval property of the tmrTimer timer to 250, the tmrTimer_Timer() procedure is automatically executed every 250 milliseconds:

```
Private Sub tmrTimer_Timer()

    If gRotateFlag = 1 Then
        imgCurrentMoon.Picture = _
                imgMoon(gCurrentMoon).Picture
        gCurrentMoon = gCurrentMoon + 1

        If gCurrentMoon = 8 Then
            gCurrentMoon = 0
        End If

    End If

End Sub
```

If you haven't clicked the Start button, gRotateFlag is still equal to 0, and the statements in the If gRotateFlag = 1 block are not executed. If you have clicked the Start button, gRotateFlag is equal to 1, and the statements in the If gRotateFlag = 1 block are executed.

The code in the If statement assigns the Picture property of the control array of images to the Picture property of the imgCurrentMoon image:

```
imgCurrentMoon.Picture= _
    imgMoon(CurrentMoon).Picture
```

For example, when the gCurrentMoon variable is equal to 0, the Picture property of the 0th element in the control array is assigned to the Picture property of imgCurrentMoon. This causes the image MOON01.ICO to be displayed (because imgMoon(0).Picture contains the MOON01.ICO picture).

The next statement in the If block increases the variable gCurrentMoon:

```
gCurrentMoon = gCurrentMoon + 1
```

The next time the tmrTimer_Timer() procedure is executed (that is, after 250 milliseconds), the variable gCurrentMoon is already updated, pointing to the next element in the control array of images.

The next statements in the tmrTimer_Timer() procedure examine whether the value of gCurrentMoon is equal to 8. If it is, the 8th element in the array was displayed already, so you need to reset gCurrentMoon to 0:

```
If gCurrentMoon = 8 Then
                gCurrentMoon = 0
End If
```

Animation

The Moon program illustrates how easy it is to write animation programs in Visual Basic. You can enhance the Moon program so its animation performance is more impressive.

Enhancing the Moon Program

☐ Change the Interval property of the tmrTimer timer to 55.

☐ Change the general declarations area of the Moon program so that it looks like the following:

```
Option Explicit
Dim gRotateFlag As Integer
Dim gCurrentMoon As Integer
Dim gDirection As Integer
Dim gLeftCorner, gTopCorner As Single
Dim gWidthOfMoon, gHeightOfMoon
Dim gEnlargeShrink As Integer
```

☐ Change the Form_Load() procedure so it looks like the following:

```
Private Sub Form_Load()

    gRotateFlag = 0
    gCurrentMoon = 0
    gDirection = 1
    gLeftCorner = imgCurrentMoon.Left
    gTopCorner = imgCurrentMoon.Top
    gWidthOfMoon = 1
    gHeightOfMoon = 1
    gEnlargeShrink = 1

    imgCurrentMoon.Stretch = True

End Sub
```

☐ Change the tmrTimer_Timer() procedure so it looks like the following:

```
Private Sub tmrTimer_Timer()

    If gRotateFlag = 1 Then
       imgCurrentMoon.Picture = _
                imgMoon(gCurrentMoon).Picture
       gCurrentMoon = gCurrentMoon + 1
       If gCurrentMoon = 8 Then
          gCurrentMoon = 0
       End If
    Else
       Exit Sub
    End If
' Use the Move method to move the image.
' After the movement, the image will have new
```

```
' width (=gWidthOfMoon), and new Height
' (=gHeightOfMoon).
imgCurrentMoon.Move gLeftCorner, gTopCorner, _
            gWidthOfMoon, gHeightOfMoon
' Change the variables that the Move method uses
' for the next execution of this procedure,
gLeftCorner = gLeftCorner + 10 * gDirection
gTopCorner = gTopCorner + 10 * gDirection
gWidthOfMoon = gWidthOfMoon + 10 * gEnlargeShrink
gHeightOfMoon = gHeightOfMoon + 10 * gEnlargeShrink
' Is width of image too large?
If gWidthOfMoon > 700 Then
   gEnlargeShrink = -1
End If
' Is width of image too small?
If gWidthOfMoon < 10 Then
   gEnlargeShrink = 1
End If
' Image crosses bottom of frame?
If imgCurrentMoon.Top > frmMoon.ScaleHeight Then
   gDirection = -1
End If
 ' Image crosses top of frame?
If imgCurrentMoon.Top < 10 Then
   gDirection = 1
End If

End Sub
```

Executing the Enhanced Version of the Moon Program

☐ Execute the Moon program.

As you can see, the moon rotates on its axis and also seems to move in three dimensions!

The Code in the General Declarations Section

The general declarations section of the frmMoon form includes additional variable declarations of variables that are visible to all procedures in the form.

The Code in the *Form_Load()* Procedure

The code in the Form_Load() procedure initializes the variables.

The variables gLeftCorner and gTopCorner are initialized to the initial position of the upper-left corner of the imgCurrentMoon image:

```
gLeftCorner = imgCurrentMoon.Left
gTopCorner = imgCurrentMoon.Top
```

Also, the Stretch property of the imgCurrentMoon is set to True:

```
imgCurrentMoon.Stretch = True
```

This means that the size of the imgCurrentMoon image will change to fit within the control. This step is necessary because during the execution of the Moon program, the size of the imgCurrentMoon picture is enlarged and reduced.

The Code in the *tmrTimer_Timer()* Procedure

The first If block in the tmrTimer_Timer() procedure is the same as the earlier version, which displays one of the elements in the control array of images.

Once the image is displayed, the Move method is used to move the image so that the new location of the top-left corner of the image is at coordinate X=gLeftCorner,Y=gTopCorner.

The Move method also uses the optional width and height arguments:

```
imgCurrentMoon.Move gLeftCorner, gTopCorner, _
                    gWidthOfMoon,gHeightOfMoon
```

After the movement, the image will have a new width and height.

The statements that follow the Move statement prepare the variables for the next time the tmrTimer_Timer() procedure is executed:

```
gLeftCorner = gLeftCorner + 10 * gDirection
gTopCorner = gTopCorner + 10 * gDirection
gWidthOfMoon = gWidthOfMoon + 10 * gEnlargeShrink
gHeightOfMoon = gHeightOfMoon + 10 * gEnlargeShrink
```

Depending on the values of the variables gDirection and gEnlargeShrink, the above variables would either increase or decrease (that is, if gDirection is equal to 1, the value of gLeftCorner is increased by 10 twips; if gDirection is equal to -1, the value of gLeftCorner is decreased by 10 twips).

Next, examine the variable gWidthOfMoon to see whether it's too large or too small:

```
If gWidthOfMoon > 700 Then
   gEnlargeShrink = -1
End If

If gWidthOfMoon < 10 Then
   gEnlargeShrink = 1
End If
```

Then examine the current position of the top-left corner of the image to see whether the image crossed the bottom or the top of the form:

```
If imgCurrentMoon.Top > frmMoon.ScaleHeight Then
   gDirection = -1
End If
```

```
If imgCurrentMoon.Top < 10 Then
    gDirection = 1
End If
```

Summary

In this chapter you have learned how to use graphics controls: the line control and the shape control. You have also learned how to display picture files in the image and picture controls and to create animation by displaying and moving pictures. As demonstrated, the control array is a handy technique often used in animation.

Q&A

Q **In this chapter I learned how to use the Move method to move an image control and a picture control. Can I use the same technique to move other controls such as buttons?**

A Yes. The Move method may be used to move any object except menus. Of course, some controls (for example, the Timer control) are invisible, and it doesn't make sense to move an invisible control.

Quiz

1. How many twips are in an inch?
   a. 1440
   b. 1
   c. There is no relationship between an inch and a twip.
2. The Min property of the horizontal scroll bar in the Shape program was set to 1 at design time. Why not leave it at the default value 0?
3. What is the AutoSize property?
4. What is the difference between the Stretch property and the AutoSize property?

Exercise

Modify the MoveEye program so it beeps whenever the imgEye image reaches the top of the form.

Quiz Answers

1. a

2. In the code of the `hsbWidth_Change()` procedure of the Shape program, you set the BorderWidth property of the shape control to the current value of the scroll bar:

   ```
   shpAllShapes.BorderWidth = hsbWidth.Value
   ```

   If 0 is the minimum value the scroll bar can have, when the scroll bar is placed at its minimum position the preceding statement assigns the value 0 to the BorderWidth property of the shpAllShapes control. However, a shape control must have a minimum width of 1. Assigning 0 to the BorderWidth property of a shape control causes a runtime error.

3. When the AutoSize property is set to True, the object sizes itself to the exact dimensions of the picture file.

4. The AutoSize property is supported by a picture control and by the label control. When this property is set to True, Visual Basic adjusts the size of the control so that the control fits its content.

   The Stretch property is supported by an image control. When this property is set to True, the size of the picture is stretched to fit the size of the image control.

Exercise Answer

The image reaches the top of the form whenever its Top property is equal to 0. You can detect it by inserting the following `If` statement in the `For` loop of the `cmdMove_Click()` procedure:

```
If picEye.Top <= 0 Then
    Beep
    Exit Sub
End If
```

This `If` statement checks the value of the Top property. If the value is equal to or less than 0, the control reached the top of the form. The `Beep` statement will be executed and the `Exit Sub` statement will end the procedure.

This technique is often used to write a *bouncing* program, in which an object moves in the form in straight lines. When the object hits the side of the form, it changes direction. The code detects that the object reached the edge of the form by examining the values of the Top and Left properties.

You have completed your first week, and you now know how to write simple Visual Basic programs. This week you'll learn how to use more powerful features of Visual Basic by writing more programs that illustrate many more new concepts.

Where You're Going

In Chapter 8, "Graphics Methods," you'll learn to use the powerful graphics methods, and in Chapter 9, "The Grid Control," you'll learn to use the powerful grid control. This week you'll also learn how to display and print data, how to interface with Windows, how to take advantage of Windows, and how to access files from within your Visual Basic programs.

8

Graphics Methods

This chapter focuses on graphics methods, which are similar to the graphics controls discussed in Chapter 7, "Graphics Controls." Graphics methods are easier to use in some cases than graphic controls are.

The Points Program

The Points program, which draws points at random locations inside a form, illustrates how to draw points by using the Point method.

The Visual Implementation of the Points Program

☐ Open a new project, save the form of the project as POINTS.FRM in the directory C:\VB4PRG\CH08 directory and save the project file as POINTS.VBP in the directory C:\VB4PRG\CH08 directory.

☐ Build the frmPoints form according to the specifications in Table 8.1.

The completed form should look like the one shown in Figure 8.1.

Table 8.1. The properties table of the frmPoints form.

Object	Property	Setting
Form	**Name**	**frmPoints**
	BackColor	White
	Caption	The Points Program
	Height	4545
	Left	1080
	Top	1170
	Width	6810
Timer	**Name**	**tmrTimer**
	Interval	60
	Left	600
	Top	2400
Menu	**(See Table 8.2.)**	**(See Table 8.2.)**

Table 8.2. The menu table of the frmPoints form.

Caption	Name
&File	mnuFile
...E&xit	mnuExit
&Graphics	mnuGraphics
...&Draw Points	mnuDrawPoints
...&Clear	mnuClear

Figure 8.1.
The frmPoints form.

Entering the Code of the Points Program

☐ Enter the following code in the general declarations section of the frmPoints form:

```
' All variables MUST be declared.
Option Explicit

' A flag that determines if points will be drawn.
Dim gDrawPoints
```

☐ Enter the following code in the Form_Load() procedure of the frmPoints form:

```
Private Sub Form_Load()

    ' Disable drawing.
    gDrawPoints = 0

End Sub
```

☐ Enter the following code in the mnuClear_Click() procedure of the frmPoints form:

```
Private Sub mnuClear_Click()

    ' Disable drawing.
    gDrawPoints = 0
```

```
' Clear the form.
frmPoints.Cls
```

End Sub

☐ Enter the following code in the `mnuDrawPoints_Click()` procedure of the frmPoints form:

```
Private Sub mnuDrawPoints_Click()

' Enable drawing.
gDrawPoints = 1
```

End Sub

☐ Enter the following code in the `mnuExit_Click()` procedure of the frmPoints form:

```
Private Sub mnuExit_Click()

End
```

End Sub

☐ Enter the following code in the `tmrTimer1_Timer()` procedure of the frmPoints form:

```
Private Sub tmrTimer1_Timer()

Dim R, G, B
Dim X, Y
Dim Counter

' Is it OK to draw?
If gDrawPoints = 1 Then
    ' Draw 100 points.
    For Counter = 1 To 100 Step 1
        ' Get a random color.
        R = Rnd * 255
        G = Rnd * 255
        B = Rnd * 255
        ' Get a random (X,Y) coordinate.
        X = Rnd * frmPoints.ScaleWidth
        Y = Rnd * frmPoints.ScaleHeight
        ' Draw the point.
        frmPoints.PSet (X, Y), RGB(R, G, B)
    Next
End If
```

End Sub

☐ Save the project.

Executing the Points Program

☐ Execute the Points program.

☐ Select Draw Points from the Graphics menu.

The program responds by displaying points with random colors at random locations inside the form. (See Figure 8.2.)

Figure 8.2.
Drawing points inside a form.

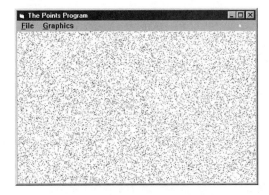

☐ Select Clear from the Graphics menu.

The program clears the form.

☐ Select Exit from the File menu to terminate the program.

How the Points Program Works

The Points program uses the PSet graphics method to draw a point inside the form and the Cls method to clear the form.

The Code in the General Declarations Section

The general declarations area of the frmPoints form declares the gDrawPoints variable. This variable serves as a flag: When it is equal to 1, drawing is enabled; when it is equal to 0, drawing is disabled.

The Code in the *Form_Load()* Procedure

The Form_Load() procedure is automatically executed when the program is started:

```
Private Sub Form_Load()

    ' Disable drawing.
    gDrawPoints = 0

End Sub
```

This procedure initializes the gDrawPoints flag to 0 to disable drawing the points.

The Code in the *mnuClear_Click()* Procedure

The mnuClear_Click() procedure is executed whenever you select Clear from the Graphics menu:

```
Private Sub mnuClear_Click()

    ' Disable drawing.
    gDrawPoints = 0

    ' Clear the form.
    frmPoints.Cls

End Sub
```

This procedure disables the drawing by setting the gDrawPoints variable to 0 and then uses the Cls method to clear the form.

DO	DON'T
DO use the Cls method to clear an object. The Cls method clears graphics generated during runtime with the graphics methods. For example, to clear the frmMyForm form, use frmMyForm.Cls.	

The Code in the *mnuDrawPoints_Click()* Procedure

The mnuDrawPoints_Click() procedure is executed whenever you select Draw Points from the Graphics menu:

```
Private Sub mnuDrawPoints_Click()

    ' Enable drawing.
    gDrawPoints = 1

End Sub
```

This procedure sets the gDrawPoints flag to 1 to enable drawing.

The Code in the *tmrTimer1_Timer()* Procedure

Because you set the Interval property of the tmrTimer timer to 60, the tmrTimer1_Timer() procedure is automatically executed every 60 milliseconds:

```
Private Sub tmrTimer1_Timer()

    Dim R, G, B
    Dim X, Y
    Dim Counter
```

```
' Is it OK to draw?
If gDrawPoints = 1 Then
    ' Draw 100 points.
    For Counter = 1 To 100 Step 1
        ' Get a random color.
        R = Rnd * 255
        G = Rnd * 255
        B = Rnd * 255
        ' Get a random (X,Y) coordinate.
        X = Rnd * frmPoints.ScaleWidth
        Y = Rnd * frmPoints.ScaleHeight
        ' Draw the point.
        frmPoints.PSet (X, Y), RGB(R, G, B)
    Next
End If
```

End Sub

The If statement examines the value of the gDrawPoints flag. If this flag is equal to 1, it means you selected Draw Points from the Graphics menu, and the code in the If block is executed.

The For loop draws 100 points. Each point is drawn with a random color and at a random location. The PSet graphics method is used to draw each point:

```
frmPoints.PSet (X, Y), RGB(R, G, B)
```

DO	DON'T
DO use the PSet graphics method to draw a point in an object.	

The *PSet* Graphics Method

As demonstrated, the PSet method draws a point at the x,y coordinate that is specified by its argument.

The PSet method has an optional argument called Step. When you're using the Step argument, the point is drawn in relation to the CurrentX,CurrentY coordinate. For example, suppose that CurrentX is equal to 100 and CurrentY is equal to 50. Upon issuing the statement

```
frmPoints.PSet Step(10, 20), RGB(R, G, B)
```

a point is drawn at location 110,70. That is, the point is drawn 10 units to the right of CurrentX and 20 units below CurrentY. After the drawing, CurrentX and CurrentY are automatically updated—CurrentX is updated to 110, and CurrentY is updated to 70. (Recall from Chapter 4, "The Mouse," that CurrentX and CurrentY are automatically updated by Visual Basic to the endpoint of the last graphic that was drawn.)

☐ Replace the code in the `tmrTimer1_Timer()` procedure with the following code:

```
Private Sub tmrTimer1_Timer()

    Dim R, G, B
    Dim X, Y
    Dim Counter
    If gDrawPoints = 1 Then
        For Counter = 1 To 100 Step 1
            R = Rnd * 255
            G = Rnd * 255
            B = Rnd * 255
            frmPoints.PSet Step(1, 1), RGB(R, G, B)
            If CurrentX >= frmPoints.ScaleWidth Then
                CurrentX = Rnd * frmPoints.ScaleWidth
            End If
            If CurrentY >= frmPoints.ScaleHeight Then
                CurrentY = Rnd * frmPoints.ScaleHeight
            End If
        Next
    End If

End Sub
```

☐ Execute the Points program, select Draw Points from the Graphics menu, and let the program run for a while.

The program now draws lines, as shown in Figure 8.3.

Figure 8.3.
Using the Step *option of the* PSet *graphics method.*

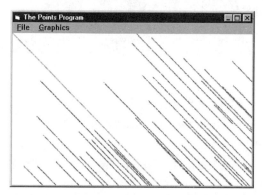

The code in the `tmrTimer1_Timer()` procedure uses the `PSet` method with the `Step` option:

```
frmPoints.PSet Step(1, 1), RGB(R, G, B)
```

Each point is drawn one unit to the right and one unit below the previous point. This explains why the points are drawn as straight diagonal lines, as shown in Figure 8.3.

The two `If` statements in this procedure check that the points are drawn within the boundaries of the form.

The *Point* Method

The Point method returns the color of a particular pixel. For example, to find the color of the pixel at location 30,40, use the following statement:

```
PixelColor = Point (30,40)
```

Although the Points program did not use the Point method, you may find some use for this method in your future projects.

Drawing Lines

You can draw lines using the Line method, which has the following syntax:

```
Line (x1,y1)-(x2,y2), color
```

where (x1,y1) is the coordinate of the starting point of the line, (x2,y2) is the coordinate of the ending point of the line, and color is the color of the line. If you omit the (x1,y1) argument, the line is drawn starting at coordinate CurrentX,CurrentY.

To see the Line method in action, add the Lines menu item to the menu system of the Points program. The new menu table of the Points program is shown in Table 8.3.

Table 8.3. The new menu table of the frmPoints form.

Caption	Name
&File	mnuFile
…&Exit	mnuExit
&Graphics	mnuGraphics
…&Draw Points	mnuDrawPoints
…&Clear	mnuClear
…&Lines	mnuLines

☐ Add the following code in the mnuLines_Click() procedure of the frmPoints form:

```
Private Sub mnuLines_Click()

    Line -(Rnd * frmPoints.ScaleWidth, _
        Rnd * frmPoints.ScaleHeight), RGB(0, 0, 0)

End Sub
```

This procedure draws one line with random width, height, and color.

☐ Execute the Points program.

☐ Select Lines from the Graphics menu.

A line is drawn in the form, as shown in Figure 8.4.

Figure 8.4.

Drawing a line with the
`Line` *method.*

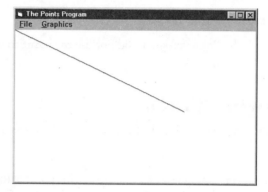

Because the `(x1,y1)` coordinate is omitted, the `Line` statement in the `mnuLines_Click()` procedure draws the line starting at coordinate CurrentX,CurrentY. The endpoint of the line is at a random location in the form. When you start the program, the initial values of CurrentX and CurrentY are 0—this explains why the line in Figure 8.4 starts at coordinate 0,0.

☐ Select Lines from the Graphics menu several times.

Each time you select Lines, a new line is drawn, starting from the endpoint of the previous line. (See Figure 8.5.)

Figure 8.5.

Drawing connected lines.

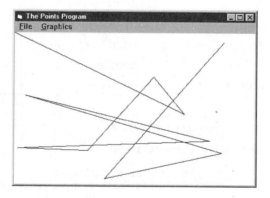

☐ Select Exit from the File menu to terminate the program.

☐ Replace the code in the `mnuLines_Click()` procedure with the following code:

```
Private Sub mnuLines_Click()
```

```
Dim Counter

For Counter = 1 To 100 Step 1
    Line -(Rnd * frmPoints.ScaleWidth, _
           Rnd * frmPoints.ScaleHeight), RGB(0, 0, 0)

Next
```

End Sub

☐ Execute the program.

☐ Select Lines from the Graphics menu.

The program draws 100 connected lines, as shown in Figure 8.6.

Figure 8.6.
*Drawing 100
connected lines.*

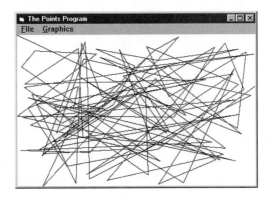

Using the *Step* Argument in the *Line* Method

The optional Step argument may be used with the Line method as follows:

```
Line (x1,y1)-Step (dX,dY), color
```

where (x1,y1) is the coordinate of the starting point, and Step (dX,dY) is an indication to Visual Basic that the endpoint of the line is at coordinate x1+dX,y1+dY. For example, the statement

```
Line (20,30)-Step(50,100), RGB(0,0,0)
```

draws a line with a starting point at coordinate 20,30 and an endpoint at coordinate 70,130.

The Step option may also be used to draw a box. The following statements draw the box shown in Figure 8.7:

```
' Line from left top corner to right top corner.
Line (100, 20)-(400,0)
```

```
' Line from right top corner to right bottom corner.
Line -Step(0, 400)
' Line from right bottom corner to left bottom ' corner.
Line -Step (-300, 0)
' Line from left bottom corner to left top corner.
Line -Step (0, -400)
```

Figure 8.7.

Drawing a box with the
Line method.

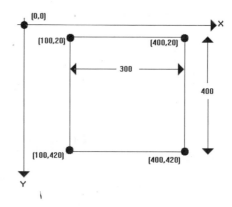

As you can see, four Line statements are needed to draw a single box! An easier way to draw a box is to use the Line method with the B option as follows:

```
Line (100,20)- (400,420), RGB(0,0,0),B
```

The first coordinate—100,20—is the coordinate of the top-left corner of the box, and the second coordinate is the coordinate of the lower-right corner of the box. The B option instructs Visual Basic to draw a box with these two corners.

If you want to fill the box, use the F option:

```
Line (100,20)-(400,420),RGB(0,255,0),BF
```

This statement draws a box and fills the box with the color RGB(0,255,0), which is green. There is no comma between the B and F options because you can't use the F option without the B option.

Filling the Box with the FillStyle Property

Another way to fill the box is to set the FillColor and FillStyle properties of the form and use the Line method with the B option and without the F option:

```
frmMyForm.FillStyle = 2
frmMyForm.FillColor = RGB(255,0,0)
frmMyForm.Line(100,20)-(400,420),RGB(0,0,0),B
```

The first statement sets the FillStyle property of the form to 2. The eight possible values of FillStyle are shown in Table 8.4. When the FillStyle property is equal to 2, the object is filled with horizontal lines. The second statement sets the FillColor property to RGB(255,0,0), which means the box is filled with the color red. Therefore, the three statements draw a box filled with red horizontal lines.

Table 8.4. The eight possible values of the FillStyle property.

Value	Description
0	Solid
1	Transparent (default setting)
2	Horizontal lines
3	Vertical lines
4	Upward diagonal lines
5	Downward diagonal lines
6	Crosshatch
7	Diagonal crosshatch

To see the meaning of each of the different FillStyles in Table 8.4 do the following:

☐ Add the Draw Box menu to the menu system of the frmPoints form. The new menu table is shown in Table 8.5.

Table 8.5. Adding the Draw Box menu to the frmPoints form.

Caption	Name
&File	mnuFile
…&Exit	mnuExit
&Graphics	mnuGraphics
…&Draw Points	mnuDrawPoints
…&Clear	mnuClear
…&Lines	mnuLines
D&raw Box	mnuDrawBox
…R&ed	mnuRed
…Gree&n	mnuGreen
…&Blue	mnuBlue
…-	mnuSep1
…&Set Style…	mnuSetStyle

☐ Add the following code in the mnuRed_Click() procedure of the frmPoints form:

```
Private Sub mnuRed_Click()

    ' Set the FillColor property of the form.
    frmPoints.FillColor = RGB(255, 0, 0)

    ' Draw the box.
    frmPoints.Line (100, 80)-Step(5000, 3000), _
                RGB(255, 0, 0), B

End Sub
```

☐ Add the following code in the mnuBlue_Click() procedure of the frmPoints form:

```
Private Sub mnuBlue_Click()

    ' Set the FillColor property of the form.to red
    frmPoints.FillColor = RGB(255, 0, 0)

    ' Draw the box.
    frmPoints.Line (100, 80)-Step(5000, 3000), _
                RGB(0, 0, 255), B

End Sub
```

☐ Add the following code in the mnuGreen_Click() procedure of the frmPoints form:

```
Private Sub mnuGreen_Click()

    ' Set the FillColor property of the form.
    frmPoints.FillColor = RGB(255, 0, 0)

    ' Draw the box.
    frmPoints.Line (100, 80)-Step(5000, 3000), _
                RGB(0, 255, 0), B

End Sub
```

☐ Add the following code in the mnuSetStyleClick() procedure of the frmPoints form:

```
Private Sub mnuSetStyle_Click()

    Dim FromUser
    Dim Instruction
    Instruction = "Enter a number between 0 and 7 " + _
                "for the FillStyle"

    ' Get from the user the desired FillStyle.
    FromUser = InputBox$(Instruction, _
                "Setting the FillStyle")
    ' Clear the form.
    frmPoints.Cls

    ' Did the user enter a valid FillStyle?
    If Val(FromUser) >= 0 And Val(FromUser) <= 7 Then
        frmPoints.FillStyle = Val(FromUser)
```

```
        Else
           Beep
           MsgBox ("Invalid FillStyle")
        End If
        ' Draw the box.
        frmPoints.Line (100, 80)-Step(5000, 3000), _
                        RGB(0, 0, 0), B

End Sub
```

Executing the Points Program

☐ Execute the Points program.

☐ Select Set Style from the Draw Box menu.

The program responds by displaying a message box, as shown in Figure 8.8.

Figure 8.8.
Entering a value for the FillStyle property.

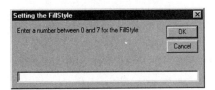

☐ Type a number between 0 and 7 and click the OK button. This number represents the FillStyle.

The program displays the box and fills it with the FillStyle entered in the previous step. Figure 8.9 shows the box when the FillStyle is set to 2 (horizontal lines).

Figure 8.9.
Experimenting with the FillStyle property.

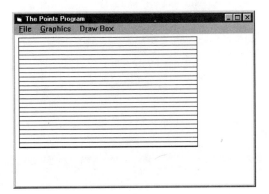

☐ Select the Red, Blue, or Green color from the Draw Box menu.

The program draws the box with the selected color.

The Code in the *mnuRed_Click()* Procedure

The mnuRed_Click() procedure is executed whenever you select Red from the Draw Box menu:

```
Private Sub mnuRed_Click()

    ' Set the FillColor property of the form.
    frmPoints.FillColor = RGB(255, 0, 0)

    ' Draw the box.
    frmPoints.Line (100, 80)-Step(5000, 3000), _
              RGB(255, 0, 0), B

End Sub
```

This procedure sets the value of the FillColor property to red, then the Line method with the B option is used to draw the box. The box is filled according to the current setting of the form's FillStyle property.

The mnuBlue_Click() and mnuGreen_Click() procedures of the frmPoints form work in a similar manner, setting the FillColor property in these procedures to blue and green.

The Code in the *mnuSetStyleClick()* Procedure

The mnuSetStyle_Click() procedure is executed whenever you select Set Style from the Draw Box menu:

```
Private Sub mnuSetStyle_Click()

    Dim FromUser
    Dim Instruction
    Instruction = "Enter a number between 0 and 7 " + _
                "for the FillStyle"

    ' Get from the user the desired FillStyle.
    FromUser = InputBox$(Instruction, _
                "Setting the FillStyle")
    ' Clear the form.
    frmPoints.Cls
    ' Did the user enter a valid FillStyle?
    If Val(FromUser) >= 0 And Val(FromUser) <= 7 Then
        frmPoints.FillStyle = Val(FromUser)
    Else
        Beep
        MsgBox ("Invalid FillStyle")
    End If
    ' Draw the box.
    frmPoints.Line (100, 80)-Step(5000, 3000), _
                RGB(0, 0, 0), B

End Sub
```

This procedure uses the InputBox$() function to get a number between 0 and 7. The form is cleared with the Cls method, and your input is checked with the If statement to see whether

the entered number is within the valid range. If the entered number is between 0 and 7, the FillStyle property is updated with this number.

The last statement in the procedure draws a box using the Line method with the B option. The box is drawn with the current setting of the FillColor and FillStyle properties of the form.

The Circles Program

Another important graphics method is the Circle method, used to draw circles. The Circles program illustrates how you may draw circles. Although you can use the Circle method to draw circles in a form, the Circles program draws circles in a picture control.

The Visual Implementation of the Circles Program

☐ Open a new project, save the form of the project as CIRCLES.FRM in the C:\VB4PRG\CH08 directory, and save the project file as CIRCLES.VBP in the C:\VB4PRG\CH08 directory.

☐ Build the frmCircles form according to the specifications in Table 8.6.

The completed form should look like the one shown in Figure 8.10.

Table 8.6. The properties table of frmCircles form.

Object	Property	Setting
Form	**Name**	**frmCircles**
	Caption	The Circles Program
	Height	4800
	Left	1080
	Top	1170
	Width	5745
Picture Box	**Name**	**picCircles**
	Height	2295
	Left	480
	Top	960
	Width	3735

continues

Table 8.6. continued

Object	Property	Setting
Command Button	**Name**	**cmdExit**
	Caption	E&xit
	FontName	System
	FontSize	10
	Height	495
	Left	2160
	Top	3840
	Width	1215
Vertical Scroll Bar	**Name**	**vsbRadius**
	Height	2295
	Left	240
	Max	100
	Min	1
	Top	960
	Value	1
	Width	255
Horizontal Scroll Bar	**Name**	**hsbCircleWidth**
	Height	255
	Left	240
	Max	10
	Min	1
	Top	3240
	Value	1
	Width	3975
Label	**Name**	**lblWidth**
	Caption	Width
	FontName	System
	FontSize	10
	Height	375
	Left	4320

Object	Property	Setting
	Top	3240
	Width	1575
Label	**Name**	**lblRadius**
	Caption	Radius
	FontName	System
	FontSize	10
	Height	375
	Left	120
	Top	480
	Width	1695

Figure 8.10.
*The frmCircles form
in design mode.*

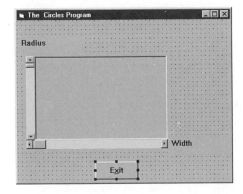

Entering the Code of the Circles Program

☐ Enter the following code in the general declarations section of the frmCircles form:

```
' All variables MUST be declared.
Option Explicit
```

☐ Enter the following code in the cmdExit_Click() procedure of the frmCircles form:

```
Private Sub cmdExit_Click()

    End

End Sub
```

☐ Enter the following code in the `hsbCircleWidth_Change()` procedure of the frmCircles form:

```
Private Sub hsbCircleWidth_Change()

    Dim X, Y, Radius

    ' Change the DrawWidth property of the picture
    ' control according to the horizontal
    ' scroll bar.
    picCircles.DrawWidth = hsbCircleWidth.Value


    ' Calculate the coordinate of the center of the
    ' circle.
    X = picCircles.ScaleWidth / 2
    Y = picCircles.ScaleHeight / 2
    ' Clear the picture box.
    picCircles.Cls
    picCircles.Circle (X, Y), vsbRadius.Value * 10, _
              RGB(255, 0, 0)


End Sub
```

☐ Enter the following code in the `hsbCircleWidth_Scroll()` procedure of the frmCircles form:

```
Private Sub hsbCircleWidth_Scroll()

Dim X, Y, Radius

    ' Change the DrawWidth property of the picture
    ' control according to the horizontal
    ' scroll bar.
    picCircles.DrawWidth = hsbCircleWidth.Value


    ' Calculate the coordinate of the center of the
    ' circle.
    X = picCircles.ScaleWidth / 2
    Y = picCircles.ScaleHeight / 2
    ' Clear the picture box.
    picCircles.Cls
    picCircles.Circle (X, Y), vsbRadius.Value * 10, _
              RGB(255, 0, 0)

End Sub
```

☐ Enter the following code in the `vsbRadius_Change()` procedure of the frmCircles form:

```
Private Sub vsbRadius_Change()

    Dim X, Y, Radius
    ' Calculate the coordinate of the center of the
    ' circle.
    X = picCircles.ScaleWidth / 2
```

```
            Y = picCircles.ScaleHeight / 2
            ' Clear the picture box.
            picCircles.Cls
            picCircles.Circle (X, Y), vsbRadius.Value * 10, _
                      RGB(255, 0, 0)

End Sub
```

☐ Enter the following code in the vsbRadius_Scroll() procedure of the frmCircles form:

```
Private Sub vsbRadius_Scroll()

    Dim X, Y, Radius
    ' Calculate the coordinate of the center of the
    ' circle.
    X = picCircles.ScaleWidth / 2
    Y = picCircles.ScaleHeight / 2
    ' Clear the picture box.
    picCircles.Cls
    picCircles.Circle (X, Y), vsbRadius.Value * 10, _
              RGB(255, 0, 0)

End Sub
```

Executing the Circles Program

☐ Execute the Circles program.

☐ Change the vertical scroll bar.

The radius of the circle displayed in the picture control changes according to the setting of the vertical scroll bar. (See Figure 8.11.)

Figure 8.11.
Changing the radius with the vertical scroll bar.

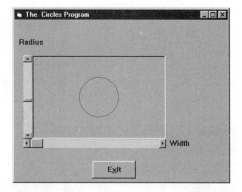

☐ Change the horizontal scroll bar to set a new value for the circle line width.

The circle is now drawn with a different line width.

How the Circles Program Works

The Circles program uses the `Circle` method to draw the circle. The radius of the circle is changed according to the vertical scroll bar position, and the width of the circle is changed according to the horizontal scroll bar position.

The Code in the *vsbRadius_Change()* Procedure

The `vsbRadius_Change()` procedure is executed whenever you change the vertical scroll bar position:

```
Private Sub vsbRadius_Change()

    Dim X, Y, Radius

    ' Calculate the coordinate of the center of the
    ' circle.
    X = picCircles.ScaleWidth / 2
    Y = picCircles.ScaleHeight / 2

    ' Clear the picture box.
    picCircles.Cls

    picCircles.Circle (X, Y), vsbRadius.Value * 10, _
              RGB(255, 0, 0)

End Sub
```

This procedure calculates the coordinate of the center point (X,Y) of the circle by calculating the coordinate of the center of the picture control (that is, the center of the circle is placed at the center of the picture control).

Then the graphics content of the picture control is cleared with the `Cls` method (erasing the previous circle, if any), and finally the circle is drawn with the `Circle` method:

```
picCircles.Circle (X, Y), vsbRadius.Value * 10, _
          RGB(255, 0, 0)
```

The radius of the circle, drawn in red, is 10 times larger than the current setting of the vertical scroll bar.

DO	DON'T

DO use the `Circle` method to draw a circle:
    `Object name.Circle _`
        `(X coord. of center, Y coord. of center), _`
      `Radius, Color`	

For example, to draw a blue circle in the frmMyForm form with the center at coordinate 1000,500 and the radius equal to 75, use the following:

```
frmMyForm.Circle (1000,500), 75, RGB(0,0,255)
```

In a similar way, the vsbRadius_Scroll() procedure draws a new circle whenever the radius vertical scroll bar is changed.

The Code in the *hsbCircleWidth_Change()* Procedure

The hsbCircleWidth_Change() procedure is executed whenever you change the horizontal scroll bar:

```
Private Sub hsbCircleWidth_Change()

    Dim X, Y, Radius

    ' Change the DrawWidth property of the picture
    ' control according to the horizontal
    ' scroll bar.
    picCircles.DrawWidth = hsbCircleWidth.Value

    ' Calculate the coordinate of the center of the
    ' circle.
    X = picCircles.ScaleWidth / 2
    Y = picCircles.ScaleHeight / 2
    ' Clear the picture box.
    picCircles.Cls
    picCircles.Circle (X, Y), vsbRadius.Value * 10, _
              RGB(255, 0, 0)

End Sub
```

This procedure changes the DrawWidth property of the picCircles picture control according to the position of the horizontal scroll bar position. The value of the DrawWidth property of the picture control determines the width of the circle drawn in the picture control. As you can see, the code in this procedure is very similar to the code in the hsbRadius_Change() procedure. However, instead of the radius changing, the DrawWidth property of the picture control is updated:

```
picCircles.DrawWidth = hsbCircleWidth.Value
```

In a similar way, the hsbCircleWidth_Scroll() procedure draws a new circle whenever the circle width is changed with the horizontal scroll bar.

Enhancing the Circles Program

As you might expect, some impressive graphics effects can be created by adding several lines of code to the Circles program.

☐ Add the Draw Style button to the frmCircles form, as shown in Figure 8.12.

☐ Give this button the following properties: The Name property should be cmdDrawStyle and the Caption property should be &Draw Style.

Figure 8.12.

Adding the Draw Style button to the Circles program.

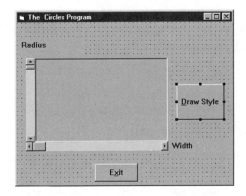

☐ Add the following code in the cmdDrawStyle_Click() procedure of the frmCircles form:

```
Private Sub cmdDrawStyle_Click()

    Dim TheStyle
    ' Get a number from the user.
    TheStyle = InputBox$("Enter DrawStyle (0-6):")

    ' Is the number between 0 and 6?
    If Val(TheStyle) < 0 Or Val(TheStyle) > 6 Then
        ' The entered number is not within the valid
        ' range.
        Beep
        MsgBox ("Invalid DrawStyle")
    Else
        ' The entered number is within the valid
        ' range, so change to DrawStyle property.
        picCircles.DrawStyle = Val(TheStyle)
    End If

End Sub
```

☐ Delete the horizontal scroll bar. (Make sure that the horizontal scroll bar is selected and press the Delete key.)

Note: In the previous version of Circles, you wrote code in the hsbWidth_Change() procedure. Now that you have deleted this control, Visual Basic has placed the procedure in the general declarations section. Therefore, after deleting the control, you can also remove its procedures from the general declarations section.

☐ Delete the hsbWidth_Change() procedure in the general declarations section. Highlight the whole procedure, including its first and last lines, and press the Delete key.

☐ Delete the lblWidth label by selecting it and pressing the Delete key.

☐ Delete the hsbWidth_Scroll() procedure in the general declarations area. Highlight the whole procedure, including its first and last lines, and press the Delete key.

☐ Set the BackColor property of the picCircles control to White. The circle will be drawn on a white background so you'll be able to see the effects of the drawing styles better.

Executing the Circles Program

☐ Execute the Circles program.

☐ Click the Draw Style button.

> *The program responds by displaying a message box that asks you to enter a number between 0 and 6.*

☐ Enter a number between 0 and 6, which represents the drawing style for the circle, and click the OK button.

☐ Play with the vertical scroll bar and see the effects that the different styles and radii have on the circle.

☐ Terminate the program by clicking the Exit button.

The DrawStyle Property

The cmdDrawStyle_Click() procedure is executed whenever you click the Draw Style button. You are asked to type a number between 0 and 6, which is assigned to the DrawStyle property of the picture control. Table 8.7 lists the seven possible values of the DrawStyle property and their meanings.

Table 8.7. The seven possible values of the DrawStyle property.

Value	Meaning
0	Solid (default value)
1	Dash (-)
2	Dot (…)
3	Dash-dot (-.-.)
4	Dash-dot-dot (-..-..-)
5	Invisible
6	Inside solid

If the DrawWidth property of the picture control is set to a value greater than 1, you will not be able to see the effects of the DrawStyle property when it's set to 2, 3, or 4. This explains why you were instructed to remove the scroll bar that changes the DrawWidth property (that is, to experiment with the DrawStyle property, the DrawWidth property must be equal to 1).

Further Enhancing the Circles Program

Now make an additional enhancement to the Circles program:

☐ Replace the code in the vsbRadius_Change() procedure with the following code:

```
Private Sub vsbRadius_Change ()

    Dim X, Y, Radius
    Static LastValue
    Dim R, G, B

    ' Generate random colors.
    R = Rnd * 255
    G = Rnd * 255
    B = Rnd * 255

    ' Calculate the coordinate of the center of the
    ' picture control.
    X = picCircles.ScaleWidth / 2
    Y = picCircles.ScaleHeight / 2

    ' If scroll bar was decrement, then clear the
    ' picture box.
    If LastValue > vsbRadius.Value Then
       picCircles.Cls
    End If

    ' Draw the circle.
    picCircles.Circle (X, Y), vsbRadius.Value * 10, _
               RGB(R, G, B)
```

```
                     ' Update LastValue for next time.
                     LastValue = vsbRadius.Value

            End Sub
```

☐ Replace the code in the vsbRadius_Scroll() procedure with the following code:

```
Private Sub vsbRadius_Scroll()

            Dim X, Y, Radius
            Static LastValue
            Dim R, G, B

            ' Generate random colors.
            R = Rnd * 255
            G = Rnd * 255
            B = Rnd * 255

            ' Calculate the coordinate of the center of the
            ' picture control.
            X = picCircles.ScaleWidth / 2
            Y = picCircles.ScaleHeight / 2

            ' If scroll bar was decremented, then clear the
            ' picture box.
            If LastValue > vsbRadius.Value Then
                picCircles.Cls
            End If

            ' Draw the circle.
            picCircles.Circle (X, Y), vsbRadius.Value * 10, _
                            RGB(R, G, B)

            ' Update LastValue for next time.
            LastValue = vsbRadius.Value

            End Sub
```

Executing the Enhanced Version of the Circles Program

☐ Execute the Circles program.

☐ Click the DrawStyle button.

> *The program responds by displaying the InputBox, which asks you to enter a number between 0 and 6.*

☐ Enter the number 2 and click the OK button.

☐ Increase the Radius scroll bar position by clicking several times on the down arrow at the bottom of the scroll bar.

> *The program responds by drawing the circles shown in Figure 8.13.*

Figure 8.13.
Drawing circles with the enhanced version of the Circles program.

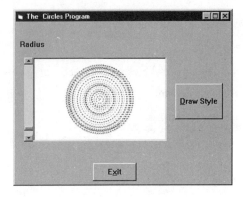

☐ Decrease the scroll bar position by clicking several times on the up arrow at the top of the scroll bar.

The program responds by drawing successively smaller circles.

☐ Terminate the program by clicking the Exit button.

The Code in the *vsbRadius_Change()* Procedure

The vsbRadius_Change() procedure is automatically executed whenever you change the scroll bar position. It starts by declaring several variables. The second variable is defined as Static:

```
Static LastValue
```

This means that the value of the LastValue variable is not initialized to 0 every time this procedure is executed (that is, this variable retains its value).

The procedure then prepares the three variables R, G, and B, updating the value of these variables with numbers that represent random colors:

```
' Generate random colors.
R = Rnd * 255
G = Rnd * 255
B = Rnd * 255
```

The procedure then calculates the coordinate of the center of the picture box control:

```
' Calculate the coordinate of the center of the
' picture control.
X = picCircles.ScaleWidth / 2
Y = picCircles.ScaleHeight / 2
```

This coordinate is used later in this procedure as the coordinate for the center of the circles.

The LastValue variable holds the Value property of the scroll bar before you changed the scroll bar position.

The If statement checks whether the current position of the scroll bar (specified by the Value property) is smaller than the last position of the scroll bar:

```
' If scroll bar was decremented, then clear the
' picture box.
If LastValue > vsbRadius.Value Then
   picCircles.Cls
End If
```

If the current Value property of the scroll bar is smaller than LastValue, you decremented the scroll bar. In this case, the Cls method is executed, which clears the picture box.

The procedure then draws the circle using the Circle method:

```
' Draw the circle.
picCircles.Circle (X, Y), vsbRadius.Value * 10, _
                   RGB(R, G, B)
```

The last thing this procedure does is update the LastValue variable. The next time this procedure is executed, the value of LastValue represents the Value property of the scroll bar before the change:

```
' Update LastValue for next time.
LastValue = vsbRadius.Value
```

When the scroll bar is incremented, the Cls method is not executed. Therefore, when incrementing the scroll bar, the already drawn circles remain onscreen.

About the *LastValue Static* Variable

An important thing to note from the preceding discussion is that the variable LastValue is declared as a Static variable:

```
Static LastValue
```

When the vsbRadius_Change() procedure is executed for the very fist time, Visual Basic sets LastValue to 0. During the execution of the vsbRadius_Change() procedure, the value of LastValue is changed to another value. The next time hsbRadius_Change() is executed, the values of nonstatic variables such as X, Y, and Radius are initialized back to 0.

However, since LastValue is declared as a Static variable, its value is not changed from the last execution of the hsbRadius_Change() procedure.

You might note the similarity between a variable declared in the general declarations area and a variable declared as Static in a procedure. In both cases, the variable retains its value for as long as the program runs. However, there is an important difference between these two types of variables:

- A variable declared in the general declarations area of a form is accessible from within *any* procedure of the form.

- A variable declared as a static variable in a procedure is accessible *only* from within the procedure that declares this variable.

For example, if you try to access the LastValue variable from within the Form_Load() procedure, you'll get an error, because you can't access LastValue outside the vsbRadius_Change() procedure.

Also, you can declare another variable called LastValue in the Form_Load() procedure. This value can be declared as a static variable or a regular nonstatic local variable, but there is no connection between the LastValue variable of the Form_Load() procedure and the LastValue variable in the vsbRadius_Change() procedure.

As you can see, declaring a static variable is a good trick to use whenever you don't want to lose the value of a variable after a procedure is terminated.

Regular nonstatic local variables and static variables are stored in your PC in different ways. For example, compare how the Radius variable (a regular nonstatic local variable in the hsbRadius_Change() procedure) and the LastValue Static variable are stored. Once Visual Basic completes the execution of the hsbRadius_Change() procedure, the value of the Radius variable is gone forever, so the memory cells (RAM bytes) used to store the Radius variable are free. However, the memory cells used for storing the LastValue Static variable are never freed; they are occupied as long as the Circles program is running. A variable declared in the general declarations area also occupies memory cells as long as the program is running.

Drawing Ellipses and Arcs

To draw ellipses and arcs, use the Circle method. Its complete syntax is as follows:

```
[object.]Circle[Step](x,y), _
                radius, _
                [color], _
                [start], _
                [end], _
                [aspect]
```

If you include the Step option, the x,y coordinate is referenced to the CurrentX,CurrentY point. For example, if CurrentX is 1000, and CurrentY is 3000, the statement

```
frmMyForm.Circle Step(10,20),80
```

draws a circle with a radius at 80 and a center at 1010,3020.

The *aspect* Argument

The aspect argument is a positive number that causes the Circle method to draw ellipses. For example, when the aspect ratio is equal to 1, the Circle method produces a perfect circle. When

the aspect ratio is greater than 1, the `Circle` method produces an ellipse stretched along the vertical axis. When the aspect ratio is less than 1, the `Circle` method produces an ellipse stretched along the horizontal axis. Figures 8.14, 8.15, and 8.16 show three ellipses with three different aspects.

Figure 8.14.

The ellipse with the `aspect` *argument equal to 1.*

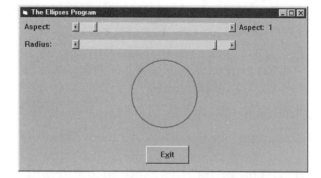

Figure 8.15.

The ellipse with the `aspect` *argument equal to 0.4.*

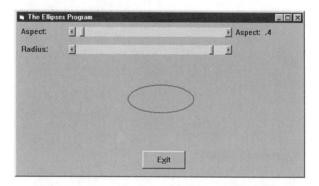

Figure 8.16.

The ellipse with the `aspect` *argument equal to 1.9.*

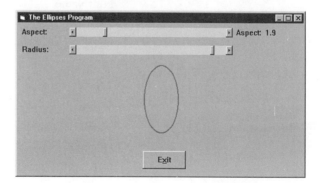

The Ellipses Program

The Ellipses program illustrates how to draw ellipses with different radii and aspects.

The Visual Implementation of the Ellipses Program

☐ Open a new project, save the form of the project as ELLIPSES.FRM in the C:\VB4PRG\CH08 directory and save the project file as ELLIPSES.VBP in the C:\VB4PRG\CH08 directory.

☐ Build the frmEllipses form according to the specifications in Table 8.8.

The completed form should look like the one shown in Figure 8.17.

Table 8.8. The properties table of the frmEllipses form.

Object	Property	Setting
Form	**Name**	**frmEllipses**
	Caption	The Ellipses Program
	Height	4545
	Left	1080
	Top	1170
	Width	8130
Command Button	**Name**	**cmdExit**
	Caption	E&xit
	FontName	System
	FontSize	10
	Height	495
	Left	3480
	Top	3480
	Width	1215
Horizontal Scroll Bar	**Name**	**hsbAspect**
	Height	255
	Left	1440
	Max	100

Object	Property	Setting
	Min	1
	Top	120
	Value	1
	Width	4575
Horizontal Scroll Bar	**Name**	**hsbRadius**
	Height	255
	Left	1440
	Max	100
	Min	1
	Top	600
	Value	1
	Width	4575
Label	**Name**	**lblInfo**
	Caption	Aspect:
	FontName	System
	FontSize	10
	Height	495
	Left	6120
	Top	120
	Width	1695
Label	**Name**	**lblAspect**
	Caption	Aspect:
	FontName	System
	FontSize	10
	Height	375
	Left	120
	Top	120
	Width	1215
Label	**Name**	**lblRadius**
	Caption	Radius:
	FontName	System

continues

Table 8.8. continued

Object	Property	Setting
	FontSize	10
	Height	375
	Left	120
	Top	600
	Width	1215

Figure 8.17.
The frmEllipses form in design mode.

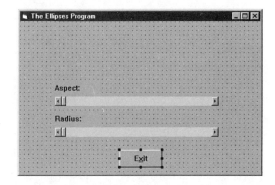

Entering the Code of the Ellipses Program

☐ Enter the following code in the general declarations sections of the frmEllipses form:

```
' All variables MUST be declared.
Option Explicit
```

☐ Enter the following code in the cmdExit_Click() procedure of the frmEllipses form:

```
Private Sub cmdExit_Click()

    End

End Sub
```

☐ Enter the following code in the Form_Load() procedure of the frmEllipses form:

```
Private Sub Form_Load()

    ' Initialize the radius and aspect scroll bars.
    hsbRadius.Value = 10
    hsbAspect.Value = 10

    ' Initialize the info label.
    lblInfo.Caption = "Aspect: 1"
```

```
' Set the DrawWidth property of the form.
frmEllipses.DrawWidth = 2
```

End Sub

☐ Enter the following code in the `hsbAspect_Change()` procedure of the frmEllipses form:

Private Sub hsbAspect_Change()

```
Dim X, Y
Dim Info
' Calculate the center of the form.
X = frmEllipses.ScaleWidth / 2
Y = frmEllipses.ScaleHeight / 2

' Clear the form.
frmEllipses.Cls

' Draw the ellipse.
frmEllipses.Circle (X, Y), hsbRadius.Value * 10, _
        RGB(255, 0, 0), , , hsbAspect.Value / 10

' Prepare the Info string.
Info = "Aspect: " + Str(hsbAspect.Value / 10)

' Display the value of the aspect.
frmEllipses.lblInfo.Caption = Info
```

End Sub

☐ Enter the following code in the `hsbAspect_Scroll()` procedure of the frmEllipses form:

Private Sub hsbAspect_Scroll()

```
Dim X, Y
Dim Info
' Calculate the center of the form.
X = frmEllipses.ScaleWidth / 2
Y = frmEllipses.ScaleHeight / 2

' Clear the form.
frmEllipses.Cls

' Draw the ellipse.
frmEllipses.Circle (X, Y), hsbRadius.Value * 10, _
        RGB(255, 0, 0), , , hsbAspect.Value / 10

' Prepare the Info string.
Info = "Aspect: " + Str(hsbAspect.Value / 10)

' Display the value of the aspect.
frmEllipses.lblInfo.Caption = Info
```

End Sub

☐ Enter the following code in the `hsbRadius_Change()` procedure of the frmEllipses form:

```
Private Sub hsbRadius_Change()

    Dim X, Y
    Dim Info

    X = frmEllipses.ScaleWidth / 2
    Y = frmEllipses.ScaleHeight / 2

    frmEllipses.Cls
    frmEllipses.Circle (X, Y), hsbRadius.Value * 10, _
            RGB(255, 0, 0), , , hsbAspect.Value / 10

    Info = "Aspect: " + Str(hsbAspect.Value / 10)

    frmEllipses.lblInfo.Caption = Info

End Sub
```

☐ Enter the following code in the `hsbRadius_Change()` procedure of the frmEllipses form:

```
Private Sub hsbRadius_Scroll()

    Dim X, Y
    Dim Info

    X = frmEllipses.ScaleWidth / 2
    Y = frmEllipses.ScaleHeight / 2

    frmEllipses.Cls
    frmEllipses.Circle (X, Y), hsbRadius.Value * 10, _
            RGB(255, 0, 0), , , hsbAspect.Value / 10

    Info = "Aspect: " + Str(hsbAspect.Value / 10)

    frmEllipses.lblInfo.Caption = Info

End Sub
```

Executing the Ellipses Program

☐ Execute the Ellipses program.

☐ Change the position of the Radius scroll bar to draw circles and ellipses with different radii.

☐ Change the position of the Aspect scroll bar to draw ellipses with different aspects.

Note that the value of the current aspect is displayed to the right of the Aspect scroll bar. When the aspect argument is equal to 1, the program draws a circle. When the aspect argument is less than 1, the program draws an ellipse stretched along the horizontal axis as shown in Figure 8.15. When the aspect argument is greater than 1, the program draws an ellipse stretched along its vertical axis, as shown in Figure 8.16.

How the Ellipses Program Works

The Ellipses program draws ellipses using the Circle method. The Value properties of the scroll bars are used as the arguments in the Circle method.

The Code in the *Form_Load()* Procedure

The Form_Load() procedure is executed when the frmEllipses form is loaded:

```
Private Sub Form_Load()

    ' Initialize the radius and aspect scroll bars.
    hsbRadius.Value = 10
    hsbAspect.Value = 10

    ' Initialize the info label.
    lblInfo.Caption = "Aspect: 1"

    ' Set the DrawWidth property of the form.
    frmEllipses.DrawWidth = 2

End Sub
```

This procedure initializes the Value properties of the scroll bars to 10 and displays the lblInfo label Aspect: 1 to the right of the Aspect scroll bar. As you will see later, the program uses one-tenth of the Value property of the Aspect scroll bar as the aspect argument in the Circle method.

For example, when the Value property of the Aspect scroll bar is 20, the Circle method uses 2 as the aspect argument, which is why this procedure sets lblInfo.Caption with Aspect: 1 after initializing the Aspect scroll bar to 10.

The last statement in this procedure sets the DrawWidth property of the form to 2:

```
frmEllipses.DrawWidth = 2
```

This causes the graphics to be drawn with a width equal to 2 units. Therefore, when using the Circle method, the ellipses are drawn with a line 2 units wide. (Although the Ellipses program sets the DrawWidth property of the form, the caption of the lblInfo label, and the Value properties of the scroll bars from within the code, you could have set these properties during design time.)

The Code in the *hsbAspect_Change()* Procedure

The hsbAspect_Change() procedure is executed whenever you change the Aspect scroll bar:

```
Private Sub hsbAspect_Change()

    Dim X, Y
    Dim Info
    ' Calculate the center of the form.
    X = frmEllipses.ScaleWidth / 2
```

```
    Y = frmEllipses.ScaleHeight / 2

    ' Clear the form.
     frmEllipses.Cls

    ' Draw the ellipse.
    frmEllipses.Circle (X, Y), hsbRadius.Value * 10, _
           RGB(255, 0, 0), , , hsbAspect.Value / 10

    ' Prepare the Info string.
    Info = "Aspect: " + Str(hsbAspect.Value / 10)

    ' Display the value of the aspect.
    frmEllipses.lblInfo.Caption = Info

End Sub
```

This procedure calculates the coordinate of the center of the form and assigns the calculated values to X and Y.

The procedure clears any previously drawn ellipses using the `Cls` method and draws the ellipse:

```
frmEllipses.Circle (X, Y), hsbRadius.Value * 10, _
           RGB(255, 0, 0), , , hsbAspect.Value / 10
```

The `radius` argument is set to the current value of the Radius scroll bar multiplied by 10, and the `aspect` argument is set as one-tenth the Value property of the Aspect scroll bar.

Note that because the two optional arguments—`start` and `end`—of the `Circle` method are not used, two commas are typed between the `color` argument and the `aspect` argument. The two commas indicate to Visual Basic that these two optional arguments are missing.

The Code in the *hsbRadius_Change()* Procedure

The `hsbRadius_Change()` procedure is automatically executed whenever you change the Radius scroll bar. It is identical to the `hsbAspect_Change()` procedure, displaying the ellipse and updating the `lblInfo` label.

Note that the code in the `hsbRadius_Scroll()` procedure is identical to the code in the `hsbRadius_Change()` procedure, and the code in the `hsbAspect_Scroll()` procedure is the same as the code in the `hsbAspect_Change()` procedure.

The Arcs Program

Now you'll write a program called Arcs. This program illustrates how to use the `Circle` method to draw arcs at different starting points and ending points. As stated, this is the complete syntax of the `Circle` method:

```
[object.]Circle[Step](x,y), _
```

```
       radius, _
      [color], _
      [start], _
        [end], _
     [aspect]
```

The start and end arguments specify the starting point and ending point of the circle. For example, if the starting point is at 0 degrees and the endpoint is at 45 degrees, only this section of the circle is drawn. Figure 8.18 shows a portion of a circle, an arc, that was drawn using the Circle method with the start argument equal to 0 degrees and the end argument equal to 45 degrees. Similarly, Figure 8.19 shows an arc with the starting point at 23 degrees and the endpoint at 180 degrees.

Figure 8.18.

Drawing a 45-degree arc.

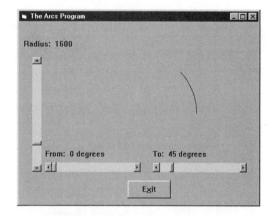

Figure 8.19.

Drawing an arc from 23 degrees to 180 degrees.

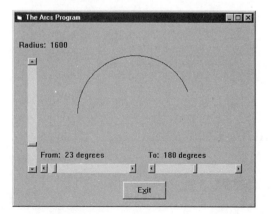

The Visual Implementation of the Arcs Program

You'll now design the form of the Arcs program.

☐ Open a new project, save the form of the project as ARCS.FRM in the C:\VB4PRG\CH08 directory and save the project file of the project as ARCS.VBP in the C:\VB4PRG\CH08 directory.

☐ Build the frmArcs form according to the specifications in Table 8.9.

The completed form should look like the one shown in Figure 8.20.

Table 8.9. The properties table of the frmArcs form.

Object	Property	Setting
Form	**Name**	**frmArcs**
	Caption	The Arcs Program
	Height	5370
	Left	1080
	Top	1170
	Width	6810
Command Button	**Name**	**cmdExit**
	Caption	E&xit
	FontName	System
	FontSize	10
	Height	495
	Left	3000
	Top	4320
	Width	1215
Horizontal Scroll Bar	**Name**	**hsbFrom**
	Height	255
	Left	720
	Max	360
	Top	3840
	Width	2655

Object	Property	Setting
Horizontal Scroll Bar	**Name**	**hsbTo**
	Height	255
	Left	3720
	Max	360
	Top	3840
	Width	2655
Vertical Scroll Bar	**Name**	**vsbRadius**
	Height	3135
	Left	360
	Max	100
	Min	1
	Top	960
	Value	10
	Width	255
Label	**Name**	**lblFrom**
	Caption	From:
	FontName	System
	FontSize	10
	Height	375
	Left	720
	Top	3480
	Width	1215
Label	**Name**	**lblTo**
	Caption	To:
	FontName	System
	FontSize	10
	Height	255
	Left	3720
	Top	3480
	Width	1215

continues

Table 8.9. continued

Object	Property	Setting
Label	**Name**	**lblRadius**
	Caption	Radius:
	FontName	System
	FontSize	10
	Height	375
	Left	120
	Top	480
	Width	1455

Figure 8.20.
The frmArcs form.

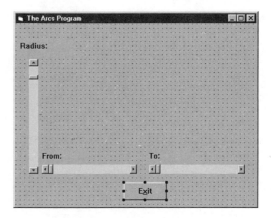

Entering the Code of the Arcs Program

☐ Enter the following code in the general declarations section of the frmArcs form:

```
' All variables MUST be declared.
Option Explicit
```

☐ Create a new procedure called DrawArc in the general declarations section of the frmArcs form. (Double-click the form to display the code window, select Procedure from the Insert menu, set the Type to Sub in the Insert Procedure dialog box, set the Scope to Public, set the Name to DrawArc, and finally click the OK button).

☐ Enter the following code in the DrawArc() procedure that you created in the previous step:

```
Public Sub DrawArc()

    Dim X, Y
```

```
Const PI = 3.14159265

' Calculate the center of the form.
X = frmArcs.ScaleWidth / 2
Y = frmArcs.ScaleHeight / 2

' Clear the form.
frmArcs.Cls

' Draw an arc.
Circle (X, Y), vsbRadius.Value * 20, , _
        hsbFrom * 2 * PI / 360, hsbTo * 2 * PI / 360

' Update the lblFrom label.
lblFrom.Caption = "From: " + Str(hsbFrom.Value) + _
              " degrees"

' Update the lblTo label.
lblTo.Caption = "To: " + Str(hsbTo.Value) + _
              " degrees"

' Update the lblRadius label.
lblRadius.Caption = "Radius: " + _
              Str(vsbRadius.Value * 20)

End Sub
```

☐ Enter the following code in the cmdExit_Click() procedure of the frmArcs form:

```
Private Sub cmdExit_Click()

    End

End Sub
```

☐ Enter the following code in the hsbFrom_Change() procedure of the frmArcs form:

```
Private Sub hsbFrom_Change()

    ' Execute the DrawArc procedure to draw the arc.
    DrawArc

End Sub
```

☐ Enter the following code in the hsbFrom_Scroll() procedure of the frmArcs form:

```
Private Sub hsbFrom_Scroll()

    ' Execute the DrawArc procedure to draw the arc.
    DrawArc

End Sub
```

☐ Enter the following code in the hsbTo_Change() procedure of the frmArcs form:

```
Private Sub hsbTo_Change()
```

```
' Execute the DrawArc procedure to draw the arc.
DrawArc

End Sub
```

☐ Enter the following code in the hsbTo_Scroll() procedure of the frmArcs form:

```
Private Sub hsbTo_Scroll()

' Execute the DrawArc procedure to draw the arc.
DrawArc

End Sub
```

☐ Enter the following code in the vsbRadius_Change() procedure of the frmArcs form:

```
Private Sub vsbRadius_Change()

' Execute the DrawArc procedure to draw the arc.
DrawArc

End Sub
```

☐ Enter the following code in the vsbRadius_Scroll() procedure of the frmArcs form:

```
Private Sub vsbRadius_Scroll()

' Execute the DrawArc procedure to draw the arc.
DrawArc

End Sub
```

Executing the Arcs Program

☐ Execute the Arcs program.

☐ Increase the radius by changing the Radius scroll bar (the vertical scroll bar).

☐ Increase the To scroll bar (the right horizontal scroll bar).

☐ Increase the From scroll bar (the left horizontal scroll bar).

As you can see, an arc is drawn starting at a point specified by the From scroll bar and ending at a point specified by the To scroll bar.

Note that the arc is drawn counterclockwise. For example, Figure 8.19 shows an arc that starts at 23 degrees and ends at 180 degrees. In Figure 8.21, an arc is drawn starting at 180 degrees and ending at 23 degrees.

Figure 8.21.
An arc drawn from 180 degrees to 23 degrees.

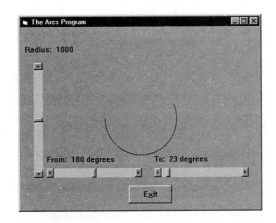

☐ Click the Exit button to terminate the program.

How the Arcs Program Works

The Arcs program uses the `Circle` method to draw the arcs.

The Value properties of the Radius scroll bar, From scroll bar, and To scroll bar are used as the arguments for the `Circle` method.

The Code in the *DrawArc()* Procedure

The `DrawArc()` procedure is executed whenever you change the Radius scroll bar, From scroll bar, or To scroll bar. It defines the `PI` constant as the numeric equivalent of π:

```
Const PI = 3.14159265
```

The center of the form is calculated:

```
X = frmArcs.ScaleWidth / 2
Y = frmArcs.ScaleHeight / 2
```

And the form is cleared with the `Cls` method:

```
frmArcs.Cls
```

The arc is drawn using the `Circle` method:

```
Circle (X, Y), vsbRadius.Value * 20, , _
            hsbFrom* 2*PI/360, hsbTo*2*PI/360
```

Again, this is the complete syntax of the `Circle` method:

```
[object.]Circle[Step](x,y), _
                   radius, _
```

```
            [color], _
            [start], _
              [end], _
           [aspect]
```

The center of the arc is given by the (x,y) argument, and the radius of the arc is given by the Value property of the vsbRadius scroll bar multiplied by 20.

At design time, the Min property of the vsbRadius scroll bar was set to 1, and its Max property was set to 100, so it takes 100 clicks to move the scroll bar position from its minimum position to its maximum position.

You multiply the Value property by 20 to get the radius argument of the Circle method; therefore, it can have any value between 20 and 2000.

The Color property is not supplied, so just type a comma indicating that the Circle method does not include the color argument. The program therefore uses the ForeColor property of the form, which is black by default.

The next two arguments of the Circle method are the start and end arguments, which must be given in radians. At design time, the Min properties of the From and To scroll bars were set to 1, and the Max properties of these scroll bars were set to 360. Therefore, each of these scroll bars is divided into 360 parts with each part representing one degree. To convert degrees to radians, use this formula:

```
Radians = Degrees * 2 * PI /360
```

For example, 360 degrees is equivalent to $2 \times \pi$ radians:

```
360*2*P/360=2*PI=2*3.14159265=  6.2831853
```

This explains why this procedure supplies the start and end properties of the Circle method as the Value properties of the From and To scroll bars multiplied by $2 \times \pi/360$.

The last argument of the Circle method is the optional aspect argument, which isn't used in this procedure. Because the aspect argument is the last argument, there is no need to type a comma after the end argument.

The last thing this procedure does is display the Radius label, the From label, and the To label:

```
lblFrom.Caption="From: "+hsbFrom.Value+ _
                " degrees"

lblTo.Caption = "To: " + hsbTo.Value+ _
                " degrees"

lblRadius.Caption = "Radius: " + _
                Str(vsbRadius.Value * 20)
```

This enables you to see the current values of the scroll bars.

The Code in the *hsbFrom_Change()* Procedure

The hsbFrom_Change() procedure is automatically executed whenever you change the From scroll bar:

```
Private Sub hsbFrom_Change()

    ' Execute the DrawArc procedure to draw the arc.
    DrawArc

End Sub
```

This procedure executes the DrawArc() procedure, which draws the arc according to the new value of the hsbFrom scroll bar.

In a similar manner, the hsbTo_Change() and the vsbRadius_Change() procedures of the frmArcs form execute the DrawArc() procedure whenever you change these scroll bars.

The hsbFrom_Scroll(), hsbTo_Scroll(), and the vsbRadius_Scroll() procedures also execute the DrawArc() procedure.

More About the *start* and *end* Arguments of the *Circle* Method

You may also supply negative values for the start and end arguments of the Circle method. When the start argument is negative, Visual Basic draws a straight line from the center of the arc to the start point of the arc. And when the endpoint is negative, Visual Basic draws a straight line from the center of the arc to the endpoint of the arc. For example, Figure 8.22 shows an arc that was drawn with the following statement:

```
Circle(X,Y),1000, ,-25*2*PI/360,-45*2*PI/360
```

Figure 8.22.
*Drawing an arc from -25
degrees to -45 degrees.*

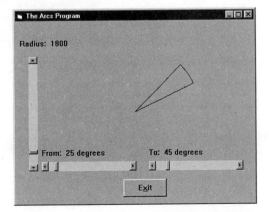

Figure 8.23 shows an arc that was drawn with the following statement:

```
Circle(X,Y),1000, ,-45*2*PI/360,-25*2*PI/360
```

Figure 8.23.
Drawing an arc from -45 degrees to -25 degrees.

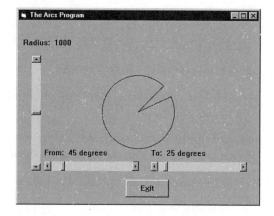

Figure 8.24 shows an arc that was drawn with the following statement:

```
Circle(X,Y),1000, ,45*2*PI/360,-25*2*PI/360
```

Figure 8.24.
Drawing an arc from -45 degrees to 25 degrees.

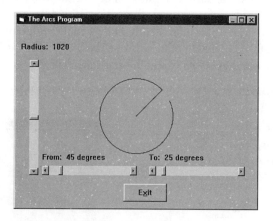

Figure 8.25 shows an arc that was drawn with the following statement:

```
Circle(X,Y),1000, ,-45*2*PI/360,25*2*PI/360
```

Figure 8.25.

Drawing an arc from 45 degrees to –25 degrees.

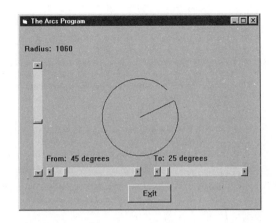

You can experiment with the start and end arguments of the Circle method in the DrawArc() procedure as follows:

☐ To draw arcs as shown in Figures 8.22 and 8.23, change the Circle method in the DrawArc() procedure to this:

```
Circle (X, Y), vsbRadius.Value * 20, , _
        -hsbFrom* 2*PI/360, -hsbTo*2*PI/360
```

☐ To draw arcs as shown in Figure 8.24, change the Circle method in the DrawArc() procedure to this:

```
Circle (X, Y), vsbRadius.Value * 20, , _
        -hsbFrom* 2*PI/360, hsbTo*2*PI/360
```

☐ To draw arcs as shown in Figure 8.25, change the Circle method in the DrawArc() procedure to this:

```
Circle (X, Y), vsbRadius.Value * 20, , _
        hsbFrom* 2*PI/360, -hsbTo*2*PI/360
```

The AutoRedraw Property

The AutoRedraw property causes the graphics to be redrawn automatically whenever you need to do so. The default setting of the AutoRedraw property of the frmArcs is False.

Use the following steps to see the effects of the AutoRedraw property:

☐ Execute the Arcs program.

☐ Draw an arc by changing the Radius, From, and To scroll bars.

☐ Minimize the Arcs program by clicking the icon on the top-right corner of the Arcs window.

The program responds by minimizing the window of the Arcs program and showing it as an icon.

☐ Restore the window of the Arcs program to its original size.

The Arcs window is displayed without the arc because the Redraw property of the form is currently set to False.

☐ Terminate the program and change the AutoRedraw property of the frmArcs form in the properties window to True.

Now repeat the above experiment (draw an arc, minimize the window, and restore the original size of the window). As you can see, this time the program automatically redraws the arc because the AutoRedraw property of the form is set to True.

The *Form_Paint()* Procedure

You can use the Form_Paint() procedure to draw five horizontal lines as follows:

☐ Set the AutoRedraw property of the frmArcs form to False.

☐ Add the following code in the Form_Paint() procedure of the frmArcs form:

```
Private Sub Form_Paint()

    ' Draw 5 horizontal lines
    frmArcs.Line (100, 100)-(1000, 100)
    frmArcs.Line (100, 200)-(1000, 200)
    frmArcs.Line (100, 300)-(1000, 300)
    frmArcs.Line (100, 400)-(1000, 400)
    frmArcs.Line (100, 500)-(1000, 500)

End Sub
```

The Form_Paint() procedure is executed whenever Visual Basic needs to paint the form. Because Visual Basic paints the form when it's made visible at the program startup, the Form_Paint() procedure is executed when you start the program. If you drag the window of the Arcs program or cover it with a window of another application and then expose the Arcs window again, Visual Basic will automatically execute the Form_Paint() procedure because the window needs to be repainted.

In general, you can use the Form_Paint() procedure as a focal point in the program to perform the drawings, serving the same role as the AutoRedraw property. The advantage of setting AutoRedraw to True is that you don't have to insert code in the Form_Paint() procedure that redraws your drawings (that is, AutoRedraw does the redrawing automatically).

The disadvantage of setting the AutoRedraw property to True is that it consumes memory used to save current drawings; on slow PCs, the redrawing that occurs when AutoRedraw is set to True may cause noticeable delays in running the program.

Summary

In this chapter you have learned how to use the graphics methods PSet, Cls, Point, Line, and Circle. You have also learned how to draw ellipses and arcs.

Q&A

Q What is the advantage and disadvantage of using graphics methods versus graphic controls?

A The advantage of using graphics methods is that these methods enable you to draw complicated graphics with a small amount of code. For example, the graphics shown in Figure 8.13 are easy to do with graphics methods.

The disadvantage of using graphics methods is that you can examine the results only during runtime. When you use graphic controls, you can see how the form looks at design time.

Quiz

1. The last graphics method used in a hypothetical program was this:

   ```
   PSet (100,20) RGB(255,255,255)
   ```

   If the next statement executed in this program is this:

   ```
   PSet Step (-5,10) RGB(255,255,255)
   ```

   at what coordinate will the point be drawn?

2. BUG BUSTER: What is wrong with the following code?

   ```
   Line (100,20)-Step(300,400),RGB(0,255,0),F
   ```

3. The Point method is used for which of the following:

   a. Drawing a point

   b. There is no such thing as the Point method in Visual Basic.

   c. Finding the color of a pixel

4. If you set the AutoRedraw property of a form to True, what happens?

Exercise

Write a program using the Circle method that displays circles at random locations all over the form when you start the program.

Quiz Answers

1. Because the last point was drawn at coordinate 100,20, after the drawing CurrentX is equal to 100 and CurrentY is equal to 20.

   Executing this statement:

   ```
   PSet Step (-5,10) RGB(255,255,255)
   ```

   causes the point to be drawn 5 units to the left of CurrentX. In the Y direction, the point is drawn 10 units below CurrentY. Therefore, the point is drawn at coordinate 100–5,20+10, or 95,30.

2. You can't use the F option without the B option. This is the correct syntax:

   ```
   Line (100,20)-Step(300,400),RGB(0,255,0),BF
   ```

3. c

4. The form on which a graphics method is drawn is automatically redrawn whenever you need to do so.

Exercise Answer

Use the following steps:

☐ Open a new project, save the form of the project as CIRCLES2.FRM, and save the project file of the project as CIRCLES2.VBP.

☐ Build the frmCircles form according to the specifications in Table 8.10.

Table 8.10. The properties table of frmCircles form.

Object	Property	Setting
Form	Name	frmCircles2
	Caption	The Circles2 Program
	Height	4425
	Left	1035
	Top	1140
	Width	7485

☐ Enter the following code in the general declarations section of the frmCircles form:

```
'All variables MUST be declared.
Option Explicit
```

8

☐ Enter the following code in the Form_Paint() procedure of the frmCircles form:

```
Private Sub Form_Paint()

    Dim I
    For I = 1 To 100 Step 1
        frmCircles2.DrawWidth = Int(Rnd * 10) + 1
        frmCircles2.ForeColor = _
              QBColor(Int(Rnd * 15))
      Circle (Rnd * frmCircles2.ScaleWidth, _
             Rnd * frmCircles2.ScaleHeight), _
             Rnd * frmCircles2.ScaleHeight / 2
    Next

End Sub
```

The Form_Paint() procedure draws 100 circles with random width and at random locations.

WEEK
2

The Grid Control

In some applications it is necessary to display text in rows and columns (that is, in tables). You can do this by displaying the text line by line, calculating the required locations where the text should be displayed, and using the Print method to display the text. However, Visual Basic includes the *grid control*, which enables you to create tables easily. In this chapter you learn how to use the grid control.

The Table Program

You'll now write the Table program, which is an example of a program that uses the grid control.

☐ Open a new project, save the form of the project as frmTable in the C:\VB4PRG\CH09 directory, and save the project file as TABLE.VBP in the C:\VB4PRG\CH09 directory.

Because the grid control is an OCX, or custom control, before you can place it in a form, you must first make sure it's included in your project. The toolbox in Figure 9.1 shows the icon of the grid control. (The exact location of the grid icon in the toolbox window may be different on your system.)

Figure 9.1.
*The icon of the grid control
in the toolbox.*

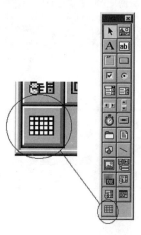

If the grid control does not appear in the toolbox, add it as follows:

☐ Select Custom Controls from the Tools menu.

Visual Basic responds by displaying the Custom Controls dialog box.

As you can see, the Custom Controls dialog box lists check boxes with names of various custom controls. The custom controls with a ✔ in their check boxes are currently included in the project.

☐ Scroll the list of custom controls until you see the check box of the Microsoft Grid Control and make sure that it has a ✓ in it. If it doesn't, place one there by clicking it. (See Figure 9.2.)

Figure 9.2.
Placing a ✓ in the Microsoft Grid Control check box.

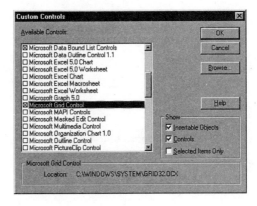

☐ Click the OK button of the Custom Controls dialog box.

Visual Basic responds by closing the Custom Controls dialog box.

Note: If you do not see the grid control in the Available Controls list, as shown in Figure 9.2, then click the Browse button and select the Grid.OCX file from the C:\WINDOWS\SYSTEM directory. If you are using 32-bit Windows, select the GRID32.OCX file, and if you are using 16-bit Windows, select the GRID16.OCX file.

Now that you've made sure the grid control is included in the project, you can use the following steps to place it in the frmTable form:

☐ Select the frmTable form by clicking anywhere in the form or by selecting frmTable in the project window and clicking the View Form button.

Visual Basic responds by displaying the frmTable form.

☐ Double-click the icon of the grid control in the Toolbox.

Visual Basic responds by placing the grid control in the frmTable form. (See Figure 9.3.)

Figure 9.3.

Placing the grid control in a form.

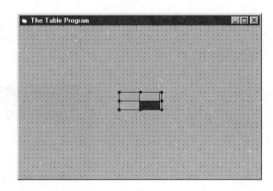

Set up the frmTable form as follows:

☐ Set the Name property of the form to frmTable.

☐ Set the Caption property of the frmTable form to The Table Program.

☐ Set the Name property of the grid control to grdTable.

☐ Set the Rows property of grdTable to 13.

☐ Set the Cols property of grdTable to 5.

☐ Enlarge the grdTable grid control vertically and horizontally by dragging its handles.

The enlarged grid control should look like the one shown in Figure 9.4.

Figure 9.4.

The enlarged grid control.

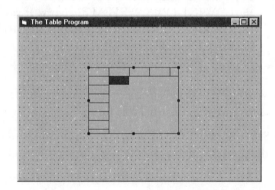

☐ Place a command button in the frmTable form below the grid control, set the Name property of the command button to cmdExit, and set the caption of the command button to E&xit.

☐ Enter the following code in the general declarations section of the frmTable form:

```
' All variables MUST be declared.
Option Explicit
```

☐ Add the following code in the Form_Load() procedure of the frmTable form:

```
Private Sub Form_Load ()

    ' Set the current row to row #0.
    grdTable.Row = 0

    ' Write into Row #0, Col #1
    grdTable.Col = 1
    grdTable.Text = "Electricity"

    ' Write into Row #0, Col #2
    grdTable.Col = 2
    grdTable.Text = "Water"

    ' Write into Row #0, Col #3
    grdTable.Col = 3
    grdTable.Text = "Transportation"

    ' Write into Row #0, Col #4
    grdTable.Col = 4
    grdTable.Text = "Food"

    ' Set the current Column to column #0.
    grdTable.Col = 0

    ' Write into Row #1, Col #0
    grdTable.Row = 1
    grdTable.Text = "Jan."

    ' Write into Row #2, Col #0
    grdTable.Row = 2
    grdTable.Text = "Feb."

    ' Write into Row #3, Col #0
    grdTable.Row = 3
    grdTable.Text = "Mar."

    ' Write into Row #4, Col #0
    grdTable.Row = 4
    grdTable.Text = "Apr."

    ' Write into Row #5, Col #0
    grdTable.Row = 5
    grdTable.Text = "May."

    ' Write into Row #6, Col #0
    grdTable.Row = 6
    grdTable.Text = "Jun."
```

```
' Write into Row #7, Col #0
grdTable.Row = 7
grdTable.Text = "Jul."

' Write into Row #8, Col #0
grdTable.Row = 8
grdTable.Text = "Aug."

' Write into Row #9, Col #0
grdTable.Row = 9
grdTable.Text = "Sep."

' Write into Row #10, Col #0
grdTable.Row = 10
grdTable.Text = "Oct."

' Write into Row #11, Col #0
grdTable.Row = 11
grdTable.Text = "Nov."

' Write into Row #12, Col #0
grdTable.Row = 12
grdTable.Text = "Dec."
```

End Sub

☐ Add the following code in the cmdExit_Click() procedure of the frmTable form:

```
Private Sub cmdExit_Click ()

    End

End Sub
```

Although you haven't finished writing the Table program yet, execute it:

☐ Execute the Table program.

The program displays the grid control, as shown in Figure 9.5.

Figure 9.5.

The Table program with column and row headings in the grid control.

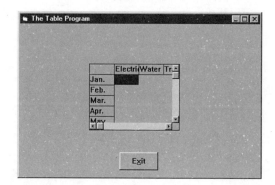

☐ Click the horizontal and vertical scroll bars of the grid control to see other cells of the grid control or use the arrow keys to move from cell to cell.

As you can see, the grid control has a total of 13 rows (including the top heading row) and a total of 5 columns (including the left heading column). That's because during design time you set the Rows property of grdTable to 13 and the Cols property of grdTable to 5.

☐ Terminate the program by clicking the Exit button.

Because the default BackColor property of the grid control is gray, its grid lines aren't visible. Complete the following steps see the grid lines:

☐ Set the BackColor property of the grdTable control to White.

☐ Make sure the GridLines property of the grdTable control is set to True.

The Code in the *Form_Load()* Procedure

The Form_Load() procedure is executed when the frmTable form is loaded at startup. The code in this procedure sets the current row to 0:

```
' Set the current row to row #0.
grdTable.Row = 0
```

Note: The grid control has both a property called Row and a property called Rows. When typing code, be sure not to confuse the two!

Note: The grid control has both a property called Col and a property called Cols. When typing code, be sure not to confuse the two!

Once the active row is set to 0, the procedure writes into the cell Row #0,Col #1 as follows:

```
' Write into Row #0, Col #1
grdTable.Col = 1
grdTable.Text = "Electricity"
```

That is, the procedure makes Row #0 the active row, sets Column #1 as the active column, and sets the Text property of the grid control to Electricity. Visual Basic places the text in the cell at Row #0,Col #1.

In a similar manner, the procedure sets the Text properties of Row #0,Col #2, Row #0,Col #3, and Row #0,Col #4 to Water, Transportation, and Food. For example, to set the Text property of the cell in Row #0,Col #4, the following statements are used:

```
' Write into Row #0, Col #4
grdTable.Col = 4
grdTable.Text = "Food"
```

There is no need to set the Row property to 0 again because it retains its value.

Once the four row headings are written, the procedure sets the Text property of the left column. For example, to set the Text property of the cell at Row #1,Col #0, the following statements are used:

```
' Set the current Column to column #0.
grdTable.Col = 0

' Write into Row #1, Col #0
grdTable.Row = 1
grdTable.Text = "Jan."
```

In a similar manner, the rest of the cells in the left column are filled with the rest of the months.

Note: The grid control displays information in a tabular format. You can move from cell to cell by using the arrow keys or the scroll bars, but you can't enter information directly into the cells.

Changing the Cell Width

As you can see from Figure 9.5, the width of the cells are not wide enough. For example, the word *Electricity* does not fit within its cell. You can use the following steps to widen the cell during runtime:

☐ Add a procedure to the frmTable form by highlighting frmTable in the project window, clicking the View Code button in the project window, and selecting Procedure from the Insert menu.

☐ Name the new procedure SetColWidth.

Visual Basic creates a new procedure called SetColWidth in the general declarations area of the frmTable form.

☐ Enter the following code in the SetColWidth() procedure:

```
Public Sub SetColWidth ()

    Dim Counter
```

```
For Counter = 0 To 4 Step 1
    grdTable.ColWidth(Counter) = 1300
Next
```

End Sub

The code you typed in the SetColWidth() procedure uses a For loop to change the ColWidth property of each of the columns to 1,300 twips. As implied by its name, the ColWidth property determines the width of the column. That is, grdTable.ColWidth(0) determines the width of column 0, grdTable.ColWidth(1) determines the width of column 1, grdTable.ColWidth(2) determines the width of column 2, and so on.

☐ Add the SetColWidth statement to the end of the Form_Load() procedure. The Form_Load() procedure should now look like this:

Sub Form_Load ()

```
.................................................
... No change to this section of the procedure ...
.................................................

    SetColWidth
```

End Sub

☐ Execute the Table program.

The window of the Table program now looks like the one shown in Figure 9.6.

Figure 9.6.
Making the columns wider.

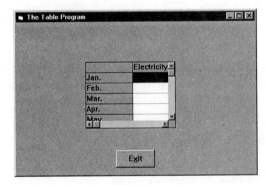

☐ Use the arrow keys or the scroll bars to move from cell to cell.

As you can see from Figure 9.7, all the columns changed their widths—they are now wider than the original width.

325

Figure 9.7.
Widening all the columns.

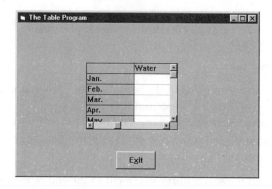

☐ Terminate the program and enlarge the grdTable grid control by dragging its handles until it looks like the one shown in Figure 9.8.

Figure 9.8.
Enlarging the size of the grid control at design time.

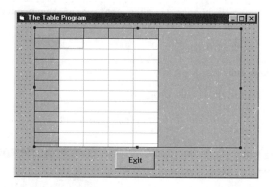

As you can see, the total area of the grid control is larger, but the cell widths are still at their default widths. This is because you can widen the cell only during runtime.

☐ Execute the Table program.

The grid control now looks like the one shown in Figure 9.9. As you can see, the total area of the grid control is larger and the width of each of the cells is greater.

☐ Experiment with the grid control by using the arrow keys or the scroll bars to move from cell to cell.

☐ Terminate the program.

Figure 9.9.

*The enlarged grid control
with widened cells at
runtime.*

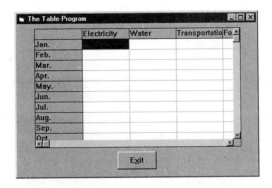

Changing the Cell Height

You can use the following steps to change the height of the cells only during runtime:

☐ Add a new procedure to the frmTable form by highlighting frmTable in the project window, clicking the View Code button in the project window, and selecting Procedure from the Insert menu.

☐ Name the new procedure SetRowHeight.

> *Visual Basic creates the* SetRowHeight() *procedure in the general declarations section of the frmTable form.*

☐ Enter the following code in the SetRowHeight() procedure:

```
Public Sub SetRowHeight ()

    Dim Counter

    For Counter = 0 To 12 Step 1
        grdTable.RowHeight(Counter) = 500
    Next

End Sub
```

The RowHeight property determines the height of the cell. The SetRowHeight() procedure uses a For loop to set the height of each of the rows to 500 twips.

☐ Add the SetRowHeight statement to the end of the Form_Load() procedure.

The Form_Load() procedure should now look like this:

```
Private Sub Form_Load ()

    ............................................
    ... No change to this section of the procedure ...
    ............................................

    SetColWidth
    SetRowHeight

End Sub
```

☐ Execute the Table program.

The cells of the grid control now look like the ones shown in Figure 9.10.

Figure 9.10.
*Increasing the height
of rows.*

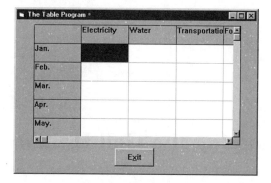

The Scroll Bars of the Grid Control

You have probably noticed that Visual Basic automatically adds horizontal and vertical scroll bars whenever the cells won't fit within the area of the grid control. This is because you left the default value of the ScrollBars property of the grdTable grid control to 3-Both. If you don't want these scroll bars to appear, either set the ScrollBars property of the grid control to 0-None at design time or issue the following statement from within the program:

```
grdTable.ScrollBars = 0
```

If you want the grid to have only a horizontal scroll bar, either set the ScrollBars property of the grid control to 1-Horizontal at design time or issue the following statement from within the program:

```
grdTable.ScrollBars = 1
```

If you want the grid control to have only a vertical scroll bar, set the ScrollBars property to 2-Vertical.

> **Note:** No matter how you set the ScrollBars property of the grid control, you are always able to move from cell to cell using the arrow keys.

Setting the Rows and Cols Properties During Runtime

During design time, you set the Rows property of the grid control to 13 and the Cols property to 5 so the grid control has a total of 5 columns and 13 rows.

Sometimes, the number of rows and columns is known only during runtime. For example, you can set up the Table program to give you the option of displaying only the electricity and water bills for each month. If you choose to display only these two columns, your program has to change the number of columns to three (one for the left column heading, one for the Electricity heading, and one for the Water heading). To change the number of columns during runtime to three, use the following statement:

```
grdTable.Cols = 3
```

If you need to change the number of rows during runtime, use the following statement:

```
grdTable.Rows = n
```

where *n* is the number of rows (including the top heading row).

Filling the Rest of the Cells of the Table Program

Use the following steps to fill the rest of the cells of the Table program:

☐ Add a new procedure to the general declarations section of the frmTable form.

☐ Name the new procedure FillCells.

> *Visual Basic responds by adding the* FillCells() *procedure to the general declarations area. You'll write the code of this procedure in the next area.*

☐ Add the FillCells statement to the end of the Form_Load() procedure.

The Form_Load() procedure should now look as follows:

```
Private Sub Form_Load ()

    ...............................................
    ... No change to this section of the procedure ...
    ...............................................

    SetColWidth
    SetRowHeight
    FillCells

End Sub
```

The Code in the *FillCells()* Procedure

☐ Add the following code in the FillCells() procedure to the general section:

```
Public Sub FillCells ()

    Dim RowCounter, ColCounter

    For ColCounter = 1 To 4 Step 1
        grdTable.Col = ColCounter
        For RowCounter = 1 To 12 Step 1
            grdTable.Row = RowCounter
            grdTable.Text = "Unknown"
        Next
    Next

End Sub
```

The two For loops set the Text property for each of the cells of the grdTable to Unknown. The outer For loop counts from 1 to 4, and the inner For loop counts from 1 to 12. These two For loops set the Text property of all the cells in the grid (except the left heading column and the top row heading) to Unknown.

☐ Execute the Table program.

The cells of the grid control are all filled with the text Unknown. *(See Figure 9.11.)*

☐ Terminate the Table program.

Figure 9.11.
Filling the cells of the grid control with text.

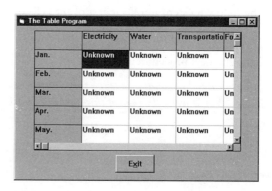

☐ To fill a specific cell with specific data, add the following statements to the end of the FillCells() procedure:

```
Public Sub FillCells ()

    ...........................................
    ... No change to this section of the procedure ...
    ...........................................
```

```
' Fill the Electricity bill for January.
grdTable.Row = 1
grdTable.Col = 1
grdTable.Text = "$100.00"

' Fill the Electricity bill for February.
grdTable.Row = 2
grdTable.Col = 1
grdTable.Text = "$50.00"

' Fill the Water bill for February.
grdTable.Row = 2
grdTable.Col = 2
grdTable.Text = "$75.00"
```

End Sub

The code that you added to the FillCells() procedure fills three cells in the grid control by setting the Row and Col properties with the required row number and column number, then setting the Text property of the cell with the desired text.

☐ Execute the Table program.

As you can see, the three cells are filled with the text $100.00, $50.00, and $75.00. (See Figure 9.12.)

Figure 9.12.
Filling three cells in the grid.

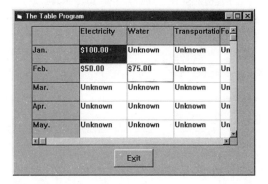

The SetStartCol, SetStartRow, SetEndCol, and SetEndRow Properties

To select a range of cells, you can use the SetStartCol, SetStartRow, SetEndCol, and SetEndRow properties. Use the following steps to see these properties in action:

☐ Add a Clear button, as shown in Figure 9.13. Give this command button the following properties: The Name property should be cmdClear and the Caption property should be &Clear.

The Grid Control

Figure 9.13.
Adding a Clear button.

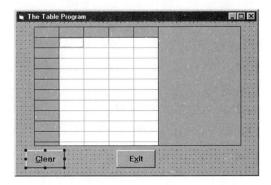

☐ Add the following code in the cmdClear_Click() procedure of the frmTable form:

```
Private Sub cmdClear_Click ()

    ' Select from Row #1, Col #1.
    grdTable.SelStartCol = 1
    grdTable.SelStartRow = 1

    ' End selection at bottom right cell.
    grdTable.SelEndCol = grdTable.Cols - 1
    grdTable.SelEndRow = grdTable.Rows - 1

    ' Set FillStyle to 1 (fill them all).
    grdTable.FillStyle = 1

    ' Fill all the cells with null.
    grdTable.Text = ""

End Sub
```

☐ Execute the Table program.

☐ Click the Clear button.

The program responds by clearing all the cells in the grid control.

The Code in the *cmdClear_Click()* Procedure

The cmdClear_Click() procedure is executed whenever you click the Clear button. The procedure sets a range of cells. The starting cell is declared with the following statements:

```
grdTable.SelStartCol = 1
grdTable.SelStartRow = 1
```

The ending cell is declared with the following statements:

```
grdTable.SelEndCol = grdTable.Cols - 1
grdTable.SelEndRow = grdTable.Rows - 1
```

The default value of the FillStyle is 0-Single. The procedure sets the FillStyle property of the grdTable grid control to 1:

```
grdTable.FillStyle = 1
```

Once the FillStyle property is set to 1, filling the Text property of a cell affects all the cells that are currently selected. Therefore, the following statement clears all the cells included in the selected range:

```
grdTable.Text = ""
```

If after clearing the cells you need to fill only a single cell, you have to unselect the selected cells. For example, to fill the cell at Row #2,Col #3, use the following statements:

```
' Set the selected cell to Row #2, Col #3.
grdTable.SelStartCol = 3
grdTable.SelStartRow = 2
grdTable.SelEndCol = 3
grdTable.SelEndRow = 2

' Fill the Text property of the cell.
grdTable.Text = "$34.00"
```

In other words, the selected range is the single cell at Row #2,Col #3.

Note that the mnuClear_Click() procedure uses the Cols and Rows properties to determine the number of columns and rows. This means that these properties may serve two roles:

- Use the Cols and Rows properties to determine the number of columns and rows. For example, the following statement updates the variable NumOfColumns with the number of columns in the grid control:

  ```
  NumOfColumns = grdTable.Cols
  ```

  The following statement updates the variable NumOfRows with the number of rows in the grid control:

  ```
  NumOfRows = grdTable.Rows
  ```

- Use the Cols and Rows properties to set the number of columns and rows.

  For example, to build a grid control with 10 columns, set the Cols property of the grid control to 10 at design time or use the following statement in your program:

  ```
  grdTable.Cols = 10
  ```

  To build a grid control with 8 rows, set the Rows property of the grid control to 8 at design time or use the following statement in your program:

  ```
  grdTable.Rows = 8
  ```

Aligning Text in the Cells

The cells in Row #0—the top row—are used to store the headings of the columns, and the cells in the left column are used to store the heading of the rows. These cells are called fixed rows and fixed columns because as you scroll in the grid control, these cells are always fixed in their position. However, you can scroll up and down or left and right in all the other cells in the grid control. Appropriately, these cells are called *non-fixed cells*.

To align the non-fixed columns in a grid control, use the ColAlignment property. The possible settings of the ColAlignment property are shown in Table 9.1.

Table 9.1. The possible settings of the ColAlignment property.

Setting for the ColAlignment Property	Description
0	Left-aligned (default setting)
1	Right-aligned
2	Centered

Use the following steps to see the ColAlignment property in action:

☐ Add the Align command button, as shown in Figure 9.14.

☐ Give the Align button the following properties: The Name property should be cmdAlign and the Caption property should be &Align.

Figure 9.14.
Adding the Align button.

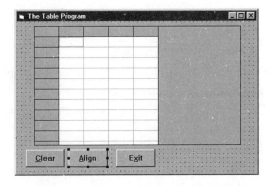

☐ Add the following code in the cmdAlign_Click() procedure of the frmTable form:

```
Private Sub cmdAlign_Click ()
```

```
Dim ColCounter

' Center the text in the cells.
For ColCounter = 1 To (grdTable.Cols - 2) Step 1
    grdTable.ColAlignment(ColCounter) = 2
Next
```

End Sub

This procedure sets the ColAlignmnent property to 2 for all the non-fixed columns except the extreme right column. As specified in Table 9.1, when the ColAlignment property is set to 2, the text is centered.

☐ Execute the Table program.

☐ Click the Align button.

> *As you can see, the text is centered in all the non-fixed cells except the ones in the extreme right column.*

The reason for not centering the text in the extreme right column is to demonstrate that you can assign different values to the ColAlignment property for different columns. That is, in this example, the non-fixed columns, 1 to 11, have their ColAlignment property set to 2 (centered), while the ColAlignment property for Column 12 remains at its default alignment, which is 0 (left-aligned).

To align the fixed columns and fixed rows, you have to use the FixedAlignment property. The FixedAlignment property can have the settings listed in Table 9.2.

Table 9.2. The possible settings of the FixedAlignment property.

Setting for the FixedAlignment Property	Description
0	Left-aligned (default setting)
1	Right-aligned
2	Centered
3	Use the same alignment used in the non-fixed column of this column

You can use the FixedAlignment property to align the text in a fixed column to a different alignment than the non-fixed cells below the heading. For example, if you set the FixedAlignment property of Column 1 to 1 (right-aligned), the text alignment of the cells below this heading can be set with the ColAlignment property to any of the values listed in Table 9.1.

As indicated in Table 9.2, if you set the FixedAlignment property to 3, the alignment of the text in the column heading is the same as the alignment of the text in the non-fixed cells in that column.

To center the text in the extreme left column (Column 0), use the following statement:

```
grdTable.FixedAlignment(0) = 2
```

To center the Electricity and Water headings (Column 1 and Column 2), use the following statements:

```
grdTable.FixedAlignment(1) = 2
grdTable.FixedAlignment(2) = 2
```

The TV Program

The TV program further explores additional features and properties of the grid control.

The Visual Implementation of the TV Program

☐ Open a new project, save the form of the project as TV.FRM in the C:\VB4PRG\CH09 directory, and save the project file as TV.VBP in the C:\VB4PRG\CH09 directory.

The TV program needs a BMP file called TV.BMP. Now you can use your artistic talent to draw the BMP picture, as shown in Figure 9.15.

Figure 9.15.
The TV.BMP picture.

Note: The following steps describe how to use Paintbrush to create a small BMP picture file, called TV.BMP, that will be used in the TV program. If you want, you can use a different drawing program—you just need to create a small BMP file that is approximately 80 pixels by 80 pixels.

☐ Start Paintbrush.

☐ Draw a picture similar to the one shown in Figure 9.15. (When drawing the picture, use colors so the TV program looks attractive.)

☐ Move the picture to the upper-left corner of the window of Paintbrush. (See Figure 9.16.)

Figure 9.16.
Moving the picture to the upper-left corner of the window.

The coordinate of the cursor

Move the cursor to here and take note of the coordinate

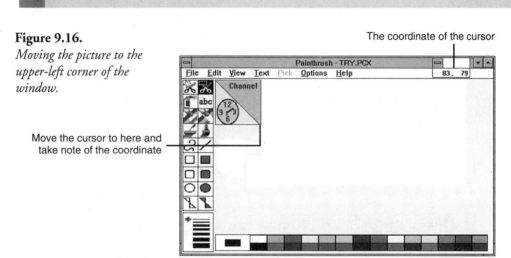

☐ Select Cursor Position from the View menu.

This causes Paintbrush to display the current coordinate of the cursor in the upper-right corner of the window. (See Figure 9.16.) Use this coordinate in the following steps:

☐ Place the cursor at the lower-right corner of the picture and note the cursor coordinate—the first number of the cursor coordinate represents the width of the picture and the second number represents the height of the picture.

☐ Copy the picture to the Clipboard (select the square scissors tool of Paintbrush, enclose the picture with the dashed square, and select Copy from the Edit menu).

Your picture is now stored in the Clipboard.

☐ Select New from the File menu. (It doesn't matter whether you save the current picture to the disk.)

☐ Select Image Attribute from the Option menu of Paintbrush.

☐ Select the Pels radio button because you are about to enter new dimensions in pixels.

☐ In the Width text box, type the width of the picture.

☐ In the Height text box, type the height of the picture.

☐ Click the OK button.

   Paintbrush responds by changing the dimensions of the drawing area according to the width and height you supplied in the previous steps.

☐ Select Paste from the Edit menu.

   Your picture is copied from the Clipboard to Paintbrush.

☐ Select Save As from the File menu and save the file as TV.BMP.

Why did you go through this exercise? Because you need the TV.BMP picture as a small file that contains only the picture you drew, not the whole drawing area of Paintbrush.

Now go back to Visual Basic.

☐ Build the frmTV form according to the specifications in Table 9.3.

The completed form should look like the one shown in Figure 9.17.

Note: Table 9.3 instructs you to place a grid control in the frmTV form. If the icon of the grid control does not appear in your toolbox window (as shown back in Figure 9.1), then you have to add the grid control to the project as described in the beginning of this chapter.

Table 9.3. The properties table of the frmTV form.

Object	Property	Setting
Form	**Name**	**frmTV**
	Caption	The TV Program
	Height	4545
	Left	1080
	Top	1170
	Width	6810
Command Button	**Name**	**cmdExit**
	Caption	E&xit
	FontName	System

Object	Property	Setting
	FontSize	10
	Height	495
	Left	240
	Top	3360
	Width	1095
Picture Box	**Name**	**picTV**
	AutoSize	-1-True
	Height	1230
	Left	120
	Picture	C:\VB4PRG\CH09\TV.BMP
	Top	120
	Visible	False
	Width	1290
MSGrid	**Grid**	**grdTV**
	Height	3735
	Left	1800
	Top	240
	Width	4575
	rows	24
	cols	10

Figure 9.17.
The frmTV form in design mode.

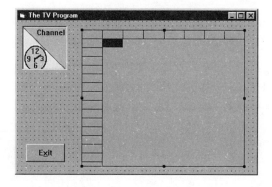

Entering the Code of the TV Program

☐ Enter the following code in the general declarations section of the frmTV form:

```
' All variables MUST be declared.
Option Explicit
```

☐ Enter the following code in the Form_Load() procedure of the frmTV form:

```
Private Sub Form_Load ()

    ' Make the upper left cell the active cell.
    grdTV.Row = 0
    grdTV.Col = 0

    ' Change the width and height of the cell to the
    ' width and height of the picTV picture.
    grdTV.ColWidth(0) = picTV.Width
    grdTV.RowHeight(0) = picTV.Height

    ' Place the picture into the cell.
    grdTV.Picture = picTV.Picture

End Sub
```

☐ Enter the following code in the cmdExit_Click() procedure of the frmTV form:

```
Private Sub cmdExit_Click()

    End

End Sub
```

Executing the TV Program

☐ Execute the TV program.

The TV program contains a picture in the 0,0 cell of the grid control, as shown in Figure 9.18.

Figure 9.18.
The TV program with a picture in its 0,0 cell.

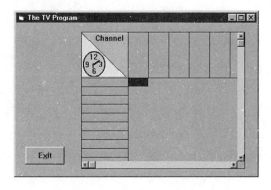

The Code in the *Form_Load()* Procedure

The Form_Load() procedure is executed when the form is loaded at startup. The procedure makes the 0,0 cell the active cell:

```
grdTV.Row = 0
grdTV.Col = 0
```

and changes the width and height of the cell's Picture property to the width and height of the TV.BMP picture:

```
grdTV.ColWidth(0) = picTV.Width
grdTV.RowHeight(0) = picTV.Height
```

The last thing this procedure does is place the picture in the cell:

```
grdTV.Picture = picTV.Picture
```

Note that the Visible property of the TV.BMP picture was set to False during design time. This is why the picture is not shown on the left side of the form at runtime.

Updating the Fixed Rows and Columns

You can now add the TV schedule as follows:

☐ Create a new procedure and name it AddSchedule.

☐ Enter the following code in the AddSchedule() procedure:

```
Public Sub AddSchdule ()
    grdTV.Row = 0
    grdTV.Col = 1
    grdTV.Text = "Ch 1"
    grdTV.Col = 2
    grdTV.Text = "Ch 2"
    grdTV.Col = 3
    grdTV.Text = "Ch 3"
    grdTV.Col = 4
    grdTV.Text = "Ch 4"
    grdTV.Col = 5
    grdTV.Text = "Ch 5"
    grdTV.Col = 6
    grdTV.Text = "Ch 6"
    grdTV.Col = 7
    grdTV.Text = "Ch 7"
    grdTV.Col = 8
    grdTV.Text = "Ch 8"
    grdTV.Col = 9
    grdTV.Text = "Ch 9"
    grdTV.Col = 0
    grdTV.Row = 1
    grdTV.Text = "7:00 AM"
    grdTV.Row = 2
    grdTV.Text = "8:00 AM"
```

```
        grdTV.Row = 3
        grdTV.Text = "9:00 AM"
        grdTV.Row = 4
        grdTV.Text = "10:00 AM"
        grdTV.Row = 5
        grdTV.Text = "11:00 AM"
        grdTV.Row = 6
        grdTV.Text = "12:00 PM"
        grdTV.Row = 7
        grdTV.Text = "1:00 PM"
        grdTV.Row = 8
        grdTV.Text = "2:00 PM"
        grdTV.Row = 9
        grdTV.Text = "3:00 PM"
        grdTV.Row = 10
        grdTV.Text = "4:00 PM"
End Sub
```

☐ Add the statement `AddSchedule` to the `Form_Load()` procedure. The `Form_Load()` procedure should now looks as follows:

```
Private Sub Form_Load ()

        ........................................
        ... No change to this section of the ...
        ... procedure.                       ...
        ........................................

        ' Add the schedule.
        AddSchedule

End Sub
```

☐ Execute the TV program.

>   *The fixed rows and columns are filled with the times and channel numbers. (See Figure 9.19.)*

Figure 9.19.

The TV program with its fixed rows and columns filled.

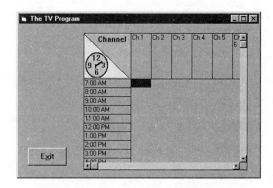

The Clip Property

To fill each of the cells, you have to set the active cell with the Row and Column properties and then set the Text property to the required text. For example, to fill Row #1,Col #1 with Good morning, you can use the following code:

```
grdTV.Row = 1
grdTV.Col = 1
grdTV.Text = "Good morning"
```

Another way to fill the cells is to use the Clip property. Use the following steps to see the Clip property in action:

☐ Add the Fill Cells button to the form, as shown in Figure 9.20.

☐ Give the command button the following properties: The Name property should be cmdFillCells and the Caption property should be &Fill Cells.

Figure 9.20.
Adding the Fill Cells button.

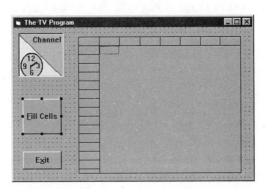

☐ Add the following code in the cmdFillCells_Click() procedure of the frmTV form:

```
Private Sub cmdFillCells_Click ()

Dim ColCounter
Dim TextToSpread as String

' Set width of all non-fixed columns to 2,000
' twips.
For ColCounter = 1 To grdTV.Cols - 1 Step 1
    grdTV.ColWidth(ColCounter) = 2000
Next

' Define a selected area.
grdTV.SelStartRow = 1
grdTV.SelStartCol = 1
grdTV.SelEndRow = 3
grdTV.SelEndCol = 4
```

```
' Into Row #1, Col #1
TextToSpread = "Good morning"

' Into Row #1, Col #2.
TextToSpread = TextToSpread + Chr(9)

' Into Row #1, Col #3.
TextToSpread = TextToSpread+"News in the morning"

' Into Row #2, Col #3
TextToSpread = TextToSpread +Chr(13)+Chr(9)+Chr(9)
TextToSpread = TextToSpread + "Gone with the wind"

' Spread the text.
grdTV.Clip = TextToSpread

End Sub
```

Executing the TV Program

☐ Execute the TV program.

☐ Click the Fill Cells button.

The program responds by filling the following cells (See Figure 19.21.):

```
            Col #1            Col #2                Col #3
Row#1 [Good morning] [News in the morning] [    (blank)     ]
Row#2 [  (blank)   ] [      (blank)      ] [Gone with the wind]
```

Figure 9.21.
The TV program after clicking the Fill Cells button.

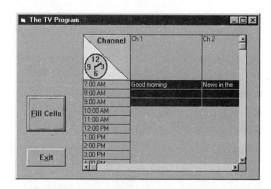

The Code in the *cmdFillCells_Click()* Procedure

The cmdFillCells_Click() procedure is executed whenever you click the Fill Cells button.

The procedure sets the width of all the non-fixed cells to 2,000 twips:

```
For ColCounter = 1 To grdTV.Cols - 1 Step 1
    grdTV.ColWidth(ColCounter) = 2000
Next
```

9

Then the procedure defines a selection area:

```
grdTV.SelStartRow = 1
grdTV.SelStartCol = 1
grdTV.SelEndRow = 3
grdTV.SelEndCol = 4
```

The selected area is as follows:

```
        Col #1 Col #2 Col #3 Col #4
Row #1  [ X  ] [ X  ] [ X  ] [ X  ]
Row #2  [ X  ] [ X  ] [ X  ] [ X  ]
Row #3  [ X  ] [ X  ] [ X  ] [ X  ]
```

The procedure prepares a string variable called TextToSpread that spreads its contents over the selected cells.

The string Good morning will be placed in the cell Row #1,Col #1:

```
' Into Row #1, Col #1
TextToSpread = "Good morning"
```

The string News in the morning will be placed in the cell Row #1,Col #2. Because this cell is to the right of the cell Row #1,Col #1, you need to include the tab character, which is Chr(9):

```
' Into Row #1, Col #2.
TextToSpread = TextToSpread + Chr(9)
TextToSpread = TextToSpread+"News in the morning"
```

The next cell to be filled is Row #2,Col #3. Because the current cell is at Row #1,Col #2, you need to include the carriage return character, which is Chr(13). This brings you to Row #2,Col #1. To place the text in Row #2,Col #3, two tab characters are needed:

```
' Into Row #2, Col #3
TextToSpread = TextToSpread +Chr(13)+Chr(9)+Chr(9)
TextToSpread = TextToSpread+"Gone with the wind"
```

Now that the string TextToSpread is ready, the Clip property is used to actually place the content of the string in the cells:

```
' Spread the text.
grdTV.Clip = TextToSpread
```

DO	DON'T

DO use the following steps to place text at various cells of a grid control:

☐ Select the area in the grid.

☐ Prepare a string.

☐ Use the tab character, Chr(9), to move one cell to the right and use the carriage return character, Chr(13), to move to the beginning of the next row.

☐ Use the Clip property to place the contents of the string in the cells.

Adding Pictures to Non-Fixed Cells

Adding pictures to non-fixed cells is done the same way as adding pictures to fixed cells. For example, suppose that at 8:00 a.m. there is a dog show on Channel 1.

To add a picture of a dog to this cell, you can generate a picture of a dog (using Paintbrush or another program), save the picture as a small BMP file, and place a picture control somewhere in the form. Be sure that the Visible property of the picture control is set to False.

The following code places the dog picture in the 8:00 AM,Ch1 cell:

```
grdTV.Row = 2
grdTV.Col = 1
grdTV.ColWidth(1) = picDog.Width
grdTV.RowHeight(2) = picDog.Height
grdTV.Picture = picDog.Picture
```

This code can be placed in the `cmdFillCells_Click()` procedure.

Figure 9.22 shows the cell at Row #2,Col #1 with a picture of a dog.

Figure 9.22.

Placing the dog in the Row #2,Col #1 cell.

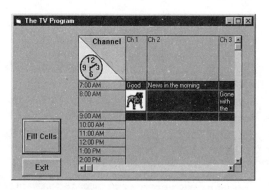

Of course, placing the dog picture in the cell is not enough to tell what show is on. To place the text The Dog Show in the cell, set the Text property of the cell. The following code places the dog picture and the name of the show in the cell:

```
grdTV.Row = 2
grdTV.Col = 1
```

```
grdTV.ColWidth(1) = picDog.Width + 1000
grdTV.RowHeight(2) = picDog.Height
grdTV.Picture = picDog.Picture
grdTV.Text = "The Dog Show"
```

Note that the ColWidth property of the cell is set to

```
grdTV.ColWidth(1) = picDog.Width + 1000
```

making room for the added text.

The resultant cell is shown in Figure 9.23.

Figure 9.23.
Placing text and graphics in a non-fixed cell.

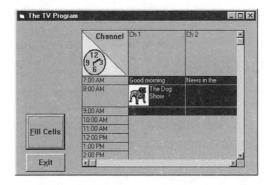

Note: You can place graphics and text in both fixed and non-fixed cells.

Removing Pictures from Cells

To remove a picture from a cell, use the LoadPicture() function without any argument. For example, to remove the dog picture from the cell, use the following statements:

```
grdTV.Row = 2
grdTV.Col = 1
grdTV.Picture = LoadPicture()
```

Adding Rows During Runtime

You can add rows to the grid control during runtime by using the AddItem method. For example, the following statements insert a row at Row 2:

```
ContentsOfCells = "7:30 AM" + Chr(9) + "gardening"
grdTV.AddItem ContentsOfCells, 2
```

The first argument of the AddItem method specifies the contents of the cells, and the second argument specifies the row number. The above statements fill two cells, so the text to be inserted includes the tab character between the text content of the cells.

Removing Rows During Runtime

You can remove rows from a grid control during runtime using the RemoveItem method. The following statement removes Row 2:

```
grdTV.RemoveItem 2
```

The argument of the RemoveItem method contains the number of the row to be removed.

Summary

In this chapter you have learned how to use the grid control, a powerful control that lets you present data (text and graphics) in a professional and pleasing way. You have learned how to insert text in the cells, how to align the text, how to insert pictures in the cells, and how to remove and add rows during runtime.

Q&A

Q Can I place more than one grid control in a form?

A Yes. You can place many grid controls in a form. (Just as you can place many command buttons and other controls in a form.)

Q Figure 9.23 shows that the text The Dog Show added to the cell is left-aligned. Can I place the text in different text alignments?

A Yes. The text may be centered or right-aligned. For example, the following code places the dog picture and the text in the cell. The text is centered:

```
grdTV.Row = 2
grdTV.Col = 1
grdTV.ColWidth(1) = picDog.Width + 1000
grdTV.RowHeight(2) = picDog.Height
grdTV.Picture = picDog.Picture
grdTV.ColAlignment(1) = 2
grdTV.Text = "The Dog Show"
```

As discussed in this chapter, the ColAlignment property can align the text to any of the alignments shown in Table 9.1.

Q **The properties table of the grid control includes a property called GridLines, which can be set to either True or False. What does this property do?**

A The default setting of this property is True. This causes the grid control to appear with visible grid lines. If you set the value of this property to False, the grid control is shown without visible grid lines. Experiment with this property (and other properties of the grid control, such as the ForeColor property) to see the effects.

Quiz

1. The height of the cells can be changed only during runtime.

    a. True
    b. False

2. The width of the cells can be changed only during runtime.

    a. True
    b. False

3. Which property should you set to change the height of a cell?

    a. RowHeight
    b. ColWidth
    c. You can't change the height of a cell

4. Which property should you set to change the width of a cell?

    a. RowHeight
    b. ColWidth
    c. You can't change the width of a cell

5. What code will remove a picture from a cell?

Exercises

1. Suppose that the Clip property is used to place text in cells, as shown in the following table:

    ```
            Col#1    Col#2     Col#3
    Row #1    A     (Blank)      C
    Row #2    D     (Blank)   (Blank)
    Row #3    E       F          G
    ```

    What should the contents be of the string that places text in these cells?

2. Write a program that displays a multiplication table.

Quiz Answers

1. a

2. a

3. a

4. b

5. Make the cell you're removing the picture from the current active cell, then use LoadPicture() with no argument. For example, to remove the picture from the cell at Row #4,Col #7, use the following:

```
grdTV.Row = 4
grdTV.Col = 7
grdTV.Picture = LoadPicture()
```

Exercise Answers

1. First select the area with the following statements:

```
' Select the area.
grdTV.SelStartRow = 1
grdTV.SelStartCol = 1
grdTV.SelEndRow = 3
grdTV.SelEndCol = 3
```

Then update a string variable as follows:

```
TheContents = "A" + Chr(9) + "C" + Chr(13) + _
              "D" + Chr(9) + Chr(9) + Chr(13) + _
              "E" + "F" + "G"
```

Finally, issue the following statement:

```
grdMyGrid.Clip TheContents
```

2. There are several ways to build such a program. The grid control should appear as follows:

```
    0   1   2   3   ...
0   0   0   0   0   ...
1   0   1   2   3   ...
2   0   1   4   6   ...
3   0   3   6   9   ...
.   .   .   .   .   ...
.   .   .   .   .   ...
.   .   .   .   .   ...
```

Try to write the program by yourself, and experiment with it by placing pictures in the cells. (The Visual Basic package comes with plenty of icons.)

When implementing the program, calculate the Text property of the non-fixed cells

by doing the multiplication. For example, the text that may be placed in the cell Row #2,Col #3 can be calculated as follows:

```
Dim X, Y
grdMultiply.Row = 2
grdMultiply.Col = 0
X = Val(grdMultiply.Text)
grdMultiply.Row = 0
grdMultiply.Col = 3
Y = Val(grdMultiply.Text)
grdMultiply.Row = 2
grdMultiply.Col = 3
grdMultiply.Text = X*Y
```

Try to implement a loop that goes through all the rows and columns and fills all the cells of the grid control.

Displaying and
Printing

In this chapter you'll learn how to display and print information, how to display text in different fonts, how to format numbers, dates, and times, and how to send data (text and graphics) to the printer.

Fonts

There are two types of fonts: scaleable and nonscaleable. A *scaleable font* is created using mathematical formulas. For example, the basic B character is defined only once. All other sizes of the B character are produced from the basic character by enlarging or shrinking the basic B. On the other hand, a *nonscaleable font* is stored as a bitmap. Larger and smaller fonts of the same character are stored as different bitmaps.

Using Different Fonts in Your Programs

When you display text in a form, you have to choose its font. Selecting the proper font is an important job. Will your user have this type of font on his/her system? If the user of your program does not have the font installed, Windows chooses a font that most closely resembles the required font. However, if your user doesn't have a large selection of fonts, Windows might choose a font that is larger than the font you intended to use, which could mess up your form by producing overlapped text.

The easiest way to overcome this problem is to use only the most common fonts, such as the fonts shipped with the original Windows package. Or your program can examine the file WIN.INI in the Windows directory. This file has a section that starts with the heading [fonts]. All the currently installed fonts are listed under this heading. Your program can examine this section and decide which font should be used.

The FontTransparent Property

The form and the picture control support the FontTransparent property. When FontTransparent is False (the default), the text is displayed with a background indicated by the BackColor property. For example, if the BackColor property of a form is set to blue, the text is displayed on the form with a blue background.

Figure 10.1 shows a form with a bitmap picture in it. That is, the Picture property of the form was set so that the form has a BMP file in it. You can display text in the form by using the Print method. The following Form_Click() procedure is automatically executed when you click in the form:

```
Private Sub Form_Click()

    ' Set the FontTransparent property to True.
    frmMyForm.FontTransparent = True

    ' Display text.
    frmMyForm.Print "Testing…"

    ' Set the FontTransparent property to False.
    frmMyForm.FontTransparent = False

    ' Display text.
    frmMyForm.Print "Testing…"

End Sub
```

Figure 10.1.
The frmMyForm form.

10

The code in this procedure sets the FontTransparent property of the form to True and uses the Print method to display the text Testing…. The procedure then sets the FontTransparent property of the form to False and again displays the text Testing….

As shown in Figure 10.2, the first line in the form displays the text Testing… with the original background of the bitmap picture. The second line of text in Figure 10.2 displays the text Testing… with a white background. The background is white because the FontTransparent property of the form is set to False and the BackColor property of the form is set to White.

Figure 10.2.
Displaying text with the FontTransparent property set to True and False.

The ShowFont Program

The ShowFont program illustrates the various font properties available in Visual Basic.

The Visual Implementation of the ShowFont Program

☐ Open a new project, save the form of the project as SHOWFONT.FRM in the C:\VB4PRG\CH10 directory and save the project file as SHOWFONT.VBP in the C:\VB4PRG\CH10 directory.

☐ Build the frmShowFont form according to the specifications in Table 10.1.

The completed form should look like the one shown in Figure 10.3.

Table 10.1. The properties table of frmShowFont form.

Object	Property	Setting
Form	**Name**	**frmShowFont**
	Caption	The ShowFont Program
	Height	4830
	Left	1080
	Top	1170
	Width	6810
Check Box	**Name**	**chkBold**
	Caption	&Bold
	FontName	MS Sans Serif
	Height	495
	Left	2400
	Top	2880
	Width	1215
TextBox	**Name**	**txtTest**
	FontName	MS Sans Serif
	Height	2055
	Left	360
	MultiLine	-1-True
	ScrollBars	3-Both
	Top	240
	Width	5895

Object	Property	Setting
Command Button	**Name**	**cmdExit**
	Caption	E&xit
	Height	495
	Left	4800
	Top	3360
	Width	1215
Check Box	**Name**	**chkItalic**
	Caption	&Italic
	FontName	MS Sans Serif
	Height	495
	Left	2400
	Top	3480
	Width	1335
Check Box	**Name**	**chkStrike**
	Caption	&Strike
	FontName	MS Sans Serif
	Height	495
	Left	240
	Top	2880
	Width	1215
Check Box	**Name**	**chkUnderline**
	Caption	&Underline
	FontName	MS Sans Serif
	Height	495
	Left	240
	Top	3480
	Width	1455
Menu	**(See Table 10.2.)**	**(See Table 10.2.)**

Table 10.2. The menu table of the frmShowFont form.

Caption	Name
&Fonts	mnuFonts
…Courier	mnuCourier
…MS Sans Serif	mnuMSSansSerif
&Size	mnuSize
…1&0 Points	mnu10Points
…1&2 Points	mnu12Points

Figure 10.3.
The frmShowFont form.

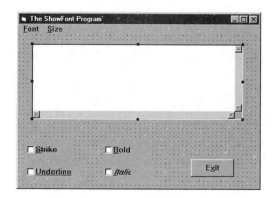

Entering the Code of the ShowFont Program

☐ Enter the following code in the general declarations section of the frmShowFont form:

```
' All variables MUST be declared.
Option Explicit
```

☐ Enter the following code in the chkBold_Click() procedure of the frmShowFont form:

```
Private Sub chkBold_Click()

' Update the FontBold property of the text
' box with the Value property of the
' chkBold check box.
txtTest.FontBold = chkBold.Value

End Sub
```

☐ Enter the following code in the chkItalic_Click() procedure of the frmShowFont form:

```
Private Sub chkItalic_Click()
```

```
' Update the FontItalic property of the
' text box with the Value property
' of the chkItalic check box.
txtTest.FontItalic = chkItalic.Value
```

End Sub

☐ Enter the following code in the chkStrike_Click() procedure of the frmShowFont form:

Private Sub chkStrike_Click()

```
' Update the FontStrikethru property
' of the text box with the  Value property
' of the chkStrike check box.
txtTest.FontStrikethru = chkStrike.Value
```

End Sub

☐ Enter the following code in the chkUnderline_Click() procedure of the frmShowFont form:

Private Sub chkUnderline_Click()

```
' Update the FontUnderline property
' of the text box with the Value
' property of the chkUnderline check box.
txtTest.FontUnderline = chkUnderline.Value
```

End Sub

☐ Enter the following code in the cmdExit_Click() procedure of the frmShowFont form:

Private Sub cmdExit_Click()

```
    End
```

End Sub

☐ Enter the following code in the mnu10Points_Click() procedure of the frmShowFont form:

Private Sub mnu10Points_Click()

```
' Set the size of the font to 10 points.
txtTest.FontSize = 10
```

End Sub

☐ Enter the following code in the mnu12Points_Click() procedure of the frmShowFont form:

Private Sub mnu12Points_Click()

```
' Set the size of the font to 12 points.
txtTest.FontSize = 12
```

End Sub

☐ Enter the following code in the `mnuCourier_Click()` procedure of the frmShowFont form:

```
Private Sub mnuCourier_Click()

    ' Set the font name to Courier.
    txtTest.FontName = "Courier"

End Sub
```

☐ Enter the following code in the `mnuMSSansSerif_Click()` procedure of the frmShowFont form:

```
Private Sub mnuMSSansSerif_Click()

    ' Set the font name to MS Sans Serif.
    txtTest.FontName = "MS Sans Serif"

End Sub
```

☐ Save the project.

Executing the ShowFont Program

☐ Execute the ShowFont program.

☐ Type something in the text box. (See Figure 10.4.)

The text you typed appears with the default font (the font set during design time).

Figure 10.4.
The default font of the ShowFont program.

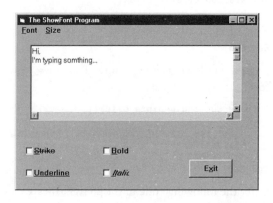

☐ Place a ✔ in the Bold check box.

The program responds by changing the font in the text box to bold. (See Figure 10.5.)

Figure 10.5.
*Checking the Bold
check box.*

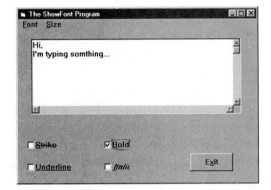

☐ Place a ✓ in the Italic check box.

> *The program responds by changing the text in the text box to italic. Since the Bold check box is also checked, the text is bold and italic. (See Figure 10.6.)*

Figure 10.6.
*Checking the Bold and Italic
check boxes.*

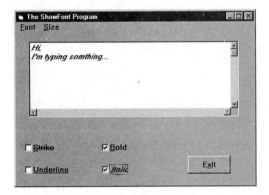

☐ Click the Bold check box and the Italic check box to uncheck them.

> *The program responds by removing the bold and italic from the text in the text box.*

☐ Place a ✓ in the Strike check box.

> *The program responds by displaying the text in the text box as strikethrough text. (See Figure 10.7.)*

☐ Click the Strike check box to uncheck this check box.

> *The program responds by removing the strikethrough font from the text.*

Figure 10.7.
Checking the Strike check box.

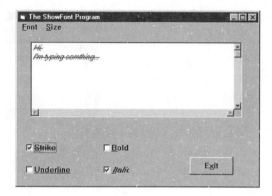

☐ Place a ✓ in the Underline check box.

The program responds by underlining the text in the text box. (See Figure 10.8.)

Figure 10.8.
Checking the Underline check box.

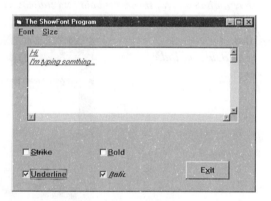

☐ Change the font name by selecting a font from the Font menu.

The program responds by changing the text in the text box to the font you selected.

☐ Change the font size by selecting a size from the Size menu.

The program responds by changing the text in the text box to the point size you selected. Figure 10.9 shows the text box after setting the size to 12 points.

☐ Click the Exit button to terminate the program.

Figure 10.9.
Setting the FontSize
property to 12 points.

How the ShowFont Program Works

The ShowFont program changes the font properties of the text box according to your selections.

The Code in the *chkBold_Click()* Procedure

The chkBold_Click() procedure is automatically executed when you click the chkBold check box:

```
Private Sub chkBold_Click()

    ' Update the FontBold property of the
    ' text box with the Value
    ' property of the chkBold check box.
    txtTest.FontBold = chkBold.Value

End Sub
```

When the Value property of chkBold is True (that is, checked), the FontBold property of the text box is set to True; when the Value property of chkBold is False (that is, unchecked), the FontBold property of the text box is set to False.

The chkItalic_Click(), chkStrike_Click(), and chkUnderline_Click() procedures work the same way to change the txtTest text box:

> The chkItalic_Click() procedure sets the FontItalic property to True or False.
>
> The chkStrike_Click() procedure sets the FontStrike property to True or False.
>
> The chkUnderline_Click() procedure sets the FontUnderline property to True or False.

The Code in the *mnu10Points_Click()* Procedure

The `mnu10Points_Click()` procedure is executed when you select 10 Points from the Size menu:

```
Private Sub mnu10Points_Click()

    ' Set the size of the font to 10 points.
    txtTest.FontSize = 10

End Sub
```

This procedure sets the FontSize property of the txtTest text box to 10. The `mnu12Points_Click()` procedure works the same way to set the FontSize property of the text box to 12.

The Code in the *mnuCourier_Click()* Procedure

The `mnuCourier_Click()` procedure is executed when you select Courier from the Font menu:

```
Private Sub mnuCourier_Click()

    ' Set the font name to Courier.
    txtTest.FontName = "Courier"

End Sub
```

This procedure sets the FontName property of the txtTest text box to Courier. The `mnuMSSansSerif_Click()` procedure works the same way to set the FontName property to MS Sans Serif.

WYSIWYG

WYSIWYG is an abbreviation for "what you see is what you get." WYSIWYG refers to the capability of a program to produce a hard copy on the printer that is an exact replica of what's on the screen. Producing 100 percent WYSIWYG programs requires careful programming because users can have different printers, monitors, fonts, and so forth.

The Fonts Program

The Fonts program illustrates how your program can make a decision about the available fonts in the system. The technique used by the Fonts program can be used to produce programs with WYSIWYG capability.

The Visual Implementation
of the Fonts Program

☐ Open a new project, save the form of the program as FONTS.FRM in the C:\VB4PRG\CH10 directory and save the project file as FONTS.VBP in the C:\VB4PRG\CH10 directory.

☐ Build the frmFonts form according to the specifications in Table 10.3.

The completed form should look like the one shown in Figure 10.10.

Table 10.3. The properties table of the frmFonts form.

Object	Property	Setting
Form	**Name**	**frmFonts**
	Caption	The Fonts Program
	Height	5160
	Left	1080
	Top	1170
	Width	6810
Command Button	**Name**	**cmdExit**
	Caption	E&xit
	FontName	System
	FontSize	10
	Height	495
	Left	5160
	Top	2640
	Width	1215
Combo Box	**Name**	**cboFontsScreen**
	Height	315
	Left	480
	Sorted	-1-True
	Style	2-Dropdown List
	Top	720
	Width	2415

continues

Table 10.3. continued

Object	Property	Setting
Combo Box	**Name**	**cboFontsPrinter**
	Height	315
	Left	3960
	Sorted	-1-True
	Style	2-Dropdown List
	Top	720
	Width	2415
Command Button	**Name**	**cmdNumberOfFonts**
	Caption	&Number of Fonts
	FontName	System
	FontSize	10
	Height	495
	Left	2280
	Top	3120
	Width	2175
Label	**Name**	**lblScreen**
	Caption	Available Screen Fonts:
	FontName	System
	FontSize	10
	Height	255
	Left	480
	Top	480
	Width	2535
Label	**Name**	**lblPrinter**
	Caption	Available Printer Fonts:
	FontName	System
	FontSize	10
	Height	255
	Left	3960
	Top	480
	Width	2535

Object	Property	Setting
Label	**Name**	**lblSample**
	Caption	Aa Bb Cc Dd Ee Ff
	Alignment	2-Center
	BorderStyle	1-Fixed Single
	FontName	MS Sans Serif
	FontSize	10
	Height	495
	Left	240
	Top	4080
	Width	6135
Label	**Name**	**lblSampleInfo**
	Caption	Sample:
	FontName	System
	FontSize	10
	Height	255
	Left	240
	Top	3720
	Width	975

Figure 10.10.
The frmFonts form.

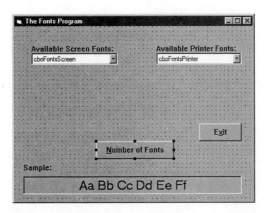

Entering the Code of the Fonts Program

☐ Enter the following code in the general declarations section of the frmFonts form:

```
' All variables MUST be declared.
Option Explicit

Dim gNumOfScreenFonts
Dim gNumOfPrinterFonts
```

☐ Enter the following code in the cboFontsScreen_Click() procedure of the frmFonts form:

```
Private Sub cboFontsScreen_Click()

    ' User selected a new screen font. Change the
    ' font of the label in accordance with the
    ' user's font selection.
    lblSample.FontName = cboFontsScreen.Text

End Sub
```

☐ Enter the following code in the cmdExit_Click() procedure of the frmFonts form:

```
Private Sub cmdExit_Click()

    End

End Sub
```

☐ Enter the following code in the cmdNumberOfFonts_Click() procedure of the frmFonts form:

```
Private Sub cmdNumberOfFonts_Click()

    'Display the number of screen fonts in the
    ' system.
    MsgBox "Number of Screen fonts:" + _
        Str(gNumOfScreenFonts)

    'Display the number of printer fonts in the
    ' system.
    MsgBox "Number of Printer fonts:" + _
        Str(gNumOfPrinterFonts)

End Sub
```

☐ Enter the following code in the Form_Load() procedure of the frmFonts form:

```
Private Sub Form_Load()

    Dim I

    ' Calculate the number of screen fonts.
    gNumOfScreenFonts = Screen.FontCount - 1

    ' Calculate the number of printer fonts.
    gNumOfPrinterFonts = Printer.FontCount - 1
```

```
' Fill the items of the combo box with the
' screen fonts.
For I = 0 To gNumOfScreenFonts - 1 Step 1
    cboFontsScreen.AddItem Screen.Fonts(I)
Next

' Fill the items of the combo box with the
' printer fonts.
For I = 0 To gNumOfPrinterFonts - 1 Step 1
    cboFontsPrinter.AddItem Printer.Fonts(I)
Next

' initialize the text of the combo box
' to item #0.
cboFontsScreen.ListIndex = 0
' Initialize the label font to value of the
' combo box.
lblSample.FontName = cboFontsScreen.Text

End Sub
```

10

Executing the Fonts Program

☐ Execute the Fonts program.

☐ Click the Number of Fonts button.

The program responds by displaying the number of available screen fonts and the number of available printer fonts.

☐ Click the down-arrow icon of the combo box on the left.

As indicated by the label above this combo box, the list in the box includes all the available screen fonts on your system. (See Figure 10.11.)

Figure 10.11.

Choosing the Univers Condensed screen font.

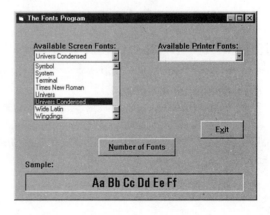

The sample label at the bottom of the form changes its font according to your selection.

369

☐ Select a font from the combo box on the right.

As indicated by the label above this combo box, the list in the box includes all the available printer fonts in your system.

The program responds by displaying all the available printer fonts. (See Figure 10.12.)

Figure 10.12.
Displaying the printer fonts.

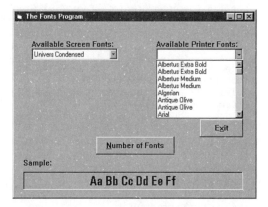

Note: The text in the Sample label doesn't change when you select new fonts from the combo box on the right because that combo box represents the printer fonts.

How the Fonts Program Works

The Fonts program extracts the available screen and printer fonts and displays them in combo boxes.

The Code in the General Declarations Section

The code in the general declarations section of the program declares two variables:

```
Dim gNumOfScreenFonts
Dim gNumOfPrinterFonts
```

These variables represent the number of available screen fonts and printer fonts. Because these variables are declared in the general declarations section, they are visible in all the procedures of the form.

The Code in the *Form_Load()* Procedure

The `Form_Load()` procedure is executed when the form is loaded:

```
Private Sub Form_Load()

    Dim I

    ' Calculate the number of screen fonts.
    gNumOfScreenFonts = Screen.FontCount - 1

    ' Calculate the number of printer fonts.
    gNumOfPrinterFonts = Printer.FontCount - 1

    ' Fill the items of the combo box with the
    ' screen fonts.
    For I = 0 To gNumOfScreenFonts - 1 Step 1
        cboFontsScreen.AddItem Screen.Fonts(I)
    Next

    ' Fill the items of the combo box with the
    ' printer fonts.
    For I = 0 To gNumOfPrinterFonts - 1 Step 1
        cboFontsPrinter.AddItem Printer.Fonts(I)
    Next

    ' initialize the text of the combo box
    ' to item #0.
    cboFontsScreen.ListIndex = 0
    ' Initialize the label font to value of the
    ' combo box.
    lblSample.FontName = cboFontsScreen.Text

End Sub
```

You can get the number of available screen fonts by using the FontCount property of the screen:

```
' Calculate the number of screen fonts.
gNumOfScreenFonts = Screen.FontCount
```

Similarly, you can get the number of available printer fonts by using the FontCount property of the printer:

```
' Calculate the number of printer fonts.
gNumOfPrinterFonts = Printer.FontCount -1
```

DO	DON'T

DO use the FontCount property to find the number of available screen fonts. For example, to assign the number of available screen fonts to the variable `gNumOfScreenFonts`, use the following:

```
gNumOfScreenFonts = Screen.FontCount
```

10

DO   **DON'T**

DO use the FontCount property to find the number of available printer fonts. For example, to assign the number of available printer fonts to the variable `gNumOfPrinterFonts`, use the following:

```
gNumOfPrinterFonts = Printer.FontCount
```

The `Form_Load()` procedure then fills the item of the cboFontsScreen combo box with the screen fonts:

```
' Fill the items of the combo box with the
' screen fonts.
For I = 0 To gNumOfScreenFonts - 1 Step 1
    cboFontsScreen.AddItem Screen.Fonts(I)
Next
```

This procedure fills the items of the cboFontsPrinter combo box with the printer fonts:

```
' Fill the items of the combo box with the
' printer fonts.
For I = 0 To gNumOfPrinterFonts - 1 Step 1
    cboFontsPrinter.AddItem Printer.Fonts(I)
Next
```

The available fonts are extracted by using the Fonts property.

Note: To extract the screen fonts, use the Fonts property. For example, to assign the first available font of the screen to a string variable called `CurrentScreenFont`, use the following:

```
CurrentScreenFont = Screen.Fonts(0)
```

Note: To extract the printer fonts, use the Fonts property. For example, to assign the ninth available font of the printer to a string variable called `CurrentPrinterFont`, use the following:

```
CurrentPrinterFont = Printer.Fonts(8)
```

The procedure then initializes the cboFontScreen combo box to the first item:

```
cboFontsScreen.ListIndex = 0
```

The text font in the lblSample label is changed according to the Text property of the screen's font combo box:

```
lblSample.FontName = cboFontsScreen.Text
```

The Code in the *cboFontsScreen_Click()* Procedure

The code in the cboFontsScreen_Click() procedure is executed when you select a new screen font from the cboFontsScreen combo box (the Available Screen Fonts combo box on the left):

```
Private Sub cboFontsScreen_Click()

    ' User selected a new screen font. Change the
    ' font of the label in accordance with the
    ' user's font selection.
    lblSample.FontName = cboFontsScreen.Text

End Sub
```

The procedure changes the font of the lblSample label to the font you selected.

The Code in the *cmdNumberOfFonts_Click()* Procedure

The cmdNumberOfFonts_Click() procedure is automatically executed when you click the Number of Fonts button:

```
Private Sub cmdNumnerOfFonts_Click()

    'Display the number of screen fonts in the
    'system.
    MsgBox "Number of Screen fonts:" + _
         Str(gNumOfScreenFonts)

    'Display the number of printer fonts in the
    ' system.
    MsgBox "Number of Printer fonts:" + _
         Str(gNumOfPrinterFonts)

End Sub
```

The procedure displays the number of available screen fonts and the number of available printer fonts using the MsgBox statements. The number of available fonts is stored in the variables gNumOfScreenFonts and gNumOfPrinterFonts. These variables were updated in the Form_Load() procedure.

The *Print* Method

The `Print` method can be used to print in a form or a picture control. To display the text `Testing…` in the frmMyForm form, use the following statement:

```
frmMyForm.Print "Testing…"
```

To display the text `Testing…` in the picMyPicture picture control, use the following statement:

```
picMyPicture.Print "Testing…"
```

The semicolon (;) is used to instruct Visual Basic to place the text on the same line. For example, use the following two statements:

```
frmMyForm.Print "This is line number 1 and ";
frmMyForm.Print "it continues…"
```

to produce this output:

```
This is line number 1 and it continues…
```

The following statement produces the same output:

```
frmMyForm.Print _
  "This is line ";"number 1";" and it continues…"
```

Clearing Text

You can use the `Cls` method to clear text that was written in a form or a picture control. For example, to clear the frmMyForm form, use the following:

```
frmMyForm.Cls
```

To clear the picMyPicture picture control, use the following:

```
picMyPicture.Cls
```

The `Cls` method clears text as well as graphics drawn with a graphics method.

Placing Text at a Specified Location

To place text at a specified location, update the CurrentX and CurrentY properties. For example, to place the text `Testing` in the frmMyForm form at Column 5, Row 6, use the following:

```
frmMyForm.CurrentX = 5
frmMyForm.CurrentY = 6
frmMyForm.Print "Testing"
```

Similarly, to place the text `Testing` in the picMyPicture picture control at Column 11, Row 10, use the following:

```
picMyPicture.CurrentX = 11
picMyPicture.CurrentY = 10
picMyPicture.Print "Testing"
```

The Index Program

The Index program illustrates how you can use the TextHeight and TextWidth properties to display text at any desired location; they are used to determine the height and width of text. For example, the height of the text AaBbCc is assigned to the variable HeightOfabc as follows:

```
HeightOfabc = frmMyForm.TextHeight("AaBbCc")
```

The returned value of the TextHeight property is given in the same units as indicated by the ScaleMode property.

The TextHeight property is useful when you want to calculate the CurrentY for a certain line. For example, to calculate CurrentY for the tenth row, use the following:

```
CurrentY = frmMyForm.TextHeight("AaBbCc")*9
```

The TextWidth property returns the width of the text. For example, to calculate the width of the text Index, use this statement:

```
WidthOfIndex = frmMyForm.TextWidth("Index")
```

The TextHeight and TextWidth properties return the height and width of the text according to the current value of the FontSize property.

The Visual Implementation of the Index Program

☐ Open a new project, save the form as INDEX.FRM in the C:\VB4PRG\CH10 directory and save the project file as INDEX.VBP in the C:\VB4PRG\CH10 directory.

☐ Build the frmIndex form according to the specifications in Table 10.4 and Table 10.5.

The completed form should look like the one shown in Figure 10.13.

Table 10.4. The properties table of frmIndex form.

Object	Property	Setting
Form	Name	frmIndex
	BackColor	White
	Caption	The Index Program
	Height	4830
	Left	1080
	Top	1170
	Width	6810
Menu	(See Table 10.5.)	(See Table 10.5.)

Table 10.5. The menu table of the frmIndex form.

Caption	Name
&File	mnuFile
...&Display Index	mnuDisplayIndex
...&Erase Chapter 2	mnuEraseCh2
...&Clear Text	mnuClearText
...-	mnuSep1
...E&xit	mnuExit

Figure 10.13.
The frmIndex form.

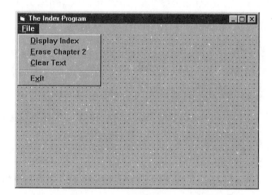

Entering the Code of the Index Program

☐ Enter the following code in the general declarations section of the frmIndex form:

```
' All variables MUST be declared.
Option Explicit
Dim gDots
```

☐ Enter the following code in the Form_Load() procedure of the frmIndex form:

```
Private Sub Form_Load()

    gDots = String$(84, ".")

End Sub
```

☐ Enter the following code in the mnuClear_Click() procedure of the frmIndex form:

```
Private Sub mnuClear_Click()

    ' Clear the form.
    frmIndex.Cls

End Sub
```

Enter the following code in the mnuDisplayIndex_Click() procedure of the frmIndex form:

```
Private Sub mnuDisplayIndex_Click()

    frmIndex.Cls

    ' Heading should be displayed 100 twips from
    ' the top.
    CurrentY = 100

    ' Place the heading at the center of the row.
    CurrentX = (frmIndex.ScaleWidth - _
                frmIndex.TextWidth("Index")) / 2
    frmIndex.FontUnderline = True

    frmIndex.Print "Index"

    ' Display the chapters.
    frmIndex.FontUnderline = False
    CurrentY = frmIndex.TextHeight("VVV") * 2
    CurrentX = 100
    Print "Chapter 1" + gDots + "The world"
    CurrentY = frmIndex.TextHeight("VVV") * 3
    CurrentX = 100
    Print "Chapter 2" + gDots + "The chair"
    CurrentY = frmIndex.TextHeight("VVV") * 4
    CurrentX = 100
    Print "Chapter 3" + gDots + "The mouse"
    CurrentY = frmIndex.TextHeight("VVV") * 5
    CurrentX = 100
    Print "Chapter 4" + gDots + "The end"

End Sub
```

Enter the following code in the mnuEraseCh2_Click() procedure of the frmIndex form:

```
Private Sub mnuEraseCh2_Click()

    Dim LengthOfLine
    Dim HeightOfLine

    ' Erase the line by placing a box with white
    ' background over the line.
    CurrentY = frmIndex.TextHeight("VVV") * 3
    CurrentX = 100
    LengthOfLine = frmIndex.TextWidth("Chapter 2" + _
                gDots + "The chair")
    HeightOfLine = frmIndex.TextHeight("C")
    frmIndex.Line -Step(LengthOfLine, HeightOfLine), _
                RGB(255, 255, 255), BF

End Sub
```

10

☐ Enter the following code in the `mnuExit_Click()` procedure of the frmIndex form:

```
Private Sub mnuExit_Click()

    End

End Sub
```

Executing the Index Program

☐ Execute the Index program.

☐ Select Display Index from the File menu.

The program responds by displaying the index shown in Figure 10.14.

Figure 10.14.
Displaying the index.

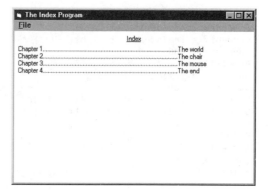

☐ Select Erase Chapter 2 from the File menu.

The program responds by erasing the Chapter 2 line. (See Figure 10.15.)

Figure 10.15
Erasing Chapter 2.

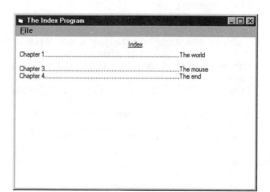

☐ Select Clear Text from the File menu.

The program responds by erasing the text from the form.

How the Index Program Works

The Index program displays text with the Print method. You can display the text at any location by updating the CurrentX and CurrentY properties.

The Code in the General Declarations Section

The code in the general declarations section of the frmIndex form declares the variable gDots. This variable, therefore, is visible in all the procedures of the frmIndex form.

The Code in the *Form_Load()* Procedure

The Form_Load() procedure is automatically executed when the frmIndex form is loaded:

```
Private Sub Form_Load()

    gDots = String$(84, ".")

End Sub
```

This procedure stores 84 dots in the gDots variable.

The Code in the *mnuClear_Click()* Procedure

The mnuClear_Click() procedure is automatically executed when you select Clear Text from the File menu:

```
Private Sub mnuClear_Click()

    ' Clear the form.
    frmIndex.Cls

End Sub
```

This procedure uses the Cls method to clear the form.

The Code in the *mnuDisplayIndex_Click()* Procedure

The mnuDisplayIndex_Click() procedure is automatically executed when you select Display Index from the File menu. It clears the text (if any) from the form and then updates CurrentY with 100. This causes text to be displayed 100 twips from the top:

```
frmIndex.Cls
CurrentY = 100
```

Because the text Index should be displayed at the center of the form (see Figure 10.15), the CurrentX property is updated as follows:

```
CurrentX = (frmIndex.ScaleWidth - _
            frmIndex.TextWidth("Index")) / 2
```

The following procedure sets the FontUnderline property to True and uses the Print method to display the text Index:

```
frmIndex.FontUnderline = True
frmIndex.Print "Index"
```

The rest of the text is displayed as non-underlined text, so the FontUnderline property is set to False:

```
frmIndex.FontUnderline = False
```

The CurrentY property is updated for the Chapter 1 line as follows:

```
CurrentY = frmIndex.TextHeight("VVV") * 2
```

and the CurrentX property is updated to 100 twips so that the line starts 100 twips from the left of the form:

```
CurrentX = 100
```

Now that CurrentX and CurrentY are updated, the Print method is used to display the text:

```
Print "Chapter 1" + Dots + "The world"
```

The rest of the lines are displayed in a similar manner.

If you omit the name of the object before the Print method, the Print method displays text in the currently active form. Therefore, this statement:

```
frmIndex.Print "Index"
```

produces the same result as this statement:

```
Print "Index"
```

Similarly, in this procedure the CurrentX and CurrentY properties were updated without preceding these properties with the form name. When you omit the name of the object, Visual Basic updates the properties of the currently active form. For example, if the currently active form is frmIndex, the following two statements are identical:

```
frmIndex.CurrentY = 100
```

```
CurrentY = 100
```

The Code in the *mnuEraseCh2_Click()* Procedure

The mnuEraseCh2_Click() procedure is executed when you select Erase Chapter 2 from the File menu:

```
Private Sub mnuEraseCh2_Click()

    Dim LengthOfLine
    Dim HeightOfLine

    ' Erase the line by placing a box with white
    ' background over the line.
    CurrentY = frmIndex.TextHeight("VVV") * 3
    CurrentX = 100
    LengthOfLine = frmIndex.TextWidth("Chapter 2" + _
                   gDots + "The chair")
    HeightOfLine = frmIndex.TextHeight("C")
    frmIndex.Line -Step(LengthOfLine, HeightOfLine), _
                  RGB(255, 255, 255), BF

End Sub
```

This procedure sets the CurrentX and CurrentY properties to the location where the Chapter 2 line starts and then draws a box with a white background. The width of the box is calculated using the TextWidth property.

Displaying Tables

You can use the Print method to display tables in a form or a picture control. Complete the following steps to see how to do this:

☐ Add the Table menu and Display Table menu item to the menu of the Index program. The new menu table is shown in Table 10.6.

Table 10.6. The menu table of the frmIndex form.

Caption	Name
&File	mnuFile
…&Display Index	mnuDisplayIndex
…&Erase Chapter 2	mnuEraseCh2
…&Clear text	mnuClear
…-	mnuSep1
…E&xit	mnuExit
&Table	mnuTable
…&Display Table	mnuDisplayTable

☐ Add the following code in the mnuDisplayTable_Click() procedure of the frmIndex form:

```
Private Sub mnuDisplayTable_Click()

    ' Clear the form.
    frmIndex.Cls
    ' Set the FontName and FontSize properties.
    frmIndex.FontName = "MS Sans Serif"
    frmIndex.FontSize = 10
    ' Display the heading.
    frmIndex.Print "Chapter", "Description", "Page"
    ' Display a blank line.
    frmIndex.Print
    ' Display the table.
    frmIndex.Print "1", "The world", "1"
    frmIndex.Print "2", "The chair", "12"
    frmIndex.Print "3", "The mouse", "42"
    frmIndex.Print "4", "The end", "100"

End Sub
```

Executing the Enhanced Version of the Index Program

☐ Execute the enhanced version of the Index program.

☐ Select Display Table from the Table menu.

The program responds by displaying the table shown in Figure 10.16.

Figure 10.16.

Displaying the table of the Index program.

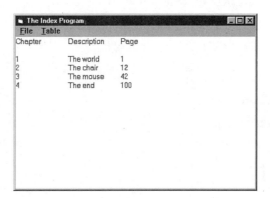

☐ Select Exit from the File menu to terminate the program.

The code in the mnuDisplayTable_Click() procedure uses the Print method with commas:

```
frmIndex.Print "Chapter", "Description", "Page"
```

This causes the first string—"Chapter"—to be displayed starting at Column 0. The second string—"Description"—is displayed starting at Column 14, and the third string—"Page"—is displayed starting at Column 28. The commas are an indication to Visual Basic to change printing zones. By default, Visual Basic defines each printing zone as 13 characters.

Note: To print strings that start at different printing zones, use the Print method and type commas between the strings. For example, use the following statements:

```
Print "abc", "def", "ghj"
Print "nop", "qrs", "tuv"
Print "ABC", "DEF", "GHI"
```

to produce the following output:

```
abc         def         ghj
nop         qrs         tuv
ABC         DEF         GHI
```

Defining New Printing Zones

You can define new printing zones by using the Tab() function.

☐ Replace the code in the mnuDisplayTable_Click() procedure with the following code:

```
Private Sub mnuDisplayTable_Click()

    ' Clear the form.
    frmIndex.Cls

    ' Set the FontName and FontSize properties.
    frmIndex.FontName = "MS Sans Serif"
    frmIndex.FontSize = 10
    frmIndex.Print Tab(5); "Chapter"; Tab(20); _
            "Description"; Tab(50); "Page"

    ' Display a blank line.
    frmIndex.Print

    ' Display the table.
    frmIndex.Print Tab(5); "1"; Tab(20); _
                "The world"; Tab(50); "1"

    frmIndex.Print Tab(5); "2"; Tab(20); _
                "The chair"; Tab(50); "12"

    frmIndex.Print Tab(5); "3"; Tab(20); _
                "The mouse"; Tab(50); "42"

    frmIndex.Print Tab(5); "4"; Tab(20); _
                "The end"; Tab(50); "100"

End Sub
```

☐ Execute the Index program.

☐ Select Display Table from the Table menu.

The program responds by displaying the table, as shown in Figure 10.17.

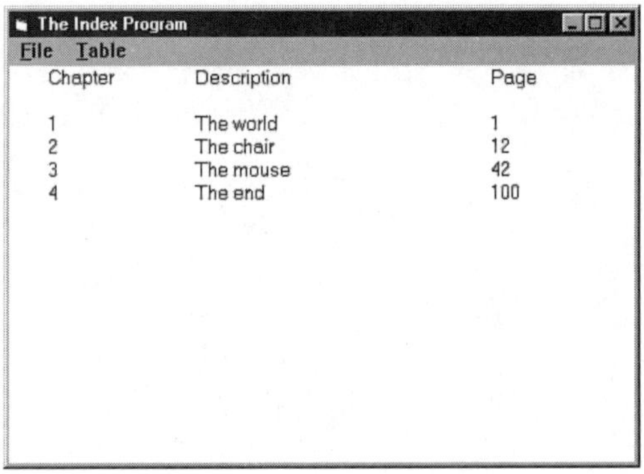

Figure 10.17.

Using the Tab() *function.*

Chapter	Description	Page
1	The world	1
2	The chair	12
3	The mouse	42
4	The end	100

The Tab() function causes the text to be displayed at the columns indicated by the argument of the Tab() function. For example, the following statement displays the Chapter 1 line:

```
frmIndex.Print Tab(5); "1"; Tab(20); _
          "The world"; Tab(50); "1"
```

The first argument of the Print method is Tab(5); this sets CurrentX at Column 5. The semicolon (;) instructs Visual Basic to stay on the current line.

The second argument of the Print method is "1"; this causes the text 1 to be displayed at Column 5.

The third argument of the Print method is Tab(20); this sets CurrentX to Column 20. The semicolon (;) instructs Visual Basic to stay on the same line. Therefore, the fourth argument (the string "The world") is displayed starting at Column 20.

As you can see, the Tab() function enables you to display text at any column you want.

Formatting Numbers, Dates, and Times

The Format$() function is used to display numbers, dates, and times in different ways. The next two sections explain how the Format$() function works.

Formatting Numbers

You can have control over the way Visual Basic displays numbers by using the Format$() function. The Format$() function has two arguments: the first argument is the number to be

displayed, and the second argument serves as a format instruction. For example, to display the number 45.6 with leading and trailing zeros, use the following statement:

```
Print Format$(45.6, "000000.00")
```

This is the result:

```
000045.60
```

That is, the number 45.6 contains two digits to the left of the decimal point and one digit to the right of the decimal point. The second argument contains `000000.00`. This means there should be six digits to the left of the decimal point and two digits to the right of the decimal point. Because 45.6 has two digits to the left of the decimal point, Visual Basic inserts four leading zeros. And because 45.6 has one digit to the right of the decimal point, Visual Basic inserts one trailing zero.

This feature is used to display numbers in a column where the decimal points are placed one under the other, as in the following:

```
000324.45
000123.40
123546.67
000004.90
132123.76
```

Formatting Dates and Times

You can use the following statement to display today's date:

```
Print Format$(Now, "m/d/yy")
```

For example, if today's date is July 4, 1995, the preceding statement produces this output:

```
7/4/95
```

The Now function is used in the first argument of the Format$() function to supply the date, and m/d/yy is supplied as the format indicator to format the date to month/day/year. Note that Visual Basic updates Now according to the setting of your PC's date and time.

You can display the date in other formats. For example, use the following statement:

```
Print Format$(Now, "dddd, mmmm dd, yyyy")
```

to produce this output:

```
Sunday, April 11, 1993
```

and use the following statement:

```
Print Format$(Now, "mmmm-yy")
```

385

to produce this output:

```
April-93
```

The Now function can also be used to display the current time. For example, you can use this statement:

```
Print Format$(Now, "h:mm:ss a/p")
```

to produce this output:

```
4:23:00 a
```

The Print Program

The Print program demonstrates how easy it is to send data to the printer with the PrintForm method.

The Visual Implementation of the Print Program

☐ Open a new project, save the form of the project as PRINT.FRM in the C:\VB4PRG\CH10 directory and save the project file as PRINT.VBP in the C:\VB4PRG\CH10 directory.

☐ Build the frmPrint form according to the specifications in Table 10.7.

The complete form should look like the one shown in Figure 10.18.

Table 10.7. The properties table of frmPrint form.

Object	Property	Setting
Form	Name	frmPrint
	BackColor	Make it white
	Caption	The Print Program
	Height	4545
	Left	1080
	Top	1170
	Width	6810
Command Button	Name	cmdExit
	Caption	E&xit
	FontName	System

Object	Property	Setting
	Height	495
	Left	5040
	Top	3480
	Width	1215
CommandButton	**Name**	**cmdPrint**
	Caption	&Print
	FontName	System
	Height	1095
	Left	120
	Top	2880
	Width	1215

Figure 10.18.
The frmPrint form.

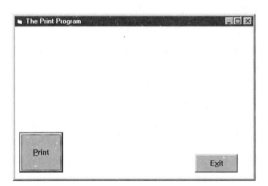

Entering the Code of the Print Program

☐ Enter the following code in the general declarations section of the frmPrint form:

```
' All variables MUST be declared.
Option Explicit
```

☐ Enter the following code in the cmdExit_Click() procedure of the frmPrint form:

```
Private Sub cmdExit_Click()

    End

End Sub
```

☐ Enter the following code in the cmdPrint_Click() procedure of the frmPrint form:

```
Private Sub cmdPrint_Click()

    ' Print.
    Printer.Print "Testing… 1 2 3…Testing"
    Printer.EndDoc

End Sub
```

Executing the Print Program

☐ Make sure your printer is ready to print.

☐ Execute the Print program.

☐ Click the Print button.

The program responds by using the printer to print this text:

```
"Testing… 1 2 3…Testing"
```

How the Print Program Works

The Print program uses the Print method to send data to the printer. The EndDoc method sends the "start printing" command to the printer device.

The Code in the *cmdPrint_Click()* Procedure

The cmdPrint_Click() procedure is executed when you click the Print button:

```
Private Sub cmdPrint_Click()

    ' Print.
    Printer.Print "Testing… 1 2 3…Testing"
    Printer.EndDoc

End Sub
```

The Print method is used with the Printer object. The argument of the Print method, Testing… 1 2 3… Testing, is printed as soon as the EndDoc method is executed.

Enhancing the Print Program

The Print method sends the text that appears as its argument to the printer. Now enhance the Print program so you can print the contents of the frmPrint form:

☐ Replace the cmdPrint_Click() procedure with the following code:

```
Private Sub cmdPrint_Click()

    ' Print the form's contents.
    frmPrint.PrintForm
    Printer.EndDoc

End Sub
```

☐ Save the project.

Executing the Enhanced Version of the Print Program

☐ Execute the enhanced version of the Print program.

☐ Click the Print button.

The program responds by printing the form's contents.

☐ Click the Exit button to terminate the program.

The Code in the Enhanced Version of the *cmdPrint_Click()* Procedure

The PrintForm method sends to the printer the content of the form, pixel by pixel:

```
frmPrint.PrintForm
```

The last thing that this procedure does is execute the EndDoc method, causing the printer to print the data it received.

DO	DON'T

DO use the PrintForm method to send the content of the form to the printer. For example, to send the contents of the frmMyForm to the printer, use the following statement:

```
frmMyForm.PrintForm
```

In previous versions of Visual Basic, the AutoDraw property of the form you want to print must be set to True for the PrintForm method to work properly.

10

Printing Several Pages

You can print several pages using the NewPage property. Visual Basic keeps track of the number of pages printed by updating the Page property. Use the following steps to print several pages:

☐ Replace the code in the cmdPrint_Click() procedure with the following code:

```
Private Sub cmdPrint_Click()

    Printer.Print "This is page number " + Str(Printer.Page)
    Printer.NewPage
    Printer.Print "This is page number " + Str(Printer.Page)
    Printer.EndDoc

End Sub
```

☐ Execute the Print program.

☐ Click the Print button.

The program responds by printing two pages. The first page is printed with This is page number 1 *and the second page is printed with* This is page number 2.

☐ Click the Exit button to terminate the program.

The cmdPrint_Click() procedure prints the string:

This is page number + Printer.Page

The Page property contains the current page number. Because this is the first printed page, Visual Basic automatically updates this property with 1.

The procedure then declares a new page by using the NewPage method:

Printer.NewPage

and sends this string to the printer:

This is page number + Printer.Page

Because the value of the Page property is currently 2, the printer prints the text:

This is page number 2

Printing Images, Picture Controls, and Graphics

To print pictures, you can place bitmaps in images and picture controls and then print the form with the PrintForm method. In other words, whatever is placed inside the form will be sent to the printer.

Printing with Better Quality

The Print program illustrates how easy it is to send data to the printer with the Print method (text) and the PrintForm method (contents of the form). Your monitor's resolution determines the best resolution that the hard copy produced by PrintForm can have. To get a better resolution, your program can use the PSet, Line, and Circle methods described below.

Generally, you draw in the Printer object just as you draw in a form. Therefore, you can set the CurrentX and CurrentY properties of the Printer object, as in this statement:

```
Printer.CurrentX = 0
Printer.CurrentY = 0
```

and you can use properties such as the following:

```
Printer.ScaleLeft
Printer.ScaleTop
Printer.Width
Printer.Height
```

To help you position text at specific locations, your program can use the TextHeight and TextWidth properties.

☐ Replace the code in the cmdPrint_Click() procedure with the following code:

```
Private Sub cmdPrint_Click()

    Printer.DrawWidth = 4
    Printer.Line (1000, 1000)-Step(1000, 1000)
    Printer.Circle (3000, 3000), 1000
    Printer.EndDoc

End Sub
```

The procedure sets the DrawWidth property of the printer to 4, draws a line and a circle, and then executes the EndDoc method. The output is shown in Figure 10.19.

As you can see, the preceding code is no different from the code that draws in a form or a picture control.

Figure 10.19.
Drawing a line and a circle with the Printer object.

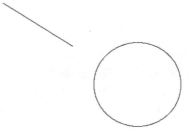

Summary

In this chapter you have learned how to set text to the desired font by changing the FontName, FontSize, FontBold, FontItalic, FontStrike, FontUnderline, and FontTransparent properties.

You have also learned how to extract the Screen and Printer fonts with the Fonts property, how to extract the number of available fonts with the FontCount property, and how to use the TextWidth and TextHeight properties and the Tab() function.

This chapter discusses how to send data (text and graphics) to the printer using two techniques:

1. The PrintForm method, which sends the contents of the form, pixel by pixel, to the printer.

2. The Print and graphics methods, such as the following:

```
Printer.Print "Abc"
Printer.Line -(1000.1000)
Circle (400,500),800
Printer.EndDoc
```

Q&A

Q I want to write a program that has the WYSIWYG capability. How can I make sure that the user chooses only these screen fonts that have corresponding printer fonts?

A The Fonts program illustrates how you can extract the screen and printer fonts using the Fonts property. To achieve WYSIWYG, you must make sure that the screen fonts you use are available for the printer. This is easily accomplished by building a list that contains the screen fonts using the Fonts property of the screen. Then build another list that contains the printer fonts by using the Fonts property of the printer. Now that you have the two lists, you can create a third list that contains only the fonts that appear in both lists. Your program should let the user choose a font from the third list only.

Quiz

1. When you set the FontTransparent property to True and then display text in a form with the Print method, which of the following happens?

    a. The text will be drawn in white.

    b. The text will not be visible.

    c. The text is displayed with the same background as the form.

2. The FontCount property is used to do which of the following?

   a. Assign a counting number to the fonts.
   b. There's no such thing.
   c. Extract the number of available fonts.

3. The Fonts property is used to do which of the following?

   a. Extract the names of available fonts.
   b. Assign a new font.
   c. Remove a font.

4. WYSIWYG means having the capability to do which of the following?

   a. Speak a foreign language.
   b. Print a hard copy that is an exact replica of the screen.
   c. No meaning, just rubbish.

5. What does the TextHeight property return?

6. What does the TextWidth property return?

7. Which of the following should you use to print the contents of a form?

   a. The Print screen key.
   b. The `Print` method.
   c. The `PrintForm` method.

Exercise

Write a program that asks the user to enter his/her date of birth. The program should respond by displaying the day of the week when this happy event occurred.

Quiz Answers

1. c

2. c

3. a

4. b

5. The TextHeight property returns the height of the characters specified in the argument.

6. The TextWidth property returns the width of the characters specified in the argument.

7. c

Exercise Answer

One possible solution is the following:

☐ Build a form with a command button called Enter Birthday and a command button called Find Day Of Week.

The code in the cmdEnterBirthday_Click() should display an input box that asks the user to enter the data. For example, the following statement can be used:

```
UserDate = InputBox("Enter date")
```

The code in the cmdFindDayOfWeek should include this statement:

```
Print "Day of Week:", Format$(UserDate, "dddd")
```

Interfacing with Windows

The programs you write with Visual Basic are Windows programs, so you are entitled to use the standard Windows features. In this chapter you'll learn to use two of them: the Clipboard interface and idle loops.

The Clipboard Object

The Visual Basic programs that you write can use the Windows Clipboard. The Clipboard is used to transfer data, which can be text or pictures.

The Clip Program

You'll now write a program called Clip, which enables you to type text in a text box and perform the standard Windows editing manipulations. The program has a standard Edit menu that you can use to copy, cut, and paste text.

The Visual Implementation of the Clip Program

☐ Start a new project.

☐ Save the form of the project as CLIP.FRM in the C:\VB4PRG\CH11 directory and save the project file as CLIP.VBP in the C:\VB4PRG\CH11 directory.

☐ Build the form of the Clip program according to the specifications in Table 11.1 and Table 11.2.

The completed form should look like the one shown in Figure 11.1.

Table 11.1. The properties table of the Clip program.

Object	Property	Setting
Form	**Name**	**frmClip**
	Caption	The Clip Program
	Height	4830
	Left	1080
	Top	1170
	Width	6810

Object	Property	Setting
Text Box	**Name**	**txtUserArea**
	Height	2775
	Left	0
	MultiLine	-1-True
	ScrollBars	3-Both
	Text	(empty)
	Top	0
	Width	4215
Menu	**(See Table 11.2.)**	**(See Table 11.2.)**

Table 11.2. The menu table of the Clip program.

Caption	Name	Shortcut
&File	mnuFile	None
...E&xit	mnuExit	None
&Edit	mnuEdit	None
...&Copy	mnuCopy	Ctrl+C
...Cu&t	mnuCut	Ctrl+X
...&Paste	mnuPaste	Ctrl+V

Figure 11.1.
The frmClip form.

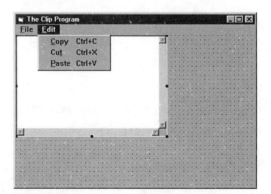

Entering the Code of the Clip Program

☐ Enter the following code in the general declarations section of the frmClip form:

```
' All variables MUST be declared.
Option Explicit
```

☐ Enter the following code in the Form_Resize() procedure:

```
Private Sub Form_Resize()

    ' Make the text box cover the entire form area.
    txtUserArea.Width = frmClip.ScaleWidth
    txtUserArea.Height = frmClip.ScaleHeight

End Sub
```

☐ Enter the following code in the mnuCopy_Click() procedure:

```
Private Sub mnuCopy_Click()

    ' Clear the clipboard.
    Clipboard.Clear
    ' Transfer to the clipboard the currently
    ' selected text of the text box.
    Clipboard.SetText txtUserArea.SelText

End Sub
```

☐ Enter the following code in the mnuCut_Click() procedure:

```
Private Sub mnuCut_Click()

    ' Clear the clipboard.
    Clipboard.Clear
    ' Transfer to the clipboard the currently
    ' selected text of the text box.
    Clipboard.SetText txtUserArea.SelText
    ' Replace the currently selected text of the
    ' text box with null.
    txtUserArea.SelText = ""

End Sub
```

☐ Enter the following code in the mnuPaste_Click() procedure:

```
Private Sub mnuPaste_Click()

    ' Replace the currently selected area of the
    ' text box with the content of the clipboard.
    ' If nothing is selected in the text box,
    ' transfer the text of the clipboard to the text
    ' box at the current location of the cursor.
    txtUserArea.SelText = Clipboard.GetText()

End Sub
```

Enter the following code in the `mnuExit_Click()` procedure:

```
Private Sub mnuExit_Click()

    End

End Sub
```

Executing the Clip Program

☐ Execute the Clip program and note its many features (even though you wrote only a small amount of code).

☐ Experiment with the copy, cut, and paste operations of the program. Try to copy text from one part of the text box to another. Try to copy text to and from another Windows program. For example, try to copy text to and from Word for Windows or Write, a word processing program that is shipped with Windows.

☐ Select Exit from the File menu to terminate the program.

How the Clip Program Works

The Clip program uses the `Form_Resize()` procedure to fill the entire form area with the text box and `mnuCopy_Click()`, `mnuCut_Clip()`, and `mnuPaste_Click()` to perform standard editing manipulations.

The Code in the *Form_Resize()* Procedure

The `Form_Resize()` procedure is automatically executed whenever the form pops up and whenever the size of the form changes.

Throughout the program, the text box should fill the entire area of the form. Therefore, this is a good place to put the code that causes the text box to cover the entire area of the form. You do this by changing the Width and Height properties of the text box to the ScaleWidth and ScaleHeight properties of the form:

```
Private Sub Form_Resize()

    ' Make the text box cover the entire form area.
    txtUserArea.Width = frmClip.ScaleWidth
    txtUserArea.Height = frmClip.ScaleHeight

End Sub
```

The Code in the *mnuCopy_Click()* Procedure

The `mnuCopy_Click()` procedure is executed whenever you select Copy from the Edit menu:

```
Private Sub mnuCopy_Click()

    ' Clear the clipboard.
    Clipboard.Clear
    ' Transfer to the clipboard the currently
    ' selected text of the text box.
    Clipboard.SetText txtUserArea.SelText

End Sub
```

Copy means copy the highlighted text of the text box into the Clipboard.

The first statement in this procedure clears the Clipboard:

```
Clipboard.Clear
```

Then the selected area in the text box is copied to the Clipboard:

```
Clipboard.SetText txtUserArea.SelText
```

DO	DON'T

DO use the `Clear` method to clear the Clipboard:
```
Clipboard.Clear
```
DO copy selected text from a text box to the Clipboard by using the following:
```
Clipboard.SetText Name of text box.SelText
```
For example, to copy the highlighted (selected) text of the txtUserArea text box to the Clipboard, use the following:
```
Clipboard.SetText txtUserArea.SelText
```

The Code in the *mnuCutClick()* Procedure

The `mnuCut_Click()` procedure is executed whenever you select Cut from the Edit menu:

```
Private Sub mnuCut_Click()

    ' Clear the clipboard.
    Clipboard.Clear
    ' Transfer to the clipboard the currently
    ' selected text of the text box.
    Clipboard.SetText txtUserArea.SelText
```

```
' Replace the currently selected text of the
' text box with null.
txtUserArea.SelText = ""
```

End Sub

Cut means copy the highlighted text to the Clipboard and delete the highlighted text.

The first statement in this procedure clears the Clipboard:

```
Clipboard.Clear
```

Then the highlighted text of the text box is copied to the Clipboard:

```
Clipboard.SetText txtUserArea.SelText
```

The last thing the procedure does is delete the currently highlighted text in the text box:

```
txtUserArea.SelText = ""
```

The Code in the *mnuPaste_Click()* Procedure

The mnuPaste_Click() procedure is executed whenever you select Paste from the Edit menu:

Private Sub mnuPaste_Click()

```
    ' Replace the currently selected area of the
    ' text box with the content of the clipboard.
    ' If nothing is selected in the text box,
    ' transfer the text of the clipboard to the text
    ' box at the current location of the cursor.
    txtUserArea.SelText = Clipboard.GetText()
```

End Sub

Paste means replace the highlighted area of the text box with the contents of the Clipboard. If the text box doesn't have highlighted text in it, the contents of the Clipboard are inserted in the text box at the current cursor location. This is accomplished with the following statement:

```
txtUserArea.SelText = Clipboard.GetText()
```

DO	**DON'T**

DO use the following statement to paste the contents of the Clipboard to a text box:
```
Name of text box.SelText = Clipboard.GetText()
```

For example, to paste the contents of the Clipboard to a text box called txtUserArea, use the following:
```
txtUserArea.SelText = Clipboard.GetText()
```

The SelLength Property

The SelLength property is defined as a long variable, and it contains the number of characters that are currently highlighted. Although the Clip program doesn't use this property, you might find a use for it in your future Visual Basic projects.

For example, to determine the number of characters that are currently selected in txtMyTextBox, use the following statement:

```
NumberOfCharacters = txtMyTextBox.SelLength
```

Transferring Pictures to and from the Clipboard: The AnyData Program

The Clip program demonstrates how to transfer text between the Clipboard and a text box. The Clipboard is also capable of accepting pictures from picture holder controls. The AnyData program illustrates this capability.

The Visual Implementation of the AnyData Program

☐ Start a new project.

☐ Save the form of the project as ANYDATA.FRM in the C:\VB4PRG\CH11 directory, and save the project file as ANYDATA.VBP in the C:\VB4PRG\CH11 directory.

☐ Build the form according to the specifications in Table 11.3 and Table 11.4.

The completed form should look like the one shown in Figure 11.2.

Table 11.3. The properties table of the AnyData program.

Object	Property	Setting
Form	**Name**	**frmAnyData**
	Caption	The AnyData Program
	Height	4830
	Left	1080
	Top	1170
	Width	6810

Object	Property	Setting
Picture Box	**Name**	**picMyPicture**
	Height	3135
	Left	120
	Tag	The picMyPicture
	Top	720
	Width	2775
List Box	**Name**	**lstList**
	Height	1035
	Left	3720
	Tag	The lstList
	Top	1200
	Width	1215
Combo Box	**Name**	**cboList**
	Height	315
	Left	5160
	Tag	The cboList
	Top	1320
	Width	1215
Text Box	**Name**	**txtUserArea**
	Height	855
	Left	3840
	MultiLine	-1-True
	ScrollBars	3-Both
	Tag	The txtUserArea
	Text	(empty)
	Top	3000
	Width	2655
Menu	**(See Table 11.4.)**	**(See Table 11.4.)**

Table 11.4. The menu table of the AnyData program.

Caption	Name	Shortcut
…E&xit	mnuExit	
&Edit	mnuEdit	
…&Copy	mnuCopy	Ctrl+C
…Cu&t	mnuCut	Ctrl+X
…&Paste	mnuPaste	Ctrl+V

Figure 11.2.
The frmAnyData form.

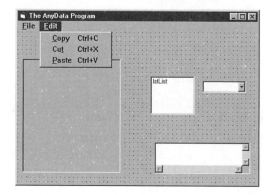

Entering the Code of the AnyData Program

☐ Enter the following code in the general declarations section of the frmAnyData form:

```
' All variables must be declared.
Option Explicit
```

☐ Enter the following code in the Form_Load() procedure:

```
Private Sub Form_Load()

    ' Fill three items inside the combo box.
    cboList.AddItem "Clock"
    cboList.AddItem "Cup"
    cboList.AddItem "Bell"

    ' Fill three items inside the list control.
    lstList.AddItem "One"
    lstList.AddItem "Two"
    lstList.AddItem "Three"

End Sub
```

☐ Enter the following code in the picMyPicture_GotFocus() procedure:

```
Private Sub picMyPicture_GotFocus()

    ' Change the BorderStyle so that user will be
    ' able to tell that the picture control got the
    ' focus (i.e., selected).
    picMyPicture.BorderStyle = 1

End Sub
```

☐ Enter the following code in the picMyPicture_LostFocus() procedure:

```
Private Sub picMyPicture_LostFocus()

    ' Change the BorderStyle so that user will be
    ' able to tell that the picture control lost the
    ' focus (i.e., not selected).
    picMyPicture.BorderStyle = 0

End Sub
```

☐ Enter the following code in the mnuCopy_Click() procedure:

```
Private Sub mnuCopy_Click()

    ' Clear the clipboard.
    Clipboard.Clear
    ' Find which is the currently active control, and
    ' copy its highlighted content to the clipboard.
    If TypeOf Screen.ActiveControl Is TextBox Then
        Clipboard.SetText Screen.ActiveControl.SelText
    ElseIf TypeOf Screen.ActiveControl Is ComboBox Then
        Clipboard.SetText Screen.ActiveControl.Text
    ElseIf TypeOf Screen.ActiveControl Is PictureBox Then
        Clipboard.SetData Screen.ActiveControl.Picture
    ElseIf TypeOf Screen.ActiveControl Is ListBox Then
        Clipboard.SetText Screen.ActiveControl.Text
    Else
        ' Do nothing
    End If

End Sub
```

☐ Enter the following code in the mnuCut_Click() procedure:

```
Private Sub mnuCut_Click()

    'Execute the mnuCopy_Click() procedure
    mnuCopy_Click
    ' Find which is the currently highlighted control,
    ' and remove its highlighted content.
    If TypeOf Screen.ActiveControl Is TextBox Then
        Screen.ActiveControl.SelText = ""
    ElseIf TypeOf Screen.ActiveControl Is ComboBox Then
        Screen.ActiveControl.Text = ""
```

```
    ElseIf TypeOf Screen.ActiveControl Is PictureBox Then
        Screen.ActiveControl.Picture = LoadPicture()
    ElseIf TypeOf Screen.ActiveControl Is ListBox Then
        If Screen.ActiveControl.ListIndex >= 0 Then
            Screen.ActiveControl.RemoveItem _
                    Screen.ActiveControl.ListIndex
        End If
    Else
        ' Do nothing
    End If

End Sub
```

☐ Enter the following code in the mnuPaste_Click() procedure:

```
Private Sub mnuPaste_Click()

    ' Find which is the currently active control and
    ' paste the content of the clipboard to it.
    If TypeOf Screen.ActiveControl Is TextBox Then
        Screen.ActiveControl.SelText = Clipboard.GetText()
    ElseIf TypeOf Screen.ActiveControl Is ComboBox Then
        Screen.ActiveControl.Text = Clipboard.GetText()
    ElseIf TypeOf Screen.ActiveControl Is PictureBox Then
        Screen.ActiveControl.Picture = Clipboard.GetData()
    ElseIf TypeOf Screen.ActiveControl Is ListBox Then
        Screen.ActiveControl.AddItem Clipboard.GetText()
    Else
        ' Do nothing
    End If

End Sub
```

☐ Enter the following code in the mnuExit_Click() procedure:

```
Private Sub mnuExit_Click()

    End

End Sub
```

Executing the AnyData Program

☐ Execute the AnyData program.

The AnyData program lets you copy, cut, and paste data from and to the Clipboard. The data can be either text or pictures.

Use the following steps to copy a picture from Paintbrush to the picture box of the AnyData program:

☐ Start Paintbrush while AnyData is still running.

☐ Draw something in Paintbrush.

☐ Copy a portion of your drawing to the Clipboard by selecting it and then choosing Copy from the Paintbrush Edit menu. (For example, in Figure 11.3, the portion of the picture that includes the man's head was copied to the Clipboard.)

☐ Switch to the AnyData program.

☐ Make the picMyPicture picture control the active control by clicking in the picture. You can tell that the picture box is selected by observing its borders. If it has a border, it is selected.

☐ Select Paste from the Edit menu.

The AnyData program responds by transferring the picture in the Clipboard into picMyPicture. (See Figure 11.4.)

Figure 11.3.
Using Paintbrush to draw a picture that will be copied to the AnyData program.

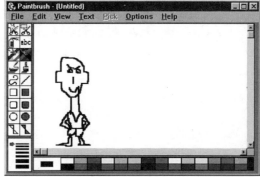

Figure 11.4.
Copying a picture to the AnyData program.

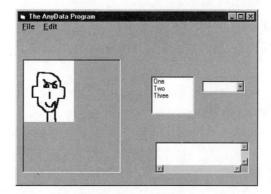

☐ The AnyData program also lets you copy, cut, and paste text to and from the text box, list box, and combo box controls of the program. Experiment with these controls for a while. You can't paste pictures into the text box, list box, or combo box, and you can't paste text into the picture box.

Before pasting data into an object, you must select the object by clicking it. You can tell which object is selected as follows:

- When a text box is selected, Visual Basic places a blinking cursor in it.
- When a combo box is selected, Visual Basic places a blinking cursor on the currently selected item.
- When a list box is selected, Visual Basic places a dashed rectangle around the selected item in the list box.

How the AnyData Program Works

The AnyData program uses the `mnuCopy_Click()`, `mnuCut_Click()`, and `mnuPaste_Click()` procedures to transfer text and pictures to or from the Clipboard.

The Code in the *Form_Load()* Procedure

The `Form_Load()` procedure is automatically executed when you start the program:

```
Private Sub Form_Load()

    ' Fill three items inside the combo box.
    cboList.AddItem "Clock"
    cboList.AddItem "Cup"
    cboList.AddItem "Bell"

    ' Fill three items inside the list control.
    lstList.AddItem "One"
    lstList.AddItem "Two"
    lstList.AddItem "Three"

End Sub
```

The code in this procedure fills three items in the combo box and three items in the list box.

The Code in the *picMyPicture_GotFocus()* Procedure

The `picMyPicture_GotFocus()` procedure is executed whenever the picture box gets the focus (that is, whenever you select the picture):

```
Private Sub picMyPicture_GotFocus()

    ' Change the BorderStyle so that user will be
    ' able to tell that the picture control got the
    ' focus (i.e., selected).
    picMyPicture.BorderStyle = 1

End Sub
```

When you select the picture box, Visual Basic doesn't automatically give you any visible indication that the picture box has been selected, as it does for the text box, combo box, and list box. The code you typed in the picMyPicture_GotFocus() procedure changes the BorderStyle property of the picture box so you can tell that the picture box is selected. Setting the BorderStyle property of the picture box to 1 places a border around the picture control.

The Code in the *picMyPicture_LostFocus()* Procedure

The picMyPicture_LostFocus() procedure is executed whenever the picture box is not selected (that is, loses the focus):

```
Private Sub picMyPicture_LostFocus()

    ' Change the BorderStyle so that user will be
    ' able to tell that the picture control lost the
    ' focus (i.e., not selected).
    picMyPicture.BorderStyle = 0

End Sub
```

The code in this procedure sets the BorderStyle property to 0, which removes the border around the picture control; this shows you that the picture box is not selected.

The Code in the *mnuCopy_Click()* Procedure

The mnuCopy_Click() procedure is executed whenever you select Copy from the Edit menu. The code in this procedure clears the Clipboard and copies the highlighted contents of the control to the Clipboard:

```
Private Sub mnuCopy_Click()

    ' Clear the clipboard.
    Clipboard.Clear
    ' Find which is the currently active control, and
    ' copy its highlighted content to the clipboard.
    If TypeOf Screen.ActiveControl Is TextBox Then
        Clipboard.SetText Screen.ActiveControl.SelText
    ElseIf TypeOf Screen.ActiveControl Is ComboBox Then
        Clipboard.SetText Screen.ActiveControl.Text
    ElseIf TypeOf Screen.ActiveControl Is PictureBox Then
        Clipboard.SetData Screen.ActiveControl.Picture
    ElseIf TypeOf Screen.ActiveControl Is ListBox Then
        Clipboard.SetText Screen.ActiveControl.Text
    Else
        ' Do nothing
    End If

End Sub
```

The Clipboard is cleared with the following statement:

```
' Clear the clipboard.
Clipboard.Clear
```

To copy the contents of the control to the Clipboard, you must first decide which control is currently active. You do this with a series of `If TypeOf` statements.

The first `If TypeOf` statement checks whether the currently active control is the text box. If this is the case, the contents of the highlighted text in the text box are copied to the Clipboard:

```
Clipboard.SetText Screen.ActiveControl.SelText
```

If the currently active control is the combo box, the highlighted text in the combo box is copied to the Clipboard:

```
Clipboard.SetText Screen.ActiveControl.Text
```

If the currently active control is the picture box, the picture in the picture box is copied to the Clipboard:

```
Clipboard.SetData Screen.ActiveControl.Picture
```

Finally, if the currently active control is the list box, the highlighted text in the list box is copied to the Clipboard:

```
Clipboard.SetText Screen.ActiveControl.Text
```

> **Note:** The value `Screen.ActiveControl` represents the currently active control. Visual Basic automatically updates this variable for you. As you can see, `Screen.ActiveControl` is useful when you need to perform operations on the currently active control.

The Code in the *mnuCut_Click()* Procedure

The `mnuCut_Click()` procedure is executed whenever you select Cut from the Edit menu:

```
Private Sub mnuCut_Click()

    'Execute the mnuCopy_Click() procedure
    mnuCopy_Click
    ' Find which is the currently highlighted control,
    ' and remove its highlighted content.
    If TypeOf Screen.ActiveControl Is TextBox Then
        Screen.ActiveControl.SelText = ""
    ElseIf TypeOf Screen.ActiveControl Is ComboBox Then
        Screen.ActiveControl.Text = ""
```

```
    ElseIf TypeOf Screen.ActiveControl Is PictureBox Then
       Screen.ActiveControl.Picture = LoadPicture()
    ElseIf TypeOf Screen.ActiveControl Is ListBox Then
       If Screen.ActiveControl.ListIndex >= 0 Then
          Screen.ActiveControl.RemoveItem _
                Screen.ActiveControl.ListIndex
       End If
    Else
       ' Do nothing
    End If

End Sub
```

Cut is defined as copying the selected data to the Clipboard and deleting the data that was copied. Therefore, the first statement in this procedure executes the `mnuCopy_Click()` procedure:

```
'Execute the mnuCopy_Click() procedure
mnuCopy_Click
```

To delete the data, a series of `If TypeOf` statements is executed. Each `If TypeOf` statement determines the currently active control and clears the data that was copied.

If the currently active control is the text box, the text copied from this control is cleared with the following statement:

```
Screen.ActiveControl.SelText = ""
```

Similarly, the text copied from the combo box is cleared with the following statement:

```
Screen.ActiveControl.Text = ""
```

To clear the picture box, the `LoadPicture()` function is used:

```
Screen.ActiveControl.Picture = LoadPicture()
```

The `LoadPicture()` loads a picture into a picture box. The argument of `LoadPicture()` specifies which picture file to load. Because the preceding statement did not specify the name of the picture file to be loaded, the `LoadPicture()` function clears the current picture from the picture box, which is exactly what you want it to do.

If the currently active control is the list box, the copied text (which is the highlighted item in the list) is cleared with the `RemoveItem` statement:

```
ElseIf TypeOf Screen.ActiveControl Is ListBox Then
If Screen.ActiveControl.ListIndex >= 0 Then
Screen.ActiveControl.RemoveItem _
     Screen.ActiveControl.ListIndex
End If
```

Before removing the item, the code checks that `ListIndex` is greater or equal to 0. `ListIndex` is the currently selected item in the list, and you want to make sure that there is currently a selected item in the list box (that is, when `ListIndex` is equal to –1, no item is currently selected in the list box).

The Code in the *mnuPaste_Click()* Procedure

The mnuPaste_Click() procedure is executed whenever you select Paste from the Edit menu:

```
Private Sub mnuPaste_Click()

    ' Find which is the currently active control and
    ' paste the content of the clipboard to it.
    If TypeOf Screen.ActiveControl Is TextBox Then
        Screen.ActiveControl.SelText = Clipboard.GetText()
    ElseIf TypeOf Screen.ActiveControl Is ComboBox Then
        Screen.ActiveControl.Text = Clipboard.GetText()
    ElseIf TypeOf Screen.ActiveControl Is PictureBox Then
        Screen.ActiveControl.Picture = Clipboard.GetData()
    ElseIf TypeOf Screen.ActiveControl Is ListBox Then
        Screen.ActiveControl.AddItem Clipboard.GetText()
    Else
        ' Do nothing
    End If

End Sub
```

Like the mnuCopy_Click() and mnuCut_Click() procedures, this procedure determines the currently active control with a series of If TypeOf statements.

If the currently active control is the text box, the text of the Clipboard is copied into the text box:

```
Screen.ActiveControl.SelText = Clipboard.GetText()
```

If the currently active control is the combo box, the text of the Clipboard is copied into the combo box:

```
Screen.ActiveControl.Text = Clipboard.GetText()
```

If the currently active control is the picture box, the picture in the Clipboard is copied to the picture box using GetData():

```
Screen.ActiveControl.Picture = Clipboard.GetData()
```

Finally, if the currently active control is the list box, the text in the Clipboard is added as a new item to the list:

```
Screen.ActiveControl.AddItem Clipboard.GetText()
```

Using *GetFormat()* to Determine the Type of Data in the Clipboard

As demonstrated, the Clipboard is capable of holding text as well as pictures. To examine what type of data the Clipboard currently holds, you can use GetFormat().

For example, the following statement determines whether the data in the Clipboard is text:

```
If Clipboard.GetFormat(vbCFText) Then
...........................................
... GetFormat() returned True, so indeed ...
... the clipboard holds text.           ...
...........................................
End If
```

If the Clipboard currently holds text, `GetFormat(vbCFText)` returns True.

To decide whether the Clipboard currently holds a bitmap, use the following:

```
If Clipboard.GetFormat(vbCFBitmap) Then
...........................................
... GetFormat() returned True, so indeed ...
... the clipboard holds bit map.        ...
...........................................
End If
```

`GetFormat(vbCFBitmap)` returns True if the Clipboard currently holds a bitmap.

Idle Time

During the execution of your Visual Basic program, there are many times when no code of your program is executed. These periods of time are called *idle time*. For example, suppose you write a program, called the Beep program, that has a Beep button in it. When you click this button, the program beeps 100 times. Until you click the button, your program is sitting idle, not executing any of your code. Once you click the button, the corresponding procedure is executed. During the execution of this procedure, your program is not in idle time any more. Upon completing the execution of the event procedure, your program is again in idle time, waiting for you to press the Beep button again (or press a different button or select a menu item).

During idle times, you are able to switch to other Windows programs. For example, in the Beep program discussed, when the program is in idle time, you can switch to another Windows program. But if you click the beep button, you cannot switch to other Windows programs while the program is beeping 100 times.

The Count Program

Now you'll write the Count program, which counts numbers from 1 to 999.

The Visual Implementation of the Count Program

☐ Start a new project.

☐ Save the form of the project as COUNT.FRM in the C:\VB4PRG\CH11 directory and save the project as COUNT.VBP in the C:\VB4PRG\CH11 directory.

☐ Build the form of the Count program according to the specifications in Table 11.5.

The completed form should look like the one shown in Figure 11.5.

Table 11.5. The properties table of the Count program.

Object	Property	Setting
Form	**Name**	**frmCount**
	Caption	The Count Program
	Height	4545
	Left	1080
	Top	1170
	Width	3120
Command Button	**Name**	**cmdExit**
	Caption	E&xit
	FontName	System
	FontSize	10
	Height	855
	Left	240
	Top	3240
	Width	2655
Command Button	**Name**	**cmdPause**
	Caption	&Pause
	FontName	System
	FontSize	10
	Height	975
	Left	1680
	Top	2160
	Width	1215

Object	Property	Setting
Command Button	**Name**	**cmdStart**
	Caption	&Start
	FontName	System
	FontSize	10
	Height	975
	Left	240
	Top	2160
	Width	1215
Label	**Name**	**lblResult**
	Alignment	2-Center
	BorderStyle	1-Fixed Single
	Height	1335
	Left	360
	Top	360
	Width	2415

Figure 11.5.
The frmCount form.

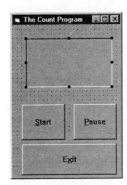

Entering the Code of the Count Program

☐ Enter the following code in the general declarations section of the frmCount form:

```
' All variables MUST be declared.
Option Explicit
```

☐ Enter the following code in the cmdExit_Click() procedure:

```
Private Sub cmdExit_Click()

    End

End Sub
```

☐ Enter the following code in the cmdStart_Click() procedure:

```
Private Sub cmdStart_Click()

    Dim Counter As Integer
    Counter = 1
    ' Count from 1 to 999
    Do While Counter < 1000
        lblResult.Caption = Str$(Counter)
        Counter = Counter + 1
    Loop

End Sub
```

Note: At this point, you are not instructed to attach any code to the cmdPause_Click() procedure.

Executing the Count Program

☐ Execute the Count program.

☐ Click the Start button.

The program seems to do nothing for a while, and then the number 999 is displayed. Depending on how fast your PC is, it may take several seconds until it displays the number 999.

By reading the code in the cmdStart_Click() procedure, you might expect to see the program display all the numbers from 1 to 999 during the counting. To understand why the program doesn't do this, look at the statements that are supposed to display the numbers:

```
Private Sub cmdStart_Click()

    Dim Counter As Integer
    Counter = 1
    ' Count from 1 to 999
    Do While Counter < 1000
        lblResult.Caption = Str$(Counter)
        Counter = Counter + 1
    Loop

End Sub
```

This is the statement responsible for changing the caption of the label:

```
lblResult.Caption = Str$(Counter)
```

However, Visual Basic is able to refresh the screen (repaint the screen) only during idle time (that is, after the procedure is completed and the program returns to idle time). This is why the label doesn't display the numbers while counting is in progress.

Keep in mind that clicking the Exit button during the counting does not terminate the program because your program can recognize clicking only during idle times. Once the counting is done, your program returns to idle time and responds to the clicking on the Exit button.

Note: Your PC might be so fast that to appreciate the previous discussion, you'll have to replace the statement

```
Do While Counter < 1000
```

in the `cmdStart_Click()` procedure with the statement

```
Do While Counter < 10000
```

That is, a fast computer will be able to execute the `Do While` loop 1000 times in a very short time, and you will not be able to see that the loop was executed.

Modifying the Count Program

Use the following steps to modify the Count program so the label displays each number from 1 to 999 during the counting:

☐ Add the following statement in the `cmdStart_Click()` procedure:

```
lblResult.Refresh
```

Now the `cmdStart_Click()` procedure looks like this:

```
Private Sub cmdStart_Click()

Dim Counter As Integer

Counter = 1
' Count from 1 to 999
Do While Counter < 1000
   lblResult.Caption = Str$(Counter)

   lblResult.Refresh

   Counter = Counter + 1
Loop

End Sub
```

The Refresh method causes an immediate refreshing of the screen.

DO	DON'T

DO use the Refresh method to cause immediate paint refreshing of an object:

`object.Refresh`

For example, to refresh the lblResult object, use the following statement:

`lblResult.Refresh`

Executing the Modified Count Program

☐ Execute the modified version of the Count program.

Now the label displays each number from 1 to 999 during the counting. Notice that clicking the Exit button during the counting still does not terminate the program. Why? During the execution of the cmdStart_Click() *procedure, your program is not in idle time.*

Enhancing the Count Program

Now enhance the Count program so that it will respond to mouse clicking during the counting. You will need to write a procedure called Main(), which will be the first procedure executed when you start the program.

Instruct Visual Basic to execute the Main() procedure on startup as follows:

☐ Select Options from the Tools menu.

Visual Basic responds by displaying the Options dialog box.

☐ Click the Project tab.

Currently, the Startup Form field is set to frmCount. However, you want the Main() procedure to be the first procedure executed when you start the Count program. Change the Startup Form field to Main() as follows:

☐ Set the Startup Form field of the Project Options dialog box to Sub Main and then click the OK button. (See Figure 11.6.)

When you start the Count program, the first procedure that will be executed is Main().

Figure 11.6.
*Setting the Startup Form
field to Sub Main.*

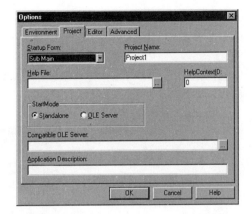

Now write the `Main()` procedure. Visual Basic requires `Main()` to be in a separate module (that is, not in the frmCount form). Therefore, add a new module to the project:

☐ Select Module from the Insert menu.

*Visual Basic responds by adding a new module to the project window. The default name of
the newly added module is Module1.BAS. (Examine the project window by selecting
Project from the View menu.)*

Now save the newly added module as COUNTM.BAS:

☐ Make sure that Module1.BAS is highlighted in the project window and select Save File
As from the File menu.

Visual Basic responds by displaying the Save File As dialog box.

☐ Save the newly added module file as COUNTM.BAS in the C:\VB4PRG\CH11
directory.

Your project window should now contain the COUNT.FRM and COUNTM.BAS files.

Now add a procedure called `Main()` in the module COUNTM.BAS:

☐ Make sure COUNTM.BAS is highlighted in the project window.

☐ Click the View Code button in the project window (because you are about to add a
procedure in the code module COUNTM.BAS).

☐ Select Procedure from the Insert menu.

Visual Basic responds by displaying the Insert Procedure dialog box.

☐ Type Main in the Name field of the New Procedure dialog box, make sure the Type is set to Sub and that the Scope is set to Public (see Figure 11.7), and finally click the OK button.

Visual Basic responds by adding the Main() procedure in the COUNTM.BAS module. The Main() procedure is shown in Figure 11.8.

Figure 11.7.

Adding the Main() proce-dure to the COUNTM.BAS module.

Figure 11.8.

The Main() procedure.

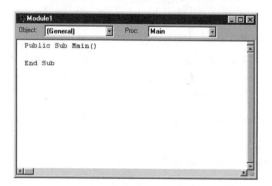

☐ Add the following code in the general declarations section of the COUNTM.BAS module:

```
'  All variables MUST be declared.
Option Explicit
' Declare a global variable so that it is visible in
' all the procedures of all the modules and forms.
Global ggFlag As Integer
```

☐ Add the following code in the Main() procedure of the COUNTM.BAS module:

```
Public Sub Main()

    Dim Counter As Integer

    ' Show the form.
    frmCount.Show
```

```
' Count from 1 to 999, then start counting
' all over again.
Do While DoEvents()
    If ggFlag = 1 Then
        Counter = Counter + 1
        frmCount.lblResult.Caption = Str$(Counter)
        If Counter = 999 Then
            Counter = 1
        End If
    End If
Loop
```

End Sub

☐ Add the following code in the general declarations section of the frmCount form:

```
' All variables MUST be declared.
Option Explicit
```

☐ Add the following code in the cmdPause_Click() procedure of the frmCount form by selecting Project from the View menu, selecting the frmCount form in the project window, clicking the View Form button, and finally double-clicking the Pause button of the frmCount form:

Private Sub cmdPause_Click()

```
    ' Set the flag to 0 to disable counting.
    ggFlag = 0
```

End Sub

☐ Change the code in the cmdStart_Click() procedure of the frmCount form so that it looks like this:

Private Sub cmdStart_Click()

```
    ' Set the flag to 1 to enable counting.
    ggFlag = 1
```

End Sub

☐ Add the following code in the Form_Load() procedure of the frmCount form:

Private Sub Form_Load()

```
    ' Set the flag to 0 to disable counting.
    ' (You must click the Start button to start
    ' counting).
    ggFlag = 0
```

End Sub

Executing the Enhanced Count Program

☐ Execute the Count program.

This program counts from 1 to 999 and then starts counting again. Each number is displayed in the label during counting.

☐ Click the Pause button.

As you can see, you can click the Pause button to pause the counting!

☐ Click the Start button to continue counting.

☐ While the Count program is counting, start Paintbrush and manipulate and resize the windows of Paintbrush and the Count programs so that the Count form is shown with the Paintbrush window onscreen. (See Figure 11.9.) As you can see, you can draw with Paintbrush, and the Count program continues to count.

Figure 11.9.
Executing the Count program and Paintbrush together.

The *Main()* Procedure

The Main() procedure is the first procedure that is executed when you start the program. Therefore, the first statement in this procedure is responsible for showing the frmCount form:

```
' Show the form.
frmCount.Show
```

DO	DON'T

DO use the Show method as the first statement in the Main() procedure to show the form. Because the Main() procedure is the first procedure that is executed when you start the program, the form isn't loaded automatically.

The `Do While DoEvents()` loop in `Main()` is called the idle loop:

```
Do While DoEvents()
    If ggFlag = 1 Then
    Counter = Counter + 1
    frmCount.lblResult.Caption = Str$(Counter)
        If Counter = 999 Then
            Counter = 1
        End If
    End If
Loop
```

The logic flow diagram of the `Do While DoEvents()` loop is shown in Figure 11.10. Notice that the program stays in an endless loop.

Figure 11.10.

The `Do While`
`DoEvents()` *loop.*

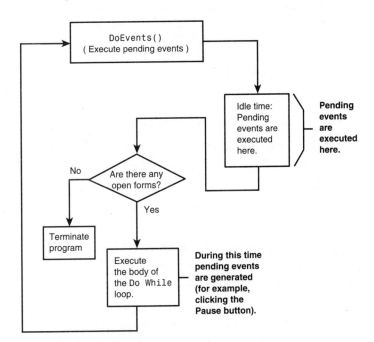

Terminating the Endless Loop

The top block in Figure 11.10 is the `DoEvents()` block. This function returns the number of the currently open forms. If you close the frmCount form, there are no open forms in the program, and `DoEvents()` returns 0. This causes the loop to terminate, which terminates the program.

Executing the Body of the *Do While DoEvents()* Loop

As shown in Figure 11.10, if there is an open form, the body of the Do While DoEvents() loop is executed.

The first statement in the loop is an If statement that checks the value of ggFlag. Assuming that you already clicked the Start button, which sets the value of this flag to 1, the statements of the If block are executed, increasing the Counter variable and updating the Caption property of the lblResult label.

During the execution of the body of the Do While loop, the program is not in idle time. This means that the program can't act on certain events that occur during the execution of the body of the Do While loop. For example, if you click the Pause button during the execution of the Do While loop, the program can't respond to this event. Events that occur while the program is not in idle time are called *pending events*. For example, clicking the Pause button while the program executes the body of the Do While loop causes a pending event.

The Do While loop contains the following statement:

```
frmCount.lblResult.Caption = Str$(Counter)
```

This statement causes a pending event, because the caption of the lblResult label can be refreshed only during idle time.

As shown in Figure 11.10, once the body of the Do While loop is executed, the program again executes the DoEvents() function.

The *DoEvents()* Function

To cause the program to act on the pending events, you must force the program to be in idle time; you do this by using the DoEvents() function.

The program acts on any pending events while it's in idle time. Refreshing the lblResult label is a pending event that occurred while the program executed the body of the Do While loop. Also, if you click the Pause button during the execution of the Do While loop, the program acts on this pending event. Once the program finishes acting on the pending events, it returns to the Do While loop and the whole process starts again.

> **Note:** The `DoEvents()` function in the `Do While DoEvents()` loop serves two purposes:
> - The returned value from `DoEvents()` is the number of currently open forms. The loop is terminated when there are no more open forms.
> - The `DoEvents()x` function forces the program to be in idle time so Windows can act on all pending events.

The Code in the General Declarations Section

The code in the general declarations section of the COUNTM.BAS module includes the following statement:

```
' Declare a global variable that is visible in
' all procedures in all the modules and forms.
Global ggFlag As Integer
```

Declaring the ggFlag variable in the general declarations section of the COUNTM.BAS module means that it is visible by all procedures in all modules and forms. Indeed, the ggFlag variable is updated in the procedures Form_Load(), cmdStart_Click(), and cmdPause_Click() of the frmCount form and used in the Main() procedure of the COUNTM.BAS module.

The Code in the *cmdPause_Click()* Procedure

The cmdPause_Click() procedure of the frmCount form is executed during idle time if you click the Pause button during the execution of the Do While DoEvents() loop. The code in this procedure sets the global variable ggFlag to 0 so that the counting process in the Main() procedure is disabled:

```
Private Sub cmdPause_Click()

    ' Set the flag to 0 to disable counting.
    ggFlag = 0

End Sub
```

The Code in the *cmdStart_Click()* Procedure

The code in the cmdStart_Click() procedure sets ggFlag to 1 to enable the counting process in the Main() procedure.

Summary

In this chapter you have learned how your Visual Basic program can take advantage of the standard Windows features. You have learned how to copy, cut, and paste text and pictures to and from the Clipboard; how to use the `Refresh` method to request an immediate refreshing of objects; and how to write code that is executed during idle time.

Q&A

Q **I understand the usefulness of copy, cut, and paste as explained in this chapter. Can I use copy, cut, and paste in a slightly different way?**

A You can use them any way you like. However, the programs you write with Visual Basic are designed to work in the Windows environment. As such, your users expect the copy, cut, and paste operations to work in a certain known and acceptable manner, as described in this chapter.

Quiz

1. What does the value `Screen.ActiveControl` represent?

2. `GetFormat()` is used to do which of the following?

    a. Find the type of data that the Clipboard currently holds.
    b. Format the hard drive.
    c. Format the disk (floppy or hard drive).

3. What does the `Refresh` method do?

Exercise

As demonstrated in the AnyData program, if the Clipboard contains text, you can't paste its contents to the picture box; if the Clipboard contains a picture, you can't paste its contents to the text box, list box, or combo box.

Enhance the AnyData program so that the Paste item in the Edit menu is disabled whenever the paste operation doesn't make sense.

Quiz Answers

1. The currently active control.

2. a

3. It causes an immediate refreshing of the screen.

Exercise Answer

The code of the program needs to determine whether to enable/disable the paste operation. A good focal point to insert such code is in the mnuEdit_Click() procedure.

The following code enables or disables the Paste item in the Edit menu by comparing the data type of the Clipboard contents with the data type of the currently active control:

```
Private Sub mnuEdit_Click()

    ' Start by enabling the Cut and Copy menus.
    mnuCut.Enabled = True
    mnuCopy.Enabled = True

    ' Initially, disable the Paste menu.
    mnuPaste.Enabled = False

    ' Is the currently active control a text box?
    If TypeOf Screen.ActiveControl Is TextBox Then
        ' Does the clipboard hold text?
        If Clipboard.GetFormat(vbCFText) Then
            ' It is Ok to paste.
            mnuPaste.Enabled = True
        End If

    ' Is the currently active control a combo box?
    ElseIf TypeOf Screen.ActiveControl Is ComboBox Then
        ' Does the clipboard hold text?
        If Clipboard.GetFormat(vbCFText) Then
            ' It is OK to paste.
            mnuPaste.Enabled = True
        End If

    ' Is the currently active control a list box?
    ElseIf TypeOf Screen.ActiveControl Is ListBox Then
    ' Does the clipboard hold text?
        If Clipboard.GetFormat(vbCFText) Then
            ' It is OK to paste.
            mnuPaste.Enabled = True
        End If

    ' Is the currently active control a picture box?
    ElseIf TypeOf Screen.ActiveControl Is PictureBox Then
        ' Does the clipboard hold bit map?
        If Clipboard.GetFormat(vbCFBitmap) Then
            ' It is OK to paste.
            mnuPaste.Enabled = True
        End If
    Else
    ' We checked all the valid possibilities!
    ' The user is trying to paste incompatible data types!
    ' Paste should be disabled!
    ' Do nothing (i.e., leave the Paste menu gray.

    End If

End Sub
```

11

It's a good idea to include such code in your programs. If you don't, your user might try to paste text into a picture box and will not understand why the paste operation isn't working. Adding the above procedure prevents your user from trying to perform paste operations that don't make sense.

The Keyboard

In this chapter you'll learn how your program can respond to keyboard events, how to detect whether a key was pressed or released, and how to manipulate the input data that comes from the keyboard.

The Keyboard Focus

As stated in previous chapters, the current object that has the keyboard focus is the object that responds to keyboard inputs. When a control has the keyboard focus, it changes its appearance in some way. For example, when a command button has the focus, a dashed rectangle appears around its caption. When a scroll bar has the focus, its thumb blinks.

The Keyboard Events

Three keyboard events correspond to keyboard activities: KeyDown, KeyUp, and KeyPress.

The *KeyDown* Event

The KeyDown event occurs when you press down any of the keys on the keyboard. For example, if you press a key while a command button called cmdPushMe has the focus, the cmdPushMe_KeyDown() procedure is executed.

The *KeyUp* Event

The KeyUp event occurs when you release any of the keys on the keyboard. For example, if you release a key while a command button called cmdPushMe has the focus, the cmdPushMe_KeyUp() procedure is executed.

The *KeyPress* Event

The KeyPress event occurs when you press a key that has a corresponding ASCII character. For example, if you press the A key while a command button called cmdPushMe has the focus, the cmdPushMe_KeyPress() procedure is executed. If you press F1, the KeyPress event does not occur because the F1 key has no corresponding ASCII character.

The Keys Program

The Keys program illustrates how the three keyboard events are used in a program.

The Visual Implementation
of the Keys Program

☐ Open a new project, save the form of the project as KEYS.FRM in the C:\VB4PRG\CH12 directory and save the project file as KEYS.VBP in the C:\VB4PRG\CH12 directory.

☐ Build the form of the project according to the specifications in Table 12.1.

The completed form should look like the one shown in Figure 12.1.

Table 12.1. The properties table of the frmKeys form.

Object	Property	Setting
Form	**Name**	**frmKeys**
	Caption	The Keys Program
	Height	4545
	Left	1080
	Top	1170
	Width	6810
Command Button	**Name**	**cmdExit**
	Caption	E&xit
	FontName	System
	Height	495
	Left	4440
	Top	3120
	Width	1215
Command Button	**Name**	**cmdPushMe**
	Caption	&Push Me
	FontName	System
	FontSize	10
	Height	495
	Left	120
	Top	1200
	Width	1215

continues

Table 12.1. continued

Object	Property	Setting
Label	Name	lblInfo
	Alignment	2-Center
	BorderStyle	1-Fixed Single
	FontName	System
	FontSize	10
	Height	495
	Left	360
	Top	240
	Width	6015

Figure 12.1.
The frmKeys form.

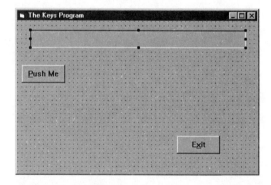

Entering the Code of the Keys Program

☐ Enter the following code in the general declarations section of the frmKeys form:

```
' All variables MUST be declared.
Option Explicit
```

☐ Enter the following code in the cmdExit_Click() procedure of the frmKeys form:

```
Private Sub cmdExit_Click ()

    End

End Sub
```

☐ Enter the following code in the cmdPushMe_KeyDown() procedure of the frmKeys form:

```
Private Sub cmdPushMe_KeyDown (KeyCode As Integer, _
                      Shift As Integer)

    lblInfo.Caption = "A key was pressed. KeyCode=" + _
```

```
Str(KeyCode) + " Shift=" + _
Str(Shift)
```

End Sub

Executing the Keys Program

☐ Execute the Keys program.

☐ Click the Push Me button.

The Keys program responds by placing a dashed rectangle around the caption of the Push Me button, indicating that the Push Me button now has the keyboard focus. Press the Tab key several times and note that the keyboard focus switches from one button to another as you press the Tab key.

☐ Make sure that the Push Me button has the focus, then press the A key.

The Keys program responds by displaying the ASCII code of the A key in the lblInfo label, as shown in Figure 12.2.

Figure 12.2.
Pressing the A key.

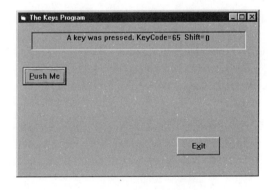

☐ Press other keys on the keyboard and notice that the lblInfo label displays the code of the key that was pressed.

☐ Press the Num Lock key and notice that the program reports that the key corresponding to the value 144 was pressed. The correlations between the displayed numbers and the pressed keys are explained later in this chapter.

☐ Press the Shift key, press the Ctrl key (while holding down the Shift key), and then press the Alt key (while holding down the Shift and Ctrl keys).

The lblInfo label reports that Shift is equal to 1, 3, and then 7. The correlation between these numbers and the Shift, Ctrl, and Alt keys is explained later in this chapter.

☐ Click the Exit button to terminate the Keys program.

How the Keys Program Works

The Keys program uses the KeyDown event to respond to keys that are pressed on the keyboard.

The Code in the *cmdPushMe_KeyDown()* Procedure

The cmdPushMe_KeyDown() procedure is executed when the Push Me button has the focus and you press any key on the keyboard:

```
Private Sub cmdPushMe_KeyDown (KeyCode As Integer, _
                              Shift As Integer)

   lblInfo.Caption = "A key was pressed. KeyCode=" + _
                  Str(KeyCode) + " Shift=" + _
                  Str(Shift)

End Sub
```

The cmdPushMe_KeyDown() procedure has two arguments. The first argument, called KeyCode, is an integer that represents the pressed key. The second argument represents the state of the Shift, Ctrl, and Alt keys.

To determine which key was pressed, you can compare the value of the first argument (KeyCode) with Visual Basic keyboard constants. For example, if the user pressed the Num Lock key, then the value of KeyCode will equal the constant vbKeyNumlock. Similarly, if the user pressed the F1 key, then the value of KeyCode will equal vbKeyF1; if the user pressed the Z key, the value of KeyCode will be vbKeyZ; if the user pressed the Home key, the value of KeyCode will be vbKeyHome, and so on.

Table 12.2 lists the meanings of the values for the cmdPushMe_KeyDown() procedure's second argument. For example, when the value of the second argument is equal to 3, it means that both the Shift and Ctrl keys are pressed and the Alt key is not pressed.

Table 12.2. The possible values of the second argument of the cmdPushMe_KeyDown() procedure.

Value of the Second Argument	Alt Status	Ctrl Status	Shift Status
0	Not pressed	Not pressed	Not pressed
1	Not pressed	Not pressed	Pressed
2	Not pressed	Pressed	Not pressed
3	Not pressed	Pressed	Pressed
4	Pressed	Not pressed	Not pressed
5	Pressed	Not pressed	Pressed

Value of the Second Argument	Alt Status	Ctrl Status	Shift Status
6	Pressed	Pressed	Not pressed
7	Pressed	Pressed	Pressed

The code in the `cmdPushMe_KeyDown()` procedure assigns a string representing the values of the two arguments to the Caption property of the lblInfo label:

```
lblInfo.Caption = "A key was pressed. KeyCode=" + _
                  Str(KeyCode) + " Shift=" + _
                  Str(Shift)
```

The `Str()` function is used because the Caption property is a string and the `KeyCode` and `Shift` variables are integers. `Str(KeyCode)` converts the integer `KeyCode` to a string, and `Str(Shift)` converts the integer `Shift` to a string.

Detecting a Released Key

As you have seen, you can use the two arguments of the `KeyDown` event to detect any pressed key. The `KeyUp` event has the same two arguments as the `KeyDown` event; however, the `KeyDown` event occurs when you press a key down, and the `KeyUp` event occurs when you release the key. The `KeyPress` event can also be used to detect a pressed key, but it detects only ASCII keys.

To see the `KeyUp` event in action, enter the following code in the `cmdPushMe_KeyUp()` procedure of the frmKeys form:

```
Private Sub cmdPushMe_KeyUp (KeyCode As Integer, _
                             Shift As Integer)

  lblInfo.Caption = "A key was released. KeyCode=" + _
                    Str(KeyCode) + " Shift=" + _
                    Str(Shift)

End Sub
```

☐ Execute the Keys program.

☐ Click the Push Me button.

> *The Keys program responds by displaying a dashed rectangle around the Push Me button, indicating that this button now has the keyboard focus.*

☐ Press a key.

> *The Keys program responds by displaying a number corresponding to the key pressed.*

☐ Release the key.

> *The Keys program responds by displaying the value of the released key.*

12

☐ Click the Exit button to terminate the Keys program.

The `cmdPushMe_KeyUp()` procedure has the same arguments as the `cmdPushMe_KeyDown()` procedure, but `cmdPushMe_KeyDown()`'s arguments report which key was pressed down, and `cmdPushMe_KeyUp()`'s arguments report which key was released.

Detecting an ASCII Key

To detect that the user pressed an ASCII key, you can use the `KeyPress` event. To see the `KeyPress` event in action, follow these steps:

☐ Enter the following code in the `cmdPushMe_KeyPress()` procedure of the frmKeys form:

```
Private Sub cmdPushMe_KeyPress (KeyAscii As Integer)

    Dim Char

    Char = Chr(KeyAscii)

    lblInfo.Caption = "KeyAscii =" + _
                      Str(KeyAscii) + _
                      " Char=" + Char

End Sub
```

☐ Comment out the code in the `cmdPushMe_KeyDown()` procedure (that is, type an apostrophe at the beginning of the statements in the `cmdPushMe_KeyDown()` procedure).

☐ Execute the Keys program.

☐ Click the Push Me button.

> *The Keys program responds by displaying a dashed rectangle around the Push Me button, indicating that this button now has the keyboard focus.*

☐ Press the A key and continue holding it down.

> *The Keys program responds to the pressing of the A key by displaying the ASCII value of the key, which is 97 for lowercase a or 65 for uppercase A.*

☐ Press F1 and continue holding it down.

> *The Keys program does not display any value in the lblInfo label because F1 does not have an ASCII code, so the KeyPress event doesn't occur when you press the F1 key.*

☐ Click the Exit button to terminate the Keys program.

The Code in the *cmdPushMe_KeyPress()* Procedure

The cmdPushMe_KeyPress() procedure is executed whenever you press an ASCII key. This procedure has one argument, which represents the ASCII value of the pressed key.

The Chr() function converts the integer KeyAscii to a character:

```
Char = Chr(KeyAscii)
```

Now the variable Char holds the character of the key that was pressed. For example, if the user pressed the Z key, now Char holds the character Z. The last statement in the cmdPushMe_KeyPress() procedure assigns a string to the Caption property of the lblInfo label:

```
lblInfo.Caption = "KeyAscii =" + _
                  Str(KeyAscii) + _
                  " Char=" + Char
```

Therefore, the user sees the character that was typed, as well as the ASCII value of the character.

Intercepting Keys with the *Form_KeyPress()* Procedure

A form can have the keyboard focus if there are no controls in it or if its controls are disabled. However, in most programs, a form does have some enabled controls in it, so the Form_KeyDown(), Form_KeyUp(), and Form_KeyPress() procedures are not executed.

To force the execution of these procedures even when the form does not have the keyboard focus, set the KeyPreview property of the form to True. To see the effect of the KeyPreview property, follow these steps:

☐ Set the KeyPreview property of the frmKeys form to True.

☐ Comment out the code in the cmdPushMe_KeyDown(), cmdPushMe_KeyUp(), and cmdPushMe_KeyPress() procedures.

☐ Enter the following code in the Form_KeyPress() procedure:

```
Private Sub Form_KeyPress (KeyAscii As Integer)

    Dim Char

    Char = Chr(KeyAscii)

    lblInfo.Caption = "KeyAscii =" + _
                      Str(KeyAscii) + _
                      " Char=" + Char

End Sub
```

☐ Execute the Keys program.

☐ Press any ASCII key and note that the lblInfo label displays the pressed key no matter which control has the keyboard focus. (That's because earlier you set the KeyPreview property of the frmKeys form to True.)

In a similar way, you can use the Form_KeyDown() procedure and the Form_KeyUp() procedure to trap pressed keys, even if the form doesn't have the keyboard focus. However, don't forget to set the KeyPreview property of the form to True.

The KeyPreview property enables the program to preview (or trap) the keyboard events. This enables you to write code that responds to key pressing regardless of which control has the keyboard focus.

The Upper Program

The Upper program illustrates how your program can trap ASCII keys.

The Visual Implementation of the Upper Program

☐ Start a new project, save the form of the project as UPPER.FRM in the C:\VB4PRG\CH12 directory and save the project file as UPPER.VBP in the C:\VB4PRG\CH12 directory.

☐ Build the frmUpper form according to the specifications in Table 12.3.

The completed form should look like the one shown in Figure 12.3.

Table 12.3. The properties table of the frmUpper form.

Object	Property	Setting
Form	**Name**	**frmUpper**
	Caption	The Upper Program
	Height	4545
	Left	1080
	Top	1170
	Width	6810
Text Box	**Name**	**txtUserArea**
	Height	1335
	Left	360

Object	Property	Setting
	ScrollBars	3-Both
	Text	(empty)
	Top	360
	Width	5895
Command Button	**Name**	**cmdExit**
	Caption	E&xit
	FontName	System
	FontSize	10
	Height	495
	Left	5040
	Top	3240
	Width	1215

Figure 12.3.
The frmUpper form.

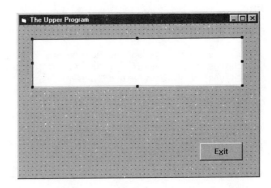

Entering the Code of the Upper Program

☐ Enter the following code in the general declarations section of the frmUpper form:

```
' All variables MUST be declared.
Option Explicit
```

☐ Enter the following code in the cmdExit_Click() procedure of the frmUpper form:

```
Private Sub cmdExit_Click ()

    End

End Sub
```

Executing the Upper Program

☐ Execute the Upper program.

☐ Type something in the text box.

☐ Try to press the Enter key to move to the next line.

> *As you can see, the Upper program refuses to move to the next line in the text box because the MultiLine property of the txtUserArea text box is currently set to False. Note that every time you press Enter, the PC beeps, alerting you that you pressed an illegal key.*

☐ Click the Exit button to exit the program.

Trapping the Enter Key

As demonstrated, the PC beeps whenever you press an illegal key. You can trap the event and fool the Upper program as follows:

☐ Enter the following code in the txtUserArea_KeyPress() procedure of the frmUpper form:

```
Private Sub txtUserArea_KeyPress (KeyAscii As Integer)

    ' If the user pressed the Return key (the Enter key),
    ' change the value of KeyAscii to 0 (null character).
    If KeyAscii = vbKeyReturn Then
        KeyAscii = 0
    End If

End Sub
```

☐ Execute the Upper program.

☐ Type something in the text box.

☐ Press Enter.

> *As you can see, the text box does not let you move to the next line, but the PC doesn't beep when you press Enter.*

☐ Terminate the Upper program by clicking the Exit button.

The Code in the *txtUserArea_KeyPress()* Procedure

The txtUserArea_KeyPress() procedure is executed whenever you press an ASCII key. The code in this procedure checks whether you pressed the Return key (the Enter key). If you pressed the Enter key, the code in this procedure changes the value of the KeyAscii argument to 0 (the null character). Therefore, the txtUserArea text box "thinks" you pressed the 0 (null) key. This is why the PC doesn't beep when you press Enter.

The code in the `txtUserArea_KeyPress()` procedure demonstrates that this procedure is executed before the text box has a chance to process the pressed key.

Modifying the Upper Program

Modify the Upper program as follows:

☐ Change the MultiLine property of the txtUserArea text box to True.

☐ Execute the Upper program.

☐ Type something in the text box and press Enter.

> *As you can see, the text box does not let you move to the next line because the Enter key is blocked by the code in the `txtUserArea_KeyPress()` procedure. That is, when you press the Enter key, the code you wrote in the `txtUserArea_KeyPress()` procedure changes the value of the `KeyAscii` argument to 0, which makes the text box think you didn't press a key.*

☐ Click the Exit button to terminate the Upper program.

Converting ASCII Characters to Uppercase

In some programs, you may want the text that the user types to appear in uppercase or lowercase only. To see how you accomplish this, change the code in the `txtUserArea_KeyPress()` procedure so that it looks like the following:

```
Private Sub txtUserArea_KeyPress (KeyAscii As Integer)

    Dim Char

    Char = Chr(KeyAscii)
    KeyAscii = Asc(UCase(Char))

End Sub
```

☐ Execute the Upper program.

☐ Type something in the text box.

> *As you can see, whatever you type appears in uppercase letters regardless of the status of the Shift or Caps Lock keys.*

☐ Click the Exit button to terminate the Upper program.

The code in the `txtUserArea_KeyPress()` procedure uses the `Chr()` function to convert the pressed key to a character:

```
Char = Chr(KeyAscii)
```

12

Then the character is converted to uppercase using the UCase() function, which returns the uppercase character of its argument. For example, the returned value of UCase("a") is *A*, and the returned value of UCase("A") is also *A*.

The txtUserArea_KeyPress() procedure converts the returned value of UCase() to an integer using the Asc() function:

```
KeyAscii = Asc( UCase(Char) )
```

The Asc() function returns an integer that represents the ASCII value of its argument.

The argument of the txtUserArea_KeyPress() procedure contains an integer that represents the ASCII value of the pressed key. This integer is converted to a character, the character is converted to uppercase, and the ASCII value of the uppercase character is assigned to the KeyAscii argument. Therefore, the text box thinks the user pressed an uppercase key.

The Cancel Property

The Cancel property is used to provide a response to pressing the Esc key. To see the Cancel property in action, follow these steps:

☐ Execute the Upper program.

☐ Press the Esc key.

> *As you can see, no matter what has the keyboard focus, the Upper program does not respond to the Esc key.*

☐ Click the Exit button to exit the Upper program.

☐ Change the Cancel property of the Exit button to True.

☐ Execute the Upper program.

☐ Press the Esc key on your keyboard.

> *No matter which control has the focus, the program responds to the Esc key as if the Exit key was pressed. This is because you set the Cancel property of the Exit button to True.*

In a similar manner, if you set the Default property of the Exit button to True, the program responds to pressing the Enter key the same way it responds to clicking the Exit button, regardless of which control has the focus.

The Tab Program

Windows programs let you move from control to control by pressing the Tab key (that is, moving the keyboard focus from control to control by pressing Tab). Pressing Shift+Tab moves the keyboard focus in the reverse order. The Tab program illustrates how the Tab order works.

☐ Start a new project, save the form of the project as TAB.FRM in the C:\VB4PRG\CH12 directory and save the project file as TAB.VBP in the C:\VB4PRG\CH12 directory.

☐ Implement the frmTab form according to the specifications in Table 12.4.

The completed form should look like the one shown in Figure 12.4.

Table 12.4. The properties table of the frmTab form.

Object	Property	Setting
Form	**Name**	**frmTab**
	Caption	The Tab Program
	Height	4545
	Left	1080
	Top	1170
	Width	6810
Command Button	**Name**	**Command1**
	Caption	Command1
	FontName	System
	FontSize	10
	Height	495
	Left	240
	TabIndex	0
	Top	480
	Width	1215
Command Button	**Name**	**Command2**
	Caption	Command2
	FontName	System
	FontSize	10
	Height	495
	Left	240
	TabIndex	1
	Top	1080
	Width	1215

continues

12

Table 12.4. continued

Object	Property	Setting
Command Button	**Name**	**Command3**
	Caption	Command3
	FontName	System
	FontSize	10
	Height	495
	Left	240
	TabIndex	2
	Top	1680
	Width	1215
Command Button	**Name**	**Command4**
	Caption	Command4
	FontName	System
	FontSize	10
	Height	495
	Left	240
	TabIndex	3
	Top	2280
	Width	1215
Command Button	**Name**	**Command5**
	Caption	Command5
	FontName	System
	FontSize	10
	Height	495
	Left	240
	TabIndex	4
	Top	2880
	Width	1215
Command Button	**Name**	**Command6**
	Caption	Command6
	FontName	System
	FontSize	10

Object	Property	Setting
	Height	495
	Left	1560
	TabIndex	5
	Top	480
	Width	1215
Command Button	**Name**	**Command7**
	Caption	Command7
	FontName	System
	FontSize	10
	Height	495
	Left	1560
	TabIndex	6
	Top	1080
	Width	1215
Command Button	**Name**	**Command8**
	Caption	Command8
	FontName	System
	FontSize	10
	Height	495
	Left	1560
	TabIndex	7
	Top	1680
	Width	1215
Command Button	**Name**	**Command9**
	Caption	Command9
	FontName	System
	FontSize	10
	Height	495
	Left	1560
	TabIndex	8
	Top	2280
	Width	1215

continues

Table 12.4. continued

Object	Property	Setting
Command Button	**Name**	**Command10**
	Caption	Command10
	FontName	System
	FontSize	10
	Height	495
	Left	1560
	TabIndex	9
	Top	2880
	Width	1215
Command Button	**Name**	**cmdExit**
	Caption	E&xit
	FontName	System
	FontSize	10
	Height	495
	Left	1560
	TabIndex	10
	Top	3480
	Width	1215
Check Box	**Name**	**Check1**
	Caption	Check1
	FontName	System
	FontSize	10
	Height	495
	Left	3840
	TabIndex	11
	Top	360
	Width	1215
Check Box	**Name**	**Check2**
	Caption	Check2
	FontName	System
	FontSize	10

Object	Property	Setting
	Height	495
	Left	3840
	TabIndex	12
	Top	960
	Width	1215
Check Box	**Name**	**Check3**
	Caption	Check3
	FontName	System
	FontSize	10
	Height	495
	Left	3840
	TabIndex	13
	Top	1560
	Width	1215
Horizontal Scroll Bar	**Name**	**HScroll1**
	Height	255
	Left	3480
	Max	50
	TabIndex	14
	Top	2520
	Width	2895

12

Figure 12.4.

The frmTab form.

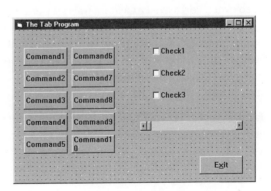

Entering the Code of the Tab Program

☐ Enter the following code in the general declarations section of the frmTab form:

```
' All variables MUST be declared.
Option Explicit
```

☐ Enter the following code in the cmdExit_Click() procedure of the frmTab form:

```
Private Sub cmdExit_Click ()

    End

End Sub
```

Executing the Tab Program

☐ Execute the Tab program.

☐ Move the focus from one control to another by pressing the Tab key or the arrow keys. Note that when the scroll bar has the focus, the left- and right-arrow keys are used for changing the thumb's position on the scroll bar.

☐ Click the Exit button to terminate the program.

The TabIndex Property

The TabIndex property determines the order in which controls receive the keyboard focus. For example, if the keyboard focus is currently on a control that has its TabIndex property set to 5, pressing Tab moves the keyboard focus to the control that has its TabIndex set to 6. If the keyboard focus is currently on a control that has its TabIndex property set to 5, pressing Shift+Tab moves the keyboard focus back to the control that has its TabIndex set to 4.

The Tab order works in a circular manner: if the control that currently has the keyboard focus is the control with the highest TabIndex value, pressing Tab moves the keyboard focus to the control that has its TabIndex property set to 0. Similarly, if the control that currently has the keyboard focus is the control that has its TabIndex property set to 0, pressing Shift+Tab moves the keyboard focus to the control with the highest TabIndex. Some controls, such as a label control, cannot accept the keyboard focus.

Visual Basic sets the TabIndex property with sequential numbers. That is, the TabIndex property of the first control placed in the form is set to 0, the TabProperty of the second control placed in the form is set to 1, and so on. However, you can change the value of the TabIndex property so that the Tab order is appropriate to your program.

The Focus Program

The Focus program demonstrates how your program can detect when a control gets or loses the keyboard focus.

The Visual Implementation of the Focus Program

☐ Open a new project, save the form of the project as FOCUS.FRM in the C:\VB4PRG\CH12 directory and save the project file as FOCUS.VBP in the C:\VB4PRG\CH12 directory.

☐ Build the frmFocus form according to the specifications in Table 12.5.

The completed form should look like the one shown in Figure 12.5.

Table 12.5. The properties table of the frmFocus form.

Object	Property	Setting
Form	**Name**	**frmFocus**
	Caption	The Focus Program
	Height	4545
	Left	1080
	Top	1170
	Width	6810
Command Button	**Name**	**cmdExit**
	Caption	E&xit
	FontName	System
	FontSize	10
	Height	495
	Left	5040
	Top	3360
	Width	1215
Text Box	**Name**	**txtUserArea**
	Height	1575
	Left	2760
	MultiLine	-1-True

continues

449

Table 12.5. continued

Object	Property	Setting
	Top	480
	Width	3375
	Text	(empty)
Command Button	**Name**	**cmdLoad**
	Caption	&Load
	FontName	System
	FontSize	10
	Height	495
	Left	240
	Top	360
	Width	1215
Command Button	**Name**	**cmdSave**
	Caption	&Save
	FontName	System
	FontSize	10
	Height	495
	Left	240
	Top	960
	Width	1215
Label	**Name**	**lblInfo**
	Alignment	2-Center
	BackColor	Black
	BorderStyle	1-Fixed Single
	FontName	System
	FontSize	10
	ForeColor	White
	Height	855
	Left	600
	Top	3000
	Width	3735

Object	Property	Setting
Label	**Name**	**lblTitle**
	Caption	Lost or Got the Focus?
	FontName	System
	FontSize	10
	Height	375
	Left	600
	Top	2640
	Width	2655

Figure 12.5.
The frmFocus form.

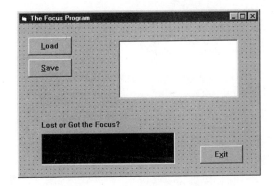

Entering the Code of the Focus Program

☐ Enter the following code in the general declarations section of the frmFocus form:

```
' All variables must be declared.
Option Explicit
```

☐ Enter the following code in the cmdExit_Click() procedure of the frmFocus form:

```
Private Sub cmdExit_Click ()

    End

End Sub
```

☐ Enter the following code in the txtUserArea_GotFocus() procedure of the frmFocus form:

```
Private Sub txtUserArea_GotFocus ()

    lblInfo.Caption = "txtUserArea got the focus"

End Sub
```

☐ Enter the following code in the txtUserArea_LostFocus() procedure of the frmFocus
form:

```
Private Sub txtUserArea_LostFocus ()

   lblInfo.Caption = "txtUserArea lost the focus"

End Sub
```

Executing the Focus Program

☐ Execute the Focus program.

☐ Move the keyboard focus to the textUserArea text box by clicking in the text box or using
the Tab key or arrow keys.

When you move the focus to the text box, the lblInfo label displays the following message:

```
txtUserArea got the focus
```

☐ Move the keyboard focus away from the txtUserArea text box by clicking the Save or
Load buttons or using the Tab or arrow keys.

When you move the focus away from the text box, the lblInfo label displays the following
message:

```
txtUserArea lost the focus
```

☐ Exit the program by clicking the Exit button.

How the Focus Program Works

The Focus program uses the GotFocus and LostFocus events to detect whether the text box got
or lost the keyboard focus.

The Code in the *txtUserArea_GotFocus()*
Procedure

The txtUserArea_GotFocus() procedure is executed whenever you move the focus to the text
box:

```
Private Sub txtUserArea_GotFocus ()

   lblInfo.Caption = "txtUserArea got the focus"

End Sub
```

This procedure sets the Caption property of the lblInfo label to a string indicating that the text box got the focus.

The Code in the *txtUserArea_LostFocus()* Procedure

The `txtUserArea_LostFocus()` procedure is executed whenever you move the focus away from the text box:

```
Private Sub txtUserArea_LostFocus ()

  lblInfo.Caption = "txtUserArea lost the focus"

End Sub
```

This procedure sets the Caption property of the lblInfo label to a string indicating that the text box lost the focus.

Summary

In this chapter, you have learned how to determine which key was pressed using the KeyDown, KeyUp, and KeyPress events. You have learned that when the KeyPreview property of a form is set to True, the Form_KeyDown(), Form_KeyUp(), and Form_KeyPress() procedures are executed no matter which control in the form has the focus.

You have also learned that the Tab order is determined by the TabIndex property and that the GotFocus and LostFocus events occur whenever a control loses or gets the keyboard focus.

12

Q&A

Q **Which event should I use to trap key pressing: KeyDown or KeyPress?**

A If your code is written to trap ASCII keys, you should use the KeyPress event because this event occurs only when an ASCII key is pressed. If your code is written to trap any key (ASCII and non-ASCII), you need to use the KeyDown event.

Quiz

1. The KeyPress event occurs whenever you do what?
2. The KeyDown event occurs whenever you do what?
3. The KeyUp event occurs whenever you do what?
4. What happens once the KeyPreview property of a form is set to True?

Exercises

1. Change the Upper program so that whenever you press *a* or *A* on the keyboard, the text box thinks you pressed the *b* or *B* keys.

2. Add code to the Tab program so it is terminated whenever you press Shift+Alt+F1.

Quiz Answers

1. Whenever you press an ASCII key on the keyboard.

2. Whenever you press any key on the keyboard.

3. Whenever you release a key.

4. Once the KeyPreview property of a form is set to True, the various keyboard event procedures of the form, such as `Form_KeyDown()`, `Form_KeyUp()`, and `Form_KeyPress()`, are executed (no matter which control in the form has the focus).

Exercise Answers

1. The solution to this exercise is as follows:

   ☐ Enter the following code in the `txtUserArea_KeyPress()` procedure of the frmUpper form:

   ```
   Private Sub txtUserArea_KeyPress (KeyAscii As Integer)

       If KeyAscii = Asc("a") Then
          KeyAscii = Asc("b")
       End If

       If KeyAscii = Asc("A") Then
          KeyAscii = Asc("B")
       End If

   End Sub
   ```

   ☐ Save the project.

   ☐ Execute the Upper program.

   ☐ Type the word Alabama in the text box.

   The text that you'll see in the text box is Blbbbmb. (Each *A* is replaced with *B*, and each *a* is replaced with *b*.)

   ☐ Click the Exit button to terminate the program.

   The first `If` statement checks whether the pressed key is the A key, and if so, it changes the `KeyAscii` value to the ASCII value of *B*. Similarly, the second `If` statement checks whether the pressed key is the *a* key. If it is, the value of KeyAscii is changed to the ASCII value of *b*.

2. The solution to this exercise is as follows:

☐ Set the KeyPreview property of the frmTab form to True.

☐ Enter the following code in the Form_KeyDown() procedure:

```
Private Sub Form_KeyDown (KeyCode As Integer, _
                            Shift As Integer)

    If Shift = 5 And KeyCode = vbKeyF1 Then
        End
    End If

End Sub
```

☐ Save the project.

☐ Execute the Tab program.

☐ Press Shift+Alt+F1 to terminate the program.

The Form_KeyDown() procedure is executed whenever you press down a key.

The If condition in the following code is satisfied when you press the Shift, Alt, and F1 keys simultaneously:

```
If Shift = 5 And KeyCode = vbKeyF1 Then
```

That is, when Shift is equal to 5, it means that the Shift key and the Alt key are currently pressed (see Table 12.2), and when KeyCode is equal to vbKeyF1, the F1 key is pressed. The End statement under the If condition terminates the program.

12

File-System
Controls

This chapter focuses on using *file-system controls* to write a program that lets you select a file from a drive. There are three file-system controls: the Drive list box, the Directory list box, and the File list box.

In a typical program that allows you to select files from drives, these three controls are used in combination. When you need to select a file, a dialog box including the three controls is displayed onscreen. (See Figure 13.1.) You can then select the desired file by selecting a drive from the Drive list box, a directory from the Directory list box, and a file from the File list box.

Figure 13.1.

The three file-system controls.

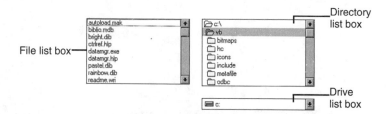

Note: In Chapter 6, "Dialog Boxes," you learned how to use the Common Dialog control to display an Open File dialog box and a Save As dialog box. As you know from Chapter 6, incorporating the Common Dialog control in your programs is very easy and convenient.

So why should you learn how to use the file-system controls? As you'll see in this chapter, they give more control over how the dialog box that displays the directories and files looks and performs. For example, if you ever want to write a program that displays directories and files like the File Manager program of Windows, you could use the file-system controls.

The Size Program

You'll now write a program, called Size, that includes the three file-system controls in it. You can use it to select a file from a drive and display the size of the selected file.

The Size program should do the following:

- When you start the program, a file selection form is displayed onscreen, as shown in Figure 13.2. As you can also see in Figure 13.2, the Size program's form also includes a combo box, called File Type, below the File list box. This combo box lets you select a file type from a list.

Figure 13.2.
The Size program.

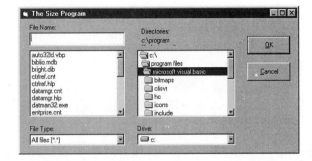

- When you select a drive from the Drive list box, the Directory list box displays that drive's directories.

- When you select a directory from the Directory list box, the File list box displays that directory's files.

- When you select a file from the File list box, the selected filename is displayed in the File Name text box.

- When you click the OK button, the size of the selected file is displayed. (See Figure 13.3.)

- When you click the Cancel button, the program terminates.

- When you select a file type from the File Type combo box, the File list box displays only files of the type you selected. For example, if you select Text files (*.TXT), only files with the extension .TXT are displayed in the File list box.

Figure 13.3.
Displaying the size of the selected file.

The Visual Implementation of the Size Program

☐ Start a new project.

☐ Save the form of the project as SIZE.FRM in the C:\VB4PRG\CH13 directory, and save the project file as SIZE.VBP in the C:\VB4PRG\CH13 directory.

☐ Build the form according to the specifications in Table 13.1.

The completed form should look like the one shown in Figure 13.2.

> **Note:** Figure 13.4 shows the locations of the three file-system controls in the toolbox window. The exact locations vary from edition to edition.

Figure 13.4.
The locations of the file-system controls' icons in the toolbox window.

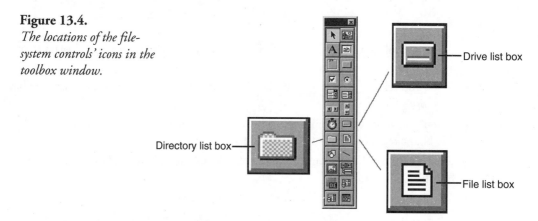

Table 13.1. The properties table of the Size program.

Object	Property	Value
Form	**Name**	**frmSize**
	Caption	The Size Program
	Height	4020
	Left	1200
	Top	1740
	Width	7890
Label	**Name**	**lblFileName**
	Caption	File Name:
	Height	255
	Left	240
	Top	120
	Width	1095

Object	Property	Value
Text Box	**Name**	**txtFileName**
	Text	(empty)
	Height	375
	Left	240
	Top	360
	Width	2655
File List Box	**Name**	**filFiles**
	Height	1785
	Left	240
	Top	840
	Width	2655
Label	**Name**	**lblFileType**
	Caption	File Type:
	Height	255
	Left	240
	Top	2880
	Width	1095
Combo Box	**Name**	**cboFileType**
	Style	2-Dropdown List
	Left	240
	Top	3120
	Width	2655
Label	**Name**	**lblDirectories**
	Caption	Directories:
	Height	255
	Left	3360
	Top	240
	Width	1215

continues

Table 13.1. continued

Object	Property	Value
Label	Name	lblDirName
	Caption	(empty)
	Height	255
	Left	3360
	Top	480
	Width	1215
Directory List Box	Name	dirDirectory
	Height	1830
	Left	3240
	Top	840
	Width	2775
Command Button	Name	cmdOK
	Caption	&OK
	Default	True
	Height	495
	Left	6360
	Top	480
	Width	1215
Label	Name	lblDrive
	Caption	Drive:
	Height	255
	Left	3240
	Top	2880
	Width	1095
Drive List Box	Name	drvDrive
	Height	315
	Left	3240
	Top	3120
	Width	2775

Object	Property	Value
Command Button	**Name**	**cmdCancel**
	Caption	&Cancel
	Cancel	True
	Height	495
	Left	6360
	Top	1200
	Width	1215

Entering the Code of the Size Program

☐ Enter the following code in the general declarations section of the frmSize form:

```
' All variables MUST be declared.
Option Explicit
```

☐ Enter the following code in the Form_Load() procedure:

```
Private Sub Form_Load ()

    ' Fill the cboFileType combo box.
    cboFileType.AddItem "All files (*.*)"
    cboFileType.AddItem "Text files (*.TXT)"
    cboFileType.AddItem "Doc files (*.DOC)"

    ' Initialize the cboFileType combo box to
    ' item #0. (i.e. All files *.*)
    cboFileType.ListIndex = 0

    ' Update the lblDirName label with the path.
    lblDirName.Caption = dirDirectory.Path

End Sub
```

☐ Enter the following code in the drvDrive_Change() procedure:

```
Private Sub drvDrive_Change ()

    ' The next statement may cause an error so we
    ' set an error trap.
    On Error GoTo DriveError

    ' Change the path of the directory list box to
    ' the new drive.
    dirDirectory.Path = drvDrive.Drive
    Exit Sub
```

```
DriveError:
    ' An error occurred! So tell the user and
    ' restore the original drive.
    MsgBox "Drive error!", vbExclamation, "Error"
    drvDrive.Drive = dirDirectory.Path
    Exit Sub

End Sub
```

☐ Enter the following code in the dirDirectory_Change() procedure:

```
Private Sub dirDirectory_Change ()

    ' A directory was just selected by the user so
    ' update the path of the file list box
    ' accordingly.
    filFiles.Path = dirDirectory.Path

    ' Also update the lblDirName label.
    lblDirName.Caption = dirDirectory.Path

End Sub
```

☐ Enter the following code in the cboFileType_Click() procedure:

```
Private Sub cboFileType_Click ()

    ' Change the Pattern of the file list box
    ' according to the File Type that the user
    ' selected.
    Select Case cboFileType.ListIndex
    Case 0
        filFiles.Pattern = "*.*"
    Case 1
        filFiles.Pattern = "*.TXT"
    Case 2
        filFiles.Pattern = "*.DOC"
    End Select

End Sub
```

☐ Enter the following code in the filFiles_Click() procedure:

```
Private Sub filFiles_Click ()

    ' Update the txtFileName text box with the file
    ' name that was just selected.
    txtFileName.Text = filFiles.FileName

End Sub
```

☐ Enter the following code in the cmdOK_Click() procedure:

```
Private Sub cmdOK_Click ()

Dim PathAndName As String
Dim FileSize As String
```

```
Dim Path As String

' If no file is selected, tell the user and
' exit this procedure.
If txtFileName.Text = "" Then
    MsgBox "You must first select a file!"
    Exit Sub
End If

'Make sure that Path ends with backslash (\).
If Right(filFiles.Path, 1) <> "\" Then
    Path = filFiles.Path + "\"
Else
    Path = filFiles.Path
End If

'Extract the Path and Name of the selected file.
If txtFileName.Text = filFiles.FileName Then
    PathAndName = Path + filFiles.FileName
Else
    PathAndName = txtFileName.Text
End If

' The next statement may cause an error so we
' set an error trap.
On Error GoTo FileLenError

'Get the file size of the file.
FileSize = Str(FileLen(PathAndName))

'Display the size of the file.
MsgBox "Size of "+PathAndName+": "+FileSize+" bytes"
Exit Sub

FileLenError:
' There was an error, so display error message
' and exit.
MsgBox "Cannot find size of " + PathAndName
Exit Sub

End Sub
```

☐ Enter the following code in the `filFiles_DblClick()` procedure:

```
Private Sub filFiles_DblClick ()

    ' Update the txtFileName text box with the file
    ' name that was just double clicked.
    txtFileName.Text = filFiles.FileName

    'Execute the cmdOK_Click() procedure.
    cmdOK_Click

End Sub
```

13

☐ Enter the following code in the cmdCancel() procedure:

```
Private Sub cmdCancel_Click ()

    End

End Sub
```

Executing the Size Program

☐ Execute the Size program and experiment with the various controls that appear onscreen.

While you run the program, notice the following features:

- As soon as you select a drive from the Drive list box, its directories appear in the Directory list box.

- If you choose a drive that is not ready, an error message appears and the Drive list box is restored to its original value. For example, if the Drive list box currently displays the C: drive and you try to change it to the A: drive while there is no disk in the A: drive, an error message appears and the Drive list box is restored to its original value (C:).

- To select a directory from the Directory list box, you need to double-click the desired directory.

- As soon as you select a directory from the Directory list box, its files appear in the File list box and the directory name appears above the Directory list box.

- As soon as you highlight a file in the File list box, its filename is displayed in the File Name text box.

- After you select a file type from the File Type combo box, the File list box displays only files of the type you selected. You cannot type in the text area of the combo box because the Style property of the combo box was set to Dropdown list at design time.

- When you click the OK button, a message appears that displays the file size of the selected file.

- Instead of selecting a file from the File list box, you can type its filename in the File Name text box.

- Pressing Enter is the same as clicking the OK button because you set the Default property of the OK button to True at design time.

- Pressing Esc is the same as pushing the Cancel button because you set the Cancel property of the Cancel button to True at design time.

☐ Click the Cancel button to terminate the Size program.

How the Size Program Works

Like other controls, the file-system controls have event procedures. The code in these procedures determines how the controls interact with each other.

The Code in the *Form_Load()* Procedure

When you start the program, the Form_Load() procedure is executed. In this procedure, the cboFileType combo box and the lblDirName label are initialized:

```
Private Sub Form_Load ()

    ' Fill the cboFileType combo box.
    cboFileType.AddItem "All files (*.*)"
    cboFileType.AddItem "Text files (*.TXT)"
    cboFileType.AddItem "Doc files (*.DOC)"

    ' Initialize the cboFileType combo box to
    ' item #0. (i.e. All files *.*)
    cboFileType.ListIndex = 0

    ' Update the lblDirName label with the path.
    lblDirName.Caption = dirDirectory.Path

End Sub
```

The AddItem method is used three times to fill the cboFileType combo box with three items: All Files (*.*), Text Files (*.TXT), and Doc Files (*.DOC).

Then the ListIndex property of the cboFileType combo box is set to 0. This sets the currently selected item of the combo box to item 0, or All Files (*.*).

Finally, the caption of the lblDirName label is set to the Path property of the Directory list box. The initial value of the Path property is the current directory, so when you start the program, the lblDirName label displays the name of the current directory.

The Code in the *drvDrive_Change()* Procedure

Whenever you change a drive in the Drive list box, the drvDrive_Change() procedure is executed. The code in this procedure updates the Path property of the Directory list box with the new drive that was selected:

```
Private Sub drvDrive_Change ()

    ' The next statement may cause an error so we
    ' set an error trap.
    On Error GoTo DriveError

    ' Change the path of the directory list box to
    ' the new drive.
```

13

```
    dirDirectory.Path = drvDrive.Drive
    Exit Sub

DriveError:
    ' An error occurred! So tell the user and
    ' restore the original drive.
    MsgBox "Drive error!", vbExclamation, "Error"
    drvDrive.Drive = dirDirectory.Path
    Exit Sub

End Sub
```

Before the procedure executes the command that changes the Path property of the Directory list box, an error trap is set. The error trap is required because changing the path of the Directory list box may cause an error. For example, if you changed the Drive list box to drive A: and drive A: is not ready, changing the path of the Directory list box to A: will cause an error. To avoid a runtime error, an error trap is set with the following statement:

```
On Error Goto DriveError
```

If an error occurs now during the execution of this statement:

```
dirDirectory.Path = drvDrive.Drive,
```

Visual Basic gives control to the code below the DriveError label. The code below the DriveError label displays an error message and restores the original value of the drive with the following statement:

```
drvDrive.Drive = dirDirectory.Path
```

Note that dirDirectory.Path still contains the original drive value because the statement that caused the error was not executed.

If the drive you selected is ready, then no error occurs. The path of the Directory list box is changed to the selected drive, and as a result, the Directory list box lists the directories of the selected drive.

The Code in the *dirDirectory_Change()* Procedure

Whenever you change a directory in the Directory list box, the dirDirectory_Change() procedure is executed. The code in this procedure updates the Path property of the File list box and the Caption property of the lblDirName label with the new directory:

```
Private Sub dirDirectory_Change ()

    ' A directory was just selected by the user so
    ' update the path of the file list box
    ' accordingly.
    filFiles.Path = dirDirectory.Path

    ' Also update the lblDirName label.
```

```
lblDirName.Caption = dirDirectory.Path
```

End Sub

As a result of updating the Path property of the File list box with the selected directory, the File list box displays the files of that directory.

The Code in the *cboFileType_Click()* Procedure

Whenever you make a selection from the cboFileType combo box, the cboFileType_Click() procedure is executed. The code in this procedure updates the Pattern property of the File list box according to the file type you selected:

Private Sub cboFileType_Click ()

```
' Change the Pattern of the file list box
' according to the File Type that the user
' selected.
Select Case cboFileType.ListIndex
Case 0
    filFiles.Pattern = "*.*"
Case 1
    filFiles.Pattern = "*.TXT"
Case 2
    filFiles.Pattern = "*.DOC"
End Select
```

End Sub

To determine which item in the cboFileType combo box you selected, a Select Case is used. Recall that the Form_Load() procedure filled the cboFileType combo box with three items: All Files (*.*), Text Files (*.TXT), and Doc Files (*.DOC). Depending on which item you select from the combo box, a different Case statement is executed. For example, if you select the second item in the combo box (Text Files (*.TXT)), the following statement is executed:

```
filFiles.Pattern = "*.TXT"
```

As a result, the File list box displays only files with the .TXT extension.

13

The Code in the *filFiles_Click()* Procedure

Whenever you highlight a file in the filFiles File list box, the filFiles_Click() procedure is executed. The code in this procedure updates the txtFileName text box with the name of the selected file:

Private Sub filFiles_Click ()

```
' Update the txtFileName text box with the file
' name that was just selected.
txtFileName.Text = filFiles.FileName
```

End Sub

The Code in the *cmdOK_Click()* Procedure

When you click the OK button, the cmdOK_Click() procedure is executed. The code of this
procedure displays the file size of the currently selected file onscreen :

```
Private Sub cmdOK_Click ()

    Dim PathAndName As String
    Dim FileSize As String
    Dim Path As String

    ' If no file is selected, tell the user and
    ' exit this procedure.
    If txtFileName.Text = "" Then
        MsgBox "You must first select a file!"
        Exit Sub
    End If

    'Make sure that Path ends with backslash (\).
    If Right(filFiles.Path, 1) <> "\" Then
        Path = filFiles.Path + "\"
    Else
        Path = filFiles.Path
    End If

    'Extract the Path and Name of the selected file.
    If txtFileName.Text = filFiles.FileName Then
        PathAndName = Path + filFiles.FileName
    Else
        PathAndName = txtFileName.Text
    End If

    ' The next statement may cause an error so we
    ' set an error trap.
    On Error GoTo FileLenError

    'Get the file size of the file.
    FileSize = Str(FileLen(PathAndName))

    'Display the size of the file.
    MsgBox "Size of "+PathAndName+": "+FileSize+" bytes"
    Exit Sub

FileLenError:
    ' There was an error, so display error message
    ' and exit.
    MsgBox "Cannot find size of " + PathAndName
    Exit Sub

End Sub
```

The first thing the procedure does is check whether you selected a file by comparing the Text
property of the txtFileName text box with null. If txtFileName.Text is null, a message is
displayed and the procedure is terminated:

```
If txtFileName.Text = "" Then
   MsgBox "You must first select a file!"
   Exit Sub
End If
```

After your code makes sure that the user selected a file, the Path variable is updated with the path of the selected file. The Right() function is used to make sure the rightmost character of the selected file's path is the backslash character (\). If it isn't, a backslash is added to the Path variable:

```
If Right(filFiles.Path, 1) <> "\" Then
   Path = filFiles.Path + "\"
Else
   Path = filFiles.Path
End If
```

After the Path variable is ready, the PathAndName variable can be updated. As implied by its name, the PathAndName variable should contain the full name of the file (that is, path and name). The PathAndName variable is updated with an If statement:

```
If txtFileName.Text = filFiles.FileName Then
   PathAndName = Path + filFiles.FileName
Else
   PathAndName = txtFileName.Text
End If
```

This If statement checks whether the currently highlighted file in the File list box is the same as the contents of the File Name text box. If the filename in the text box is not the same as the currently highlighted file, it means that you manually typed the path and name of the file, so the PathAndName variable is updated with whatever you typed. However, if the filename in the text box is the same as the currently highlighted file, the variable PathAndName is updated with the string Path + filFiles.FileName.

After the PathAndName variable is updated, the FileLen() function can be used to find the size of the file. However, since the FileLen() function may cause a runtime error (for example, if you typed a name of a file that doesn't exist), an error trap is set with the following statement:

```
On Error GoTo FileLenError
```

If an error occurs during the execution of the following statement:

```
FileSize = Str(FileLen(PathAndName))
```

Visual Basic gives control to the statement below the FileLenError label, which displays an error message and terminates the procedure:

```
FileLenError:
   MsgBox "Cannot find size of " + PathAndName
   Exit Sub
```

13

However, if the `FileLen()` function does not cause an error, the size of the file is displayed onscreen and the procedure is terminated:

```
MsgBox "Size of "+PathAndName+": "+FileSize+" bytes"
Exit Sub
```

The Code in the *filFiles_DblClick()* Procedure

When you double-click on a file in the File list box, the `filFiles_DblClick()` procedure is executed. The code of this procedure updates the File Name text box with the name of the file that was doubled-clicked and executes the `cmdOK_Click()` procedure:

```
Private Sub filFiles_DblClick ()

  ' Update the txtFileName text box with the file
  ' name that was just double clicked.
  txtFileName.Text = filFiles.FileName

  'Execute the cmdOK_Click() procedure.
  cmdOK_Click

End Sub
```

The Code in the *cmdCancel_Click()* Procedure

When you click the Cancel button, the `cmdCancel_Click()` procedure is executed. The code of this procedure terminates the program:

```
Private Sub cmdCancel_Click ()

    End

End Sub
```

The Attribute Properties of the File List Box

A file can have any of the following four attributes:

- Read-only: When the read-only attribute of a file is set, the file can only be read (that is, it cannot be erased or overwritten).
- Hidden: When the hidden attribute of a file is set, the DIR command of DOS does not display the file.
- System: DOS system files (files that are part of the operating system) have their system attribute set. A system file cannot be erased or overwritten.

- Archive: When the DOS BACKUP command (and other backup utilities) backs up a file, the archive attribute of the file is set. This attribute is used as a flag to indicate that the file was backed up. As soon as the file is modified, the archive attribute is automatically reset by DOS to indicate that the file was modified and therefore needs to be backed up. The archive attribute can be used by a backup utility to perform incremental backup (that is, to back up only files that were modified since the last backup).

The attribute properties of a File list box determine which files are displayed in the File list box, depending on the attributes of the files. The attribute properties of a File list box are ReadOnly, Archive, Normal, System, and Hidden. Each of these properties can be set to either True or False. For example, to display just the read-only files, you need to set the attribute properties of the filMyFiles File list box as follows:

```
filMyFiles.ReadOnly = True
filMyFiles.Archive  = False
filMyFiles.Normal   = False
filMyFiles.System   = False
filMyFiles.Hidden   = False
```

The Select Program

The Size program illustrates how to create a form that lets you select files from a drive. Because many programs need such a form, it is a good idea to create a general-purpose Select a File dialog box form that could be used by many projects. The Select program illustrates how to create and use a general-purpose Select a File dialog box. Before you start writing the Select program, specify what it should do:

☐ When you start the program, a menu bar with a File menu title appears. (See Figure 13.5.)

☐ The File menu has two items: Select File and Exit. (See Figure 13.6.)

☐ When you choose Select File from the File menu, the Select a File dialog box appears. (See Figure 13.7.)

☐ After selecting a file from the Select a File dialog box, the dialog box closes and the name of the selected file is displayed.

☐ When you select Exit from the File menu, the program terminates.

Figure 13.5.
The Select program.

Figure 13.6.
The File menu of the Select program.

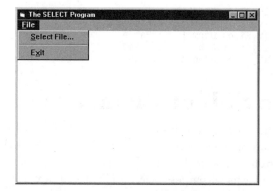

Figure 13.7.
The Select a File dialog box.

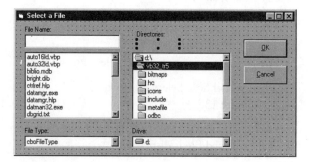

The Visual Implementation of the Select Program

☐ Start a new project.

☐ Save the form of the project as SELECT.FRM in the C:\VB4PRG\CH13 directory, and save the project file as SELECT.VBP in the C:\VB4PRG\CH13 directory.

☐ Build the form according to the specifications in Table 13.2.

The completed form should look like the one shown in Figure 13.5.

Table 13.2. The properties table of the frmSelect form.

Object	Property	Value
Form	**Name**	**frmSelect**
	BackColor	White
	Caption	The Select Program
Menu	**(See Table 13.3.)**	**(See Table 13.3.)**

Table 13.3. The menu table of the frmSelect form.

Caption	Name
&File	mnuFile
...&Select File...	mnuSelectFile
...-	mnuSep1
...E&xit	mnuExit

You now have to create another form and name it GETFILE.FRM—it will be used as a general-purpose Select a File dialog box.

The GETFILE.FRM form is almost identical to the SIZE.FRM form that you designed earlier in the Size program. So instead of creating the GETFILE.FRM form from scratch, you'll copy the SIZE.FRM file onto GETFILE.FRM and then add the GETFILE.FRM form to the SELECT.VBP project. Here is how you do that:

☐ Use the Windows File Manager or the DOS prompt to copy the file SIZE.FRM onto GETFILE.FRM.

Now add the GETFILE.FRM file to the SELECT.VBP project as follows:

☐ Switch back to Visual Basic.

☐ Select Add File from the File menu and then select the GETFILE.FRM file.

Visual Basic responds by adding the GETFILE.FRM file to the SELECT.VBP project.

At this point, the GETFILE.FRM form is identical to the SIZE.FRM form. You have to change the Name property and Caption property of the GETFILE.FRM form as follows:

13

☐ Select the GETFILE.FRM form by highlighting GETFILE.FRM in the SELECT.VBP window and then clicking the View Form button.

☐ Change the Name property of the GETFILE.FRM form from frmSize to frmGetFile.

☐ Change the Caption property of the GETFILE.FRM form from The Size Program to Select a File.

> *The visual implementation of the frmGetFile form is completed. The frmGetFile form should now look like the one shown in Figure 13.7.*

Entering the Code of the Select Program

The Select program has two forms: frmSelect and frmGetFile. The following sections listing the procedures of these forms.

Entering the Code of the frmSelect Form

☐ Enter the following code in the general declarations section of the frmSelect form:

```
' All variables MUST be declared.
Option Explicit
```

☐ Enter the following code in the Form_Load() procedure of the frmSelect form:

```
Private Sub Form_Load ()

    ' Load the frmGetFile dialog box
    '(without displaying it).
    Load frmGetFile

    ' Initialize the cboFileType combo box of the
    ' frmGetFile dialog box.
    frmGetFile.cboFileType.AddItem "All files (*.*)"
    frmGetFile.cboFileType.AddItem "Text files (*.TXT)"
    frmGetFile.cboFileType.AddItem "Doc files   (*.DOC)"
    frmGetFile.cboFileType.ListIndex = 0

End Sub
```

☐ Enter the following code in the mnuSelectFile_Click() procedure of the frmSelect form:

```
Private Sub mnuSelectFile_Click ()

    ' Set the Caption property of frmGetFile.
    frmGetFile.Caption = "Select a file"

    ' Display the frmGetFile form as a modal dialog
    ' box.
    frmGetFile.Show 1

    ' Display the name of the selected file on the
    ' screen.
```

```
        If frmGetFile.Tag = "" Then
            MsgBox "No file was selected!"
        Else
            MsgBox "You selected " + frmGetFile.Tag
        End If

    End Sub
```

☐ Enter the following code in the mnuExit_Click() procedure of the frmSelect form:

```
Private Sub mnuExit_Click ()
    End
End Sub
```

Entering the Code of the frmGetFile Form

Although you haven't typed any code yet in the frmGetFile form, the frmGetFile form already has code in it because you created the frmGetFile form from the frmSize form when you copied the file SIZE.FRM onto the file GETFILE.FRM.

☐ Edit the code in the Form_Load() procedure of the frmGetFile form so that it looks as follows:

```
Private Sub Form_Load ()

    ' Update the Directory lblDirName label with the
    ' path value of the directory list box.
    lblDirName.Caption = dirDirectory.Path

End Sub
```

☐ The code in the drvDrive_Change() procedure of the frmGetFile form is the same as the code in the frmSize form, so you don't have to modify it. Just make sure that it looks as follows:

```
Private Sub drvDrive_Change()

    ' The next statement may cause an error so we
    ' set an error trap.
    On Error GoTo DriveError

    ' Change the path of the directory list box to
    ' the new drive.
    dirDirectory.Path = drvDrive.Drive
    Exit Sub

DriveError:
    ' An error occurred! So tell the user and
    ' restore the original drive.
    MsgBox "Drive error!", vbExclamation, "Error"
    drvDrive.Drive = dirDirectory.Path
    Exit Sub

End Sub
```

13

☐ The code in the `dirDirectory_Change()` procedure of the frmGetFile form is the same as the code in the frmSize form, so you don't have to modify it. Just make sure that it looks as follows:

```
Private Sub dirDirectory_Change()

    ' A directory was just selected by the user so
    ' update the path of the file list box
    ' accordingly.
    filFiles.Path = dirDirectory.Path

    ' Also update the lblDirName label.
    lblDirName.Caption = dirDirectory.Path

End Sub
```

☐ Edit the code in the `cboFileType_Click()` procedure of the frmGetFile form so that it looks as follows:

```
Private Sub cboFileType_Click ()

    Dim PatternPos1 As Integer
    Dim PatternPos2 As Integer
    Dim PatternLen As Integer
    Dim Pattern As String

    ' Find the start position of the pattern in the
    ' cbboFileType combo box.
    PatternPos1 = InStr(1, cboFileType.Text, "(") + 1

    ' Find the end position of the pattern in the
    ' cbboFileType combo box.
    PatternPos2 = InStr(1, cboFileType.Text, ")") - 1

    ' Calculate the length of the Pattern string.
    PatternLen = PatternPos2 - PatternPos1 + 1

    ' Extract the Pattern portion of the cboFileType
    ' combo box.
    Pattern=Mid(cboFileType.Text,PatternPos1,PatternLen)

    ' Set the Pattern of the filFiles file listbox to the
    ' selected pattern.
    filFiles.Pattern = Pattern

End Sub
```

☐ The code in the `filFiles_Click()` procedure of the frmGetFile form is the same as the code in the frmSize form, so you don't have to modify it. Just make sure that it looks as follows:

```
Private Sub filFiles_Click()

    ' Update the txtFileName text box with the file
    ' name that was just selected.
    txtFileName.Text = filFiles.FileName

End Sub
```

☐ Edit the code in the `cmdOK_Click()` procedure of the frmGetFile form so that it looks as follows:

```
Private Sub cmdOK_Click ()

Dim PathAndName As String
Dim Path As String

' If no file is selected, tell the user and
' exit this procedure.
If txtFileName.Text = "" Then
 MsgBox "No file is selected!", vbExclamation, "Error"
 Exit Sub
End If

' Make sure that Path ends with backslash (\).
If Right(filFiles.Path, 1) <> "\" Then
   Path = filFiles.Path + "\"
Else
   Path = filFiles.Path
End If

' Extract the Path and Name of the selected
' file.
If txtFileName.Text = filFiles.FileName Then
   PathAndName = Path + filFiles.FileName
Else
   PathAndName = txtFileName.Text
End If

' Set the tag property of the frmGetFile dialog
' box to the selected file path and name.
frmGetFile.Tag = PathAndName

' Hide the frmGetFile dialog box.
frmGetFile.Hide

End Sub
```

☐ The code in the `filFiles_DblClick()` procedure of the frmGetFile form is the same as the code in the frmSize form, so you don't have to modify it. Just make sure that it looks as follows:

```
Private Sub filFiles_DblClick()

   ' Update the txtFileName text box with the file
   ' name that was just double clicked.
   txtFileName.Text = filFiles.FileName

   'Execute the cmdOK_Click() procedure.
   cmdOK_Click

End Sub
```

☐ Edit the code in the cmdCancel_Click() procedure of the frmGetFile form so that it looks as follows:

```
Private Sub cmdCancel_Click ()

    ' Set the tag property of the form to null.
    frmGetFile.Tag = ""

    ' Hide the frmGetFile dialog box.
    frmGetFile.Hide

End Sub
```

Executing the Select Program

☐ Execute the Select program.

After you choose Select File from the File menu, the Select a File dialog box appears onscreen as a modal form. So as long as the dialog box is open, you can't select other forms in the program. If you click the mouse in the frmSelect form while the dialog box is displayed, you hear a beep.

☐ Experiment with the various controls of the Select a File dialog box.

☐ Terminate the Select program by selecting Exit from the File menu.

How the Select Program Works

The Select program uses the frmGetFile form as a modal dialog box. The program's code displays the frmGetFile form whenever it needs a filename from you.

The frmSelect Form's Procedures

The next two sections explain the code in the Form_Load() and mnuSelectFile_Click() procedures for the frmSelect form.

The Code in the *Form_Load()* Procedure

When you start the program, the Form_Load() procedure of the frmSelect form is executed. In this procedure, the frmGetFile dialog box is loaded, and the cboFileType combo box of the dialog box is initialized:

```
Private Sub Form_Load ()

    ' Load the frmGetFile dialog box
    '(without displaying it).
    Load frmGetFile
```

```
' Initialize the cboFileType combo box of the
' frmGetFile dialog box.
frmGetFile.cboFileType.AddItem "All files (*.*)"
frmGetFile.cboFileType.AddItem "Text files (*.TXT)"
frmGetFile.cboFileType.AddItem "Doc files  (*.DOC)"
frmGetFile.cboFileType.ListIndex = 0
```

End Sub

The frmGetFile dialog box is loaded into memory with the Load statement. Loading the form does not display it. The form is loaded into memory so that later other procedures can show the dialog box without delays.

After the frmGetFile dialog box is loaded, the procedure initializes the cboFileType combo box of the frmGetFile dialog box. The cboFileType combo box is filled with three items: All Files (*.*), Text Files (*.TXT), and Doc Files (*.DOC); later when the frmGetFile dialog box is displayed, you can set the File Type combo box to either *.*, *.TXT, or *.DOC.

The Code in the *mnuSelectFile_Click()* Procedure

When you choose Select File from the File menu, the mnuSelectFile_Click() procedure is executed. The code in this procedure displays the frmGetFile form as a modal dialog box, then uses the output of the dialog box to find which file you selected from the dialog box. The output of the dialog box (that is, the name of the selected file) is provided in the Tag property of the frmGetFile form:

```
Private Sub mnuSelectFile_Click ()

    ' Set the Caption property of frmGetFile.
    frmGetFile.Caption = "Select a file"

    ' Display the frmGetFile form as a modal dialog
    ' box.
    frmGetFile.Show 1

    ' Display the name of the selected file on the
    ' screen.
    If frmGetFile.Tag = "" Then
        MsgBox "No file was selected!"
    Else
        MsgBox "You selected " + frmGetFile.Tag
    End If

End Sub
```

The first statement of the procedure sets the Caption property of the frmGetFile form to Select a file:

```
frmGetFile.Caption = "Select a file"
```

Then the frmGetFile form is displayed onscreen as a modal dialog box by using the Show method with its style equal to 1:

```
frmGetFile.Show 1
```

The code in the frmGetFile form updates the Tag property of frmGetFile with the name of the file that you select. If you don't select a file (for example, you push the Cancel button), the code of the frmGetFile sets the Tag property of frmGetFile to null.

After you select a file from the frmGetFile form, the name of the selected file, if any, is displayed onscreen :

```
If frmGetFile.Tag = "" Then
   MsgBox "No file was selected!"
Else
   MsgBox "You selected " + frmGetFile.Tag
End If
```

If frmGetFile.Tag is null, you didn't select a file, and the message No file was selected! is displayed. However, if frmGetFile.Tag is not null, the selected file (that is, frmGetFile.Tag) is displayed.

The frmGetFile Form's Procedures

The following sections explain the code in the frmGetFile form's procedures.

The Code in the *Form_Load()* Procedure

Whenever the frmGetFile form is loaded, the Form_Load() procedure of the frmGetFile form is executed. The code of this procedure updates the lblDirName label with the path value of the Directory list box:

```
Private Sub Form_Load ()

    ' Update the Directory lblDirName label with the
    ' path value of the Directory list box.
    lblDirName.Caption = dirDirectory.Path

End Sub
```

The Code in the *drvDrive_Change()* Procedure

The code in this procedure is the same as the code in the Size program's drvDrive_Change() procedure.

The Code in the *dirDirectory_Change()* Procedure

The code in this procedure is the same as the code in the Size program's drvDirectory_Change() procedure.

The Code in the *cboFileType_Click()* Procedure

Whenever you make a selection from the cboFileType combo box, the cboFileType_Click() procedure is executed. The code in this procedure updates the Pattern property of the File list box:

```
Private Sub cboFileType_Click ()

    Dim PatternPos1 As Integer
    Dim PatternPos2 As Integer
    Dim PatternLen As Integer
    Dim Pattern As String

    ' Find the start position of the pattern in the
    ' cbboFileType combo box.
    PatternPos1 = InStr(1, cboFileType.Text, "(") + 1

    ' Find the end position of the pattern in the
    ' cbboFileType combo box.
    PatternPos2 = InStr(1, cboFileType.Text, ")") - 1

    ' Calculate the length of the Pattern string.
    PatternLen = PatternPos2 - PatternPos1 + 1

    ' Extract the Pattern portion of the cboFileType
    ' combo box.
    Pattern=Mid(cboFileType.Text,PatternPos1,PatternLen)

    ' Set the Pattern of the filFiles file listbox to the
    ' selected pattern.
    filFiles.Pattern = Pattern

End Sub
```

The Text property of the cboFileType combo box (cboFileType.Text) contains the file type you selected. To find the pattern of the selected file type, the procedure extracts the pattern portion from cboFileType.Text. For example, if cboFileType.Text is equal to Text Files (*.TXT), the pattern portion is *.TXT.

The procedure finds the position of the first character of the pattern portion from cboFileType.Text by locating the first parenthesis and adding 1 to it:

```
PatternPos1 = InStr(1, cboFileType.Text, "(" ) + 1
```

Similarly, the procedure finds the position of the last character of the pattern portion locating the second parenthesis and subtracting 1 from it:

```
PatternPos2 = InStr(1, cboFileType.Text, ")") - 1
```

The length of the Pattern string is calculated by subtracting `PatternPos1` from `PatternPos2` and adding 1 to the result:

```
PatternLen = PatternPos2 - PatternPos1 + 1
```

Finally, the pattern portion is extracted by using the `Mid()` function:

```
Pattern= Mid(cboFileType.Text, PatternPos1, PatternLen)
```

The last statement of the procedure assigns the extracted pattern to the Pattern property of the filFiles File list box:

```
filFiles.Pattern = Pattern
```

As a result, the File list box displays only files with the same pattern as the extracted pattern.

The Code in the *filFiles_Click()* Procedure

The code in this procedure is the same as the code in the Size program's `filFiles_Click()` procedure.

The Code in the *cmdOK_Click()* Procedure

When you push the OK pushbutton, the `cmdOK_Click()` procedure is executed:

```
Private Sub cmdOK_Click ()

    Dim PathAndName As String
    Dim Path As String

    ' If no file is selected, tell the user and
    ' exit this procedure.
    If txtFileName.Text = "" Then
     MsgBox "No file is selected!", vbExclamation, "Error"
     Exit Sub
    End If

    ' Make sure that Path ends with backslash (\).
    If Right(filFiles.Path, 1) <> "\" Then
        Path = filFiles.Path + "\"
    Else
        Path = filFiles.Path
    End If

    ' Extract the Path and Name of the selected
    ' file.
```

```
If txtFileName.Text = filFiles.FileName Then
   PathAndName = Path + filFiles.FileName
Else
   PathAndName = txtFileName.Text
End If

' Set the tag property of the frmGetFile dialog
' box to the selected file path and name.
frmGetFile.Tag = PathAndName

' Hide the frmGetFile dialog box.
frmGetFile.Hide
```

End Sub

As you can see, this procedure is very similar to the Size program's cmdOK_Click() procedure. The first thing it does is check whether you selected a file by comparing the Text property of the txtFileName text box with null. If txtFileName.Text is null, a message is displayed and the procedure is terminated:

```
If txtFileName.Text = "" Then
  MsgBox "No file is selected!", vbExclamation, "Error"
  Exit Sub
End If
```

After the code makes sure that the user selected a file, the Path variable is updated with the path (directory name) of the selected file. The Right() function is used to make sure the rightmost character of the selected file's path is the backslash character (\). If it isn't, the backslash is added to the Path variable:

```
If Right(filFiles.Path, 1) <> "\" Then
   Path = filFiles.Path + "\"
Else
   Path = filFiles.Path
End If
```

The preceding If statement is necessary because when you select a file from the root directory of a drive, filFiles.Path contains the letter drive of the selected root directory and the backslash character (for example, C:\). However, when you select a file that isn't in the root directory, filFiles.Path contains the pathname of the selected directory without the backslash character at the end (for example, C:\TRY instead of C:\TRY\). Therefore, the preceding If statement ensures that no matter which directory you select, the Path variable will always terminate with the backslash character.

After the Path variable is ready, the PathAndName variable can be updated. As implied by its name, the PathAndName variable should contain the full name of the file (that is, path and name). The PathAndName variable is updated with an If statement:

```
If txtFileName.Text = filFiles.FileName Then
   PathAndName = Path + filFiles.FileName
Else
   PathAndName = txtFileName.Text
End If
```

13

This `If` statement checks whether the currently highlighted file in the File list box is the same as the contents of the File Name text box. If the filename in the text box is not the same as the currently highlighted file, it means that you manually typed the path and name of the file, so the `PathAndName` variable is updated with whatever you typed. However, if the filename in the text box is the same as the currently highlighted file, the variable `PathAndName` is updated with the string `Path + filFiles.FileName`.

Once the variable `PathAndName` is updated, its value is assigned to the Tag property of the frmGetFile form:

```
frmGetFile.Tag = PathAndName
```

The Tag property of the form is used to store the output of the frmGetFile form. The procedure that displayed the frmGetFile form "knows" which file you selected by using `frmGetFile.Tag`.

The last statement in the procedure removes the frmGetFile form from the screen by using the `Hide` method:

```
frmGetFile.Hide
```

After executing this statement, the frmGetFile is removed from the screen, and control is given back to the procedure that displayed the frmGetFile form.

The Code in the *filFiles_DblClick()* Procedure

The code in this procedure is the same as the code in the Size program's `filFiles_DblClick()` procedure.

The Code in the *cmdCancel_Click()* Procedure

When you click the Cancel button, the `cmdCancel_Click()` procedure is executed:

```
Private Sub cmdCancel_Click ()

  ' Set the tag property of the form to null.
  frmGetFile.Tag = ""

  ' Hide the frmGetFile dialog box.
  frmGetFile.Hide

End Sub
```

Recall that the Tag property of the frmGetFile form is used to store the path and name of the file you selected. Because you clicked the Cancel button, this procedure assigns null to the Tag property:

```
frmGetFile.Tag = ""
```

The last statement in the procedure removes the frmGetFile form from the screen by using the Hide method:

```
frmGetFile.Hide
```

After executing this statement, the frmGetFile is removed from the screen, and control is given back to the procedure that displayed the frmGetFile form.

Summary

In this chapter you have learned how to use the file-system controls to write programs that let you select files. You have also learned how to write a general-purpose GetFile form that can be used by any program that requires you to select files.

Q&A

Q **How can I add the GETFILE.FRM form of the Select program to other projects?**

A Let's say you have a project called AnyProj. Use the following steps to add the GETFILE.FRM form to the AnyProj project:

☐ Open the AnyProj project.

☐ Select Add File from the File menu, then select the GETFILE.FRM file.

Quiz

1. What is the purpose of the first line in the following code?

```
On Error GoTo DriveError
dirDirectory.Path = "A:"
Exit Sub
DriveError:
MsgBox "Drive error!", 48, "Error"
drvDrive.Drive = dirDirectory.Path
Exit Sub
```

2. What happens after the following statement is executed?

```
filFiles.Pattern = "*.BAT"
```

3. What happens after the following statement is executed?

```
filFiles.Path = dirDirectory.Path
```

4. What happens after the following statement is executed?

```
dirDirectory.Path = "D:"
```

13

Exercise

Enhance the Select program so that the File Type combo box of the GetFile dialog box also includes the file type Batch Files (*.BAT).

Quiz Answers

1. The purpose of the first line of the code:

   ```
   On Error GoTo DriveError
   ```

   is to set an error trap so that if a runtime error occurs on the following lines, the error will be trapped.

2. After the statement `filFiles.Pattern = "*.BAT"` is executed, the filFiles File list box displays only files that have the .BAT extension.

3. After the statement `filFiles.Path = dirDirectory.Path` is executed, the filFiles list box displays the files of the directory currently selected in the dirDirectory Directory list box.

4. After the statement `dirDirectory.Path = "D:"` is executed, the dirDirectory Directory list box displays the directories of the D: drive.

Exercise Answer

To enhance the Select program so that the File Type combo box of the Select a File dialog box includes the file type Batch Files (*.BAT), you need to add the following statement to the `Form_Load()` procedure of the frmSelect form:

```
frmGetFile.cboFileType.AddItem "Batch files (*.BAT)"
```

After adding this statement, the `Form_Load()` procedure should look like the following:

```
Private Sub Form_Load ()

    ' Load the frmGetFile dialog box
    '(without displaying it).
    Load frmGetFile

    ' Initialize the File Type combo box of the
    ' frmGetFile dialog box.
    frmGetFile.cboFileType.AddItem "All files (*.*)"
    frmGetFile.cboFileType.AddItem "Text files (*.TXT)"
    frmGetFile.cboFileType.AddItem "Doc files  (*.DOC)"
    frmGetFile.cboFileType.AddItem "Batch files (*.BAT)"
    frmGetFile.cboFileType.ListIndex = 0

End Sub
```

14

Accessing Files

Many programs need to read and write data to disk files. In this chapter you'll learn how to create files, how to read data from files, and how to write data to files.

There are three ways to access files in Visual Basic:

- Random access
- Sequential access
- Binary access

This chapter teaches you how to use each of these file access techniques to manipulate files.

Random Access Files

A *random access file* is like a database. It is made up of records of identical size. Each record is made up of fields that store data. Figure 14.1 shows a random access file with two fields per record. The first field is a 5-byte string that corresponds to a person's name. The second field is a 2-byte string that corresponds to a person's age. Each record in this file is 7 bytes—the first sequence of 7 bytes makes up the first record, the second sequence of 7 bytes makes up the second record, and so on. Each record stores data about a specific person (that is, the person's name and age).

Figure 14.1.
A random access file.

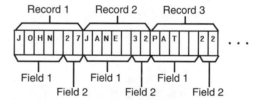

The Phone Program

The Phone program illustrates how to create and manipulate random access files. The program lets you maintain a database file called PHONE.DAT that keeps records of people and their phone numbers.

The Visual Implementation of the Phone Program

☐ Start a new project.

☐ Save the form of the project as PHONE.FRM in the C:\VB4PRG\CH14 directory and save the project file as PHONE.VBP in the C:\VB4PRG\CH14 directory.

☐ Build the form according to the specifications in Table 14.1.

The completed form should look like the one shown in Figure 14.2.

Table 14.1. The properties table of the Phone program.

Object	Property	Value
Form	**Name**	**frmPhone**
	Caption	(empty)
	MaxButton	False
	Height	3555
	Left	1530
	Top	1875
	Width	6705
Text Box	**Name**	**txtName**
	Text	(empty)
	FontName	System
	FontSize	10
	Height	285
	Left	840
	MaxLength	40
	Top	120
	Width	4335
Text Box	**Name**	**txtPhone**
	Text	(empty)
	FontName	System
	FontSize	10
	Height	285
	Left	840
	MaxLength	40
	Top	720
	Width	4335

continues

14

Table 14.1. continued

Object	Property	Value
Text Box	**Name**	**txtComments**
	Text	(empty)
	FontName	System
	FontSize	10
	Height	1455
	Left	120
	MaxLength	100
	MultiLine	True
	ScrollBars	2-Vertical
	Top	1560
	Width	5055
Command Button	**Name**	**cmdNew**
	Caption	New
	FontName	System
	FontSize	10
	Height	495
	Left	5280
	Top	120
	Width	1215
Command Button	**Name**	**cmdNext**
	Caption	Next
	FontName	System
	FontSize	10
	Height	495
	Left	5280
	Top	600
	Width	1215

Object	Property	Value
Command Button	**Name**	**cmdPrevious**
	Caption	Previous
	FontName	System
	FontSize	10
	Height	495
	Left	5280
	Top	1080
	Width	1215
Command Button	**Name**	**cmdExit**
	Caption	Exit
	FontName	System
	FontSize	10
	Height	495
	Left	5280
	Top	2520
	Width	1215
Label	**Name**	**lblComments**
	Caption	Comments:
	FontName	System
	FontSize	10
	Height	255
	Left	120
	Top	1320
	Width	975
Label	**Name**	**lblPhone**
	Caption	Phone:
	FontName	System
	FontSize	10
	Height	255
	Left	120

14

continues

Table 14.1. continued

Object	Property	Value
	Top	720
	Width	615
Label	**Name**	**lblName**
	Caption	Name:
	FontName	System
	FontSize	10
	Height	255
	Left	120
	Top	120
	Width	615

Figure 14.2.
The form of the Phone program.

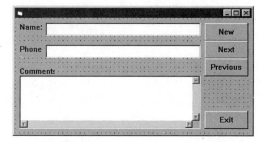

Entering the Code of the Phone Program

As you'll soon see, besides the PHONE.FRM form that you designed, the Phone program also needs a program module (you'll soon see what it's for). Therefore, you need to create a program module. Here is how you do that:

☐ Create a new program module by selecting Module from the Insert menu.

Visual Basic responds by creating a new module and displaying its code window. As you can see from the title of the new module's code window, Visual Basic named the new module Module1.

Save the new module as PHONE.BAS:

☐ Select Save File As from the File menu and save the file as PHONE.BAS in the C:\VB4PRG\CH14 directory.

Now the Module1 module is saved in the file PHONE.BAS.

☐ Enter the following code in the general declarations section of the Module1 module:

```
' All variables must be declared.
Option Explicit

' Declare a user-defined type that corresponds to a
' record in the file PHONE.DAT.
Type PersonInfo
    Name        As String * 40
    Phone       As String * 40
    Comments    As String * 100
End Type
```

That's all the code you need to type in the Module1 module. In the following steps you'll enter code in the frmPhone form.

☐ Enter the following code in the general declarations section of the frmPhone form:

```
' All variables must be declared.
Option Explicit

' Declare variables that should be visible in all
' the procedures of the form.
Dim gPerson As PersonInfo
Dim gFileNum As Integer
Dim gRecordLen As Long
Dim gCurrentRecord As Long
Dim gLastRecord As Long
```

☐ Create a new procedure in the frmPhone form and name it SaveCurrentRecord.

☐ Enter the following code in the SaveCurrentRecord() procedure:

```
Public Sub SaveCurrentRecord()

    ' Fill gPerson with the currently displayed data.
    gPerson.Name = txtName.Text
    gPerson.Phone = txtPhone.Text
    gPerson.Comments = txtComments.Text

    ' Save gPerson to the current record.
    Put #gFileNum, gCurrentRecord, gPerson

End Sub
```

☐ Create a new procedure in the frmPhone form and name it ShowCurrentRecord.

☐ Enter the following code in the ShowCurrentRecord() procedure:

```
Public Sub ShowCurrentRecord()

    ' Fill gPerson with the data of the current
    ' record.
    Get #gFileNum, gCurrentRecord, gPerson

    ' Display gPerson.
    txtName.Text = Trim(gPerson.Name)
    txtPhone.Text = Trim(gPerson.Phone)
    txtComments.Text = Trim(gPerson.Comments)
```

14

```
' Display the current record number in the
' caption of the form.
 frmPhone.Caption= "Record " + _
                   Str(gCurrentRecord) + "/" + _
                   Str(gLastRecord)
```

End Sub

☐ Enter the following code in the Form_Load() procedure:

Private Sub Form_Load()

```
' Calculate the length of a record.
gRecordLen = Len(gPerson)

' Get the next available file number.
gFileNum = FreeFile

' Open the file for random-access. If the file
' does not exist then it is created.
Open "PHONE.DAT" For Random As gFileNum Len = gRecordLen

' Update gCurrentRecord.
gCurrentRecord = 1

' Find what is the last record number of
' the file.
gLastRecord = FileLen("PHONE.DAT") / gRecordLen

' If the file was just created
' (i.e. gLastRecord=0) then update gLastRecord
' to 1.
If gLastRecord = 0 Then
   gLastRecord = 1
End If

' Display the current record.
ShowCurrentRecord
```

End Sub

☐ Enter the following code in the cmdNew_Click() procedure:

Private Sub cmdNew_Click()

```
' Save the current record.
SaveCurrentRecord

' Add a new blank record.
gLastRecord = gLastRecord + 1
gPerson.Name = ""
gPerson.Phone = ""
gPerson.Comments = ""
Put #gFileNum, gLastRecord, gPerson
```

```
' Update gCurrentRecord.
gCurrentRecord = gLastRecord

' Display the record that was just created.
ShowCurrentRecord

' Give the focus to the txtName field.
txtName.SetFocus
```

End Sub

☐ Enter the following code in the cmdNext_Click() procedure:

Private Sub cmdNext_Click()

```
' If the current record is the last record,
' beep and display an error message. Otherwise,
' save the current record and skip to the
' next record.
If gCurrentRecord = gLastRecord Then
   Beep
   MsgBox "End of file!", vbExclamation
Else
   SaveCurrentRecord
   gCurrentRecord = gCurrentRecord + 1
   ShowCurrentRecord
End If

' Give the focus to the txtName field.
txtName.SetFocus
```

End Sub

☐ Enter the following code in the cmdPrevious_Click() procedure:

Private Sub cmdPrevious_Click()

```
' If the current record is the first record,
' beep and display an error message. Otherwise,
' save the current record and go to the
' previous record.
If gCurrentRecord = 1 Then
   Beep
   MsgBox "Beginning of file!", vbExclamation
Else
   SaveCurrentRecord
   gCurrentRecord = gCurrentRecord - 1
   ShowCurrentRecord
End If

' Give the focus to the txtName field.
txtName.SetFocus
```

End Sub

14

☐ Enter the following code in the cmdExit_Click() procedure:

```
Private Sub cmdExit_Click()

    ' Save the current record.
    SaveCurrentRecord

    ' Close the file.
    Close #gFileNum

    ' End the program.
    End

End Sub
```

Executing the Phone Program

☐ Execute the Phone program.

While you run the program, notice the following features:

- The first time you execute the program, the database is empty and a blank record appears onscreen. This Record is record 1 of 1, as indicated in the caption of the program's window. The program lets you type the person's name and phone number and comments about the person. (See Figure 14.3.) You can move from one field to another by using the mouse or pressing the Tab key.

- To add a new record, click the New button and a new blank record will appear. The form's caption displays the new record's record number and the total number of records. (See Figure 14.4.)

- Once you have a few records in the database, you can move from one record to another by using the Next and Previous buttons. When you click the Next button, the next record is displayed; clicking the Previous button displays the previous record.

☐ Click the Exit button to terminate the Phone program.

Figure 14.3.

The first record in the Phone program.

Figure 14.4.

*The Phone program after
you add a new record.*

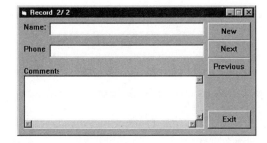

All the records you added to the database are stored in the file PHONE.DAT. If you execute
the program again, you will see the records you entered.

As you can see, you can't delete a record or search for a record in the Phone program. Later in
this chapter, you will enhance the program so you can delete records and search for records.

How the Phone Program Works

The Phone program opens the file PHONE.DAT as a random access file with the fields Name,
Phone, and Comments. If the file does not exist, the program creates it.

Declaring a User-Defined Type

The code you typed in the general declarations section of the Module1 module declares a user-
defined type that corresponds to the fields of a record in the PHONE.DAT file:

```
' Declare a user-defined type that corresponds to a
' record in the file PHONE.DAT.
Type PersonInfo
    Name        As String * 40
    Phone       As String * 40
    Comments    As String * 100
End Type
```

The declared type is called `PersonInfo`, and it is made up of three variables: `Name` (a 40-character
string), `Phone` (a 40-character string), and `Comments` (a 100-character string). Each of these strings
corresponds to a field in the PHONE.DAT file.

Later, the Phone program will use a variable of the type `PersonInfo` to write (and read) data to
the PERSON.DAT file.

Note that `PersonInfo` is declared in the general declarations area of the Module1 module, not
in the general declarations area of the frmPhone form.

The General Declarations Section of the frmPhone Form

In the general declarations section of the frmPhone form, the variables that should be visible in all the form's procedures are declared:

```
' Declare variables that should be visible in all
' the procedures of the form.
Dim gPerson As PersonInfo
Dim gFileNum As Integer
Dim gRecordLen As Long
Dim gCurrentRecord As Long
Dim gLastRecord As Long
```

The variable gPerson is declared as type PersonInfo. Because the user-defined type PersonInfo consists of three variables (that is, Name, Phone, and Comments), the variable gPerson also consists of three variables: gPerson.Name, gPerson.Phone, and gPerson.Comments. The variable gPerson is used to hold a record's data.

Opening the PHONE.DAT File

Before data can be written to or read from a file, the file must be opened. The code responsible for opening the PHONE.DAT file is in the Form_Load() procedure:

```
Private Sub Form_Load()

    ' Calculate the length of a record.
    gRecordLen = Len(gPerson)

    ' Get the next available file number.
    gFileNum = FreeFile

    ' Open the file for random-access. If the file
    ' does not exist then it is created.
    Open "PHONE.DAT" For Random As gFileNum Len = gRecordLen

    ' Update gCurrentRecord.
    gCurrentRecord = 1

    ' Find what the last record number of
    ' the file is.
    gLastRecord = FileLen("PHONE.DAT") / gRecordLen

    ' If the file was just created
    ' (i.e. gLastRecord=0) then update gLastRecord
    ' to 1.
    If gLastRecord = 0 Then
        gLastRecord = 1
    End If

    ' Display the current record.
    ShowCurrentRecord

End Sub
```

When you open a file for random access, you need to specify the record size of the file and a file number. So before opening the file, the Form_Load() procedure extracts these values with the following two statements:

```
gRecordLen = Len(gPerson)
gFileNum = FreeFile
```

The first statement uses the Len() function to extract the length of the variable gPerson. Because the variable gPerson corresponds to the fields of the PHONE.DAT file, its length is the same as the length of a record.

The second statement uses the FreeFile function to get a file number that is not already in use. As stated previously, when you open a file, you need to specify a file number used to identify the opened file. Subsequent statements that perform operations on this file need this file number to tell Visual Basic on which file to perform the operation.

Now that the variables gRecordLen and gFileNum are updated, the procedure opens the PHONE.DAT file for random access with the following statement:

```
Open "PHONE.DAT" For Random As gFileNum Len = gRecordLen
```

If the PHONE.DAT file does not exist, the Open statement creates it. So the first time you execute the Phone program, the file PHONE.DAT is created in the same directory the Phone program is executed from. When you finish developing the Phone program, you'll create the file PHONE.EXE. If you save the PHONE.EXE file in, for example, the C:\TRY directory and then later execute the PHONE.EXE program from the C:\TRY directory, the PHONE.DAT file will be created in the C:\TRY directory. However, during design time (when you execute the Phone program from Visual Basic), the PHONE.DAT file is created in the Visual Basic directory.

After the file PHONE.DAT is opened, the procedure updates the variables gCurrentRecord and gLastRecord.

The variable gCurrentRecord is used to store the record number of the currently displayed record. Since initially record number 1 should be displayed, gCurrentRecord is initialized to 1:

```
gCurrentRecord = 1
```

The variable gLastRecord is used to store the record number of the last record in the file (that is, the total number of records). This value is calculated by dividing the total file length by the length of a record:

```
gLastRecord = FileLen("PHONE.DAT") / gRecordLen
```

However, there is one special case for which this calculation does not work. If the file was just created, FileLen() returns 0 and the above calculation yields a value of 0 for gLastRecord. To make sure that gLastRecord is not assigned a value of 0, use an If statement:

14

```
If gLastRecord = 0 Then
    gLastRecord = 1
End If
```

This `If` statement checks to see whether `gLastRecord` is 0. If it is, the `If` statement changes it to 1.

The last statement in the `Form_Load()` procedure executes the procedure `ShowCurrentRecord()`:

```
' Display the current record.
ShowCurrentRecord
```

The procedure `ShowCurrentRecord` displays the data of the record specified by the variable `gCurrentRecord`. Since `gCurrentRecord` is now equal to 1 after executing the preceding statement, the data of record number 1 is displayed.

The Code in the *ShowCurrentRecord()* Procedure

The code in the `ShowCurrentRecord()` procedure displays the data of the record specified by the variable `gCurrentRecord`:

```
Public Sub ShowCurrentRecord()

    ' Fill gPerson with the data of the current
    ' record.
    Get #gFileNum, gCurrentRecord, gPerson

    ' Display gPerson.
    txtName.Text = Trim(gPerson.Name)
    txtPhone.Text = Trim(gPerson.Phone)
    txtComments.Text = Trim(gPerson.Comments)

    ' Display the current record number in the
    ' caption of the form.
    frmPhone.Caption= "Record " + _
                    Str(gCurrentRecord) + "/" + _
                    Str(gLastRecord)

End Sub
```

The first statement of the procedure uses the `Get` statement to fill the variable `gPerson` with the data of the current record:

```
Get #gFileNum, gCurrentRecord, gPerson
```

The `Get` statement takes three parameters: The first parameter specifies the file number of the file (the number specified when the file was opened), the second parameter specifies the record number of the record to be read, and the third parameter specifies the name of the variable that is filled with the data read from the record.

For example, if gCurrentRecord is currently equal to 5 after executing the preceding statement, the variable gPerson contains the data of record number 5. That is, gPerson.Name, gPerson.Phone, and gPerson.Comments contain the data stored in the fields Name, Phone, and Comments of record number 5.

After the variable gPerson is filled with the data of the current record, its contents are displayed by updating the txtName, txtPhone, and txtComments text boxes:

```
txtName.Text = Trim(gPerson.Name)
txtPhone.Text = Trim(gPerson.Phone)
txtComments.Text = Trim(gPerson.Comments)
```

Note that the text boxes are assigned with the trimmed values of the gPerson variable. That's because the text boxes shouldn't contain any trailing blanks. For example, if the current record in the database contains the name JOHN SMITH in the Name field, after you execute the Get statement the variable gPerson.Name contains these characters:

```
"JOHN SMITH............................."
```

Since the Name field was defined as 40 characters and JOHN SMITH is only 10 characters, Visual Basic added 30 trailing blanks to the field when the record was stored. These trailing blanks should not appear in the text box, so the Trim() function was used.

The last statement of the procedure displays the current record number in the form's caption:

```
frmPhone.Caption= "Record " + _
                Str(gCurrentRecord) + "/" + _
                Str(gLastRecord)
```

For example, if the current value of gCurrentRecord is 5 and the value of gLastRecord is 15, the preceding statement sets the form's caption to Record 5/15.

The Code in the *cmdNext_Click()* Procedure

Whenever you click the Next button, the cmdNext_Click() procedure is executed. The code in this procedure is responsible for displaying the contents of the next record:

```
Private Sub cmdNext_Click()

' If the current record is the last record,
' beep and display an error message. Otherwise,
' save the current record and skip to the
' next record.
If gCurrentRecord = gLastRecord Then
    Beep
    MsgBox "End of file!", vbExclamation
Else
    SaveCurrentRecord
    gCurrentRecord = gCurrentRecord + 1
    ShowCurrentRecord
End If
```

503

```
' Give the focus to the txtName field.
txtName.SetFocus
```

End Sub

The first statement of the procedure is an `If` statement that checks whether `gCurrentRecord` is equal to `gLastRecord`. If `gCurrentRecord` is equal to `gLastRecord` (that is, there is no next record), your PC beeps and displays a message—`End of file!`—informing you that the current record is the end of the file:

```
Beep
MsgBox "End of file!", vbExclamation
```

If, however, `gCurrentRecord` is not equal to `gLastRecord`, the following statements are executed:

```
SaveCurrentRecord
gCurrentRecord = gCurrentRecord + 1
ShowCurrentRecord
```

The first statement executes the `SaveCurrentRecord()` procedure, which saves the contents of the text boxes txtName, txtPhone, and txtComments in the PHONE.DAT file. The second statement increments the variable `gCurrentRecord` by 1 so it points to the next record. The third statement executes the procedure `ShowCurrentRecord()` so the text boxes txtName, txtPhone, and txtComments display the record that equals the new value of `gCurrentRecord`.

The last statement of the procedure uses the `SetFocus` method to set the keyboard focus to the txtName text box:

```
txtName.SetFocus
```

After the preceding statement is executed, the cursor appears in the txtName text box.

The Code in the *SaveCurrentRecord()* Procedure

The `SaveCurrentRecord()` procedure is responsible for saving the contents of the text boxes txtName, txtPhone, and txtComments in the record specified by `gCurrentRecord`:

Public Sub SaveCurrentRecord()

```
  ' Fill gPerson with the currently displayed data.
  gPerson.Name = txtName.Text
  gPerson.Phone = txtPhone.Text
  gPerson.Comments = txtComments.Text

  ' Save gPerson to the current record.
  Put #gFileNum, gCurrentRecord, gPerson
```

End Sub

The first three statements of the procedure fill the gPerson variable with the contents of the three text boxes:

```
gPerson.Name = txtName.Text
gPerson.Phone = txtPhone.Text
gPerson.Comments = txtComments.Text
```

After the gPerson variable is filled, the procedure executes the Put statement to store the contents of the gPerson variable in record number gCurrentRecord of the file:

```
Put #gFileNum, gCurrentRecord, gPerson
```

The Put statement takes three parameters: The first parameter specifies the file number of the file (the number specified when the file was opened), the second parameter specifies the record number that is being saved, and the third parameter specifies the name of the variable whose contents will be saved in the record.

Adding a New Record to the PHONE.DAT File

The cmdNew_Click() procedure is responsible for adding a new record to the PHONE.DAT file. It is executed whenever you click the New button:

```
Private Sub cmdNew_Click()

   ' Save the current record.
   SaveCurrentRecord

   ' Add a new blank record.
   gLastRecord = gLastRecord + 1
   gPerson.Name = ""
   gPerson.Phone = ""
   gPerson.Comments = ""
   Put #gFileNum, gLastRecord, gPerson

   ' Update gCurrentRecord.
   gCurrentRecord = gLastRecord

   ' Display the record that was just created.
   ShowCurrentRecord

   ' Give the focus to the txtName field.
   txtName.SetFocus

End Sub
```

The first statement of the procedure executes the SaveCurrentRecord() procedure so the current record (that is, the contents of the text boxes) is saved in the PHONE.DAT file. After saving the current record, the procedure adds a new blank record to the file with the following statements:

```
gLastRecord = gLastRecord + 1
gPerson.Name = ""
```

```
gPerson.Phone = ""
gPerson.Comments = ""
Put #gFileNum, gLastRecord, gPerson
```

The first statement increments gLastRecord so it points to the number of the new record, then the gPerson variable is set to null, and finally the Put statement is used to create the new record. The number of the new record is gLastRecord, and its contents are the contents of the gPerson variable (that is, null).

After creating the new blank record, the gCurrentRecord variable is updated so it points to the new record:

```
gCurrentRecord = gLastRecord
```

Then the ShowCurrentRecord() procedure is executed so the record that was just created is displayed:

```
ShowCurrentRecord
```

The last statement of the procedure uses the SetFocus method to set the keyboard focus to the txtName text box:

```
txtName.SetFocus
```

After the preceding statement is executed, the cursor appears in the txtName text box.

The Code in the *cmdPrevious_Click()* Procedure

Whenever you click the Previous button, the cmdPrevious_Click() procedure is executed. The code in this procedure is responsible for displaying the contents of the previous record:

```
Private Sub cmdPrevious_Click()

  ' If the current record is the first record,
  ' beep and display an error message. Otherwise,
  ' save the current record and go to the
  ' previous record.
  If gCurrentRecord = 1 Then
    Beep
    MsgBox "Beginning of file!", vbExclamation
  Else
    SaveCurrentRecord
    gCurrentRecord = gCurrentRecord - 1
    ShowCurrentRecord
  End If

  ' Give the focus to the txtName field.
  txtName.SetFocus

End Sub
```

The first statement of the procedure is an `If` statement that checks whether `gCurrentRecord` is equal to 1. If it is (that is, there is no previous record), your PC beeps and displays a message—`Beginning of file!`—informing you that the current record is the beginning of the file:

```
Beep
MsgBox "Beginning of file!", vbExclamation
```

If, however, `gCurrentRecord` is not equal to 1, the following statements are executed:

```
SaveCurrentRecord
gCurrentRecord = gCurrentRecord - 1
ShowCurrentRecord
```

The first statement executes the `SaveCurrentRecord()` procedure to save the contents of the text boxes txtName, txtPhone, and txtComments in the PHONE.DAT file. The second statement decrements the variable `gCurrentRecord` by 1 so it points to the previous record. The third statement executes the procedure `ShowCurrentRecord` so the text boxes txtName, txtPhone, and txtComments display the record that equals the new value of `gCurrentRecord`.

The last statement of the procedure uses the `SetFocus` method to set the keyboard focus to the txtName text box:

```
txtName.SetFocus
```

After executing this statement, the cursor appears in the txtName text box.

The Code in the *cmdExit_Click()* Procedure

The `cmdExit_Click()` procedure is executed whenever you click the Exit button. The code in this procedure saves the current record in the PHONE.DAT file, closes the PHONE.DAT file, and terminates the program:

```
Private Sub cmdExit_Click()

    ' Save the current record.
    SaveCurrentRecord

    ' Close the file.
    Close #gFileNum

    ' End the program.
    End

End Sub
```

The `Close` statement, `Close #gFileNum`, closes the file. As you can see, it takes one parameter that specifies the file number of the file to be closed.

You really don't have to use the `Close` statement in the `cmdExit_Click()` procedure because the last statement in the `cmdExit_Click()` procedure is `End`, which closes all files, if any, that were opened with the `Open` statement. As you know, the `End` statement also terminates the program.

The Close statement was included in the cmdExit_Click() procedure to illustrate how you can close a file without using the End statement (that is, without terminating the program).

Enhancing the Phone Program

You'll now enhance the Phone program by adding a Search button and a Delete button. The Search button enables you to search for a particular name, and the Delete button enables you to delete records:

☐ Add a command button to the frmPhone form and set its properties as follows:

Object	Property	Value
Command Button	**Name**	**cmdSearch**
	Caption	Search
	Height	495
	Left	5280
	Top	1560
	Width	1215

☐ Add another command button to the frmPhone form and set its properties as follows:

Object	Property	Value
Command Button	**Name**	**cmdDelete**
	Caption	Delete
	Height	495
	Left	5280
	Top	2040
	Width	1215

When you finish setting the properties of the two new buttons, the frmPhone form should look like the one shown in Figure 14.5.

Figure 14.5.

The frmPhone form after you add the Search and Delete buttons.

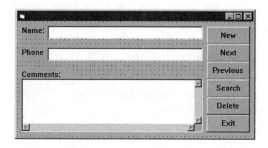

☐ Enter the following code in the cmdSearch_Click() procedure:

```
Private Sub cmdSearch_Click()

Dim NameToSearch As String
Dim Found As Integer
Dim RecNum As Long
Dim TmpPerson As PersonInfo

' Get the name to search from the user.
NameToSearch = InputBox("Search for:", "Search")

' If the user did not enter a name, exit
' from this procedure.
If NameToSearch = "" Then
   ' Give the focus to the txtName field.
   txtName.SetFocus
   ' Exit this procedure.
   Exit Sub
End If

' Convert the name to be searched to upper case.
NameToSearch = UCase(NameTosearch)

' Initialize the Found flag to False.
Found = False

' Search for the name that the user entered.
For RecNum = 1 To gLastRecord
  Get #gFileNum, RecNum, TmpPerson
  If NameToSearch=UCase(Trim(TmpPerson.Name)) Then
     Found = True
     Exit For
  End If
Next

' If the name was found, display the record
' of the found name.
If Found = True Then
   SaveCurrentRecord
   gCurrentRecord = RecNum
   ShowCurrentRecord
Else
    MsgBox "Name " + NameToSearch + " not found!"
End If

' Give the focus to the txtName field.
txtName.SetFocus

End Sub
```

☐ Enter the following code in the cmdDelete_Click() procedure:

```
Private Sub cmdDelete_Click()

Dim DirResult
Dim TmpFileNum
```

```
Dim TmpPerson As PersonInfo
Dim RecNum As Long
Dim TmpRecNum As Long

' Before deleting get a confirmation from the user.
If MsgBox("Delete this record?", vbYesNo) = vbNo Then
    ' Give the focus to the txtName field.
    txtName.SetFocus
    ' Exit the procedure without deleting.
    Exit Sub
End If

' To physically delete the current record of PHONE.DAT,
' all the records of PHONE.DAT, except the
' current record, are copied into a temporary file
' (PHONE.TMP) and then the file PHONE.TMP is copied into
' PHONE.DAT:

' Make sure that PHONE.TMP does not exist.
If Dir("PHONE.TMP") = "PHONE.TMP" Then
    Kill "PHONE.TMP"
End If

' Create PHONE.TMP with the same format
' as PHONE.DAT.
TmpFileNum = FreeFile
Open "PHONE.TMP" For Random As TmpFileNum Len = gRecordLen

' Copy all the records from PHONE.DAT
' to PHONE.TMP, except the current record.
RecNum = 1
TmpRecNum = 1
Do While RecNum < gLastRecord + 1
    If RecNum <> gCurrentRecord Then
        Get #gFileNum, RecNum, TmpPerson
        Put #TmpFileNum, TmpRecNum, TmpPerson
        TmpRecNum = TmpRecNum + 1
    End If
    RecNum = RecNum + 1
Loop

' Delete PHONE.DAT.
Close gFileNum
Kill "PHONE.DAT"

' Rename PHONE.TMP into PHONE.DAT.
Close TmpFileNum
Name "PHONE.TMP" As "PHONE.DAT"

' Re-open PHONE.DAT.
gFileNum = FreeFile
Open "PHONE.DAT" For Random As gFileNum Len = gRecordLen

' Update the value of LastRecord.
gLastRecord = gLastRecord - 1

' Make sure that gLastRecord is not 0.
```

```
If gLastRecord = 0 Then gLastRecord = 1

' Make sure gCurrentRecord is not out of range.
If gCurrentRecord > gLastRecord Then
   gCurrentRecord = gLastRecord
End If

' Show the current record.
ShowCurrentRecord

' Give the focus to the txtName field.
txtName.SetFocus

End Sub
```

☐ Execute the Phone program and experiment with the Search and Delete buttons.

The Code in the *cmdSearch_Click()* Procedure

Whenever you click the Search button, the cmdSearch_Click() procedure is executed. This procedure lets you search for a particular name.

The procedure begins by using the InputBox() function to get a name from you. The name you enter is stored in the variable NameToSearch:

```
NameToSearch = InputBox("Search for:", "Search")
```

The InputBox() function returns null if you click the Cancel button of the Search Input Box, so an If statement is used. If you click the Cancel button, the procedure is terminated:

```
If NameToSearch = "" Then
   ' Give the focus to the txtName field.
   txtName.SetFocus
   ' Exit this procedure.
   Exit Sub
End If
```

After the variable NameToSearch is updated, the UCase() function is used to convert it to uppercase:

```
NameToSearch = UCase(NameToSearch)
```

This conversion is necessary because the search for the name shouldn't be case sensitive (that is, even if you type john, the record containing the name JOHN should be found).

To search for the name you entered, a For loop is used:

```
' Initialize the Found flag to False.
Found = False

' Search for the name that the user entered.
For RecNum = 1 To gLastRecord
  Get #gFileNum, RecNum, TmpPerson
  If NameToSearch=UCase(Trim(TmpPerson.Name)) Then
```

```
      Found = True
      Exit For
   End If
Next
```

This `For` loop uses the `Get` statement to read the records of the file, record after record, into the variable `TmpPerson`. After it reads each record, an `If` statement is used to see whether the record that was just read contains the name being searched for. The `If` statement compares the value of the variable `NameToSearch` with the value of `UCase(Trim(TmpPerson.Name))`. The `UCase()` function is used so the search won't be case sensitive, and the `Trim()` function gets rid of leading or trailing blanks in the Name field.

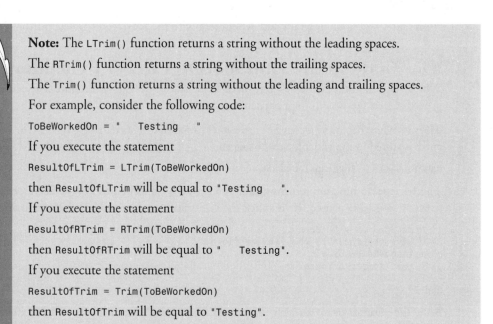

Note: The `LTrim()` function returns a string without the leading spaces.

The `RTrim()` function returns a string without the trailing spaces.

The `Trim()` function returns a string without the leading and trailing spaces.

For example, consider the following code:

`ToBeWorkedOn = "   Testing   "`

If you execute the statement

`ResultOfLTrim = LTrim(ToBeWorkedOn)`

then `ResultOfLTrim` will be equal to `"Testing   "`.

If you execute the statement

`ResultOfRTrim = RTrim(ToBeWorkedOn)`

then `ResultOfRTrim` will be equal to `"   Testing"`.

If you execute the statement

`ResultOfTrim = Trim(ToBeWorkedOn)`

then `ResultOfTrim` will be equal to `"Testing"`.

If a record with its Name field equal to `NameToSearch` is found, the variable `Found` is set to True and the `For` loop is terminated. After the `For` loop ends, the procedure displays the results of the search:

```
If Found = True Then
   SaveCurrentRecord
   gCurrentRecord = RecNum
   ShowCurrentRecord
Else
    MsgBox "Name " + NameToSearch + " not found!"
End If
```

If the search was successful, the current record is saved and the found record is displayed. If, however, the search failed, a not found! message is displayed.

The Code in the *cmdDelete_Click()* Procedure

Whenever you click the Delete button, the cmdDelete_Click() procedure deletes the current record. It uses the following four steps to delete the current record from the PHONE.DAT file:

1. Create an empty temporary file (PHONE.TMP).
2. Use a For loop to copy all the records in PHONE.DAT (record after record), except the current record, into the file PHONE.TMP.
3. Erase the file PHONE.DAT.
4. Rename the file PHONE.TMP as PHONE.DAT.

Sequential Access Files

Random files are accessed record by record, but *sequential files* are accessed line by line. That is, when you write data into a sequential file, you write lines of text into the file. When you read data from a sequential file, you read lines of text from the file. The fact that sequential files are accessed line by line makes them ideal for use in applications that manipulate text files.

You can open a sequential file in one of three ways: output, append, or input.

Opening a Sequential File for Output

To create a sequential file, you need to open a file for output. After the file is created, you can use output commands to write lines to the file. The following sample code creates the file TRY.TXT:

```
' Get a free file number.
FileNum = FreeFile

' Open the file TRY.TXT for output (i.e. create it).
Open "TRY.TXT" For Output As FileNum
```

If the file TRY.TXT does not exist, this code creates it. If the file does exist, this code erases the old file and creates a new one.

Note that in the preceding code, the file to be opened, TRY.TXT, was specified without a path. When a path isn't specified, the file is opened in the current directory. For example, if the current directory is C:\PROGRAMS, the following two statements will do the same thing:

```
Open "TRY.TXT" For Output As FileNum
Open "C:\PROGRAMS\TRY.TXT" For Output As FileNum
```

Because opening a file for output creates the file, it will be empty. To write text into the file, you can use the Print # statement. The following example creates the file TRY.TXT and writes the contents of the text box txtMyText into the file:

```
' Get a free file number.
FileNum = FreeFile

' Open TRY.TXT for output (i.e. create TRY.TXT).
Open "TRY.TXT" For Output As FileNum

' Write the contents of the text box txtMyText into the file TRY.TXT.
Print #FileNum, txtMyText.Text

' Close the file.
Close FileNum
```

In the preceding code, two parameters are passed to the Print # statement: The first parameter is the file number, and the second parameter is the string to be written into the file.

Opening a Sequential File for Append

Opening a sequential file for append is similar to opening it for output; however, when you open a file for append, it isn't erased if the file already exists. Rather, subsequent output commands append new lines to the opened file. For example, suppose that the file TRY.TXT already exists and contains the following two lines:

```
THIS IS LINE NUMBER 1
THIS IS LINE NUMBER 2
```

To append a new line to the file TRY.TXT, you can use the following code:

```
' Get a free file number.
FileNum = FreeFile

' Open TRY.TXT for append.
Open "TRY.TXT" For Append As FileNum

' Add new text to the file.
Print #FileNum, "THIS IS A NEW TEXT"

' Close the file.
Close FileNum
```

After executing this code, the file TRY.TXT contains three lines:

```
THIS IS LINE NUMBER 1
THIS IS LINE NUMBER 2
THIS IS A NEW TEXT
```

If you execute the same code again, the file TRY.TXT will contain four lines:

```
THIS IS LINE NUMBER 1
THIS IS LINE NUMBER 2
THIS IS A NEW TEXT
THIS IS A NEW TEXT
```

Opening a Sequential File for Input

To read the contents of a sequential file, you need to open a file for input. Once a file is opened for input, you can use the Input() function to read the entire contents of the file into a text box or a string variable.

The following example opens the file TRY.TXT for input and uses the Input() function to read the contents of the file into the text box txtMyText:

```
' Get a free file number.
FileNum = FreeFile

' Open TRY.TXT for input.
Open "TRY.TXT" For Input As FileNum

' Read all the contents of the file into the text
' box txtMyText.
txtMyText.Text = Input(LOF(FileNum), FileNum)

' Close the file.
Close FileNum
```

The Input() function takes two parameters: The first parameter specifies the number of bytes to be read from the file, and the second parameter specifies the file number.

Because the purpose of the preceding code is to read the entire contents of the file, the first parameter of the Input() function was specified as LOF(FileNum). The LOF() function returns the total length of the file in bytes.

The *Write #* and *Input #* Statements

In the preceding examples, the Input() function and the Print # statement were used to read data from and write data to a sequential file, but you can also use the Write # and Input # statements.

The Write # statement lets you write a list of variables (strings or numeric) to a file. The following example creates the file TRY.TXT and stores the contents of the string variable MyString and the contents of the numeric variable MyNumber into the file:

```
' Get a free file number.
FileNum = FreeFile

' Create the file TRY.TXT.
Open "TRY.TXT" For Output As FileNum

' Write the contents of the variables MyString and
' MyNumber into the file.
Write #FileNum, MyString, MyNumber

' Close the file.
Close FileNum
```

14

The first parameter of the Write # statement is the file number. The rest of the parameters are the variables that will be written into the file. Because only two variables are written into the file in the preceding example, there are only two parameters after the first parameter.

The Input # statement lets you read data from a file that contains the contents of a list of variables. The following code reads the contents of the file created in the preceding example:

```
' Get a free file number.
FileNum = FreeFile

' Open the file TRY.TXT for input.
Open "TRY.TXT" For Input As FileNum

' Read the contents of the file into the variables
' MyString and MyNumber.
Input #FileNum, MyString, MyNumber

' Close the file.
Close FileNum
```

The first parameter of the Input # statement is the file number. The rest of the parameters are the variables that will be filled with the contents of the file. The order in which the variables are placed in the Input # statement must match the order in which they were originally stored in the file with the Write # statement.

Binary Access Files

Random files are accessed record by record and sequential files are accessed line by line, but *binary files* are accessed byte by byte. Once you open a file for binary access, you can read from and write to any byte location in the file. This ability to access any desired byte in the file makes binary access the most flexible.

Opening a File for Binary Access

Before you can access a file in a binary mode (byte by byte), you must first open a file for binary access. The following sample code opens the file TRY.DAT for binary access:

```
' Get a free file number.
FileNum = FreeFile

' Open the file TRY.DAT for binary access.
Open "TRY.DAT" For Binary As FileNum
```

If the file TRY.DAT does not already exist, the preceding Open statement creates it.

Writing Bytes into a Binary File

After a file is opened for binary access, the Put # statement can be used to write bytes to any byte location in the file. The following sample code writes the string THIS IS A TEST into the file TRY.DAT, starting at byte location 100:

```
' Fill the string variable MyString with the
' string "THIS IS A TEST".
MyString = "THIS IS A TEST"

' Get a free file number.
FileNum = FreeFile

' Open the file TRY.DAT for binary access.
Open "TRY.DAT" For Binary As FileNum

' Write the string variable MyString, starting at
' byte location 100.
Put #FileNum,100, MyString

' Close the file.
Close FileNum
```

The Put # statement takes three parameters: The first parameter is the file number, the second parameter is the byte location where the writing starts, and the third parameter is the name of the variable whose contents will be written into the file. In the preceding example, the variable whose contents are written into the file is a string variable, but you could use other types of variables, such as numeric.

After the Put # statement is executed, the position of the file is automatically set to the next byte after the last byte that was written. For example, in the preceding sample code, after the 14 characters of the string THIS IS A TEST are written into the file starting at position 100, the position of the file is automatically set to 114. So if another Put # statement is executed without specifying the byte location, the writing of this new Put # statement starts at byte location 114. The following sample code illustrates how the file position is updated automatically after a Put # statement:

```
' Get a free file number.
FileNum = FreeFile

' Open the file TRY.DAT for binary access.
Open "TRY.DAT" For Binary As FileNum

' Write the string "12345" starting at byte
' location 20 of the file.
MyString = "12345"
Put #FileNum, 20, MyString

' At this point the file position is set at byte
' location 25, so if the next Put # statement will
' not specify a byte location, then the writing of
```

14

```
' the next Put # statement will be performed at byte
' location 25.

' Write the string "67890" without specifying a byte
' location.
MyString = "67890"
Put #FileNum, , MyString

' Close the file.
Close FileNum
```

Note that the second Put # statement in the preceding code did not specify a byte location (that is, the second parameter is not specified—there is a blank between the first comma and second comma).

Reading Bytes from a Binary File

After a file is opened for binary access, the Get # statement can be used to read bytes from any byte location in the file. The following sample code reads 15 characters, starting at byte location 40, of the file TRY.DAT:

```
' Get a free file number.
FileNum = FreeFile

' Open the file TRY.DAT for binary access.
Open "TRY.DAT" For Binary As FileNum

' Initialize the MyString string to 15 blanks. '
MyString = String(15, " ")

' Read 15 characters from the file, starting at byte
' location 40.
Get #FileNum, 40, MyString

' Close the file.
Close FileNum
```

As you can see, the Get # statement takes three parameters: The first parameter is the file number, the second parameter is the byte location where the reading will start, and the third parameter is the name of the variable that will be filled with the data from the file. The number of bytes read from the file is determined by the size of the variable filled with the data. Because the variable MyString was initialized to 15 blanks in the preceding code, the Get # statement reads only 15 characters.

Summary

In this chapter you have learned how to create files, how to write data to files, and how to read data from files. You have also learned that there are three types of files: random, sequential, and

binary. Random files are accessed record by record and are useful in database applications. Sequential files are accessed line by line and are ideal for use with text files. Binary files are the most flexible because they are accessed byte by byte.

Q&A

Q Why are random files considered random?

A The word *random* is used because once a file is opened for random access, the program can access any record in the file. In other words, the program can read and write records in a random order (first Record 7, then Record 3, then Record 9, and so on).

Q In the Phone program, the file PHONE.DAT was opened for random access with the following statement:

```
Open "PHONE.DAT" For Random As gFileNum Len = gRecordLen
```

The name of the file, PHONE.DAT, was specified without a path. What directory was the file opened in?

A Because no path was specified, the file is opened in the current directory. The question is What is the current directory? Say that you create an .EXE file PHONE.EXE from the Phone program and save the file PHONE.EXE in the C:\MYDIR directory. When you execute the C:\MYDIR\PHONE.EXE program, the current directory is C:\MYDIR by default. This means that the file PHONE.DAT is opened in C:\MYDIR.

Quiz

1. Assume there is a user-defined data type that is defined as follows:

```
Type EmployeeInfo
   Name As String * 40
   Age  As Integer
End Type
```

Then what does the following code do?

```
Dim FileNum As Integer
Dim Employee As EmployeeInfo
FileNum = FreeFile
Open "EMPLOYEE.DAT" For Random As FileNum Len=Len(Employee)
Employee.Name = "JOHN SMITH"
Employee.Age = 32
Put FileNum, 5, Employee
```

2. Assume there is a user-defined data type that is defined as follows:

```
Type EmployeeInfo
   Name As String * 40
   Age  As Integer
End Type
```

Then what does the following code do?

```
Dim FileNum As Integer
Dim Employee As EmployeeInfo
FileNum = FreeFile
Open "EMPLOYEE.DAT" For Random As FileNum Len=Len(Employee)
Get #FileNum, 10, Employee
MsgBox "The age of  "+ _
       Trim(Employee.Name)+ _
       " is " + Str(Employee.Age)
```

3. What does the following code do?

```
FileNum = FreeFile
Open "TRY.TXT" For Output As FileNum
Print #FileNum, txtMyText.Text
Close FileNum
```

4. What do the following statements do?

```
FileNum = FreeFile
Open "C:\TRY\TRY.TXT" For Append As FileNum
```

5. What does the following code do?

```
FileNum = FreeFile
Open "INFO.TXT" For Append As FileNum
Print #FileNum, txtMyText.Text
Close FileNum
```

6. What does the following code do?

```
FileNum = FreeFile
Open "TRY.TXT" For Input As FileNum
txtMyText.Text = Input(LOF(FileNum), FileNum)
Close FileNum
```

7. What does the following code do?

```
FileNum = FreeFile
Open "TRY.DAT" For Binary As FileNum
MyString = "THIS IS A TEST"
Put #FileNum, 75, MyString
Close FileNum
```

8. What does the following code do?

```
FileNum = FreeFile
Open "TRY.DAT" For Binary As FileNum
MyString = String(20, " ")
Get #FileNum, 75, MyString
MsgBox "MyString="+MyString
Close FileNum
```

Exercises

1. Wave (WAV) files are standard sound files used in Windows. The sampling rate of a WAV file is saved as an integer value starting at byte location 25 of the file. Write a program that displays the sampling rate of the file C:\WINDOWS\TADA.WAV. (The file TADA.WAV is included with Windows.) Hint: Use binary access.

2. Write a program that displays the contents of the file C:\AUTOEXEC.BAT in a text box. Hint: Use sequential access.

Quiz Answers

1. The code stores the name JOHN SMITH and his age (32) in record number 5 of the file EMPLOYEE.DAT:

```
' Declare variables.
Dim FileNum As Integer
Dim Employee As EmployeeInfo
' Get a free file number.
FileNum = FreeFile

' Open the file EMPLOYEE.DAT.
Open "EMPLOYEE.DAT" For Random As FileNum Len=Len(Employee)

' Fill the variable Employee.
Employee.Name = "JOHN SMITH"
Employee.Age = 32

' Store the contents of the variable Employee in
' record number 5 of the file.
Put FileNum, 5, Employee
```

2. The code displays the name of the person and his age from record number 10:

```
Dim FileNum As Integer
Dim Employee As EmployeeInfo

' Get a free file number.
FileNum = FreeFile

' Open the file EMPLOYEE.DAT.
Open "EMPLOYEE.DAT" For Random As FileNum Len=Len(Employee)

' Fill the variable Employee with the contents of
' record number 10 of the file.
Get #FileNum, 10, Employee

' Display the contents of the Employee variable.
MsgBox "The age of  "+ Trim(Employee.Name)+ " is "+Str(Employee.Age)
```

14

3. The code creates the file TRY.TXT and writes the contents of the txtMyText text box into the file:

```
' Get a free file number.
FileNum = FreeFile

' Create the file TRY.TXT.
Open "TRY.TXT" For Output As FileNum

' Write the contents of the text box txtMyText into
' the file TRY.TXT.
Print #FileNum, txtMyText.Text

' Close the file.
Close FileNum
```

4. These statements open the file C:\TRY\TRY.TXT for sequential append.

If the file does not exist, it is created. If it does exist, subsequent output statements append new data to the file.

5. The code appends the contents of the txtMyText text box to the file INFO.TXT:

```
' Get a free file number.
FileNum = FreeFile

' Open the file INFO.TXT for append.
Open "INFO.TXT" For Append As FileNum

' Add the contents of the text box txtMyText to the
' end of INFO.TXT.
Print #FileNum, txtMyText.Text

' Close the file.
Close FileNum
```

6. The code reads the contents of the file TRY.TXT into the txtMyText text box:

```
' Get a free file number.
FileNum = FreeFile

' Open the file TRY.TXT for input.
Open "TRY.TXT" For Input As FileNum

' Read all the contents of TRY.TXT into the text
' box txtMyText.
txtMyText.Text = Input(LOF(FileNum), FileNum)

' Close the file.
Close FileNum
```

7. The code writes the string THIS IS A TEST into the file TRY.DAT, starting at byte location 75:

```
' Get a free file number.
FileNum = FreeFile

' Open the file TRY.DAT for binary access.
Open "TRY.DAT" For Binary As FileNum

' Fill the string variable MyString.
MyString = "THIS IS A TEST"

' Write the string variable MyString into the file,
' starting at byte location 75.
Put #FileNum, 75, MyString

' Close the file.
Close FileNum
```

8. The code reads 20 bytes from the file TRY.DAT, starting at byte location 75. The code then displays these 20 bytes:

```
' Get a free file number.
FileNum = FreeFile

' Open the file TRY.DAT for binary access.
Open "TRY.DAT" For Binary As FileNum

' Initialize the MyString string to 20 blanks.
MyString = String(20, " ")

' Read 20 characters from the file, starting at byte
' location 75. Only 20 characters are read because
' the length of MyString is 20 characters.
Get #FileNum, 75, MyString

' Display MyString.
MsgBox "MyString="+MyString

' Close the file.
Close FileNum
```

Exercise Answers

1. One possible solution to this exercise is to open the TADA.WAV file for binary access and read an integer value starting at byte number 25 of the file. After the value is read into an integer variable, the value of the variable can be displayed using a message box. The following code does this:

```
Dim SamplingRate As Integer
Dim FileNum As Integer

' Get a free file number.
FileNum = FreeFile
```

```
' Open the file C:\WINDOWS\MEDIA\TADA.WAV for binary access.
' NOTE: It is assumed that the TADA.WAV file
' resides in C:\WINDOWS\MEDIA
Open "C:\WINDOWS\MEDIA\TADA.WAV" For Binary As FileNum

' Read the sampling rate into the integer variable
' SamplingRate, starting at byte location 25.
Get #FileNum, 25, SamplingRate

' Close the file.
Close FileNum

' Display the sampling rate.
MsgBox "The sampling rate of TADA.WAV is " + _
       Str(SamplingRate)
```

You can place this code in the `Click` event procedure of a command button. After you run the program and click the command button, the following message should be displayed (assuming that your TADA.WAV was recorded at a sampling rate of 22050Hz):

```
The sampling rate of TADA.WAV is 22050
```

2. Because the file C:\AUTOEXEC.BAT is a text file, a good way to open it is with sequential access. The following code opens the file C:\AUTOEXEC.BAT for input and reads the contents of the file into a text box. The code is placed in the `Form_Load()` procedure of the program's form:

```
Private Sub Form_Load()

   ' Get a free file number.
   FileNum = FreeFile

   ' Open the file C:\AUTOEXEC.BAT for input.
   Open "C:\AUTOEXEC.BAT" For Input As FileNum

   ' Read all the contents of AUTOEXEC.BAT into the
   ' text box txtMyText.
   txtMyText.Text = Input(LOF(FileNum), FileNum)

   ' Close the file.
   Close FileNum

End Sub
```

3

This is your final week! This week you'll learn about some of the most sophisticated features of Visual Basic—features that make it famous!

Where You're Going

This week, you'll learn how to use the data control, which enables your Visual Basic programs to interface with databases such as Access, Paradox, FoxPro, and dBase. You'll also learn how to create multiple-document interface applications, how to use popular third-party OLE controls such as the spin and switch OLE controls, and more.

This week you'll also learn how to perform sprite animation by using the powerful sprite OLE control, which enables you to create professional animation programs with great ease. You'll write programs that utilize WinG technology, and you will also be introduced to the fascinating world of 3D virtual reality.

This week you'll also learn how to write programs that play sound through a sound card as well as through the PC speaker (for users who do not own a sound card).

In Chapter 21, "Multimedia," you'll learn how to play MIDI files (synthesized music files), movies files, and CD audio.

Arrays, OLE, and Other Topics

In this chapter you'll learn about miscellaneous topics in Visual Basic that have not been covered in previous chapters.

ASCII Files

As you develop your programs, you might find it useful to print a hard copy of the form's properties table and the program's code. Visual Basic saves the properties table and the code in the form file. For example, the form file MYFORM.FRM contains the properties table and the code of the form frmMyForm.

Take a look at the OPTION.FRM file that you developed in Chapter 2, "Properties and Controls."

☐ Start Notepad (usually in the Accessories group of Windows) or any other word processor capable of loading ASCII files.

☐ Select Open from the File menu of Notepad and load the file C:\VB4PRG\CH02\OPTION.FRM.

The OPTION.FRM file looks like this:

```
VERSION 4.00
Begin VB.Form frmOption
    BackColor       =   &H000000FF&
    Caption         =   "The Option Program"
    ClientHeight    =   4140
    ClientLeft      =   1140
    ClientTop       =   1515
    ClientWidth     =   6690
    Height          =   4545
    Left            =   1080
    LinkTopic       =   "Form1"
    ScaleHeight     =   4140
    ScaleWidth      =   6690
    Top             =   1170
    Width           =   6810
    Begin VB.CommandButton cmdExit
        Caption         =   "E&xit"
        BeginProperty Font
            name            =   "System"
            charset         =   0
            weight          =   700
            size            =   9.75
            underline       =   0   'False
            italic          =   0   'False
            strikethrough   =   0   'False
        EndProperty
        Height          =   1095
        Left            =   4800
        TabIndex        =   6
```

```
            Top             =    1200
            Width           =    1215
         End
         Begin VB.CheckBox chkSound
            BackColor       =    &H000000FF&
            Caption         =    "&Sound"
            BeginProperty Font
               name         =    "System"
               charset      =    0
               weight       =    700
               size         =    9.75
               underline    =    0    'False
               italic       =    0    'False
               strikethrough =   0    'False
            EndProperty
            ForeColor       =    &H00FFFFFF&
            Height          =    495
            Left            =    3000
            TabIndex        =    5
            Top             =    1440
            Width           =    1215
         End
         Begin VB.CheckBox chkMouse
            BackColor       =    &H000000FF&
            Caption         =    "&Mouse"
            BeginProperty Font
               name         =    "System"
               charset      =    0
               weight       =    700
               size         =    9.75
               underline    =    0    'False
               italic       =    0    'False
               strikethrough =   0    'False
            EndProperty
            ForeColor       =    &H00FFFFFF&
            Height          =    495
            Left            =    3000
            TabIndex        =    4
            Top             =    960
            Width           =    1215
         End
         Begin VB.CheckBox chkColors
            BackColor       =    &H000000FF&
            Caption         =    "&Colors"
            BeginProperty Font
               name         =    "System"
               charset      =    0
               weight       =    700
               size         =    9.75
               underline    =    0    'False
               italic       =    0    'False
               strikethrough =   0    'False
            EndProperty
            ForeColor       =    &H00FFFFFF&
            Height          =    495
```

```
         Left            =   3000
         TabIndex        =   3
         Top             =   480
         Width           =   1215
      End
      Begin VB.OptionButton optLevel3
         BackColor       =   &H000000FF&
         Caption         =   "Level &3"
         BeginProperty Font
            name         =   "System"
            charset      =   0
            weight       =   700
            size         =   9.75
            underline    =   0   'False
            italic       =   0   'False
            strikethrough =  0   'False
         EndProperty
         ForeColor       =   &H00FFFFFF&
         Height          =   495
         Left            =   360
         TabIndex        =   2
         Top             =   1440
         Width           =   1215
      End
      Begin VB.OptionButton optLevel2
         BackColor       =   &H000000FF&
         Caption         =   "Level &2"
         BeginProperty Font
            name         =   "System"
            charset      =   0
            weight       =   700
            size         =   9.75
            underline    =   0   'False
            italic       =   0   'False
            strikethrough =  0   'False
         EndProperty
         ForeColor       =   &H00FFFFFF&
         Height          =   495
         Left            =   360
         TabIndex        =   1
         Top             =   960
         Width           =   1215
      End
      Begin VB.OptionButton optLevel1
         BackColor       =   &H000000FF&
         Caption         =   "Level &1"
         BeginProperty Font
            name         =   "System"
            charset      =   0
            weight       =   700
            size         =   9.75
            underline    =   0   'False
            italic       =   0   'False
            strikethrough =  0   'False
         EndProperty
         ForeColor       =   &H00FFFFFF&
```

```
            Height          =    495
            Left            =    360
            TabIndex        =    0
            Top             =    480
            Width           =    1215
         End
         Begin VB.Label lblChoice
            Alignment       =    2    'Center
            BorderStyle     =    1    'Fixed Single
            BeginProperty Font
               name            =    "System"
               charset         =    0
               weight          =    700
               size            =    9.75
               underline       =    0    'False
               italic          =    0    'False
               strikethrough   =    0    'False
            EndProperty
            Height          =    1455
            Left            =    360
            TabIndex        =    7
            Top             =    2280
            Width           =    3015
         End
      End
End
Attribute VB_Name = "frmOption"
Attribute VB_Creatable = False
Attribute VB_Exposed = False
Option Explicit


Private Sub chkColors_Click()

        If chkColors.Value = 1 Then
           frmOption.BackColor = QBColor(13)
        Else
           frmOption.BackColor = QBColor(14)
        End If

        UpdateLabel

End Sub


Private Sub chkMouse_Click()

    UpdateLabel

End Sub


Private Sub chkSound_Click()
```

```
            If chkSound.Value = 1 Then
                Beep
            End If
            UpdateLabel

    End Sub


    Private Sub cmdExit_Click()

        End

    End Sub

    Private Sub optLevel1_Click()

        UpdateLabel

    End Sub


    Private Sub optLevel2_Click()

        UpdateLabel

    End Sub


    Private Sub optLevel3_Click()

        UpdateLabel

    End Sub


    Public Sub UpdateLabel()

        ' Declare the variables
        Dim Info
        Dim LFCR

        LFCR = Chr(13) + Chr(10)

        ' Sound
        If chkSound.Value = 1 Then
            Info = "Sound: ON"
        Else
            Info = "Sound: OFF"
        End If
```

```
' Mouse
If chkMouse.Value = 1 Then
    Info = Info + LFCR + "Mouse: ON"
Else
    Info = Info + LFCR + "Mouse: OFF"
End If

' Colors
If chkColors.Value = 1 Then
    Info = Info + LFCR + "Colors: ON"
Else
    Info = Info + LFCR + "Colors: OFF"
End If

' Level 1
If optLevel1.Value = True Then
    Info = Info + LFCR + "Level:1"
End If

' Level 2
If optLevel2.Value = True Then
    Info = Info + LFCR + "Level:2"
End If

' Level 3
If optLevel3.Value = True Then
    Info = Info + LFCR + "Level:3"
End If

lblChoice.Caption = Info

End Sub
```

As you can see, OPTION.FRM is a regular ASCII file.

The first line of the ASCII file OPTION.FRM indicates which version of Visual Basic was used to generate the file:

```
VERSION 4.00
```

The next lines in the ASCII file describe the form and the controls in the form (that is, the properties table). Only those properties that were changed from their default values are listed. The lines after the properties table are the code of the program. The ASCII file of the form can be useful for documenting programs.

Understanding the format of the ASCII files can also be useful for programmers who write programs that generate the ASCII files automatically (that is, you can write a program that asks you several questions, and based on your answers, the program generates the ASCII file of the form). Naturally, Visual Basic has no way of knowing who generated the ASCII file. However, the file must be in strict compliance with the format that Visual Basic expects.

Arrays

If your program uses arrays, it must declare them. The declaration of the array specifies the array's name and the number of elements it can hold.

Just like with other variables, if you declare an array in the general declarations section of a form, the array is visible by all procedures and functions in the form. If you declare an array in a separate module and precede the declaration statement with the `Global` keyword, the array is visible by all the forms of the project.

Data Types

As you might have noticed by now, Visual Basic supports several data types. Table 15.1 lists the various data types and the range of values of the data Visual Basic supports. For example, when you declare a variable as an integer, you can use the following statement:

```
Dim Counter As Integer
```

The following statement yields identical results:

```
Dim Counter%
```

That is, the character `%` is a short notation for `As Integer`. An integer variable has the range −32,768 to 32,767. Each integer occupies 2 bytes of memory.

Similarly, you can declare the long variable `Number` as follows:

```
Dim Numbers As Long
```

The following statement is another syntax notation for declaring the `Number` variable `As Long`:

```
Dim Numbers&
```

That is, the character `&` is a short notation for `As Long`. A long variable has the range −2,147,483,648 to 2,147,483,647. Each long variable occupies 4 bytes of memory.

The double variable `MyVariable` is declared as follows:

```
Dim MyVariable As Double
```

which is the same as this:

```
Dim MyVariable#
```

A double variable can be a positive or negative number and occupies 8 bytes of memory. The ranges of positive and negative values for each data type are specified in Table 15.1.

Table 15.1. The data types that Visual Basic supports.

Data Type	Number of Bytes	Shortcut Notation	Range
Integer	2	%	–32,768 to 32,767
Long	4	&	–2,147,483,648 to 2,147,483,647
Single-positive	4	!	1.401298E-45 to 3.402823E38
Single-negative	4	!	–3.402823E38 to –1.401298E–45
Double	8	#	4.94065645841247D–24 positive 1.79769313486232D308
Double-negative	8	#	1.79769313486232D308 to –4.94065645841247D–324
Currency	8	@	–922337203685477.5808 to 922337203685466.5807
String	Depends	$	In Windows 3.1 or earlier, a string can hold up to approximately 65,000 charaters. In other newer operating systems, strings can support up to 2 billion characters.
Variant	Date, time, floating point, or string.	(none)	Range of date: from January 1, 0000 to December 31, 9999

Note that the last item in Table 15.1 describes a variable of the type `Variant`, which can be a date, time, floating point (for example, 1234.5678), or string. When you declare a variable as follows:

```
Dim I As Integer
```

Visual Basic creates a variable called `I` as an integer. However, if you declare a variable as follows:

```
Dim I
```

Visual Basic creates this variable as a variant variable. That is, Visual Basic doesn't know whether the `I` variable will serve as a string, an integer, a long, or other type. Later in the program, Visual Basic will figure out how to treat the variable by looking at the statement that uses the variable. For example, if Visual Basic encounters this statement:

```
I = "My String"
```

then Visual Basic knows the variable should be treated as a string. However, if Visual Basic encounters this statement:

```
I = 2 + 3
```

then Visual Basic knows the variable should be treated as an integer.

The advantage of using variant variables is that the same variable can serve as several types of data. For example, it is okay to have the following statements in the same procedure:

```
Dim I
I = 2 + 3
I = "My String"
```

That is, as a variant data type, I serves as an integer and then as a string.

The disadvantage of using variant data types is that Visual Basic programs that use them can sometimes run more slowly than programs that specifically indicate the variables' data types. For example, a For loop will be executed faster when the counter variable of the loop is declared as an integer. Of course, if the For loop has to count more than 32,767 times, then you must use a long variable in the For counter (because an integer variable has a maximum value of 32,767). A For loop with a long variable as its counter variable will be executed a bit slower than a For loop with an integer.

Of course you can write the For loop with a variant variable. In this case, the For loop will be executed slower than it would with an integer or a long variable. To declare a variable as variant, you use a statement such as this:

```
Dim HisVariant
```

However, you can also use the following statement to declare a variant variable:

```
Dim HisVariant As Variant
```

The Arrays Program

The Arrays program illustrates how you declare arrays in Visual Basic.

The Visual Implementation of the Arrays Program

☐ Open a new project, save the form of the project as ARRAYS.FRM in the C:\VB4PRG\CH15 directory, and save the project file as ARRAYS.VBP in the C:\VB4PRG\CH15 directory.

☐ Build the frmArrays form according to the specifications in Table 15.2.

The completed form should look like the one shown in Figure 15.1.

Table 15.2. The properties table of the frmArrays form.

Object	Property	Setting
Form	**Name**	**frmArrays**
	Caption	The Arrays Program
	FontName	System
	FontSize	10
	Height	4425
	Left	1035
	Top	1140
	Width	7485
Command Button	**Name**	**cmdArray1**
	Caption	Array&1
	FontName	System
	FontSize	10
	Height	495
	Left	3360
	Top	720
	Width	1215
Command Button	**Name**	**cmdArray2**
	Caption	Array&2
	FontName	System
	Font Size	10
	Height	495
	Left	3360
	Top	1320
	Width	1215
Command Button	**Name**	**cmdExit**
	Caption	E&xit
	FontName	System
	FontSize	10
	Height	495
	Left	5880
	Top	3360
	Width	1215

Figure 15.1.

The frmArrays form.

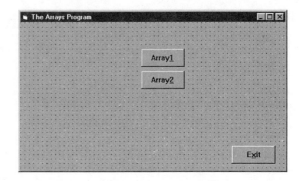

Entering the Code of the Arrays Program

☐ Enter the following code in the general declarations section of the frmArrays form:

```
' All variables MUST be declared.
Option Explicit
' Declare  the array.
' The first element of the array is gArray2(10).
' The last element of the array is gArray2(20).
Dim gArray2(10 To 20)  As Integer
```

☐ Enter the following code in the cmdArray1_Click() procedure of the frmArrays form:

```
Private Sub cmdArray1_Click()

    Dim Counter

    ' Declare the array.
    ' The first element of the array is Array1(1).
    ' The last element of the array is Array1(10).
    Static Array1(1 To 10)  As String

    ' Fill 3 elements of the array.
    Array1(1) = "ABC"
    Array1(2) = "DEF"
    Array1(3) = "GHI"

    ' Clear the form.
    frmArrays.Cls

    ' Display 3 elements of the array.
    Print "Here are the elements of Array1[]:"
    For Counter = 1 To 3 Step 1
        Print "Array1(" + Str(Counter) + ") =" + _
                Array1(Counter)
    Next

End Sub
```

☐ Enter the following code in the cmdArray2_Click() procedure of the frmArrays form:

```
Private Sub cmdArray2_Click()

    Dim Counter

    ' Fill 3 elements of the array.
    gArray2(11) = 234
    gArray2(12) = 567
    gArray2(13) = 890

    ' Clear the form.
    frmArrays.Cls

    ' Display 3 elements of the array.
    Print "Here are the elements of gArray2[]:"
    For Counter = 11 To 13 Step 1
        Print "gArray2(" + Str(Counter) + ") = "; _
                    Str(gArray2(Counter))
    Next

End Sub
```

☐ Enter the following code in the cmdExit_Click() procedure of the frmArrays form:

```
Private Sub cmdExit_Click()

    End

End Sub
```

Executing the Arrays Program

☐ Execute the Arrays program.

☐ Click the Array1 button.

> *The Arrays program responds by displaying the elements of* Array1(). *(See Figure 15.2.)*

☐ Click the Array2 button.

> *The Arrays program responds by displaying the elements of* gArray2(). *(See Figure 15.3.)*

☐ Click the Exit button to exit the Arrays program.

Figure 15.2.

Displaying the elements of Array1( ).

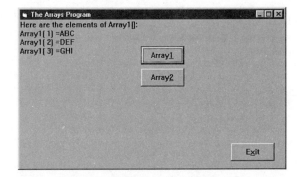

Figure 15.3.

Displaying the elements of gArray2( ).

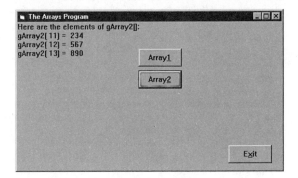

How the Arrays Program Works

The Arrays program declares the arrays Array1() and gArray2(). When you click the Array1 button, the program fills three elements of the array and displays them in the Array1() array; when you click the Array2 button, the program fills three elements of the gArray2() array and displays them.

The Code in the General Declarations Section

The code in the general declarations section declares the gArray2() array:

```
Dim gArray2(10 To 20)  As Integer
```

The array is declared As Integer, which means its elements are integers. The numbers in the parentheses indicate that the first element of the array is gArray(10), the second element is gArray(11), and so on. The last element of the array is gArray(20).

Because the gArray2() array is declared in the general declarations section of the form, it is visible in all procedures and functions of the form.

The Code in the *cmdArray1_Click()* Procedure

The cmdArray1_Click() procedure is automatically executed whenever you click the Array1 button:

```
Private Sub cmdArray1_Click()

    Dim Counter

    ' Declare the array.
    ' The first element of the array is Array1(1).
    ' The last element of the array is Array1(10).
    Static Array1(1 To 10)  As String

    ' Fill 3 elements of the array.
    Array1(1) = "ABC"
    Array1(2) = "DEF"
    Array1(3) = "GHI"

    ' Clear the form.
    frmArrays.Cls

    ' Display 3 elements of the array.
    Print "Here are the elements of Array1[]:"
    For Counter = 1 To 3 Step 1
        Print "Array1(" + Str(Counter) + ") =" + _
                Array1(Counter)
    Next

End Sub
```

This procedure declares the Array1() array as follows:

```
Static Array1(1 To 10) As String
```

Note that because Array1() is declared in the procedure, you must declare it as static. That is, an array must be declared either in the general declarations section or as static in a procedure.

The first element of the array is Array1(1), the second element of the array is Array1(2), and so on. The last element of the array is Array1(10).

The procedure then fills three elements in the array and clears the form with the Cls method:

```
Array1(1) = "ABC"
Array1(2) = "DEF"
Array1(3) = "GHI"
frmArrays.Cls
```

Finally, the procedure displays the first three elements of the array with a For loop:

```
Print "Here are the elements of Array1[]:"
For Counter = 1 To 3 Step 1
    Print "Array1(" + Str(Counter) + ") =" + _
            Array1(Counter)
Next
```

The Code in the *cmdArray2_Click()* Procedure

The cmdArray2_Click() procedure is executed whenever you click the Array2 button:

```
Private Sub cmdArray2_Click()

    Dim Counter

    ' Fill 3 elements of the array.
    gArray2(11) = 234
    gArray2(12) = 567
    gArray2(13) = 890

    ' Clear the form.
    frmArrays.Cls

    ' Display 3 elements of the array.
    Print "Here are the elements of gArray2[]:"
    For Counter = 11 To 13 Step 1
        Print "gArray2(" + Str(Counter) + ") = "; _
                    Str(gArray2(Counter))
    Next

End Sub
```

This procedure is similar to the cmdArray1_Click() procedure. Because the gArray2() array is declared in the general declarations section of the form, this array is visible in this procedure.

The Upper and Lower Bounds of Arrays

As illustrated in the Arrays program, the first and last elements of the array are specified in the declaration of the array. For example, this declaration declares an array of long numbers:

```
Dim MyArray (0 to 35) As Long
```

The first element (the lower bound) is MyArray(0), and the last element in the array is MyArray(35) (the upper bound). As a shortcut, you can also declare arrays as follows:

```
Dim MyArray(35) As long
```

The preceding notations are interpreted by Visual Basic as follows: The first element of the array is MyArray(0), the second element is MyArray(1), and so on. The last element of the array is MyArray(35). The disadvantage of using this shortcut notation for the declaration is that the lower bound of the array is 0 by default. In other words, you have to remember that element number 0 is the first element, element number 1 is the second element, and so on.

The Array's Size

Basically, the maximum size of the array depends on the operating system. As you know, Windows uses virtual memory. That is, when all the available memory (RAM) is used, Windows

starts using the hard drive as RAM. When space in the hard drive is used as RAM, that portion of the hard drive is called virtual memory.

For example, if a PC with 16 megabytes of RAM used all 16MB, Windows will start using hard drive space as RAM. As you know, RAM uses integrated circuit chips that store bytes electronically, so storing data to RAM and reading data from RAM is performed very fast. On the other hand, the hard drive is a mechanical device and requires an actual mechanical rotation of its parts. This means that storing and reading data from the hard drive is much slower than storing and reading data from RAM. So if you are using huge arrays and your PC has used all the available RAM, Windows will start using hard drive space as RAM, and the program will slow down. Again, your program will experience performance problems only if your PC has used all the available RAM.

Multidimensional Arrays

The Arrays program used a one-dimensional array. In Visual Basic, you can declare multidimensional arrays. For example, the following statement declares a two-dimensional array:

```
Static MyArray (0 To 3, 1 To 4 )
```

These are the elements of the preceding array:

```
MyArray(0,1) MyArray(0,2) MyArray(0,3) MyArray(0,4)
MyArray(1,1) MyArray(1,2) MyArray(1,3) MyArray(1,4)
MyArray(2,1) MyArray(2,2) MyArray(2,3) MyArray(2,4)
MyArray(3,1) MyArray(3,2) MyArray(3,3) MyArray(3,4)
```

In a similar way, you can declare a three-dimensional array:

```
Dim MyArray ( 1 To 3, 1 To 7, 1 To 5)
```

The following code uses two For loops to fill all the elements of a two-dimensional array with the value 3:

```
Static MyArray (1 To 10, 1 To 10) As Integer
Dim Counter1, Counter2
For Counter1 = 1 To 10
    For Counter2 = 1 To 10
        MyArray(Counter1, Counter2) = 3
    Next Counter2
Next Counter1
```

Typically, you'll use one-dimensional arrays, although you may find two-dimensional arrays are more convenient to use in some situations. Occasionally, you might even find that using three-dimensional arrays is useful. However, using an array with more than three dimensions makes the program very hard to understand and debug.

Dynamic Arrays

When declaring arrays, you have to be careful not to consume too much memory. For example, this declaration declares an array with 10,001 elements:

```
Static MyArray (10000) As long
```

Because each element is defined as Long, and a long variable occupies four bytes of memory (as shown in Table 15.1), the MyArray() array requires 40,004 (10,001×4) bytes of memory. This might not sound like a lot of memory, but if you have 10 such arrays in your program, these arrays consume 400,040 (40,004×10) bytes of memory! Therefore, always try to set the size of your arrays to the minimum your program requires. Sometimes, however, the size of the arrays can be determined only during runtime. In these cases, you can use the ReDim (redimensioning) statement that Visual Basic supports. An array that changes its size during runtime is called a *dynamic array*.

The following code illustrates how to redimension an array:

```
Private Sub Command1_Click()

    Dim Counter

    ' Declare Array1 as a dynamic array.
    Dim Array1() As Integer

    ' Assign the size of the dynamic array.
    ReDim Array1(1 To 15) As Integer

    For Counter = 1 To 15 Step 1
        Array1(Counter) = Counter
    Next Counter

    ' Assign a new size to the dynamic array.
    ReDim Array1(1 To 5) As Integer

End Sub
```

The procedure declares Array1() as a dynamic array. Note that the declaration of a fixed array is different from the declaration of a dynamic array. That is, when you declare a dynamic array, its size isn't specified in the declaration.

The next statement in the preceding code assigns a size to the array by using the ReDim statement:

```
ReDim Array1(1 To 15) As Integer
```

This ReDim statement assigns 15 elements to the array. The elements in the array are defined as integers.

The For loop fills the 15 elements of the array, then the ReDim statement is used again to redimension the array:

```
ReDim Array1(1 To 5)  As Integer
```

After executing the second ReDim statement, the Array1() array has only five elements. Therefore, you can use this technique to change the size of your arrays during runtime and conserve memory. In the preceding code, Array1() required 30 (15×2) bytes. However, after the execution of the second ReDim statement, the size of Array1() was changed to five elements, and from that point on, Array1() occupied only 10 (5×2 = 10) bytes.

It is important to understand that once the ReDim statement is executed, the values that were stored in the array are lost forever! If you want to preserve some of the values of the array, you must use the Preserve keyword. The Arrays2 program illustrates how you can accomplish this.

The Arrays2 Program

You'll now implement the Arrays2 program. The Arrays2 program illustrates how you can redimension arrays from within your Visual Basic programs.

The Visual Implementation of the Arrays2 Program

☐ Start a new project, save the new form of the form as ARRAYS2.FRM in the C:\VB4PRG\CH15 directory, and save the project file as ARRAYS2.VBP in the C:\VB4PRG\CH15 directory.

☐ Build the frmArray form according to the specifications in Table 15.3.

The completed form should look like the one shown in Figure 15.4.

Table 15.3. The properties table of the frmArray form.

Object	Property	Setting
Form	**Name**	**frmArray**
	Caption	The Arrays2 Program
	Height	4425
	Left	1035
	Top	1140
	Width	7485

continues

Table 15.3. continued

Object	Property	Setting
Command Button	Name	cmdFill10
	Caption	Fill &10 Elements
	FontName	System
	FontSize	10
	Height	495
	Left	3240
	Top	1320
	Width	3855
Command Button	Name	cmdOnly5
	Caption	Cut to &5 Elements
	FontName	System
	FontSize	10
	Height	495
	Left	3240
	Top	1920
	Width	3855
Combo Box	Name	cboElements
	FontName	System
	FontSize	10
	Height	360
	Left	1080
	Text	(empty)
	Top	1320
	Width	1215
Command Button	Name	cmdExit
	Caption	E&xit
	FontName	System
	FontSize	10
	Height	495
	Left	5880
	Top	3240
	Width	1215

Figure 15.4.
The frmArray form of the Arrays2 program.

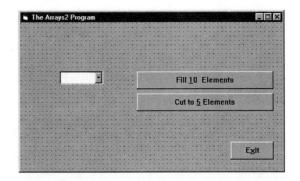

Entering the Code of the Arrays2 Program

☐ Enter the following code in the general declarations section of the frmArray form:

```
' All variables MUST be declared.
Option Explicit
' Declare a dynamic array.
Dim gTheArray() As Integer
```

☐ Enter the following code in the cmdExit_Click() procedure of the frmArray form:

```
Private Sub cmdExit_Click()

    End

End Sub
```

☐ Enter the following code in the cmdFill10_Click() procedure of the frmArray form:

```
Private Sub cmdFill10_Click()

    ' Set the size of the array.
    ReDim gTheArray(1 To 10) As Integer
    Dim Counter
    ' Fill the elements of the array.
    For Counter = 1 To 10 Step 1
        gTheArray(Counter) = Counter
    Next Counter
    ' Clear the combo box.
    cboElements.Clear
    ' Fill the items of the combo box.
    For Counter = 0 To 9 Step 1
        cboElements.AddItem _
            Str(gTheArray(Counter + 1))
    Next Counter

End Sub
```

☐ Enter the following code in the cmdOnly5_Click() procedure of the frmArray form:

```
Private Sub cmdOnly5_Click()

    ' Set the size of the array.
    ReDim Preserve gTheArray(1 To 5) As Integer
    Dim Counter
    ' Clear the combo box.
    cboElements.Clear
    ' Fill the items of the combo box.
    For Counter = 0 To 4 Step 1
        cboElements.AddItem _
              Str(gTheArray(Counter + 1))
    Next Counter

End Sub
```

Executing the Arrays2 Program

☐ Execute the Arrays2 program.

☐ Click the Fill 10 Elements button.

The Arrays2 program responds by filling the combo box with 10 elements. You can see these 10 elements by clicking the right-arrow button on the combo box to drop down the list. (See Figure 15.5.)

☐ Click the Cut to 5 Elements button.

The Arrays2 program responds by eliminating five elements in the combo box. You can see the five elements that are left in the combo box by clicking the right-arrow button on the combo box to drop down the list. (See Figure 15.6.)

Figure 15.5.
Filling the combo box with 10 items.

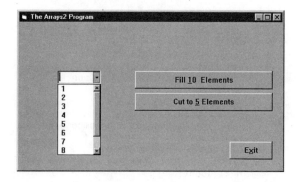

Figure 15.6.
Preserving five elements of the array.

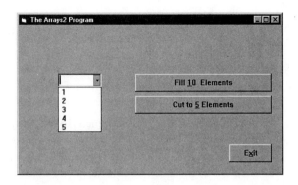

☐ Click the Exit button to exit the program.

How the Arrays2 Program Works

The Arrays2 program fills an array and then fills the items in the combo box with the elements of the array. As you'll soon see, the array is then redimensioned with the Preserve keyword, which retains the values of the elements that remain in the array.

The Code in the General Declarations Section

The code in the general declarations section of the frmArray form declares a dynamic array:

```
Dim gTheArray() As Integer
```

Visual Basic interprets this statement as a declaration of a dynamic array, because the parentheses that follow the name of the array are empty.

The Code in the *cmdFill10_Click()* Procedure

The cmdFill10_Click() procedure is automatically executed whenever you click the Fill 10 Elements button:

```
Private Sub cmdFill10_Click()

    ' Set the size of the array.
    ReDim gTheArray(1 To 10) As Integer
    Dim Counter
    ' Fill the elements of the array.
    For Counter = 1 To 10 Step 1
        gTheArray(Counter) = Counter
    Next Counter
    ' Clear the combo box.
```

```
cboElements.Clear
' Fill the items of the combo box.
For Counter = 0 To 9 Step 1
    cboElements.AddItem _
            Str(gTheArray(Counter + 1))
Next Counter
```

End Sub

The procedure uses the ReDim statement to set the size of the array to 10 elements:

```
ReDim gTheArray(1 To 10) As Integer
```

The elements of the array are filled using a For loop:

```
For Counter = 1 To 10 Step 1
gTheArray(Counter) = Counter
Next Counter
```

The elements in the combo box are cleared, then a For loop is used to fill 10 items in the combo box. The items in the combo box correspond to the elements of the array:

```
cboElements.Clear
For Counter = 0 To 9 Step 1
    cboElements.AddItem _
        Str(gTheArray(Counter + 1))
Next Counter
```

Note that the first item in the combo box is item number 0, and the first element of the array is element number 1. Also, the last item of the combo box is item number 9, and the last element of the array is element number 10.

The Code in the *cmdOnly5_Click()* Procedure

The cmdOnly5_Click() procedure is automatically executed whenever you click the Cut to 5 Elements button:

Private Sub cmdOnly5_Click()

```
    ' Set the size of the array.
    ReDim Preserve gTheArray(1 To 5) As Integer
    Dim Counter
    ' Clear the combo box.
    cboElements.Clear
    ' Fill the items of the combo box.
    For Counter = 0 To 4 Step 1
        cboElements.AddItem _
                Str(gTheArray(Counter + 1))
    Next Counter
```

End Sub

The procedure uses the ReDim statement to change the size of the array to five elements:

```
ReDim Preserve gTheArray(1 To 5) As Integer
```

The Preserve keyword causes the first five elements of the array to retain their original values. The procedure then clears the items in the combo box and fills five elements in the combo box:

```
cboElements.Clear
For Counter = 0 To 4 Step 1
    cboElements.AddItem _
        Str(TheArray(Counter + 1))
Next Counter
```

Use the following steps to see the effect of the Preserve keyword:

☐ Remove the Preserve keyword from the ReDim statement. That is, change the ReDim statement in the cmdOnly5_Click() procedure so that it looks like this:

```
ReDim gTheArray(1 To 5) As Integer
```

☐ Execute the Arrays2 program and check its proper operation. That is, click the Fill 10 Elements button, open the combo list, and check that the list is filled with 10 items (each item corresponds to an element of the array). Click the Cut to 5 Elements button, open the combo list, and check that the list is filled with five items (each item corresponds to an element of the array). Because you removed the Preserve keyword, the elements of the array are all zeros.

☐ Click the Exit button to terminate the Arrays2 program.

Arrays That Exceed 64KB

The size of the arrays can exceed 64KB. An array that exceeds 64KB is called a *huge array*. You do not have to use any special declaration for huge arrays. Generally speaking, huge arrays are handled the same way as non-huge arrays—the only exception is that if the huge array is declared as a string, all the elements in the array must have the same number of characters in each element.

The Vary Program

As you saw in previous chapters, sometimes you create procedures and functions in your projects by selecting Procedure from the Insert menu of Visual Basic. When you create your own procedure or function, you can design it so it has arguments.

In Visual Basic you can pass arguments to a function by one of two methods: by reference or by value. The difference between these two methods is illustrated with the Vary program.

15

The Visual Implementation of the Vary Program

☐ Start a new project, save the form of the project as VARY.FRM in the C:\VB4PRG\CH15 directory, and save the project file as VARY.VBP in the C:\VB4PRG\CH15 directory.

☐ Build the frmVary form according to the specifications in Table 15.4.

The completed form should look like the one shown in Figure 15.7.

Table 15.4. The properties table of the frmVary form.

Object	Property	Setting
Form	**Name**	**frmVary**
	Caption	The Vary Program
	Height	4425
	Left	1035
	Top	1140
	Width	7485
Command Button	**Name**	**cmdDoIt**
	Caption	&Do It
	Height	1335
	Left	1920
	Top	1680
	Width	1575
Command Button	**Name**	**cmdExit**
	Caption	E&xit
	Height	495
	Left	6000
	Top	3240
	Width	1215
Label	**Name**	**lblInfo**
	Alignment	2-Center
	BorderStyle	1-Fixed Single
	Caption	(empty)

Object	Property	Setting
	FontName	System
	FontSize	10
	Height	495
	Left	1560
	Top	720
	Width	2415

Figure 15.7.
The frmVary form.

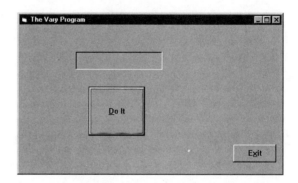

Entering the Code of the Vary Program

☐ Enter the following code in the general declarations section of the frmVary form:

```
' All variables MUST be declared.
Option Explicit
```

☐ Enter the following code in the cmdDoIt_Click() procedure of the frmVary form:

```
Private Sub cmdDoIt_Click()

    Dim V As Integer
    Dim Result As Integer

    V = 3
    Result = VSquare(V)
    lblInfo.Caption = "V=" + Str(V) + "    4*4=" _
                                    + Str(Result)

End Sub
```

☐ Enter the following code in the cmdExit_Click() procedure of the frmVary form:

```
Private Sub cmdExit_Click()

    End

End Sub
```

553

☐ Create a new function in the frmArray form and name it VSquare. That is, display the code window, display the Insert Procedure dialog box by selecting Procedure from the Insert menu, set the Type option to Function, set the Name to VSquare, and click the OK button.

Visual Basic responds by adding the VSquare() *function.*

☐ Change the first line of the VSquare() function as follows:

```
Public Function VSquare(ByVal V As Integer)

End Function
```

☐ Enter the following code in the VSquare() function:

```
Public Function VSquare(ByVal V As Integer)

    V = 4
    VSquare = V * V

End Function
```

Executing the Vary Program

☐ Execute the Vary program.

☐ Click the Do It button.

The Vary program responds by displaying the values in the lblInfo label, as shown in Figure 15.8.

☐ Click the Exit button to exit the Vary program.

Figure 15.8.
The Vary program, when passing the V *variable to the* ByVal *function.*

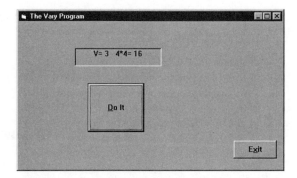

How the Vary Program Works

The Vary program passes a variable to a function by value (ByVal), which is explained in the following sections.

The Code in the *cmdDoIt_Click()* Procedure

The cmdDoIt_Click() procedure is automatically executed whenever you click the Do It button:

```
Private Sub cmdDoIt_Click()

    Dim V As Integer
    Dim Result As Integer

    V = 3
    Result = VSquare(V)
    lblInfo.Caption = "V=" + Str(V) + "    4*4=" _
                                  + Str(Result)

End Sub
```

The procedure sets the value of the V variable to 3, then executes the VSquare() function. VSquare() returns the result of 4×4.

The procedure then displays the value of V and the returned value from VSquare() in the lblInfo label.

The Code in the *VSquare()* Function

The VSquare() function is called by the cmdDoIt_Click() procedure:

```
Public Function VSquare(ByVal V As Integer)

    V = 4
    VSquare = V * V

End Function
```

This function sets the value of V to 4, then sets the value of VSquare to V×V. The important thing to note is that the V variable is passed to the function ByVal. This means that this procedure creates a new copy of a variable called V. There are no connections between the variable V in the calling procedure cmdDoIt_Click() and the variable V in the VSquare() function. This explains why the value of V displayed in the lblInfo label is 3 and not 4. (See Figure 15.8.) So when you pass a variable to a function ByVal, the value of the passed variable doesn't change in the calling procedure.

Modifying the Vary Program

You'll now modify the Vary program.

☐ Change the VSquare() function so that it looks like the following (note that the first line of the function is modified):

```
Public Function VSquare(V As Integer)

    V = 4
```

```
        VSquare = V * V

    End Function
```

☐ Execute the Vary program.

☐ Click the Do It button.

The Vary program responds by displaying values in the lblInfo label, as shown in Figure 15.9.

Figure 15.9.

The Vary program when passing the variable V by reference.

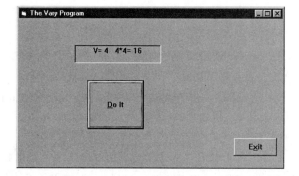

Note that now the variable is not passed by value to the VSquare() function; it is passed by reference. Passing an argument by reference means that the passed variable is the same variable in the calling procedure and the called function. Therefore, when passing V by reference, the V variable in the cmdDoIt_Click() procedure is the same V variable used in the VSquare() function. This explains why the value of V is displayed in the lblInfo label as 4. (See Figure 15.9.)

Readers familiar with the C programming language may recognize that passing an argument by reference is the equivalent of passing the address of the variable in C. If you are not familiar with C and find the concept a little confusing, just note the difference between the two methods of passing arguments:

- When you're passing an argument by value (ByVal), the called function is not able to change the value of the passed variable in the calling procedure. For example, in the Vary program, even though the VSquare() function sets the value of V to 4, the value of V in the cmdDoIt_Click() procedure remains 3.

- When you're passing an argument by reference, the called function and the calling procedure are using the same variable. For example, in the modified version of the Vary program, the VSquare() function sets the value of V to 4, and this value is displayed in the lblInfo label by the cmdDoIt_Click() procedure.

Modifying the Vary Program Again

☐ Change the first line of the VSquare() function and the contents of the VSquare() function so that it looks like this:

```
Public Function VSquare(VV As Integer)

    VV = 4
    VSquare = VV * VV

End Function
```

☐ Execute the Vary program.

☐ Click the Do It button.

The Vary program again responds, as shown in Figure 15.9.

☐ Terminate the program by clicking the Exit button.

As you can see, you changed the name of the variable in the VSquare() function from V to VV. However, this did not affect the way the program works because the variable V was passed by reference! So, although the variable is called VV in the VSquare() function, it is the same variable passed by the calling procedure (that is, V and VV are the same variable). As you can see, passing variables by reference can be tricky.

Note: To further understand the concept of passing variables by reference, take a look at Figure 15.10.

In Figure 15.10, certain cells in RAM are used for storing the V variable of the cmdDoIt_Click() procedure. Because the cmdDoIt_Click() procedure passed the V variable by reference to the VSquare() function, the VSquare() function uses the passed variable by using the same cells in RAM.

So, the cmdDoIt_Click() procedure uses the RAM area that stores the V variable, and the VSquare() function uses the RAM area that stores the VV variable, but in either case, V and VV are the same variable.

Figure 15.10.
Passing variables by reference.

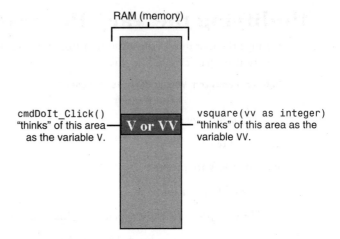

OLE

Object linking and embedding (OLE) is an important Windows topic available in Visual Basic. (The topic OLE deserves a whole book.)

OLE is so powerful that you can think of it as a separate software package included with your Visual Basic package. The rest of this chapter serves as a brief introduction to OLE.

What Is OLE?

OLE is the abbreviation for *object linking and embedding.* A program that includes OLE capability can communicate data (text and graphics) to other Windows applications that are OLE based.

To see an example of OLE in action, suppose that you have to tell your user to modify a certain BMP file. One way to do this (although not the best way) is to write a Visual Basic program that lets your user draw and modify BMP pictures. However, writing your own graphics program can take a long time, and you'll have to teach your user how to use your graphics program for drawing and modifying BMP files.

The solution is to tell your user to load the BMP picture by using a well-known drawing program, such as Paintbrush or Paint, and then modifying the picture. Since your user is using Windows, he or she will most likely know how to use Paintbrush, Paint, or another drawing program that comes with Windows.

So how will you tell your user to use Paintbrush (or Paint)? You can write a simple Visual Basic program that lists a sequence of steps telling your user to start Paintbrush, load a certain BMP file, and then modify the BMP picture by using the Paintbrush (or Paint) tools. A more elegant way to tell your user to use Paintbrush or Paint is to use OLE control, as the UsePB program demonstrates.

The icon of the OLE control in the tools window of Visual Basic is shown in Figure 15.11.

Figure 15.11.
The OLE control.

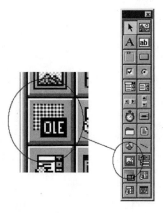

The UsePB Program

The UsePB program illustrates how an OLE-based Visual Basic program can be used as a *front-end application*, which is an application used in front of all the other applications. That is, when you start the front-end application, you see menus and icons that enable you to perform word processing, spreadsheet work, and other common tasks. When you click the word processor icon, a word processor program starts just as if the word processor's icon was clicked from the Windows Program Manager. The UsePB program lets your user use Paintbrush (or Paint) for loading a BMP picture and modifying it.

The Visual Implementation of the UsePB Program

☐ Start a new project, save the form of the project as USEPB.FRM in the C:\VB4PRG\CH15 directory, and save the project file as USEPB.VBP in the C:\VB4PRG\CH15 directory.

☐ Change the properties of the form as follows: The Name property should be frmUsePB and the Caption property should be The UsePB Program.

Adding the OLE Control to the frmUsePB Form

Now add the OLE control to the frmUsePB form:

☐ Double-click the OLE icon in the toolbox.

Visual Basic responds by placing the OLE control in the form and displaying the Insert Object dialog box. (See Figure 15.12.)

Figure 15.12.
The Insert Object dialog box.

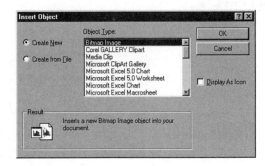

As you can see, the Insert Object dialog box displays a list of objects that can be embedded in the UsePB program.

☐ Select the item Bitmap Image from the list of objects, then click the OK button.

☐ Save the project.

Executing the UsePB Program

You'll now execute the UsePB program and see OLE in action:

☐ Execute the UsePB program.

The window of the UsePB program appears, as shown in Figure 15.13.

Figure 15.13.
The UsePB program.

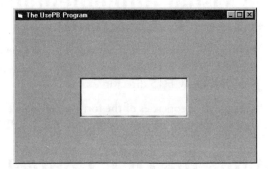

☐ Double-click the OLE control.

The program responds by displaying the Paint program. (See Figure 15.14.)

Figure 15.14.

The Paint program, which is executed after you double-click the OLE control.

☐ Draw something with the Paint program.

☐ Terminate the Paint program.

> *Control is returned to the UsePB program, and as you can see, the portion of the picture that fits in the OLE control is displayed. You can now double-click the OLE control again to pop up the Paint program.*

☐ Experiment with the UsePB program, then click the icon on the upper-left corner of UsePB's window and select Close from the System menu that pops up.

Summary

In this chapter you have learned about the FRM file that contains the description of the form in an ASCII format, how to declare and use arrays, and how to pass arguments by reference and ByVal. This chapter also introduces the OLE topic.

Q&A

Q Should I pass arguments ByVal or by reference?

A As you'll learn in Chapter 20, "Sprite Animation and WinG" (which deals with DLLs), sometimes it is not up to you to decide whether a variable should be passed ByVal or by reference. DLLs are functions written by others, and, therefore, you must pass the arguments as specified by the authors of the DLL functions.

When you write your own Visual Basic functions, you can design them in such a way that the variables must be passed ByVal or by reference. Generally speaking, the easiest and safest way to pass arguments to a function is by value (ByVal). However, there are applications in which passing arguments by reference might be more convenient.

Quiz

1. A file with the .FRM file extension is which of the following?

   a. A file that describes the form and its procedures in an ASCII format.

   b. A file that comes with Notepad.

2. The following declaration is used to declare an array:

   ```
   Dim OurArray (7) As integer
   ```

   Is the following statement correct?

   ```
   OurArray(12) = 32
   ```

3. Is the variable `MyVariable` in the following statement passed `ByVal` or by reference?

   ```
   Result = Calculate( MyVariable)
   ```

   a. ByVal

   b. By reference

   c. There is no way to answer this question just by looking at this statement.

4. Is the variable `MyVariable` in the following function passed `ByVal` or by reference?

   ```
   Function Calculate (MyVariable)
           ..........
           ..........
           ..........
   End Function
   ```

   a. By reference

   b. ByVal

   c. There is no way to answer this question just by looking at this statement.

5. Is the variable `MyVariable` in the following function passed `ByVal` or by reference?

   ```
   Function Calculate (ByVal MyVariable)
           ..........
           ..........
           ..........
   End Function
   ```

   a. By reference

   b. ByVal

   c. There is no way to answer this question just by looking at this statement.

Exercise

Write a loop that declares a two-dimensional array. The loop should fill the elements of the array with an integer that represents the multiplication of its two indexes. For example, the element (3,5) should contain the value 3×5 = 15.

Quiz Answers

1. a
2. No; the subscript of the array can be any value between 0 and 7.
3. b
4. a
5. b

Exercise Answer

Here is one possible solution:

```
Static TheArray (1 To 5, 1 To 5 )As Integer
Dim I, J
For I = 1 To 5 Step 1
    For J = 1 To 5 Step 1
        TheArray(I,J) = I*J
    Next J
Next I
```

The Data Control
and SQL

This chapter shows you how to use the data control, a powerful control supplied with the Visual Basic package. *Data controls* enable you to write programs that access databases such as Microsoft Access, dBASE, Btrieve, Paradox, and FoxPro.

This chapter also shows you how to use SQL statements to manipulate databases.

The Data Program

The Data program illustrates how easy it is to access data from within your Visual Basic programs using the data control. Figure 16.1 shows the data control in the toolbox.

Figure 16.1.
The data control.

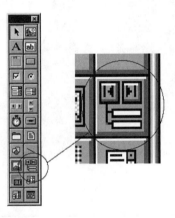

Creating the Database and the Table

The Data program communicates with a database. Therefore, to see the data control in action, you must first create a database. In this chapter you'll create a database by using a software utility, the Data Manager, that comes with Visual Basic. The database you'll create with the Data Manager (or another database manager program, such as Microsoft Access, FoxPro, dBASE III, dBASE IV, Btrieve, or Paradox) is called TEST.MDB, and it has one table called Parts.

You can now build the Parts table using the Data Manager, which is another program capable of producing a database file that is compatible with Visual Basic's data control.

The next sections in this chapter show you how to build the database using the Data Manager of Visual Basic.

☐ Start a new project in Visual Basic.

☐ Select Data Manager from the Add Ins menu of Visual Basic.

Visual Basic responds by displaying the Data Manager window shown in Figure 16.2.

Figure 16.2.
The Data Manager window.

☐ Select New Database from the File menu of the Data Manager. (See Figure 16.3.)

> *The Data Manager responds by displaying the New Database dialog box, which lets you save the new database as an Access MDB file.*

Figure 16.3.
Creating a new database with the Data Manager.

☐ Save the new database as TEST.MDB in the C:\VB4PRG\CH16 directory.

> *The Data Manager responds by saving the new database as an Access database file called TEST.MDB, and the window shown in Figure 16.4 is displayed.*

If you are unfamiliar with databases and tables, just remember that a database is a collection of data. For example, a factory can store its inventory data in a database. The database itself is a collection of tables. For example, the database INVENTRY.MDB may include a table called Parts, which lists parts numbers in the inventory, another table called Shipping, which lists shipping transactions, and so on.

Figure 16.4.
The TEST.MDB database window.

So the TEST.MDB database should include one or more tables. As shown in Figure 16.4, the TEST.MDB database does not include any tables right now, so your job is to create a new table called Parts.

☐ Click the New button of the TEST.MDB window.

> *As expected, Visual Basic responds by displaying the Add Table window shown in Figure 16.5.*

Figure 16.5.
The Add Table window.

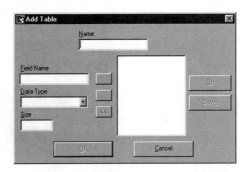

You'll now use the window shown in Figure 16.5 to construct the Parts table.

☐ In the Name box type Parts (the name of the table).

☐ In the Field Name box type PartNum (the name of the first field in the Parts table).

☐ Set the data type to Text, because the PartNum field is composed of text.

☐ Set the size to 10. (The PartNum field can hold a maximum of 10 characters.)

The Add Table window should now look as shown in Figure 16.6.

Figure 16.6.
Designing the first field of the Parts table.

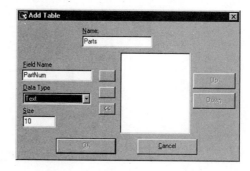

Okay, now it's time to add the field to the table:

☐ Click the button to the right of the Field Name box.

> *The Data Manager responds by copying the name of the field to the list of fields, as shown in Figure 16.7. The Add Table window now waits for you to enter the next field.*

Figure 16.7.
The PartNum field added to the Parts table.

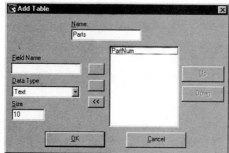

☐ In the Field Name box type Description.

☐ Set the data type to Text.

☐ Set the size to 20.

The Add Table window should now look as shown in Figure 16.8.

☐ Click the button to the right of the Field Name box.

> *The Data Manager responds by copying the name of the field to the list of fields shown in Figure 16.9. The Add Table window now waits for you to enter the next field.*

You have finished designing the Parts table.

Figure 16.8.
Adding the Description field.

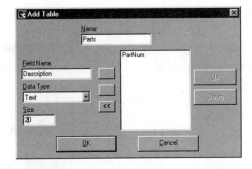

Figure 16.9.
The PartNum field and Description fields added to the Parts table.

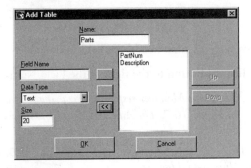

☐ Click the OK button of the Add Table window.

> *The Data Manger responds by displaying the window shown in Figure 16.10. As shown, the TEST.MDB database now contains the Parts table.*

Figure 16.10.
The TEST.MDB database with the Parts table included.

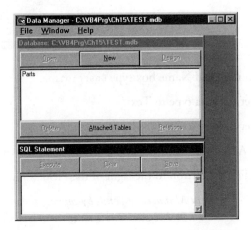

☐ Click the Parts item in the TEST.MDB database window.

If you want to add another table to the database, click the New button. If you want to modify the design of the Parts table, click the Design button. At this point, however, you want to enter data into the Parts table.

☐ Click the Parts item, then click the Open button.

The Data Manager responds by displaying the Parts table, ready to accept data. (See Figure 16.11.)

Figure 16.11.
The Parts table, ready to accept data.

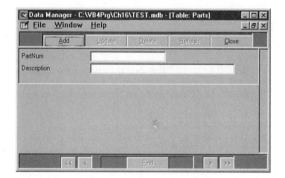

☐ Click the Add button.

☐ Type PC100 in the PartNum field.

☐ Type PC 100 Megahertz in the Description field.

The Parts table should now look as shown in Figure 16.12.

Figure 16.12.
The Parts table with the first record in it.

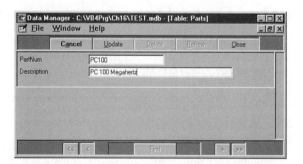

What you see in Figure 16.12 is called a record. That is, the Parts table is composed of records, and the first record contains the PC100 part number.

☐ Click the Update button to actually enter the data into the table.

☐ Click the Add button to display the next record (that is, record number 2, which is currently empty).

☐ Type RAM40 in the PartNum field of record number 2.

☐ Type 40 nanoseconds RAM in the Description field of record number 2.

☐ Click the Update button.

The last record you'll enter is record number 3.

☐ Click the Add button.

> *The Data Manager responds by displaying record number 3, ready for you to edit.*

☐ Type KEY101 in the PartNum field.

☐ Type 101 keys keyboard in the Description field.

☐ Click the Update button.

☐ Click the Close button.

☐ Select Exit from the Data Manager's File menu.

What have you accomplished so far? You have created the TEST.MDB database in the C:\VB4PRG\CH16 directory, and you have attached a table called Parts to the TEST database. The Parts table consists of two fields: PartNum and Description. You have also added three records to the Parts table.

The Visual Implementation of the Data Program

☐ Start a new project in Visual Basic, save the form of the project as C:\VB4PRG\CH16\DATA.FRM, and save the project file of the project as C:\VB4PRG\CH16\DATA.VBP.

☐ Place the data control in the form, as shown in Figure 16.13.

You can move, enlarge, and shrink the data control just as you would any other control.

☐ Move the data control to the lower part of the form and enlarge the data control by dragging its handles. The enlarged data control is shown in Figure 16.14.

The default name that Visual Basic assigns to the data control is Data1.

☐ Change the Name property of the form to frmData and the Caption property of the form to The Data Program.

Figure 16.13.

Placing the data control in the form.

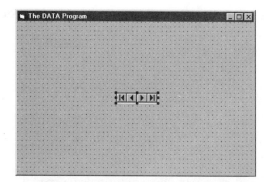

Figure 16.14.

Enlarging the data control.

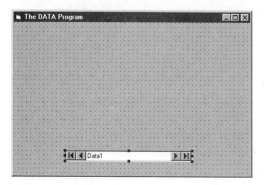

Specifying an Access Database

Now enter the name and path of the database file that will communicate with the Data1 data control. Specifying a non-Access database is a little different from specifying an Access database. The TEST database you created with the Data Manager at the beginning of this chapter is an Access database. (That is, the files generated by Visual Basic's Data Manager are compatible with the Microsoft Access database manager program.)

Use the following steps to enter the name and path of an Access database:

☐ Make sure the data control is selected and select Properties from the View menu.

   Visual Basic responds by displaying the properties window of the data control.

☐ Click the DatabaseName property in the properties table of the data control and then click the three-dots icon on the DatabaseName property line.

   Visual Basic responds by displaying the DatabaseName dialog box shown in Figure 16.15.

Figure 16.15.
The DatabaseName dialog box.

☐ Select the C:\VB4PRG\CH16\TEST.MDB file that you created with the Data Manager and click the Open button.

Okay, now the Data1 control knows it should control the TEST.MDB database.

☐ Click the data control's RecordSource property in the properties table, then click the down-arrow icon to display a list of all the tables in the TEST database.

> *Visual Basic responds by letting you select from a list box a table that contains all the tables in the TEST database. Because you created just one table—the Parts table—the list contains only that table. However, if the TEST database had several tables, the drop-down list would show all of them and you would select one from the list.*

☐ Select the Parts table from the RecordSource property list.

Placing a Text Box to Hold the Data

Now you'll place a text box in the frmData form. This text box serves as a placeholder for the PartNum field.

☐ Place a text box control in the frmData form, as shown in Figure 16.16.

☐ Set the text box's Name property to txtPartNumber and leave its Text property empty.

☐ Place a label control in the frmData form, as shown in Figure 16.16.

☐ Set the label's Name property to lblPartNumber and its Caption property to Part Number:.

☐ Set the Name property of the Text box to txtPartNumber and delete the text from the Text property of this text box.

☐ Add the E&xit command button (cmdExit) to the frmData form, as shown in Figure 16.16.

Add the following code in the `cmdExit_Click()` procedure of the frmData form:

```
Private Sub cmdExit_Click()

     End

End Sub
```

Figure 16.16.

Placing a text box, a label, and a command button in the frmData form.

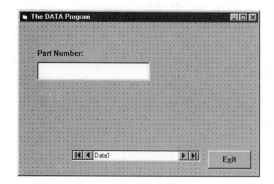

16

The txtPartNumber text box you placed in the form will be used to display and edit the contents of the PartNum field. Now tell Visual Basic which data control is associated with this text box:

Set the DataSource property of the txtPartNumber text box in the properties window to Data1. (Recall that Data1 is the name of the data control.)

Because you have only one data control in the form, the DataSource property's drop-down list contains only one item: Data1.

Now tell Visual Basic that this text box should hold the contents of the PartNum field:

Set the DataField property of the txtPartNumber text box to PartNum.

Save the project.

DO	DON'T

DO save your work, because if you have made an error in the preceding steps, it might cause Windows to crash and all the work that you have done so far would be lost. However, if you save your work, you can restart Windows, start Visual Basic, load the DATA.VBP project, and correct the mistake. This advice is valid for any project, but it is particularly valid for projects that include databases, OLE, DDE, and other powerful Visual Basic/Windows features.

Executing the Data Program

Note: Before you execute the Data program in Windows 3.1, you must first make sure the DOS program SHARE.EXE is loaded.

To load the SHARE.EXE program, you must exit Windows, then type the following statement at the DOS command line:

```
C:\DOS\SHARE.EXE  {Enter}
```

This statement assumes that your SHARE.EXE file is in C:\ DOS.

Many users prefer to add the following line to their AUTOEXEC.BAT file:

```
C:\DOS\SHARE.EXE
```

☐ Execute the Data program.

> *The Data program responds by displaying the window shown in Figure 16.17. As you can see, the part number you entered in Access appears in the text box!*

Figure 16.17.
The Data program.

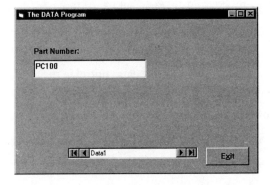

☐ Click the arrow icons of the Data1 data control and notice that the contents of the text box change with the contents of the PartNum field. Each click of the inner-right arrow of the Data1 data control causes the record in the table to advance one record; each click of the inner-left arrow of the Data1 data control causes the record to retreat one record. Clicking the rightmost arrow of the Data1 control causes the text box to display the PartNum contents of the very last record, and clicking the leftmost arrow of the Data1 control causes the text box to display the PartNum contents of the very first record.

☐ Experiment with the Data program, then click the Exit button to terminate the Data program.

As shown in Figure 16.17, the text in the Data1 data control displays the text Data1. This is the default name of the Caption property of Data1. You can set the Caption property of Data1 at design time to TEST.MDB or any other text appropriate to your application. Or you can change the Caption property of Data1 during runtime. For example, you can set the Caption property of Data1 to Database:TEST Table:Parts with the following statement:

```
Data1.Caption = "Database:TEST Table:Parts"
```

Disabling the Text Box

Note that the text box holding the contents of the PartNum field is currently enabled. That is, you can click in the text box and change its contents. For example, try the following experiment:

☐ Execute the Data program.

☐ Change the PartNum contents of the first record from PC100 to PC200.

☐ Click the inner-right arrow icon of the data control to display the second record.

☐ Click the inner-left arrow icon of the data control to display the first record.

As you can see, you are able to change the contents of the table!

☐ Click the Exit button to terminate the Data program.

☐ Execute the Data program again.

As you can see, the PartNum field contains the data you modified in the previous steps.

☐ Change the contents of the PartNum field back to PC100.

☐ Click the inner-right arrow icon to advance to the next record, then click the inner-left arrow icon to display the first record, and check that the PartNum field now contains the value PC100.

☐ Click the Exit button to terminate the program.

There are additional "database considerations" that must be incorporated into a Visual Basic program that includes the data control. For example, during the design of your tables, you can design the table so that the PartNum field is the key field. This means that the Parts table must not have more than one record with the same value for PartNum—the value of the PartNum field must be unique. Because this chapter concentrates on Visual Basic programming and not on database design, simplify the Data program by disabling the text box containing the contents of the PartNum field:

☐ Set the Enabled property of the txtPartNumber text box to False.

☐ Save the project.

577

☐ Execute the Data program.

☐ Check that the txtPartNumber text box displays the contents of the PartNum field and that the contents cannot be modified.

☐ Experiment with the Data program, then click the Exit button to terminate the program.

Enhancing the Data Program

Now enhance the Data program by adding to the frmData form another text box, shown in Figure 16.18, that will contain the contents of the Description field:

☐ Add a label to the frmData form with its Name property set to lblDescription and its Caption property set to Description:.

☐ Add a text box to the frmData form and set its properties as follows: The Name property should be txtDescription, the Text property should be empty, and the Enabled property should be False.

Figure 16.18.

The Data program with the Description text box added.

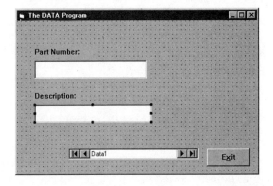

Of course, if you execute the Data program now, only the txtPartNumber text box will display the contents of its field. The txtDescription text box will not display the contents of its field in the Parts table because you haven't instructed Visual Basic to associate the text box with the corresponding field in the Parts table.

☐ Set the DataSource property of the txtDescription text box to Data1.

☐ Set the DataField property of the txtDescription text box to Description.

☐ Save the project.

Executing the Enhanced Data Program

☐ Execute the Data program.

The Data program appears, as shown in Figure 16.19.

Figure 16.19.
The Data program, with two text boxes that correspond to two fields.

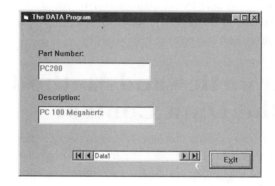

☐ Click the arrows of the Data1 data control to move from record to record.

As you can see, the contents of the two text boxes correspond to the contents of the two fields in the Parts table.

☐ Click the Exit button to terminate the program.

Adding Logical Fields to the Table of the Database

In a similar manner, you can design the Parts table with a Boolean (logical) field. For example, you could add the field InStock. When the value of the InStock field is True, it means that the part number is available in stock. If InStock is equal to False, the part number is not in stock.

You can then place a check box in the form and correlate its Value property with the InStock field of the Parts table (just as you correlated the Part Number and Description text boxes with the fields of the Parts table).

Remember to use the following steps when correlating a check box with a field of the Parts table:

☐ Set the DataSource property of the check box to Data1.

☐ Set the DataField property of the check box to the logical field of the Parts table.

579

Using Bound Controls

The Data program illustrates how a text box is used to bind the data of a table. A control used to display the contents of a field is called a *bound control*. Therefore, a text box control and a check box control can be used in a program as bound controls. In a similar manner, you can add a field to the Parts table that contains a BMP file, then add a picture control or an image control to the frmData form that corresponds to the picture field in the Parts table. Picture controls and image controls can also serve as bound controls.

Properties and Methods of the Data Control

The Data program illustrates how your Visual Basic program can display the contents of a table's fields. As you might expect, the data control has many more properties and methods that enable you to manipulate the database in almost any conceivable way. Some of these properties and methods are discussed in the following sections.

The *Refresh* Method

You can use the Refresh method to update the bound controls with the most recent values of the table's fields. For example, if the database is in a file server connected to your PC through a LAN (local area network), and another user on a different station changed a field's values in the table, the current values on your screen haven't been updated with those changes. To update the screen with the most recent values, use the following statement:

```
Data1.Refresh
```

The Exclusive Property

If you want your program to be the only program that can access the database, you have to set the Exclusive property of the data control to True, as shown in the following statement:

```
Data1.Exclusive = True
```

Setting the Exclusive property to True prevents all other programs from accessing the database.

The default value of the Exclusive property is False. To return to its default value, use the following statement:

```
Data1.Exclusive = False
```

If the database is already open and you change the Exclusive property, then you must execute the Refresh method to make the change effective:

```
Data1.Exclusive = False
Data1.Refresh
```

Working with a database with the Exclusive property set to True makes access to the database much faster (at the expense of other users, who have to wait until you are kind enough to set the Exclusive property back to False).

The ReadOnly Property

Once you modify the contents of a field, you can click the arrows of the Data1 data control to move to the next record. The changes you made to the previous record are automatically saved. To see the automatic saving in action, try the following experiment:

☐ Execute the Data program.

☐ Change the contents of any of the fields of the first record.

☐ Click the inner-right arrow of the Data1 data control to move to the next record, which saves the new data.

☐ Click the Exit button to terminate the Data program.

☐ Start the Data program again.

As you can see, the record appears with the value you updated. This means that the changes you made to the database in the previous execution of the Data program were saved.

If you want your program to just read records, set the ReadOnly property of the data control to True. For example, modify the Form_Load() procedure so that it looks like this:

```
Private Sub Form_Load()

    Data1.ReadOnly = True
    Data1.Refresh

End Sub
```

☐ Enable the text box that holds the contents of a field.

☐ Save the project.

☐ Execute the Data program.

☐ Change the contents of any of the fields in the first record.

The program responds by changing the contents of the field, but as you'll see in the next step, it does not change the value in the table.

☐ Click the inner-right arrow of the Data1 data control to move to the next record.

☐ Click the inner-left arrow of the Data1 data control to return to the previous record.

The field was not changed because the ReadOnly property was set to True.

To set the ReadOnly property back to its default value of False, change the `Form_Load()` procedure so that it looks like this:

```
Private Sub Form_Load()

    Data1.ReadOnly = False
    Data1.Refresh

End Sub
```

☐ Try the previous experiment again and notice that now you can change the contents of the fields in the table.

Again, if you change properties (such as the ReadOnly property) after the database is already open, you must use the Refresh method to make the change to the property effective.

Note: You must set the ReadOnly property of Data1 to False to perform the experiments with the properties and methods described in the next sections.

Typically you'll design the application so that the bound control's Enabled property matches the ReadOnly property. For example, if the table is set as read-only, you must set the Enabled property of the bound controls to False to let your user know that the database is in a read-only state. If you enable the bound controls and the database is read-only, your user might not realize that the data he or she is modifying on the screen isn't being transferred to the database.

Using SQL (Structured Query Language) Statements

Your program can use SQL statements to select only a set of records that comply with a certain condition. Do the following steps to see a SQL statement in action:

☐ Add the Select command button, as shown in Figure 16.20.

☐ Set the Name property of the Select button to cmdSelect and the Caption property to &Select.

Figure 16.20.

Adding the Select button.

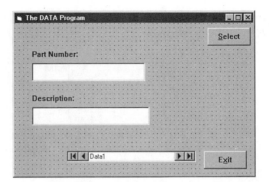

16

☐ Add the following code in the cmdSelect_Click() procedure of the frmData form:

```
Private Sub cmdSelect_Click()

    Data1.RecordSource = "Select * from Parts where PartNum = 'PC100' "

    Data1.Refresh

End Sub
```

The preceding procedure uses the standard SQL Select statement to select all the records from the Parts table that satisfy the condition PartNum = 'PC100'. To make the SQL request effective, the Refresh method is executed.

☐ Save the project.

☐ Execute the Data program.

☐ Make sure the PartNum of the first record is PC100.

☐ Click the arrows of the Data1 data control to browse from record to record.

As you can see, you are able to browse through all the records.

☐ Click the Select button.

Because there is only one record that satisfies the SQL statement, the Data program displays only this record, as shown in Figure 16.21.

Clicking the arrow of the Data1 data control doesn't display any other records because only one record satisfies the SQL selection. The SQL statement filtered out all the records that didn't satisfy the SQL requirement.

☐ Exit the Data program by clicking the Exit button.

Figure 16.21.
Clicking the Select button to select the PC100 record.

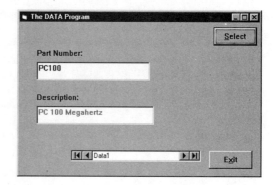

You can use SQL statements to select any group of records. For example, suppose you added the InStock field to the Parts field (a field that indicates whether the part number exists in stock). You can then change the cmdSelect_Click() procedure so that it looks like this:

```
Private Sub cmdSelect_Click()

    Data1.RecordSource = "Select * from Parts where InStock = True "
    Data1.Refresh

End Sub
```

When you click the Select button, the Data program will display only those records that have their InStock field equal to True.

Generally speaking, the syntax of the SQL statements is simple, but this book does not teach SQL syntax. You should know, however, that SQL statements can manipulate databases and tables in almost any conceivable way.

The *AddNew* Method

You can add a new record at runtime by using the AddNew method:

☐ Add the New Record button, as shown in Figure 16.22. Set its Name property to cmdAddRecord and its Caption property to &Add Record.

☐ Add the following code in the cmdAddRecord_Click() procedure of the frmData form:

```
Private Sub cmdAddRecord_Click()

    Data1.Recordset.AddNew

End Sub
```

The AddNew method is applied to the RecordSet property of Data1. (The RecordSet property is discussed later in this chapter.)

Figure 16.22.
Adding the New Record button to the frmData form.

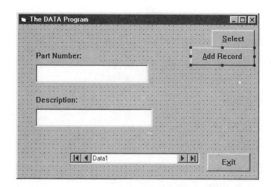

In the following experiment, you are going to fill the fields of the Parts table with data.

☐ Set the Enable property of the txtPartNumber text box to True.

☐ Set the Enable property of the txtDescription text box to True.

☐ Save the project.

☐ Execute the Data program.

☐ Click the Add Record button.

> *The Data program responds by displaying a blank record (that is, all the bound controls are empty).*

☐ Fill the contents of the bound controls with new values, but remember that the PartNum field is a key field, so you can't add a part number that already exists in the table.

The data control saves the new record once you move the record pointer (that is, click the inner arrow of the Data1 data control to the next or previous record).

☐ Exit the program by clicking the Exit button.

The *Delete* Method

To delete a record, you can use the Delete method:

☐ Add the Delete button and place this button below the Add Records button.

☐ Set the Delete button's Name property to cmdDelete and its Caption property to &Delete.

☐ Add the following code in the cmdDelete_Click() procedure of the frmData form:

```
Private Sub cmdDelete_Click()

    Data1.Recordset.Delete
    Data1.Recordset.MoveNext

End Sub
```

☐ Save the project.

☐ Execute the Data program.

☐ Use the arrow buttons of the Data1 data control to move the record pointer to the record you want to delete.

☐ Click the Delete button.

> *The Data program responds by deleting the record.*

☐ Practice with the Delete and Add Record buttons for a while, then click the Exit button to terminate the Data program.

Like the AddNew method, the Delete method is used on the RecordSet property of the Data1 data control.

> **Note:** In the Data program, you can delete records very easily! You simply click the Delete button.
>
> Naturally, in a real-world application you have to use a verification step. When you click the Delete button, a message box pops up, asking whether you really want to delete the record. The record will be deleted if you click the Yes button in the message box.

The *MoveNext* Method

In the cmdDelete_Click() procedure, the MoveNext method was executed after the Delete method:

Data1.RecordSet.MoveNext

The MoveNext method moves the record pointer to the next record. The MoveNext method has the same effect as clicking the inner-right arrow of the data control.

The *MovePrevious* Method

The MovePrevious method moves the record pointer to the previous record. You can use the MovePrevious method as follows:

```
Data1.RecordSet.MovePrevious
```

The MovePrevious method has the same effect as clicking the inner-left arrow of the data control.

The *MoveLast* Method

The MoveLast method moves the record pointer to the very last record. You can use the MoveLast method as follows:

```
Data1.RecordSet.MoveLast
```

The MoveLast method has the same effect as clicking the rightmost arrow of the data control.

The *MoveFirst* Method

The MoveFirst method moves the record pointer to the very first record. You can use the MoveFirst method as follows:

```
Data1.RecordSet.MoveFirst
```

The MoveFirst method has the same effect as clicking the leftmost arrow of the data control.

The RecordSet Property

You can think of the RecordSet property of the data control as the current records your program can access. For example, if you don't set a filter by issuing a SQL statement, the RecordSet property represents all the records in the Parts table. Because the data control can represent a database with several tables, you can use SQL statements to create a RecordSet that represent records from several tables.

As demonstrated in the previous sections, many of the methods are applied to the RecordSet property (for example, Data1.RecordSet.Delete, Data1.RecordSet.AddNew, and Data1.RecordSet.MoveNext).

The following steps illustrate how your program can determine the number of records in the record set:

☐ Add the Count Records button, as shown in Figure 16.23.

Figure 16.23.

Adding the Count Records button to the frmData form.

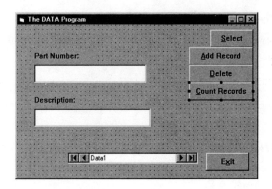

☐ Set the Name property of the Count Records button to cmdCountRecords and its Caption property to &Count Records.

☐ Add the following code in the cmdCountRecords_Click() procedure:

```
Private Sub cmdCountRecords_Click()

    Data1.RecordSet.MoveLast
    MsgBox Data1.Recordset.RecordCount

End Sub
```

The cmdCountRecords_Click() procedure moves the record pointer to the last record of the record set, then the RecordCount method counts all the records up to the current record. Since the MoveLast method moved the record pointer to the last record of the RecordSet (which represents the Parts table), RecordCount returns the total number of records in the Parts table.

☐ Save the project.

☐ Execute the Data program.

☐ Click the Count Records button.

> *The Data program responds by displaying the total number of records in the RecordSet (which represents the total number of records in the Parts table).*

☐ Delete and add records by clicking the Add Record and Delete buttons, then click the Count Records button to see whether the number of total records in the table increases and decreases accordingly.

☐ Terminate the Data program by clicking the Exit button.

Note: You should be aware of certain "standard" database users' interfaces. Once you add a new record, a blank record is created. If you then fill the contents of the key field, the new record will indeed be added to the table. However, if you just added a new record and then moved the record pointer to a different record, the blank record won't be added to the table.

Also, once you modify a record, the change will take effect only after you move the record pointer.

The Value Property

You can extract the contents of the fields by examining the corresponding properties of the bound controls. For example, you can determine the contents of the PartNum field of the current record by examining the Text property of the txtPartNumber text box. The following code illustrates how to display the contents of the current record's PartNum field whenever you click the form:

☐ Add the following code in the `Form_Click()` procedure of the frmData form:

```
Private Sub Form_Click()

    MsgBox "Part number: " + txtPartNumber.Text

End Sub
```

☐ Save the project.

☐ Execute the Data program.

☐ Click the form.

> *The Data program responds by displaying the contents of the current record's PartNum field.*

☐ Click the Exit button to terminate the program.

Sometimes you might want to know the contents of a field that doesn't have a corresponding bound control in the form. In these cases, you can use the Value property. To see how it works, do the following:

☐ Change the code in the Form_Click() procedure so that it looks like this:

```
Private Sub Form_Click()

    Dim MyString As String

    MyString = Data1.Recordset.Fields("PartNum").Value
    MsgBox MyString

End Sub
```

☐ Save the project.

☐ Execute the Data program.

☐ Click the form.

> *The Data program responds by displaying a message box with the contents of the current record's PartNum field.*

☐ Click the Exit button to terminate the program.

The code in the Form_Click() procedure assigns the Value property of the current record's PartNum field to the MyString variable. Then this string is displayed by using the MsgBox statement.

In a similar manner, you can extract the Value property of the other fields in the database. For example, to assign the Value property of the current record's Description field to the MyString variable, you can use the following statement:

```
MyString = Data1.RecordSet.Fields("Description").Value
```

The EOF and BOF Properties

Your program can use the EOF (end of file) and BOF (beginning of file) properties to determine whether the current record is valid. For example, while your program is displaying a particular record, another workstation (another PC in the LAN) could delete that record. In this case, the record pointer would be pointing to an invalid record. Your program can determine the validity of the pointer as follows:

```
If Data1.RecordSet.EOF = False AND Data1.RecordSet.BOF=False Then
    ..................................
    ... The record pointer points ...
    ... to a valid record.        ...
    ..................................
End If
```

The above If…End If block of statements checks whether the record pointer is pointing to a valid record by checking whether both the EOF and the BOF properties are False.

As shown in Table 16.1, any other combination of values for the EOF and BOF properties, such as both properties being True, means that the record pointer is pointing to an invalid record.

Table 16.1. The BOF and EOF properties.

BOF	EOF	Comment
False	False	Valid record
False	True	Invalid record
True	False	Invalid record
True	True	Invalid record

What Else Can the Data Control Do?

The properties and methods this chapter introduces are the basic properties and methods of the data control, and you can use them to display and modify the contents of the tables' fields. However, the data control supports many more features that enable Visual Basic to manipulate databases in almost any way (for example, building a database, modifying the structures of tables). In fact, Visual Basic's data control is so powerful that you could think of it as a separate programming package included with the Visual Basic package. Although the data control can handle databases other than the Access database, it uses the same software engine that powers the Access program, so it makes sense to assume that for faster, bug-free operations, the Access database is the easiest database platform to use.

Summary

In this chapter you have learned about the data control supplied with the Visual Basic package, how to assign properties to the data control, and how to assign properties to the bound controls that display the contents of the tables' fields.

You have also learned how to refresh the data, issue SQL statements, and delete and add records to the tables.

Q&A

Q Is it possible to place more than one data control in a form?

A Yes. You can place several data controls in a form. Make sure to set the DatabaseName and RecordSource properties of each of the data controls to the corresponding database and tables each of them represents.

Quiz

1. When using an Access database, the DatabaseName property of a data control is a string that specifies which of the following?

   a. The name of the required table
   b. The name of the required database
   c. The name of the bound control

2. When using an Access database, the RecordSource property of a data control is a string that specifies which of the following?

   a. The name of the required table in the database
   b. The contents of the SQL statement
   c. The name of the field

3. A scroll bar can be a bound control.

   a. False
   b. True

4. What is the ReadOnly property used for?

5. What is the AddNew method used for?

6. What is the Delete method used for?

7. What is the MoveNext method used for?

Exercise

Suppose that the Parts table includes the InStock Boolean field. Write a SQL statement so the Data1 control accesses only those records that have their InStock fields equal to No.

Quiz Answers

1. b

2. Both a and b

3. a

4. The ReadOnly property is used to prevent your program from changing the contents of the table's field from within your Visual Basic program.

5. The AddNew method is used for adding a record.

6. The Delete method is used for deleting a record.

7. The MoveNext method is used for moving the record pointer to the next record.

Exercise Answer

☐ Change the code in the cmdSelect_Click() procedure so it looks like the following:

```
Private Sub cmdSelect_Click()

    Data1.RecordSource = "Select * from Parts where InStock = False "
    Data1.Refresh

End Sub
```

☐ Execute the Data program.

☐ Click the Select button.

☐ Click the arrows of the Data1 data control.

As you can see, only those records that have their InStock field equal to No are displayed.

16

Multiple-
Document
Interface

This chapter focuses on developing multiple-document interface (MDI) programs. An *MDI program* contains several documents, each with its own window, contained in a single parent form. Some well-known MDI applications are programs such as Word for Windows, Microsoft Excel, and others.

Your First MDI Program: The Pictures Program

The Pictures program illustrates how to create an MDI program. The key to designing impressive MDI programs with Visual Basic is understanding how to manipulate the various forms of the program.

Creating the Pictures Project

Build an MDI project called Pictures.vbp that consists of a parent form called Pictures.frm and three child forms: Picture1.frm, Picture2.frm, and Picture3.frm.

To create the Pictures project, follow these steps:

☐ Create a new project by selecting New Project from the File menu.

Visual Basic responds by opening a new project and displaying a blank form. The default name of the form file is Form1.frm and the default name of the project file is Project1.vbp. This is no different than creating a typical new (non-MDI) project.

Every MDI program has one parent form. Use the following step to create the parent form:

☐ Select MDI Form from the Insert menu.

Visual Basic responds by displaying a blank form with the default name MDIForm1. (See Figure 17.1.) This blank form is the parent form.

See how the project window looks at this point:

☐ Select Project from the View menu.

Visual Basic responds by displaying the project window shown in Figure 17.2. As shown, the project window contains the following: Form1.frm, a standard (non-MDI) blank form, and MDIForm1.frm, the blank parent form.

Figure 17.1.
The blank MDI form.

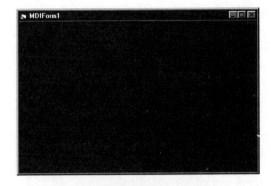

Figure 17.2.
*The project window with
default form filenames.*

17

Note the little icons to the left of each file in the project window. These icons are indicators of the type of file. The standard form (Form1.frm) has an icon that looks like a form standing on its edge. The parent form's (MDIForm1.frm) icon looks like a form standing on its edge with a little form next to it.

Your Visual Basic program can have only one parent form. Use the following steps to see this for yourself:

☐ Open the Insert menu.

> *As you can see, the MDI Form item is gray (not available because you already have a parent MDI window in the project).*

So what do you have so far? As indicated by the project window, you have one parent form (MDIForm1.frm) and one standard form (Form1.frm). Use the following steps to convert the standard form to a child form:

☐ Highlight Form1.frm in the project window.

☐ Click the View Form button in the project window.

☐ Change the MDIChild property of Form1 to True.

Now take a look at the project window (select Project from the View menu). Form1.frm now appears as a child form (it has the MDI icon next to its name in the project window). To tell the difference between the parent form and the child form, take a look at their icons. Both have an icon of a large form standing on its edge next to a little form. However, the little form is dimmed in the parent form's icon (MDIForm1.frm), and the large form is dimmed in the child form's icon (Form1.frm). (See Figure 17.3.)

Figure 17.3.

The difference between the parent form's icon and the child form's icon.

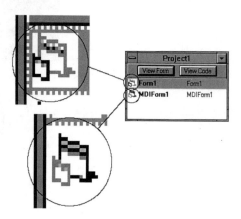

The MDI program that you are currently building is called Pictures. Therefore, a more appropriate name for the child form is Picture1.frm. Use the following steps to change its name from Form1.frm to Picture1.frm:

☐ Highlight Form1.frm in the project window.

☐ Select Save File As from the File menu.

   Visual Basic responds by displaying the Save File As dialog box.

☐ Save the file as C:\VB4PRG\CH17\Picture1.frm.

Now that Visual Basic has saved the child form as Picture1.frm, take a look at the project window. The child form's name was changed to Picture1.frm.

Currently, the name of the parent form is MDIForm1.frm. Use the following steps to change its name to Pictures.frm:

☐ Highlight MDIForm1.frm in the project window.

☐ Select Save File As from the File menu.

   Visual Basic responds by displaying the Save File As dialog box.

☐ Save the parent form as C:\VB4PRG\CH17\Pictures.frm.

Take a look at the project window. The parent form's name, MDIForm1.frm, was changed to Pictures.frm.

Currently, the project name is Project1.vbp (as shown by the title of the project window in Figure 17.2). Use the following steps to change the name of the project from Project1.vbp to Pictures.vbp:

☐ Select Save Project As from the File menu.

  Visual Basic responds by displaying the Save Project As dialog box.

☐ Save the project as C:\VB4PRG\CH17\Pictures.vbp.

The project window now has the title Pictures. It should look like the one in Figure 17.4.

Figure 17.4.

The project window with the project name Pictures, one parent form called Pictures.frm, and one child form called Picture1.frm.

MDI programs usually have more than one child form. Use the following steps to add two more child windows:

☐ Select Form from the Insert menu.

  Visual Basic responds by adding a standard form called Form2.frm to the project window.

☐ Select Form from the Insert menu again.

  Visual Basic responds by adding a standard form called Form3.frm to the project window.

The project window now has one parent form (Pictures.frm), one child form (Picture1.frm), and two new standard forms (Form2.frm and Form3.frm). Of course, you need these two new standard forms to be child forms, not standard forms, so change Form2.frm and Form3.frm from standard forms to child forms:

☐ Highlight Form2.frm in the project window and click the View Form button in the project window (so you'll have access to the properties window of Form2.frm).

☐ Change the MDIChild property of Form2.frm to True.

☐ Highlight Form3.frm in the project window and click the View Form button in the project window.

☐ Change the MDIChild property of Form3.frm to True.

Currently, the two newly added child forms are called Form2.frm and Form3.frm (the default names that Visual Basic assigned to these forms). Use the following steps to change their filenames:

☐ Highlight Form2.frm in the project window.

☐ Select Save File As from the File menu and save the form as C:\VB4PRG\CH17\Picture2.frm.

☐ Highlight Form3.frm in the project window.

☐ Select Save File As from the File menu and save the form as C:\VB4PRG\CH17\Picture3.frm.

You now have a project called Pictures.vbp with a parent form called Pictures.frm and three child forms: Picture1.frm, Picture2.frm, and Picture3.frm. The complete project window is shown in Figure 17.5.

Figure 17.5.

The complete project window of the Pictures project.

☐ Select Save Project from the File menu to save the project.

Changing the Properties of the Child Forms

Now you will change several properties of the forms. Use the following steps to change the properties of the child form Picture1.frm:

☐ Select the Picture1 form by highlighting Picture1.frm in the project window, then clicking the View Form button in the project window.

☐ Select Properties from the View menu and change the properties of the Picture1.frm form as follows: Change the Caption property of Picture1.frm to The Picture 1 Child and change the Name property of Picture1.frm to frmPicture1.

Now change the properties of the other child forms:

☐ Change the Caption property of Picture2.frm to The Picture 2 Child.

□ Change the Name property of Picture2.frm to frmPicture2.

□ Change the Caption property of Picture3.frm to The Picture 3 Child.

□ Change the Name property of Picture3.frm to frmPicture3.

Changing the Properties of the Parent Form

To change the properties of Pictures.frm (the parent form), highlight Pictures.frm in the project window and click the View Form button. (This gives you access to the properties window of Pictures.frm.)

□ Change the Caption property of Pictures.frm to I am the parent window.

□ Change the Name property of Pictures.frm to frmPictures.

□ To save the work that you've done so far, select Save project from the File menu.

The Visual Implementation of the Pictures Program

An MDI program has several properties tables—one for the parent form and one for each of the child forms.

The Visual Implementation of the Parent Form

□ Build the frmPictures form according to the specifications in its properties table (Table 17.1) and menu table (Table 17.2).

The completed form should look like the one shown in Figure 17.6.

Table 17.1. The properties table of the parent form Pictures.frm.

Object	Property	Setting
Form	**Name**	**frmPictures**
	Caption	I am the parent window
	Height	4545
	Left	1080
	Top	1170
	Width	6810
Menu	**(See Table 17.2.)**	**(See Table 17.2.)**

Note: You already set the properties of the parent form according to Table 17.1 in the previous steps. Just build the menu of the parent form according to Table 17.2. Make sure to attach the menu of Table 17.2 to the Pictures form—that is, select the Pictures form, then select Menu Editor from the Window menu.

Table 17.2. The menu table of the parent form Pictures.frm.

Caption	Name
&File	mnuFile
...E&xit	mnuExit
&Show Pictures	mnuShow
...Show Picture &1	mnuShowPicture1
...Show Picture &2	mnuShowPicture2
...Show Picture &3	mnuShowPicture3
...- (separator)	mnuSep1
...Show &All Pictures	mnuShowAll
...&Clear All Pictures	mnuClearAll

Figure 17.6.
The parent form in design mode.

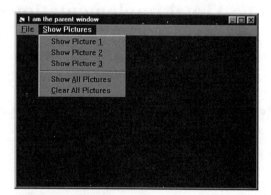

The Visual Implementation of the Child Forms

Because the Pictures project contains three child forms, there are three separate properties tables.

The Visual Implementation of frmPicture1

☐ Build the frmPicture1 form according to the specifications in its properties table (Table 17.3) and menu table (Table 17.4).

The completed form should look like the one shown in Figure 17.7.

Note: You already set some of the properties listed in Table 17.3 in the previous steps.

Note: Table 17.3 instructs you to set the Picture property of the imgClub image control to C:\VB\BITMAPS\ASSORTED\CLUB.BMP.

If your Visual Basic directory doesn't contain this BMP file, use a different BMP file. For example, you can use Paint, Paintbrush, or another drawing program to draw your own small BMP pictures.

Table 17.3. The properties table of the frmPicture1 form.

Object	Property	Setting
Form	**Name**	**frmPicture1**
	MDIChild	True
	Caption	The Picture 1 Child
	BackColor	(yellow)
	Height	3945
	Left	1080
	Top	1170
	Width	3060
Image	**Name**	**imgClub**
	Stretch	True
	Picture	C:\VB\BITMAPS\ASSORTED\CLUB.BMP
	Height	1335
	Left	840
	Top	840
	Width	1215

continues

Table 17.3. continued

Object	Property	Setting
Command Button	Name	**cmdClose**
	Caption	&Close
	FontName	System
	FontSize	10
	Height	495
	Left	840
	Top	2400
	Width	1215
Menu	**(See Table 17.4.)**	**(See Table 17.4.)**

Table 17.4. The menu table of the frmPicture1 form.

Caption	Name
&File	mnuFile
…&Close	mnuClose
&Beep	mnuBeep
…Beep &Once	mnuBeepOnce
…Beep &Twice	mnuBeepTwice

Figure 17.7.
The frmPicture1 form in design mode.

The Visual Implementation of frmPicture2

☐ Build the frmPicture2 form according to the specifications in its properties table. (See Table 17.5.)

The completed form should look like the one shown in Figure 17.8.

 Note: The frmPicture2 form does not have a menu.

Table 17.5. The properties table of the frmPicture2 form.

Object	Property	Setting
Form	**Name**	**frmPicture2**
	MDIChild	True
	Caption	The Picture 2 Child
	BackColor	(yellow)
	Height	3600
	Left	1035
	Top	1605
	Width	3105
Image	**Name**	**imgCup**
	Picture	C:\VB\BITMAPS\ASSORTED\CUP.BMP
	Stretch	True
	Height	1095
	Left	960
	Top	480
	Width	975
Command Button	**Name**	**cmdClose**
	Caption	&Close
	FontName	System
	FontSize	10
	Height	495
	Left	840
	Top	2160
	Width	1215

17

Figure 17.8.
The frmPicture2 form in design mode.

The Visual Implementation of frmPicture3

☐ Build the frmPicture3 form according to the specifications in its properties table. (See Table 17.6.)

The completed form should look like the one shown in Figure 17.9.

Note: The frmPicture3 form does not have a menu.

Table 17.6. The properties table of the frmPicture3 form.

Object	Property	Setting
Form	Name	frmPicture3
	MDIChild	True
	Caption	The Picture 3 Child
	BackColor	(yellow)
	Height	3405
	Left	·1065
	Top	1905
	Width	2970
Image	Name	imgBell
	Picture	C:\VB\BITMAPS\ASSORTED\BELL.BMP
	Stretch	True
	Height	1455
	Left	840
	Top	360
	Width	1215

Object	Property	Setting
Command Button	**Name**	**cmdClose**
	Caption	&Close
	Height	495
	Left	840
	Top	2040
	Width	1215

Figure 17.9.
The frmPicture3 form in design mode.

Entering the Code of the Pictures Program

You enter the code of the Pictures program in the various forms included in the program. Therefore, the code of the parent form is typed in the procedures of frmPictures, the code of the Picture1 child form is typed in the procedures of frmPicture1, and so on.

Entering the Code of the Parent Form

☐ Enter the following code in the general declarations section of the frmPictures form:

```
' Each variable MUST be declared.
Option Explicit
```

☐ Enter the following code in the MDIForm_Load() procedure of the frmPictures form:

```
Private Sub MDIForm_Load()

    ' Upon starting the program, show the three
    ' children.
    frmPicture1.Show
    frmPicture2.Show
    frmPicture3.Show

End Sub
```

☐ Enter the following code in the mnuExit_Click() procedure of the frmPictures form:

```
Private Sub mnuExit_Click()

    ' The user selected Exit from the menu,
    ' so terminate the program.
    End

End Sub
```

☐ Enter the following code in the mnuShowAll_Click() procedure of the frmPictures form:

```
Private Sub mnuShowAll_Click()

    ' The user selected Show All from the menu,
    ' so show all the children.
    frmPicture1.Show
    frmPicture2.Show
    frmPicture3.Show

End Sub
```

☐ Enter the following code in the mnuShowPicture1_Click() procedure of the frmPictures form:

```
Private Sub mnuShowPicture1_Click()

    ' The user selected Show Picture 1 from the
    ' menu, so show PICTURE1.
    frmPicture1.Show

End Sub
```

☐ Enter the following code in the mnuShowPicture2_Click() procedure of the frmPictures form:

```
Private Sub mnuShowPicture2_Click()

    ' The user selected Show Picture 2 from
    ' the menu, so show PICTURE2.
    frmPicture2.Show

End Sub
```

☐ Enter the following code in the mnuShowPicture3_Click() procedure of the frmPictures form:

```
Private Sub mnuShowPicture3_Click()

    ' The user selected Show Picture 3 from the
    ' menu, so show PICTURE3.
    frmPicture3.Show

End Sub
```

□ Enter the following code in the mnuClearAll_Click() procedure of the frmPictures form:

```
Private Sub mnuClearAll_Click()

    ' The user selected Clear All from the Show
    ' Picture menu, so unload the children.
    Unload frmPicture1
    Unload frmPicture2
    Unload frmPicture3

End Sub
```

Entering the Code of the frmPicture1 Form

□ Enter the following code in the general declarations section of the frmPicture1 form:

```
' Each variable MUST be declared.
Option Explicit
```

□ Enter the following code in the cmdClose_Click() procedure of the frmPicture1 form:

```
Private Sub cmdClose_Click()

    ' The user clicked the Close button of PICTURE1,
    ' so unload PICTURE1.
    Unload frmPicture1

End Sub
```

□ Enter the following code in the mnuBeepOnce_Click() procedure of the frmPicture1 form:

```
Private Sub mnuBeepOnce_Click()

    ' The user selected Beep Once from the menu,
    ' so beep once.
    Beep

End Sub
```

□ Enter the following code in the mnuBeepTwice_Click() procedure of the frmPicture1 form:

```
Private Sub mnuBeepTwice_Click()

    ' First beep.
    Beep

    MsgBox "Beep Again"

    ' Second beep.
    Beep

End Sub
```

☐ Enter the following code in the `mnuClose_Click()` procedure of the frmPicture1 form:

```
Private Sub mnuClose_Click()

    Unload frmPicture1

End Sub
```

Entering the Code of the frmPicture2 Form

☐ Enter the following code in the general declarations section of the frmPicture2 form:

```
' Each variable MUST be declared.
Option Explicit
```

☐ Enter the following code in the `cmdClose_Click()` procedure of the frmPicture2 form:

```
Private Sub cmdClose_Click()

    ' The user clicked the Close button,
    ' so unload PICTURE2.
    Unload frmPicture2

End Sub
```

Entering the Code of the frmPicture3 Form

☐ Enter the following code in the general declarations section of the frmPicture3 form:

```
' Each variable MUST be declared.
Option Explicit
```

☐ Enter the following code in the `cmdClose_Click()` procedure of the frmPicture3 form:

```
Private Sub cmdClose_Click()

    ' The user clicked the Close button,
    ' so unload PICTURE3.
    Unload frmPicture3

End Sub
```

Executing the Pictures Program

☐ Execute the Pictures program.

When you execute the Pictures program, the parent form pops up, as shown in Figure 17.10. The child forms are contained in the parent form.

☐ Drag the child forms by dragging the title of the forms.

As you can see, the child forms can be dragged anywhere inside the parent form, but they cannot be dragged outside the parent form.

The user can minimize each child form as he or she would any standard form (by clicking the icon on the upper-left corner of each child form and selecting Minimize from the system menu that pops up). Figure 17.11 shows the Pictures program after minimizing two child forms, Picture1 and Picture2. As shown, the minimized forms appear as icons at the bottom of the parent form.

Figure 17.10.
The Pictures program.

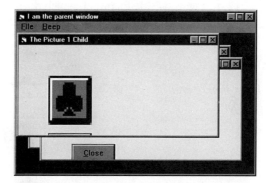

Figure 17.11.
Minimizing children in an MDI program.

The Menus of the Parent and Child Forms

Experiment with the Pictures program and note that the menu bar of the parent form is displayed and available as long as the currently active child form doesn't have a menu. To see how this works, try the following experiments:

☐ Make Picture2 the active form by clicking it or selecting Show Picture 2 from the Show Pictures menu.

Because Picture2 doesn't have a menu, the menu bar displays the parent form's menu.

☐ Make Picture3 the active form by clicking it or selecting Show Picture 3 from the Show Pictures menu.

Because Picture3 does not have a menu, the menu bar displays the parent form's menu.

611

However, if the currently active child form has a menu, the menu bar that appears contains the child form's menu:

☐ Make Picture1 the active form by clicking it or selecting Show Picture 1 from the Show Picture menu. Because Picture1 has a menu, the menu bar that appears in the parent form is the menu of Picture1. (See Figure 17.12.) Compare Figure 17.11 with Figure 17.12. In Figure 17.11, Picture 3, which doesn't have a menu, is the active window, so the menu bar displays the parent form's menu.

Figure 17.12.
The menu of the parent form when frmPicture1 is the active form.

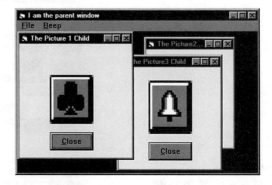

☐ Play with the Pictures program and study its features and behavior—minimize and maximize the child forms, select items from the various menus, and so forth.

The Code of the Parent Form

The code in the procedures of the parent form contains the code corresponding to events related to the parent form. For example, selecting Show All Pictures from the Show Pictures menu of the parent form causes the execution of the mnuShowAll_Click() procedure.

The Code in the *MDIForm_Load()* Procedure

The Pictures program consists of an MDI parent form and three child forms. When you start the program, the form that is loaded is the parent MDI form frmPictures. The procedure that corresponds to loading the parent form is called MDIForm_Load():

```
Private Sub MDIForm_Load()

    ' Upon starting the program, show the three
    ' children.
    frmPicture1.Show
    frmPicture2.Show
    frmPicture3.Show

End Sub
```

Because the Pictures program is an MDI program, the MDI parent form is loaded when you start the program. You can take advantage of this and perform initializations and start-up tasks in the MDIForm_Load() procedure.

The code in the MDIForm_Load() procedure of the frmPictures form displays the three child forms by using the Show method.

For example, to display the frmPicture1 child form, the MDIForm_Load() procedure uses the following statement:

```
frmPicture1.Show
```

The Code in the *mnuClearAll_Click()* Procedure

The mnuClearAll_Click() procedure of the frmPictures parent form is executed whenever you select Clear All Pictures from the Show Pictures menu:

```
Private Sub mnuClearAll_Click()

    ' The user selected Clear All from the Show
    ' Picture menu, so unload the children.
    Unload frmPicture1
    Unload frmPicture2
    Unload frmPicture3

End Sub
```

To remove a child form, use the Unload statement. For example, to remove the frmPicture1 child form, the mnuClearAll_Click() procedure uses the following statement:

```
Unload frmPicture1
```

The Code in the *mnuExit_Click()* Procedure

The mnuExit_Click() procedure of the frmPictures parent form is executed whenever you select Exit from the File menu. This procedure terminates the program by executing the End statement.

The Code in the *mnuShowAll_Click()* Procedure

The mnuShowAll_Click() procedure of the frmPictures parent form is executed whenever you select Show All Pictures from the Show Pictures menu:

```
Private Sub mnuShowAll_Click()

    ' The user selected Show All Pictures from the menu,
    ' so show all the children.
    frmPicture1.Show
```

17

613

```
frmPicture2.Show
frmPicture3.Show
```

End Sub

This procedure uses the Show method for each of the child forms.

The Code in the *mnuShowPicture1_Click()* Procedure

The mnuShowPicture1_Click() procedure of the frmPictures parent form is executed whenever you select Show Picture 1 from the Show Pictures menu:

Private Sub mnuShowPicture1_Click()

```
' The user selected Show Picture 1 from the
' menu, so show PICTURE1.
frmPicture1.Show
```

End Sub

This procedure uses the Show method to display the frmPicture1 child form.

In a similar manner, the mnuShowPicture2_Click() and mnuShowPicture3_Click() procedures are executed whenever you select Show Picture 2 and Show Picture 3 from the Show Pictures menu. Again, these procedures use the Show method for displaying the corresponding child form.

The Code in the frmPicture1 Child Form

The procedures of the frmPicture1 child form contain the code corresponding to events related to the frmPicture1 form. For example, clicking the Close button (cmdClose) of frmPicture1 causes the execution of the cmdClose_Click() procedure.

The Code in the *mnuBeepOnce_Click()* Procedure

The mnuBeepOnce_Click() procedure is executed whenever you select Beep Once from the Beep menu of the frmPicture1 form. Therefore, this procedure contains the Beep statement:

Private Sub mnuBeepOnce_Click()

```
' The user selected Beep Once from the menu,
' so beep once.
Beep
```

End Sub

The Code in the *mnuBeepTwice_Click()* Procedure

The mnuBeepTwice_Click() procedure is executed whenever you select Beep Twice from the Beep menu of the frmPicture1 form. Therefore, this procedure contains two Beep statements. In between the beeps, a message box is inserted.

```
Private Sub mnuBeepTwice_Click()

    ' First beep.
    Beep

    MsgBox "Beep Again"

    ' Second beep.
    Beep

End Sub
```

The Code in the *cmdClose_Click()* Procedure

The cmdClose_Click() procedure is executed whenever you click the Close button in the frmPicture1 form:

```
Private Sub cmdClose_Click()

    ' The user clicked the Close button of PICTURE1,
    ' so unload PICTURE1.
    Unload frmPicture1

End Sub
```

The form is unloaded with the following statement:

```
Unload frmPicture1
```

The Code in the frmPicture2 and frmPicture3 Child Forms

Child forms frmPicture2 and frmPicture3 each have a Close button. When you click them, the cmdClose_Click() procedure is executed. To close the frmPicture2 and frmPicture3 forms, the cmdClose_Click() procedure uses the Unload statement. This statement is used to close frmPicture2:

```
Unload frmPicture2
```

And this statement is used to close frmPicture3:

```
Unload frmPicture3
```

17

Which Form Is Loaded First?

The Pictures program comprises an MDI parent form and its three child forms. As previously stated, a Visual Basic program can contain only one MDI form; however, it's possible to design a program that has one MDI form and several standard forms. Add a standard form to the Pictures program:

☐ Select Form from the Insert menu.

> *Visual Basic responds by adding a standard form to the project window.*

Use the following steps to save the newly added standard form:

☐ Make sure the new form is highlighted in the project window.

☐ Select Save File As from the File menu.

> *Visual Basic responds by displaying the Save File As dialog box.*

☐ Save the newly added form as C:\VBPROG\CH17\Standard.frm.

☐ Build the Standard.frm according to the specifications in Table 17.7.

The completed form should look like the one shown in Figure 17.13.

☐ Select Save Project from the File menu to save your work.

Table 17.7. The properties table of Standard.frm.

Object	Property	Setting
Form	**Name**	**frmStandard**
	Caption	I am a standard form
	BackColor	(gray)
Command Button	**Name**	**cmdExit**
	Caption	E&xit
Command Button	**Name**	**cmdSwitch**
	Caption	&Switch to the MDI form

☐ Add the following code to the cmdSwitch_Click() procedure of the frmStandard form:

```
Private Sub cmdSwitch_Click()

    ' Show the parent form.
    frmPictures.Show

End Sub
```

Figure 17.13.
The frmStandard form.

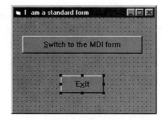

☐ Add the following code to the `cmdExit_Click()` procedure of the frmStandard form:

```
Private Sub cmdExit_Click()

    End

End Sub
```

The Pictures.vbp project now contains the following forms:

- An MDI parent form (Pictures.frm) and its three child forms (Picture1.frm, Picture2.frm, Picture3.frm)
- The frmStandard form

Which form is loaded when you start the program: the MDI parent form or the frmStandard form? At design time, you decide which form will be loaded by updating the Project Options window.

Use the following step to update the Project Options window:

☐ Select Options from the Tools menu, then click the Project tab of the Options dialog box.

Visual Basic responds by displaying the Project Options dialog box. (See Figure 17.14.) As shown in Figure 17.14, the content of the Startup Form field is frmPicture1. This means that the child form frmPicture1 is loaded when you start the program. But since frmPicture1 is a child of frmPictures, both the parent form frmPictures and the child form frmPicture1 are loaded.

Use the following steps to change which form is loaded when you start the program:

☐ Change the content of the Startup Form field of the Project Options dialog box to frmStandard. (Click the down-arrow icon to the right of the Startup Form field and select the frmStandard form from the drop-down list.)

☐ Now execute the Pictures program. As you can see, frmStandard is loaded when you start the program.

Figure 17.14.
The Options dialog box with the Project tab selected.

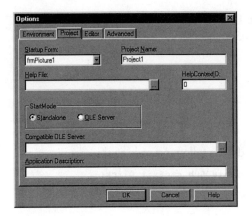

Switching Between Forms at Runtime

At runtime, you can switch between the frmStandard and frmPictures forms by clicking the cmdSwitch button in the frmStandard form. The code in the cmdSwitch_Click() procedure is executed whenever you click this button:

```
Private Sub cmdSwitch_Click()

    ' Show the parent form.
    frmPictures.Show

End Sub
```

The statement frmPictures.Show in this procedure displays the MDI parent form.

☐ Execute the program.

As you can see, the frmStandard form is loaded when you start the program.

☐ Switch to the MDI form by clicking the Switch to the MDI form button.

The program responds by displaying the MDI form.

In a similar way, you can add code to the MDI parent form or any of the child forms that would cause the program to switch from the MDI form to the standard form. For example, you can add a command button in the frmPicture1 form with the caption Switch to the standard form and insert the following statement in the button's Click procedure:

```
frmStandard.Show
```

The Window List Menu

Many professional MDI programs include a Window menu. If you own the Word for Windows program, take a look at its Window menu. (See Figure 17.15.) The Window menu contains a list of all the child forms that the parent form currently contains. If you don't have the Word for Windows program, then look at any other MDI application you have (for example, Excel, Access).

Figure 17.15.
The Window menu of Word for Windows.

Adding a Window List Menu to the Parent Window

Now you'll add a Window list menu to the parent window frmPictures of the Pictures program with the following steps:

☐ Select the frmPictures parent form and add a menu item called Window. (Make sure the frmPictures parent form is selected. Select Menu Editor from the Tools menu and add the Window item, as shown in Figure 17.16.)

☐ Place a ✓ in the WindowList box in the Menu Editor dialog box, as shown in Figure 17.16. Before you do this, make sure the Window menu item is selected because that's where you want to add the WindowList feature.

That's all! The frmPictures parent form now has a Window list menu.

Figure 17.16.
Adding a Window list menu.

☐ Select Save Project from the File menu.

☐ Execute the Pictures program and select the Window menu. The Window menu should list the three child forms. (See Figure 17.17.)

☐ Experiment with the Window menu. For example, close the frmPicture1 child and note that the list in the Window menu is updated.

Also note that in the Window menu, a check mark appears next to the child form that is currently active. For example, in Figure 17.17, frmPicture3 has a check mark next to it in the window list, so it is the active window.

Figure 17.17.
The Window menu of the Pictures program.

Adding a Window List Menu to a Child Form

In the preceding steps, you added a Window list menu to the frmPictures parent form. A Window list menu can also be added to a child form. In many applications, it is convenient to have the Window menu in the child forms as well as in the parent form. Use the following steps to add a Window list menu to the frmPicture1 child form:

☐ Select the frmPicture1 form and add a menu item called Window. (Select the frmPicture1 form, select Menu Editor from the Tools menu, and add the Window item to the menu of frmPicture1.)

☐ Make sure the Window menu item is selected, then place a ✓ in the WindowList check box in the Menu Editor dialog box. (See Figure 17.18.)

☐ Select Save project from the File menu.

Figure 17.18.

Adding the Window list menu to the frmPicture1 form.

☐ Execute the Pictures program.

☐ Click the Switch to the MDI button.

> *The Pictures program responds by displaying the MDI form.*

☐ Make the frmPicture3 child form the active form.

> *As you can see from Figure 17.19, the menu that appears is the menu of the frmPictures parent form because the frmPicture3 child form doesn't have a menu of its own.*

☐ Make the frmPicture1 child form the active form.

> *As you can see from Figure 17.20, the menu that appears is the menu of the frmPicture1 child form (because the frmPicture1 child form does have its own menu). Note that the Window menu you added to the menu of frmPicture1 appears in Figure 17.20.*

Figure 17.19.

The menu of the Pictures program when frmPicture3 is the active window.

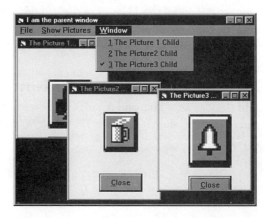

Figure 17.20.
The menu of the Pictures program when frmPicture1 is the active window.

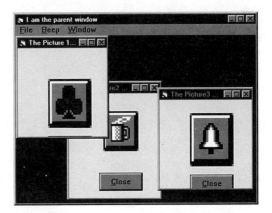

Note: The Window menu feature can save you a lot of programming work. Each item in it represents a child form, and the active child form has a check mark next to it. Also, the items in the Window menu are updated automatically. For example, if you close a child form, the corresponding menu item in the Window menu is removed. And the beauty of it is that you didn't have to write a single line of code to do all this! All you had to do was place a check mark in the WindowList check box when you designed the Window menu.

Adding Cascade, Tile, and Arrange Icons Items to the Window Menu

Sometimes it is useful to add items to the Window menu of an MDI application that help you arrange the child windows. The following sections explain how to add the Cascade, Tile, and Arrange Icons items to the Window menu.

The Visual Implementation of the Window Menu

☐ Add the Cascade, Tile, and Arrange Icons items to the Window menu of the frmPictures parent form, as shown in Table 17.8. The Menu Editor dialog box is shown in Figure 17.21.

Table 17.8. The menu table of the Window menu.

Caption	Name	Shortcut
&Cascade	mnuCascade	Shift+F5
&Tile	mnuTile	Shift+F4
&ArrangeIcons	mnuArrangeIcons	none

Figure 17.21.
Adding items to the Window menu.

☐ Save the project and then execute the Pictures program.

☐ Make the frmPicture2 child form the active menu.

> *As you can see in Figure 17.22, the Window menu now contains the Cascade, Tile, and Arrange Icons items. Of course, none of these items function because you haven't written any code yet that accomplishes these tasks.*

☐ Terminate the Pictures program by selecting Exit from the File menu.

Figure 17.22.
The Window menu of the Pictures program.

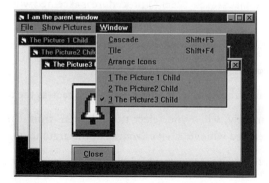

Attaching Code to the Cascade, Tile, and Arrange Icons Menu Items

☐ You'll now add code that is executed whenever you select Cascade, Tile, or Arrange Icons from the Window menu.

☐ Add the following code to the mnuCascade_Click() procedure of the frmPictures parent form:

```
Private Sub mnuCascade_Click()

    ' The user selected Cascade from the Window menu.
    frmPictures.Arrange vbCascade

End Sub
```

☐ Add the following code to the mnuTile_Click() procedure of the frmPictures form:

```
Private Sub mnuTile_Click()

    ' The user selected Tile from the Window menu.
    frmPictures.Arrange vbTileHorizontal

End Sub
```

☐ Add the following code to the mnuArrangeIcons_Click() procedure of the frmPictures form:

```
Private Sub mnuArrangeIcons_Click()

    ' The user selected Arrange Icons from the
    ' Window menu.
    frmPictures.Arrange vbArrangeIcons

End Sub
```

How the Window Menu Items Work

The mnuCascade_Click() procedure is executed whenever you select Cascade from the Window menu of the Pictures program.

The code in this procedure consists of the following statement:

```
frmPictures.Arrange vbCascade
```

It uses the Arrange method with vbCascade as the argument to cascade the child forms.

Similarly, when you select the Tile item from the Window menu, the Arrange method is executed with vbTileHorizontal as the argument:

```
frmPictures.Arrange vbTileHorizontal
```

And when you select the Arrange Icons item from the Window menu, the `Arrange` method is executed with `vbArrangeIcons` as the argument:

```
frmPictures.Arrange vbArrangeIcons
```

☐ Select Save Project from the File menu.

☐ Execute the Pictures program, click the Switch to the MDI form button, and resize and rearrange the three child forms by dragging their captions and the edges of their windows.

After scrambling the child forms, the Pictures program should look like the one in Figure 17.23.

Figure 17.23.
The child forms, after you've scrambled them in the MDI parent form.

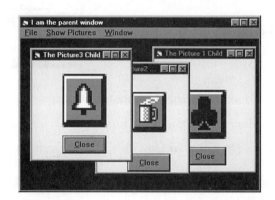

☐ Make frmPicture2 or frmPicture3 the active form so the menu of the frmPictures parent form will appear.

☐ Select Cascade from the Window menu.

The Pictures program responds by cascading the child forms as shown in Figure 17.24.

Figure 17.24.
The child forms, after you've cascaded Cascade from the Window menu.

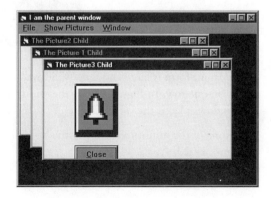

☐ Select Tile from the Window menu.

The Pictures program responds by tiling the child forms, as shown in Figure 17.25.

Figure 17.25.
The child forms, after you've selected Tile from the Window menu.

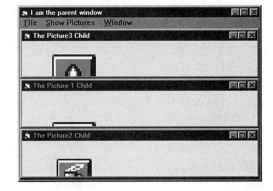

To see the Arrange Icons feature in action, follow these steps:

☐ Minimize the three child forms.

The three minimized child forms are shown in Figure 17.26.

Figure 17.26.
The three minimized child forms.

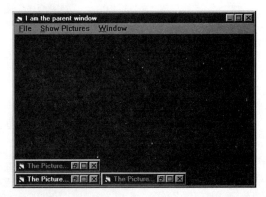

If the parent form is large enough, Windows will be able to place the minimized child forms on one row. In Figure 17.26, the width of the parent form was not wide enough, so Windows placed the minimized child forms on two rows.

☐ Close one of the minimized child forms so that the remaining two look like those shown in Figure 17.27.

Figure 17.27.
The two remaining mini-mized child forms.

So take a look at Figure 17.27: There are two minimized child forms spread over two rows. But the width of the parent window is wide enough to place two minimized windows. You can instruct Windows to rearrange the icons by selecting Arrange Icons form the Window menu.

☐ Make sure the frmPicture1 icon isn't highlighted, then select Arrange Icons from the Window menu.

> *The Pictures program responds by arranging the minimized child forms, as shown in Figure 17.28.*

Figure 17.28.
The two minimized child forms, rearranged on a single row.

☐ Experiment with the Pictures program and then terminate the program.

> **Note:** In Windows 95 the Arrange Icons feature doesn't seem to be very important because the minimized child windows are always at the bottom of the parent window on one or more rows.

However, in Windows 3.1 and Windows NT, you can place the minimized child windows anywhere in the MDI parent window. In this case, the Arrange Icons feature is more useful than in Windows 95.

The *vbTileVertical* Constant

In the preceding section you have learned that the Arrange method can be executed with the vbCascade, the vbTileHorizontal, and the vbArrangeIcons arguments.

There is also a fourth argument, vbTileVertical. When the Arrange method is used with the vbTileVertical argument, the child forms are arranged as shown in Figure 17.29.

Figure 17.29.

Arranging the child forms vertically.

You added the Cascade, Tile, and Arrange Icons items to the Window menu of the parent form. Of course, since the frmPicture1 has its own Window menu, you'll have to add these menu items and their codes to the frmPicture1 child form.

For example, you can add the Cascade item to the Window menu of the frmPicture1 form, then add the following code to the mnuCascade_Click() procedure of the frmPicture1 form:

```
Private Sub mnuCascade_Click()

    ' The user selected Cascade from the Window menu.
    frmPictures.Arrange vbCascade

End Sub
```

Designing a Text Editor Program

Now you'll build an MDI program called TextEd. This program illustrates how a text editor program can be designed as an MDI program in which each child form represents a new document.

The Visual Implementation of the TextEd Program

☐ Open a new project by selecting New Project from the File menu.

☐ Create an MDI parent form by selecting MDI Form from the Insert menu.

Your project window should now contain a standard form, Form1.frm, and an MDI parent form, MDIForm1.frm.

☐ Save the standard form as C:\VB4PRG\CH17\Template.frm by highlighting Form1.frm in the Project menu, selecting Save File As from the File menu, and saving the file as C:\VB4PRG\CH17\Template.frm.

☐ Save the MDI parent form as C:\VB4PRG\CH17\TextEd.frm by highlighting MDIForm1.frm in the Project menu, selecting Save File As from the File menu, and saving the file as C:\VB4PRG\CH17\TextEd.frm.

☐ Save the project file of the project as C:\VB4PRG\CH17\TEXTED.VBP by selecting Save Project As from the File menu and saving the project as C:\VB4PRG\CH17\TEXTED.VBP.

Your project window should now contain the following items:

- A standard form Template.frm.
- An MDI parent form TextEd.frm.

Now you'll convert the non-MDI form Template.frm to an MDI child form and change its properties:

☐ Build the Template.frm form according to the specifications in Table 17.9.

The completed form should look like the one shown in Figure 7.30.

Figure 17.30.
The frmTemplate form in design mode.

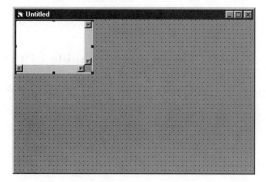

Note that once you change the MDIChild property of Template.frm to True (as specified in Table 17.9), the icon that appears in the project window to the left of Template.frm indicates that this form is a child form.

Table 17.9. The properties table of the Template.frm child form.

Object	Property	Setting
Form	**Name**	**frmTemplate**
	MDIChild	True
	Caption	Untitled
	Height	4545
	Left	1080
	Top	1170
	Width	6810
Text Box	**Name**	**txtUserArea**
	Text	(empty)
	MultiLine	True
	ScrollBars	3-Both
	Height	1455
	Left	0
	Top	0
	Width	2175

Now build the parent form of the project:

☐ Build the MDI parent form according to the specifications in Table 17.10.

The completed form should look like the one shown in Figure 7.31.

Table 17.10. The properties table of the MDI parent form frmTextEd.

Object	Property	Setting
Form	**Name**	**frmTextEd**
	Caption	My Text Editor
	Height	4710
	Left	1035

Object	Property	Setting
	Top	1140
	Width	7486
Menu	**(See Table 17.11.)**	**(See Table 17.11.)**

Table 17.11. The menu table of the MDI parent form TextEd.frm.

Caption	Procedure Name
&File	mnuFile
...&New	mnuNew
...E&xit	mnuExit

Figure 17.31.
The frmTextEd form in design mode.

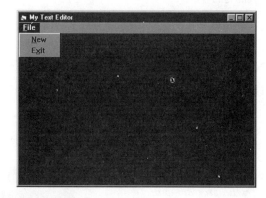

You'll now set the Startup Form field of the frmTextEd form.

☐ Select Options from the Tools menu.

> *Visual Basic responds by displaying the Options dialog box.*

☐ Click the Project tab of the Options dialog box, set the Startup Form field to frmTextEd, and click the OK button.

☐ Save the project by selecting Save Project from the File menu.

Entering the Code of the TextEd Program

☐ Enter the following code in the general declarations section of the frmTextEd parent form:

```
' Variables MUST be declared.
Option Explicit
```

☐ Enter the following code in the mnuNew_Click() procedure of the frmTextEd parent form:

```
Private Sub mnuNew_Click()

    ' Declare a variable for the instance form
    ' as a copy of the form frmTemplate.
    Dim frmNewForm As New frmTemplate
    ' Show the instance form.
    frmNewForm.Show

End Sub
```

☐ Enter the following code in the mnuExit_Click() procedure of the frmTextEd form:

```
Private Sub mnuExit_Click()

    End

End Sub
```

☐ Save the project by selecting Save Project from the File menu.

Executing the TextEd Program

The TextEd program isn't finished yet, but see what you have accomplished so far.

☐ Execute the TextEd program.

The parent form frmTextEd pops up. (See Figure 17.32.)

Figure 17.32.
The TextEd program with no documents in it.

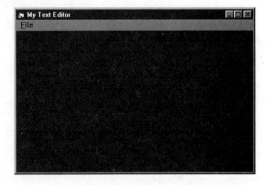

☐ Select New from the File menu.

A new child form pops up. (See Figure 17.33.) You can now type text in the text box. As you can see, the text box area isn't big enough! But don't worry about it—you'll fix this problem soon.

Figure 17.33.
The TextEd program with one document in it.

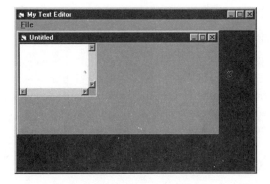

☐ Select New from the File menu several more times.

> *The program displays the child forms, as shown in Figure 17.34.*

Figure 17.34.
The TextEd program with several documents in it.

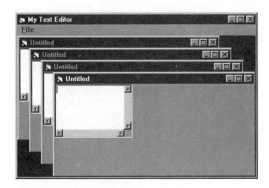

☐ Terminate the program by selecting Exit from the File menu.

The Code in the *mnuNew_Click()* Procedure

The mnuNew_Click() procedure is executed whenever you select New from the File menu:

```
Private Sub mnuNew_Click()

    ' Declare a variable for the instance form
    ' as a copy of the form frmTemplate.
    Dim frmNewForm As New frmTemplate
    ' Show the instance form.
    frmNewForm.Show

End Sub
```

This is the first statement in the procedure:

```
Dim frmNewForm As New frmTemplate
```

This statement declares a variable called frmNewForm as a new *instance*, or copy, of the child form frmTemplate. This means that, for all purposes, you can refer to frmNewForm as a form with the same properties as the frmTemplate form you designed at design time. In other words, you create a copy of the frmTemplate form. Once the frmNewForm is created, you can use it in the program just like any other form.

For example, the second statement in the mnuNew_Click() procedure causes the newly created form to pop up by using the following statement:

```
frmNewForm.Show
```

Every time you select New from the File menu, a new instance is created that is a copy of the frmTemplate form.

DO   DON'T

DO use the following statement to declare a new form variable that is a copy of an existing form:

```
Dim [Name Of the new variable] As New [Name of existing form]
```

For example, to declare the variable frmNewForm that is a copy of the frmTemplate form, use the following:

```
Dim frmNewForm As New frmTemplate
```

Adjusting the Text Box Size According to the Form Size

The text box should fill the entire child form area. Therefore, no matter how big or small the child form is, the text box should always cover the whole child form. You can do this by using the Resize event.

The *Resize* Event

The Resize event occurs whenever the form pops up and whenever the size of the form is changed. Therefore, the Form_Resize() procedure is a focal point that is executed whenever the form size changes. This is a good place to resize the text box according to the form size.

☐ Enter the following code in the Form_Resize() procedure of the frmTemplate child form:

```
Private Sub Form_Resize()

    Me.txtUserArea.Height = Me.ScaleHeight
    Me.txtUserArea.Width = Me.ScaleWidth

End Sub
```

The first statement in the Form_Resize() procedure assigns the ScaleHeight property of the current form to the Height property of the text box. Similarly, the second statement of the Form_Resize() procedure assigns the ScaleWidth property of the current form to the Width property of the text box. Therefore, the text box has the size of the current form.

The *Me* Reserved Word

The Me reserved word used in the two statements of Form_Resize() is a Visual Basic reserved word. It is a variable containing the name of the form where the code is currently executed.

For example, in the TextEd program, there may be several instances of the frmTemplate form in the parent form. When the size of one of these forms is changed, Visual Basic executes the Form_Resize() procedure and automatically updates the Me variable with the name of the instance that was resized. It is the responsibility of Visual Basic to maintain and update the value of the Me variable with the instance where code is currently executed.

Interestingly enough, if you omit the Me word in the statements of the Form_Resize() procedure, the program still works because when you omit the name of the form, it has the same effect as substituting Me for the name of the form.

Changing the Caption Property of a Form

Another useful feature in Visual Basic is the ActiveForm property, which specifies the currently active form. If there is currently no active child form, the ActiveForm property specifies the most recently active child form.

To illustrate how useful the ActiveForm property is, enhance the TextEd program so that you can change the Caption property of the child forms at runtime.

☐ Add the Assign Name menu to the parent form, as shown in Figure 17.35.

Figure 17.35.
Adding the Assign Name
menu to the parent form.

Entering the Code in the *mnuAssignName_Click()* Procedure

☐ Enter the following code in the mnuAssignName_Click() procedure of the frmTextEd parent form:

```
Private Sub mnuAssignName_Click()

    ' Declare a string variable
    Dim DocumentName As String

    ' Get from the user the name of the document
    DocumentName = InputBox("Document name:", "Assign Name")

    ' Change the Caption property of the currently
    ' active (or last active)form.
    frmTextEd.ActiveForm.Caption = DocumentName

End Sub
```

Executing the TextEd Program Again

☐ Execute the TextEd program.

☐ Select New from the File menu.

A new child document appears.

☐ Select the Assign Name menu.

The program responds by displaying the input box, as shown in Figure 17.36.

Figure 17.36.
*Entering the document
name by using an input box.*

☐ Type Document Number 1 in the input box and click the OK button.

>   *The program responds by changing the Caption property of the currently active child form
>   from Untitled to Document Number 1. (See Figure 17.37.)*

Figure 17.37.
*The new document with its
new caption.*

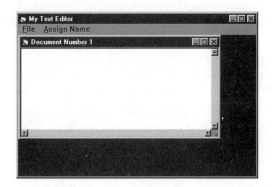

☐ Add several more new documents by selecting New from the File menu.

☐ You can switch to other child documents and change their names by selecting the Assign
Name menu.

The Code in the *mnuAssignName_Click()* Procedure

The mnuAssignName_Click() procedure is automatically executed whenever you select the Assign
Name menu:

```
Private Sub mnuAssignName_Click()

    ' Declare a string variable
    Dim DocumentName As String

    ' Get from the user the name of the document
    DocumentName = InputBox("Document name:", "Assign Name")

    ' Change the Caption property of the currently
    ' active (or last active)form.
    frmTextEd.ActiveForm.Caption = DocumentName

End Sub
```

The first statement in this procedure declares `DocumentName` as a string variable. The second statement displays the input box shown in Figure 17.36. Your input is assigned to the `DocumentName` string variable:

```
DocumentName = InputBox("Enter Document name:", "Assign Name")
```

The last statement in the procedure assigns the contents of the `DocumentName` variable to the Caption property of the currently active child form:

```
frmTextEd.ActiveForm.Caption = DocumentName
```

Visual Basic automatically maintains and updates the `ActiveForm` variable. So when the `mnuAssignName_Click()` procedure is executed, `ActiveForm` is already updated with the value of the currently active form (to which you're assigning a new name).

Note: The properties of the currently active or the most recently active child form can be changed by using the ActiveForm property as follows:

```
[ParentForm].ActiveForm.[Property to be changed] = Value
```

For example, to change the Caption property of the currently active child form of the frmTextEd parent form to DocumentName, use this statement:

```
frmTextEd.ActiveForm.Caption = DocumentName
```

Note: The TextEd program currently has a little bug in it. Can you tell what it is?

If you execute the program and select the AssignName menu without selecting New from the File menu, the program crashes. Why? There aren't any child forms in the parent form. The `mnuAssignName_Click()` procedure tries to change the Caption property of a child form that doesn't exist.

The answer to the second exercise at the end of this chapter tells you how to fix this bug.

Creating a Toolbar

Many Windows programs include a toolbar, which is an area containing controls you can select. Figure 17.38 shows the toolbar of the popular Microsoft Word for Windows program. Typically, the controls on the toolbar are included in programs to provide quick access to the most commonly used operations. The controls on the toolbar may be images, command

buttons, scroll bars, and so on. For example, clicking the disk image on the toolbar of Word for Windows has the same effect as selecting Save from the File menu of the Word program.

Figure 17.38.
The toolbar of Microsoft Word for Windows.

Note: In some Windows literature, the toolbar is called a ribbon bar or a control bar.

The Visual Implementation of the Toolbar and the Status Bar

Now you'll add a toolbar and a status bar to the TextEd program. The complete TextEd form with its toolbar and status bar is shown in Figure 17.39.

Figure 17.39.
The toolbar and the status bar in the TextEd program.

☐ Select the MDI parent form.

☐ Double-click the image icon of the toolbox.

Visual Basic responds by displaying an error box. (See Figure 17.40.)

Why is Visual Basic unhappy with your action? Because you tried to place a control that doesn't support the Align property in the MDI parent form. (If you examine the properties window of the image control, you'll see that this control doesn't support the Align property.) The only control that supports the Align property is the picture control.

Figure 17.40.

The error message displayed when you try to place a control in the MDI parent form.

☐ Click the OK button of the error message.

☐ Double-click the picture icon of the toolbox.

Visual Basic responds by placing the picture control on the MDI form, as shown in Figure 17.41. You will place the toolbar icons in this picture control. If you try to drag the picture control to another location in the MDI parent form, Visual Basic refuses to honor your request.

Figure 17.41.

Placing the toolbar in the MDI parent form.

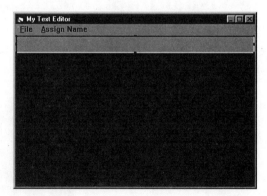

Now you'll prepare the area where the icons of the status bar are located. (The status bar serves the same purpose as the toolbar, but the toolbar is at the top of the form and the status bar is at the bottom.)

☐ Double-click the picture icon of the toolbox again.

Visual Basic responds by placing a picture control below the picture control you placed in the previous step. (See Figure 17.42.)

Figure 17.42.
Placing a second picture control in the MDI parent form.

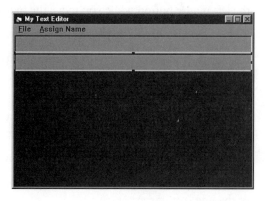

17

As shown in Figure 17.39, the status bar is located at the bottom of the form, so you need to reposition the second picture control you placed:

☐ Make sure the second picture control is selected and change its Align property to 2-Align Bottom.

Visual Basic responds by positioning the picture control at the bottom of the form. (See Figure 17.43.)

Figure 17.43.
Placing the status bar in the MDI parent form.

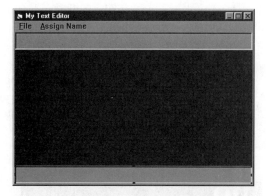

Now you'll place controls on the toolbar and the status bar, as shown in Figure 17.39.

Use the following steps to place the disk image on the toolbar:

☐ Click (do not double-click) the image icon in the toolbox.

Visual Basic responds by highlighting the image icon in the toolbox.

☐ Place the mouse cursor in the toolbar area (the top picture control) and click and hold the left mouse button while you move the mouse.

Visual Basic responds by placing the image control in the toolbar area.

☐ Change the Picture property of the image control to C:\VB\ICONS\COMPUTER\DISK03.ICO. (If your VB directory doesn't have this ICO file, use any other ICO file.)

☐ Change the Stretch property of the image control to True so you can stretch the image to any desired size, as long as it fits in the toolbar area.

☐ Change the Name property of the image to imgSave.

☐ Enlarge the area of the toolbar (which is the picture control) so you can enlarge the area of the imgSave image control.

You can now place the other controls shown in Figure 17.39 in the toolbar and the status bar. (The globe shown on the status bar in Figure 17.39 is an image control with its Picture property set to C:\VB\ICONS\ELEMENTS\EARTH.ICO.) Again, if you don't have this ICO file, then use a different one.

☐ Change the Name property of the command button on the toolbar to cmdExit.

☐ Change the Caption property of the cmdExit button to E&xit.

The visual implementation of the toolbar and status bar is done. Now you'll attach code to some of the controls on the toolbar.

> **Note:** You haven't been instructed to change the properties of the other controls you placed on the toolbar and status bar. You have been instructed to place these controls on the toolbar and the status bar just so you could see how this task is done.

DO ——————————————————— DON'T

DON'T double-click the control when you want to place controls in the toolbar and in the status bar. Simply click the control in the toolbox, then click the left mouse button where you want the control and drag the mouse.

Entering the Code of the Toolbar Icons

Attaching code to the icons and controls of the toolbar and status bar is done the same way as attaching code to regular controls.

The Code in the *imgSave_Click()* Procedure

Use the following steps to enter code in the imgSave_Click() procedure, which is automatically executed whenever you click the disk icon on the toolbar:

☐ Make sure the parent form is selected.

☐ Double-click the disk image on the toolbar.

> *Visual Basic responds by displaying the* imgSave_Click() *procedure. Enter the* Beep *statement in this procedure:*

```
Private Sub imgSave_Click()

    Beep

End Sub
```

Saving files is the subject of another chapter, so for simplicity, the concept is demonstrated by inserting the Beep statement instead of statements that save files. In other words, during the execution of the program, whenever you click the disk icon, you'll hear a beep instead of actually saving the file.

☐ Double-click the Exit button and add the following code in the cmdExit_Click() procedure:

```
Private Sub cmdExit_Click()

    End

End Sub
```

☐ Select Save Project from the File menu to save the TextEd project.

Executing the TextEd Program After Adding the Toolbar and Status Bar

☐ Execute the TextEd program.

> *The TextEd form should pop up, as shown in Figure 17.44.*

☐ Click the disk icon on the toolbar.

> *The program beeps when you click this icon.*

Figure 17.44.

The TextEd program with no documents in it.

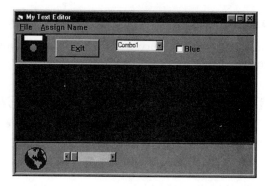

☐ Select New from the File menu several times.

The program responds by creating a new document (a new child form) every time you click the New item. (See Figure 17.45.)

Figure 17.45.

The TextEd program with new documents in its parent window.

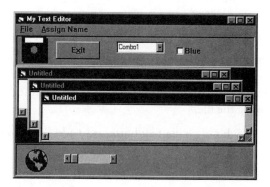

☐ Click the Exit button to terminate the program.

Attaching Code to the Other Controls of the Toolbar and Status Bar

You can now attach code to the other controls on the toolbar and status bar. You type code in the procedures of the scroll bars just as you would for procedures of regular scroll bars in non-MDI forms.

It is possible to have more than one toolbar or status bar. For example, in Figure 17.38, Word for Windows is shown with two toolbars. The top toolbar contains icons such as the disk icon, and the lower toolbar contains tools such as a list box for font styles. Take a look at Figure 17.42—before you converted the second toolbar to a status bar, you had two toolbars in the program.

Summary

In this chapter you have learned how to write multiple-document interface (MDI) programs. MDI programs include one parent form and at least one child form. You have learned how to display (show) the child forms, how to unload child forms, and how to use the powerful Window list menu that helps you maneuver and arrange child forms in the parent form.

You have also learned how to create instances (copies) of a child form at runtime, how to change the properties of the instances at runtime, how to build a toolbar and status bar, and how to attach code to the controls of these bars.

Q&A

Q I want to design an MDI program that doesn't load any of its child forms when I start the program. Is it possible?

A Yes. By default, Visual Basic initializes the Startup Form field of the Project Options window with the name of the first child form. For example, in the Pictures program, the default Startup Form is frmPicture1. So when you start the program, the MDI parent form and the child form frmPicture1 are loaded. If you want only the parent MDI form to be loaded, set the Startup Form field to the parent MDI form.

You can try this procedure by making the following changes to the Pictures program:

☐ Set the Startup Form field of the Pictures project to frmPictures by selecting Options from the Tools window, clicking the Project tab, and then setting the Startup Form field.

☐ Remove the statements in the MDIForm_Load() procedure. (These statements cause all the child forms to be displayed.)

When you start the Pictures program, the parent form is shown without any of its child forms.

Q If the currently active child form has a menu, the menu of the parent form changes to the child form's menu. Is it possible to design the program so that the menu of the parent form remains unchanged, and the child form's menu appears on the window of the child form?

A No. That's how MDI programs work! Generally speaking, it is best to accept the rules and standards of MDI, because your users expect the MDI program to work in an acceptable, known way. After all, one of the main advantages of using Windows programs is that the user-interface aspect of all Windows programs are well known and accepted by millions of happy users.

Quiz

1. How many MDI parent forms can a Visual Basic program have?
   a. 255
   b. No limit
   c. 1
   d. Depends on the number of child forms

2. A program contains the following forms: an MDI parent form and its child forms and two standard forms. Which form is loaded when you start the program?
   a. The MDI parent form
   b. The form mentioned in the Startup Form field of the Project Options window
   c. Depends on the code in the `Form_Load()` procedure

3. What is the difference between a toolbar and a status bar?
   a. They're the same thing—it's just different terminology.
   b. The toolbar is at the top of the MDI parent form, and the status bar is at the bottom.
   c. Status bars are not supported by Visual Basic. (They are supported by Word for Windows only.)

Exercises

1. Enhance the Window menu of the Pictures program by adding the Tile Vertical item.

2. Enhance the TextEd program as follows:
   - Add a new menu to the TextEd parent form called Color. This menu should have two items in it: Green and Gray.
   - When you select Green or Gray from the Color menu, the currently active child document should change its background color to the selected color.

Quiz Answers

1. c
2. b
3. b

Exercise Answers

1. To enhance the Pictures program, perform the following steps:

   ☐ Highlight the frmPictures parent form and select Menu Editor from the Tools menu.

   ☐ Add the menu item Tile Vertical to the Window menu of the frmPictures form.

   ☐ Add the following code in the mnuTileVertical_Click() procedure of the frmPictures form:

   ```
   Private Sub mnuTile_Click()

       ' The user selected Tile from the Window menu.
       frmPictures.Arrange vbTileVertical

   End Sub
   ```

   The mnuTileVertical_Click() procedure causes the child forms to be arranged vertically, as shown in Figure 17.29.

2. To enhance the TextEd program, perform the following steps:

   ☐ Add the following items to the menu of the TextEd parent form:

Caption	Procedure name
&Color	mnuColor
...&Green	mnuGreen
...G&ray	mnuGray

   ☐ Enter the following code in the mnuGray_Click() procedure:

   ```
   Private Sub mnuGray_Click()


       frmTextEd.ActiveForm.txtUserArea.BackColor = _
                           QBColor(8)

   End Sub
   ```

   ☐ Enter the following code in the mnuGreen_Click() procedure:

   ```
   Private Sub mnuGreen_Click()

       frmTextEd.ActiveForm.txtUserArea.BackColor = _
                           QBColor(2)

   End Sub
   ```

17

(Note that the ActiveForm property is used as a substitute for the child form name in the preceding two procedures.)

☐ Save the project.

☐ Execute the program.

☐ Select New from the File menu several times.

☐ Change the color of the currently active child form by selecting an item from the Color menu.

☐ Experiment with the program, then select Exit from the File menu to terminate the program.

This implementation is not finished, because if you select a color from the Color menu while there is no child document in the parent form, the program will crash. One solution is to declare a variable called ggNumberOfChildren in the general declarations section of a new module as follows:

☐ Select Module from the Insert menu.

Visual Basic responds by adding a new module to the project. The default name that Visual Basic assigns to the new module is Module1.bas.

☐ Select Save File As from the File menu and save the new module file as C:\VB4PRG\CH17\TextEd.bas.

☐ Add the following statement in the general declarations section of the TextEd.bas module:

```
Option Explicit
Public ggNumberOfChildren
```

This statement declares the ggNumberOfChildren public variable in a separate module, so it is visible by all the other modules (if any) and forms of this project. The objective is to maintain the value of ggNumberOfChildren so that this variable will always indicate the number of child forms in the parent form.

☐ Modify the code in the mnuNew_Click() procedure of the frmTextEd parent form as follows:

```
Private Sub mnuNew_Click()

    ' Declare a variable for the instance form
    ' as a copy of the form frmTemplate.
    Dim frmNewForm As New frmTemplate

    ' Show the instance form.
    frmNewForm.Show


    ' For exercise #2 chapter 17
    ggNumberOfChildren = ggNumberOfChildren + 1

End Sub
```

When you select New from the File menu, the code in the mnuNew_Click() procedure should increase ggNumberOfChildren. Initially, ggNumberOfChildren is 0, but every time you select New from the File menu, it is increased by one.

Also, you have to add code to the mnuForm_Unload() procedure of the frmTemplate child form as follows:

```
Private Sub Form_Unload(Cancel As Integer)

    ggNumberOfChildren = ggNumberOfChildren - 1

End Sub
```

The Form_Unload() procedure of the frmTemplate child form is automatically executed whenever you unload a child form. For example, if you select New from the File menu three times, the current value of ggNumberOfChildren is 3. Now suppose that you click the system icon of one of the child forms and select Close to close the child form. Visual Basic automatically executes the Form_Unload() procedure of the frmTemplate child form, which means that the value of ggNumberOfChildren is now 3–1=2.

Now modify the mnuGreen_Click() and the mnuGray_Click() procedures of the frmTextEd parent form so that they will look like this:

```
Private Sub mnuGreen_Click()
    If ggNumberOfChildren > 0 Then
        frmTextEd.ActiveForm.txtUserArea.BackColor = _
                              QBColor(2)
    End If
End Sub

Private Sub mnuGray_Click()
    If ggNumberOfChildren > 0 Then
        frmTextEd.ActiveForm.txtUserArea.BackColor = _
                              QBColor(8)
    End If

End Sub
```

As you can see, an If statement is executed to check whether ggNumberOfChildren is greater than 0. If it isn't, the background color of the child form is not changed (because there is no child form in the parent form).

As this chapter explains, you have to use the same If statement (with the ggNumberOfChildren variable) for determining whether the code in the mnuAssignName_Click() procedure of the frmTextEd parent form should be executed. That is, if there is no child form in the parent form, then the statements in the mnuAssignName_Click() procedure shouldn't be executed.

Therefore, modify the mnuAssignName_Click() procedure of the frmTextEd parent form as follows:

```
Private Sub mnuAssignName_Click()

    ' Declare a string variable
    Dim DocumentName As String

If ggNumberOfChildren > 0 Then
        ' Get from the user the name of the document
    DocumentName = InputBox("Document name:", "Assign Name")
    ' Change the Caption property of the currently
    ' active (or last active)form.
    frmTextEd.ActiveForm.Caption = DocumentName
End If

End Sub
```

Sending Keystrokes, the Spin Control, and the Switch Control

In this chapter you'll learn about three different topics.

In the first section you'll learn how to send keystrokes from within your program to other Windows programs, and you'll also learn how to send keystrokes to yourself. These features are helpful when building demo programs and other applications.

In the second section you'll learn how to use the Spin control, which helps you set up an easy-to-use, attractive user-interface device.

In the third section you'll learn how to use the switch control, which also improves your user-interface mechanism. This section also discusses binary-counting notation.

In this chapter you'll also learn about distributing your Visual Basic programs to your users. Remember—your user does not need to own the Visual Basic package. This means that there are certain considerations that you have to take into account when distributing your programs.

Emulating Keystrokes: The Source and Dest Programs

You can write a Visual Basic program that sends keystrokes to another Windows application. You'll now write two programs: Source and Dest. As implied by their names, Source serves as the *source program* where keystrokes are generated, and Dest is the *destination program* that receives the keystrokes.

The Visual Implementation of the Source Program

☐ Start a new project and save the project form as C:\VB4PRG\CH18\SOURCE.FRM and the project file as C:\VB4PRG\CH18\SOURCE.VBP.

☐ Build the frmSource form according to the specifications in Table 18.1.

The completed form should look like the one shown in Figure 18.1.

Table 18.1. The properties table of the frmSource form.

Object	Property	Setting
Form	**Name**	**frmSource**
	Caption	The Source Program
	Height	3765
	Left	1080
	Top	1170
	Width	3030
Text Box	**Name**	**txtUserArea**
	Height	1335
	Left	360
	MultiLine	–1-True
	ScrollBars	3-Both
	Top	120
	Width	2175
Command Button	**Name**	**cmdSend**
	Caption	&Send
	FontName	System
	FontSize	10
	Height	495
	Left	840
	Top	1680
	Width	1215
Command Button	**Name**	**cmdExit**
	Caption	E&xit
	FontName	System
	FontSize	10
	Height	495
	Left	840
	Top	2640
	Width	1215

Figure 18.1.
The frmSource form in design mode.

Entering the Code of the frmSource Form

☐ Enter the following code in the general declarations section of the frmSource form:

```
' All variables MUST be declared.
Option Explicit
```

☐ Enter the following code in the Form_Load() procedure of the frmSource form:

```
Private Sub Form_Load()

    Dim ID

    ' Execute the destination program.
    ID = Shell("DEST.exe", 1)

End Sub
```

☐ Enter the following code in the cmdSend_Click() procedure of the frmSource form:

```
Private Sub cmdSend_Click()

    ' Make the destination program the active program.
    AppActivate "The Dest Program"

    ' Send characters to the destination program.
    SendKeys txtUserArea.Text, True

End Sub
```

☐ Enter the following code in the cmdExit_Click() procedure of the frmSource form:

```
Private Sub cmdExit_Click()

    End

End Sub
```

☐ Save the project.

☐ Create the Source.EXE file by selecting Make EXE File from the File menu of Visual Basic and saving the file as Source.EXE in the C:\VB4PRG\EXE directory.

You cannot execute the Source program yet! Why? The Source program requires the Dest program to work, so now you'll implement the Dest program.

The Visual Implementation of the Dest Program

☐ Start a new project, save the new form as DEST.FRM in the C:\VB4PRG\CH18 directory and save the new project file as DEST.VBP in the C:\VB4PRG\CH18 directory.

☐ Build the frmDest form according to the specifications in Table 18.2. When you finish building the form, it should look like the one shown in Figure 18.2.

Table 18.2. The properties table of the frmDest form.

Object	Property	Setting
Form	Name	frmDest
	Caption	The Dest Program
	Height	2475
	Left	4800
	Top	1860
	Width	2985
Command Button	Name	cmdDisplayMessage
	Caption	&Display Message
	FontName	System
	FontSize	10
	Height	495
	Left	120
	Top	360
	Width	2655
Command Button	Name	cmdExit
	Caption	E&xit
	FontName	System

continues

18

Table 18.2. continued

Object	Property	Setting
	FontSize	10
	Height	495
	Left	840
	Top	1200
	Width	1215

Figure 18.2.
*The frmDest form
in design mode.*

Entering the Code of the Dest Program

☐ Type the following code in the general declarations section of the frmDest form:

```
' All variables must be declared
Option Explicit
```

☐ Type the following code in the cmdDisplayMessage_Click() procedure of the frmDest form:

```
Private Sub cmdDisplayMessage_Click()

    MsgBox "Display Message was clicked"

End Sub
```

☐ Type the following code in the cmdExit_Click() procedure of the frmDest form:

```
Private Sub cmdExit_Click()

    End

End Sub
```

You'll now create the Dest program.

☐ Select Make EXE File from the File menu of Visual Basic and save the program as Dest.EXE in the C:\VB4PRG\EXE directory. Make sure the Source program is in the same directory as the Dest program.

Executing the Source and Dest Programs

You'll now execute the Dest program.

☐ Terminate Visual Basic by selecting Exit from the File menu of Visual Basic.

☐ Execute the Dest program by displaying the C:\VB4PRG\EXE directory and double-clicking the Dest item.

> *Windows responds by executing the Dest program and displaying the window shown in Figure 18.3.*

Figure 18.3.
The Dest program.

☐ Click the Display Message button of the Dest program.

> *Dest responds by displaying the message box shown in Figure 18.4.*

Figure 18.4.
The message box displayed after you click the Display Message button.

☐ Click the Exit button of the Dest program to terminate the program.

As you can see, the Dest program is very simple—you click its Display Message button to display a message box. The point of the Source and Dest programs is to illustrate how you can click the Display Message button of the Dest program from within the Source program! Use the following steps to see how this is accomplished:

☐ Make sure that the Dest program isn't running.

☐ Execute the Source program.

> *Windows responds by executing the Source program and displaying the windows shown in Figure 18.5. As soon as you execute Source, Windows executes the Dest program as well.*

☐ Minimize all programs except the Source and Dest programs so you can see their windows better.

Figure 18.5.
The Source and Dest programs.

☐ Type %{S} in the Source text box.

☐ Click the Send button of the Source program.

> *As you can see, the Dest program responds as if you had clicked its Display Message button; in other words, you clicked the Display Message button of the Dest program from within the Source program.*

☐ Experiment with the Source and Dest programs and then terminate them.

How the Source Program Works

The code in the Source program executes the Dest program by using the Shell() function and the SendKeys statement to send characters to the Dest program.

The Code in the *Form_Load()* Procedure

The Form_Load() procedure is executed when the frmSource form is loaded:

```
Private Sub Form_Load()

    Dim ID
    ' Execute the destination program.
    ID = Shell("DEST.exe", 1)

End Sub
```

This procedure uses the Shell() function to execute the Dest program. The first argument of the Shell() function is a string containing the name of the program to be executed.

The second argument is an optional argument that specifies the window style of the program to be executed. A value of 1 means that the program to be executed will be shown with a normal window. The preceding Shell() function assumes that the Dest program is in either the current directory or a directory mentioned in the DOS path.

The Code in the *cmdSend_Click()* Procedure

The `cmdSend_Click()` procedure is executed whenever you click the Send button:

```
Private Sub cmdSend_Click()

    ' Make the destination program the active program.
    AppActivate "The Dest Program"

    ' Send characters to the destination program.
    SendKeys txtUserArea.Text, True

End Sub
```

This procedure makes the Dest program the active application with the `AppActivate` statement:

```
AppActivate "The Dest Program"
```

The argument of the `AppActivate` statement is the title of the program to be activated. You must supply this argument exactly as it appears in the window title of the program to be activated. When you start the Dest program, the window title that appears is `The Dest Program`.

For example, if you supply `The Dest.EXE Program` as the argument of the `AppActivate` statement, you get a runtime error because the text `.EXE` doesn't appear in the Dest program's title.

However, the `AppActivate` argument is not case-sensitive. For example, you could use the following statement to activate the Dest program:

```
ThE DeSt PrOgRaM
```

The second statement in the `cmdSend_Click()` procedure sends characters to the currently active application with the `SendKeys` statement:

```
SendKeys txtUserArea.Text, True
```

The characters that are sent are the contents of the `txtUserArea`. It is important to understand that these characters are transferred to the currently active application. This explains why you activated the Dest program before issuing the `SendKeys` statement.

After sending the keys to Dest.EXE, the active program is still the Dest program. You can add the following statement after the `SendKeys` statement in the `cmdSend_Click()` procedure of the frmSource form:

```
AppActivate "The Source Program"
```

This statement makes Source the active program.

The *SendKeys* Statement

As demonstrated in the Source and Dest programs, the `SendKeys` statement is used to send characters to the currently active program. The `True` argument causes these keys to be processed before the program returns to the cmdSend_Click() procedure. This means that the Source program yields to the program receiving the characters, letting it execute its code. If you supply False as the second argument of the SendKeys statement, control is returned to the Source program immediately after the characters are sent.

You can send special keys using the codes specified in Table 18.3. For instance, to send the Alt+D key, use %{D}.

When you press Alt+D in Dest, you get the same result as when you click the Display Message button because the Caption property of the Display Message button was set at design time to &Display Message.

Table 18.3. The code for special keys when used with the SendKeys statement.

Key	Use in SendKeys
Shift	+
Ctrl	^ (Above the 6 key)
Alt	%
Backspace	{BACKSPACE}
Break	{BREAK}
CapsLock	{CAPLOCKS}
Clear	{CLEAR}
Del	{DELETE}
Down Arrow	{DOWN}
End	{END}
Enter	{ENTER}
Esc	{ESCAPE}
Help	{HELP}
Home	{HOME}
Ins	{INSERT}
Left Arrow	{LEFT}
Num Lock	{NUMLOCK}
Page Down	{PGDN}
Page Up	{PGUP}

Key	Use in SendKeys
Print Screen	{PRTSC}
Right Arrow	{RIGHT}
Scroll Lock	{SCROLLLOCK}
Tab	{TAB}
Up Arrow	{UP}
F1	{F1}
...	...
...	...
...	...
F16	{F16}

Sending Keystrokes to Yourself: The MySelf Program

The SendKeys statement sends the keys to the currently active program. What happens when the currently active program is the Source program? As you might expect, the keys are sent to themselves!

Does sending keystrokes to your program have any practical uses? Sure. For example, you can build a demo program or a tutorial program that demonstrates what happens when a sequence of keystrokes is pressed. The MySelf program demonstrates how a Visual Basic program can send keystrokes to itself.

The Visual Implementation of the MySelf Program

☐ Start a new project and save the project form as C:\VB4PRG\CH18\MYSELF.FRM and the project file as C:\VB4PRG\CH18\MYSELF.VBP.

☐ Build the frmMySelf form according to the specifications in Table 18.4.

The completed form should look like the one shown in Figure 18.6.

Table 18.4. The properties table of the frmMySelf form.

Object	Property	Setting
Form	**Name**	**frmMySelf**
	Caption	The MySelf Program
	Height	4545
	Left	1080
	Top	1170
	Width	3210
Command Button	**Name**	**cmdBeep**
	Caption	&Beep
	FontName	System
	FontSize	10
	Height	495
	Left	840
	Top	480
	Width	1215
Command Button	**Name**	**cmdSend**
	Caption	&Send
	FontName	System
	FontSize	10
	Height	495
	Left	840
	Top	2640
	Width	1215
Text Box	**Name**	**txtUserArea**
	Height	1215
	Left	840
	MultiLine	True
	Text	(empty)
	Top	1200
	Width	1215

Object	Property	Setting
Command Button	**Name**	**cmdExit**
	Caption	E&xit
	FontName	System
	FontSize	10
	Height	495
	Left	840
	Top	3360
	Width	1215

Figure 18.6.
The frmMySelf form in design mode.

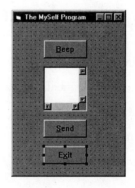

Entering the Code of the frmMySelf Form

☐ Enter the following code in the general declarations section of the frmMySelf form:

```
' All variables MUST be declared.
Option Explicit
```

☐ Enter the following code in the cmdSend_Click() procedure of the frmMySelf form:

```
Private Sub cmdSend_Click()

    ' Make sure this program is the active program.
    AppActivate "The MySelf Program"

    ' Send the text to this program that is
    ' currently in the text box.
    SendKeys txtUserArea.Text, True

End Sub
```

☐ Enter the following code in the cmdBeep_Click() procedure of the frmMySelf form:

```
Private Sub cmdBeep_Click()

    Beep
    MsgBox "The Beep button was clicked"

End Sub
```

☐ Enter the following code in the cmdExit_Click() procedure of the frmMySelf form:

```
Private Sub cmdExit_Click()

    End

End Sub
```

Executing the MySelf Program

☐ Select Make EXE File from the File menu of Visual Basic and save the program as MySelf.EXE in the C:\VB4PRG\EXE directory.

☐ Select Exit from the File menu of Visual Basic to terminate Visual Basic.

☐ Execute the MySelf program.

☐ Click the Beep button.

   The PC should beep.

☐ Press Alt+B.

   The PC should beep because the caption of the Beep button is &Beep.

☐ Type %{B} in the text box of the MySelf program and click the Send button.

   The PC should beep!

☐ Experiment with the MySelf program and then terminate the program.

The Code in the *cmdSend_Click()* Procedure

The cmdSend_Click procedure is executed whenever you click the Send button:

```
Private Sub cmdSend_Click()

    ' Make sure this program is the active program.
    AppActivate "The MySelf Program"

    ' Send the text to this program that is
    ' currently in the text box.
    SendKeys txtUserArea.Text, True

End Sub
```

The first statement in this procedure makes sure the currently active program is the MySelf program. (This statement is really not necessary because even if you omit this statement, the currently active program is the MySelf program. This statement is included just to emphasize that you are sending keystrokes to yourself.)

The second statement in this procedure executes the SendKeys statement to send whatever characters are in the text box.

If you type %{B} in the text box, this text is translated as Alt+B (as shown in Table 18.3), which is the same as clicking the &Beep button.

The code in the cmdBeep_Click() procedure contains the Beep and MsgBox statements, which causes the PC to beep and display a message box.

Using OLE Controls

One of the advantages of Visual Basic is that it enables you to use OLE controls. An *OLE control* is a separate software module. Take a look at Visual Basic's toolbox. It includes controls such as scroll bars, command buttons, check boxes, and so on, but you can add more controls. You'll now learn how to add the spin OLE control to your toolbox window and build a program that uses it.

Utilizing OLE controls from within your Visual Basic program is a very important and powerful feature. No matter what project you are working on, chances are that the particular feature that you are looking for is not included in the off-the-shelf box of Visual Basic. In this case, you can do one of the following:

- Incorporate the feature you are looking for by writing Visual Basic code.
- Use a programming language such as Visual C++ to write a DLL or an OLE control by yourself, and then incorporate the DLL or OLE control you designed into your Visual Basic program.
- Use an off-the-shelf OLE control from a third-party vendor.

Let's review these three options:

Writing Visual Basic code to incorporate a particular feature that is not included with the off-the-shelf package of Visual Basic is not always a practical solution. Why? The particular feature you are trying to incorporate may require a very large amount of Visual Basic code. This means that you'll spend a lot of time writing the code. And guess what? When you finish writing the code, you may discover that the program is too slow. That is, Visual Basic is a relatively easy programming language to learn and to use. But this programming language has its limits! If you try to use Visual Basic for designing very complicated programming tasks, sooner or later you'll find that you are using the wrong programming language.

One solution is to write your own OLE control with a programming language such as Visual C++. Once you finish writing the code of the OLE control, you can use the OLE control from within your Visual Basic programs. However, before writing an OCX by yourself, do a little research! In many cases you may find that the particular OCX you want to build by yourself is already available as an off-the-shelf component for a reasonable price. Therefore, your job as a Visual Basic programmer is to search for the OCX that can do the job for you, and then incorporate the OCX into your Visual Basic project. This is the trend in modern modular programming nowadays. That is, do not try to reinvent the wheel! Visual Basic was specifically designed in a such a way so that you can "plug" off-the-shelf software modules into it.

The rest of the programs in this chapter use third-party OLE controls. It is highly recommended that even if you currently do not own these OLE controls, you should read the material of these programs. This way, you'll gain an understanding of how you can enhance the power of your Visual Basic by using inexpensive, powerful off-the-shelf OLE controls.

Note: In the "old" days, a programmer designed DOS programs from start to finish. That is, the programmer had to design the user-interface mechanism of the program, the printer interface, and *all* the other aspects of the program. In modern modular programming environment such as Windows, many of the "old" programming tasks are the responsibility of Windows. For example, as a programmer, you don't really care what type of printer your user uses. As long as Windows accepts the printer, the printer should work fine with your programs. A similar modularity exists within a modern programming language such as Visual Basic. When designing a project, try to concentrate your efforts on *your* project. If a certain OLE control is available, use it so that you can go on with the development of your project.

The SpinMe Program

You'll now write the SpinMe program. This program utilizes the TegSpin3.OCX control. Note the character 3 that appears in the filename TEGSPIN3.OCX. The 3 means that this OLE control was designed for 32-bit Windows (for example, Windows 95 and Windows NT). But what if you are developing 16-bit Windows applications? In this case you should not use the TegSpin3.OCX control. Instead, use the TegSpin1.OCX control. The TegSpin1.OCX control was designed for 16-bit Windows (for example, Windows 3.1*x*).

You are now going to build a program called SpinMe. When you finish building the program, you'll generate the EXE file of the program, SPINME.EXE.

If you want to distribute your SpinMe program to other users, you'll have to distribute the SpinMe.EXE file as well as other files. You own the Visual Basic package, so you can develop Visual Basic programs. Your user, however, doesn't necessarily own the Visual Basic package. But if you distribute the SpinMe.EXE file, you'll have to distribute additional files that will enable your user to execute the SpinMe program even if your user doesn't own Visual Basic.

So which files should you distribute with the SpinMe.EXE file? When your programs use OLE controls (as the SpinMe program does), you have to distribute the OCX files your programs use. Of course, you must comply with the software licensing agreement of the particular OCX you want to distribute with your application. In addition, you have to distribute the runtime modules of Visual Basic that come with your Visual Basic package. Consult the software licensing agreement of Visual Basic to determine which files you are allowed to distribute together with your application.

> **Note:** The SpinMe program uses the TegoSpin?.OCX control. The TegoSpin?.OCX control is part of the TegoSoft OLE Control Kit, which is a collection of various powerful OLE controls. You can find information about the TegoSoft OLE Control Kit by reading the TegoSoft disk offer at the end of this book.

The Specifications of the SpinMe Program

Before writing the SpinMe program, review its specifications:

☐ When you execute the SpinMe program, the window shown in Figure 18.7 appears.

Figure 18.7.
The SpinMe program.

Each spin control consists of two buttons. In Figure 18.7 you see a spin control on the left side of the window that has two buttons. One button has a picture of an arrow pointing up, and the other button has a picture of an arrow pointing down.

Note: The spin control has two buttons—the up button and the down button.

To illustrate the concept of a spin control, the SpinMe program includes another spin control shown on the right side of the window in Figure 18.7. However, the up button of this spin control has a picture of a lamp in its ON state, and the down button has a picture of a lamp in its OFF state. The two spin controls serve identical purposes in the SpinMe program, but they are included to illustrate the capability of the spin control to display different pictures on its up and down buttons. Which picture should you attach to the buttons of the spin control? It depends on the application you are building. You'll get a better idea of which pictures you should attach to the buttons of the spin control later in this chapter.

☐ Place the mouse cursor on the up-arrow button of the spin control and hold down the left mouse button.

The SpinMe program responds by displaying the values of a counter at the top of the SpinMe window. (See Figure 18.8.)

As long as the spin control's up button is pressed down, this button flashes to indicate that the spin control spins upward.

Figure 18.8.
The counter label at the top of the SpinMe window.

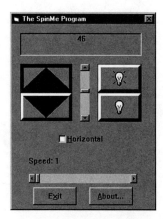

☐ Now place the mouse cursor on the spin control's down button and hold down the left mouse button.

Now the counter counts downward. As long as the spin control's down button is pressed down, the button flashes.

As stated, the spin control on the right performs the same tasks as the spin control on the left.

☐ Experiment with the spin control on the right side of the window. Press the up and down buttons and note that the counter either increases or decreases, depending on which button you click.

As you can see, the spin control is an attractive tool for getting users' input.

Two scroll bars are included in the SpinMe program to illustrate the spin control features. The horizontal scroll bar lets you experiment with the spin control by changing the flashing speed—you can program the rate at which the counter is changing. For example, you can set the horizontal scroll bar to its extreme left position to make the spin control flash every 500 milliseconds (0.5 seconds).

The vertical scroll bar is incorporated into the SpinMe program to illustrate the 3D appearance of the spin control. For example, in Figure 18.8, the vertical scroll bar is in its middle position. This makes the spin control look somewhat three-dimensional.

☐ Move the thumb of the vertical scroll bar to its lowest position.

As shown in Figure 18.9, now the spin controls have more of a 3D border around them.

Figure 18.9.
The vertical scroll bar at its maximum value.

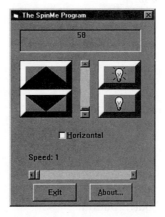

☐ Move the thumb of the vertical scroll bar to its highest position.

As shown in Figure 18.10, now the spin controls have no border around them.

Figure 18.10.
The vertical scroll bar at its minimum value.

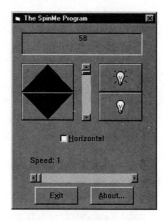

The SpinMe program also includes a Horizontal check box.

☐ Click to place a check mark in the Horizontal check box.

> *The SpinMe program responds by displaying the spin controls horizontally, as shown in Figure 18.11.*

Figure 18.11.
The spin controls in their horizontal position.

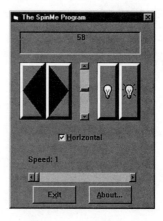

☐ Click the About… button.

> *The SpinMe program responds by displaying the About message box shown in Figure 18.12.*

Figure 18.12.
The About message box of the SpinMe program.

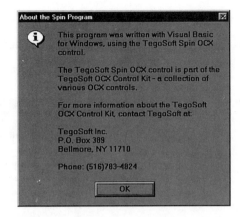

☐ Experiment with the SpinMe program and then click its Exit button to terminate the program.

The Visual Implementation of the frmSpinMe Form

You'll now build the frmSpinMe form.

☐ Start a new project, save the new form as SpinMe.FRM in the C:\VB4PRG\CH18 directory and save the project file as SpinMe.VBP in the C:\VB4PRG\CH18 directory.

The SpinMe project uses the spin OLE control, so first you must add the spin control into the SpinMe.VBP project. Take a look at Figure 18.13, which shows the toolbox window with the spin OLE control in it.

Figure 18.13.
The icon of the spin OLE control in the toolbox window.

If your toolbox window doesn't include the spin OCX icon, you have to add it as follows:

☐ Select Custom Controls from the Tools menu.

Visual Basic responds by displaying the Custom Controls window shown in Figure 18.14.

Figure 18.14.

The Custom Controls window, which is used for adding OLE controls to your project.

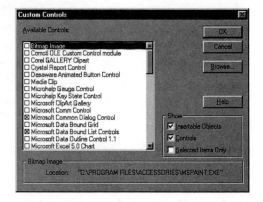

The Available Controls list in the Custom Controls window includes the OLE controls previously registered in your system. In Figure 18.14, the Microsoft Common Dialog Control, an OLE control, is listed. This means that the control is already registered in your system. Furthermore, because an × appears to the left of this OCX item, the OLE control appears in the toolbox of the project.

☐ If you are using 32-bit Windows, click the Browse button of the Custom Controls window and select the TegSpin3.OCX file from the \Windows\System directory; for 16-bit Windows, select the TegSpin1.OCX file from the \Windows\System directory.

Visual Basic responds by adding the spin OLE control to the list of available controls.

☐ Close the Custom Controls window.

As you can see, the toolbox window now includes the spin OLE control.

☐ Build the frmSpinMe form according to the specifications in Table 18.5. When you finish building the form, it should look like the one shown in Figure 18.15. Table 18.5 instructs you to set the PictureSpinDown and PictureSpinUp properties of the TegoSpin1 control to the LightOn.ICO and LightOff.ICO icons. If you don't have these icons, use other ICO files.

Table 18.5. The properties table of the frmSpinMe form.

Object	Property	Setting
Form	**Name**	**frmSpinMe**
	BorderStyle	3-Fixed Dialog
	Caption	The SpinMe Program
	Height	5430
	Left	1080
	MaxButton	0-False
	MinButton	0-False
	Top	1170
	Width	4095
Check Box	**Name**	**chkHorizontal**
	Caption	&Horizontal
	FontName	System
	FontSize	10
	Height	495
	Left	1320
	Top	2880
	Width	1455
Vertical Scroll Bar	**Name**	**vsbBevel**
	Height	1575
	Left	1920
	Max	10
	Min	1
	Top	1080
	Value	5
	Width	255
Horizontal Scroll Bar	**Name**	**hsbSpeed**
	Height	255
	Left	480
	Max	500
	Min	1

continues

Table 18.5. continued

Object	Property	Setting
	Top	4080
	Value	1
	Width	3015
Command Button	**Name**	**cmdAbout**
	Caption	&About...
	FontName	System
	FontSize	10
	Height	495
	Left	2160
	Top	4440
	Width	1215
Command Button	**Name**	**cmdExit**
	Caption	E&xit
	FontName	System
	FontSize	10
	Height	495
	Left	600
	Top	4440
	Width	1215
Label	**Name**	**lblSpeed**
	Caption	Speed: 1
	FontName	System
	FontSize	10
	Height	375
	Left	480
	Top	3600
	Width	1455

Object	Property	Setting
Label	**Name**	**lblCounter**
	Alignment	2-Center
	BorderStyle	1-Fixed Single
	FontName	System
	FontSize	10
	Height	615
	Left	240
	Top	240
	Width	3375
TegoSoft Spin	**Name**	**TegoSpin1**
	Height	1575
	Left	2400
	Top	1080
	Width	1215
	BevelWidth	5
	Interval	1
	PictureSpinUp	C:\VB\ICONS \MISC\LIGHTON.ICO
	PictureSpinDown	C:\VB\ICONS \MISC\LIGHTOFF.ICO
TegoSoft Spin	**Name**	**TegoSpin2**
	Height	1560
	Left	240
	Top	1080
	Width	1455
	BevelWidth	5
	Interval	1

18

Figure 18.15.
The frmSpinMe form in design mode.

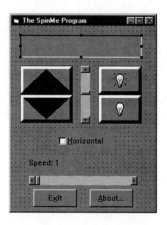

Entering the Code of the SpinMe Program

You'll now enter the code of the SpinMe program.

The Code in the General Declarations Section

You'll now enter the code of the general declarations section of the form.

☐ Type the following code in the general declarations section of the frmSpinMe form:

```
Option Explicit
Public gCounter
```

The gCounter variable is declared in the general declarations section, so it is accessible from any procedure. This variable is used to hold the value of the counter.

The Code in the *cmdExit_Click()* Procedure

You'll now attach code to the Click event of the Exit button.

☐ Type the following code in the cmdExit_Click() procedure of the frmSpinMe form:

```
Private Sub cmdExit_Click()

    End

End Sub
```

This code terminates the SpinMe program.

The Code in the *chkHorizontal_Click()* Procedure

You'll now attach code to the Horizontal check box. When you click to place a check mark in

the Horizontal check box, the two spin controls are aligned horizontally; when the Horizontal check box isn't checked, the two spin controls are aligned vertically.

☐ Type the following code in the chkHorizontal_Click() procedure of the frmSpinMe form:

```
Private Sub chkHorizontal_Click()

    TegoSpin1.Horizontal = chkHorizontal.Value
    TegoSpin2.Horizontal = chkHorizontal.Value

End Sub
```

This procedure sets the Horizontal property of the spin controls to the Value property of the Horizontal check box. So when the Value property of the check box is equal to 0 (the check box is not checked), the Horizontal properties of the spin controls are set to 0, which displays them vertically. And when the check box is checked (Value property is 1), the Horizontal properties of the spin controls are set to 1, which displays them horizontally.

The Code in the *SpinDown* Event of the Spin Control

The SpinDown event occurs whenever you click the down button of the spin control. When the spin control is displayed vertically, the down button is the bottom button; when the spin control is displayed horizontally, the down button is the right button.

☐ Type the following code in the TegoSpin1_SpinDown() procedure of the frmSpinMe form:

```
Private Sub TegoSpin1_SpinDown()

    gCounter = gCounter - 1

    If gCounter < 0 Then
        gCounter = 0
        TegoSpin1.Flash = False
    Else
        TegoSpin1.Flash = True
    End If

    lblCounter.Caption = Str(gCounter)

End Sub
```

This statement in the code decreases the value of gCounter by 1:

```
gCounter = gCounter - 1
```

Since you want gCounter to be in the range of 0 to 100, an If statement is executed to make sure that gCounter is not decreased below 0:

```
If gCounter < 0 Then
```

18

```
    gCounter = 0
    TegoSpin1.Flash = False
Else
    TegoSpin1.Flash = True
End If
```

The code under the If statement is executed whenever the value of gCounter is less than 0. In this case, the gCounter variable is set to 0 and the Flash property of the spin control is set to False. You set the Flash property to False because once you decrease the counter to 0, you don't want the user to see the spin control flash when the down button is decreased. That is, the user will notice that the spin control doesn't decrease the value of the counter once it reaches 0.

The caption of the lblCounter label is then updated with the value of gCounter:

```
lblCounter.Caption = Str(gCounter)
```

The Code in the *SpinUp* Event of the Spin Control

Whenever you click the spin control's up button, the SpinUp event occurs. When the spin control is displayed vertically, the up button is the top button; when the spin control is displayed horizontally, the up button is the left button.

☐ Type the following code in the TegoSpin1_SpinUp() procedure of the frmSpinMe form:

```
Private Sub TegoSpin1_SpinUp()

    gCounter = gCounter + 1

    If gCounter > 100 Then
        gCounter = 100
        TegoSpin1.Flash = False
    Else
        TegoSpin1.Flash = True
    End If

    lblCounter.Caption = Str(gCounter)

End Sub
```

The code in this procedure is very similar to the code in the TegoSpin1_SpinDown() procedure. However, now the gCounter variable is increased with this statement:

```
gCounter = gCounter + 1
```

An If statement is then executed to make sure the value of gCounter doesn't exceed 100:

```
If gCounter > 100 Then
    gCounter = 100
    TegoSpin1.Flash = False
Else
    TegoSpin1.Flash = True
End If
```

Note that when the gCounter reaches its maximum value of 100, the Flash property of the spin control is set to False to indicate that the counter can't be increased once it reaches 100.

The Code in the *SpinDown* and *SpinUp* Events of the Left Spin Control

The spin control on the left side of the window (TegoSpin2) serves the same purpose as the spin control on the right side of the window (TegoSpin1). The only reason for including two spin controls in the program is to illustrate that the spin control can be placed with the default pictures of arrows (TegoSpin2) or with customized pictures such as the light bulbs in the TegoSpin1 control. So the code you attach to the second spin control is identical to the code you attach to the first spin control.

☐ Type the following code in the TegoSpin2_SpinDown() procedure of the frmSpinMe form:

```
Private Sub TegoSpin2_SpinDown()

        TegoSpin1_SpinDown

End Sub
```

In other words, you execute the code in the TegoSpin1_SpinDown() procedure.

☐ Type the following code in the TegoSpin2_SpinUp() procedure of the frmSpinMe form:

```
Private Sub TegoSpin2_SpinUp()

    TegoSpin1_SpinUp

End Sub
```

In other words, you execute the code in the TegoSpin1_SpinUp() procedure.

Assigning Pictures to the Spin Control

Although you attached an icon (ICO) picture to the spin control, you can also set the SpinPictureUp and SpinPictureUp properties of the spin control to BMP files. You can draw small BMP files with Paintbrush, for example, then during design time or runtime set the picture properties of the spin control to the BMP pictures you drew.

This is a very useful feature because you can draw any picture you like. If you set the StretchPicture property of the spin control to False, the picture you assign to the picture properties will not stretch—they will appear in the size you originally drew. If you set the StretchPicture property of the spin control to True, the picture will be stretched to accommodate the size of the spin control.

Assigning pictures to the spin control makes your program very easy to use. Suppose you're designing a program that lets your user set the speed of a certain process; for example, you are designing an animation program and you want your user to be able to control the speed of the animation. In such cases, you can incorporate a spin control. The picture on the up button, which increases the animation speed, could be a rabbit. And the picture on the down button, which decreases the animation speed, could be a turtle.

The Code in the *Change* Event of the Horizontal Scroll Bar

You'll now attach code to the horizontal scroll bar's Change event, which occurs whenever you change its thumb position. The horizontal scroll bar position determines how fast the buttons of the spin control flash when the buttons are clicked. The horizontal scroll bar is usually not included, but it's been added in the SpinMe program so you can see the spin control in action with various flashing speeds.

☐ Type the following code in hsbSpeed_Change() procedure of the frmSpinMe form:

```
Private Sub hsbSpeed_Change()

    TegoSpin1.Interval = hsbSpeed.Value
    TegoSpin2.Interval = hsbSpeed.Value
    lblSpeed.Caption = "Speed:" + Str(hsbSpeed.Value)

End Sub
```

The code in this procedure sets the Interval properties of the spin control to the Value property of the horizontal scroll bar:

```
TegoSpin1.Interval = hsbSpeed.Value
TegoSpin2.Interval = hsbSpeed.Value
```

For example, if the horizontal scroll bar is set to 100, then the Interval properties of the spin controls are set to 100. This means that while the buttons of the spin controls are pressed down, the SpinUp or SpinDown events occur every 100 milliseconds.

The caption label above the horizontal scroll bar is updated so you can see the current setting of the horizontal scroll bar:

```
lblSpeed.Caption = "Speed:" + Str(hsbSpeed.Value)
```

The Code in the *Scroll* Event of the Horizontal Scroll Bar

The hsbSpeed_Scroll() procedure is executed whenever you drag the thumb of the horizontal scroll bar.

☐ Type the following code in the hsbSpeed_Scroll() procedure of the frmSpinMe form:

```
Private Sub hsbSpeed_Scroll()

    TegoSpin1.Interval = hsbSpeed.Value
    TegoSpin2.Interval = hsbSpeed.Value
    lblSpeed.Caption = "Speed:" + Str(hsbSpeed.Value)

End Sub
```

The code in this procedure is the same as the code in the hsbSpeed_Change() procedure.

The Code in the *Change* Event of the Vertical Scroll Bar

The horizontal scroll bar determines the amount of 3D appearance that the spin control will have. Although you won't usually include this scroll bar in your programs, it is used here so you can see the 3D feature of the spin control in action.

☐ Type the following code in the vsbBevel_Change() procedure of the frmSpinMe form:

```
Private Sub vsbBevel_Change()

    TegoSpin1.BevelWidth = vsbBevel.Value
    TegoSpin2.BevelWidth = vsbBevel.Value

End Sub
```

The code in this procedure sets the BevelWidth property of the spin control to the Value property of the vertical scroll bar. When the BevelWidth property of the spin control is set to 0, the spin control's borders aren't 3D. A value of 10 (the maximum) means that the spin control has a 3D border that is 10 pixels wide.

The Code in the *Scroll* Event of the Vertical Scroll Bar

☐ Type the following code in the vsbBevel_Scroll() procedure of the frmSpinMe form:

```
Private Sub vsbBevel_Scroll()

    TegoSpin1.BevelWidth = vsbBevel.Value
    TegoSpin2.BevelWidth = vsbBevel.Value

End Sub
```

The code in this procedure is the same as the code in the vsbBevel_Change() procedure. When you drag the thumb of the vertical scroll bar, you can immediately see the 3D changes in the spin control.

The Code in the *Click* Event of the About Button

You'll now attach code to the Click event of the About... button. The cmdAbout_Click() procedure is automatically executed whenever you click the About... button.

☐ Type the following code in the cmdAbout_Click() procedure of the frmSpinMe form:

```
Private Sub cmdAbout_Click()

Dim Title
Dim Msg
Dim CR

CR = Chr(13) + Chr(10)

' The title of the About message box.
Title = "About the Spin Program"

' Prepare the message of the About message box.
Msg = "This program was written with Visual "
Msg = Msg + "Basic for Windows, using the "
Msg = Msg + "TegoSoft Spin OCX control. "
Msg = Msg + CR + CR
Msg = Msg + "The TegoSoft Spin OCX control "
Msg = Msg + "is part of the TegoSoft OCX Control "
Msg = Msg + "Kit - a collection of various OCX controls. "
Msg = Msg + CR + CR
Msg = Msg + "For more information about the "
Msg = Msg + "TegoSoft OCX Control Kit, contact TegoSoft "
Msg = Msg + "at:"
Msg = Msg + CR + CR
Msg = Msg + "TegoSoft Inc." + CR
Msg = Msg + "P.O. Box 389" + CR
Msg = Msg + "Bellmore, NY 11710"
Msg = Msg + CR + CR
Msg = Msg + "Phone: (516)783-4824"

' Display the About message box.
MsgBox Msg, vbInformation, Title

End Sub
```

The code in this procedure displays the message box shown in Figure 18.12.

☐ Save your project.

Executing the SpinMe Program

☐ Experiment with the SpinMe program and get familiar with the behavior of the spin control during runtime.

Just like any other control, the spin control can be enabled and disabled. To disable the spin control during runtime, use the following statement:

```
MySpin.Enabled = True
```

To enable the spin control during runtime, use the following statement:

```
MySpin.Enabled = False
```

You can also enable or disable the spin control during design time as follows:

☐ During design time right-click the spin control.

> *Visual Basic responds by displaying a menu.*

☐ Select Properties from the menu.

> *Visual Basic responds by displaying a Properties dialog box. You can now set various properties of the control, including its Enabled property.*

☐ Experiment with the Properties dialog box by selecting different tabs and setting various properties of the spin control.

The Switch Control

18

Windows is a very sophisticated operating system used on personal computers. As you know, the personal computer is mainly composed of electronic components (called integrated circuits, or *chips*). This means that the PC is basically composed of nonmoving parts. While the CPU (the main chip of the PC) is processing data and instructions, there are no wheels turning in the CPU chip—everything is accomplished electronically.

Nevertheless, some parts of the PC are mechanical moving parts. For example, the hard drive has a motor, and when you load data from the hard drive, it is actually rotating. The fan and keyboard are also mechanical moving parts. Some mechanical moving parts are necessary in the PC, but a moving part has a finite lifetime and can eventually break! However, as technology progresses, the number of moving parts in electronic equipment is reduced, making the product more reliable.

Now take a look at the Windows user interface. You might notice "primitive" tools, such as the famous hourglass representing the mouse cursor during wait time, the command button that looks like a mechanical push button, the scroll bar that looks like a mechanical slide switch, and so on. These mechanical look-alike controls are used in Windows to let you feel you are working in the real world with real tools rather than clicking pixels on the screen. So in Windows, a control that resembles a mechanical tool makes your application more appealing. You'll now write a program called MySwitch, which illustrates how you can incorporate a "mechanical switch" (that never breaks) into your Windows programs.

The Specifications of the MySwitch Program

Before writing the MySwitch program, take a look at the specifications of the program.

☐ When you execute the MySwitch program, the window shown in Figure 18.16 appears.

As you can see in Figure 18.16, the upper-left corner of the window has a switch that serves as the Exit switch to terminate the application.

Figure 18.16.
The MySwitch program.

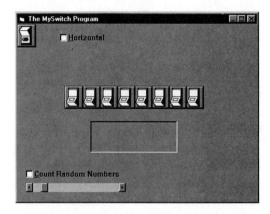

The switch control can be displayed horizontally or vertically. In Figure 18.16, the Exit switch is displayed vertically.

☐ Click to place a check mark in the Horizontal check box to display the Exit switch horizontally.

MySwitch responds by displaying the Exit switch horizontally, as shown in Figure 18.17.

Figure 18.17.
Displaying the Exit switch horizontally.

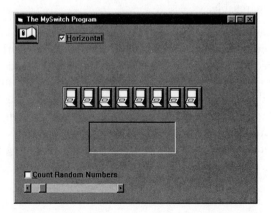

The Horizontal check box isn't usually included in your programs, but it's incorporated into the MySwitch program to illustrate that the switch control can be displayed horizontally or vertically.

The window of the MySwitch program contains eight additional switches. Each switch represents a bit in a byte. If you are not familiar with bits and bytes used in *binary-counting notation*, note the following:

A byte consists of 8 bits; each bit can be 0 or 1. So the following are examples of bytes:

```
00000000
01010101
11111111
11111100
00000001
```

But `00211111` is an invalid byte because bits can only be 0 or 1, not 2 or anything else.

But who uses bits and bytes? As it turns out, your PC does. In fact, everything your PC does, including counting, is performed by manipulating bits and bytes. For example, when a byte is equal to `00000000`, the PC equates the byte to 0; when a byte is equal to `00000001`, the PC thinks of the byte as equal to 1.

Use the following steps to convert a byte to a decimal number:

☐ Take the first bit from the right and multiply it by 1.

☐ Multiply the second bit from the right by 2.

☐ Multiply the third bit from the right by 4 (2×2).

☐ Multiply the fourth bit from the right by 8 (2×2×2).

☐ Multiply the fifth bit from the right by 16 (2×2×2×2).

☐ Multiply the sixth bit from the right by 32 (2×2×2×2×2).

☐ Multiply the seventh bit from the right by 64 (2×2×2×2×2×2).

☐ Multiply the eighth bit from the right by 128 (2×2×2×2×2×2×2).

☐ Add the results of all the multiplication steps to calculate the value of the byte.

Try calculating the value of the following byte:

```
Byte = 10000011
```

The result of the formula is this:

```
1+
1*2+
0*2*2+
0*2*2*2+
```

18

```
0*2*2*2*2+
0*2*2*2*2*2+
0*2*2*2*2*2*2+
1*2*2*2*2*2*2*2

=

1+
2+
0+
0+
0+
0+
0+
128

=

131
```

So the binary number 10000011 is the same as the decimal number 131.

Now take a look at Figure 18.18. The eight switches are arranged as the byte 10000011.

Figure 18.18.

The switches arranged to represent the binary number 10000011, which equals the decimal number 131.

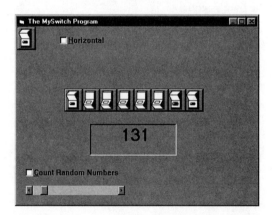

A switch with its lamp ON represents a bit equal to 1, and an OFF switch represents a bit equal to 0.

When you click the eight switches to arrange them as 10000011, the label displays the value 131. You can set the eight switches to any other combination, and the MySwitch program will display the corresponding decimal value of the byte.

Now that you know the MySwitch program can perform the serious task of converting a binary number to a decimal number, have some fun with the MySwitch program:

☐ Click to place a ✔ in the Count Random Numbers check box.

MySwitch responds by setting the eight switches randomly and displaying the corresponding decimal numbers. To slow down or accelerate the process of setting the eight switches, play with the scroll bar below the Count Random Numbers check box.

As you can see, the eight switches just keep blinking in a random order like the lights on a Christmas tree.

> **Note:** The switch control is helpful in many applications. For example, you can place a switch on the upper-left corner of the window so you have an Exit switch to terminate the program.
>
> Naturally, you can use the switch control when you want your user to choose between two states. For example, suppose you are giving your user the option to execute your program with or without the use of a sound card. In this case, you can add a switch so the user can click it to select either of these choices.

The Visual Implementation of the frmMySwitch Form

Follow these steps to build the frmMySwitch form:

☐ Start a new project, save the new form as MySwitch.FRM in the C:\VB4PRG\CH18 directory and save the new project file as MySwitch.VBP in the C:\VB4PRG\CH18 directory.

The MySwitch project uses the TegoSoft switch OLE control which is part of the TegoSoft OLE Control Kit (see TegoSoft Disk offer at the end of this book).

☐ Select Custom Controls from the tools window.

☐ Click the Browse button and select the \Windows\System\TegoSW(16 or 32).OCX file (16 if you are using 16-bit Windows and 32 if you are using 32-bit Windows).

☐ Close the Custom Controls dialog box.

As you can see, your toolbox window now includes the switch (ON/OFF) icon. (See Figure 18.19.)

Figure 18.19.
The icon of the switch (ON/OFF) OLE control.

☐ Build the frmMySwitch form according to the specifications in Table 18.6. When you finish building the form, it should look like the form shown in Figure 18.20.

Table 18.6 instructs you to place an array of switches called swBinary. When you place the first switch, set its name to swExit. This is the Exit switch on the upper-left corner of the window, not part of the array of eight switches. Place a switch in the form and set its Name property to swBinary. Then place another switch and set its Name property to swBinary. Visual Basic displays a dialog box asking whether you want to create an array of controls. Click the Yes button. So the first swBinary switch you place is swBinary(0) because its Index property is equal to 0, and the second switch in the array is swBinary(1) because its Index property is 1. Keep placing switches in the form and setting their Name properties to swBinary. Visual Basic automatically sets their Index properties.

Table 18.6. The properties table of the frmMySwitch form.

Object	Property	Setting
Form	**Name**	**frmMySwitch**
	Caption	The MySwitch Program
	Height	5220
	Left	1080
	Top	1170
	Width	6810
Check Box	**Name**	**chkHorizontal**
	Caption	&Horizontal
	FontName	System

Object	Property	Setting
	Font Size	10
	Height	495
	Left	1200
	Top	120
	Width	1575
Check Box	**Name**	**chkCountRandom**
	Caption	&Count Random Numbers
	FontName	System
	FontSize	10
	Height	495
	Left	240
	Top	3720
	Width	2775
Horizontal Scroll Bar	**Name**	**hsbSpeed**
	Height	255
	LargeChange	100
	Left	240
	Max	1000
	Min	1
	SmallChange	10
	Top	4320
	Value	100
	Width	2775
Timer	**Name**	**tmrTimer**
	Left	360
	Top	2400
Label	**Name**	**lblResult**
	Alignment	2-Center
	BorderStyle	1-Fixed Single
	FontName	MS Sans Serif
	FontSize	24
	Height	855

continues

Table 18.6. continued

Object	Property	Setting
	Left	2040
	Top	2640
	Width	2415
Switch	**Name**	**swExit**
	Height	630
	Left	0
	Top	0
	Width	525
	Value	-1-True
Switch	**Name**	**swBinary**
	Height	630
	Index	0
	Left	4680
	Top	1680
	Width	525
Switch	**Name**	**swBinary**
	Height	630
	Index	1
	Left	4200
	Top	1680
	Width	525
Switch	**Name**	**swBinary**
	Height	630
	Index	2
	Left	3720
	Top	1680
	Width	525

Object	Property	Setting
Switch	**Name**	**swBinary**
	Height	630
	Index	3
	Left	3240
	Top	1680
	Width	525
Switch	**Name**	**swBinary**
	Height	630
	Index	4
	Left	2760
	Top	1680
	Width	525
Switch	**Name**	**swBinary**
	Height	630
	Index	5
	Left	2280
	Top	1680
	Width	525
Switch	**Name**	**swBinary**
	Height	630
	Index	6
	Left	1800
	Top	1680
	Width	525
Switch	**Name**	**swBinary**
	Height	630
	Index	7
	Left	1320
	Top	1680
	Width	525

18

Figure 18.20.

The frmMySwitch form in design mode.

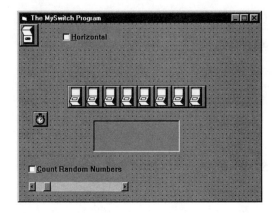

Entering the Code of the MySwitch Program

You'll now enter the code of the MySwitch program.

The Code in the General Declarations Section

☐ Type the following code in the general declarations section of the frmMySwitch form:

```
' Force variable declarations
Option Explicit
```

The Code in the *Load* Event

You'll now attach code to the Load event of the frmMySwitch. The Form_Load() procedure is executed whenever the MySwitch program starts.

☐ Type the following code in the Form_Load() procedure of the frmMySwitch form:

```
Private Sub Form_Load()

    tmrTimer.Interval = hsbSpeed.Value
    Randomize

End Sub
```

The code in this procedure sets the Interval property of the timer to the Value property of the hsbSpeed scroll bar. As you'll soon see, the speed at which random numbers are displayed is determined by the Interval property of the Timer.

The Randomize statement is executed because the Rnd statement is used to generate random numbers. The Randomize statement causes Rnd to generate different random numbers for each execution of the program. This is known as generating a new *seed number* from which the Rnd statement will generate random numbers.

The Code in the *Click* Event of the Exit Switch

You'll now attach code to the Click event of the Exit switch. The swExit_Click() procedure is executed whenever you click the Exit switch.

☐ Type the following code in the swExit_Click() procedure of the frmMySwitch:

```
Private Sub swExit_Click()

    End

End Sub
```

So the program terminates whenever you click the Exit switch.

The Code in the *Click* Event of the Horizontal Check Box

You'll now attach code to the Click event of the Horizontal check box. When you place a check mark in the Horizontal check box, the Exit switch is displayed horizontally. When you remove the check mark from the Horizontal check box, the Exit switch is displayed vertically.

☐ Type the following code in the chkHorizontal_Click() procedure:

```
Private Sub chkHorizontal_Click()

    If chkHorizontal.Value = 1 Then
        swExit.Horizontal = True
    Else
        swExit.Horizontal = False

    End If

End Sub
```

The code in this procedure sets the Horizontal property of the Exit switch according to the state of the Horizontal check box.

The Code in the *Change* Event of the Horizontal Scroll Bar

You'll now attach code to the Change event of the horizontal (Speed) scroll bar. The Change event occurs whenever you change the position of the hsbSpeed scroll bar.

☐ Type the following code in the hsbSpeed_Change() procedure:

```
Private Sub hsbSpeed_Change()

    tmrTimer.Interval = hsbSpeed.Value

End Sub
```

The code in this procedure sets the Interval property of the timer to the Value property of the Speed scroll bar.

The Code in the *Click* Event of the Binary Switches

During design time you placed an array of eight switches in the frmMySwitch form:

```
swBinary(0)
swBinary(1)
swBinary(2)
swBinary(3)
swBinary(4)
swBinary(5)
swBinary(6)
swBinary(7)
```

When you click any of these eight switches, the swBinary_Click() procedure is executed. The parameter of the swBinary_Click() procedure is Index. This means that if you click the swBinary(0) switch, the swBinary_Click() procedure is executed with Index equal to 0. If you click the swBinary(1) switch, the swBinary_Click() procedure is executed with Index equal to 1, and so on.

☐ Type the following code in the swBinary_Click() procedure:

```
Private Sub swBinary_Click(Index As Integer)

    Dim Result

    Result = 0

    If swBinary(0).Value = True Then
        Result = Result + 1
    End If

    If swBinary(1).Value = True Then
        Result = Result + 2
    End If

    If swBinary(2).Value = True Then
        Result = Result + 2 * 2
    End If

    If swBinary(3).Value = True Then
        Result = Result + 2 * 2 * 2
    End If

    If swBinary(4).Value = True Then
        Result = Result + 2 * 2 * 2 * 2
    End If

    If swBinary(5).Value = True Then
        Result = Result + 2 * 2 * 2 * 2 * 2
```

```
    End If

    If swBinary(6).Value = True Then
        Result = Result + 2 * 2 * 2 * 2 * 2 * 2
    End If

    If swBinary(7).Value = True Then
        Result = Result + 2 * 2 * 2 * 2 * 2 * 2 * 2
    End If

    lblResult.Caption = Str(Result)
```

End Sub

The code in this procedure doesn't use the Index parameter. Instead, a series of If statements are executed. Take a look at the first If statement:

```
If swBinary(0).Value = True Then
    Result = Result + 1
End If
```

The Value property of swBinary(0) is examined. If the switch is turned to ON, the variable Result is increased by 1. This complies with the formula of calculating the decimal value because swBinary(0) is the rightmost switch. So if its Value property is equal to False (the switch is set to OFF), Result is not incremented. If the switch is set to ON, Result is incremented by 1.

The next If statement increases Result by 2 if the swBinary(1) is set to ON:

```
If swBinary(1).Value = True Then
    Result = Result + 2
End If
```

In a similar manner, the rest of the If statements increment Result according to the Value property of the rest of the switches.

The last statement updates the Caption property of the lblResult label with the contents of the Result variable:

```
lblResult.Caption = Str(Result)
```

So when you click any of the switches, the label is updated to display the decimal value corresponding to the binary number represented by the eight switches.

The Code in the *Timer* Event of the Timer

You'll now attach code to the Timer event of the timer. The tmrTimer_Timer() procedure is executed periodically. The Interval property of the timer determines how often the tmrTimer_Timer() procedure is executed.

☐ Type the following code in the tmrTimer_Timer() procedure:

```
Private Sub tmrTimer_Timer()
```

```
Dim Counter

If chkCountRandom.Value = 1 Then
        For Counter = 0 To 7
            swBinary(Counter).Value = Int(2 * Rnd)
        Next

    swBinary_Click (0)

End If
```

End Sub

An `If` statement is executed to determine whether the code in the `tmrTimer_Timer()` procedure should be executed:

```
If chkCountRandom.Value = 1 Then

    .........................
    ... Generate random number
    ... and random states for the switches
    .........................

End If
```

So if the Count Random Numbers check box is not checked, the code under the `If` statement is not executed.

If you place a check mark in the Count Random Numbers check box, the code under the `If` statement is executed to set the swBinary switches to random states. The lblResult label displays the decimal number corresponding to the binary number represented by the swBinary switches.

A `For` loop is then executed as follows:

```
For Counter = 0 To 7
    swBinary(Counter).Value = Int(2 * Rnd)
Next
```

The `Rnd` statement generates a number greater than or equal to 0 but less than 1. You multiply `Rnd` by 2, so 2×Rnd can be a number greater than 0 but less than 2.

The `Int()` function converts the 2×Rnd number to an integer, so `Int(2×Rnd)` returns a number that can be either 0 or 1.

Therefore, the Value property of the swBinary switches is assigned a number that can be either 0 or 1. When the Value property of the switch control is equal to False, or 0, the switch is in its OFF position. When the Value property of the switch is equal to any number not equal to 0 (for example, -1, 1, 2, 3), the switch is in its ON state. So the `For` loop places the eight switches in either ON or OFF states.

The last statement executes the `swBinary_Click()` procedure:

```
swBinary_Click (0)
```

In the swBinary_Click() procedure you added code that examines the states of the eight switches and updates the label with the corresponding decimal value.

Why did you supply 0 as the argument of the swBinary_Click() procedure? Since the swBinary switches are an array of controls, the swBinary_Click() procedure expects an argument indicating which switch was clicked. For example, when swBinary(0) is clicked, the argument of the swBinary_Click() procedure is equal to 0. In this case, it doesn't matter which switch is clicked—you just want the swBinary_Click() procedure to be executed so that the lblResult label will be updated. But since the swBinary_Click() procedure expects an argument, you must supply one.

Note: Just like any other control, you can disable the switch control by setting its Enabled property to False as follows:

```
swMySwitch.Enabled = False
```

Figure 18.21 shows the rightmost switch disabled.

To enable the switch control during runtime, use the following statement:

```
swMySwitch.Enabled = True
```

During design time you can enable or disable the switch control by right-clicking the control. Visual Basic will display the Properties dialog box so you can enable or disable the switch control.

18

Figure 18.21.
The rightmost switch is disabled.

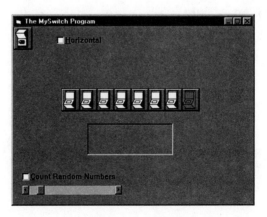

Summary

In this chapter, you have learned how to use the Shell() function to execute the destination application from within the source application, how to send data from the source application to the destination application, and how to send keystrokes to yourself.

In this chapter you have also learned how to use the spin and switch controls, which were designed to make your Windows programs attractive and easy to use.

Q&A

Q When will I want to use the feature of one application sending keystrokes to another application?

A There are many situations where this capability of sending keystrokes from one application to another is useful. For example, you can build a very complicated program that uses other pieces of hardware such as a CD-ROM drive, sound card, scanner, and so on. Because of its complexity, you may have to test the program by trying different ways to execute the program. In such a case, you might consider using another program that will serve as the source program. The source program will periodically send keystrokes to the destination program. So instead of hiring someone to test the destination program, you can build a tester program that will do the testing for you automatically.

Other applications might send keystrokes to a destination program for educational or demo purposes. For example, an automatic demo program that serves as the destination program is executed according to keystrokes sent to it from a source program.

Q When will I want to use the spin control?

A The spin control is typically used in applications that let you set a certain value from a predetermined set of values. In the SpinMe program, you can select a value by displaying a counter that increases or decreases as you click the spin control's buttons. Or you could construct a program that lets you view and select pictures while you click the spin control's buttons.

Remember, one of the main advantages of Windows is its impressive graphic user-interface mechanism. Your users expect your Windows program to include easy-to-use, attractive user-interface mechanisms. Sure, you can perform the same tasks that the spin control does by using a regular scroll bar, but the program is more interesting visually when the spin control is used.

Q When will I want to use the switch control?

A The switch control can be used as an Exit switch. For example, place a switch on the upper-left corner of the window; when you click it, the program terminates.

Also, when you give the user the choice of selecting between two states, the switch control is an ideal candidate for getting the user's input.

Quiz

1. What does the `Shell()` function provide?
   a. A good seafood dinner
   b. A means to execute any program from within a Visual Basic program
   c. There is no such thing
2. Spin control is used when you want to create some type of rotation in your program.
   a. True
   b. False

Exercise

What should you type in the text box of the MySelf program so that clicking the Send button terminates the program?

Quiz Answers

1. b
2. b (The spin control is used when you want the program to perform a certain task continuously for as long as the user keeps the button of the spin control down.)

Exercise Answer

Use the following steps to terminate the program:

☐ Type `&{x}` in the text box.

☐ Click the Send button.

The sequence `%{x}` is translated to Alt+X. (Refer to Table 18.3.)

The caption of the Exit button is E&xit, so pressing Alt+X terminates the program. Typing `%{x}` in the text box and clicking the Send button causes the program to send the Alt+X keystroke to itself, which has the same effect as clicking the Exit button.

WEEK
3

Sound
Programming

In this chapter you'll learn how to write Visual Basic programs that play WAV sound files. You'll learn how to play WAV files through a sound card, and you'll also learn how to play them through the PC speaker without any additional hardware or drivers. You'll also learn how to detect whether the PC has a sound card in it—if it does, you can play the WAV file through the sound card; if it doesn't, you can play the WAV file through the PC speaker.

Note: In the first section of this chapter you'll write a program called MyWAV that requires a sound card. It is recommended that you read this section even if you don't have a sound card in your PC. This way, you'll learn what it takes to play and record sound files from within your Visual Basic programs.

In the second section you'll learn how to play sound files through the PC speaker. Every PC has a small speaker, and in this chapter you'll learn how you can play sound files (speech and music) through it. You'll also learn that you can perform animation (moving text and graphics) simultaneously and in synchronization with sound playback through the PC speaker.

The programs require the use of the TegoSoft advanced multimedia OLE control (see the disk offer at the end of this book). It is highly recommended that you read the material in this chapter even if you do not own the multimedia control, so that you gain an understanding of what it takes to design multimedia applications with Visual Basic.

What Is a WAV File?

A *WAV file* is a file that contains a recording. Basically, a WAV file is similar to a recording you make with a tape recorder. However, the recording is saved into a cassette when you use a tape recorder and into a file when you record WAV files (for example, MySong.WAV).

You can purchase disks or CDs that contain WAV files recorded by others or you can record your own WAV files by using a sound card. Inexpensive sound cards can cost less than $100.

DO	**DON'T**

DO read the software license agreement to see whether you are allowed to distribute the WAV files with your applications when you purchase a CD or a disk with WAV files.

Figure 19.1 shows a schematic of a sound card installed in a PC. A microphone and a set of speakers are attached to the sound card. When you play WAV files, the sound is played through the speakers.

Figure 19.1.
A sound card.

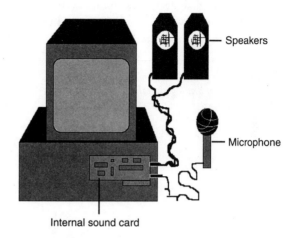

The Process of Recording

Here is how the WAV file is constructed by the sound card: When you speak into the microphone, an electronic circuit on the sound card converts the incoming air waves to a continuous electrical signal called an *analog signal.* An example of an analog recording signal is shown in Figure 19.2.

Figure 19.2.
An analog recording signal.

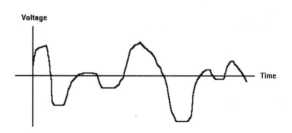

So if you store the analog signal shown in Figure 19.2 and apply it to a speaker at a later time, the speaker will play the same sound that was recorded. This technology of recording and playing is used in, for example, the record playing industry. The analog signal is etched by the record manufacturer on the record. The etched groove on the record has the same shape as the analog signal produced by the recording.

When you play a record, the record player moves a needle over the etched grooves of the record, the needle movement generates the original analog signal, and this analog signal is fed to a speaker that plays the sound.

A PC is a digital machine, so it cannot directly read or save analog signals. The analog recording needs to be converted to a digital recording for PCs. The PC's sound card converts the analog signal to a *digital signal,* as shown in Figure 19.3.

Figure 19.3.

Converting an analog signal to a digital signal.

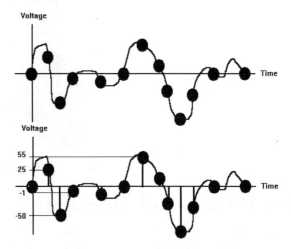

As shown in Figure 19.3, the sound card samples the incoming analog signal at various times. For example, at time 0, the sound card senses the incoming analog signal and discovers that its amplitude is 0. Then the sound card senses the incoming analog signal again and discovers that at the time of the second sampling, the amplitude of the analog signal is 25. The value of the sampled signal at the next sampling is -50. So, to the sound card, the incoming signal looks like this:

```
0
25
-50
-1
. . .
. . .
. . .
```

The sound card then converts the signals as follows:

```
A sample of value 0 is converted to a byte with a value of 128.
A sample of value 1 is converted to a byte with a value of 129.
A sample of value 2 is converted to a byte with a value of 130.
A sample of value 3 is converted to a byte with a value of 131.
. . . . . . . . . . . . . . . . . . . .
. . . . . . . . . . . . . . . . . . . .
. . . . . . . . . . . . . . . . . . . .
```

```
A sample of value -1 is converted to a byte with a value of 127.
A sample of value -2 is converted to a byte with a value of 126.
A sample of value -3 is converted to a byte with a value of 125.
....................
....................
....................
```

So, for example, if the sound card samples the following signals:

```
0
-1
0
1
2
...
...
...
```

the sound card creates a WAV file with the following values in it:

```
128,127,128,129,130,...
```

Before the values of the samples are written into the WAV file, various overhead bytes are written at the beginning of the WAV file. These overhead bytes are later used by the sound card as instructions for how to play the WAV file. For example, at the beginning of the WAV file, some of the bytes indicate the *sampling rate* at which the recording was performed.

Sampling Rate

In the previous section you learned the principle of recording a WAV file. The sound card samples the incoming analog signal at regular time intervals. What is this time interval? Say, for example, that the sound card samples the incoming analog signal every minute. As you can imagine, a recording sampled at 1-minute intervals isn't worth much. The sound card would miss a lot of sound information between the samples! So what sampling rate should the sound card use? There are several "standard" sampling rates at which sound cards record WAV files. The sampling rate is expressed in units of *hertz* (Hz). For example, if the sound card samples a signal every 60 seconds, the sampling rate in hertz is calculated as follows:

```
Sampling Rate = 1/60 = 0.0166Hz
```

This is a very low sampling rate, and in almost all cases the recording it produces is useless. If the sound card samples a signal every millisecond (0.001 second), the sampling rate is calculated as follows:

```
Sampling Rate = 1/0.001 = 1000Hz.
```

As it turns out, a sampling rate of 1000Hz is also too low. When recording WAV files, the sampling rates used are the following:

11,025 Hz (11KHz)
22,050 Hz (22KHz)
44,100 Hz (44KHz)

Note that 11,025Hz is commonly known as 11 *kilohertz* (KHz), not as 11.025KHz.

As you might have guessed, the higher the sampling rate (the more samplings the sound card takes each second), the better the quality of the recording. An 8KHz (8000Hz) recording produces a telephone-like quality, an 11KHz recording produces a tape recorder quality, a 22KHz recording produces a fairly good recording for speech and music, and a 44KHz recording produces a CD-like quality.

Which sampling rate should you use? It depends on the particular application you're developing. Naturally, if the application you are writing is to demonstrate your singing ability, you want the recording to be as good as possible, so you want to record with a 44KHz sampling rate.

Note that when you are recording at 44KHz, the WAV file contains 44100 bytes for each second of recording. Therefore, when you record at 44KHz, 2 seconds of recording requires 44100×2=88200 bytes, and so on. On the other hand, when you record at a sampling rate of 22KHz, 1 second of recording requires 22050 bytes, 2 seconds of recording requires 22050×2=44100 bytes, and so on. In other words, as you increase the sampling rate, the recording quality is better, but the size of the resulting WAV file increases.

Mono and Stereo Recording

So far in this chapter, only mono WAV files have been discussed. Some sound cards have the ability to record stereo WAV files. A *stereo recording* records two separate recordings. For example, the sound picked up from the left side of the room is recorded as one recording, and the sound picked up from the right side of the room is recorded as a second recording.

The WAV file of a stereo recording is constructed as follows: Suppose that the samples picked up from the left side of the room are 127, 128, and 126, and the samples picked up from the right side of the room are 127, 126, and 125. The resulting bytes in the WAV file are the following:

```
LEFT  RIGHT  LEFT  RIGHT  LEFT  RIGHT
 127   127   128   126    126   125
```

In other words, the samples are written one after another, one sample from the left channel followed by one sample from the right channel.

Of course the quality of a stereo recording is better than that of a mono recording, but the size of the stereo WAV file is double the size of the mono WAV file. If you record a mono WAV file with a 44KHz sampling rate for 1 second, the resulting WAV file needs 44100 bytes for the mono recording. For a stereo recording, the WAV file needs 88200 bytes for this recording (44100 bytes for the left channel and 44100 bytes for the right channel).

8-Bit and 16-Bit Recording

There is another factor to consider besides mono and stereo recording when you record WAV files. As previously stated, the sound card samples the analog incoming signal and assigns a value to the sample. The range of the sample can be from 0 to 255, with 128 representing the middle point. This means that each sample can be expressed as a byte. A byte consists of 8 bits, hence the expression 8-bit recording.

Some sound cards have the capability of recording so that each sample is composed of 2 bytes. Since each byte is composed of 8 bits, this type of recording is called 16-bit recording. The 16-bit recording produces better quality because the samples have better resolution. For example, suppose the sound card senses that the amplitude of the incoming analog signal is 32.5 units. Because the sound card must assign an integer to the resulting sample, the sound card rounds the amplitude. So an incoming analog signal with an amplitude of 32.5 produces the same sample as an analog signal with an amplitude of 32.4. If, however, the sound card can record with the 16-bit technique, a better resolution can be achieved than with an 8-bit recording. When performing 8-bit recording, the range of the incoming analog signal is broken into 256 distinct parts, but it is broken into about 65,000 parts when performing a 16-bit recording.

So should you use the 8-bit or 16-bit recording technique? As you can imagine, the WAV file for a 16-bit recording is larger than that for an 8-bit recording.

In a 16-bit recording each sample occupies 2 bytes. So here are the first three samples (3 bytes) of an 8-bit mono recording:

```
BYTE1 = Represents sample #1
BYTE2 = Represents sample #2
BYTE3 = Represents sample #3
```

Here are the first three samples (6 bytes) of a 16-bit mono recording (each sample occupies 2 bytes):

```
BYTE1 = Represents sample #1
BYTE2 = Represents sample #1

BYTE3 = Represents sample #2
BYTE4 = Represents sample #2

BYTE5 = Represents sample #3
BYTE6 = Represents sample #3
```

The MyWAV Program

You'll now write a program called MyWAV. This program lets you load a WAV file, record into the WAV file, and play the WAV file. Before writing the MyWAV program, review its specifications.

When you start the MyWAV program, the window shown in Figure 19.4 appears. (In Exercise 1 of this chapter you'll add code that performs animation. For now, simply ignore the animation and pictures displayed during the execution of the MyWAV program.)

Figure 19.4.
The MyWAV program.

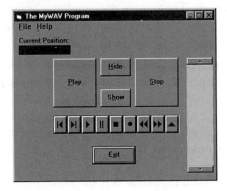

You can now select Open from the File menu to load a WAV file. (See Figure 19.5.) The Open dialog box (when executing the program in Windows 95) is shown in Figure 19.6. You can now load the WAV files.

Figure 19.5.
The File menu of the MyWAV program.

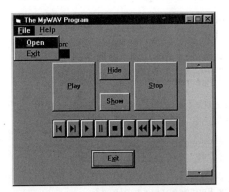

Figure 19.6.
Loading a WAV file.

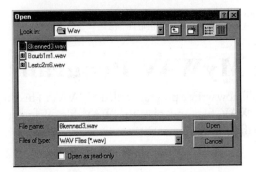

Once you select a WAV file, the caption of the program's window indicates the name of the WAV file that was opened. (See Figure 19.7.)

Figure 19.7.

The caption of the MyWAV window indicating which WAV file was selected.

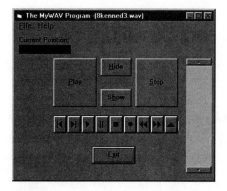

You can now use the various buttons of the multimedia control. Figure 19.8 shows the multimedia control and its buttons.

Figure 19.8.

The multimedia OLE control.

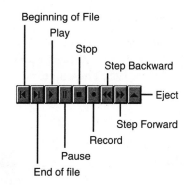

The multimedia control has nine buttons and can play a variety of multimedia devices. In Chapter 21, "Multimedia," you'll learn that the same control is used for playing MIDI files (synthesized music files), CD audio, and movie AVI files. Therefore, some of the buttons have different purposes when you use the multimedia control on different devices. When the multimedia control is used for playing WAV files (as in the MyWAV program), the first button from the left is the Beginning of File button. This button rewinds the WAV file to the beginning of the file. The second button from the left places the current position at the end of the WAV file. The third button is the Play button, the fourth button is the Pause button, the fifth button is the Stop button, and the sixth button is the Record button.

The three buttons on the right of the multimedia control don't apply to playing WAV files. Take a look at the extreme right button of the multimedia control (the Eject button). This button is used, for example, when you play CD audio. Clicking the Eject button causes the CD-ROM drive to eject the disc. However, the Eject button has no purpose when you play WAV files, so it is dimmed when you play WAV files. The Step Backward and Step Forward buttons are used when you play movie AVI files (as you'll learn in Chapter 21). These buttons let you move forward and backward to different frames of a movie.

You can now play the WAV file through the sound card by clicking the Play button of the multimedia control. You can stop and pause the playback and even record sound by clicking the Record button and speaking into the microphone.

Providing Custom Multimedia Buttons

In many cases you will want to provide buttons that are more user friendly than the multimedia control's buttons. For example, instead of letting the user play the WAV file by clicking the third button of the multimedia control, you can place your own Play button in the form. When the user clicks the Play button, the WAV file will be played. Similarly, you can place other buttons that perform the same tasks as the multimedia control's buttons.

The MyWAV program has two such buttons: the Play button and the Stop button. So once the user loads a WAV file, he or she can play the WAV file either by using the multimedia control's buttons or by using your Play and Stop buttons.

The Hide and Show buttons of the MyWAV program let you hide and show the multimedia control. For example, after you click the Hide button, the multimedia control becomes invisible, as shown in Figure 19.9. These buttons are used to illustrate that the MyWAV program doesn't have to display the multimedia control during runtime.

Figure 19.9.

Making the multimedia control invisible.

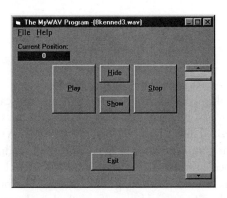

The MyWAV program has a label control in its upper-left corner that displays the current position of the playback. For example, in Figure 19.9, the current position of the WAV file is 0, which means that the WAV file is at the beginning of the file. When you play the WAV file, the label displays its current position during the playback. In Figure 19.10, the current position is at 2135 milliseconds (2.135 seconds) from the beginning of the file.

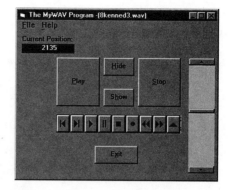

Figure 19.10.
*The label in the upper-left
corner of the window
displays the current position
of the WAV file.*

The MyWAV program also displays a vertical scroll bar. This scroll bar changes its position randomly during the playback. Its purpose is mostly cosmetic, to illustrate the important concept of the multimedia control's StatusUpdate event (as you'll see later in this chapter).

Now that you know what the MyWAV program is supposed to do you can try it yourself.

The Visual Implementation of the MyWAV Program

You'll now visually implement the frmMyWAV form of the MyWAV program.

☐ Select New Project from the File menu and save the new form as MyWAV.FRM in the C:\VB4PRG\CH19 directory and the new project file as MyWAV.VBP in the C:\VB4PRG\CH19 directory.

19

The MyWAV program uses the TegoSoft Multimedia OLE control, so you need to add this control to your project.

Note: The multimedia OLE control is part of the TegoSoft OLE Control Kit—a collection of powerful and sophisticated OLE controls. You can purchase the TegoSoft OLE Control Kit directly from TegoSoft, Inc. (See disk offer at the end of this book.)

☐ Select Custom Controls from the Tools menu of Visual Basic.

Visual Basic responds by displaying the Custom Controls dialog box.

☐ Click the Browse button, then select the TegMM(16 or 32).OCX file from the \Windows\System directory (depending on whether you're using 32-bit or 16-bit Windows).

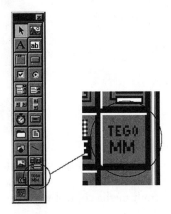

After you select the OCX file, the toolbox window includes the multimedia OLE control, as shown in Figure 19.11.

Figure 19.11.
The icon of the multimedia OLE control in the toolbox.

☐ Build the frmMyWAV form according to the specifications in Table 19.1. When you finish building the form, it should look like the one shown in Figure 19.12.

Table 19.1 instructs you to place the common dialog OLE control in the form. To add it to your project, select Custom Controls from the Tools menu, click the Browse button, and select the COMDLG(16 or 32).OCX file from the \Windows\System directory (16 for 16-bit Windows or 32 for 32-bit Windows). The COMDLG(16 or 32).OCX files came with your Visual Basic package and were installed in your hard drive when you installed the Visual Basic program.

Table 19.1. The properties table of the frmMyWAV form.

Object	Property	Setting
Form	**Name**	**frmMyWAV**
	Caption	The MyWAV Program
	Height	4710
	Left	1020
	Top	1140
	Width	5700
Vertical Scroll Bar	**Name**	**vsbNothing**
	Enabled	0-False
	Height	3135
	Left	4800
	Max	100

Object	Property	Setting
	Top	720
	Width	735
Command Button	**Name**	**cmdShow**
	Caption	S&how
	Height	495
	Left	2400
	Top	1560
	Width	855
Command Button	**Name**	**cmdHide**
	Caption	&Hide
	Height	495
	Left	2400
	Top	720
	Width	855
Command Button	**Name**	**cmdStop**
	Caption	&Stop
	Height	1335
	Left	3360
	Top	720
	Width	1215
Command Button	**Name**	**cmdPlay**
	Caption	&Play
	Height	1335
	Left	1080
	Top	720
	Width	1215
Command Button	**Name**	**cmdExit**
	Caption	E&xit
	Height	495
	Left	2160
	Top	3120
	Width	1215

19

continues

Table 19.1. continued

Object	Property	Setting
Common Dialog	**Name**	**CMDialog1**
	CancelError	True
	Left	1080
	Top	3120
Multimedia	**Name**	**Tegomm1**
	Height	495
	Left	1080
	Top	2280
	Width	3510
Label	**Name**	**lblPosition**
	Alignment	2-Center
	BackColor	Black
	Caption	(empty)
	ForeColor	White
	Height	255
	Left	120
	Top	360
	Width	1455
Label	**Name**	**lblCurrentPosition**
	Caption	Current Position:
	Height	255
	Left	120
	Top	120
	Width	1575
Menu	**(See Table 19.2.)**	**(See Table 19.2.)**

Table 19.2. The menu table of the frmMyWAV form.

Caption	Name
&File	mnuFile
...&Open	mnuOpen
...E&xit	mnuExit
&Help	mnuHelp
...&About...	mnuAbout

Figure 19.12.
*The frmMyWAV form in
design mode.*

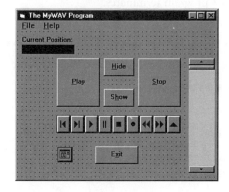

Entering the Code of the MyWAV Program

You'll now enter the code of the MyWAV program.

The Code in the General Declarations Section

You'll now type the code of the general declarations section.

☐ Enter the following code in the general declarations section of the frmMyWAV form:

```
' Force variable declarations
Option Explicit
```

☐ The code in this procedure forces variable declarations. Therefore, you must declare
variables before using them in the program.

The Code in the *Click* Event of the Exit Button

You'll now attach code to the Click event of the Exit button.

☐ Type the following code in the cmdExit_Click() procedure of the frmMyWAV form:

```
Private Sub cmdExit_Click()

    End

End Sub
```

The code in this procedure executes the End statement. When you click the Exit button, the MyWAV program terminates.

The Code in the *Click* Event of the Exit Menu Item

☐ Type the following code in the mnuExit_Click() procedure of the frmMyWAV form:

```
Sub mnuExit_Click()

    cmdExit_Click

End Sub
```

The code in this procedure terminates the MyWAV program whenever you select Exit from the File menu. As you can see, you execute the same code you use when you click the Exit button.

The Code in the *Click* Event of the Hide Button

You'll now attach code to the Click event of the Hide button.

☐ Type the following code in the cmdHide_Click() procedure of the frmMyWAV form:

```
Private Sub cmdHide_Click()

    Tegomm1.Visible = False

End Sub
```

The code in this procedure sets the Visible property of the multimedia control to False. So when you click the Hide button, the multimedia control becomes invisible. This button won't usually be incorporated into your program, but it's included here to illustrate that you can make the multimedia control invisible during runtime. So if you want to immediately make the multimedia control invisible without using the Hide button, use the following statement in the Form_Load() procedure:

```
Tegomm1.Visible = False
```

The Code in the *Click* Event of the Show Button

You'll now attach code to the Click event of the Show button.

☐ Type the following code in the cmdShow_Click() procedure of the frmMyWAV form:

```
Sub cmdShow_Click()

    Tegomm1.Visible = True

End Sub
```

The code in this procedure sets the Visible property of the multimedia control to True. So when you click the Show button, the multimedia control becomes visible. Again, the Show button was included in the MyWAV program to illustrate the Visible property, but typically you won't include it in your programs.

The Code in the *Click* Event of the Open Menu Item

You'll now attach code to the Click event of the Open menu item. When you select Open from the File menu, the MyWAV program displays an Open dialog box that lets you select a WAV file. The code that you'll now attach is used frequently to select a file with the Open menu.

☐ Type the following code in the mnuOpen_Click() procedure:

```
Sub mnuOpen_Click()

    ' Selecting a file (with the common dialog box)

    ' Set an error trap
    On Error GoTo OpenError

    ' Set the items of the File Type list box
    CMDialog1.Filter = _
        "All Files (*.*) ¦ *.* ¦WAV Files (*.wav)¦*.wav"

    ' Set the default File Type
    CMDialog1.FilterIndex = 2

    ' Display the common dialog box
    CMDialog1.Action = 1

    ' Remove the error trap
    On Error GoTo 0

    ' Open the selected file
    Tegomm1.DeviceType = "WaveAudio"
    Tegomm1.FileName = CMDialog1.Filename
    Tegomm1.Command = "Open"
    If Tegomm1.Error > 0 Then
```

19

```
        cmdPlay.Enabled = False
        cmdStop.Enabled = False
        frmMyWAV.Caption = _
            "The MyWAV Program - (No file is loaded)"

        MsgBox "Can't open " + CMDialog1.Filename, vbCritical, "Error"

    Else
        cmdPlay.Enabled = True
        cmdStop.Enabled = True
        frmMyWAV.Caption = _
            "The MyWAV Program -(" + CMDialog1.Filetitle + ")"
    End If

    ' Exit this procedure
    Exit Sub

OpenError:
    ' The user pressed the Cancel key of the common dialog

    ' Exit this procedure
    Exit Sub

End Sub
```

The code in the following statement sets an error trap:

```
On Error GoTo OpenError
```

So if an error occurs when you select a file, the program immediately jumps to the `OpenError` line of this procedure:

```
OpenError:
    Exit Sub
```

During design time you set the CancelError property of the common dialog control to True. This means that if you click the Cancel button of the Open dialog box, an error occurs (and because you set the error trap, the program will immediately jump to the `OpenError` line).

The common dialog box is then prepared with these statements:

```
CMDialog1.Filter = _
        "All Files (*.*) ¦ *.* ¦WAV Files (*.wav)¦*.wav"

CMDialog1.FilterIndex = 2
```

Then the Open dialog box is displayed as follows:

```
CMDialog1.Action = 1
```

Once you select a file, the program proceeds with the statement after the `CMDialog1.Action = 1` statement. Because there is no need to trap errors anymore, the error trap is removed:

```
On Error GoTo 0
```

The DeviceType property of the multimedia control determines what type of medium is being played. When playing WAV files through the sound card, you have to set the DeviceType property to WaveAudio:

```
Tegomm1.DeviceType = "WaveAudio"
```

Then the FileName property of the multimedia control is set as follows:

```
Tegomm1.FileName = CMDialog1.Filename
```

Recall that you selected the WAV file by using the Open dialog box, and the selected file is saved as the Filename property of the CMDialog1 control.

Finally, the Open command is issued as follows:

```
Tegomm1.Command = "Open"
```

An If…Else statement is then executed to examine whether the Open command was executed successfully:

```
If Tegomm1.Error > 0 Then
    ........................................
    ... An error occurred during
    ... the execution of the last command
    ........................................
Else
    ........................................
    ... No error occurred during
    ... the execution of the last command
    ........................................
End If
```

The code under the If statement is executed if an error occurred during the last execution of a command by the multimedia control. Because the last command executed by the multimedia control was the Open command, the If statement indicates whether there was an error during the execution of the Open command. An error could occur if the FileName property of the multimedia control was set with an invalid WAV file, if the sound card isn't functioning, or if one of the sound card's drivers is missing.

The code under the If statement disables the Play and Stop buttons:

```
cmdPlay.Enabled = False
cmdStop.Enabled = False
```

The Caption property of the program's window is set to indicate that no WAV file is loaded:

```
frmMyWAV.Caption = _
    "The MyWAV Program - (No file is loaded)"
```

A message box is then displayed to indicate that the selected file can't be opened:

```
MsgBox "Can't open " + CMDialog1.Filename, vbCritical, "Error"
```

> **Note:** The preceding code disables the Play and Stop buttons that you placed in the form. But what about the Play and Stop buttons of the multimedia control? You don't have to disable or enable its buttons because the multimedia control takes care of this automatically. For example, if the WAV file was not opened successfully, the multimedia control does not enable its own Play and Stop buttons.

The code under the Else statement is executed if the Open command was executed successfully. This code enables the Play and Stop buttons that you placed in the form:

```
cmdPlay.Enabled = True
cmdStop.Enabled = True
```

The Caption property of the form is changed so that you can see which WAV file is open:

```
frmMyWAV.Caption = _
        "The MyWAV Program -(" + CMDialog1.Filetitle + ")"
```

Finally, the procedure is terminated with the Exit Sub statement.

The Code in the *Click* Event of the cmdPlay Button

You'll now attach code to the Click event of the cmdPlay button.

☐ Type the following code in the cmdPlay_Click() procedure:

```
Sub cmdPlay_Click()

    Tegomm1.Command = "Play"

End Sub
```

The code in this procedure starts the playback by issuing the Play command to the multimedia control.

> **Note:** As stated, after issuing the Open command, you can examine the Error property to see whether the WAV file was opened successfully. If the Error property is greater than 0, it means that the WAV file wasn't opened successfully. There could be many reasons why the WAV file wasn't opened successfully; for example, the specified WAV file doesn't exist or one of the sound card's drivers is missing.
>
> Sometimes, after issuing the Open command, the Error property reports that no error occurred, yet no sound is played! This could happen if, for example, you had all the necessary sound card drivers but the sound card itself was missing. You can

detect this situation by issuing the Play command, then examining the Error property. If the Error property is greater than 0, it means that an error occurred during the playback.

It's usually enough to examine the Error property after issuing the Open command to see whether you have a sound card. However, you can also perform a sound card test by issuing the following statements:

```
Tegomm1.TimeFormat = Sample
Tegomm1.From = 0
Tegomm1.To   = 1
Tegomm1.Command = "Play"
If Tegomm1.Error > 0 Then
    ...........................
    ... Error. Playback failed.
    ...........................
End If
```

The preceding statements tell the multimedia card to consider units in samples (not in milliseconds) and then to play one sample. The next statements examine the Error property. So if the sound card didn't play the sample, you can inform the user that something is wrong with the sound card. If everything is OK with the sound card, it will play the sample. However, the user won't hear the playback because it's so short, so he or she won't even notice that the sound card test was performed.

The Code in the *Click* Event of the cmdStop Button

You'll now attach code to the Click event of the cmdStop button.

☐ Type the following code in the cmdStop_Click() procedure:

```
Sub cmdStop_Click()

    Tegomm1.Command = "Stop"

End Sub
```

The code in this procedure stops the playback by issuing the Stop command to the multimedia control.

The Code in the *Form_Load()* Procedure

You'll now attach code to the Form_Load event of the frmMyWAV form.

☐ Type the following code in the Form_Load() procedure:

```
Sub Form_Load()

    Tegomm1.UpdateInterval = 250

End Sub
```

The code in this procedure sets the UpdateInterval property of the multimedia control to 250. This means that from now on the Tegomm1_StatusUpdate() procedure will be executed automatically every 250 milliseconds (0.25 seconds). Later in this chapter you'll write the code of the Tegomm1_StatusUpdate() procedure.

The Code in the *Done* Event of the Multimedia Control

You'll now attach code to the Done event of the multimedia control.

☐ Type the following code in the Tegomm1_Done() procedure:

```
Sub Tegomm1_Done()

    If Tegomm1.Position = Tegomm1.Length Then
        Tegomm1.Command = "Prev"
    End If

End Sub
```

The Position property of the multimedia control indicates the current position of the WAV file. The Length property of the multimedia control indicates the length of the WAV file. So if the Position property is equal to the Length property, you know that the Done event occurred because the WAV file was played in its entirety. Therefore, the code under the If statement is executed when the WAV file is played in its entirety. In other words, the Done event occurs whenever the multimedia control finishes executing commands. The If statement in the Tegomm1_Done() procedure checks whether the Done event occurred because the Play command was executed and the playback position reached the end of the WAV file.

The code under the If statement issues the Prev command:

```
Tegomm1.Command = "Prev"
```

This causes the WAV file to rewind itself to the beginning of the file so it's ready the next time you click the Play button.

Note: If you write a program that plays the WAV file automatically in an endless loop (the WAV file is played all over again when it reaches the end of the file), use the following code:

```
Sub Tegomm1_Done()

    If Tegomm1.Position = Tegomm1.Length Then
        Tegomm1.Command = "Prev"
        Tegomm1.Command = "Play"
    End If

End Sub
```

That is, once the WAV file is played in its entirety, you rewind the WAV file and then play it again.

The Code in the *StatusUpdate* Event of the Multimedia Control

In the `Form_Load()` procedure you set the UpdateInterval property of the multimedia control to 250 to automatically execute the `Tegomm1_StatusUpdate()` procedure every 250 milliseconds.

☐ Type the following code in the `Tegomm1_StatusUpdate()` procedure:

```
Sub Tegomm1_StatusUpdate()

    If Tegomm1.Mode = 526 Then
        lblPosition.Caption = Str(Tegomm1.Position)
        vsbNothing.Value = Int(Rnd * 100)
    End If

End Sub
```

The code in this procedure updates the Caption property of the lblPosition label with the value of the multimedia control's Position property:

```
lblPosition.Caption = Str(Tegomm1.Position)
```

So every 250 milliseconds the lblPosition label displays the current position of the WAV file. (The default units are milliseconds, so the Position property and other properties, such as the Length property, are in milliseconds. However, you can set the TimeFormat property of the multimedia control to other units, such as samples. When the TimeFormat property is set to Samples, the units of the Position and Length properties are samples.)

19

This is the second statement in the Tegomm1_StatusUpdate() procedure:

```
vsbNothing.Value = Int(Rnd * 100)
```

The preceding statement sets the Value property of the vsbNothing scroll bar to a random number between 0 and 99. The only reason this statement is included is to show that the Tegomm1_StatusUpdate() procedure is indeed executed automatically every 250 milliseconds—during the playback of the WAV file, you'll see the scroll bar's position change to random values. You can examine the Mode property to see whether playback is in progress:

```
If Tegomm1.Mode = 526 Then
    .............
    ... Playback is in progress.
    .............
End If
```

The Code in the *Click* Event of the About Menu Item

When you click the About item in the Help menu, the About dialog box appears, as shown in Figure 19.13.

Figure 19.13.
The About dialog box of the MyWAV program.

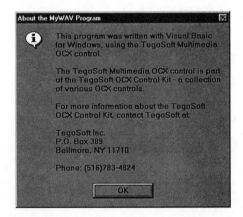

☐ Type the following code in the cmdAbout_Click() procedure of the frmMyWAV program:

```
Private Sub mnuAbout_Click()

    Dim Title
    Dim Msg
    Dim CR
```

```
CR = Chr(13) + Chr(10)

' Prepare the title of the About message box.
Title = "About the MyWAV Program"
Msg = "This program was written with Visual "
Msg = Msg + "Basic for Windows, using the "
Msg = Msg + "TegoSoft Multimedia OCX control. "
Msg = Msg + CR + CR
Msg = Msg + "The TegoSoft Multimedia OCX control "
Msg = Msg + "is part of the TegoSoft OCX Control "
Msg = Msg + "Kit - a collection of various OCX controls. "
Msg = Msg + CR + CR
Msg = Msg + "For more information about the "
Msg = Msg + "TegoSoft OCX Control Kit, contact TegoSoft "
Msg = Msg + "at:"
Msg = Msg + CR + CR
Msg = Msg + "TegoSoft Inc." + CR
Msg = Msg + "P.O. Box 389" + CR
Msg = Msg + "Bellmore, NY 11710"
Msg = Msg + CR + CR
Msg = Msg + "Phone: (516)783-4824"

' Display the About message box.
MsgBox Msg, vbInformation, Title

End Sub
```

The code in this procedure displays the message box shown in Figure 19.13.

☐ Experiment with the MyWAV program and then click its Exit button to terminate the program.

Playing WAV Files Through the PC Speaker: The Speaker Program

In this part of the chapter you'll learn how to use the Speaker program, which lets you play WAV files through the PC speaker (so you don't need a sound card). Before designing the Speaker program, review its specifications.

☐ When you execute the Speaker program, the window shown in Figure 19.14 appears.

Figure 19.14.
The Speaker program.

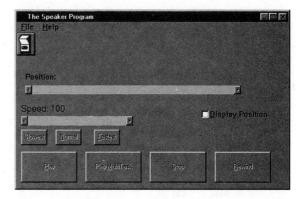

Note: The Speaker program uses the TegoSoft speaker OLE control. The 16-bit speaker OLE control works on any 16-bit Windows operating system (for example, Windows 3.1, Windows for Workgroups 3.11).

The current version of the 32-bit speaker OLE control works on Windows 95 but not on Windows NT. So if you want to use the 32-bit OLE control, use it on Windows 95.

Note: The Speaker program uses the TegoSoft speaker OLE control. The speaker OLE control is part of the TegoSoft OLE Control Kit—a collection of powerful and sophisticated OLE controls. You can purchase the TegoSoft OLE Control Kit directly from TegoSoft, Inc. (See disk offer at the end of this book.)

It is highly recommended that even if you do not own the speaker OLE control, you read the material on the Speaker program. This way, you'll gain an understanding of how the PC speaker (that every PC has) can be used from within your Visual Basic programs.

The Speaker program has two menus: File and Help. (See Figures 19.15 and 19.16.)

Figure 19.15.
The File menu of the Speaker program.

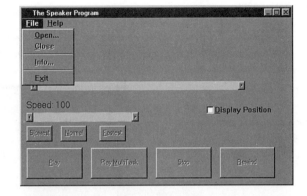

Figure 19.16.
The Help menu of the Speaker program.

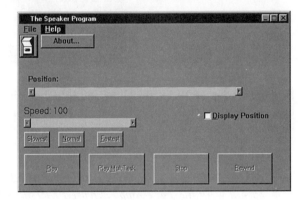

19

☐ Select Open from the File menu.

Speaker.EXE responds by displaying the Open dialog box shown in Figure 19.17.

Figure 19.17.
The Open dialog box.

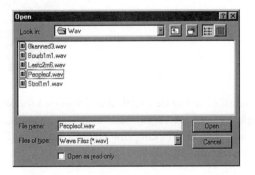

☐ Select a WAV file. (For example, select the Peopleof.WAV file.)

Speaker.EXE responds by opening the WAV file and displaying the name of the WAV file in the caption of the program's window. (See Figure 19.18.)

Figure 19.18.

The program's caption with the name of the opened WAV file.

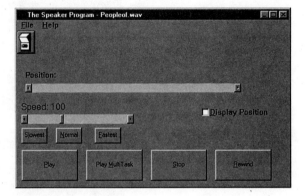

Note that in Figure 19.15, the Close and Info menu items of the File menu are not available because a WAV file hasn't been loaded yet. However, now that a WAV file is open, these menu items are available.

☐ Select the Info item from the File menu.

Speaker.EXE responds by displaying a dialog box that displays information about the opened WAV file. For example, Figure 19.19 shows the Information dialog box of the Peopleof.WAV file.

Figure 19.19.

The Information dialog box.

Take a look at Figure 19.19. It tells you that the WAV filename is Peopleof.WAV. This WAV file says People of Earth, your attention please…. The file has 53,261 samples, and the WAV file was recorded at a sampling rate of 22,050Hz. The WAV file was recorded as an 8-bit, mono WAV file (one channel means that the WAV file was recorded as a mono recording).

Note: Some sound cards can play WAV files that were recorded as stereo and as 16-bit recordings.

The PC speaker can only play WAV files that were recorded as 8-bit mono recordings.

The Speaker program lets you play the WAV file by either clicking the Play button or clicking the Play MultiTask button.

☐ Click the Play button.

Speaker.EXE responds by playing the WAV file through the PC speaker. Note that during the playback, the mouse cursor becomes an hourglass.

☐ When the playback is over, click the Play MultiTask button.

Speaker.EXE responds by again playing the WAV file through the PC speaker. Note that during this playback the mouse is available. The Play MultiTask button causes the program to play through the PC speaker, but you can perform other operations during the playback. You can, for example, stop the playback by clicking the Stop button.

☐ Click to place a check mark in the Display Position check box.

☐ Click the Play MultiTask button.

Speaker.EXE responds by playing the WAV file through the PC speaker. During the playback, the upper horizontal scroll bar displays the current position of the WAV file. Also, the label above the position scroll bar displays the current position in units of samples and milliseconds.

The Speaker program also lets you change the playback speed.

☐ Set the Speed scroll bar (the lower horizontal scroll bar) to various positions and then click the Play or Play MultiTask button.

Speaker.EXE responds by playing the WAV file at the speed you set with the Speed scroll bar.

☐ Select About... from the Help menu to display the About dialog box.

Speaker.EXE responds by displaying the dialog box shown in Figure 19.20.

19

Figure 19.20.

The About dialog box of the Speaker program.

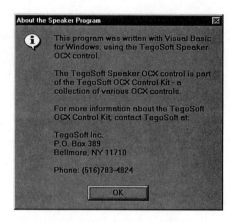

☐ Experiment with the Speaker program and then click its Exit switch on the upper-left corner of the window to terminate the program.

The Visual Implementation of the Speaker Program

You'll now visually implement the frmSpeaker form of the Speaker program.

☐ Select New Project from the File menu and save the new form as SPEAKER.FRM in the C:\VB4PRG\CH19 directory and the new project file as SPEAKER.VBP in the C:\VB4PRG\CH19 directory.

The Speaker program uses the TegoSoft speaker OLE control, so you need to add this control to your project. Make sure that the TegSPKR3.OCX file (if you are using 32-bit Windows) or the TegSPKR1.OCX file (if you are using 16-bit Windows) is in the \Windows\System directory and add it to your project as follows:

☐ Select Custom Controls from the Tools menu of Visual Basic.

Visual Basic responds by displaying the Custom Controls dialog box.

☐ Click the Browse button, and then select the TegSPKR(3 or 1).OCX file from the \Windows\System directory (use 3 for 32-bit Windows or 1 for 16-bit Windows).

After you select the OCX file, the toolbox window includes the speaker OLE control, as shown in Figure 19.21.

Figure 19.21.
The icon of the speaker OLE control in the toolbox.

☐ Build the frmSpeaker form according to the specifications in Table 19.3. When you finish building the form, it should look like the one shown in Figure 19.22.

Table 19.3 instructs you to place the common dialog OLE control in the form. To add it to your project, select Custom Controls from the Tools menu, click the Browse button, and select the COMDLG(32 or 16).OCX file from the \Windows\System directory (32 for 32-bit Windows or 16 for 16-bit Windows). The COMDLG(32 or 16).OCX files came with your Visual Basic package and were installed in your hard drive when you installed the Visual Basic program. Add the TegoSoft switch OLE control used in the Speaker program to the project in the same way.

Table 19.3. The properties table of the frmSpeaker form.

Object	Property	Setting
Form	**Name**	**frmSpeaker**
	Caption	The Speaker Program
	Height	4920
	Left	990
	Top	1140
	Width	7695

continues

Table 19.3. continued

Object	Property	Setting
Check Box	**Name**	**chkDisplayPosition**
	Caption	&Display Position
	FontName	System
	FontSize	10
	Height	375
	Left	5160
	Top	2040
	Width	1935
Timer	**Name**	**Timer1**
	Interval	250
	Left	4200
	Top	240
Horizontal Scroll Bar	**Name**	**hsbPosition**
	Enabled	0-False
	Height	240
	Left	240
	Max	100
	Top	1440
	Width	6015
Command Button	**Name**	**cmdFast**
	Caption	&Fastest
	Height	435
	Left	2160
	Top	2640
	Width	735
Command Button	**Name**	**cmdNormal**
	Caption	&Normal
	Height	435
	Left	1080
	Top	2640
	Width	735

Object	Property	Setting
Command Button	**Name**	**cmdSlow**
	Caption	S&lowest
	Height	435
	Left	120
	Top	2640
	Width	735
Horizontal Scroll Bar	**Name**	**hsbSpeed**
	Height	255
	Left	120
	Max	200
	Min	50
	Top	2280
	Value	100
	Width	3135
Command Button	**Name**	**cmdRewind**
	Caption	&Rewind
	Height	855
	Left	5520
	Top	3240
	Width	1575
Command Button	**Name**	**cmdPlayMultitask**
	Caption	Play &MultiTask
	Height	855
	Left	1920
	Top	3240
	Width	1575
Command Button	**Name**	**cmdStop**
	Caption	&Stop
	Height	855
	Left	3720
	Top	3240
	Width	1575

19

continues

Table 19.3. continued

Object	Property	Setting
Command Button	**Name**	**cmdPlay**
	Caption	&Play
	Height	855
	Left	120
	Top	3240
	Width	1575
Label	**Name**	**lblPosition**
	Caption	Position:
	FontName	System
	FontSize	10
	Height	255
	Left	240
	Top	1080
	Width	5895
Label	**Name**	**lblSpeed**
	Caption	Speed: 100
	FontName	MS Sans Serif
	FontSize	12
	Height	300
	Left	120
	Top	1920
	Width	1935
TegoSoft Switch	**Name**	**swExit**
	Height	630
	Left	0
	Top	0
	Width	525
	Value	-1-True
Common Dialog	**Name**	**CommonDialog1**
	Left	1560
	Top	0
	CancelError	-1-True

Object	Property	Setting
TegoSoft Speaker	Name	TegoSpeaker1
	Height	600
	Left	600
	Top	0
	Width	930
Menu	(See Table 19.4.)	(See Table 19.4.)

Table 19.4. The menu table of the frmSpeaker form.

Caption	Name
&File	mnuFile
...&Open...	mnuOpen
...&Close	mnuClose
...-	mnuSep1
...&Info...	mnuInfo
...-	mnuSep2
...E&xit	mnuExit
&Help	mnuHelp
...About...	mnuAbout

19

Figure 19.22.
The frmSpeaker form in design mode.

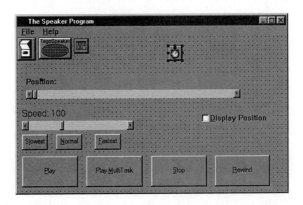

Entering the Code of the Speaker Program

You'll now enter the code of the Speaker program.

The Code in the General Declarations Section

☐ Enter the following code in the general declarations section of the frmSpeaker form:

```
' Force variable declarations
Option Explicit
```

The code in this procedure forces you to declare variables before using them in the program.

The Code in the *Load* Event

You'll now attach code to the Load event of the frmSpeaker form. The Form_Load() procedure is executed when you start the Speaker program.

☐ Type the following code in the Form_Load() procedure of the frmSpeaker form:

```
Private Sub Form_Load()

    TegoSpeaker1.Visible = False

    ' Disable menu items and buttons that should
    ' be disabled when no WAV file is open yet.
    mnuClose_Click

End Sub
```

The code in this procedure sets the Visible property of the Speaker control to False because this control should be invisible during runtime.

The code in this procedure also executes the mnuClose_Click() procedure:

```
' Disable menu items and buttons that should
' be disabled when no WAV file is open yet.
mnuClose_Click
```

When no WAV file is loaded, certain buttons, such as the Play button, should be disabled. As you'll see in the next section, the code you'll attach to the Click event of the Close menu performs these disable operations.

The Code in the *Click* Event of the Close Menu Item

You'll now attach code to the Click event of the Close menu item.

☐ Type the following code in the mnuClose_Click() procedure of the frmSpeaker form:

```
Private Sub mnuClose_Click()

    ' Close the WAV file.
    TegoSpeaker1.Close

    ' No WAV file is now open, so disable
    ' the Speed, Close, Info, Play, Stop,
    ' and Rewind controls.
    hsbSpeed.Enabled = False
    cmdSlow.Enabled = False
    cmdFast.Enabled = False
    cmdNormal.Enabled = False
    mnuClose.Enabled = False
    mnuInfo.Enabled = False
    cmdPlay.Enabled = False
    cmdPlayMultitask.Enabled = False
    cmdStop.Enabled = False
    cmdRewind.Enabled = False

    Me.Caption = "The Speaker Program"

End Sub
```

The code in this procedure executes the Close command:

```
' Close the WAV file.
TegoSpeaker1.Close
```

If there is currently an open WAV session, selecting the Close menu item closes the WAV file. Then the controls that should be disabled when no WAV session is open are disabled as follows:

```
' No WAV file is now open, so disable
' the Speed, Close, Info, Play, Stop,
' and Rewind controls.
hsbSpeed.Enabled = False
cmdSlow.Enabled = False
cmdFast.Enabled = False
cmdNormal.Enabled = False
mnuClose.Enabled = False
mnuInfo.Enabled = False
cmdPlay.Enabled = False
cmdPlayMultitask.Enabled = False
cmdStop.Enabled = False
cmdRewind.Enabled = False
```

Finally, the Caption property of the program's window is updated:

```
Me.Caption = "The Speaker Program"
```

The Code in the *Click* Event of the Exit Menu Item

Whenever you select the Exit menu item, the program terminates.

19

☐ Type the following code in the `mnuExit_Click()` procedure of the frmSpeaker form:

```
Private Sub mnuExit_Click()

        Unload Me

End Sub
```

The code in this procedure unloads the frmSpeaker form, which causes the Speaker program to terminate.

The Code in the *Click* Event of the Exit Switch

The switch in the upper-left corner of the program's window is the Exit switch. You can terminate the Speaker program by clicking this switch.

☐ Type the following code in the `swExit_Click()` procedure of the frmSpeaker form:

```
Private Sub swExit_Click()

    Dim Title
    Dim Question
    Dim Response

    ' If the user turned the swExit switch OFF,
    ' confirm that the user wants to exit the
    ' program, and if so, exit the program.
    If swExit.Value = False Then
       Title = "Exit Program"
       Question = "Are you sure you want to exit?"
       Response = MsgBox(Question, vbYesNo + vbQuestion, Title)
       If Response = vbYes Then
          Unload Me
       Else
          swExit.Value = True
       End If
    End If

End Sub
```

The code in this procedure is executed when you click the Exit switch. This code displays a message box that asks whether you want to terminate the program. If you click the Yes button, the program terminates.

The Code in the *Click* Event of the Open Menu Item

When you select the Open item from the File menu, the Speaker program displays an Open dialog box that lets you select a WAV file. You'll now enter the code that is executed whenever you select Open from the File menu.

☐ Type the following code in the mnuOpen_Click() procedure of the frmSpeaker form:

```
Private Sub mnuOpen_Click()

    ' Set an error trap to detect the clicking
    ' of the Cancel key of the Open dialog box.
    On Error GoTo OpenError

    ' Fill the items of the File Type list box of
    ' the Open dialog box.
    CommonDialog1.Filter = _
        "All Files (*.*)¦*.*¦Wave Files (*.wav)¦*.wav"

    ' Set the default File Type to Wave Files (*.wav).
    CommonDialog1.FilterIndex = 2

    ' Display the Open dialog box.
    CommonDialog1.Action = 1

    ' Remove the error trap.
    On Error GoTo 0

    ' Open the WAV file that the user selected.
    TegoSpeaker1.Open CommonDialog1.FileName

    ' If Open command failed, exit this procedure.
    If TegoSpeaker1.GetErrorCode <> 0 Then
        MsgBox "Cannot open " + CommonDialog1.FileName, 0, "ERROR"
        MsgBox TegoSpeaker1.GetErrorMessage
        mnuClose_Click
        Exit Sub
    End If

    ' Display the name of the WAV file (without the path).
    Me.Caption = _
        "The Speaker Program - " + CommonDialog1.FileTitle

    ' A WAV file is now open, so enable
    ' the Speed, Close, Info, Play, Stop,
    ' and Rewind controls.
    hsbSpeed.Enabled = True
    cmdSlow.Enabled = True
    cmdFast.Enabled = True
    cmdNormal.Enabled = True
    mnuClose.Enabled = True
    mnuInfo.Enabled = True
    cmdPlay.Enabled = True
    cmdPlayMultitask.Enabled = True
    cmdStop.Enabled = True
    cmdRewind.Enabled = True

    ' Set the Speed scrollbar to normal speed.
    hsbSpeed.Value = 100

    ' Exit the procedure.
    Exit Sub
```

19

```
OpenError:
    ' The user clicked the Cancel button of the
    ' Open File dialog box.
    Exit Sub

End Sub
```

The code in this procedure sets an error trap:

```
' Set an error trap to detect the clicking
' of the Cancel key of the Open dialog box.
On Error GoTo OpenError
```

Recall that during design time you set the CancelError property of the common dialog control to True. This means that if you click the Cancel button while the Open dialog box is displayed, an error is generated. If an error occurs or you click the Cancel button, the program immediately executes the statements following the OpenError statement at the end of this procedure.

The common dialog box is then prepared as follows:

```
' Fill the items of the File Type list box of
' the Open dialog box.
CommonDialog1.Filter = _
         "All Files (*.*)¦*.*¦Wave Files (*.wav)¦*.wav"

' Set the default File Type to Wave Files (*.wav).
CommonDialog1.FilterIndex = 2
```

Then the dialog box is displayed as an Open dialog box:

```
' Display the Open dialog box.
CommonDialog1.Action = 1
```

Now that the Open dialog box is displayed, you can remove the error trap:

```
' Remove the error trap.
On Error GoTo 0
```

The path and filename of the WAV file you selected is stored as the FileName property of the common dialog box. You then open the selected WAV file by using the Open method as follows:

```
' Open the WAV file that the user selected.
TegoSpeaker1.Open CommonDialog1.FileName
```

You then execute an If statement to examine whether the WAV file was opened successfully:

```
' If Open command failed, exit this procedure.
If TegoSpeaker1.GetErrorCode <> 0 Then
   MsgBox "Cannot open " + CommonDialog1.FileName, 0, "ERROR"
   MsgBox TegoSpeaker1.GetErrorMessage
   mnuClose_Click
   Exit Sub
End If
```

The GetErrorCode method returns the code corresponding to an error. If the value returned from the GetErrorCode method is 0, no error occurs. If the GetErrorCode method returns a value other than 0, an error occurs and the code under the If statement is executed.

The code under the If statement displays two message boxes. The first message box simply tells you that there is an error:

```
MsgBox "Cannot open " + CommonDialog1.FileName, 0, "ERROR"
```

The second message box tells you the reason for the error:

```
MsgBox TegoSpeaker1.GetErrorMessage
```

That is, the GetErrorMessage method returns a string explaining the nature of the error.

Then the mnuClose_Click() procedure is executed to disable all the buttons that can't be used when no WAV file is loaded:

```
mnuClose_Click
```

Finally, the procedure is terminated:

```
Exit Sub
```

If no errors occurred, the statements that follow the If…End If block are executed. Because a WAV file was successfully opened, the Caption property of the program's window is set so that you can tell which WAV file was opened:

```
' Display the name of the WAV file (without the path).
Me.Caption = _
        "The Speaker Program - " + CommonDialog1.FileTitle
```

19

Because a WAV file is open now, the controls you should use are enabled as follows:

```
' A WAV file is now open, so enable
' the Speed, Close, Info, Play, Stop,
' and Rewind controls.
hsbSpeed.Enabled = True
cmdSlow.Enabled = True
cmdFast.Enabled = True
cmdNormal.Enabled = True
mnuClose.Enabled = True
mnuInfo.Enabled = True
cmdPlay.Enabled = True
cmdPlayMultitask.Enabled = True
cmdStop.Enabled = True
cmdRewind.Enabled = True
```

The Value property of the Speed control is then set to 100:

```
' Set the Speed scrollbar to normal speed.
hsbSpeed.Value = 100
```

During the execution of the Speaker program, you can increase or decrease the playback speed by changing the Speed scroll bar. A value of 100 means that the playback speed is normal. A value of 101 means that the playback speed is 1 percent faster than the normal speed, and so on. For example, when the Value property of the Speed scroll bar is 90 percent, the playback speed is 10 percent slower than the normal speed. You'll correlate the Value property of the Speed scroll bar with the speaker control later in this chapter.

The Code in the *Click* Event of the Fastest Button

When you click the Fastest button, the cmdFast_Click() procedure is executed.

☐ Type the following code in the cmdFast_Click() procedure of the frmSpeaker form:

```
Private Sub cmdFast_Click()

        hsbSpeed.Value = hsbSpeed.Max

End Sub
```

The code in this procedure sets the Value property of the Speed scroll bar to its Max property. So clicking the Fastest button has the same effect as moving the thumb of the Speed scroll bar to its extreme-right position.

The Code in the *Click* Event of the Normal Button

When you click the Normal button, the cmdNormal_Click() procedure is executed.

☐ Type the following code in the cmdNormal_Click() procedure of the frmSpeaker form:

```
Private Sub cmdNormal_Click()

        hsbSpeed.Value = 100

End Sub
```

The code in this procedure sets the Value property of the Speed scroll bar to 100. So clicking the Normal button has the same effect as moving the thumb of the Speed scroll bar so that its Value property is equal to 100.

The Code in the *Click* Event of the Slowest Button

When you click the Slowest button, the cmdSlow_Click() procedure is executed.

☐ Type the following code in the cmdSlow_Click() procedure of the frmSpeaker form:

```
Private Sub cmdSlow_Click()

        hsbSpeed.Value = hsbSpeed.Min

End Sub
```

The code in this procedure sets the Value property of the Speed scroll bar to its Min property. So clicking the Slowest button has the same effect as moving the thumb of the Speed scroll bar to its extreme left position.

The Code in the *Change* Event of the Speed Scroll Bar

You'll now attach code to the Change event of the Speed scroll bar. The Change event occurs whenever you change the position of the Speed scroll bar. Also, since the code you attached to the Slowest, Normal, and Fastest buttons changes the Value property of the Speed scroll bar, the hsbSpeed_Change() procedure is executed whenever you click any of these buttons.

☐ Type the following code in the hsbSpeed_Change() procedure of the frmSpeaker form:

```
Private Sub hsbSpeed_Change()

    lblSpeed.Caption = "Speed: " + Str(hsbSpeed.Value)

    TegoSpeaker1.SetSpeed hsbSpeed.Value

End Sub
```

The code in this procedure uses the SetSpeed method of the speaker control. The parameter you supplied to the SetSpeed method is the Value property of the Speed control. Therefore, the playback speed is determined by the Value property of the speed control. The following examples explain how the parameter of the SetSpeed method changes the playback speed.

The following statement will set the playback speed to 10 percent faster than the normal speed (that is, 110 percent of the normal speed):

```
TegoSpeaker1.SetSpeed 110
```

The following statement will set the playback speed to the normal, 100 percent, playback speed:

```
TegoSpeaker1.SetSpeed 100
```

The following statement will set the playback speed to 10 percent less than the normal speed (that is, 90 percent of the normal speed):

```
TegoSpeaker1.SetSpeed 90
```

The following statement will set the playback speed to twice, or 200 percent of, the normal speed:

```
TegoSpeaker1.SetSpeed 200
```

The following statement will set the playback speed to half, or 50 percent, of the normal speed:

```
TegoSpeaker1.SetSpeed 50
```

19

The Code in the *Scroll* Event of the Speed Scroll Bar

You'll now attach code to the Scroll event of the Speed scroll bar. When you drag the thumb of the Speed scroll bar, the Scroll event occurs.

☐ Type the following code in the hsbSpeed_Scroll() procedure of the frmSpeaker form:

```
Private Sub hsbSpeed_Scroll()

    hsbSpeed_Change

End Sub
```

The code in this procedure executes the hsbSpeed_Change() procedure.

The Code in the *Click* Event of the Play Button

When you click the Play button, the Speaker program should play the currently open WAV file through the PC speaker. You'll now write the code that accomplishes this task.

☐ Type the following code in the cmdPlay_Click() procedure:

```
Private Sub cmdPlay_Click()

chkDisplayPosition.Value = 0

' Play from the beginning of the WAV file until
' the end of the WAV file without multitasking,
' and disable the mouse during playback.
TegoSpeaker1.Play 0, -1, 0, False

End Sub
```

The code in the cmdPlay_Click() procedure sets the Value property of the DisplayPosition check box to 0 (to remove the check mark from this check box). This is done because during the playback, the Position scroll bar will not move to indicate the current playback position. In other words, the code that executes the playback doesn't permit the Position scroll bar to change position. Therefore, the Display Position check box is unchecked so that you won't wonder why the position scroll bar doesn't move during the playback even though the check box is checked.

This statement plays the loaded WAV file through the PC speaker:

```
TegoSpeaker1.Play 0, -1, 0, False
```

This statement uses the Play method of the speaker control to play the WAV file from the current playback position to the end of the WAV file.

The Play method of the speaker control takes four parameters:

- From: This parameter specifies the starting position of the playback (in units of samples). If you specify -1, the playback starts from the current playback position.

- `To`: This parameter specifies the end position of the playback (in units of samples). If you specify -1, the end position of the playback will be the end of the WAV file.
- `TaskInterval`: This parameter specifies the time slice (in milliseconds) of the playback. When this parameter is set to 0 (as in the `cmdPlay_Click()` procedure), the program is suspended while the playback is in progress so you can't perform any other operations. If, however, this parameter is set to a value greater than 0, then the playback is performed in a multitasking mode. For example, if you set this parameter to 300, the program will play the WAV file for 300 milliseconds, and then the program will yield control to Windows so that other tasks can be performed, the next 300 milliseconds of the WAV file will be played, the program will yield control to Windows again, and so on.
- `EnableMouse`: This parameter can be set to either True or False. When this parameter is set to True, the mouse is enabled during playback. If, however, this parameter is set to False, the mouse is disabled during playback. (When the mouse is disabled, the mouse does not generate `Click` events.)

Note: To produce the best playback quality, you should set the third parameter of the `Play` method (`TaskInterval`) to 0 and the fourth parameter (`EnableMouse`) to False.

The Code in the *Click* Event of the Play MultiTask Button

You'll now attach code to the Play MultiTask button.

☐ Type the following code in the `cmdPlayMultitask_Click()` procedure of the frmSpeaker form:

```
Private Sub cmdPlayMultitask_Click()

        TegoSpeaker1.Play -1, -1, 300, True

End Sub
```

The code in this procedure plays the WAV file from location 0 to the end of the WAV file. However, every 300 milliseconds, the speaker control will let Windows perform other tasks. For example, if you click the Play MultiTask button, then click the Stop button, after 300 milliseconds the speaker control will let Windows perform other tasks. Windows knows that there is a pending event (the clicking of the Stop button) and will act on it. That is, Windows will instruct the Speaker program to execute the `cmdStop_Click()` procedure to end the playback. Note that the last parameter of the `Play` method is set to True. This means that the mouse is available during the playback, so you can move it and click the Stop button.

The Code in the *Click* Event of the Stop Button

You'll now attach code to the Click event of the Stop button. If there is a playback in progress, you can click the Stop button to stop the playback if it's being done in a multitasking mode.

☐ Type the following code in the cmdStop_Click() procedure of the frmSpeaker form:

```
Private Sub cmdStop_Click()

        TegoSpeaker1.Stop

End Sub
```

The code in this procedure executes the Stop method to stop the playback.

The Code in the *Click* Event of the Rewind Button

When you click the Rewind button, the WAV file is rewound to the beginning of the file.

☐ Type the following code in the cmdRewind_Click() procedure of the frmSpeaker form:

```
Private Sub cmdRewind_Click()

        TegoSpeaker1.Seek 0

End Sub
```

The code in this procedure places the current position of the WAV file at the beginning of the file (at sample number 0). Of course, you can supply other values to the Seek method. For example, if you have an application where the length of the WAV file is 10,000 bytes and you want to place the current position of the WAV file at sample number 1234, use the following statement:

```
TegoSpeaker1.Seek 1234
```

The Code in the *Click* Event of the About... Menu Item

You'll now attach code to the Click event of the About... menu item.

☐ Type the following code in the mnuAbout_Click() procedure of the frmSpeaker form:

```
Private Sub mnuAbout_Click()

    Dim Title
    Dim Msg
    Dim CR

    CR = Chr(13) + Chr(10)

    ' The title of the About message box.
    Title = "About the Speaker Program"
```

```
' Prepare the message of the About message box.
Msg = "This program was written with Visual "
Msg = Msg + "Basic for Windows, using the "
Msg = Msg + "TegoSoft Speaker OCX control. "
Msg = Msg + CR + CR
Msg = Msg + "The TegoSoft Speaker OCX control "
Msg = Msg + "is part of the TegoSoft OCX Control "
Msg = Msg + "Kit - a collection of various OCX controls. "
Msg = Msg + CR + CR
Msg = Msg + "For more information about the "
Msg = Msg + "TegoSoft OCX Control Kit, contact TegoSoft "
Msg = Msg + "at:"
Msg = Msg + CR + CR
Msg = Msg + "TegoSoft Inc." + CR
Msg = Msg + "P.O. Box 389" + CR
Msg = Msg + "Bellmore, NY 11710"
Msg = Msg + CR + CR
Msg = Msg + "Phone: (516)783-4824"

' Display the About message box.
MsgBox Msg, vbInformation, Title

End Sub
```

The code in this procedure displays a message box with information on the speaker OLE control.

The Code in the *Click* Event of the Info Menu Item

You'll now attach code to the Click event of the File menu's Info item. This code extracts various information about the WAV file and displays the information with a message box.

☐ Type the following code in the mnuInfo_Click() procedure of the frmSpeaker form:

```
Private Sub mnuInfo_Click()

Dim Title
Dim Msg
Dim CRLF

CRLF = Chr(13) + Chr(10)

' The title of the Info message box.
Title = "WAV File Information"

' Prepare the message for the Info message box.
Msg = "File Name: " + TegoSpeaker1.GetWavFilename
Msg = Msg + CRLF
Msg = _
    Msg + _
    "File Length: " + _
    Str(TegoSpeaker1.GetLength) + _
    " samples."
```

19

```
Msg = Msg + CRLF
Msg = _
    Msg + _
    "Sampling Rate: " + _
    Str(TegoSpeaker1.GetSamplingRate) + _
    " Hz."

Msg = Msg + CRLF
Msg = Msg + "Number of Bits Per Sample: " + Str(TegoSpeaker1.GetNumBits)
Msg = Msg + CRLF
Msg = _
    Msg + _
    "Number of Channels: " + _
    Str(TegoSpeaker1.GetNumChannels)

' Display the Info message box.
MsgBox Msg, vbInformation, Title

End Sub
```

The code in this procedure sets the value of the CRLF variable to the carriage return plus line feed characters:

```
CRLF = Chr(13) + Chr(10)
```

The string displayed with the message box has several CRLF characters in it. So when the string is displayed, every CRLF causes the characters that follow it in the string to be displayed on a new line.

The Title variable is set as follows:

```
' The title of the Info message box.
Title = "WAV File Information"
```

The Title variable is later used as the Title parameter of the MsgBox statement.

The Msg string that will be displayed with the message box is then prepared:

```
' Prepare the message for the Info message box.
Msg = "File Name: " + TegoSpeaker1.GetWavFilename
Msg = Msg + CRLF
```

In the preceding statements Msg is assigned the name of the loaded WAV file. Note that the GetWavFilename method returns the name of the loaded WAV file.

The Msg variable is then assigned a string that describes the length of the WAV file:

```
Msg = _
    Msg + _
    "File Length: " + _
    Str(TegoSpeaker1.GetLength) + _
    " samples."
```

In the preceding statement the GetLength method is used to extract the length of the WAV file in units of samples.

Then the sampling rate is extracted with the `GetSamplingRate` method:

```
Msg = Msg + CRLF
Msg = _
    Msg + _
    "Sampling Rate: " + _
    Str(TegoSpeaker1.GetSamplingRate) + _
    " Hz."
```

The number of bits per sample is extracted with the `GetNumBits` method:

```
Msg = Msg + CRLF
Msg = Msg + "Number of Bits Per Sample: " + Str(TegoSpeaker1.GetNumBits)
```

The number of bits per sample is 8 for an 8-bit recording and 16 for a 16-bit recording. As stated previously, you can play only 8-bit recordings with the PC speaker.

The number of channels is extracted with these statements:

```
Msg = Msg + CRLF
Msg = _
    Msg + _
    "Number of Channels: " + _
    Str(TegoSpeaker1.GetNumChannels)
```

The number of channels is 1 for a mono WAV file and 2 for a stereo WAV file. As stated previously, you can play only mono recordings with the PC speaker.

Finally, the `Msg` string you prepared is displayed with the `MsgBox` statement:

```
' Display the Info message box.
MsgBox Msg, vbInformation, Title
```

The Code in the *Done* Event of the Speaker Control

You'll now attach code to the `Done` event of the speaker control.

☐ Type the following code in the `TegoSpeaker1_Done()` procedure of the frmSpeaker form:

```
Private Sub TegoSpeaker1_Done()

If TegoSpeaker1.GetPosition = TegoSpeaker1.GetLength Then

    TegoSpeaker1.Seek 0

End If

End Sub
```

The code in this procedure uses an `If` statement to examine whether the current position of the WAV file is equal to the length of the WAV file. If so, the code under the `If` statement is executed.

The code under the `If` statement places the current position of the WAV file at the beginning of the WAV file:

```
TegoSpeaker1.Seek 0
```

The `Done` event occurs whenever the speaker control finishes executing a certain operation. The `If` statement makes sure the `Done` event occurs because the WAV file was played in its entirety. You place the current position of the WAV file at the beginning because you want to rewind it whenever the entire WAV file is played. Then the WAV file is ready for the next time it's played.

The Code in the *Timer* Event of the Timer

When you play WAV files in a multitasking mode, you can perform animation such as moving text and graphics while the playback is in progress. The code in the `Timer1_Timer()` procedure illustrates this capability. While playback is in progress in a multitasking mode, the code in the `Timer1_Timer()` procedure is executed, which updates the Position scroll bar and the Position label. So during the playback, you can see the current position of the WAV file. However, rather than update the Position label and Position scroll bar, as in the Speaker program, you can write code that changes pictures.

☐ Type the following code in the `Timer1_Timer()` procedure of the frmSpeaker form:

```
Private Sub Timer1_Timer()

Dim Length
Dim Position

Length = TegoSpeaker1.GetLength
Position = TegoSpeaker1.GetPosition

If chkDisplayPosition.Value = 1 And Length > 0 Then
        hsbPosition.Value = (Position / Length) * 100

    lblPosition.Caption = _
        "Sample: " + Str(Position) + _
        "   Time: " + _
        Str(Int(Position * 1000 / TegoSpeaker1.GetSamplingRate))

End If

End Sub
```

The code in this procedure sets the value of the `Length` variable to the length of the WAV file:

```
Length = TegoSpeaker1.GetLength
```

And the current position of the WAV file is assigned to the `Position` variable:

```
Position = TegoSpeaker1.GetPosition
```

If the Display Position check box is checked and `Length` is greater than 0, the code under the `If` statement is executed. In other words, the code is executed if you request it by checking the check box and if the Length property is greater than 0, which indicates that a WAV file is loaded.

Here is the code of the `If` block:

```
If chkDisplayPosition.Value = 1 And Length > 0 Then

    hsbPosition.Value = (Position / Length) * 100

    lblPosition.Caption = _
        "Sample: " + Str(Position) + _
        "  Time: " + _
        Str(Int(Position * 1000 / TegoSpeaker1.GetSamplingRate))

End If
```

The Value property of the Position scroll bar is updated with the current position of the WAV file as follows:

```
hsbPosition.Value = (Position / Length) * 100
```

The Position scroll bar is divided into 100 units (as you set it during design time, Min = 0 and Max = 100).

So this product:

```
(Position/Length) * (100)
```

represents the current position of the WAV file in percents.

The Position label is then updated as follows:

```
        lblPosition.Caption = _
            "Sample: " + Str(Position) + _
            "  Time: " + _
            Str(Int(Position * 1000 / TegoSpeaker1.GetSamplingRate))
```

The currently played sample is displayed with the value of the `Position` variable, and the current position in milliseconds is displayed with this formula:

```
Current position in milliseconds = Position*1000/Sampling Rate
```

Note: Windows comes with a program called Sound Recorder that lets you load a WAV file and then increase its volume.

When you play WAV files through the PC speaker, you may have to first increase the volume of the WAV file because the PC speaker doesn't have electronic amplifier circuitry. As stated, you can use the Windows Sound Recorder program to increase the volume of your WAV files, or you can use the wave OLE control, which lets you write programs that enable you to increase or decrease the volume of your WAV files. See the first question in the Q&A section at the end of this chapter to learn more about the wave OLE control.

Summary

In this chapter you have learned how to play WAV files through both the sound card and the PC speaker. You have also learned how to determine whether the PC has a sound card installed in it, so you can direct the sound to the sound card or the PC speaker. When you play WAV files through the PC speaker, you don't need any additional hardware or drivers.

Q&A

Q **I want to perform sound tricks such as producing an echo, increasing and decreasing the volume and playback speed, performing Cut, Copy, and Paste with sound sections, and so on. Can it be done?**

A You can perform practically any sound trick with the TegoSoft wave OLE control (part of the TegoSoft OLE Control Kit). For example, you can record and then save your recording as a new WAV file, you can record your own voice and then change the WAV file so it will sound like a different person, you can design a professional Wave Editor program, and so on. Because the wave OLE control lets you read and write each and every sample of the WAV files, you can add your own code, such as Fourier transform code, filtering, and sound processing (digital signal processing), and modify the WAV files in the most sophisticated way you can think of.

Using the wave OLE control is very similar to using the multimedia control, so it can enhance the sound capabilities of your Visual Basic programs.

Q **When will I want to use the PC speaker for playing WAV files?**

A You'll want to use the PC speaker when your program detects that your user doesn't have a sound card. However, the PC speaker is useful in many situations where a sound card is already installed. For example, you can write a program that sends audio messages to the PC speaker while the sound card is playing, so you're using the PC speaker as a "second" sound card. Naturally, the sound quality of the PC speaker isn't as good as the sound card's, but in many situations the PC speaker's sound quality is acceptable.

Quiz

1. What code should you write to disable the Play button of the multimedia control when the WAV file is not opened successfully?

2. There are two properties that must be set before issuing the `Play` command to the multimedia control. What are they?

3. To play WAV files through the PC speaker, what do you need to do?
   a. Install drivers
   b. Install an external speaker
   c. None of the above

4. It is possible to play WAV files through the PC speaker and to display animation during the playback.
   a. True
   b. False

Exercise

Enhance the MyWAV program so that an animation show is displayed during the playback.

Quiz Answers

1. You don't have to write any code. The multimedia control automatically disables and enables its own buttons.

2. The DeviceType property and the FileName property.

3. c (To play through the PC speaker, you don't need any drivers. Every PC is equipped with a small speaker, so you don't need to install a speaker.)

4. a

Exercise Answer

You can add an animation show to the MyWAV program as follows:

☐ Place an image control in the form.

☐ Set the Name property of the image control to imgAnimation.

☐ Modify the `Tegomm1_StatusUpdate()` procedure so that it looks like this:

```
Private Sub Tegomm1_StatusUpdate()

Static FrameNumber

Dim Path

Path = App.Path
If Right(Path, 1) <> "\" Then
    Path = Path + "\"
End If

If Tegomm1.Mode = 526 Then
    lblPosition.Caption = Str(Tegomm1.Position)
    vsbNothing.Value = Int(Rnd * 100)

    Select Case FrameNumber
    Case 0
    imgAnimation.Picture = LoadPicture(Path + "Dance1.BMP")
    Case 1
    imgAnimation.Picture = LoadPicture(Path + "Dance2.BMP")
    Case 2
    imgAnimation.Picture = LoadPicture(Path + "Dance3.BMP")
    Case 3
    imgAnimation.Picture = LoadPicture(Path + "Dance4.BMP")
    Case 4
    imgAnimation.Picture = LoadPicture(Path + "Dance5.BMP")

    End Select
    FrameNumber = FrameNumber + 1
    If FrameNumber >= 5 Then
        FrameNumber = 0
    End If

End If

End Sub
```

The code in this procedure declares a static variable:

```
Static FrameNumber
```

and a local variable:

```
Dim Path
```

The Path variable is then updated with the name of the directory from which the program is executed:

```
Path = App.Path
If Right(Path, 1) <> "\" Then
    Path = Path + "\"
End If
```

An `If` statement is then executed to see whether playback is in progress:

```
If Tegomm1.Mode = 526 Then
    ................................
    ... Yes, playback is in progress.
    ................................
End If
```

The code in the `If` statement updates the lblPosition label:

```
lblPosition.Caption = Str(Tegomm1.Position)
```

and the Value property of the scroll bar is assigned a random number:

```
vsbNothing.Value = Int(Rnd * 100)
```

An animation code is then executed. A `Select Case` is executed to examine the value of the `FrameNumber` variable. When you execute the `Tegomm1_StatusUpdate()` procedure for the first time, `FrameNumber` is equal to 0. Therefore, the first `Case` is satisfied:

```
Case 0
imgAnimation.Picture = LoadPicture(Path + "Dance1.BMP")
```

The preceding code sets the Picture property of the imgAnimation image control to the Dance1.BMP pictures that should be in the same directory from which the program is executed.

The statement after the `Select Case` block then increases the value of `FrameNumber`:

```
FrameNumber = FrameNumber + 1
If FrameNumber >= 5 Then
    FrameNumber = 0
End If
```

On the next execution of `Tegomm1_StatusUpdate()`, `FrameNumber` is equal to 1, so the code under the `Case 1` statement is executed:

```
Case 1
imgAnimation.Picture = LoadPicture(Path + "Dance2.BMP")
```

So now the Dance2.BMP picture is executed.

Then `FrameNumber` is increased by 1 again. This process repeats itself, which means that the following sequence of pictures are displayed:

```
Dance1.BMP
Dance2.BMP
Dance3.BMP
Dance4.BMP
Dance5.BMP
Dance1.BMP
Dance2.BMP
....
....
....
```

19

Figure 19.23 shows the window of the enhanced version of the MyWAV program.

Figure 19.23.

The MyWAV program with the animation show in it.

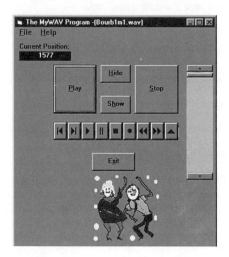

Sprite Animation, WinG, and 3D Virtual Reality

In this chapter you'll learn how to create professional, powerful animation with Visual Basic using a new technology called WinG (pronounced *Win-Gee*). The animation that you'll create uses the so-called *sprite animation*, another concept this chapter introduces.

The chapter concludes with a discussion of 3D virtual-reality applications.

What Is WinG?

Windows is an operating system that uses a graphics interface. Unlike the old DOS version, in Windows you use graphics objects such as command buttons, scroll bars, and check boxes. As you know, Windows can also display pictures such as BMP files.

However, Windows was not designed to perform animation. If you try to move graphics objects, such as the image and picture controls, you'll soon realize that a lot of flickering occurs. In fact, some of the best games for the PC are designed for DOS, not for Windows. Why? In a sophisticated PC game, there is typically a lot of animation (moving graphics objects). So until lately, PC game designers stayed away from Windows because it produced terrible results when performing animation.

The *G* in WinG stands for *games* or *graphics*. WinG is a new technology that enhances the capabilities of Windows to process graphics so you can create great animation. In this chapter you'll learn how to use Visual Basic to do this.

In the rest of this chapter you'll learn about sprites and animation and how to use the sprite control. The sprite control uses WinG technology.

What Is the Sprite Control?

The sprite control is similar to the standard picture and image controls of Visual Basic—it enables you to display a picture. However, the sprite control is much more powerful than these controls because of the following two features:

- The sprite control enables you to move, enlarge, shrink, and animate pictures quickly and efficiently.

- The sprite control has a transparency feature so you can display a picture that has transparent sections. The background displayed behind the transparent sections of the picture won't be erased.

Take a look at the following examples that illustrate the transparency feature of the sprite control:

Suppose you have two pictures, one of a man (Figure 20.1) and one of a room (Figure 20.2).

Figure 20.1.
A picture of a man.

Figure 20.2.
A picture of a room.

Suppose you want to write a program that uses these two pictures. Your program will display the picture of the man over the picture of the room. The room will serve as the background for the man. Your program can then move the picture of the man to create the illusion that the man is moving in the room. If you try to design this program with a standard picture or image control, you will have a problem: The picture control and the image control don't have a transparency feature. So when you place the picture of the man over the picture of the room, parts of the man picture that should be transparent will hide the background, as shown in Figure 20.3.

Figure 20.3.
Displaying a picture of a man over a picture of a room (using a picture or an image control).

20

In Figure 20.3, the man picture doesn't have any transparent sections, so it completely erases part of the background picture of the room. However, if you use two sprite controls rather than two picture controls, the resultant picture would look like the one shown in Figure 20.4.

Figure 20.4.

Displaying a picture of a man over a picture of a room (using sprite controls).

As shown in Figure 20.4, the problem is solved! Whatever is under the transparent parts of the man picture, or *sprite*, isn't erased. Your program can now move the man sprite in the room to effectively give the illusion of a moving man in a room.

So the sprite control lets you display pictures, as the standard picture and image controls do, but the sprite control has a transparency feature. It also enables you to move, enlarge, shrink, and animate pictures quickly and efficiently. This efficiency and speed is accomplished by using WinG technology.

> **Note:** The sprite OLE control is part of the TegoSoft OLE Control Kit—a collection of various powerful and sophisticated OLE controls. You can purchase the TegoSoft OLE Control Kit directly from TegoSoft, Inc. (See disk offer at the end of this book.)
>
> Even if you do not own the sprite OLE control, it is highly recommended that you read the material in this chapter. This way you'll gain an understanding of what it takes to develop some of the most sophisticated animation and 3D virtual reality programs for Windows.

The Sprite Program

In the following sections you'll write a program called Sprite.EXE that illustrates how to use the sprite OLE control. But before you start writing the Sprite program, let's review its specifications.

☐ When you execute the Sprite program, the window shown in Figure 20.5 appears.

The main window of the Sprite program appears, as shown in Figure 20.5, and the Sprite program displays an animation show with background music.

Figure 20.5.
The main window of the Sprite program.

The animation show of the Sprite program shows a man moving in a room. As you can see, the man moves counterclockwise around the room. The program shows three walls of the room: One wall has a window, one wall has a door, and one wall has a picture hanging on it.

Figures 20.6 through 20.9 show four snapshots of the animation show.

Note that during the animation, as the man gets closer to the screen, he becomes larger, as he gets farther away from the screen, he becomes smaller. The man is walking around the room in an endless loop. No matter where he is in the room, he never hides part of the background room. As soon as he moves to a new spot, the area of the room previously hidden by the man's picture become visible again.

20

Figure 20.6.
Snapshot 1 of the animation show.

Figure 20.7.
Snapshot 2 of the animation show.

Figure 20.8.
Snapshot 3 of the animation show.

Figure 20.9.
Snapshot 4 of the animation show.

Depending on the direction the man is moving, a different view of him is displayed. In Figure 20.5, the man is moving toward you so his front is displayed. In Figure 20.6, the man is moving left to right so you see his right profile. In Figure 20.7, the man is moving away from you so his back is displayed. In Figure 20.8, the man is moving right to left so you see his left profile. Notice that the man is smaller than he is in Figure 20.5 because he's farther away.

The animation show in the Sprite program uses two sprite controls. One sprite control is used for the background picture of the room and the other is used for the picture of the man. The Sprite program performs the animation show by simply moving the man sprite over the room sprite.

The Sprite program has a File menu and a Help menu. (See Figure 20.10.) When you select Exit from the File menu, the program is terminated. When you select About… from the Help menu, the About message box shown in Figure 20.11 is displayed.

Figure 20.10.
The Help menu of the Sprite program.

Figure 20.11.

The About message box of the Sprite program.

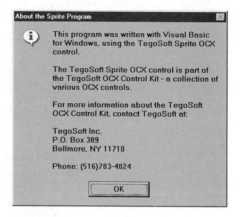

About the Sprite Program

This program was written with Visual Basic for Windows, using the TegoSoft Sprite OCX control.

The TegoSoft Sprite OCX control is part of the TegoSoft OCX Control Kit - a collection of various OCX controls.

For more information about the TegoSoft OCX Control Kit, contact TegoSoft at:

TegoSoft Inc.
P.O. Box 389
Bellmore, NY 11710

Phone: (516)783-4824

OK

☐ Terminate the Sprite program by selecting Exit from the File menu.

Now that you know what the Sprite program is supposed to do, start writing this program.

Using Bitmap Files for the Sprites

Before you start the visual implementation of the Sprite program, you need to prepare several bitmap files (BMP files) that will be used by the program. These bitmap files will serve as the pictures for the program's sprites. To create BMP files for your sprites, you can use any painting program that can create 256-color, 8-bit BMP files (for example, Paintbrush, Paint). The sprite control will not accept any other formats of BMP files.

Note: When you create a BMP file used for a sprite control, you must save the BMP file as a 256-color, 8-bit BMP file.

You can use the Paintbrush program (or the Paint program) shipped with Windows to create 256-color, 8-bit BMP files. Save the file using the following steps:

☐ Start Paintbrush (or Paint), and then select Save As from the File menu of Paintbrush (or Paint).

Paintbrush (or Paint) will display the Save As dialog box.

☐ Set the Save File As Type list box of the Save As dialog box to 256 Color bitmap (*.BMP).

☐ Click the OK button of the Save As dialog box.

Paintbrush (or Paint) will save your BMP file as a 256-color, 8-bit BMP file. Note that in Windows 3.1, if you select Save from the File menu (instead of Save As), Paintbrush will save the BMP file as a 16-color bitmap, so use the Save As menu item when you want to save a BMP file to be used for a sprite.

In the following sections you'll learn how to prepare the BMP files that are needed by the Sprite program. These sample BMP files are supplied with the Sprite.OCX control (see disk offer at the end of this book). Even if you do not own the Sprite.OCX control, it is recommended that you keep reading the material. This way, you'll gain an understanding of what it takes to create sprite BMP files with a drawing program such as Paintbrush or Paint.

The Sprite program uses nine BMP files: BGND.BMP, MAN0.BMP, MAN1.BMP, MAN2.BMP, MAN3.BMP, MMAN0.BMP, MMAN1.BMP, MMAN2.BMP, and MMAN3.BMP.

The BGND.BMP file is used as the picture for the background sprite (a picture of a room). To see the BGND.BMP picture, follow these steps:

☐ Start the Paintbrush (or Paint) program of Windows (or any other drawing program that can load BMP files).

☐ Select Open from the File menu of Paintbrush and then select the file BGND.BMP.

   Paintbrush responds by opening the BGND.BMP file.

Because BGND.BMP will serve as the background picture, it doesn't have any transparent sections. That is, you'll never place the BGND.BMP picture over another picture.

Now examine the BMP files used for the man sprite. Unlike the picture used for the background, the picture of the man sprite should have transparent sections. To create a sprite that has transparent sections, you need to use two BMP files. One BMP file specifies the picture of the sprite, and the other BMP file (called the *mask* BMP file) specifies which parts of the picture are transparent. The two bitmap files of the man picture, MAN0.BMP and MMAN0.BMP, illustrate how this transparency feature works. MAN0.BMP contains the picture of the sprite, and MMAN0.BMP (the mask BMP file) specifies which sections of the picture are transparent. To see the MAN0.BMP and MMAN0.BMP pictures, follow these steps:

☐ Select Open from the File menu of Paintbrush and then select the file MAN0.BMP.

   Paintbrush responds by opening the MAN0.BMP file. (See Figure 20.12.)

Figure 20.12.
The MAN0.BMP file.

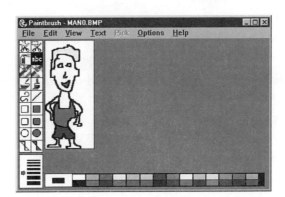

As you can see, the MAN0.BMP bitmap is a regular, small picture. Now take a look at the mask bitmap of the MAN0.BMP picture:

☐ Select Open from the File menu of Paintbrush and then select the file MMAN0.BMP.

Paintbrush responds by opening the MMAN0.BMP file. (See Figure 20.13.)

Figure 20.13.
*The MMAN0.BMP file
(the mask bitmap of the
MAN0.BMP bitmap).*

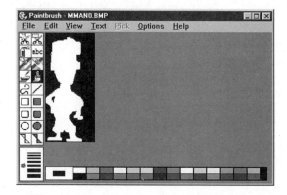

As you can see, the MMAN0.BMP picture has the same size and shape as MAN0.BMP, but the MMAN0.BMP picture has only two colors: black and white. The black areas represent the transparent sections of the picture, and the white areas represent the opaque sections.

When you create two BMP files for a sprite that has transparent sections, follow these steps:

☐ Use any painting program that can create 256-color, 8-bit BMP files.

☐ Before drawing the picture of the sprite, set the width and height of the BMP file so your picture will fit inside it. For example, the width of MAN0.BMP is 90 pixels and the height is 197 pixels. (In Paintbrush you set the height and width of the BMP file by selecting Image Attributes from the Options menu, and in Paint you set the height and width of the BMP file by selecting Attributes from the Image menu.)

☐ Draw the picture.

☐ Select Save As from the File menu and save the BMP file as a 256-color, 8-bit BMP file. Name the BMP file with any name you wish (for example, MyPic.BMP), but don't use more than seven letters for the filename.

Next you have to create the mask BMP file. At first glance, it looks as if generating the mask file is a lot of work, but it's actually very easy and quick.

☐ Select Save As from the File menu again, but this time name the BMP file M*xxxx*.BMP (where *xxxx* is the name of the first BMP file you created). For example, if the name of

the first BMP file is MyPic.BMP, then the name of the mask BMP file should be MMyPic.BMP.

You'll now modify the BMP file to make its transparent sections black and its opaque sections white, as shown in Figure 20.13.

☐ Use the tools of your painting program to fill all the areas of the picture that you want to be transparent with a color not used in the picture. For example, in the MAN0.BMP picture, gray is not used. So click the gray color from the color palette, then click the Fill tool (in the left column, fourth row from the top of the Paintbrush toolbox), and finally click in an area of the MMAN0.BMP picture that you want to be transparent. Your MMAN0.BMP picture should now look like the one shown in Figure 20.14.

Figure 20.14.

Filling a transparent area with gray.

☐ The lower-left section of the picture isn't filled with gray yet, so fill it in, too. Now the MMAN0.BMP picture should look like the one shown in Figure 20.15.

Figure 20.15.

Filling all the transparent areas with gray.

You can now replace all the colors of the picture with white. Here is how you replace the red areas of the picture with white:

☐ Right-click white from the color palette, which makes white the background color. So the red color you erase will be replaced with white.

☐ Click red from the colors palette because you are now going to replace it.

☐ Select the erase color tool (in the left column, third row from the top in the Paintbrush toolbox).

☐ Erase all the red from the picture by dragging the mouse over the picture.

As you drag the mouse, each red area under the mouse cursor is replaced by white. When you drag the mouse over an area that isn't red, that section does not change.

After erasing the entire picture with the erase color tool, the MMAN0.BMP picture looks like the one shown in Figure 20.16.

You can make the area to be color-erased larger by selecting the thickness from the scale on the lower-left area of the Paintbrush window. With just a few drags of your mouse, you can erase all the red from the entire picture. The man's shirt was red in the MAN0.BMP picture, but now it's white because you replaced the red area of the picture with white.

Figure 20.16.

The MMAN0.BMP picture after you've erased the red areas.

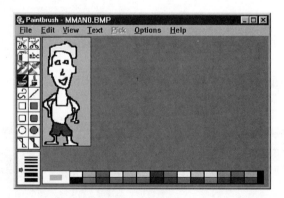

☐ Click blue from the color palette to replace the blue area of the MMAN0.BMP picture and drag the mouse over the entire MMAN0.BMP picture.

As shown in Figure 20.17, now the picture has no red or blue in it.

☐ Click yellow in the color palette and erase the yellow area from the picture. (See Figure 20.18.)

Figure 20.17.
The MMAN0.BMP picture after you've erased the red and blue areas.

Figure 20.18.
The MMAN0.BMP picture after you've erased the red, blue, and yellow areas.

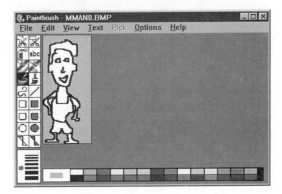

☐ Click black in the color palette and erase the black areas from the picture. (See Figure 20.19.)

Figure 20.19.
The MMAN0.BMP picture after you've erased the red, blue, yellow, and black areas.

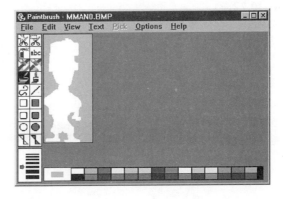

☐ Now replace gray with black. Click black in the color palette, select the fill tool, and fill all the areas currently painted gray with black. (See Figure 20.20.)

Figure 20.20.
The final MMAN0.BMP mask picture.

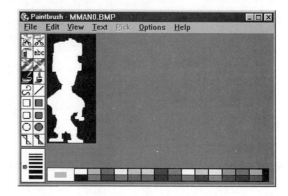

☐ Save the bitmap as a 256-color, 8-bit BMP file.

Figures 20.21 and 20.22 show the MAN1.BMP picture and its mask file, MMAN1.BMP.

Figure 20.21.
The MAN1.BMP picture.

Figure 20.22.
The MMAN1.BMP mask file for MAN1.BMP.

Figures 20.23 and 20.24 show the MAN2.BMP picture and its mask file, MMAN2.BMP.

Figure 20.23.
The MAN2.BMP picture.

Figure 20.24.
*The MMAN2.BMP mask
file for MAN2.BMP.*

Figures 20.25 and 20.26 show the MAN3.BMP picture and its mask file, MMAN3.BMP.

Figure 20.25.
The MAN3.BMP picture.

Figure 20.26.
*The MMAN3.BMP mask
file for MAN3.BMP.*

Playing a WAV File During
the Sprite Program

In addition to the BMP files needed for the sprites, the Sprite program also needs a WAV file
to play background music while the animation show is in progress.

☐ Make sure that the directory from which the Sprite program is executed contains the
nine BMP files used during the animation.

☐ Copy any WAV file that contains music into the directory from which the Sprite program is executed.

The Visual Implementation of the Sprite Program

You'll now visually implement the Sprite program.

Note: Instead of following a properties table, in this chapter you'll be instructed to design the program by following a set of step-by-step instructions. This will help you understand the sprite control better.

☐ Start a new project.

☐ Save the form of the project as C:\VB4PRG\CH20\SPRITE.FRM and save the project file as C:\VB4PRG\CH20\SPRITE.VBP.

☐ Add the TegoSoft multimedia OLE control to the project. Select Custom Controls from the Tools menu, click the Browse button of the Custom Controls dialog box, then select the TegoSoft multimedia control from the C:\WINDOWS\SYSTEM directory. (The 16-bit filename is TegoMM16.OCX and the 32-bit filename is TegoMM32.OCX.) The OCX file of the TegoSoft multimedia control must reside in your Windows system directory.

☐ Repeat the previous step to add the TegoSoft Sprite OLE control to the project. (The 16-bit filename is TegSpr16.OCX and the 32-bit filename is TegSpr32.OCX.)

☐ Set the properties of the SPRITE.FRM form as follows:

Property	Setting
Name	frmSprite
Caption	The Sprite Program
ScaleMode	3-Pixel

Note: When you're designing a form with sprites, it is convenient to set the ScaleMode property of the form to Pixel because the methods and properties of the sprite control use pixel units for specifying width, height, and location.

☐ Place a TegoSoft sprite OLE control in the form. Its icon in Visual Basic's toolbox window is shown in Figure 20.27.

Your form should now look like the one shown in Figure 20.28.

Figure 20.27.
The icon of the TegoSoft sprite OLE control.

Figure 20.28.
The frmSprite form with a blank sprite control in it.

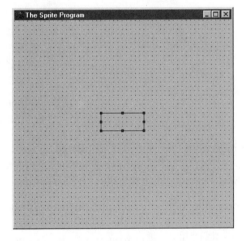

The sprite you placed in the form will serve as the background sprite (that is, it will contain the picture of the room).

Note: When you design a form that contains sprite controls, the first sprite you have to place in the form is the background sprite.

☐ Set the properties of the blank sprite control as follows:

Property	Setting
Name	sprBack
AutoSize	True
Left	0
Top	0
Transparent	False
SpriteFileName	BGND.BMP

Your frmSprite form should now look like the one shown in Figure 20.29.

Figure 20.29.

The frmSprite form after you set the properties of the sprBack sprite control.

In the preceding step you were instructed to set the SpriteFileName property of the sprBack sprite to BGND.BMP. The SpriteFileName property specifies the filename of the sprite's BMP file. The picture of this BMP file will be displayed in the sprite.

In the preceding step you were also instructed to set the AutoSize property of the sprBack sprite control to True. As a result, the sprBack sprite control automatically sized itself to fit the exact size of the BMP file of the sprite. In most cases, the AutoSize property of the background sprite should be set to True.

In the preceding step you were also instructed to set the Transparent property of the sprBack sprite control to False. This means that the sprBack sprite will not have any transparent sections since it will serve as the background sprite.

The next thing you have to do is size the form so that it will be the same size as the sprBack sprite. As shown in Figure 20.29, the form isn't the same size as the sprBack sprite control.

☐ Drag the edges of the form so it will enclose the picture of the background. The code you'll enter assumes that the upper-left corner of the sprBack sprite control is at the upper-left corner of the form. Therefore, after dragging and sizing the form, make sure that the Left and Top properties of the sprBack are set to 0.

Your frmSprite form should now look like the one shown in Figure 20.30.

Figure 20.30.

The frmSprite form after you've resized it.

Now that the background of the animation show is finished, add the star of the show, the man, to the form:

☐ Place another sprite control in the form and set the properties of this sprite control as follows:

Property	Setting
Name	sprMan
Left	144
Top	136
SpriteHeight	73
SpriteWidth	49
Transparent	True
SpriteFileName	MAN0.BMP

Your frmSprite form should now look like the one shown in Figure 20.31.

Figure 20.31.
The frmSprite form after you add the sprMan sprite.

In the preceding step, you were instructed to set the SpriteFileName property of the sprMan sprite to MAN0.BMP. The SpriteFileName property of the sprite control specifies the filename of the sprite's BMP file. MAN0.BMP has a mask bitmap called MMAN0.BMP, but you don't have to specify the mask BMP filename because the sprite control knows that it's M*xxxx*.BMP (where *xxxx* is the sprite's filename). For example, if you set the SpriteFileName to C:\TRY\MyPic.BMP, then the sprite control knows that the filename of the mask bitmap is C:\TRY\MMyPic.BMP.

In the preceding step you set the Transparent property of the sprMan control to True because the sprMan sprite has transparent sections. Indeed, as shown in Figure 20.31, the sprMan sprite has transparent sections (for example, the area between the man's legs). The sprite control knows which sections of the picture should be transparent or opaque, based on the mask BMP file of the MAN0.BMP file.

Another control you have to add to the form before you can start writing the code of the animation show is the Timer control. As you'll see later, you will attach the code that performs the animation show to the timer control.

☐ Add a timer control to the form and set its Name property to Timer1 and its Interval property to 50.

Your frmSprite form should now look as shown in Figure 20.32.

As you know, the timer control is invisible at runtime, so it really doesn't matter where you place it.

☐ Save your work by selecting Save Project from the File menu.

Figure 20.32.
*The frmSprite form after
you add the Timer control.*

Note: There is still one more control you have to add to the frmSprite form: the multimedia control. However, you are not instructed to add the multimedia control to the form now because you are concentrating on the sprite animation aspect of the program. Once the animation aspect of the program is done, you'll use the multimedia control to add background music to the show.

The Sprite Control in Design Time Versus Runtime

If you try to execute the Sprite program now, you won't see any pictures in the form—instead, you will see a blank form. Why? You need to write some code to display a sprite control in runtime mode. This code is necessary because the sprite control is not a regular picture control. The sprite control uses WinG technology, which requires code to display the picture of the sprite.

The only purpose of setting the properties of the sprites in design time is to set the initial sizes and positions of the sprite controls and to see how the background and foreground sprites look. However, it is important to understand that the actual setting of the SpriteFileName property during design time has no effect in runtime. In fact, the SpriteFileName property isn't used at runtime.

Experimenting with a sprite control during design time can also help you determine how it should change its position and size during the animation show. To see how useful it can be to experiment with a sprite control during design time, try the following experiment:

20

As shown in Figure 20.32, the current size and position of the sprMan sprite control makes the man look as if he is standing in the back of the room. Suppose you want to make the man look as if he is moving away from the back wall toward you. To create this illusion, all you have to do is stretch the bottom edge of the sprMan sprite downward. The more you stretch the bottom edge of the sprMan sprite downward, the closer the man will look to you.

☐ Stretch the bottom edge of the sprMan sprite downward by dragging the mouse.

As you can see, the man seems to get closer as you stretch the bottom edge of the sprMan downward. (See Figures 20.33 and 20.34.)

Figure 20.33.
Stretching the bottom edge of the sprMan downward.

Figure 20.34.
Stretching the bottom edge of the sprMan even farther.

To create the illusion that the man is getting closer and closer, you need to stretch the sprite's width as well as its height. That is, as the man gets closer he should seem taller as well as wider. The code you'll write later to make the man move toward you will stretch both the height and width of the sprMan sprite.

By moving the sprMan sprite to various positions in the form, you can create various illusions. For example, to make the man look as if he is standing on the edge of the window, you can move the sprMan sprite to the position shown in Figure 20.35.

Figure 20.35.

Making the man stand on the edge of the window.

To restore the original size and position of the sprMan sprite, do the following:

☐ Set the properties of the sprMan sprite control as follows:

Property	Setting
Left	144
Top	136
SpriteHeight	73
SpriteWidth	49

☐ Make sure your frmSprite form now looks like the one in Figure 20.31. The code that performs the animation show assumes that the initial position and size of the sprMan sprite control are as shown in Figure 20.31.

Again, the only purpose of setting the properties of the sprites in design time is to set the initial sizes and positions of the sprite controls, to see how the background and foreground sprites look, and to experiment by changing the sizes and positions of the sprite controls.

The actual setting of the SpriteFileName property during design time has no effect in runtime. As you'll soon see, the SpriteFileName property is not used at runtime.

20

Entering the Code of the Sprite Program

When you write the code that displays the sprite controls at runtime, you use WinG technology. WinG technology enhances the standard graphics capabilities of Windows and makes your graphics operations perform better. You don't draw directly to the screen with WinG technology. Rather, you first draw into memory (into WinG) and then transfer the contents of WinG into the screen. The transfer of the WinG contents into the screen is very efficient and very fast. This transfer is also called "slamming"—that is, you are slamming the contents of WinG into the screen.

In the following sections you'll write code that uses WinG technology. First, you will write code that draws the sprites in WinG, then you'll slam WinG into the screen.

The Code in the General Declarations Section

☐ Type the following code in the general declarations section of the frmSprite form:

```
' All variables must be declared.
Option Explicit

' Declare handles for the show's sprites.
Dim gBack As Long
Dim gMan0 As Long
Dim gMan1 As Long
Dim gMan2 As Long
Dim gMan3 As Long
```

☐ Save your work by selecting Save Project from the File menu.

The code in this procedure declares five general variables of type Long: gBack, gMan0, gMan1, gMan2, and gMan3. Because these variables are declared in the general declarations section of the form, you'll be able to access these variables from any procedure of the form.

The Code in the *Form_Load()* Procedure

The Form_Load() procedure of the form is executed when you start the program. Therefore, it's a good place to write various initialization code.

☐ Type the following code in the Form_Load() procedure of the frmSprite form:

```
Private Sub Form_Load()

Dim Path

' Get the name of the directory where the
' program resides.
Path = App.Path
If Right(Path, 1) <> "\" Then
    Path = Path + "\"
End If
```

```
' Initialize all the sprite controls.
sprBack.InitializeSprite Me.hWnd
sprMan.InitializeSprite Me.hWnd

' Open all the sprites that will be used in our show.
gMan0 = sprBack.OpenSprite(Path + "MAN0.bmp")
gMan1 = sprBack.OpenSprite(Path + "MAN1.bmp")
gMan2 = sprBack.OpenSprite(Path + "MAN2.bmp")
gMan3 = sprBack.OpenSprite(Path + "MAN3.bmp")
gBack = sprBack.OpenSprite(Path + "BGND.bmp")
```

End Sub

☐ Save your work by selecting Save Project from the File menu.

The first statement you typed in the `Form_Load()` procedure declares a local variable called `Path`:

```
Dim Path
```

These are the next two statements:

```
Path = App.Path
If Right(Path, 1) <> "\" Then
    Path = Path + "\"
End If
```

These statements update the variable `Path` with the name of the directory where the program is. For example, if the program is in the C:\VB4PRG\CH20 directory, the preceding statements will fill the variable `Path` with the string C:\VB4PRG\Ch20\. The reason for getting the name of the directory is so subsequent statements will know where to find files that the program uses (for example, BMP files, WAV files).

The next two statements use the `InitializeSprite()` method of the sprite control to initialize the sprBack and sprMan sprite controls:

```
sprBack.InitializeSprite Me.hWnd
sprMan.InitializeSprite Me.hWnd
```

As you can see, the hWnd property of the form is passed to the `InitializeSprite()` method. The hWnd property of the form specifies the window handle of the form. By passing the hWnd property of the form to the `InitializeSprite()` method, you are telling the sprite control that you want to draw the sprite in the form.

20

> **Note:** When you write a program that uses sprite controls, you must initialize each of the sprite controls at the beginning of the program (that is, in the `Form_Load()` procedure of the main form of the program). You initialize a sprite control by calling its `InitializeSprite()` method.
>
> The `InitializeSprite()` method takes one parameter: the handle of the window where the sprite should be drawn.

For example, the following statement initializes the sprMySprite sprite control:

```
sprMySprite.InitializeSprite Me.hWnd
```

This means that when you later slam the WinG contents into the screen, it will be slammed into the Me.hWnd window (which is the frmSprite form).

The remaining five statements of the Form_Load() procedure open all the sprites the program will use:

```
gMan0 = sprBack.OpenSprite(Path + "MAN0.bmp")
gMan1 = sprBack.OpenSprite(Path + "MAN1.bmp")
gMan2 = sprBack.OpenSprite(Path + "MAN2.bmp")
gMan3 = sprBack.OpenSprite(Path + "MAN3.bmp")
gBack = sprBack.OpenSprite(Path + "BGND.bmp")
```

Each sprite is opened by executing the OpenSprite() method of the sprite control. The returned value of the OpenSprite() method is a handle to the opened sprite.

This statement:

```
gMan0 = sprBack.OpenSprite(Path + "MAN0.bmp")
```

fills the gMan0 variable with the handle of the sprite whose bitmap file is MAN0.BMP and whose mask file is MMAN0.BMP. That is, when you open a sprite, you only have to specify its bitmap filename. The MAN0.BMP and MMAN0.BMP files contain the picture that shows the front of the man.

This statement:

```
gMan1 = sprBack.OpenSprite(Path + "MAN1.bmp")
```

fills the gMan1 variable with the handle of the sprite whose bitmap file is MAN1.BMP and whose mask file is MMAN1.BMP. The MAN1.BMP and MMAN1.BMP files contain the picture that shows the man's right profile.

This statement:

```
gMan2 = sprBack.OpenSprite(Path + "MAN2.bmp")
```

fills the gMan2 variable with the handle of the sprite whose bitmap file is MAN2.BMP and whose mask file is MMAN2.BMP. The MAN2.BMP and MMAN2.BMP files contain the picture that shows the back of the man.

This statement:

```
gMan3 = sprBack.OpenSprite(Path + "MAN3.bmp")
```

fills the gMan3 variable with the handle of the sprite whose bitmap file is MAN3.BMP and whose

mask file is MMAN3.BMP. The MAN3.BMP and MMAN3.BMP files contain the picture that shows the man's left profile.

This statement:

```
gBack = sprBack.OpenSprite(Path + "BGND.bmp")
```

fills the gBack variable with the handle of the sprite whose bitmap file is BGND.BMP. Recall that the BGND.BMP file contains the background of the animation show. Because BGND.BMP is a background bitmap with no transparent sections, it doesn't have a mask file.

So at this point, the gMan0 variable holds the handle of the sprite showing the front of the man; the gMan1 variable holds the handle of the sprite showing his right profile; the gMan2 variable holds the handle of the sprite showing the back of the man; the gMan3 variable holds the sprite showing his left profile; and the gBack variable holds the handle of the background sprite showing the room.

The five statements that open the five sprites execute the OpenSprite() method on the sprBack sprite control. However, it does not matter on which sprite control you execute the OpenSprite() method. This statement:

```
gMan0 = sprBack.OpenSprite(Path + "MAN0.bmp")
```

has the same effect as this statement:

```
gMan0 = sprMan.OpenSprite(Path + "MAN0.bmp")
```

Both of these statements fill the gMan0 variable with the handle of the sprite whose bitmap file is MAN0.BMP and whose mask bitmap file is MMAN0.BMP.

The Code in the *Form_Unload()* Procedure

The Form_Unload() procedure of the frmSprite form is executed when you close the form (when the program terminates). Therefore, the Form_Unload() procedure is a good place to write cleanup code.

☐ Type the following code in the Form_Unload() procedure of the frmSprite form:

```
Private Sub Form_Unload(Cancel As Integer)

' Close all the sprites of the show.
sprBack.CloseSprite (gBack)
sprBack.CloseSprite (gMan0)
sprBack.CloseSprite (gMan1)
sprBack.CloseSprite (gMan2)
sprBack.CloseSprite (gMan3)

End Sub
```

☐ Save your work by selecting Save Project from the File menu.

The code in the Form_Unload() procedure uses the CloseSprite() method of the sprite control to close the five sprites you opened in the Form_Load() procedure:

```
sprBack.CloseSprite (gBack)
sprBack.CloseSprite (gMan0)
sprBack.CloseSprite (gMan1)
sprBack.CloseSprite (gMan2)
sprBack.CloseSprite (gMan3)
```

As you can see, the CloseSprite() method takes one parameter: the handle of the sprite to be closed.

Notice that the preceding five statements execute the CloseSprite() method on the sprBack sprite control. However, it doesn't matter on which sprite control you execute the CloseSprite() method. This statement:

```
sprBack.CloseSprite(gMan0)
```

has the same effect as this statement:

```
sprMan.CloseSprite(gMan0)
```

Both of these statements close the sprite whose handle is gMan0.

Note: You must remember to close all the sprites when you end the program. When a sprite is open, it uses memory, so closing the sprite frees up memory. If you don't close the sprites, the memory they occupy won't be freed up even if you end the program.

The Code in the *Form_Paint()* Procedure

When you start the program, you want the sprBack and sprMan sprite controls to be displayed. You can't write the code that draws these sprite controls in the Form_Load() procedure because the form isn't open yet when the Form_Load() procedure is executed. In other words, the Form_Load() procedure is executed just before the form is displayed. A good place to write drawing code is in the Form_Paint() procedure of the form, which is automatically executed whenever there is a need to draw in the form.

☐ Type the following code in the Form_Paint() procedure of the frmSprite form:

```
Private Sub Form_Paint()

' Draw the sprBack sprite in WinG
sprBack.SpriteHandle = gBack
```

```
sprBack.DrawSprite

' Draw the sprMan sprite in WinG.
sprMan.SpriteHandle = gMan0
sprMan.DrawSprite

' Slam WinG into the screen
sprBack.SlamIt
```

End Sub

☐ Save your work by selecting Save Project from the File menu.

These are the first two statements you typed in the Form_Paint() procedure:

```
' Draw the sprBack sprite in WinG
sprBack.SpriteHandle = gBack
sprBack.DrawSprite
```

These statements draw the sprBack sprite control in WinG. The first statement:

```
sprBack.SpriteHandle = gBack
```

fills the sprBack sprite control with the gBack sprite, and the second statement:

```
sprBack.DrawSprite
```

draws the sprBack sprite in WinG. So at this point, WinG is filled with the gBack sprite. (Recall that gBack is the handle of the background sprite.)

The next two statements draw the sprMan sprite control in WinG:

```
' Draw the sprMan sprite in WinG.
sprMan.SpriteHandle = gMan0
sprMan.DrawSprite
```

The first statement:

```
sprMan.SpriteHandle = gMan0
```

fills the sprMan sprite control with the gMan0 sprite, and the second statement:

```
sprMan.DrawSprite
```

draws the sprMan sprite in WinG.

So now WinG is filled with the gBack sprite and the gMan0 sprite. (Recall that gMan0 is the handle of the sprite that shows the front of the man.)

Finally, the contents of WinG are slammed into the screen by using the SlamIt() method:

```
' Slam WinG into the screen
sprBack.SlamIt
```

20

Notice that the preceding statement executes the SlamIt() method on the sprBack sprite control. However, it doesn't matter on which sprite control you execute the SlamIt() method. This statement:

```
sprBack.SlamIt
```

has the same effect as this statement:

```
sprMan.SlamIt
```

Both of these statements slam the current contents of WinG into the screen.

Here is how the code you wrote in the Form_Paint() procedure draws the sprites on the screen:

1. The gBack sprite is placed in the sprBack sprite control and then the sprBack sprite is drawn in WinG.

2. The gMan0 sprite is placed in the sprMan sprite control and then the sprMan sprite is drawn in WinG.

3. The contents of WinG are slammed into the screen.

The order in which you draw sprites into WinG is important. First you draw the background sprite, then you draw the foreground sprite. To see your WinG drawing code in action, follow these steps:

☐ Execute the Sprite program.

The code you wrote in the Form_Paint() *procedure draws the sprBack sprite (the room) and the sprMan sprite (the man).*

☐ Terminate the Sprite program by closing its window. (You can close the program's window by pressing Alt+F4 on your keyboard.)

The Code in the *Stretch* Methods of the Sprite Control

In the next section you are going to write the code that performs the animation show, but first you should know about the StretchBottom, StretchTop, StretchLeft, and StretchRight methods of the sprite control.

The StretchBottom method stretches the bottom edge of the sprite control. For example, the following statement will stretch the bottom edge of the sprMan control by 10 pixels:

```
sprMan.StretchBottom 10
```

Stretching the bottom edge of the sprite control by 10 pixels in runtime is the same as dragging the bottom edge of the sprite control downward by 10 pixels—it increases the height of the sprite control by 10 pixels.

Similarly, the following statement will stretch the bottom edge of the sprMan control by −10 pixels:

```
sprMan.StretchBottom -10
```

Stretching the bottom edge of the sprite control by -10 pixels at runtime is the same as dragging the bottom edge of the sprite control upward by 10 pixels—it decreases the height of the sprite control by 10 pixels.

The StretchTop, StretchLeft, and StretchRight methods are similar to the StretchBottom method. Each of these methods stretches a different edge of the sprite control. When an edge is stretched by a positive amount, the sprite control size is increased. When an edge is stretched by a negative amount, the sprite control size is decreased. For example, the StretchLeft method stretches the left edge of the sprite control. Therefore, the following statement will stretch the left edge of the sprMan control by 15 pixels to increase the width of the control by 15 pixels:

```
sprMan.StretchLeft 15
```

Similarly, the following statement will stretch the left edge of the sprMan control by −15 pixels to decrease the width of the sprite control by 15 pixels:

```
sprMan.StretchLeft -15
```

The Code in the *Timer* Event

The code you wrote in the Form_Paint() procedure draws the sprBack and sprMan sprites on the screen. Of course, the sprMan sprite isn't moving yet because you haven't written the code that animates it. You'll now write the code that animates the sprMan sprite and attach the code to the Timer event of the Timer1 timer (the Timer1_Timer() procedure).

Recall that during design time you set the Interval property of the Timer1 timer control to 50. Therefore, the Timer1_Timer() procedure is automatically executed every 50 milliseconds. In each iteration of the Timer1_Timer() procedure you will move the sprMan sprite to a different position in the room, creating the illusion that the man is moving in the room.

☐ Type the following code in the Timer1_Timer() procedure of the frmSprite form:

```
Private Sub Timer1_Timer()

Static WalkingDirection

' If the program's window is currently minimized,
' exit this procedure.
If Me.WindowState = 1 Then
   Exit Sub
End If

' Draw the background sprite in WinG
sprBack.SpriteHandle = gBack
```

20

```
sprBack.DrawSprite

' Animate the sprMan Sprite control.
If WalkingDirection = 0 Then
   ' Show the man going in direction 0.
   sprMan.StretchBottom 10
   sprMan.StretchLeft 5
   sprMan.SpriteHandle = gMan0
   sprMan.DrawSprite
   If sprMan.SpriteHeight >= 210 Then
      WalkingDirection = 1
   End If
ElseIf WalkingDirection = 1 Then
   ' Show the man going in direction 1.
   sprMan.SpriteLeft = sprMan.SpriteLeft + 6
   sprMan.SpriteHandle = gMan1
   sprMan.DrawSprite
   If sprMan.SpriteLeft >= 220 Then
      WalkingDirection = 2
   End If
ElseIf WalkingDirection = 2 Then
   ' Show the man going in direction 2.
   sprMan.StretchBottom -10
   sprMan.StretchRight -5
   sprMan.SpriteHandle = gMan2
   sprMan.DrawSprite
   If sprMan.SpriteHeight <= 80 Then
      WalkingDirection = 3
   End If
ElseIf WalkingDirection = 3 Then
   ' Show the man going in direction 3.
   sprMan.SpriteLeft = sprMan.SpriteLeft - 6
   sprMan.SpriteHandle = gMan3
   sprMan.DrawSprite
   If sprMan.SpriteLeft <= 150 Then
      WalkingDirection = 0
   End If
End If

' Slam WinG into the screen.
sprBack.SlamIt

End Sub
```

☐ Save your work by selecting Save Project from the File menu.

The code in the Timer1_Timer() procedure moves the sprMan sprite control in the directions shown in Figure 20.36. When the sprMan sprite is moved in Direction 0, the sprMan sprite control contains the gMan0 sprite that shows the front of the man. When sprMan is moved in Direction 1, the sprMan sprite control contains the gMan1 sprite that shows the man's right profile. When sprMan is moved in Direction 2, the sprMan sprite control contains the gMan2 sprite that shows the back of the man. When sprMan is moved in Direction 3, the sprMan sprite control contains the gMan3 sprite that shows the man's left profile.

Figure 20.36.

The movements of the sprMan sprite control in the room.

The first statement you typed in the `Timer1_Timer()` procedure declares a static variable called `WalkingDirection`:

```
Static WalkingDirection
```

The `WalkingDirection` variable is used for storing the current direction in which the man is moving. As illustrated in Figure 20.36, the direction can be either 0, 1, 2, or 3. When the `Timer1_Timer()` procedure is executed for the first time, `WalkingDirection` is equal to 0.

The `WalkingDirection` variable is declared as static so that the value stored in it will be maintained for the next execution of the `Timer1_Timer()` procedure.

The next statement is an `If` statement:

```
If Me.WindowState = 1 Then
    Exit Sub
End If
```

This `If` statement checks whether the form is currently minimized by checking whether the value of the form's WindowState property is equal to 1. If it is, the preceding `If` statement terminates the procedure by using the `Exit Sub` statement. If the form isn't minimized, then the remaining statements of the procedure are executed.

The `Timer1_Timer()` procedure isn't executed when the form is minimized because in the Sprite program you don't want to perform the animation when the form is minimized. However, when you write other programs, you may want to execute the drawing code even when the form is minimized. In this case the animation will be displayed in the icon of the minimized window (that is, an animated icon).

The next two statements draw the background sprite in WinG:

```
' Draw the background sprite in WinG
sprBack.SpriteHandle = gBack
sprBack.DrawSprite
```

As you can see, these statements are the same as the statements you wrote in the Form_Paint() procedure. The first statement places the gBack sprite (the background sprite) in the sprBack sprite control:

```
sprBack.SpriteHandle = gBack
```

And the second statement draws the sprBack sprite control in WinG:

```
sprBack.DrawSprite
```

The next block of statements is a series of If…ElseIf statements. These statements animate the sprMan sprite control so that the sprMan sprite is displayed in a different position in each iteration of the Timer1_Timer() procedure:

```
If WalkingDirection = 0 Then
    ' Show the man going in direction 0.
    sprMan.StretchBottom 10
    sprMan.StretchLeft 5
    sprMan.SpriteHandle = gMan0
    sprMan.DrawSprite
    If sprMan.SpriteHeight >= 210 Then
        WalkingDirection = 1
    End If
ElseIf WalkingDirection = 1 Then
    ' Show the man going in direction 1.
    sprMan.SpriteLeft = sprMan.SpriteLeft + 6
    sprMan.SpriteHandle = gMan1
    sprMan.DrawSprite
    If sprMan.SpriteLeft >= 220 Then
        WalkingDirection = 2
    End If
ElseIf WalkingDirection = 2 Then
    ' Show the man going in direction 2.
    sprMan.StretchBottom -10
    sprMan.StretchRight -5
    sprMan.SpriteHandle = gMan2
    sprMan.DrawSprite
    If sprMan.SpriteHeight <= 80 Then
        WalkingDirection = 3
    End If
ElseIf WalkingDirection = 3 Then
    ' Show the man going in direction 3.
    sprMan.SpriteLeft = sprMan.SpriteLeft - 6
    sprMan.SpriteHandle = gMan3
    sprMan.DrawSprite
    If sprMan.SpriteLeft <= 150 Then
        WalkingDirection = 0
    End If
End If
```

If the static variable WalkingDirection is currently equal to 0, then the code under If WalkingDirection = 0 Then is executed:

```
If WalkingDirection = 0 Then
   ' Show the man going in direction 0.
   sprMan.StretchBottom 10
   sprMan.StretchLeft 5
   sprMan.SpriteHandle = gMan0
   sprMan.DrawSprite
   If sprMan.SpriteHeight >= 210 Then
      WalkingDirection = 1
   End If
```

This code uses the StretchBottom and StretchLeft methods of the sprite control to stretch the bottom edge of the sprMan sprite by 10 pixels and the left edge by 5 pixels:

```
sprMan.StretchBottom 10
sprMan.StretchLeft 5
```

Stretching the bottom and left edges of the sprMan sprite control in each iteration of the Timer1_Timer() procedure creates the illusion that the man is moving in Direction 0 (refer back to Figure 20.36 to see which is Direction 0).

Then the sprMan sprite control is filled with the gMan0 sprite that shows the front of the man:

```
sprMan.SpriteHandle = gMan0
```

Next the sprMan sprite control is drawn in WinG:

```
sprMan.DrawSprite
```

Finally, an If statement is used to see whether the man has reached the end of his movement in Direction 0:

```
If sprMan.SpriteHeight >= 210 Then
   WalkingDirection = 1
End If
```

If the height of the sprMan control is greater than or equal to 210, it means that the man has reached the end of his movement in Direction 0. If this is the case, the preceding If statement changes the value of the WalkingDirection static variable to 1. Therefore, on the next execution of the Timer1_Timer() procedure, the man will start moving in Direction 1.

If the static variable WalkingDirection is currently equal to 1, then the code under ElseIf WalkingDirection = 1 Then is executed:

```
ElseIf WalkingDirection = 1 Then
   ' Show the man going in direction 1.
   sprMan.SpriteLeft = sprMan.SpriteLeft + 6
   sprMan.SpriteHandle = gMan1
   sprMan.DrawSprite
   If sprMan.SpriteLeft >= 220 Then
      WalkingDirection = 2
   End If
```

20

This code moves the sprMan sprite control to the right by 6 pixels:

```
sprMan.SpriteLeft = sprMan.SpriteLeft + 6
```

Increasing the SpriteLeft property of the sprite control by 6 moves the sprite control 6 pixels to the right. Moving the sprMan sprite control to the right in each iteration of the Timer1_Timer() procedure creates the illusion that the man is moving in Direction 1. (See Figure 20.36.)

Then the sprMan sprite control is filled with the gMan1 sprite that shows his right profile:

```
sprMan.SpriteHandle = gMan1
```

Next the sprMan sprite control is drawn in WinG:

```
sprMan.DrawSprite
```

Finally, an If statement is used to see whether the man has reached the end of his movement in Direction 1:

```
If sprMan.SpriteLeft >= 220 Then
    WalkingDirection = 2
End If
```

If the SpriteLeft property of the sprMan control is greater than or equal to 220, it means that the man has reached the end of his movement in Direction 1. If this is the case, the preceding If statement changes the value of the WalkingDirection static variable to 2. Therefore, on the next execution of the Timer1_Timer() procedure, the man will start moving in Direction 2.

If the static variable WalkingDirection is currently equal to 2, then the code under ElseIf WalkingDirection = 2 Then is executed:

```
ElseIf WalkingDirection = 2 Then
    ' Show the man going in direction 2.
    sprMan.StretchBottom -10
    sprMan.StretchRight -5
    sprMan.SpriteHandle = gMan2
    sprMan.DrawSprite
    If sprMan.SpriteHeight <= 80 Then
        WalkingDirection = 3
    End If
```

This code uses the StretchBottom and StretchLeft methods of the sprite control to stretch the bottom edge of the sprMan sprite control by –10 pixels and the left edge by –5 pixels:

```
sprMan.StretchBottom -10
sprMan.StretchLeft -5
```

Stretching the bottom and left edges of the sprMan sprite control in each iteration of the Timer1_Timer() procedure creates the illusion that the man is moving in Direction 2. (See Figure 20.36.)

Then the sprMan sprite control is filled with the gMan2 sprite that shows the back of the man:

```
sprMan.SpriteHandle = gMan2
```

Next the sprMan sprite control is drawn in WinG:

```
sprMan.DrawSprite
```

Finally, an If statement is used to see whether the man has reached the end of his movement in Direction 2:

```
If sprMan.SpriteHeight <= 80 Then
   WalkingDirection = 3
End If
```

If the height of the sprMan control is less than or equal to 80, it means that the man has reached the end of his movement in Direction 2. If this is the case, the preceding If statement changes the value of the WalkingDirection static variable to 3. Therefore, on the next execution of the Timer1_Timer() procedure, the man will start moving in Direction 3.

If the static variable WalkingDirection is currently equal to 3, then the code under ElseIf WalkingDirection = 3 Then is executed:

```
ElseIf WalkingDirection = 3 Then
   ' Show the man going in direction 3.
   sprMan.SpriteLeft = sprMan.SpriteLeft - 6
   sprMan.SpriteHandle = gMan3
   sprMan.DrawSprite
   If sprMan.SpriteLeft <= 150 Then
      WalkingDirection = 0
   End If
```

This code moves the sprMan sprite control to the left by 6 pixels:

```
sprMan.SpriteLeft = sprMan.SpriteLeft - 6
```

Decreasing the SpriteLeft property of the sprite control by 6 moves the sprite control 6 pixels to the left. Moving the sprMan sprite control to the left in each iteration of the Timer1_Timer() procedure creates the illusion that the man is moving in Direction 3. (See Figure 20.36.)

Then the sprMan sprite control is filled with the gMan3 sprite that shows his left profile:

```
sprMan.SpriteHandle = gMan3
```

Next the sprMan sprite control is drawn in WinG:

```
sprMan.DrawSprite
```

Finally, an If statement is used to see whether the man has reached the end of his movement in Direction 3:

```
If sprMan.SpriteLeft <= 150 Then
   WalkingDirection = 0
End If
```

20

If the SpriteLeft property of the sprMan control is less than or equal to 150, it means that the man has reached the end of his movement in Direction 3. If this is the case, the preceding `If` statement changes the value of the `WalkingDirection` static variable to 0. Therefore, on the next execution of the `Timer1_Timer()` procedure, the man will start moving in Direction 0.

The last statement in the `Timer1_Timer()` procedure slams the contents of WinG (the sprBack sprite and the sprMan sprite) into the screen:

```
' Slam WinG into the screen.
sprBack.SlamIt
```

To see your sprite animation code in action, follow these steps:

☐ Execute the Sprite program.

The code you wrote in the `Timer1_Timer()` *procedure displays an animation show in which the man moves in the room.*

☐ Terminate the Sprite program by closing its window. (You can close the program's window by pressing Alt+F4 on your keyboard.)

Optimizing the Code That Performs the Animation Show

The code you wrote in the `Timer1_Timer()` procedure redraws the entire background sprite every time the `Timer1_Timer()` procedure is executed. However, it is not really necessary to redraw the entire background sprite; instead, you can redraw only the section of the background that the sprMan sprite overlaps. This technique will make your drawing code more efficient.

> **Note:** When you start the program, the code you wrote in the `Form_Paint()` procedure draws the entire background sprite, so you don't need to redraw it every time the `Timer1_Timer()` procedure is executed. You can redraw only the section of the background overlapped by the sprMan sprite.

As you know, the `DrawSprite` method draws the entire area of a sprite control. For example, the following statement draws the entire contents of the sprBack sprite control in WinG:

```
sprBack.DrawSprite
```

If you want to draw only a section of a sprite control in WinG, then you have to use the `PartialDraw` method. The `PartialDraw` method takes four parameters:

☐ The x coordinate of the top-left corner of the rectangular section to be drawn

☐ The y coordinate of the top-left corner of the rectangular section to be drawn

☐ The width of the rectangular section to be drawn

☐ The height of the rectangular section to be drawn

All the values of these parameters are in pixel units.

For example, the following statement draws a rectangular section of the sprBack sprite in WinG:

```
sprBack.PartialDraw 10, 20, 100, 200
```

The top-left corner of the rectangular section is at coordinates x=10,y=20, and the width and height of the rectangular section are width=100,height=200. All the units are in pixels.

To make the code in the Timer1_Timer() procedure more efficient, all you have to do is replace the statement that draws the sprBack sprite control in the Timer1_Timer() procedure:

☐ Display the code window of the Timer1_Timer() procedure.

☐ Delete this statement:

```
sprBack.DrawSprite
```

and replace it with the following statement:

```
sprBack.PartialDraw sprMan.SpriteLeft, _
                    sprMan.SpriteTop, _
                    sprMan.SpriteWidth, _
                    sprMan.SpriteHeight
```

This statement uses the PartialDraw method to partially redraw the sprBack sprite in WinG—only the section of sprBack that sprMan covers is redrawn.

To see your partial-drawing code in action, follow these steps:

☐ Execute the Sprite program.

The code in the Timer1_Timer() procedure displays the same animation show as before, but now it's faster. Depending on how fast your PC is, you may not notice the improvement in the animation speed. On a very fast PC you won't notice it, but the difference in speed can be noticeable on some PCs, so whenever possible you should redraw only a section of the background sprite.

☐ Terminate the Sprite program by closing its window. (You can close the program's window by pressing Alt+F4 on your keyboard.)

20

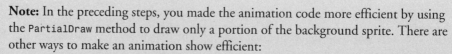

Note: In the preceding steps, you made the animation code more efficient by using the `PartialDraw` method to draw only a portion of the background sprite. There are other ways to make an animation show efficient:

☐ Set the AutoSize property of the background sprite control to True during design time (which you did during the visual implementation of the form). When the AutoSize property is set to True, the sprite control is the same size as the sprite's BMP file (that is, the sprite is not stretched). When a sprite is not stretched, the drawing is performed faster.

☐ Use a small BMP file for the background sprite. The smaller the background sprite is, the faster the animation show will be.

☐ Don't stretch the foreground sprites more than you need to. The less you stretch the foreground sprites, the faster things will move.

Enhancing the Sprite Program

You have finished writing all the sprite-related and animation-related code. In the following sections, you'll enhance the Sprite program by adding a menu and background music.

Adding a Menu to the Sprite Program

Follow these steps to add a menu to the Sprite program:

☐ Add a menu to the frmSprite form according to the specifications in Table 20.1.

Table 20.1. The menu table of the frmSprite form.

Caption	Name
&File	mnuFile
...E&xit	mnuExit
&Help	mnuHelp
...&About...	mnuAbout

☐ Type the following code in the `mnuExit_Click()` procedure:

```
Private Sub mnuExit_Click()

' Terminate the program.
Unload Me

End Sub
```

☐ Save your work by selecting Save Project from the File menu.

The code in this procedure terminates the program by unloading (closing) the form. Before the form is unloaded, the Form_Unload() procedure is executed. Recall that in the Form_Unload() procedure you wrote code that closes all the sprites that the program uses. Therefore, when you select Exit from the File menu, all the sprites will be closed and then the program will terminate.

Adding Background Music to the Sprite Program

Follow these steps to add background music to the Sprite program:

☐ Place a TegoSoft Multimedia OLE control in the form and set its properties as follows:

Property	Setting
Name	Tegomm1
Height	33
Left	88
Top	8
Width	234

Your form should now look like the one shown in Figure 20.37.

Figure 20.37.
*The frmSprite form after
adding a multimedia
control.*

☐ Add code to the beginning of the Form_Load() procedure that uses the multimedia control to open and play a WAV file. After adding this code the Form_Load() procedure should look as follows:

```
Private Sub Form_Load()

    Dim Path
```

```
' Get the name of the directory where the
' program resides.
Path = App.Path
If Right(Path, 1) <> "\" Then
   Path = Path + "\"
End If

' Open a WAV file for background music.
Tegomm1.Visible = False
Tegomm1.DeviceType = "WaveAudio"
Tegomm1.FileName = Path + "LASTC2M6.WAV"
Tegomm1.Command = "Open"

' Start playing the WAV file.
Tegomm1.Command = "Play"

' Initialize all the Sprite controls.
sprBack.InitializeSprite Me.hWnd
sprMan.InitializeSprite Me.hWnd

' Open all the sprites that will be used in our show.
gMan0 = sprBack.OpenSprite(Path + "MAN0.bmp")
gMan1 = sprBack.OpenSprite(Path + "MAN1.bmp")
gMan2 = sprBack.OpenSprite(Path + "MAN2.bmp")
gMan3 = sprBack.OpenSprite(Path + "MAN3.bmp")
gBack = sprBack.OpenSprite(Path + "BGND.bmp")

End Sub
```

☐ Save your work by selecting Save Project from the File menu.

The code you just added to the beginning of the Form_Load() procedure uses the multimedia control to open and play a WAV file:

```
' Open a WAV file for background music.
Tegomm1.Visible = False
Tegomm1.DeviceType = "WaveAudio"
Tegomm1.FileName = Path + "LASTC2M6.WAV"
Tegomm1.Command = "Open"

' Start playing the WAV file.
Tegomm1.Command = "Play"
```

The first statement hides the multimedia control by setting its Visible property to False:

```
Tegomm1.Visible = False
```

Now you can play sound in the background without having to click anything.

Then a WAV file is opened:

```
Tegomm1.DeviceType = "WaveAudio"
Tegomm1.FileName = Path + "LASTC2M6.WAV"
Tegomm1.Command = "Open"
```

The name of the WAV file to be opened is `Path + "LASTC2M6.WAV"`. Recall that the variable `Path` is filled with the name of the program's directory. For example, if the program is in the C:\VB4PRG\CH20 directory, then the preceding statements will open the C:\VB4PRG\CH20\LASTC2M6.WAV file.

The last statement you add to the `Form_Load()` procedure starts the playback of the WAV file:

```
Tegomm1.Command = "Play"
```

The Code in the *Done* Event of the Multimedia Control

The `Done` event of the multimedia control occurs when the playback of the WAV file is done. In the Sprite program you want the WAV file to play again and again in an endless loop. Therefore, the code you attach now will rewind the playback position to the beginning of the WAV file and play it again.

☐ Type the following code in the `Tegomm1_Done()` procedure:

```
Private Sub Tegomm1_Done()

    ' If playback reached the end of the WAV file,
    ' rewind the WAV file and play again.
    If Tegomm1.Position = Tegomm1.Length Then
       Tegomm1.Command = "Prev"
       Tegomm1.Command = "Play"
    End If

End Sub
```

☐ Save your work by selecting Save Project from the File menu.

An `If` statement forms the code you attached to the `Done` event of the multimedia control:

```
If Tegomm1.Position = Tegomm1.Length Then
   Tegomm1.Command = "Prev"
   Tegomm1.Command = "Play"
End If
```

This `If` statement determines whether the playback has reached the end of the file by evaluating the Position property of the multimedia control. If the value of the Position property is equal to the value of the Length property of the multimedia control, then the playback has reached the end of the file. If this is the case, the statements under the `If` statement rewind the playback position to the beginning of the file by issuing a `Prev` command and start playing the WAV file again by issuing a `Play` command:

```
Tegomm1.Command = "Prev"
Tegomm1.Command = "Play"
```

To hear the background music you've added to the program, follow these steps:

☐ Execute the Sprite program.

20

The Sprite program performs the animation show and music plays in the background. Once the playback reaches the end of the WAV file, it is rewound to the beginning of the WAV file and the playback starts again.

☐ Terminate the Sprite program by selecting Exit from the File menu.

The Code in the *Click* Event of the About... Menu Item

When you select About... from the Help menu, the Sprite program should display an About message box. You'll now write the code that accomplishes this task.

☐ Type the following code in the mnuAbout_Click() procedure:

```
Private Sub mnuAbout_Click()

Dim Title
Dim Msg
Dim CR

CR = Chr(13) + Chr(10)

' Prepare the title of the About message box.
Title = "About the Sprite Program"
Msg = "This program was written with Visual "
Msg = Msg + "Basic for Windows, using the "
Msg = Msg + "TegoSoft Sprite OCX control. "
Msg = Msg + CR + CR
Msg = Msg + "The TegoSoft Sprite OCX control "
Msg = Msg + "is part of the TegoSoft OCX Control "
Msg = Msg + "Kit - a collection of various OCX controls. "
Msg = Msg + CR + CR
Msg = Msg + "For more information about the "
Msg = Msg + "TegoSoft OCX Control Kit, contact TegoSoft "
Msg = Msg + "at:"
Msg = Msg + CR + CR
Msg = Msg + "TegoSoft Inc." + CR
Msg = Msg + "P.O. Box 389" + CR
Msg = Msg + "Bellmore, NY 11710"
Msg = Msg + CR + CR
Msg = Msg + "Phone: (516)783-4824"

' Display the About message box.
MsgBox Msg, vbInformation, Title

' Make sure that there is playback after
' the user closes the modal message box.
Tegomm1.Command = "Play"

End Sub
```

☐ Save your work by selecting Save Project from the File menu.

The code in the mnuAbout_Click() procedure uses the MsgBox statement to display an About message box. Notice that after displaying the message box, the following statement is executed:

```
' Make sure that there is playback after
' the user closes the modal message box.
Tegomm1.Command = "Play"
```

This statement issues a `Play` command to the multimedia control after the modal message box is closed, because if the playback position of the WAV file reaches the end while the message box is displayed, the `Done` event of the multimedia control won't occur and the playback of the WAV file won't start again. Therefore, a `Play` command is issued to make sure the playback resumes after the message box is closed.

Enhancing the Forward-Walking Animation

As the man moves in the room, he looks as though he's sliding on the floor. This is done to keep the program fairly simple. However, you can enhance the program so that it shows the man walking, rather than sliding, in the room by creating additional BMP and mask files. For example, as the man walks toward you, the code that displays the man should alternate the BMP picture between two BMP files. Figures 20.38 and 20.39 show two possible BMP files that can be displayed while the man is walking forward. Figure 20.38 shows the right leg in front of the left leg, and Figure 20.39 shows the left leg in front of the right leg. As you alternate these two BMP pictures, the man will appear to walk forward instead of slide forward.

Now you have to create a pair of BMP pictures for the animation in the each of the other directions. To alternate the BMP pictures, you have to declare another static variable that serves as a flag indicating which BMP picture should be displayed. For example, you can declare the static variable `FrameNumber`. This variable can be either 0 or 1. When this variable is equal to 0, the BMP picture in Figure 20.38 is displayed. Then you increase the value of `FrameNumber` to 1. At the next execution of the `Timer1_Timer()` procedure, the `FrameNumber` variable is equal to 1 so the BMP picture in Figure 20.39 is displayed. You then set `FrameNumber` back to 0 so the BMP in Figure 20.38 will be displayed at the next execution of the timer procedure.

Figure 20.38.
One BMP used for animating the man in the forward direction.

Figure 20.39.
Another BMP used for
animating the man in the
forward direction.

Note: The preceding section suggests using only two BMP pictures for the animation in the forward direction. Of course, you can make your animation as sophisticated as you want. For example, you may decide that the forward-walking animation should consist of four or more separate BMP pictures.

Three-Dimensional Sprite Animation and Virtual Reality

3D virtual reality refers to the technology in which a 3D (three-dimensional) picture is displayed on the screen and the user can "travel" inside the 3D picture. The 3D picture can be composed of many rooms, halls, and so on. The user can use the mouse or the keyboard to move from room to room. As the user moves, the 3D virtual reality program displays the appropriate picture that would have been displayed if the user were moving in a real environment.

3D virtual reality games first became popular in amusement parks, where for a small fee, the user is attached to a set of sensors and goggles. The sensors and the goggles are attached to a computer. As the user moves, the sensors detect the motion and send signals to the computer. The computer translates the signals, and based on the user's movement, the computer displays new pictures. The pictures are displayed inside the goggles. The reason for using goggles instead of a monitor is that this gives the player a sense that he/she is in a real environment.

You can create 3D virtual reality programs on your PC with Visual Basic. Instead of using the goggles, you'll use the monitor for displaying the scene. And instead of using sensors, you can use the mouse or the keyboard for "moving" inside the 3D picture.

The main requirement for creating an impressive 3D virtual reality program in Windows is that the graphics operation be performed fast. That is, the 3D virtual reality program needs to display the new views as fast the user moves the mouse (or the keyboard).

With WinG technology you can create sophisticated games and multimedia applications that are executed very quickly in Windows. For example, the TegoSoft WinG OLE control lets you draw graphics (points, lines, circles, and other shapes) by using WinG technology. The 3D floor OLE control lets you draw a 2D floor and then converts it to a 3D picture.

Furthermore, the 3D floor OLE control lets you "move" in the rooms and halls of the 3D floor by using the mouse or the keyboard and lets you design the walls and other objects inside the 3D floor. You can design your own world on the PC and let your user travel in the 3D picture.

From within your Visual Basic program you can then place sprite controls in the 3D picture and move them. As you can imagine, you can create very sophisticated games and multimedia applications by using Visual Basic and controls such as the sprite and 3D floor OLE controls. Both the WinG OLE control and the 3D floor OLE control are part of the TegoSoft OLE Control Kit. (See the disk offer at the end of this book.)

For example, as your user moves in your 3D pictures, he or she is seeing the environment as it would be viewed in the real 3D world (hence the name *3D virtual reality*). Figures 20.40 and 20.41 are examples of views your user will see as he or she is traveling in one of your 3D pictures.

Naturally, you can make your 3D pictures as interesting (and scary) as you want them to be. For example, in Figure 20.42 a sprite is shown. Your Visual Basic program can move the sprite from room to room and across the halls. Of course, as the sprite gets closer to you, it looks bigger.

By adding sound to your virtual reality applications (as discussed in Chapter 19, "Sound Programming"), you can create very impressive applications.

Figure 20.40.
A 3D picture in your virtual reality program. The user stands an the entrance of one of the rooms.

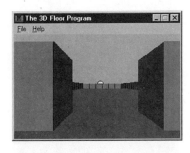

Figure 20.41.
The user "moving" inside the room.

20

Figure 20.42.
Moving sprites in the 3D pictures.

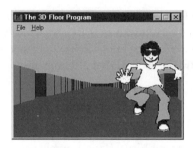

Note: When designing the 3D pictures, you start by using a regular text editor. With the text editor program you design a 2D (two-dimensional) floor such as the one shown in Figure 20.43. The 3D floor OLE control then translates the 2D drawing shown in Figure 20.43 into the 3D drawing shown in Figure 20.40.

You can place sprites inside the 3D picture by placing the appropriate symbols inside the 2D drawing (where the symbols represent the sprites). The floor OLE control will then display the sprites inside the 3D pictures according to the placement of the sprites inside the 2D drawing.

Alternatively, you can place the sprites inside the 3D pictures from within your Visual Basic code. Furthermore, you can write code that moves the sprites inside the 3D pictures. So when the user uses the mouse (or the keyboard) to move inside the 3D picture, the user will also see the sprites "walking" and moving inside the 3D picture.

Figure 20.43.
A text file used for designing the 2D drawing.

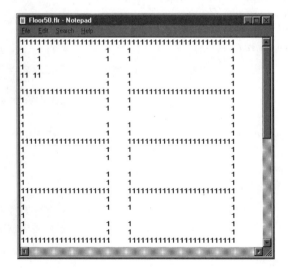

Summary

In this chapter you have written a program that uses a background sprite and a foreground sprite. In a similar manner, you can write programs that have more than two sprite controls. For example, you can enhance the Sprite program by adding another sprite control that displays another character, such as another person or an animal. There are no limits to the number of gadgets you can add to the room. You can display a sprite that has a picture of a TV in it, then display different pictures in this sprite so the TV will look as if it's playing a movie.

When you write programs that use sprites, always remember to draw the background sprite first and then draw the foreground sprites. If your animation show has more than one foreground sprite (for example, sprMan1, sprMan2, sprWoman, sprDog), then the order in which you draw the foreground sprites should be based on the distance of the sprites from your point of view. That is, the sprite that is furthest away from you should be drawn into WinG first, and the sprite that is closest to you should be drawn into WinG last.

In this chapter, the program you have written performs an animation show with the foreground sprite, but you can also animate the background sprite in other programs you write.

The chapter also briefly discusses how you can create sophisticated 3D virtual reality programs, such as DOOM.

Q&A

Q I want to create a professional cartoon movie. Can I use the sprite control?

A Yes. As you can see from the Sprite program, creating a professional cartoon movie is very easy when you use the sprite/WinG technology. After practicing by writing several animation programs of your own, you'll realize that most of your development time is spent on selecting the WAV files of the movie you're creating, writing the manuscript for your movie, and, of course, drawing the BMP pictures of your sprites.

During the playback of your cartoon movie, you'll have to change the background picture from time to time. For example, if you show a cat chasing a mouse, you have to change the background picture sprite when the mouse enters a different hole or a different room. (Naturally, you have seen this technique many times on TV.)

Quiz

1. Why do you display the background sprite and other sprites during design time?
2. How did the `PartialDraw` method make the Sprite program more efficient?
3. Explain the WinG concept in two to three sentences.
4. Can you use more than one sprite?

Exercise

Create an animation movie.

Quiz Answers

1. The background sprite is displayed during design time because you need to see how the sprite will look during runtime. You'll also be able to examine the sprite's properties and determine its initial size and location. Also, you can drag and size the sprites so you'll be able to write code that determines the sprites' maximum and minimum sizes during runtime.

2. Before the enhancement, the entire background picture was drawn into WinG, then the new location of the man was drawn into WinG, and finally the WinG contents were slammed into the screen.

   After the enhancement, the drawing sequence into WinG is as follows:

   • Only the section of the background picture currently occupied by the man is drawn into WinG.

   • The man in his new location is drawn into WinG.

   • The WinG contents are slammed into the screen.

   This technique is more efficient because you didn't draw the entire background picture into WinG for each movement of the man.

3. A picture is drawn into WinG that serves as the background picture. Then other pictures in the form of sprites are drawn into WinG. Finally, the WinG contents are slammed into the screen.

4. Yes. Simply place additional sprite controls in the form.

Exercise Answer

Follow the steps this chapter outlines to create your BMP and mask BMP files. Then create the animation program as you do in the Sprite program.

There are no limits to the amount of sophistication you can add to your movie. Generally speaking, it's best to start creating a movie with simple animation. Then you can add gadgets and other sprites. Once you are satisfied with the results, you can make your animation more realistic. For example, create walking animation by using two or more BMP pictures. You can show a grandfather clock with a swinging pendulum on the wall, for example.

21

Multimedia

In this chapter you'll learn how to add multimedia capabilities to your programs.

Multimedia technology is used in a wide range of applications, including those for business, education, and games. In this chapter you'll learn how to write Visual Basic programs that utilize various multimedia devices.

What Is Multimedia?

As the name implies, multimedia programs use several media methods to perform their functions. Sounds, animation, movies, and print style can make your programs more friendly, usable, and interesting. Adding multimedia capabilites to your program requires specialized hardware. For example, the sound card is used to play sound, the monitor is used to display movies and the CD-ROM drive is used to play CD audio.

Multimedia technology is very popular, and many PC vendors are now shipping their PCs with multimedia hardware already installed.

Typically, a multimedia set includes a sound card, a microphone, speakers, a CD-ROM drive that is capable of playing CD audio, and a monitor that is capable of displaying movies (for example, a VGA monitor).

DOS Versus Windows: Device Independence

One of the main advantages of Windows over DOS is that Windows is device independent. While DOS programs must be written to support each manufacturer's hardware device, Windows programs provide a single way to use any media device. Your programs should work on any multimedia device, regardless of the manufacturer of the device. For example, it does not matter who manufactured your sound card—if Windows recognizes the sound card, any multimedia program you write should be able to use this sound card.

Determining Your Multimedia Capabilities

Before you start to write the multimedia programs of this chapter, you need to examine the multimedia capabilities of your PC. That is, you installed the multimedia hardware, and you installed the associated multimedia software (drivers) that come with the multimedia hardware. Did Windows accept your installation?

There is a very easy way to determine the multimedia capabilities of your PC:

Start the Media Player program. Media Player usually resides inside the Accessories group. (See Figure 21.1.)

Windows responds by displaying the Media Player window shown in Figure 21.2.

Figure 21.1.

The program icon of Media Player (usually inside the Accessories group).

Figure 21.2.

The Media Player program.

 Open the Device menu of Media Player.

The Device menu of Media Player displays the names of devices that are installed on your system. (See Figure 21.3.)

Figure 21.3.

The Device menu of the Media Player program.

Now examine the various items that appear inside the Device menu of Media Player. (See Figure 21.3.) The Sound item indicates that the PC is capable of playing WAV files. The CD Audio item indicates that the PC is capable of playing CD audio. The MIDI Sequencer item indicates that the PC can play MIDI files. The Video for Windows item indicates that the PC is capable of playing movie AVI files. If you don't see any of these devices in the Device menu, something is wrong with the hardware or software installation of the devices that are missing from the Device menu.

The Video for Windows, Sound, MIDI Sequencer, and CD Audio items in the Media Player Device menu are the standard Windows multimedia devices. In addition to these devices, you can install other devices. For example, in Figure 21.3, the QuickTime for Windows item is shown as an additional multimedia device. Similarly, your Device menu may include a list of other devices in the Device menu of Media Player.

21

Note: You might encounter a situation in which a certain proprietary program is capable of playing a certain device, but that device does not appear in the Device menu of Media Player. It means that that application uses some special proprietary drivers. Even though you can play the device with that particular applications, other "normal" applications will not be able to play the device.

So the bottom line is this: Insist on seeing the multimedia device you are installing among the items of the Device menu. This will ensure that every Windows application that needs to utilize the device will be able to do so.

Note: The programs that you'll be instructed to implement in this chapter require the use of the TegoSoft multimedia OLE control and multimedia hardware such as a sound card. It is highly recommended that you read this chapter even if you do not have the TegoSoft multimedia OLE control and even if you do not have a sound card. This way, you'll gain an understanding of what it takes to create interesting multimedia applications with Visual Basic.

MIDI Files

The PlayMIDI program that you'll write in this chapter demonstrates how you can play MIDI files. MIDI files are synthesized music files. You can consider the MIDI file to be a file that contains instructions to the sound card. These instructions consist of information such as the music notes, the type of instruments to play, the tempo (the playback speed), and other information that the sound card needs in order to play the music. How does the sound card play the music? The sound card has special MIDI electronic hardware on it that enables the playback of musical instruments. For example, the sound card can generate piano sounds, violin sounds, drum sounds, and sounds of other instruments.

It is clear that the MIDI file cannot emulate human voice, nor can it emulate sounds that are not the sound of musical instruments. For example, you cannot play the sound of breaking glass with a MIDI file.

Typically, the MIDI file instructs the sound card to play several musical instruments simultaneously. In fact, you can play a MIDI file that produces music that is otherwise generated by a whole orchestra. Naturally, the more expensive the sound card, the more impressive are its MIDI capabilities.

Note: Most sound cards include the electronic circuit that enables them to play MIDI files.

Note: Unlike WAV files (which contain the actual samples of recording), MIDI files contain only the instructions that tell the sound card how to play the music. Therefore, MIDI files are very small.

So how do you obtain MIDI files? A typical programmer purchases the MIDI files. Alternatively, you can generate the MIDI files by using a special hardware that lets you "record" the MIDI file. The hardware includes a musical keyboard that is connected to the PC. As you play the keyboard, the music is stored as a MIDI file. Special MIDI software lets you manipulate the music (mixing several instruments, selecting an instrument and making its volume higher/lower, and so on).

As you can see, "recording" MIDI files is not as easy as recording WAV files. To begin with, you need special software and hardware, but more importantly, you need musical talent. Professional MIDI equipment is typically purchased in stores that specialize in selling musical instruments. Lately, computer stores have begun carrying inexpensive MIDI equipment that lets you interface the MIDI hardware to the sound card for the purpose of "recording" MIDI files.

DO	DON'T

DO make sure that the sound card you are purchasing is capable of interfacing to MIDI equipment if you plan to record MIDI files yourself using a sound card. Typically, the sound card lets you interface to MIDI equipment through the joystick port of the sound card. That is, most sound cards include a joystick port (where you can connect a joystick). When recording MIDI files, you'll connect the MIDI hardware to the joystick port of the sound card (provided that the MIDI equipment and the sound card were designed to interface with each other this way).

21

Note: When a sound card plays a MIDI file, the music is played through the speakers that are attached to the sound card (just like when you play WAV files).

Most sound cards let you play a WAV file and a MIDI file simultaneously. Typically, MIDI files are used as background music. For example, you can announce "Happy birthday, Jean" with a WAV file while a MIDI file of the song "Happy birthday to you" is played in the background.

The PlayMIDI Program

In the following sections you'll write the PlayMIDI program. The PlayMIDI program is an example of a program that lets the user play MIDI files.

Before writing the PlayMIDI program yourself, let's review its specifications.

Upon startup of the PlayMIDI program, the window shown in Figure 21.4 appears.

Figure 21.4.

The window of the PlayMIDI program.

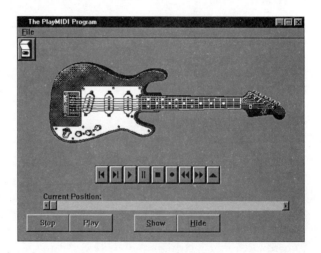

As shown in Figure 21.4, a picture of a guitar appears. This is an appropriate picture because the subject of the PlayMIDI program is playing musical instruments.

The Current Position scroll bar does not indicate any position because currently no MIDI file is open.

The PlayMIDI program has a File menu, as shown in Figure 21.5.

Figure 21.5.
The File menu of the PlayMIDI program.

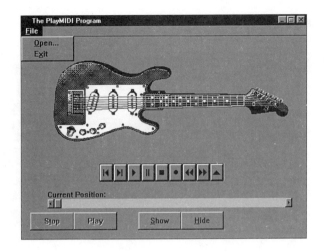

☐ To load a MIDI file, select Open from the File menu.

The PlayMIDI program responds by displaying the Open dialog box, as shown in Figure 21.6.

Figure 21.6.
The Open dialog box that appears after you select Open from the File menu.

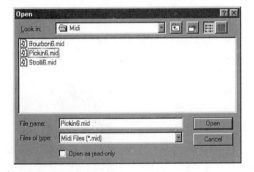

As shown in Figure 21.6, the Open dialog box lets you load a MIDI file (a file with the .MID file extension). The user can now load a MIDI file.

Figure 21.7 shows the main window of the PlayMIDI program after the user loads a MIDI file. Note that because a MIDI file is now loaded, various buttons that previously appeared dimmed are now available.

Figure 21.7.

The title of the PlayMIDI program indicates the name of the loaded MIDI file.

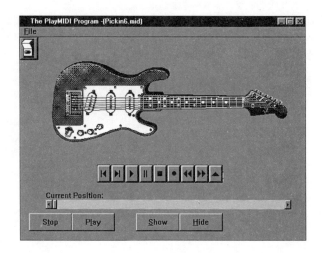

Note the Show and Hide buttons that appear inside the window of the PlayMIDI program. These buttons are implemented for the sole purpose of demonstrating that you can make the TegoSoft multimedia OLE control visible or invisible.

When the user clicks the Hide button, PlayMIDI responds by making the multimedia control invisible. (See Figure 21.8.)

When the user clicks the Show button, PlayMIDI responds by making the multimedia control visible.

Figure 21.8.

Making the multimedia control invisible.

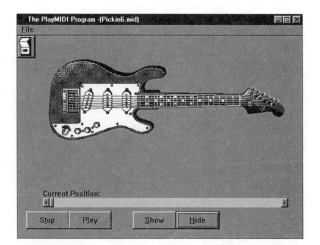

Note: Why would you want to make the multimedia control invisible? Sometimes you might want to make the visual appearance of your program more fancy. Instead of using the standard multimedia control buttons of the multimedia control, you could make your own buttons. For example, the PlayMIDI program implements the Play and Stop buttons. In a similar manner, you can implement the other buttons of the multimedia control.

Also, sometimes you might want the MIDI file to be played without the need to click any button. In such a case, you would make the multimedia control invisible, and you would not implement the Stop and Play buttons. For example, you might want to implement a program in which, upon startup of the program, a section of a MIDI file is played automatically, without requiring the user to click any button.

The user can now play the MIDI file by clicking the Play button you placed inside the form or by clicking the Play button of the multimedia control (the third button from the left on the multimedia control).

To stop the playback, the user has to click the Stop button you placed inside the form, or click the Stop button of the multimedia control (the fifth button from the left), or click the Pause button of the multimedia control (the fourth button from the left).

During the playback, the scroll bar indicates the current position of the playback. For example, Figure 21.9 shows the window of the PlayMIDI program after you play approximately half of the file.

Figure 21.9.
The scroll bar indicates that approximately half of the MIDI file has been played.

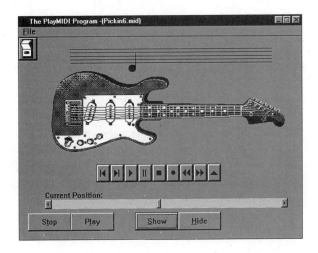

Note: In the PlayMIDI program, the scroll bar is disabled so that the user will not be able to manually scroll the current position to any desired position. Nevertheless, it is very easy to enable the scroll bar and to enable the user to start playing from any desired position.

The Visual Implementation of the PlayMIDI Program

Now that you know what the PlayMIDI program is supposed to do, you can implement it.

☐ Select New Project from the File menu, and save the new project as follows: Save the new form as C:\VB4PRG\CH21\PLAYMIDI.FRM and the new project file as C:\VB4PRG\CH21\PLAYMIDI.VBP.

The PlayMIDI program uses the multimedia control. Therefore, you have to add this OLE control to your project:

☐ Select Custom Controls from the Tools menu, Click the Browse button, and select the TegoMM??.OCX (where ?? stands for 32 if you are using 32-bit Windows, and ?? stands for 16 if you are using 16-bit Windows) file from the \Windows\System directory.

DO	**DON'T**

DO incorporate multimedia into your Windows applications. Nowadays, many people have multimedia capabilities in their PCs, and most users expect to be able to utilize the multimedia devices.

☐ Implement the frmPlayMIDI form according to the specifications in Table 21.1. When you finish implementing the form, it should look like the one shown in Figure 21.10. Table 21.1 instructs you to place the common dialog OLE control and the switch OLE control inside the frmPlayMIDI form. Select Custom control from the Tools menu, click the Browse button and add the COMDLG32.OCX file (if you are using 32-bit Windows) or the COMDLG16.OCX file (if you are using 16-bit Windows) from the \Windows\System directory. Also add the TegoSW32.OCX file (if you are using 32-bit Windows) or the TegoSW16.OCX file (if you are using 16-bit Windows) from the \Windows\System directory.

Table 21.1. The properties table of the frmPlayMIDI form.

Object	Property	Setting
Form	**Name**	**frmPlayMIDI**
	BackColor	Light Gray
	BorderStyle	1-Fixed Single
	Caption	The PlayMIDI Program
	Height	6225
	Icon	\VB\ICONS\MISC\MISC31.ICO
	Left	915
	MaxButton	0-False
	Top	570
	Width	8100
Command Button	**Name**	**cmdPlay**
	Caption	P&lay
	Enabled	0-False
	FontName	System
	FontSize	10
	Height	495
	Left	1440
	Top	4800
	Width	1215
Command Button	**Name**	**cmdStop**
	Caption	S&top
	Enabled	0-False
	FontName	System
	FontSize	10
	Height	495
	Left	240
	Top	4800
	Width	1215

continues

21

Table 21.1. continued

Object	Property	Setting
Command Button	**Name**	**cmdHide**
	Caption	&Hide
	FontName	System
	FontSize	10
	Height	495
	Left	4440
	Top	4800
	Width	1215
Command Button	**Name**	**cmdShow**
	Caption	&Show
	FontName	System
	FontSize	10
	Height	495
	Left	3240
	Top	4800
	Width	1215
Horizontal Scroll Bar	**Name**	**hsbPosition**
	Enabled	0-False
	Height	255
	Left	720
	Top	4440
	Width	6855
Image	**Name**	**imgMusic**
	Height	3090
	Left	720
	Picture	\VB4PRG\BMP\MIDI.BMP (Use a BMP picture that is appropriate for this program)
	Top	120
	Width	6900

Object	Property	Setting
Label	**Name**	**lblNowPlaying**
	Caption	Current Position:
	FontName	System
	FontSize	10
	Height	255
	Left	720
	Top	4200
	Width	3135
Multimedia	**Name**	**Tegomm1**
	Height	495
	Left	2160
	Top	3480
	Width	3510
Switch	**Name**	**swExit**
	Height	630
	Left	0
	Top	0
	Width	525
	value	-1-True
Common Dialog	**Name**	**CMDialog1**
	Left	6600
	Top	4800
	CancelError	-1-True
Menu	**(See Table 21.2.)**	**(See Figure 21.5.)**

Table 21.2. The menu table of the frmPlayMIDI form.

Caption	Name
&File	mnuFile
...&Open...	mnuOpen
...E&xit	mnuExit

21

Figure 21.10.
*The frmPlayMIDI form (in
design mode).*

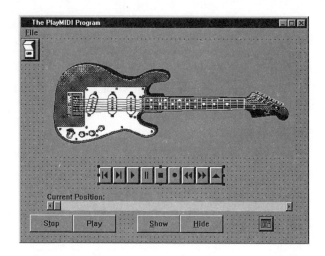

Entering the Code
of the PlayMIDI Program

You'll now enter the code of the PlayMIDI program.

Attaching Code to the *Click* Event
of the Exit Button

☐ Type the following code inside the swExit_Click() procedure of the frmPlayMIDI form:

```
Private Sub swExit_Click()

    End

End Sub
```

Attaching Code to the *Click* Event
of the Exit Menu Item

☐ Type the following code inside the mnuExit_Click() procedure of the frmPlayMIDI
form:

```
Sub mnuExit_Click()

    swExit_Click

End Sub
```

The code you typed executes the swExit_Click() procedure. Therefore, selecting the Exit item
from the File menu has the same results as clicking the Exit switch.

Attaching Code to the *Click* Event of the Hide Button

Whenever the user clicks the Hide button, the multimedia control is made invisible.

☐ Type the following code inside the cmdHide_Click() procedure of the frmPlayMIDI form:

```
Sub cmdHide_Click()

    Tegomm1.Visible = False

End Sub
```

> **Note:** The only reason you were instructed to implement the Show and Hide buttons is to demonstrate that you can make your own multimedia buttons and make the multimedia control invisible.

If you want your program to make the multimedia control invisible upon startup, execute the following statement from within the Form_Load() procedure:

```
Tegomm1.Visible = False
```

Attaching Code to the *Click* Event of the Show Button

Whenever the user clicks the Show button, the multimedia control is made visible.

☐ Type the following code inside the cmdShow_Click() procedure of the frmPlayMIDI form:

```
Sub cmdShow_Click()

    Tegomm1.Visible = True

End Sub
```

The code you typed sets the Visible property of the multimedia control to True.

Attaching Code to the *Load* Event of the Form

You'll now attach code to the Load event of the frmPlayMIDI form. The Form_Load() procedure is executed whenever the program starts.

21

☐ Type the following code inside the Form_Load() procedure of the frmPlayMIDI form:

```
Sub Form_Load()

    Tegomm1.UpdateInterval = 250

End Sub
```

The code you typed sets the UpdateInterval property of the multimedia control to 250. This means that the Tegomm1_StatusUpdate() procedure is automatically executed every 250 milliseconds. Later in this chapter you'll write the code of the Tegomm1_StatusUpdate() procedure.

Opening a MIDI File

During design time, you placed the common dialog control inside the frmPlayMIDI file. This control is used to select a MIDI file. Whenever the user clicks the Open item from the File menu, the mnuOpen_Click() procedure is executed, which uses the common dialog control for selecting a file.

☐ Type the following code inside the mnuOpen_Click() procedure.

```
Sub mnuOpen_Click()

' Selecting a file (with the common dialog box)

    ' Set an error trap
    On Error GoTo OpenError

    ' Set the items of the File Type list box
    CMDialog1.Filter = _
        "All Files (*.*) | *.* |Midi Files (*.mid)|*.mid"

    ' Set the default File Type
    CMDialog1.FilterIndex = 2

    ' Display the common dialog box
    CMDialog1.Action = 1

    ' Remove the error type
    On Error GoTo 0

    ' Open the selected file
    Tegomm1.DeviceType = "Sequencer"
    Tegomm1.FileName = CMDialog1.FileName
    Tegomm1.Command = "Open"
    If Tegomm1.Error > 0 Then
        cmdPlay.Enabled = False
        cmdStop.Enabled = False
        frmPlayMIDI.Caption = _
            "The PlayMIDI Program - (No file is loaded)"

        MsgBox _
            "Can't open " + _
            CMDialog1.FileName, _
            vbCritical, _
            "Error"
```

```
        Else
            cmdPlay.Enabled = True
            cmdStop.Enabled = True
            frmPlayMIDI.Caption = _
                "The PlayMIDI Program -(" + CMDialog1.FileTitle _
                + ")"

            hsbPosition.Min = 0
            hsbPosition.Max = Tegomm1.Length
            hsbPosition.Enabled = False
        End If

        ' Exit this procedure
        Exit Sub

    OpenError:
    ' The user pressed the Cancel key of the common dialog

        ' Exit this procedure
        Exit Sub

End Sub
```

The code you that typed lets your user select a file.

An error trap is set:

```
On Error GoTo OpenError
```

This means that if during the execution of the mnuOpen_Click() procedure an error occurs, the procedure jumps to the OpenError line.

```
OpenError:

    ' Exit this procedure
    Exit Sub
```

So if an error occurred, the procedure terminates.

The Filter property of the common dialog control is set:

```
CMDialog1.Filter = _
    "All Files (*.*) ¦ *.* ¦Midi Files (*.mid)¦*.mid"
```

This means that the user will be able to examine all the files (*.*) or just the files with the .MID file extension.

The default setting of the common dialog box is set so the user will see the files with the .MID file extension:

```
CMDialog1.FilterIndex = 2
```

Now that the settings of the common dialog control have been set, you can display the common dialog box as an Open dialog box:

```
CMDialog1.Action = 1
```

21

When the common dialog box is displayed, the user can type a name of a file that does not exist, and the user can select a file that resides on a drive that is not ready (for example, the user can select a file from the A: drive even though there is no disk inside the A: drive). The common dialog box responds by generating an error, which causes the procedure to immediately branch to the OpenError line.

Recall that during design time you set the CancelError property of the common dialog box to True. This means that if the user clicks the Cancel button of the Open common dialog box an error is generated, and again, the procedure immediately jumps to the OpenError line.

However, if the user selects a legal file, no error is generated. So after displaying the common dialog box by setting its Action property to 1, the procedure will not jump to the OpenError line if an error did not occur. Instead, if no error occurred, the mnuOpen_Click() procedure continues with its normal execution. Because there is no need to trap errors anymore, the error trapping is canceled:

```
On Error GoTo 0
```

Next, the DeviceType property of the multimedia control is set to play MIDI files:

```
Tegomm1.DeviceType = "Sequencer"
```

Note: Before playing MIDI files with the multimedia control, you have to set the DeviceType property of the multimedia control to Sequencer.

The user selects a file with the common dialog box, and the selected file is stored in the Filename property of the common dialog box. The Filename property of the multimedia control is assigned with the filename and path that the user selected with the common dialog box:

```
Tegomm1.Filename = CMDialog1.Filename
```

Note: Before playing MIDI files with the multimedia control, you have to set the Filename property of the multimedia control to the name of the MIDI file.

Next, the Open command is issued:

```
Tegomm1.Command = "Open"
```

An `If…Else` statement is executed to determine whether the Open command was carried out successfully:

```
If Tegomm1.Error > 0 Then
   cmdPlay.Enabled = False
   cmdStop.Enabled = False
   frmPlayMIDI.Caption = _
          "The PlayMIDI Program - (No file is loaded)"
   MsgBox "Can't open " + _
          CMDialog1.Filename, _
          vbCritical, _
          "Error"
Else
   cmdPlay.Enabled = True
   cmdStop.Enabled = True
   frmPlayMIDI.Caption = _
    "The PlayMIDI Program -(" + CMDialog1.Filetitle + ")"

   hsbPosition.Min = 0
   hsbPosition.Max = Tegomm1.Length
   hsbPosition.Enabled = False
End If
```

If the Error property of the multimedia control is greater than 0, it means that an error occurred during the execution of the last command of the multimedia control. The last command that was executed by the multimedia control was the Open command, so the preceding `If…Else` statement examines whether the Open command was successfully executed.

If an error occurred during the execution of the Open command, the Play and Stop buttons that you placed inside the frmPlayMIDI form are disabled:

```
cmdPlay.Enabled = False
cmdStop.Enabled = False
```

and the Caption property of the frmPlayMIDI is set as follows:

```
frmPlayMIDI.Caption = _
        "The PlayMIDI Program - (No file is loaded)"
```

Finally, a message box is displayed, telling the user that the file can't be opened:

```
MsgBox "Can't open " + _
        CMDialog1.Filename, _
        vbCritical, _
        "Error"
```

If no error occurred during the execution of the Open command, the code under the `Else` statement is executed.

The Play and Stop buttons that you placed inside the form are enabled:

```
cmdPlay.Enabled = True
cmdStop.Enabled = True
```

The Caption property of the form is set to indicate which MIDI file is open:

```
frmPlayMIDI.Caption = _
    "The PlayMIDI Program -(" + CMDialog1.Filetitle + ")"
```

The Min property of the scroll bar is set to 0:

```
hsbPosition.Min = 0
```

The Max property of the scroll bar is set to the Length property of the MIDI file:

```
hsbPosition.Max = Tegomm1.Length
```

In other words, the range of the scroll bar represents the entire range of the MIDI file. Later in this chapter you'll type code that changes the scroll bar position according to the position of the played MIDI file.

> **Note:** The length of the MIDI file is stored as the Length property of the multi-media control.

The Enabled property of the scroll bar is set to False (so that the user will not be able to manually change the position of the scroll bar):

```
hsbPosition.Enabled = False
```

Then the Exit Sub statement is executed to terminate the procedure:

```
Exit Sub
```

> **Note:** The PlayMIDI program does not let the user change the position of the MIDI file. However, you can implement your own programs that do let the user set the position of the MIDI file to any desired position by changing the scroll bar position.

Attaching Code to the *Click* Event of the Play Button

Whenever the user clicks the Play button, the MIDI file is played.

☐ Type the following code inside the `cmdPlay_Click()` procedure:

```
Sub cmdPlay_Click()

    Tegomm1.Command = "Play"

End Sub
```

The code you typed issues the `Play` command to the multimedia control.

Attaching Code to the *Click* Event of the Stop Button

Whenever the user clicks the Stop button the MIDI file stops playing.

☐ Type the following code inside the `cmdStop_Click()` procedure:

```
Sub cmdStop_Click()

    Tegomm1.Command = "Stop"

End Sub
```

The code you typed issues the `Stop` command to the multimedia control.

Attaching Code to the *StatusUpdate* Event of the Multimedia Control

Recall that during design time you set the UpdateInterval property of the multimedia control to 250. This means that the `Tegomm1_StatusUpdate()` procedure is executed automatically every 250 milliseconds.

☐ Type the following code inside the `Tegomm1_StatusUpdate()` procedure:

```
Sub Tegomm1_StatusUpdate()

    hsbPosition.Value = Tegomm1.Position

End Sub
```

The code you typed sets the Value property of the scroll bar to the Position property of the multimedia control:

```
hsbPosition.Value = Tegomm1.Position
```

As the MIDI file is played, the multimedia control automatically updates the Position property of the multimedia control. Because the `Tegomm1_StatusUpdate()` procedure is executed every 250 milliseconds, the scroll bar changes its position every 250 milliseconds.

21

Attaching Code to the *Done* Event of the Multimedia Control

You'll now attach code to the Done event of the multimedia control.

☐ Type the following code inside the Tegomm1_Done() procedure:

```
Sub Tegomm1_Done()

    If Tegomm1.Position = Tegomm1.Length Then
        Tegomm1.Command = "Prev"
    End If

End Sub
```

The Done event occurs whenever the multimedia control finishes playing. An If statement is executed to examine the reason for the occurrence of the Done event. After the Play command is issued, the MIDI file is played. Eventually the entire MIDI file will be played, and this will generate a Done event. The If statement checks whether the current position of the MIDI file is equal to the Length property of the multimedia control:

```
If Tegomm1.Position = Tegomm1.Length Then

   Tegomm1.Command = "Prev"

End If
```

If the Position property is equal to the Length property, it means that the current position (the Position property) of the MIDI file is at the end of the file, and the entire MIDI file was played.

The Prev command is issued to rewind the MIDI file, so the next time the user clicks the Play button, the MIDI file is ready to be played from its beginning.

☐ Execute the PlayMIDI program and experiment with it.

The PlayAVI Program

The PlayAVI program that you'll now write demonstrates how you can play movie AVI files, which are files that contain movies (video and audio). Your PC acts as a TV that plays movies. To play a movie AVI file, you need a PC with a 386 processor or better and a VGA monitor or better. You do not need any other hardware.

As stated at the beginning of this chapter, the Media Player program can be used to determine whether your PC is capable of playing movie AVI files.

Note: If your PC has a 386 or better CPU and a VGA monitor or better, then you'll be able to play movie AVI files, provided that you installed the movie AVI drivers (just like you have to install the appropriate drivers for playing WAV and MIDI files).

Generating Movie AVI Files

There are two ways you can obtain movie AVI files:

- Purchase a CD with movie AVI files in it.
- Generate the AVI files with a camcorder and a video capture card.

When purchasing a CD that has movie AVI files in it, read the software license agreement of the CD to make sure that you are allowed to distribute the movie AVI files with your programs.

If you want to generate the AVI files yourself, you have to install a video capture card into your PC (this costs about $400 to $600), and you have to use a camcorder. Figure 21.11 is a schematic diagram showing a camcorder connected to a video capture card inside the PC. Typically, the manufacturer of the video capture card supplies the software that converts the captured video into an AVI file (for example, you record something, and your recording is saved as the MyFilm.AVI file).

Figure 21.11.
Generating a movie AVI file using a camcorder.

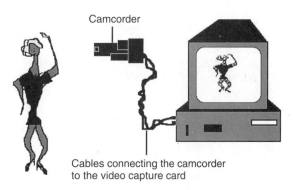

Camcorder

Cables connecting the camcorder to the video capture card

21

Using the PlayAVI Program to Play Movie AVI Files

Let's review the specifications of a Visual Basic program called PlayAVI that plays movie AVI files.

Upon startup of the PlayAVI program, the window shown in Figure 21.12 appears.

As shown in Figure 21.12, the multimedia OLE control is used for playing the AVI file.

Figure 21.12.
The window of the PlayAVI program.

Note: The PlayAVI program uses the buttons of the multimedia control as the buttons of the VCR. However, just like the PlayMIDI program that uses your Play and Stop buttons, you can make the multimedia control invisible and use your own buttons for the buttons that manipulate the playback of the AVI file.

Figure 21.13 shows the File menu of the PlayAVI program.

Here's how the PlayAVI program operates:

☐ The user selects Open item from the File menu and loads an AVI file.

PlayAVI responds by loading the AVI file, and the title of the PlayAVI window indicates which AVI file is loaded.

☐ The user clicks the Play button of the multimedia control (the third button from the left) to play the AVI file.

PlayAVI responds by playing the movie of the AVI file that was loaded. The sound of the movie is played through the sound card. In Figure 21.14, the Kennedy.AVI movie is loaded. In a similar way, you can play the other movies.

Figure 21.13.
The File menu of the PlayAVI program.

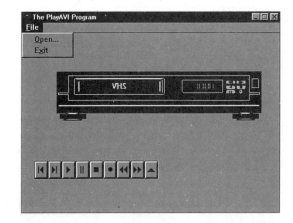

You can experiment with the PlayAVI program as follows:

☐ Experiment with the buttons of the multimedia control. In particular, click the Stop button to stop the playback, and then click the Step button (second button from the right) and the Back button (third button from the right). As you click the Step and Back buttons, you can view individual frames of the movie.

Figure 21.14.
Playing the Kennedy.AVI movie.

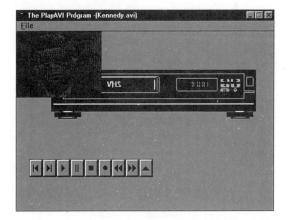

The Visual Implementation of the frmPlayAVI Form

You'll now visually design the frmPlayAVI form of the PlayAVI form.

☐ Select New Project from the File menu, and save the new project as follows: Save the new form as PlayAVI.frm in the C:\VB4PRG\CH21 directory and save the new project file as PlayAVI.VBP in the C:\VB4PRG\CH21 directory.

☐ Add the TegoSoft multimedia OLE control to your project as follows:

☐ Select Custom Control from the Tools menu, click the Browse button, and select the TegoMM??.OCX (where ?? stands for 32 if you are using 32-bit Windows, and ?? stands for 16 if you are using 16-bit Windows) file from the \Windows\System directory.

☐ Implement the frmPlayAVI form according to the specifications in Table 21.3. When you finish implementing the form, it should look like the one shown in Figure 21.15. Table 21.3 instructs you to place the common dialog OLE control inside the frmPlayAVI form. Use the Custom control dialog box (which you access from the Tools menu) to add the common dialog OLE control to your project.

Table 21.3. The properties table of the frmPlayAVI form.

Object	Property	Setting
Form	Name	frmPlayAVI
	BackColor	Light gray
	BorderStyle	1-Fixed Single
	Caption	The PlayAVI Program
	Height	5580
	Icon	\VB\ICONS\MISC\MISC41.ICO
	Left	1080
	MaxButton	0-False
	Top	420
	Width	7410
Image	Name	imgMovie
	Height	1665
	Left	840
	Picture	C:\VB4PRG\BMP\AVI.BMP (Use a BMP picture that is appropriate for this program)
	Top	840
	Width	6060
Multimedia	Name	Tegomm1
	Height	495
	Left	360
	Top	3480
	Width	3510

Object	Property	Setting
Common Dialog	**Name**	**CMDialog1**
	Left	480
	Top	2640
	CancelError	-1-True
Menu	**(See Table 21.4.)**	**(See Figure 21.13.)**

Table 21.4. The menu table of frmPlayAVI.

Caption	Name
&File	mnuFile
...&Open...	mnuOpen
...E&xit	mnuExit

Figure 21.15.
The frmPlayAVI form in design mode.

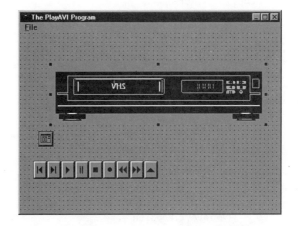

Attaching Code to the *Click* Event of the Exit Menu Item

You'll now attach code to the Exit item of the File menu.

☐ Type the following code inside the mnuExit_Click() procedure:

```
Sub mnuExit_Click()

    End

End Sub
```

Attaching Code to the *Click* Event of the Open Menu Item

You'll now attach code to the Click event of the Open menu item.

☐ Type the following code inside the mnuOpen_Click() procedure of the frmPlayAVI form:

```
Sub mnuOpen_Click ()

    ' Selecting a file (with the common dialog box)

    ' Set an error trap
    On Error GoTo OpenError

    ' Set the items of the File Type list box
    CMDialog1.Filter = _
    "All Files (*.*) ¦ *.* ¦Movie AVI Files (*.avi)¦*.avi"

    ' Set the default File Type
    CMDialog1.FilterIndex = 2

    ' Display the common dialog box
    CMDialog1.Action = 1

    ' Remove the error type
    On Error GoTo 0

    ' Open the selected file
    Tegomm1.DeviceType = "AVIVideo"
    Tegomm1.FileName = CMDialog1.Filename
    Tegomm1.Command = "Open"
    If Tegomm1.Error > 0 Then
        frmPlayAVI.Caption = _
          "The PlayAVI Program - (No file is loaded)"

        MsgBox "Can't open " + _
            CMDialog1.Filename, _
            vbCritical, _
            "Error"
    Else
        frmPlayAVI.Caption = _
    "The PlayAVI Program -(" + CMDialog1.Filetitle + ")"

    End If


''' Tegomm1.hWndDisplay = 0
Tegomm1.hWndDisplay = Me.hWnd

    ' Exit this procedure
    Exit Sub

OpenError:
    ' The user pressed the Cancel key of the common dialog

    ' Exit this procedure
    Exit Sub

End Sub
```

The code you typed is very similar to the code you typed inside the mnuOpen_Click() procedure of the frmPlayMIDI form of the PlayMIDI program. Of course, now you are opening an AVI file. Therefore, the Filter property of the common dialog box is set as follows:

```
CMDialog1.Filter = _
  "All Files (*.*) ¦ *.* ¦Movie AVI Files (*.avi)¦*.avi"
```

When opening the AVI file, you set the DeviceType property to AVIVideo:

```
Tegomm1.DeviceType = "AVIVideo"
```

The selected AVI file is assigned to the FileName property of the multimedia control:

```
Tegomm1.FileName = CMDialog1.Filename
```

Then the Open command is issued:

```
Tegomm1.Command = "Open"
If Tegomm1.Error > 0 Then
   frmPlayAVI.Caption = _
      "The PlayAVI Program - (No file is loaded)"
   MsgBox "Can't open " + _
          CMDialog1.Filename, _
          vbCritical, _
          "Error"
Else
   frmPlayAVI.Caption = _
"The PlayAVI Program -(" + CMDialog1.Filetitle + ")"
End If
```

After issuing the Open command, you set the hWndDisplay property of the multimedia control as follows:

```
''' Tegomm1.hWndDisplay = 0
Tegomm1.hWndDisplay = Me.hWnd
```

That is, you assigned the hWnd property of the frmPlayAVI form to the hWndDisplay property of the multimedia control. This means that the movie will be shown in the frmPlayAVI form. Similarly, you can display the movie in other forms. For example, your project can include another form called frmForMovie. If you want to display the movie in the frmForMovie form, use the following statement after issuing the Open command:

```
Tegomm1.hWndDisplay = frmForMovie.hWnd
```

21

Therefore, at design time you can size and place the frmForMovie form to any desired place on the screen, so that at runtime the movie will be shown at any desired place.

You can also set the hWndDisplay property to 0, as in the following:

```
Tegomm1.hWndDisplay = 0
```

The preceding statement causes the movie to be placed in its own window.

Attaching Code to the *Done* Event of the Multimedia Control

☐ Type the following code inside the Tegomm1_Done() procedure of the frmPlayAVI form:

```
Private Sub Tegomm1_Done()

    If Tegomm1.Position = Tegomm1.Length Then
       Tegomm1.Command = "Prev"
    End If

End Sub
```

The code that you typed checks if the entire AVI file was played, and if so, the AVI file is rewound with the Prev command.

☐ Execute the PlayAVI program and experiment with it.

Data CDs and Audio CDs

Many PCs have CD-ROM drives. Typically, you can use the CD-ROM drive for using data CDs as well as for using audio CDs.

A data CD is a CD that stores data. It is a standard data storage device like the hard drive, a 5.25" disk, or a 3.5" disk, but a data CD has the following special characteristics:

- Your CD-ROM drive cannot write into the data CD. You can only read the data of the data CD.
- The data CD can stores about 600MB.

Most PC users do not have the equipment to generate data CDs by themselves.

Once a CD-ROM drive is installed into your PC, it is treated like any other drive (except that you can only read data from the CD; you cannot write data into the CD).

You can access the CD-ROM drive just as you would any other drive. For example, if your CD-ROM drive is installed as a D: drive, then from the DOS prompt you can examine the directories of the data CD that was inserted into the CD-ROM drive as follows:

```
DIR D:\  {Enter}
```

Similarly, you can use the Windows 95 Explorer (or the Windows 3.1*x* File Manager) to read the contents of a data CD that was inserted into the CD-ROM drive.

You can also copy files from the data CD to your hard drive. However, the data CD is a read-only device. This means that you cannot copy files to the data CD.

Note: Once you copy a file from the data CD to your hard drive, the file on your hard drive has the read-only attribute (the r attribute). This means that you cannot modify the file.

Nevertheless, you can change the attribute of the file on your hard drive. For example, in Windows 3.1x you can use the Properties item of the File menu in File Manager. In File Manager select the file that was copied from the data CD, select Properties from the File menu of File Manager, and remove the check mark from the Read-Only check box. Now that the r attribute is removed from the file, you can modify the file. The same procedure works within Windows 95 Explorer.

Note: There are many types of CD-ROM drives. Basically, the faster the CD-ROM drive, the more expensive it is. Usually, the CD-ROM drive is categorized as double speed (2X), triple speed (3X), and nowadays, some companies manufacture the quad speed (4X) CD-ROM drive.

You should be aware that the operating system known as Windows NT 3.5 does not recognize all CD-ROM drives. Windows NT 3.5 requires that the CD-ROM drive be an SCSI CD-ROM drive. SCSI is a special interface protocol. So, for example, you can have a CD-ROM drive that is recognized by Windows other than Windows NT 3.5, but if this CD-ROM drive is not an SCSI drive, Windows NT 3.5 will report that you do not have a CD-ROM drive in your system.

If you take a look at a data CD, you'll notice that it looks just like an audio CD sold in music stores. An audio CD contains recordings, and you can play the audio only if your CD-ROM drive is capable of playing CD audio. Most CD-ROM drives are capable of using both data CDs and audio CDs.

There are several ways to listen to an audio CD:

- Typically, the CD-ROM drive has a jack that lets you plug in earphones. (See Figure 21.16.)
- Many sound card vendors sell their sound cards as a multimedia package that includes a CD-ROM drive and a sound card. The CD-ROM drive can serve as both a data CD-ROM drive and as an audio CD-ROM drive. When installing the CD-ROM drive, you have to internally connect the CD-ROM drive to the sound card. So when you play CD audio, the sound is played through the sound card. (See Figure 21.17.)

Figure 21.16.

Connecting earphones to a CD-ROM drive that is capable of playing CD audio. Typically, a volume control lets you adjust the volume.

Volume

Figure 21.17.

An internal connection between a sound card and a CD-ROM drive that is capable of playing CD audio. The sound is played through the speakers of the sound card.

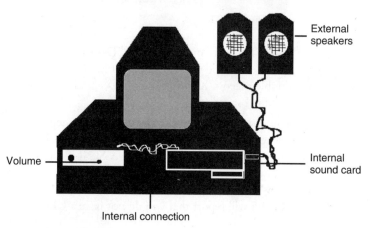

External speakers

Volume

Internal sound card

Internal connection

DO	DON'T

DO consider your selection of a CD-ROM drive based on the following factors:

- You should consider the speed of the CD-ROM drive. Ideally, you want the fastest CD-ROM drive so that you can read data CDs as quickly as possible. For example, if the data CD that you insert to the CD-ROM drive is an encyclopedia program, you want to be able to extract information from the encyclopedia as quickly as possible. Also, many programs are now sold on a data CD. When installing the program, the installation (copying files from the CD to your hard drive) will be performed faster on a fast CD-ROM drive than on a slow one. And yes, a faster CD-ROM drive costs more!

- Most CD-ROM drives can use both data CDs and audio CDs. Make sure the CD-ROM drive you are planning to purchase can use both types of CDs.

- Most CD-ROM drives let you connect the CD to the sound card so that you can hear the CD audio through the sound card.

- There are other features that may or may not be important to you. For example, some CD-ROM drives require that you use a cartridge. That is, you cannot simply insert the CD (a data CD or an audio CD) into your CD-ROM drive. Instead, you have to insert the CD into a cartridge, and then insert the cartridge into the CD-ROM drive. (This makes the process of inserting CDs into the CD-ROM drive take a little bit longer, but most users get used to it.)

- A consideration with some CD-ROM drives is the mechanical robotics capabilities. For example, in some CD-ROM drives you have to manually open and close the door of the CD-ROM drive to insert or eject a CD. Other CD-ROM drives let the software eject the CD. So instead of having to manually press a button on the CD-ROM drive, the software has an Eject button, and when you click the Eject button, the door of the CD-ROM drive opens.

- You need to decide whether you want to purchase an SCSI-type CD-ROM drive. If you plan to use Windows NT 3.5, you must purchase a CD-ROM drive that has an SCSI connection.

As you can see, there are many things to consider when purchasing a CD-ROM drive.

Note: As previously stated, the data CD is treated like a regular storage device. For example, you can execute the DOS DIR command to examine the directory of the data CD, you can use the DOS COPY command to copy files from the data CD, and so on.

However, when you insert an audio CD into your CD-ROM drive, you cannot execute the DIR, COPY, or any other command. When an audio CD is inserted into your CD-ROM drive, your CD-ROM drive simply serves as an audio CD player machine that can be remotely operated by software to play, stop, and so on.

The PlayCD Program

You'll now write the PlayCD program, which demonstrates how easy it is to write a Visual Basic program that plays CD audio.

Before writing the PlayCD program yourself, let's review its specifications.

☐ Upon startup of the PlayCD program, the window shown in Figure 21.18 appears.

Figure 21.18.
The PlayCD program.

The user can now insert an audio CD into the CD-ROM drive and play the audio CD.

To Play the audio CD, the user has to do the following:

☐ Click the Load button to load the CD.

☐ Click the Play button of the multimedia control (the third button from the left on the multimedia control).

Experiment with the program as follows:

☐ Click the Play button to start playback. Click the Stop and Pause buttons to stop and pause the playback. Click the Next button (second button from the left on the multimedia control) to advance to the next CD track. Click the Prev button (first button from the left on the multimedia control) to go back to the previous CD track.

Now that you know what the PlayCD program is supposed to do, you can write the program.

The Visual Implementation of the frmPlayCD Form

☐ Select New Project from the File menu and save the new project as follows: Save the new form as PlayCD.FRM in the C:\VB4PRG\CH21 directory and the new project file as PlayCD.VBP in the C:\VB4PRG\CH21 directory.

The PlayCD program uses the TegoSoft multimedia OLE control. Therefore, you have to add this control to your project:

☐ Select Custom Control from the Tools menu, click the Browse button, and select the TegoMM??.OCX (where ?? stands for 32 if you are using 32-bit Windows, and ?? stands for 16 if you are using 16-bit Windows) file from the \Windows\System directory.

☐ Implement the frmPlayCD form according to the specifications in Table 21.5. When you finish implementing the form, it should look like the one shown in Figure 21.19.

Table 21.5. The properties table of the frmPlayCD form.

Object	Property	Setting
Form	**Name**	**frmPlayCD**
	BackColor	Light gray
	Caption	The PlayCD Program
	Height	4950
	Left	1080
	Top	765
	Width	6810
Command Button	**Name**	**cmdExit**
	Caption	E&xit
	FontName	System
	FontSize	10
	Height	495
	Left	5280
	Top	3960
	Width	1215
Command Button	**Name**	**cmdLoad**
	Caption	&Load
	FontName	System
	FontSize	10
	Height	495
	Left	3840
	Top	3960
	Width	1215
Image	**Name**	**imgCD**
	Height	3135
	Left	240

continues

21

Table 21.5. continued

Object	Property	Setting
	Picture	\VB4PRG\BMP\CD.BMP (Use a BMP picture that is appropriate for this program)
	Top	480
	Width	6075
Multimedia	**Name**	**Tegomm1**
	Height	495
	Left	120
	Top	3960
	Width	3510

Figure 21.19.
The frmPlayCD form (in design mode).

Attaching Code to the *Click* Event of the Exit Button

You'll now attach code to the Click event of the Exit button of the frmPlayCD form.

☐ Type the following code inside the cmdExit_Click() procedure of the frmPlayCD form:

```
Sub cmdExit_Click()

    End

End Sub
```

Attaching Code to the *Click* Event of the Load Button

You'll now attach code to the Click event of the Load button.

☐ Type the following code inside the cmdLoad_Click() procedure of the frmPlayCD form:

```
Sub cmdLoad_Click()

    Tegomm1.DeviceType = "CDAudio"
    Tegomm1.Command = "Open"

End Sub
```

The code you typed sets the DeviceType property of the multimedia control to CDAudio:

```
Tegomm1.DeviceType = "CDAudio"
```

Then the Open command is issued:

```
Tegomm1.Command = "Open"
```

That's it! The PlayCD program is complete.

> **Note:** After issuing the Open command, you can use an If statement to examine the Error property to see if any errors occurred.

☐ Execute the PlayCD program and experiment with it. Note that in order to see the PlayCD program in action, you have to insert an audio CD into the CD-ROM drive, click the Load button, and then click the Play button.

> **Note:** Some CD-ROM drives are not manufactured in strict compliance with Windows. Therefore, sometimes you will find that the audio CD does not function as expected. For example, some CD-ROM drives refuse to move to another track while playback is in progress. In this case, you can place a button that will serve as the Next Track button, and attach code to it that's similar to the following:
>
> ```
> mciFormatTmsf = 10
> Tegomm1.Command = "Stop"
> Tegomm1.TimeFormat = "TMSF"
> Tegommm1.To = 3
> Tegomm1.Command = "Seek"
> Tegomm1.Command = "Play"
> ```

21

The preceding code stops the playback. Then the TimeFormat property is set to TMSF (which means tracks for the CD), the To property is set to 3, and then the Seek command is executed.

Because you set the To property to 3, the Seek command will place the current track of the CD-ROM to 3.

Finally, the Play command is issued.

Summary

In this chapter you have written some simple multimedia programs that play various multimedia devices. The PlayMIDI program illustrates how to play MIDI files, the PlayAVI program illustrates how to play movie AVI files, and the PlayCD program illustrates how to play CD audio.

Q&A

Q I would like to perform additional multimedia-related tasks. For example, in the PlayMIDI program, I want to display the total length of the MIDI file in seconds, and as the MIDI file is played, I want to display the elapsed time.

Also, I want to be able to cut, paste, and copy sections of WAV files; I want to be able to increase/decrease the volume; I want to create echo; I want to be able to record my own voice and then play it so it will sound like a different person, and I have millions of other ideas that I want to implement. Help!

A In this chapter you have only scratched the surface of multimedia programming. The multimedia control is capable of performing all the tasks you mentioned in your question, but we can't cover all these topics in this book, because every book has a limited scope. You might want to consult the book *Master Visual Basic 4,* by Gurewich and Gurewich (published by Sams Publishing), which elaborates on multimedia programming (as well as other programming topics in Visual Basic).

Q I purchased a sound card, installed it according to the manufacturer's instructions, and later checked the Device menu of Media Player. Guess what? The Sound item does not appear inside the Device menu. Nevertheless, the sound card comes with software, and that software plays WAV files without any problems! Should I insist on seeing Sound inside the Device menu of Media Player?

A Yes. This way, other Windows applications will also be able to play WAV files on your PC. That's what Windows is all about. If Windows accepts the device (and the acceptance can be tested by examining the Device menu), every Windows application should be able to use the device. So insist on seeing the Sound item in the Device menu of Media Player (so ANY Windows application will be able to utilize your sound card).

Quiz

1. The current position of the played file is given by what property of the multimedia control?

2. The length of the played file is given by what property of the multimedia control?

3. The DeviceType property of the TegoMM??.OCX control determines various media. Give some examples of values that can be assigned to the DeviceType property.

Exercises

1. Modify the PlayMIDI program so that when the file has been played in its entirety, the playback starts all over again.

2. Modify the PlayMIDI program so that an animation show is displayed during the playback.

Quiz Answers

1. Position

2. Length

3. To play WAV files through the sound card, set the DeviceType property as follows:

```
MyTegoMM.DeviceType = "WaveAudio"
```

To play MIDI files through the sound card, set the DeviceType property as follows:

```
MyTegoMM.DeviceType = "Sequencer"
```

To play AVI files, set the DeviceType property as follows:

```
MyTegoMM.DeviceType = "AVIVideo"
```

21

Exercise Answers

1. Here is the `Tegomm1_Done()` procedure of the PlayMIDI program:

```
Sub Tegomm1_Done()

    If Tegomm1.Position = Tegomm1.Length Then
        Tegomm1.Command = "Prev"
    End If

End Sub
```

When the file has been played in its entirety, the `Prev` command is issued. The next time the user plays the file, the MIDI file starts playing from the beginning.

To cause the MIDI file to automatically start playing all over again when the entire file is played, modify the `Tegomm1_Done()` procedure as follows:

```
Sub Tegomm1_Done()

    If Tegomm1.Position = Tegomm1.Length Then

        Tegomm1.Command = "Prev"
        Tegomm1.Command = "Play"

    End If

End Sub
```

When the file has been played in its entirety, you issue the `Prev` command to rewind the file, and then you issue the `Play` command to start the file playing again.

2. Modify the `Tegomm1_StatusUpdate()` procedure of the frmPlayMIDI form so that it looks as follows:

```
Private Sub Tegomm1_StatusUpdate()

Static FrameNumber

Dim Path

Path = App.Path
If Right(App.Path, 1) <> "\" Then
    Path = Path + "\"
End If

hsbPosition.Value = Tegomm1.Position

If Tegomm1.Mode = 526 Then

    FrameNumber = FrameNumber + 1
    imgMusic.Picture = _
LoadPicture(Path + "Midi" + Format(FrameNumber) + ".BMP")

    If FrameNumber = 10 Then
        FrameNumber = 0
    End If
```

```
End If
```

End Sub

The code that you typed declares a static variable:

```
Static FrameNumber
```

A local variable `Path` is assigned with the path from which the PlayMIDI program is executed:

```
Path = App.Path
If Right(App.Path, 1) <> "\" Then
    Path = Path + "\"
End If
```

The Position scroll bar is then updated with the position of the MIDI file:

```
hsbPosition.Value = Tegomm1.Position
```

An `If` statement is then executed to determine if playback is in progress:

```
If Tegomm1.Mode = 526 Then

    ............................
    ... Playback is in progress
    ............................

End If
```

That is, when the Mode property of the multimedia control is equal to 526, playback is in progress. The code of the animation is therefore written under the `If` statement.

`FrameNumber` is a static variable that indicates which frame of the animation to display. Initially, `FrameNumber` is equal to 0.

`FrameNumber` is increased by 1:

```
FrameNumber = FrameNumber + 1
```

and the Picture property of the imgMusic image is assigned with the file Midi?.BMP, where ? stands for an integer:

```
imgMusic.Picture = _
LoadPicture(Path + "Midi" + Format(FrameNumber) + ".BMP")
```

So, for example, when `FrameNumber` is equal to 1, the Midi1.BMP file is assigned to the Picture property of the imgMusic image.

The animation consists of 10 BMP files, so an `If` statement is executed to make sure that `FrameNumber` does not exceed 10:

```
    If FrameNumber = 10 Then
        FrameNumber = 0
    End If
```

So every time the `Tegomm1.StatusUpdate()` procedure is executed, a different picture is displayed. Here is the sequence of BMP pictures that are displayed during the animation:

```
Midi1.BMP
Midi2.BMP
Midi3.BMP
Midi4.BMP
Midi5.BMP
...
...
...
Midi10.BMP
Midi1.BMP
Midi2.BMP
Midi3.BMP
Midi4.BMP
Midi5.BMP
...
...
...
```

Note that the Midi?.BMP files are assumed to reside in the same directory from which the program is executed. So if you are executing the PlayMIDI program from the C:\VB4PRG\CH21 directory, make sure that the BMP files are inside this directory. Likewise, if you decide to generate an EXE file (PlayMIDI.EXE) and to save the EXE file inside the C:\VB4PRG\EXE directory, then the BMP pictures must reside inside this directory.

Bonus Day

1+

Adding Your Own Custom Property to a Form

As you know, a form has many properties (Caption, Width, Height, Background color, and so on). These properties are standard properties; every Visual Basic form has them.

In this chapter, you'll learn how to add your own custom property to a form. As you'll soon see, after you add a custom property to a form, you can use this property as if it were a regular property. That is, you can set the value of the property and read the value of the property in the same way you read and set the values of regular properties.

The STARS Program

You'll now write the STARS program. The STARS program illustrates how to write code that adds a custom property to a form.

The Visual Implementation of the STARS Program

You'll now visually implement the STARS program.

☐ Create the C:\TYVBProg\BD01 directory. (You'll save the program of this chapter into this directory.)

☐ Start a new project, save the form of the project as STARS.FRM in the C:\TYVBProg\BD01 directory, and save the project file as STARS.VBP.

☐ Build the frmStars form in accordance with Table BD1.1.

The completed form should look like the one shown in Figure BD1.1.

Table BD1.1. The properties table of frmStars form.

Object	Property	Setting
Form	**Name**	**frmStars**
	Caption	The Stars Program
	Height	4545
	Left	1080
	Top	1170
	Width	6810

Object	Property	Setting
CommandButton	**Name**	**cmdExit**
	Caption	E&xit
	Font Name	System
	Font Size	10
	Height	495
	Left	2760
	Top	3480
	Width	1215
TextBox	**Name**	**txtStars**
	Enabled	False
	Font Name	System
	Font Size	10
	Height	1575
	Left	840
	MultiLine	True
	Text	(make it empty)
	Top	360
	Width	4935

Figure BD1.1.
The frmStars form in design mode.

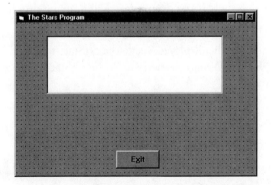

Entering the Code of the STARS Program

☐ Enter the following code inside the general declarations section of the frmStars form:

```
' All variables MUST be declared.
Option Explicit
```

☐ Enter the following code inside the cmdExit_Click() procedure of the frmStars form:

```
Private Sub cmdExit_Click ()

    End

End Sub
```

☐ Execute the STARS program to make sure that you designed the form and entered the code correctly. For example, make sure that the edit box is disabled.

☐ Click the Exit button.

The program responds by terminating itself.

Writing the Code that Adds a Custom Property to the Form

You'll now write the code that is responsible for adding a custom property to the frmStars form.

You'll name the custom property NumberOfStars, and you'll define the functionality of the NumberOfStars property as follows:

☐ The NumberOfStars property will hold a numeric number (an Integer).

☐ The value stored in the NumberOfStars property will determine how many stars (asterisks) will be displayed inside the txtStars text box. For example, if someone will set the NumberOfStars property to 7, the txtStars text box will be automatically filled with 7 stars.

Now that you know what the NumberOfStars property should do, you can implement this property.

Declaring a Variable for the NumberOfStars Property

Before you write the code that adds the NumberOfStars property to the frmStars form, you need to declare a variable for the NumberOfStars property. This variable will be used to hold the value of the NumberOfStars property.

☐ Add code to the general declarations section of the frmStars form that declares an Integer variable called gNumStars. After you write this code, the general declarations section of the frmStars form should look as follows:

```
' All variables MUST be declared.
Option Explicit

' Declare a variable for the NumberOfStars custom
' property.
Dim gNumStars As Integer
```

> **Note:** Don't get confused. The property name will be NumberOfStars. The variable name that you just declared is gNumStars. gNumStars will be used for holding the value of the NumberOfStars property.

The reason for declaring gNumStars inside the general declarations of the form is that we want gNumStars to be visible in all the procedures of the form.

Writing the Property Procedures for the NumberOfStars Custom Property

At this point you have a variable called gNumStars that will be used for storing the value of the NumberOfStars property.

Now you'll write the procedures that actually implement the NumberOfStars property.

☐ Display the Code window of the frmStars form (that is, select Project from the View menu, select frmStars inside the Project window, and then click the View Code button).

☐ Select Procedure from the Insert menu.

Visual Basic responds by displaying the Insert Procedure dialog box. (See Figure BD1.2.)

Figure BD1.2.
The Insert Procedure dialog box.

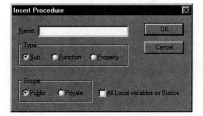

☐ Type NumberOfStars inside the Name edit box (because that's the name of the property that you are now adding).

☐ Click the Property radio button (because you are now adding a property).

☐ Make sure that the Scope is set to Public (because you want other forms and modules in the program to be able to access the NumberOfStars property of the frmStars form).

Your Insert Procedure dialog box should now look as shown in Figure BD1.3.

Figure BD1.3.

Adding the NumberOfStars property to the frmStars form.

☐ Click the OK button of the Insert Procedure dialog box.

Visual Basic responds by adding two property procedures inside the code window. They look as follows:

```
Public Property Get NumberOfStars()

End Property
```

and

```
Public Property Let NumberOfStars(vNewValue)


End Property
```

☐ Write the following code inside the Property Get NumberOfStars() procedure:

```
Public Property Get NumberOfStars()

   ' Someone is trying to get the value of
   ' the NumberOfStars custom property, so return
   ' the value of the gNumStars variable.
   NumberOfStars = gNumStars

End Property
```

The Property Get NumberOfStars() procedure is automatically executed whenever someone tries to get the value of the NumberOfStars property. The statement that you typed inside this procedure,

```
NumberOfStars = gNumStars
```

simply returns the value of the gNumStars variable. Thus, whoever tries to read the value of the NumberOfStars property is provided with the current value of the gNumStars variable.

☐ Write the following code inside the Property Let NumberOfStars() procedure:

```
Public Property Let NumberOfStars(vNewValue)

    ' Someone is trying to set the value of the
    ' NumberOfStars custom property with a new
    ' value, so set the value of gNumOfStars
    ' with the new value.
    gNumStars = vNewValue

    ' Fill the txtStars text box with X number of stars
    ' (where X is the current value of the NumberOfStars
    ' property).
    txtStars.Text = String(gNumStars, "*")

End Property
```

The Property Let NumberOfStars() procedure is automatically executed whenever someone tries to set the value of the NumberOfStars property with a new value. The first statement that you typed inside the procedure,

```
gNumStars = vNewValue
```

sets gNumStars (the variable of the NumberOfStars property) with the new value of the property. The new value of the property is vNewValue (the parameter of the procedure).

The second statement that you typed inside the procedure,

```
txtStars.Text = String(gNumStars, "*")
```

uses the String() function to fill the txtStars text box with gNumStars stars. Thus, whenever someone sets the NumberOfStars property to a certain value, the txtStars text box will be filled with a number of stars equal to the new value of the property.

For example, if someone sets the NumberOfStars property to 10, the txtStars text box will be automatically filled with 10 stars.

That's it. You have finished adding the NumberOfStars property to the frmStars form. In the following section you'll test the NumberOfStars property.

☐ Save your work! (That is, select save Project from the File menu of Visual Basic.)

Testing the NumberOfStars Property

You have finished the implementation of the NumberOfStars custom property. This means that you (or any other programmer) can now write code that uses the NumberOfStars property as if it were a regular property.

Let's test the NumberOfStars property by adding two controls to the frmNumberOfStars form: a horizontal scroll bar and a pushbutton. The code that you'll attach to the scroll bar will enable the user to set the value of the NumberOfStars property, and the code that you'll attach to the pushbutton will enable the user to read the value of the NumberOfStars property.

☐ Add a horizontal scroll bar to the frmStars form, and set its properties as follows:

Name: hsbNumStars

Max: 200

Min: 0

☐ Add a command button to the frmStars form, and set its properties as follows:

Name: cmdDisplayNumStars

Caption: Display Number of Stars

☐ Add a label control to the frmStars form, and set its properties as follows:

Name: lblNumStars

Caption: Number of Stars

Your frmStars form should now look as shown in Figure BD1.4.

Figure BD1.4.

The frmStars form after adding to it a horizontal scroll bar, a pushbutton, and a label.

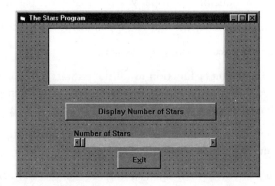

☐ Enter the following code inside the `hsbNumStars_Change()` procedure of the frmStars form:

```
Private Sub hsbNumStars_Change()

    ' Set the value of the NumberOfStars custom
    ' property to the current position of the
    ' scroll bar.
    frmStars.NumberOfStars = hsbNumStars.Value

End Sub
```

BD1

☐ Enter the following code inside the hsbNumStars_Scroll() procedure of the frmStars form:

```
Private Sub hsbNumStars_Scroll()

    ' Set the value of the NumberOfStars custom
    ' property to the current position of the
    ' scroll bar.
    frmStars.NumberOfStars = hsbNumStars.Value

End Sub
```

☐ Enter the following code inside the cmdDisplayNumStars_Click() procedure of the frmStars form:

```
Private Sub cmdDisplayNumStars_Click()

    ' Display the current value of the
    ' NumberOfStars custom property.
    MsgBox frmStars.NumberOfStars

End Sub
```

☐ Save your work!

The code that you attached to the Change event and Scroll event of the hsbNumStars scroll bar sets the value of the NumberOfStars property according to the position of the scroll bar. The code that you attached to the Click event of the cmdDisplayNumStars pushbutton uses the MsgBox statement to display the current value of the NumberOfStars property. To see this code in action, do as follows:

☐ Execute the STARS program and experiment with the horizontal scroll bar and the pushbutton.

As you can see, the text box is filled with stars in accordance with the thumb position of the scroll bar. When you click the Display Number Of Stars pushbutton, the program displays the current number of stars. Figure BD1.5 shows the STARS program when the scroll bar thumb is at the extreme right position.

Figure BD1.5.
The STARS program when the scroll bar thumb is at the rightmost position.

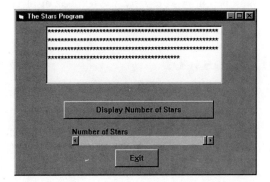

Summary

In this chapter you learned how to add a custom property to a form. As you have seen, after you complete writing the code that adds the property to the form, you can use the property just as you use other standard properties.

Q&A

Q **I added the NumberOfStars property to the frmStars form, and the Stars program works as expected. But the NumberOfStars property does not appear inside the Property window of the form.**

A From within your code, you refer to the new property as:

```
frmStars.NumberOfStars
```

But the NumberOfStars property was added to the form from within your code. So during design time, you can't see this property in the Properties window of the form. For all other purposes, the NumberOfStars property is just like any other property of the form.

Quiz

What is the result of executing the statement

```
txtStars.Text = String(gNumStars, "*")
```

when gNumStars is equal to 3?

Exercise

Currently, upon setting the NumberOfStars property of the frmStars form, the text box displays a string composed of stars. The number of stars on the string is equal to the NumberOfStars property. Modify the Stars program so that when the user sets the NumberOfStars property, the text box displays a message that indicates the value of the NumberOfStars property.

Quiz Answer

The result of executing the statement

```
txtStars.Text = String(gNumStars, "*")
```

is that the txtStars text box is filled with a string. The string is composed of 3 stars (* characters) because gNumStars (the first parameter of the String() function) is equal to 3.

Exercise Answer

Modify the `Property Let NumberOfStars()` procedure (inside the general section of the frmStars form) so that it will look as follows:

BD1

```
Public Property Let NumberOfStars(vNewValue)

    ' Someone is trying to set the value of the
    ' NumberOfStars custom property with a new
    ' value, so set the value of gNumOfStars
    ' with the new value.
    gNumStars = vNewValue

    ' Fill the txtStars text box with X number of stars
    ' (where X is the current value of the NumberOfStars
    ' property).
    'txtStars.Text = String(gNumStars, "*")
    txtStars.Text = "Number of stars = " + Str(gNumStars)

End Property
```

That is, you commented out the statement:

```
'txtStars.Text = String(gNumStars, "*")
```

and you added the following statement:

```
txtStars.Text = "Number of stars = " + Str(gNumStars)
```

Bonus Day

2+

Creating Your Own Classes

Starting with Visual Basic 4, you can create your own classes from within your Visual Basic programs. In this chapter you'll learn what is a class, how to create classes, and how to utilize your classes from within your Visual Basic programs.

What is a Class?

Before proceeding with the study of classes, let's answer the question of what is a class?

You already used classes many times in this book. For example, every time you placed a command button inside your form, you created an object. This object is an object of the class `CommandButton`. So for example, when you placed a command button and set its Name property to cmdExit, you created an object called `cmdExit`. The `cmdExit` object is of class `CommandButton`. If you placed another command button called cmdHello, you created an object `cmdHello` that also belongs to the `CommandButton` class.

Note: If you place the mouse cursor (without clicking the mouse) on an icon that appears in the Toolbox Window of Visual Basic, after a second or two, a yellow label pops up. This yellow label indicates the name of the class. For example, if you place the mouse cursor on the command-button icon inside the Toolbox, the yellow rectangle indicates the class `CommandButton`. Likewise, when you place the mouse cursor on the check box icon inside the Toolbox, the yellow rectangle indicates that the class of the check box is `CheckBox`.

After working with this book for a while, you probably realized how easy it is to program a command button. You placed it inside your form, and then you set several properties such as Caption, Name, and so on. No matter whether the button is used for the Hello button or the Exit button, the way you utilize the button is the same. Why? Because these command buttons belong to the same class. So putting it altogether, the fact that all your command buttons are objects of the same class makes your programming efforts very easy. The `CommandButton` class is a piece of software written by others. You (the programmer) don't care much about things like: Who exactly wrote the `CommandButton` class? How large is the code of the `CommandButton` class? How long did it take to develop the `CommandButton` class? All that you care about is that you'll be able to "plug" objects of the `CommandButton` class into your project.

Let's take a look, for example, at the `CheckBox` class. As you saw during the course of this book, plugging objects of class `CheckBox` (that is, incorporating check boxes) into your program is not much different from incorporating command buttons into your project. Sure, some of the property names are different, but essentially, you can say that if you know how to use the `CommandButton` class, you automatically know how to use the `CheckBox` class.

So where does all this discussion lead us? It leads to the conclusion that classes make your programming efforts very easy. Classes let you incorporate objects into your projects. And the nice thing about classes is that there is a uniform way of using them.

The MyCalc Program

You'll now design and implement the MyCalc program, a program that illustrates how to create your own class, and then utilize this class.

☐ Create the directory C:\TYVBProg\BD02. (This directory will be used to save all the work that you'll perform in this chapter.)

☐ Select New Project from the File menu of Visual Basic.

☐ Select Save Project As from the File menu of Visual Basic, save the new form as MyCalc.frm inside the C:\TYVBProg\BD02 directory, and save the new project as MyCalc.vbp inside the C:\TYVBProg\BD02 directory.

☐ Implement the frmMyCalc form according to Table BD2.1. When you complete implementing the form, the frmMyCalc form should look as shown in Figure BD2.1.

Table BD2.1. The Properties table of the frmMyCalc form.

Object	Property	Setting
Form	**Name**	**frmMyCalc**
	Caption	The MyCalc Program
	Height	4515
	Left	1080
	Top	1170
	Width	6600
TextBox	**Name**	**txtResult**
	Alignment	2 'Center
	Font name	MS Sans Serif
	Font size	13.5
	Height	855
	Left	360
	MultiLine	True
	Top	720
	Width	5895

continues

Table BD2.1. continued

Object	Property	Setting
CommandButton	**Name**	**cmdExit**
	Caption	E&xit
	Font name	MS Sans Serif
	Font size	8.25
	Height	495
	Left	2640
	Top	3360
	Width	1215
CommandButton	**Name**	**cmdMyCalculation**
	Caption	&My Calculation
	Font name	MS Sans Serif
	Font size	9.75
	Height	495
	Left	240
	Top	2520
	Width	1935
CommandButton	**Name**	**cmdHisCalculation**
	Caption	H&is Calculation
	Font name	MS Sans Serif
	Font size	9.75
	Height	495
	Left	2280
	Top	2520
	Width	1935
CommandButton	**Name**	**cmdHerCalculation**
	Caption	&Her Calculation
	Font name	MS Sans Serif
	Font size	9.75
	Height	495
	Left	4320
	Top	2520
	Width	1935

Figure BD2.1
*The frmMyCalc form
(design mode).*

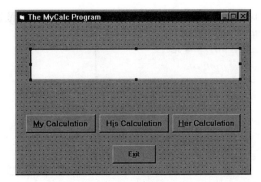

Attaching Code to the *Click* Event of the Exit Button

You'll now attach code to the `Click` event of the Exit button.

☐ Type the following code inside the `cmdExit_Click()` procedure of the frmMyCalc form:

```
Private Sub cmdExit_Click()

    Unload Me

End Sub
```

The code that you typed executes the `Unload` statement to unload the frmMyCalc form (which causes the termination of the MyCalc program).

Creating the Class File

> **Note:** The class that you'll create is called `CCalculation`. We start the name `CCalculation` with a `C`, to make it clear that `CCalculation` is a name of a class. This is not a Visual Basic requirement, but it makes your project easier to read and understand.

You'll now create a class called `CCalculation`.

☐ Select Class Module from the Insert menu of Visual Basic.

Visual Basic responds by displaying the Class1 window shown in Figure BD2.2.

Figure BD2.2.

The window that Visual Basic displays after you select Class Module from the Insert menu.

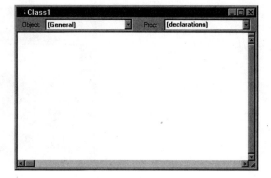

☐ Make sure that the Class1 window is selected, and then select Save File As from the File menu of Visual Basic.

Visual Basic responds by displaying the Save File As dialog box.

☐ Save the file as CCalc.cls inside the C:\TYVBProg\BD02 directory.

> **Note:** When saving the class file, save the file with a name that is appropriate to the nature of the class that you are creating. For example, as you'll soon see, the CCalculation class that you will create has to do with calculations. Hence, you were instructed to save the file as CCalc.cls.
>
> As you can see, in Visual Basic the file extension for classes is .cls.

Naming the Class

You'll now create the CCalculation class.

☐ Make sure that the Class module window is selected, and then press F4 (or select Properties from the View menu).

Visual Basic responds by displaying the properties window of the class.

☐ Use the properties window to set the Name property of the class to CCalculation as shown in Figure BD2.3.

☐ Select Save File from the File menu to save the CCalc.cls file.

You have now set the name of the class to CCalculation.

Figure BD2.3.
*Setting the Name property of
the class to* CCalculation.

Note: The class filename is CCalc.cls.

The Name property of the class is CCalculation.

Creating an Object of Class *CCalculation*

You'll now create an object of class CCalculation.

☐ Type the following code inside the cmdMyCalculation_Click() procedure of the frmMyCalc form:

```
Private Sub cmdMyCalculation_Click()

' Declare MyCalc as an object
' of class CCalculation
Dim MyCalc As New CCalculation

End Sub
```

The code that you typed creates the MyCalc object as an object of class CCalculation:

```
Dim MyCalc As New CCalculation
```

Note the syntax used to create the new object. That is, you use the Dim keyword, then the name of the object that you are creating, then you use the keywords As New, and finally you type the name of the class.

Creating the Properties of the *CCalculation* Class

Currently, the CCalculation class does not have any properties. You'll now add two properties to the CCalculation class:

☐ Make the CCalculation module window the active window.

☐ Inside the general declarations section of the class module window, type the following code:

```
Option Explicit
' Properties of the CCalculation class
Public Num1 As Long
Public Num2 As Long
```

The code that you typed inside the general declarations section of the CCalculation class declares two properties: Num1 and Num2. Thus, just like the CommandButton class that has properties such as Caption, Name, Top, and so on, the CCalculation class now has the Num1 and Num2 properties.

In the next section you'll write code that makes use of the properties of the CCalculation class.

Setting the Values of the Properties of the *MyCalc* Object

Previously, you typed code inside the cmdMyCalculation_Click() procedure that creates an object called MyCalc of class CCalculation as follows:

```
Dim MyCalc As New CCalculation
```

You'll now add code to the cmdMyCalculation_Click() procedure of the frmMyCalc form. The code that you'll add will set the Num1 and Num2 properties of the MyCalc object.

Can you guess what code you should have typed to set the Num1 and Num2 properties? Remember, the idea of all classes is to make your programming tasks easier. Well, if you were asked to type code that sets the Caption property of a command-button object called cmdMyButton, you'll type the following code:

```
cmdMyButton.Caption ="My Button"
```

In a similar way, you set the Num1 property of the MyCalc object as follows:

```
MyCalc.Num1 = 2
```

☐ Add code to the `cmdMyCalculation_Click()` procedure of the frmMyCalc form so that the procedure will look as follows:

```
Private Sub cmdMyCalculation_Click()

' Declare MyCalc as an object
' of class CCalculation
Dim MyCalc As New CCalculation

' Set the values of the Num1 and Num2 properties
' of the MyCalc object.
MyCalc.Num1 = 2
MyCalc.Num2 = 3

End Sub
```

The code that you typed sets the Num1 and Num2 properties of the `MyCalc` object as follows:

```
MyCalc.Num1 = 2
MyCalc.Num2 = 3
```

Adding a Method to the *CCalculation* Class

At this point, clicking the My Calculation button causes the creation of the `MyCalc` object of class `CCalculation`. Furthermore, the code that you typed inside the `cmdMyCalculation_Click()` procedure sets the Num1 and Num2 properties of the `MyCalc` project to 2 and 3. But at this point, you have no way to verify that indeed the Num1 and Num2 properties are set to 2 and 3. You'll now add a method to the `CCalculation` class. This method lets you perform calculations based on the values of Num1 and Num2. In particular, you'll write the `DoMultiplication` method. This method will multiply Num1 by Num2.

Here is how you add the `DoMultiplication` method to the `CCalculation` class:

☐ Make sure that the class module window is selected.

☐ Select Procedure from the Insert menu.

Visual Basic responds by displaying the Insert Procedure dialog box.

☐ Set the Insert Procedure dialog box as shown in Figure 2.4. That is, set the Name to DoMultiplication, and set the Type radio button to Function. Finally, click the OK button of the Insert Procedure dialog box.

Visual Basic responds by inserting the `DoMultiplication` *method as follows:*

```
Public Function DoMultiplication()

End Function
```

☐ Add the words As Long to the end of the first line of the DoMultiplication() method as follows:

```
Public Function DoMultiplication() As Long

End Function
```

You added the As Long words on the first line of the DoMultiplication() method, because you want the DoMultiplication() method to return a number of the type Long.

☐ Add code inside the DoMultiplication() method of the CCalculation class as follows:

```
Public Function DoMultiplication() As Long

Dim Result As Long

Result = Num1 * Num2

DoMultiplication = Result

End Function
```

The code that you typed declares Result as a local variable:

```
Dim Result As Long
```

Then, Result is assigned with the result of multiplying Num1 by Num2:

```
Result = Num1 * Num2
```

Finally, the DoMultiplication variable is assigned with the variable Result:

```
DoMultiplication = Result
```

In other words, because the name of the method is DoMultiplication, you must assign the value that will be returned by this method to the DoMultiplication variable as accomplished in the preceding statement.

Note: Of course, you can write the code of the DoMultiplication() method as follows:

```
Public Function DoMultiplication() As Long

DoMultiplication = Num1 * Num2

End Function
```

The only reason the Result variable is used is to demonstrate that the way you write code in methods is the same way you write code inside functions. You can declare local variables, you can perform calculations, and so on.

Because you declared the method as a method that returns a value (as indicated on the first line of the method), you have to assign the value that you want to be returned by the method to a variable that has the same name as the method's name.

Executing the *DoMultiplication* Method

BD2

You have created the DoMultiplication method. Now you'll have a chance to execute the DoMultiplication method.

☐ Add code to the cmdMyCalculation_Click() procedure of the frmMyCalc form. After adding the code, the cmdMyCalculation_Click() procedure should look as follows:

```
Private Sub cmdMyCalculation_Click()

' Declare MyCalc as an object
' of class CCalculation
Dim MyCalc As New CCalculation

' Set the values of the Num1 and Num2 properties
' of the MyCalc object.
MyCalc.Num1 = 2
MyCalc.Num2 = 3

' Display the result
MsgBox Str(MyCalc.DoMultiplication)

End Sub
```

The code that you typed displays the result inside a message box:

```
' Display the result
MsgBox Str(MyCalc.DoMultiplication)
```

Note that the result of the multiplication is extracted by executing the DoMultiplication method as follows:

```
MyCalc.DoMultiplication
```

☐ Select Save Project from the File menu of Visual Basic.

☐ Execute the MyCalc program.

☐ Click the My Calculation button.

MyCalc responds by displaying a message box that displays the result of multiplying 2 by 3.

☐ Experiment with the MyCalc program and then click the Exit button to terminate the MyCalc program.

Creating the *HisCalc* Object

You'll now create the HisCalc object.

☐ Type the following code inside the cmdHisCalculation_Click() procedure of the frmMyCalc form:

```
Private Sub cmdHisCalculation_Click()

' Declare HisCalc as an object
' of class CCalculation
Dim HisCalc As New CCalculation

' Set the values of the Num1 and Num2 properties
' of the HisCalc object.
HisCalc.Num1 = 20
HisCalc.Num2 = 30

' Display the result
MsgBox Str(HisCalc.DoMultiplication)

End Sub
```

The code that you typed declares the HisCalc object of class CCalculation:

```
Dim HisCalc As New CCalculation
```

You set the Num1 and Num2 properties of the HisCalc object as follows:

```
HisCalc.Num1 = 20
HisCalc.Num2 = 30
```

And then you display a message box that displays the result of the multiplication:

```
' Display the result
MsgBox Str(HisCalc.DoMultiplication)
```

Again, the result of the multiplication is extracted by executing the DoMultiplication method as follows:

```
HisCalc.DoMultiplication
```

☐ Select Save Project As from the File menu of Visual Basic, and then execute the MyCalc program.

☐ Click the His Calculation button to display the result of multiplying 20 by 30.

☐ Experiment with the MyCalc program and then click its Exit button to terminate the program.

Creating the *HerCalc* Object

You'll now create the HerCalc object, an object of class CCalculation.

☐ Type code inside the `cmdHerCalculation_Click()` procedure of the frmMyCalc form as follows:

```
Private Sub cmdHerCalculation_Click()

' Declare HerCalc as an object
' of class CCalculation
Dim HerCalc As New CCalculation

' Set the values of the Num1 and Num2 properties
' of the HerCalc object.
HerCalc.Num1 = 200
HerCalc.Num2 = 300

' Display the result
MsgBox Str(HerCalc.DoMultiplication)

End Sub
```

The code that you typed creates the `HerCalc` object:

```
Dim HerCalc As New CCalculation
```

The properties of the `HerCalc` object are set as follows:

```
HerCalc.Num1 = 200
HerCalc.Num2 = 300
```

And then the message box is displayed.

☐ Select Save Project from the File menu of Visual Basic, and then execute the MyCalc program.

☐ Experiment with the MyCalc program by clicking its My Calculation button, His Calculation button, and Her Calculation button.

Why Use Classes?

The MyCalc program demonstrated how a class called `CCalculation` is created, how two properties are declared in the `CCalculation` class, and how the `DoMultiplication` method is implemented. You then created three objects of class `CCalculation` inside the frmMyCalc form.

At first glance, it looks as if classes is a way to make programs complex without any real benefit. However, suppose that instead of the `DoMultiplication` method, you implement the `DoFourier` method, a method that performs a very complex mathematical operation (frequently used to analyze and manipulate sound files). In fact, if you are familiar with Fourier analysis, you'd realize that the `DoFourier` method requires a lot of coding that takes a significant amount of time to develop. The idea of classes is to isolate the programmer who develops a program such as the MyCalc program from complex tasks such as the `DoFourier` method. That is, implementing the

DoFourier method is a one-time investment. Once the DoFourier method is implemented (by yourself or by other programmers), it is very easy to use the class and its methods. In short, the class can be as complex as you want it to be. However, utilizing the class from within your project is in most cases as easy as utilizing the command button object of the CommandButton class.

Modifying the *CCalculation* Class

You'll now modify the CCalculation class. In particular, you'll add another property to the CCalculation class, the Result property. The Result property stores the result of multiplying the Num1 property with the Num2 property. So the procedures inside the frmMyCalc form will be able to extract the result of the multiplication as MyCalc.Result, HisCalc.Result, and HerCalc.Result (instead of using the returned value of the DoMultiplication method).

First, add the Result property to the CCalculation class as follows:

☐ Inside the general declarations section of the CCalculation class add the Result property. After adding the Result property, the general declaration section should look as follows:

```
Option Explicit

' Properties of the CCalculation class
Public Num1 As Long
Public Num2 As Long
Public Result As Long
```

Next, change the first line of the DoMultiplication method, so that it will not return a value. That is, remove the As Long words from the first line of the DoMultiplication method. Also, because the DoMultiplication method does not return a value, it is a Sub, not a Function. This means that you have to replace the word Function on the first line with the word Sub, and you also have to make sure that the word Function in the last line of the DoMultiplication method is replaced with the word Sub in the last line of the method. So the first and last lines of the DoMultiplication method will look as follows:

```
Public Sub DoMultiplication()


End Sub
```

☐ Change the code inside the DoMultiplication method so that it will look as follows:

```
    Public Sub DoMultiplication()

    Result = Num1 * Num2

    End Sub
```

The code that you typed sets the value of the Result property with the result of the multiplication Num1*Num2.

☐ Change the code inside the cmdMyCalculation_Click() procedure so that it will look as follows:

```
Private Sub cmdMyCalculation_Click()

' Declare MyCalc as an object
' of class CCalculation
Dim MyCalc As New CCalculation

' Set the values of the properties
' of the object.
MyCalc.Num1 = 2
MyCalc.Num2 = 3

MyCalc.DoMultiplication

MsgBox Str(MyCalc.Result)

End Sub
```

As you can see, you made a few modifications to the cmdMyCalculation_Click() procedure. Before you display the message box, you execute the DoMultiplication method as follows:

```
MyCalc.DoMultiplication
```

The DoMultiplication method does not return any value. But as you know (because you wrote the code of the DoMultiplication method), this method updates the Result property of the MyCalc object. Then you display the result:

```
MsgBox Str(MyCalc.Result)
```

That is, you use MyCalc.Result to extract the result of multiplying Num1 by Num2. Yes, the Result property is updated with the result because you already executed the DoMultiplication method.

Likewise, you have to modify the code inside the cmdHisCalculation_Click() and cmdHerCalculation_Click() procedures of the frmMyCalc form:

☐ Modify the code inside the cmdHisCalculation_Click() procedure so that it will look as follows:

```
Private Sub cmdHisCalculation_Click()

' Declare HisCalc as an object
' of class CCalculation
Dim HisCalc As New CCalculation

' Set the values of the properties
' of the object.
HisCalc.Num1 = 20
HisCalc.Num2 = 30

HisCalc.DoMultiplication
```

```
MsgBox Str(HisCalc.Result)
```

End Sub

☐ Modify the code inside the cmdHerCalculation_Click() procedure so that it will look as follows:

```
Private Sub cmdHerCalculation_Click()

' Declare HerCalc as an object
' of class CCalculation
Dim HerCalc As New CCalculation

' Set the values of the properties
' of the object.
HerCalc.Num1 = 200
HerCalc.Num2 = 300

HerCalc.DoMultiplication

MsgBox Str(HerCalc.Result)

End Sub
```

☐ Select Save Project from the File menu of Visual Basic to save your work.

☐ Execute the MyCalc program and verify that clicking the buttons inside the frmMyCalc form produces the expected results.

Changing the Form and its Objects from Within the Class

So far, you saw that the CCalculation class was used to make some calculations. But the CCalculation class did not change the properties of the frmMyCalc form or any of its objects in any way. Can the CCalculation class change any of the properties of the frmMyCalc form or any of its objects? Sure it can! You'll now add another method to the CCalculation class, the DisplayResult method. This method changes the Text property of the text box that you placed inside the frmMyCalc form.

☐ Make sure that the class module window is selected, and then select Procedure from the Insert menu of Visual Basic.

Visual Basic responds by displaying the Insert Procedure dialog box. (See Figure BD2.4.)

☐ Set the Name to DisplayResult, set the Sub radio button, and then click the OK button of the Insert Procedure dialog box.

Visual Basic responds by inserting the DisplayResult method in the CCalculation class.

Figure BD2.4.

The Insert Procedure dialog box.

BD2

☐ Type the following code inside the `DisplayResult` method:

```
Public Sub DisplayResult()

frmMyCalc.txtResult.Text = Str(Num1 * Num2)

End Sub
```

The code that you typed sets the Text property of the txtResult text box inside the frmMyCalc form to a string that indicates the result of multiplying Num1 and Num2.

☐ Modify the `cmdMyCalculation_Click()` procedure so that it will look as follows:

```
Private Sub cmdMyCalculation_Click()

' Declare MyCalc as an object
' of class CCalculation
Dim MyCalc As New CCalculation

' Set the values of the properties
' of the object.
MyCalc.Num1 = 2
MyCalc.Num2 = 3

MyCalc.DisplayResult

End Sub
```

The code that you typed executes the DisplayResult method on the MyCalc object.

☐ Modify the `cmdHisCalculation_Click()` procedure so that it will look as follows:

```
Private Sub cmdHisCalculation_Click()


' Declare HisCalc as an object
' of class CCalculation
Dim HisCalc As New CCalculation

' Set the values of the properties
' of the object.
HisCalc.Num1 = 20
HisCalc.Num2 = 30

HisCalc.DisplayResult

End Sub
```

877

☐ Modify the cmdHerCalculation_Click() procedure so that it will look as follows:

```
Private Sub cmdHerCalculation_Click()

' Declare HerCalc as an object
' of class CCalculation
Dim HerCalc As New CCalculation

' Set the values of the properties
' of the object.
HerCalc.Num1 = 200
HerCalc.Num2 = 300

HerCalc.DisplayResult

End Sub
```

☐ Select Save Project from the File menu, and then execute the MyCalc program.

☐ Experiment with the MyCalc program. In particular, verify that the text box displays the result of the multiplication.

☐ Click the Exit button to terminate the MyCalc program.

A Closer Examination of the *DisplayResult* Method

There is something terribly wrong with the DisplayResult method! Can you tell what is wrong with it?

Let's take a look at this method:

```
Public Sub DisplayResult()

frmMyCalc.txtResult.Text = Str(Num1 * Num2)

End Sub
```

This method has the name of the form (frmMyCalc) and the name of the text box (txtResult) hard-coded inside the code of the method! In other words, if in the future you (or somebody else) will want to use the CCalc.cls file for utilizing the CCalculation class, the class is usable *only* if the name of the form that utilizes the class is frmMyCalc, and *only* if the name of the text box inside the frmMyCalc form is txtResult. Evidently, this way of implementing the DisplayResult method defeats the whole objective of the class feature and Object Oriented Programming. That is, just as objects of class CommandButton work with any form, so should objects of class CCalculation.

Making the *DisplayResult* Method the Right Way

Ok, now that you understand that the class should be completely independent from the application in which the class is utilized, let's fix the `DisplayResult` method.

☐ Modify the `DisplayResult` method of the `CCalculation` class so that it will look as follows. Do not forget to modify the first line of the `DisplayResult` method (because now the `DisplayResult` method has a parameter).

BD2

```
Public Sub DisplayResult(TXT As TextBox)

TXT.Text = Str(Num1 * Num2)

End Sub
```

Now the `DisplayResult` method has a parameter, `TXT as TextBox`, which is an object of type `TextBox`. Yes, the code inside the frmMyCalc form will have to pass a text box object to the `DisplayResult` method.

The code inside the `DisplayResult` method sets the Text property (of the text box that was passed to `DisplayResult`) to a string that represents the result of multiplying Num1 by Num2.

☐ Modify the `cmdMyCalculation_Click()` procedure so that it will look as follows:

```
Private Sub cmdMyCalculation_Click()

' Declare MyCalc as an object
' of class CCalculation
Dim MyCalc As New CCalculation

' Set the values of the properties
' of the object.
MyCalc.Num1 = 2
MyCalc.Num2 = 3

MyCalc.DisplayResult frmMyCalc.txtResult

End Sub
```

Note how the `DisplayResult` method is executed:

`MyCalc.DisplayResult frmMyCalc.txtResult`

That is, the parameter of the `DisplayResult` method has a parameter, `frmMyCalc.txtResult`. So the `DisplayResult` method will display the result inside the txtResult text box.

☐ Modify the code of the cmdHisCalculation_Click() procedure so that it will look as follows:

```
Private Sub cmdHisCalculation_Click()

' Declare HisCalc as an object
' of class CCalculation
Dim HisCalc As New CCalculation

' Set the values of the properties
' of the object.
HisCalc.Num1 = 20
HisCalc.Num2 = 30

HisCalc.DisplayResult frmMyCalc.txtResult

End Sub
```

☐ Modify the code of the cmdHerCalculation_Click() procedure so that it will look as follows:

```
Private Sub cmdHerCalculation_Click()

' Declare HerCalc as an object
' of class CCalculation
Dim HerCalc As New CCalculation

' Set the values of the properties
' of the object.
HerCalc.Num1 = 200
HerCalc.Num2 = 300

HerCalc.DisplayResult frmMyCalc.txtResult

End Sub
```

☐ Select Save Project from the File menu of Visual Basic, and then execute the MyCalc program.

☐ Experiment with the MyCalc program. In particular, verify that clicking the buttons causes the text box to display the results of the multiplication.

The Object Browser

As your projects become more complex, you'll need a tool that lets you browse through your project files and module. Fortunately, Visual Basic comes with the Object Browser feature, which lets you browse through your project files easily. To see the Object Browser in action, do the following:

☐ While the MyCalc project is open, select Object Browser from the View menu of Visual Basic.

Visual Basic responds by displaying the Object Browser window. (See Figure BD2.5.)

Figure BD2.5.

*The Object Browser
dialog box.*

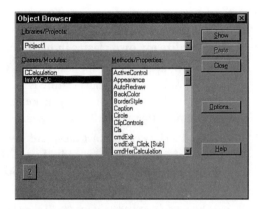

As you can see, the various methods and procedures are displayed inside the Methods/Properties list of the Object Browser dialog box.

☐ Select the CCalculation item from the Classes/Modules list.

☐ The Methods/Properties list now lists the methods and properties of the CCalculation class.

☐ Select the frmMyCalc item from the Classes/Modules list.

☐ The Methods/Properties list now lists the methods and properties of the frmMyCalc form.

☐ Click the Close button of the Object Browser to close the Object Browser dialog box.

Once you highlight a certain method or procedure that has code in it, you can click the Show button of the Object Browser dialog box. This causes Visual Basic to display the window where the code of the method/procedure that you highlighted is written. So if you have a class that has hundreds of methods/ procedures in it, the Object Browser is a convenient way to quickly locate the code that you are looking for.

Summary

In this chapter you were introduced to the powerful feature of creating and using your own classes with Visual Basic 4. In the Exercise section of this chapter, you'll explore an additional and powerful way to implement properties in a class.

As you saw in this chapter, classes let you implement reusable code. That is, once you implement a class, the class can be utilized by many applications, provided that you implemented the class in such a way that the class is completely independent from the application.

The Object Browser of Visual Basic was also discussed in this chapter.

Q&A

Q **Should I utilize my own classes in my future Visual Basic projects?**

A It depends on the particular application that you are implementing. You should be aware that just because the class feature is available in Visual Basic, this is not a reason to utilize it. If the application that you are developing does not necessitate the use of classes, do not bother yourself with classes.

Q **I developed a class called CMyClass, and saved it as CMyClass.cls. It is a wonderful, powerful, state-of-the-art code. I used this class to develop an application called MyApp. I now want to develop another application and to utilize the CMyClass class. How can I incorporate CMyClass into my new application?**

A Here is how you can utilize your CMyClass class in a new project:

☐ Create a new project.

☐ Select Add File from the File menu of Visual Basic, and select the CMyClass.cls file.

Visual Basic responds by adding the CMyClass class to the Project window. You can now use the CMyClass class just as you did in your original project.

Q **I am developing an application and need to utilize more than one class. Can I use additional classes?**

A Yes. To create additional classes in your project, select Class Module from the Insert menu. To use additional classes that you created in the past, select Add file from the File menu of Visual Basic, and select the cls file that you want to use.

Quiz

1. To create a method in a class, select _____ from the _____ menu of Visual Basic.

2. It is possible to pass an object as a parameter of a method.

    a. True

    b. False

Exercise

Follow the steps outlined in the Exercise Answer Section of this chapter to learn about another way of implementing properties in a class. As you'll see, this way of implementing properties is a very powerful one.

Quiz Answers

1. To create a method in a class, select Procedure from the Insert menu of Visual Basic.

2. a.

Exercise Answer

During the course of this chapter, you were instructed to create properties in the CCalculation class by simply declaring them inside the general declarations section of the class. For example, inside the general declarations section of the CCalculation class you declared properties as follows:

```
Option Explicit

' Properties of the CCalculation class
Public Num1 As Long
Public Num2 As Long
Public Result As Long
```

There is nothing wrong with declaring class properties in this way. The only thing is that there is a better way of creating properties for a class.

As an example, suppose that you want the CCalculation class to be able to change the BackColor property of the text box. This can be accomplished by adding a new method called ChangeBackColor() to the CCalculation class as follows:

```
Public Sub ChangeBackColor(TXT As TextBox, Color As Long)

TXT.BackColor = Color

End Sub
```

That is, from within the cmdMyCalculation_Click() procedure of the frmMyCalc form, you will write the following code:

```
MyCalc.ChangeBackColor(frmMyCalc.txtResult, RGB(255,0,0))
```

The preceding statement sets the BackColor property of the txtResult text box to RGB(255,0,0), which is the red color.

However, a better way to set the color of the text box from within the code of the frmMyCalc form is as follows:

```
MyCalc.BackColorOfTextBox = RGB(255,0,)
```

The preceding statement assumes that the CCalculation class has a property called BackColorOfTextBox.

However, you want to see an immediate action. That is, upon setting the BackColorOfTextBox property, you want the BackColor property of the txtResult text box to immediately change to the new color setting. This means that you have to implement the BackColorOfTextBox property in a different way. Here is how you implement the BackColorOfTextBox property:

☐ Make sure that the class module window is selected.

☐ Select Procedure from the Insert menu of Visual Basic.

    Visual Basic responds by displaying the Insert Procedure dialog box.

☐ Inside the Insert Procedure dialog box, set the Name to BackColorOfTextBox.

☐ Inside the Insert Procedure dialog box, set the Property radio button.

☐ Click the OK button of the Insert Procedure dialog box.

    Visual Basic responds by inserting two procedures inside the class module:

```
Public Property Get BackColorOfTextBox()

End Property
```

and

```
Public Property Let BackColorOfTextBox(vNewValue)

End Property
```

Whenever you write code inside the frmMyCalc form that sets the BackColorOfTextBox property, the `Let BackColorOfTextBox()` procedure is executed automatically.

And whenever you write code that reads the value of the BackColorOfTextBox property, the `Get BackColorOfTextBox()` procedure is executed automatically.

Let's see this in action:

☐ Add the declaration of a general variable called `Color` (as a `Long` variable) inside the general declarations section of the class module. After adding the declaration, the general declarations section of the class module should look as follows:

```
Option Explicit

' Properties of the CCalculation class
Public Num1 As Long
Public Num2 As Long
Public Result As Long

Dim Color As Long
```

As you can see, the Color long variable is declared inside the general declarations section, so this variable is accessible from every procedure of the CCalc.cls module.

☐ Inside the general declarations section of the CCalculation class add the declaration of the TheTextBox property. After adding this property, the general declarations section of the CCalculation class should look as follows:

```
Option Explicit

' Properties of the CCalculation class
Public Num1 As Long
Public Num2 As Long
Public Result As Long
Public TheTexBox As Control

Dim Color As Long
```

Note that TheTextBox was declared as Control:

```
Public TheTextBox As Control
```

☐ Add code to the Let BackColorOfTextBox() procedure as follows:

```
Public Property Let BackColorOfTextBox(vNewValue)

Color = vNewValue
TheTextBox.BackColor = Color

End Property
```

The code that you typed sets the value of the Color variable to vNewValue. That is, the code inside the frmMyCalc form will set the BackColorOfTextBox property to a certain value as follows:

```
MyCalc.BackColorOfTextBox = RGB(255,0,0)
```

As a result of executing the preceding statement, the Let BackColorOfTextBox() procedure is automatically executed, and vNewValue is equal to RGB(255,0,0). The code that you typed inside the Let BackColorOfTextBox() procedure sets the Color variable to RGB(255,0,0):

```
Color = vNewValue
```

Also, the code that you typed inside the Let BackColorOfTextBox() procedure changes the BackColor property of the text box to RGB(255,0,0):

```
TheTextBox.BackColor = Color
```

So putting it altogether, when the code inside the frmMyCalc form sets the BackColorOfTextBox property to a certain color, the text box immediately changes its back color to the color that was set.

Note: You learned that when the code inside the frmMyCalc form sets the BackColorOfTextBox property to a certain color, the text box immediately changes its BackColor property accordingly.

This is possible because you set the BackColorOfTextBox property of the CCalculation class by using the Procedure menu of the Insert menu (and as a result, Visual Basic created two special property functions).

However, note that in the current state of the CCalculation class, the BackColorOfTextBox property of the class uses the following statement:

```
TheTextBox.BackColor = Color
```

This means that prior to setting the BackColorOfTextBox property of the object, the code inside the frmMyCalc form must set the TheTextBox property of the object. This is an undesirable restriction. That is, when you implement classes, try to implement the classes in such a way that the user is not forced to set the properties in a certain order.

☐ Modify the cmdMyCalculation_Click() procedure so that it looks as follows:

```
Private Sub cmdMyCalculation_Click()

' Declare MyCalc as an object
' of class CCalculation
Dim MyCalc As New CCalculation

' Set the values of the properties
' of the object.
MyCalc.Num1 = 2
MyCalc.Num2 = 3

Set MyCalc.TheTextBox = frmMyCalc.txtResult

MyCalc.BackColorOfTextBox = RGB(255, 0, 0)

MyCalc.DisplayResult frmMyCalc.txtResult

End Sub
```

Let's take a look at the last two statements.

You set the TheTextBox property to the txtResult text box:

```
Set MyCalc.TheTextBox = frmMyCalc.txtResult
```

Note that when you set a property that stores a control, you have to use the Set keyword.

Then you set the BackColorOfTextBox property as follows:

```
MyCalc.BackColorOfTextBox = RGB(255, 0, 0)
```

☐ Modify the cmdHisCalculation_Click() procedure as follows:

```
Private Sub cmdHisCalculation_Click()

' Declare HisCalc as an object
' of class CCalculation
Dim HisCalc As New CCalculation

' Set the values of the properties
' of the object.
HisCalc.Num1 = 20
HisCalc.Num2 = 30

Set HisCalc.TheTextBox = frmMyCalc.txtResult

HisCalc.BackColorOfTextBox = RGB(0, 255, 0)


HisCalc.DisplayResult frmMyCalc.txtResult

End Sub
```

☐ Modify the cmdHerCalculation_Click() procedure as follows:

```
Private Sub cmdHerCalculation_Click()

' Declare HerCalc as an object
' of class CCalculation
Dim HerCalc As New CCalculation

' Set the values of the properties
' of the object.
HerCalc.Num1 = 200
HerCalc.Num2 = 300

Set HerCalc.TheTextBox = frmMyCalc.txtResult

HerCalc.BackColorOfTextBox = RGB(0, 0, 255)


HerCalc.DisplayResult frmMyCalc.txtResult

End Sub
```

☐ Select Save project from the File menu of Visual Basic, and then execute the MyCalc program.

☐ Experiment with the MyCalc program, and verify that clicking the buttons causes the displaying of the results of the multiplication in the text box.

In a similar way, you can add code to the Get BackColorOfTextBox() procedure as follows:

```
Public Property Get BackColorOfTextBox()

BackColorOfTextBox = Color

End Property
```

887

The `Get BackColorOfTextBox()`procedure is automatically executed whenever the code inside the frmMyCalc form reads the value of the BackColorOfTextBox property.

For example, inside the `cmdMyCalculation_Click()` procedure you can display the BackColorOfTextBox property as follows:

```
MsgBox "BackColorOfTextBox=" + _
       Str(MyCalc.BackColorOfTextBox)
```

The preceding statement causes the automatic execution of the `Get BackColorOfTextBox()` procedure (because in this statement, the BackColorOfTextBox property is extracted).

So if the BackColorOfTextBox property was previously set to `RGB(255,0,0)`, the preceding code displays a message box that displays a number that corresponds to `RGB(255,0,0)`. (Typically, the number returned from `RGB()` does not give you a clue to what color is used).

Bonus Day

3+

Creating Your Own OLE Automation Server

In this chapter you'll create your own OLE automation server. If you don't know what an OLE automation server is, don't worry. This chapter explains all the OLE terms that you'll need during the implementation of the OLE server. Note that Visual Basic 4, 32-bit professional version, is required for the implementation of the material of this chapter.

Note: This chapter assumes that you understand what classes are, and you know how to create properties and methods for a class. In other words, Bonus Day 2 of this book is a prerequisite to the material in this chapter.

What is an OLE Automation Server?

Before implementing the OLE server, let's answer the question: What is an OLE automation server?

OLE stands for object linking and embedding. An OLE server is a DLL file. For example, in this chapter you'll create a DLL file called MyOLE.DLL.

The OLE server DLL file that you'll create contains a class. That is, the DLL contains the code that declares the properties of the class, and it contains the code of the class's methods.

In the previous chapter, you implemented the CCalculation class. The class inside the MyOLE.DLL that you'll implement in this chapter is not much different from the CCalculation class that you created in the previous chapter. However, the beauty of an OLE server is that other Windows applications can utilize the class that is inside the MyOLE.DLL OLE server. In this case, the MyOLE.DLL is called the OLE server, and the program that utilizes the class inside MyOLE.DLL is called the OLE client.

Thus, you can write a Visual Basic program that will be able to use the class of the MyOLE.DLL OLE server.

Besides your own Visual Basic client programs, there are many other Windows OLE client programs that can utilize your MyOLE.DLL server. Word for Windows and Excel are just two examples of programs that can be OLE clients for your MyOLE.DLL server.

Note: In this chapter you'll design and implement an OLE server called MyOLE.DLL.

In the next chapter you'll implement a Visual Basic program that utilizes the MyOLE.DLL server. In other words, in the next chapter you'll design and implement an OLE client application.

In the previous chapter you created a class called CCalculation. So what is the difference between the CCalculation class that you implemented in the previous chapter and the class that you'll implement inside MyOLE.DLL?

The difference is that the CCalculation class that you created in the previous chapter is an integral part of the MyCalc program that uses the CCalculation class.

On the other hand, the class that is inside the MyOLE.DLL OLE server (which you'll create in this chapter) is completely independent from the client program that makes use of the class inside MyOLE.DLL.

Is it hard to create OLE server applications and OLE client applications? As you'll soon see, with Visual Basic, the job of creating your own OLE Server and client applications is very easy.

BD3

Creating the *CMyOLEClass* Class

You'll now create an OLE automation server application that contains a class called CMyOLEClass.

☐ Create the C:\TYVBProg\BD03 directory. (You'll save to this directory the work that you'll implement in this chapter.)

☐ Start Visual Basic, and then select New Project from the File menu of Visual Basic.

☐ Select Save Project from the File menu of Visual Basic, and save the project as follows: Save the form as MyOLE.frm inside the C:\TYVBProg\BD03 directory, and save the project as MyOLE.vbp inside the C:\TYVBProg\BD03 directory.

☐ Select Options from the Tools menu of Visual Basic.

  Visual Basic responds by displaying the Options dialog box.

☐ Click the Project tab of the Options dialog box.

  Visual Basic responds by displaying the Project page of the Options dialog box.

You'll now set the various options of the Project page of the Options dialog box.

☐ Set the Startup Form box Form to: Sub Main

That is, upon starting the application, the Main() procedure will be executed (not the Form_Load() procedure of the Form1 form).

☐ Set the Project Name to: MyOLE.

☐ Select the OLE Server radio button inside the StartMode group of radio buttons.

☐ Inside the Application Description box type: This is my OLE.

Your Project page of the Options dialog box should now look as shown in Figure BD3.1.

Figure BD3.1.

Setting the Project page of the Options dialog box.

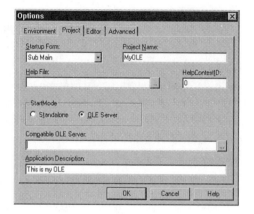

☐ Click the OK button of the Options dialog box.

Creating the *Sub Main* Procedure

In the previous section you set the Startup Form to Sub Main. This means that upon starting the OLE server application, Main() will be executed first. So you'll now create the Main() procedure:

☐ Select Module from the Insert menu of Visual Basic.

> *Visual Basic responds by inserting a new module (Module1) into the project.*

☐ Make sure that the window of Module1 is selected, select Save File As from the File menu of Visual Basic, and save the module as MyOLE.BAS inside the C:\TYVBProg\BD03 directory.

While the MyOLE.BAS module is selected, press F4 to display the properties window of the MyOLE.BAS module.

☐ Set the Name property to ModuleForMain (see Figure BD3.2).

Figure BD3.2.

Setting the Name property of the MyOLE.BAS module to ModuleForMain.

You'll now create the Sub Main() procedure inside the ModuleForMain module.

☐ Make sure the window of the ModuleForMain module is selected, and then select Procedure from the Insert menu of Visual Basic.

Visual Basic responds by displaying the Insert Procedure dialog box.

☐ Set the Insert Procedure dialog box as shown in Figure BD3.3. That is, set the Name to Main, set the Type to Sub, and set the Scope to Public.

Figure BD3.3.

Inserting the Main()
procedure inside the
ModuleForMain module.

☐ Click the OK button of the Insert procedure.

Visual Basic responds by inserting the Main() procedure to the ModuleForMain module.

☐ Type the following code inside the Main() procedure:

```
Public Sub Main()

' Here I can type the initialization code for the
' OLE server.

End Sub
```

That is, for now, you don't have to write any code inside Main(). But in your future OLE server projects, you can insert initialization code inside the Main() procedure. Even if you don't have any initialization code, you must include the Main() procedure. Recall that inside the Project page of the Options dialog box you specified the Startup Form as Sub Main (see Figure BD3.1). This means that upon starting the OLE Server application, Main() is executed.

Creating the Class of the OLE Server

So far you have only implemented the overhead code that is required for creating the OLE Server application. You'll now start implementing the class that you want the OLE server to contain.

Before implementing the class, let's take a look at the Project window:

☐ Select Project from the View menu of Visual Basic.

Visual Basic responds by displaying the Project window as shown in Figure BD3.4.

Figure BD3.4.

The Project window of the
MyOLE.vbp project.

As shown in Figure BD3.4, there are currently two files inside the Project window: MyOLE.frm is the form of the OLE server application; the other file is MyOLE.BAS, which is the module (ModuleForMain) where you implemented the Main() procedure.

> **Note:** Did you notice that you were not instructed to customize the MyOLE.frm form? Furthermore, you were not instructed to Show this form. The reason is that typically the OLE server is running in the background. That is, the end user of the client application usually does not know (or care) that he/she is using OLE automation technology. So while the client application will run, the OLE server application will run in the background, and the end user will not notice that there is an OLE server application running in the background.
>
> Nevertheless, if for some reason you want the user to know that there is an OLE server running in the background, you should customize the properties of the MyOLE.frm form, and Show it.

Now let's add another module to the project:

☐ Select Class Module from the Insert menu of Visual Basic.

   Visual Basic responds by inserting a class (Class1) module to the project.

☐ Make sure that the window of Class1 is selected, select Save File As from the File menu of Visual Basic, and save the file as MyClass.cls inside the C:\TYVBProg\BD03 directory.

☐ Make sure that the Class1 window is selected and press F4 to display the properties window of Class1.

   Visual Basic responds by displaying the properties window of Class1.

☐ Set the Name property of the class to CMyOLEClass.

☐ Set the Public property of the class to True.

☐ Set the Instancing property of the class to Createable MultiUse.

The properties window of the class should now look as shown in Figure BD3.5.

Figure BD3.5.
The properties window of the class.

Let's take a look at the Project window at this point of the development:

☐ Select Project from the View menu.

Visual Basic responds by displaying the Project window (see Figure BD3.6).

Figure BD3.6.
The Project window. (The project includes a form, a BAS module, and a class module.)

Adding Properties to the *CMyOLEClass* Class

You'll now add properties to the CMyOLEClass class.

☐ Make sure that the window of the CMyOLEClass class is selected.

☐ Inside the general declarations section of the CMyOLEClass module, type the following code:

```
Option Explicit

'Declare properties for the CMyOLEClass
Public Num1 As Long
Public Num2 As Long
```

(Make sure to type the preceding code inside the general declarations section of the class module).

Num1 and Num2 are properties of the CMyOLEClass class, because they are declared as Public variables inside the general declaration section of the class.

Thus the client application will be able to create an object of class CMyOLEClass and use these properties. For example, the client application will be able to create the object MyObject of class CMyOLEClass and to create the object HerObject of class CMyOLEClass. Then the client application will be able to set the Num1 and Num2 properties as follows:

```
MyObject.Num1 = 3
MyObject.Num2 = 6
HerObject.Num1 = 7
HerObject.Num1 = 7
```

The client application will also be able to read the properties of the objects as follows:

```
MsgBox ("Num1 property of MyObject is:" + Str(MyObject.Num1))
MsgBox ("Num2 property of MyObject is:" + Str(MyObject.Num2))
MsgBox ("Num1 property of HerObject is:" + Str(HerObject.Num1))
MsgBox ("Num2 property of HerObject is:" + Str(HerObject.Num2))
```

Creating a Read-Only Property

As you saw in the previous section, the Num1 and Num2 properties are read and write properties. That is, the client application is capable of setting these properties as well as reading these properties.

You'll now declare the Result property of the CMyOLEClass class. The Result property stores the result of multiplying Num1 by Num2. The client application will be able to read the Result property as follows:

```
MsgBox ("Result of MyObject is:" + Str(MyObject.Result))
MsgBox ("Result of HerObject is:" + Str(HerObject.Result))
```

However, you do not want the client application to be able to set the value of the Result property (because Result should be the result of multiplying Num1 by Num2). So there is a need to make the Result property a read-only property. Here is how you do that:

☐ Inside the general declaration section of the CMyOLEClass module, add the declaration of the PrivateResult property. After adding the declaration, the general declarations section of the CMyOLEClass module should look as follows:

```
Option Explicit

'Declare properties for the CMyOLEClass
Public Num1 As Long
Public Num1 As Long

Private PrivateResult As Long
```

You added the statement:

```
Private PrivateResult As Long
```

Note that PrivateResult is declared as `Private`. This means that the client application cannot access this property. The client property cannot read this property and cannot write into this property.

Now you'll add the Result property as follows:

☐ Make sure that the window of the CMyOLEClass module is selected, and then select Procedure from the Insert menu of Visual Basic.

> *Visual Basic responds by displaying the Insert Procedure dialog box.*

☐ Select the Property radio button of the Insert Procedure dialog box.

☐ Set the Name box of the Insert Procedure dialog box to Result.

☐ Make sure that the Public radio button is selected inside the Scope group of radio buttons.

Your Insert Property dialog box should now look as shown in Figure BD3.7.

Figure BD3.7.
Inserting the Result property.

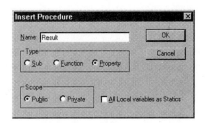

☐ Click the OK button of the insert Procedure dialog box.

> *Visual Basic responds by inserting the following two procedures into the CMyOLEClass procedure:*

```
Public Property Get Result()

End Property
```

and

```
Public Property Let Result(vNewValue)

End Property
```

☐ Add the words `As Long` to the end of the first line of the `Property Get Result()` procedure so that it will look as follows:

```
Public Property Get Result() As Long

End Property
```

You added As Long because you want this procedure to return a Long number. That is, you want the Result property to be of type Long.

☐ Add code inside the Property Get Result() procedure as follows:

```
Public Property Get Result() As Long

    Result = PrivateResult

End Property
```

The Property Get Result() procedure is automatically executed whenever the client application reads the value of the Result property. For example, whenever any of the following statements is executed inside the client application

```
MsgBox ("Result of MyObject is:" + Str(MyObject.Result))
MsgBox ("Result of HerObject is:" + Str(HerObject.Result))
```

the Get Result() procedure is automatically executed (assuming that the client application created MyObject and HerObject as objects of class CMyOLEClass).

The code that you typed inside the Get Result() procedure sets the value of the Result property to the value of PrivateResult.

You'll now add code to the Let Result() procedure. This code is automatically executed whenever the client application tries to set the value of the Result property.

☐ Add code inside the Let Result() procedure as follows:

```
Public Property Let Result(vNewValue As Long)

    ' No need to type code here

End Property
```

Make sure to add the words As Long inside the parenthesis on the first line of the Let Result() procedure.

You did not type code inside the Let Property Result() procedure that sets the value of PrivateResult to vNewValue. So if the programmer of the client application tried to use the statement

```
MyObject.Result = 33
```

the OLE Server will not change the value of PrivateResult.

> **Note:** Suppose that, for some strange reason, you decide that you want to let the client application set the value of the Result property. That is, you want the client application to be able to use the following statements:
>
> ```
> MyObject.Num1 = 3
> MyObject.Num2 = 6
> HerObject.Num1 = 7
> HerObject.Num1 = 7
> ```
>
> (where MyObject and HerObject are objects of class `CMyOLEClass`).
>
> To make the Result property a writeable property, you'll have to write the following code inside the `Let Result()` procedure:
>
> ```
> Public Property Let Result(vNewValue As Long)
>
> PrivateResult = vNewValue
>
> End Property
> ```

Adding the *DoMultiplication* Method to the *CMyOLEClass* class

You'll now add the `DoMultiplication` method of the `CMyOLEClass` class.

☐ Make sure that the window of the `CMyOLEClass` class is selected, and then select Procedure from the Insert menu of Visual Basic.

Visual Basic responds by displaying the Insert Procedure dialog box.

☐ Set the Name of the Insert Procedure dialog box to DoMultiplication, set the Type radio button to Sub, and set the Scope radio button to Public.

☐ Click the OK button of the Insert Procedure dialog box.

Visual Basic responds by inserting the `DoMultiplication` method inside the `CMyOLEClass` class.

☐ Type the following code inside the `DoMultiplication` method of the `CMyOLEClass` class:

```
Public Sub DoMultiplication()

    PrivateResult = Num1 * Num2

End Sub
```

The code that you typed sets the value of PrivateResult to the result of the multiplication of Num1 by Num2.

Note: In Exercise 1 of this chapter, you'll add another method to the class. The new method is called the DoAddition method. (And yes, you guessed it, the DoAddition method adds Num1 to Num2 and updates the PrivateResult property with the result of the addition).

The *Initialize* and *Terminate* Events

You can attach code to the Initialize and Terminate events of the CMyOLEClass class as follows:

☐ Make sure that the CMyOLEClass window is selected, set the object box to Class, and then select Initialize from the Proc box. (See Figure BD3.8.)

Figure BD3.8.

The class has two events:
Initialize and Terminate.

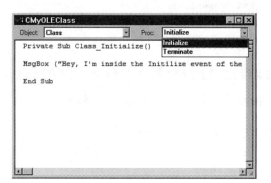

☐ Add the following code inside the Class_Initialize() procedure of the class:

```
Private Sub Class_Initialize()

MsgBox ("Hi, I'm inside the Initialize event of the Server")

End Sub
```

☐ Add the following code inside the Class_Terminate() procedure of the class:

```
Private Sub Class_Terminate()

MsgBox ("Hi, I'm inside the Terminate event of the Server")

End Sub
```

So when the client application will use the CMyOLEClass class for the very first time (when the object of class CMyOLEClass is created), the Class_Initialize() procedure will be executed automatically. And when the object of the client application will be destroyed, the Class_Terminate() procedure will be terminated.

Of course, the two message boxes that you placed are not needed. The only reason you were instructed to place these two message boxes is to provide you with proof that indeed these two procedures are executed when an object of class CMyOLEClass is created by the client application and when the client application destroys the object (as it does, for example, when the client application is terminated).

Compiling and Running *CMyOLEClass*

You completed implementing the OLE Automation server application. Here is how you compile the application:

☐ Select Save Project from the File menu of Visual Basic.

☐ Select Start With Full Compile from the Run menu. (Or press Ctrl+F5.)

If you did not make any errors entering the code, you will not get any errors and you'll see the debug window.

☐ Select End from the Run menu of Visual Basic to terminate the server application.

At this point in the development, you don't see any action. To see some action, you need to execute a client application that makes use of CMyOLEClass. You'll do so in the next chapter.

Making a DLL—The Last Thing to Do

You'll now create a DLL file for the OLE server application.

☐ Select Make OLE DLL File from the File menu of Visual Basic.

Visual Basic responds by displaying the Make OLE DLL File dialog box.

☐ Save the file as MyOLE.DLL inside the C:\TYVBProg\BD03 directory.

☐ Terminate the Visual Basic program. (Select Exit from the File menu of Visual Basic.)

Typically, a DLL should reside inside the \Windows\System directory:

☐ Copy the MyOLE.DLL file from the C:\TYVBProg\BD03 directory to your C:\Windows\System directory.

In the next chapter you'll design and implement a client application that makes use of MyOLE.DLL, the OLE Automation Server application that you created in this chapter.

Summary

In this chapter you learned what an OLE server and a client application are. You learned that an OLE server application enables the client OLE application to create objects based on the class that is declared inside the OLE server application.

Q&A

Q I've implemented the OLE server application. Now how can I use it?

A In the next chapter you'll implement an application (a client application) that utilizes the server application that you created in this chapter.

Q Can any Windows application use the OLE server application that I built in this chapter?

A Any Windows application that is capable of using an OLE server will be able to use your OLE server application.

Q Can I declare more than one class in the OLE server application?

A Yes. Select Class Module from the Insert menu of Visual Basic, and then implement the class as you implemented the CMyOLEClass class of this chapter.

Quiz

1. After you select Procedure from the Insert menu of Visual Basic, Visual Basic displays the _____ dialog box.
2. To insert a property to a class, you can _____
3. If you decide to add a property called Result to a class by using the Insert Procedure dialog box, then Visual Basic inserts two procedures to the class. What are these two procedures?

Exercises

1. Currently, the CMyOLEClass class has a single method, the DoMultiplication method. Add another method to the class, and call this new method the DoAddition method. The DoAddition method adds Num1 and Num2, and assigns the result of the addition to the PrivateResult property.
2. So far, you have three properties inside the CMyOLEClass class, and you have two methods. Use Visual Basic to quickly verify this fact.

Quiz Answers

1. After you select Procedure from the Insert menu of Visual Basic, Visual Basic displays the Insert Procedure dialog box. This dialog box is used for inserting procedures and properties.

2. To insert a property to a class, you can:

   Declare the property as Public inside the general declarations section of the class module.

   Alternatively, you can select Procedure from the Insert menu, and set the Property radio button that appears inside the Insert Procedure dialog box.

3. Here are the two procedures:

```
Public Property Get Result()

End Property
```
and
```
Public Property Let Result(vNewValue)

End Property
```

Exercise Answers

1. You'll now add the DoAddition method to the CMyOLEClass class.

   ☐ Make sure that the window of the CMyOLEClass class is selected, and then select Procedure from the Insert menu of Visual Basic.

   Visual Basic responds by displaying the Insert Procedure dialog box.

   ☐ Set the Name of the Insert Procedure dialog box to DoAddition, set the Type radio button to Sub, and set the Scope radio button to Public.

   ☐ Click the OK button of the Insert Procedure dialog box.

   Visual Basic responds by inserting the DoAddition method inside the CMyOLEClass class.

   ☐ Type the following code inside the DoAddition method of the CMyOLEClass class:

```
Public Sub DoAddition()

    PrivateResult = Num1 + Num2

End Sub
```

   The code that you typed sets the value of PrivateResult to the result of the addition of Num1 by Num2.

☐ Select Save Project from the File menu of Visual Basic.

In the next chapter you'll write a client application that makes use of the CMyOLEClass class. Therefore, if you want the client application to be able to use the DoAddition method, you have to perform the following steps:

☐ Select Make OLE DLL File form the File menu of Visual Basic.

Visual Basic responds by displaying the Make OLE DLL File dialog box.

☐ Save the file as MyOLE.DLL inside the C:\TYVBProg\BD03 directory.

☐ Terminate the Visual Basic program. (Select Exit from the File menu of Visual Basic.)

☐ Copy the MyOLE.DLL file from the C:\TYVBProg\BD03 directory to your C:\Windows\System directory.

As stated earlier, the client application that you'll write in the next chapter will make use of the MyOLE.DLL file that you created in this chapter. This means that the client application will be able to use the DoMultiplication and DoAddition methods.

2. To verifiy the properties and classes inside CMyOLEClass:

☐ Select Object Browser from the View menu of Visual Basic.

Visual Basic responds by displaying the Object Browser window as shown in Figure BD3.9.

Figure BD3.9.

The Object Browser window.

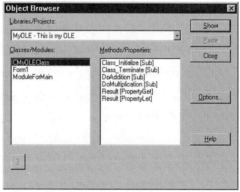

☐ Select the CMyOLEClass item.

Methods/Properties lists all the properties and methods of the class as shown in Figure BD3.9.

Bonus Day 4+

Creating Your Own OLE Automation Client

In this chapter you'll create a client OLE program. This program will utilize the MyOLE.DLL OLE server that you developed in the previous chapter. Note that Visual Basic 4, 32-bit professional version is required for the implementation of the material of this chapter.

Reviewing Client/Server OLE Automation

Before implementing the client program of this chapter, let's review the client/server OLE concept:

In the previous chapter you implemented the MyOLE.DLL OLE server. The MyOLE.DLL server contains a class (the CMyOLEClass class). Once you copy the MyOLE.DLL to the \Windows\System directory, the CMyOLEClass class is available for many Windows applications. Any Windows application that utilizes the CMyOLEClass class is called a client program of the MyOLE.DLL OLE server.

The MyClient Program

You'll now design and implement the MyClient program, a client program that utilizes the CMyOLEClass class that is included in the MyOLE.DLL file.

☐ Make sure that the MyOLE.DLL file (that you developed in the previous chapter) resides inside the C:\Windows\System directory.

☐ Start Visual Basic, and select New Project from the File menu of Visual Basic.

☐ Save the new project as follows: Save the new form as MyClient.frm inside the C:\TYVBProg\BD04 directory, and save the project file as MyClient.vbp inside the C:\TYVBProg\BD04 directory.

☐ Implement the frmMyClient form per Table BD4.1. When you complete implementing the form, it should look as shown in Figure BD4.1.

Table BD4.1. The Properties table of the frmMyClient table.

Object	Property	Setting
Form	**Name**	**frmMyClient**
	Caption	The MyClient Program
	Height	3540
	Left	1080
	Top	1170
	Width	5715

Object	Property	Setting
CommandButton	**Name**	**cmdHerMultiply**
	Caption	Her Multiply
	Font name	System
	Font size	10
	Height	495
	Left	3240
	Top	1200
	Width	1455
CommandButton	**Name**	**cmdMyMultiply**
	Caption	My Multiply
	Font name	System
	Font size	10
	Height	495
	Left	840
	Top	1200
	Width	1455
CommandButton	**Name**	**cmdExit**
	Caption	E&xit
	Font name	System
	Font size	10
	Height	495
	Left	2160
	Top	2520
	Width	1215
TextBox	**Name**	**txtResult**
	Alignment	2 'Center
	Enabled	False
	Font name	System
	Font size	10
	Height	495
	Left	720
	MultiLine	True

continues

Table BD4.1. continued

Object	Property	Setting
	Text	(make it empty)
	Top	360
	Width	3975

Figure BD4.1.
The frmMyClient form in design mode.

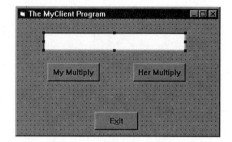

Attaching Code to the *Click* Event of the Exit button

You'll now attach code to the Click event of the Exit button.

☐ Type the following code inside the cmdExit_Click() procedure of the frmMyClient form:

```
Private Sub cmdExit_Click()

    End

End Sub
```

The code that you typed terminates the MyClient program.

Adding the MyOLE.DLL OLE Server to the Project

The MyClient program will use the CMyOLEClass class that resides inside the MyOLE.DLL OLE server. Therefore, you must first add the MyOLE.DLL OLE server to the project.

☐ Select References from the Tools menu of Visual Basic.

Visual Basic responds by displaying the References dialog box.

☐ If the This is my OLE item does not appear inside the References dialog box, click the Browse button of the References dialog box, and select the MyOLE.DLL file that resides inside the C:\Windows\System directory.

After selecting the MyOLE.DLL file, the item labelled This is my OLE appears as one of the items inside the Available References list. (See Figure BD4.2.) Recall that when you implemented the MyOLE.DLL, you set the Application Description as This is my OLE. (See Figure BD3.1 in the previous chapter.)

Figure BD4.2.

The This is my OLE item appears as an available reference.

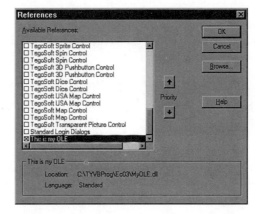

Once you include a reference to the This is My OLE OLE server, your program can use the CMyOLEClass class that is inside the MyOLE.DLL file.

☐ Make sure that the check box of the This is my OLE item in the Available References list is checked.

☐ Click the OK button of the References dialog box.

Attaching Code to the *Click* Event of the My Multiply button

You'll now attach code to the Click event of the My Multiply button.

☐ Type the following code inside the cmdMyMultiply_Click() procedure of the frmMyClient form:

```
Private Sub cmdMyMultiply_Click()

Dim MyObject As New CMyOLEClass

MyObject.Num1 = 2
```

```
MyObject.Num2 = 3

MyObject.DoMultiplication

txtResult.Text = Str(MyObject.Result)
```

End Sub

The code that you typed declares a variable as follows:

```
Dim MyObject As New CMyOLEClass
```

The variable name is `MyObject`, and the variable is of type `CMyOLEClass`. Recall that the `CMyOLEClass` is a class inside the MyOLE.DLL OLE server. Thus, `MyObject` is an object of class `CMyOLEClass`.

When you implemented the `CMyOLEClass` class, you declared three properties:

> Num1
> Num2
> Result

The following statements inside the `cmdMyMultiply_Click()` procedure set the `Num1` and `Num2` properties of the `MyObject` object:

```
MyObject.Num1 = 2
MyObject.Num2 = 3
```

When you implemented the `CMyOLEClass` class, you implemented the `DoMultiplication` method. The next statement inside the `cmdMyMultiply_Click()` procedure executes the `DoMultiplication` method:

```
MyObject.DoMultiplication
```

As you recall from the previous chapter, the `DoMultiplication` method sets the Result property with the result of the multiplication of Num1 by Num2. The next statement inside the `cmdMyMultiply_Click()` procedure updates the Text property of the text box with the value of the Result property:

```
txtResult.Text = Str(MyObject.Result)
```

☐ Select Save Project from the File menu of Visual Basic to save your work, and then execute the MyClient program.

☐ Click the MyMultiply button.

MyClient responds by displaying the message box shown in Figure BD4.3.

Figure BD4.3.

The message box that indicates that the Initialize *event of the OLE server occurs.*

When the statement:

```
Dim MyObject As New CMyOLEClass
```

is executed, an object, MyObject, of class CMyOLEClass is created. This means that the Class_Initialize() procedure of the MyOLE.DLL OLE server is executed. Recall that in the previous chapter you typed the following code inside the Class_Initialize() procedure of the class module:

```
Private Sub Class_Initialize()

MsgBox ("Hi, I'm inside the Initialize event of the Server")

End Sub
```

Indeed, you proved to yourself that whenever an object (such as MyObject) of class CMyOLEClass is created, the Class_Initialize() procedure is automatically executed.

The text box of the MyClient program is updated with the numeral 6, because you set Num1 to 2 and Num2 to 3. Hence, the text box indicates that 2*3 is 6.

When the cmdMyMultiply_Click() procedure is terminated, all the local variables of the procedure are destroyed. For example, suppose that you have the following procedure:

```
Private Sub cmdMyButton_Click()

Dim I as Integer

I = 3

End Sub
```

During the execution of the cmdMyButton_Click() procedure, the I local variable is set to 3. But when the cmdMyButton_Click() procedure is terminated, the I variable is destroyed.

When the cmdMyMultiply_Click() procedure is terminated, all its local variables are destroyed. Inside the cmdMyMultiply_Click() procedure you declared the MyObject object as a local variable. This means that when the cmdMyMultiply_Click() procedure is terminated, the MyObject object is destroyed.

Recall that inside the Class_Terminate() procedure of the CMyOLEClass class you typed the following code:

```
Private Sub Class_Terminate()
```

```
MsgBox ("Hi, I'm inside the Terminate event of the Server")
```

End Sub

This means that upon destroying the MyObject object, the Class_Terminate() procedure is executed. Indeed, when the cmdMyMultiply_Click() procedure is terminated, you see the message box shown in Figure BD4.4.

Figure BD4.4.

The message box that is displayed when an object of class CMyOLEClass is destroyed.

☐ Experiment with the My Multiply button. Note that the message box shown in Figure BD4.3 appears every time you create the MyObject object. And every time you destroy the MyObject object, the message box shown in Figure BD4.4 is displayed.

☐ Click the Exit button of the MyClient program to terminate the MyClient program.

Attaching Code to the *Click* Event of the Her Multiply button

You'll now attach code to the Click event of the Her Multiply button.

☐ Type the following code inside the Click event of the Her Multiply button:

```
Private Sub cmdHerMultiply_Click()

Dim HerObject As New CMyOLEClass

HerObject.Num1 = 20
HerObject.Num2 = 30

HerObject.DoMultiplication

txtResult.Text = Str(HerObject.Result)

End Sub
```

The code that you typed is very similar to the code that you typed inside the cmdMyMultiply_Click() procedure.

A local object, HerObject of class CMyOLEClass, is created:

```
Dim HerObject As New CMyOLEClass
```

Then the Num1 and Num2 properties of the HerObject object are set:

```
HerObject.Num1 = 20
HerObject.Num2 = 30
```

The DoMultiplication method is executed:

```
HerObject.DoMultiplication
```

And finally, the text box is updated with the result of multiplying Num1 by Num2:

```
txtResult.Text = Str(HerObject.Result)
```

☐ Select Save Project from the File menu of Visual Basic, and then execute the MyClient program.

☐ Experiment with the My Multiply and Her Multiply buttons. Note that whenever an object is created, the message box of Figure BD4.3 is displayed. And whenever an object is destroyed, the message box of Figure BD4.4 is displayed.

☐ Click the Exit button of the MyClient program to terminate the MyClient program.

Creating Static Objects

Currently, the MyClient program creates two local objects:

The MyObject object is created inside the cmdMyMultiply_Click() procedure as a local object, as follows:

```
Private Sub cmdMyMultiply_Click()

Dim MyObject As New CMyOLEClass

...
...
...

End Sub
```

And the HerObject object is created as a local object as follows:

```
Private Sub cmdHerMultiply_Click()

Dim HerObject As New CMyOLEClass

...
...
...

End Sub
```

As stated, being local objects to the procedures, the `MyObject` is destroyed whenever the `cmdMyMultiply_Click()` procedure is terminated, and the `HerObject` is destroyed whenever the `cmdHerMultiply_Click()` procedure is terminated.

You'll now create the `MyObject` and `HerObject` objects as static objects. Recall that a `Static` variable does not lose its value when the procedure is terminated.

For example, in the following procedure, `I` is declared as a `Static` variables:

```
Private Sub cmdMyButton_Click()

Static I as Integer

I = I + 1

End Sub
```

Upon executing the `cmdMyButton_Click()` procedure for the first time, `I` is set to 0. The code inside the `cmdMyButton_Click()` procedure sets the value of `I` to 0+1=1.

If the `cmdMyButton_Click()` procedure is executed again, `I` is equal to 1. Why? Because `I` was declared as `Static` variable. So during the second execution of the `cmdMyButton_Click()` procedure, `I` is increased by 1: 1+1=2. If you execute the `cmdMyButton_Click()` procedure again, `I` is equal to 2 and then its value will increase to 3.

Likewise, you can declared the `MyObject` and `HerObject` objects as `Static` objects.

☐ Modify the `cmdMyMultiply_Click()` procedure of the frmMyClient form so that it will look as follows:

```
Private Sub cmdMyMultiply_Click()

'''Dim MyObject As New CMyOLEClass
Static MyObject As New CMyOLEClass

    …
    …
    …

End Sub
```

That is, you created the `MyObject` object as a `Static` object.

☐ Modify the `cmdHerMultiply_Click()` procedure of the frmMyClient form so that it will look as follows:

```
Private Sub cmdHerMultiply_Click()

'''Dim HerObject As New CMyOLEClass
Static HerObject As New CMyOLEClass

    …
    …
    …

End Sub
```

Again, you declared the HerObject object as a Static object.

☐ Select Save Project from the File menu of Visual Basic, and then execute the MyClient program.

☐ Click the My Multiply button.

The message box of Figure BD4.3 appears. Why? Because the MyObject object was created for the first time.

☐ Click the OK button of the message box.

MyClient responds by updating the text box. However, now the message box of Figure BD4.4 does not appear. Why? Because MyObject was created as a Static variable. This means that when the cmdMyMultiply_Click() procedure is terminated, the MyObject object is not destroyed.

☐ Click the My Multiply button again.

The message box of Figure BD4.3 does not appear. Why? Because the MyObject object was created already. Being a Static variable, it was not destroyed when the cmdMyMultiply_Click() procedure was terminated in the previous step.

☐ Experiment with the My Multiply and Her Multiply buttons, and note that the message box of Figure BD4.3 appears only once for each creation of the MyObject and HerObject objects.

☐ Click the Exit button to terminate the MyClient program.

Note that the message box of Figure BD4.4 appears twice. Why? Because when you terminate the MyClient program, all the Static variables are destroyed. So the destruction of the MyObject object causes the Class_Terminate() procedure of the CMyOLEClass class to be executed, and the destruction of the HerObject object also causes the execution of the Class_Terminate() procedure of the CMyOLEClass class.

Verifying that the Result Property is a Read-Only Property

When you implemented the CMyOLEClass class in the previous chapter, you implemented the Result property in such a way that the Result property is a read-only property. You'll now add code to the cmdMyMultiply_Click() procedure of the frmMyClient form that verifies that the Result property cannot be set by the client application.

☐ Modify the cmdMyMultiply_Click() procedure so that it will look as follows:

```
Private Sub cmdMyMultiply_Click()
```

```
'''Dim MyObject As New CMyOLEClass
Static MyObject As New CMyOLEClass

MyObject.Num1 = 2
MyObject.Num2 = 3

MyObject.DoMultiplication
txtResult.Text = Str(MyObject.Result)

MyObject.Result = 100
MsgBox "MyObject.Result=" + Str(MyObject.Result)

End Sub
```

The code that you added tries to set the Result property as follows:

```
MyObject.Result = 100
```

Then, a message box is displayed so that you can see the value of Result:

```
MsgBox "MyObject.Result=" + Str(MyObject.Result)
```

☐ Save your work and then execute the MyClient program.

☐ Click the My Multiply button.

The last message box that the cmdMyMultiply_Click() procedure displays is a message box that displays the value of Result. As you can see, Result is equal to 6 (2*3). That is, the statement

```
MyObject.Result = 100
```

did not affect the value of Result (because Result is a read-only property).

Summary

In this chapter you implemented the MyClient program, which utilizes the CMyOLEClass class that you implemented in the previous chapter. As you saw during the course of this chapter, your client programs can utilize classes that were implemented in OLE servers.

Q&A

Q Can two or more client applications use the same OLE server simultaneously?

A Yes. See Exercise 1 of this chapter.

Quiz

1. Typically, you would insert code that displays a message box inside the `Class_Initialize()` and `Class_Terminate()` procedures of the OLE server class.

   a. True

   b. False

2. Setting the Result property as follows

   `HerObject.Result = 0`

   will cause the Result property of the `HerObject` object to be equal to 0.

   a. True

   b. False

Exercises

1. Demonstrate that more than one client program can utilize the OLE server at the same time.

2. In the Exercises section of the previous chapter, you implemented the `DoAddition` method of the `CMyOLEClass` class. Use the `DoAddition` method from within the MyClient program.

BD4

Quiz Answers

1. b. The message boxes were implemented for the sole purpose of "seeing" the creation and destruction of the objects during the execution of the client program. Typically, you do not include code that displays message boxes inside the `Class_Initialize()` and `Class_Terminate()` procedures of the class.

2. b. False. Because the Result property is a read-only property.

Exercise Answers

1.

   ☐ Load the MyClient project, and then select Make EXE from the File menu of Visual Basic to create the MyClient.EXE program inside the C:\TYVBProg\BD4 directory.

   ☐ Terminate the Visual Basic program.

   ☐ Execute the MyClient.EXE program.

☐ Execute another copy of the MyClient.EXE program.

So now you have two MyClient.EXE programs running at the same time.

As you can see, each program works as expected, which means that the OLE server serves the two programs.

If you implement another program called HerClient.EXE that utilizes the `CMyOLEClass` class, you'll realize that the OLE Server is capable of serving the HerClient.EXE program simultaneously with serving the MyClient.EXE program.

2.

☐ Place another text box inside the frmMyClient form and set the Name property of the text box to: txtAddResult.

☐ Inside the `cmdMyMultiply_Click()` procedure add statements that execute the `DoAddition` method, and then update the txtAddResult text box. Your `cmdMyMultiply_Click()` procedure should then look as follows:

```
Private Sub cmdMyMultiply_Click()

'''Dim MyObject As New CMyOLEClass
Static MyObject As New CMyOLEClass

MyObject.Num1 = 2
MyObject.Num2 = 3

MyObject.DoMultiplication
txtResult.Text = Str(MyObject.Result)

MyObject.DoAddition
txtAddResult.Text = Str(MyObject.Result)


End Sub
```

☐ Inside the `cmdHerMultiply_Click()` procedure, add statements that execute the `DoAddition` method, and then update the txtAddResult text box. Your `cmdHerMultiply_Click()` procedure should then look as follows:

```
Private Sub cmdHerMultiply_Click()

Dim HerObject As New CMyOLEClass

HerObject.Num1 = 20
HerObject.Num2 = 30

HerObject.DoMultiplication
txtResult.Text = Str(HerObject.Result)

HerObject.DoAddition
```

```
txtAddResult.Text = Str(HerObject.Result)
```

End Sub

☐ Save your work, execute the MyClient program, and verify that the DoAddition
  method works as expected.

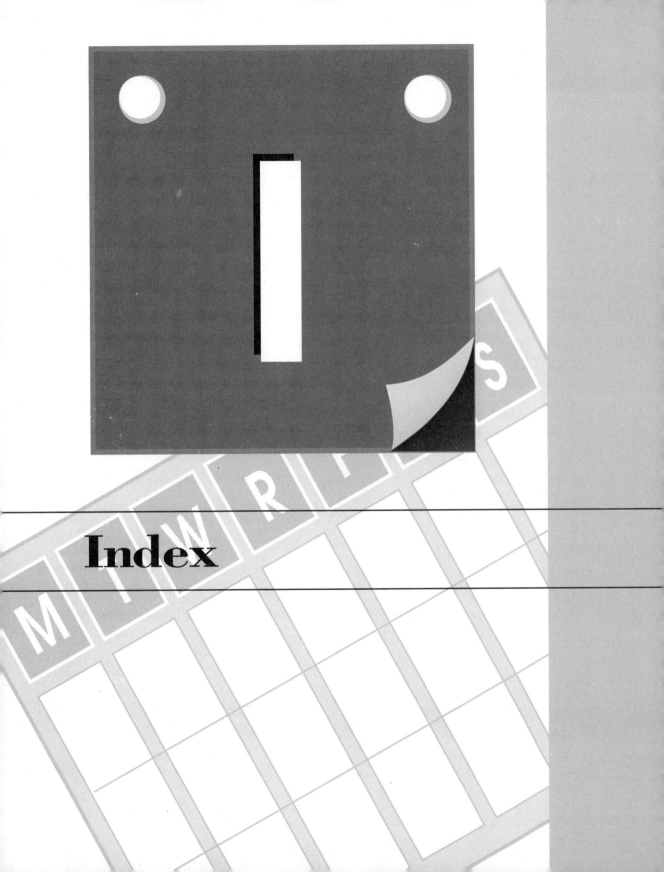

Index

Symbols

frmCommon form

mnuDisplayTable_Click ( ) procedure

procedures

SAMS
Learning
Center

SAMS
PUBLISHING

procedures

procedures

properties

SAMS
Learning
Center

SAMS
PUBLISHING

Disk Offer
from SAMS

Teach Yourself Visual Basic 4 in 21 Days

You can purchase the book's special companion disk for only $10.00. The disk contains the source code of the book's programs. (Some of the book's programs require third-party OLE controls, which are not included on this disk.)

The easiest way to order the disk is to call 1-800-428-5331 between 9:00 a.m. and 5:00 p.m. EST. For fastest service, please have your credit card available.

To order the disk by mail, send your name, address, order, and a check for the correct amount to

SAMS Publishing
Sales Department—Disk Offer
Teach Yourself Visual Basic 4 in 21 Days (0-672-30620-4D)
201 West 103rd Street
Indianapolis, IN 46290

Special Disk Offer

The Full Version of the TegoSoft OLE Control Kit

You can order the full version of the TegoSoft OLE Control Kit directly from TegoSoft, Inc.

The TegoSoft OLE Control Kit includes a variety of powerful OLE controls for Visual Basic (as well as many other programming languages that supports OLE controls).

The TegoSoft OLE Control Kit includes the following powerful OLE controls:

- ☐ An advanced multimedia OLE control (to play WAV, MIDI, CD audio, and movie files).
- ☐ A 3D virtual reality OLE control (which lets you use the mouse and keyboard to travel inside your 3D pictures).
- ☐ An advanced animation OLE control and a sprite OLE control.
- ☐ 3D controls (for example, 3D buttons, 3D spin).
- ☐ A spy OLE control (which lets you intercept Windows messages of other applications).
- ☐ Gadget OLE controls.
- ☐ A PC speaker OLE control (which enables you to play WAV files through the PC speaker without a sound card and without any drivers).
- ☐ Other powerful OLE controls.

The price of the TegoSoft OLE Control Kit is $29.95. Please add $5.00 for shipping and handling. New York State residents please add appropriate sales tax.

When ordering from outside the U.S.A., your check or money order must be in U.S. dollars and drawn from a U.S. bank.

To order, send check or money order to

> TegoSoft, Inc.
> Attn.: OCX-Kit-VB421
> Box 389
> Bellmore, NY 11710
> Phone: (516) 783-4824

Add to Your Sams Library Today with the Best Books for Programming, Operating Systems, and New Technologies

The easiest way to order is to pick up the phone and call
1-800-428-5331
between 9:00 a.m. and 5:00 p.m. EST.
For faster service please have your credit card available.

ISBN	Quantity	Description of Item	Unit Cost	Total Cost
0-672-30602-6		Programming Windows 95 Unleashed (book/CD)	$49.99	
0-672-30474-0		Windows 95 Unleashed (book/CD)	$35.00	
0-672-30611-5		Your Windows 95 Consultant	$19.99	
0-672-30685-9		Windows NT 3.5 Unleashed, Second Edition	$39.99	
0-672-30765-0		Navigating the Internet with Windows 95	$25.00	
0-672-30568-2		Teach Yourself OLE Programming in 21 Days (book/CD)	$39.99	
0-672-30448-1		Teach Yourself C in 21 Days, Bestseller Edition	$24.95	
0-672-30594-1		Programming WinSock (book/disk)	$35.00	
0-672-30655-7		Developing Your Own 32-Bit Operating System (book/CD)	$49.99	
0-672-30667-0		Teach Yourself Web Publishing with HTML in a Week	$25.00	
0-672-30737-5		The World Wide Web Unleashed, Second Edition	$39.99	
❏ 3 ½" Disk		Shipping and Handling: See information below.		
❏ 5 ¼" Disk		TOTAL		

Shipping and Handling: $4.00 for the first book, and $1.75 for each additional book. Floppy disk: add $1.75 for shipping and handling. If you need to have it NOW, we can ship product to you in 24 hours for an additional charge of approximately $18.00, and you will receive your item overnight or in two days. Overseas shipping and handling adds $2.00 per book and $8.00 for up to three disks. Prices subject to change. Call for availability and pricing information on latest editions.

201 W. 103rd Street, Indianapolis, Indiana 46290

1-800-428-5331 — Orders   1-800-835-3202 — FAX   1-800-858-7674 — Customer Service

Book ISBN 0-672-30620-4

Here's a look at just a few of the programs that you'll learn to write while reading *Teach Yourself Visual Basic 4 in 21 Days!*

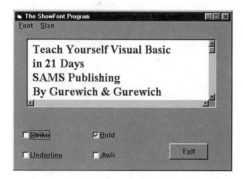

Learn how to display and print text using different fonts.

Learn how to create drawing programs.

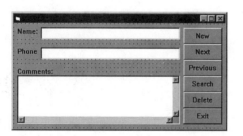

Learn how to save and extract data from files.

Learn how to write programs that play CD audio and movie AVI files.

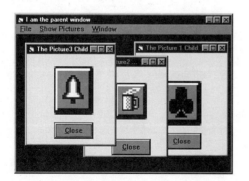

Learn how to write MDI-based programs.

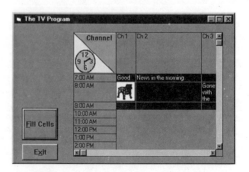

Learn how to write spreadsheet-based programs.